Lincoln in New Orleans

Lincoln in
New Orleans

The 1828–1831 Flatboat Voyages
and Their Place in History

Richard Campanella

University of Louisiana at Lafayette Press
2010

973.
7092
C

University of Louisiana at Lafayette Press
P. O. Box 40831
Lafayette, LA 70504-0831
http://ulpress.org

Printed in Canada on acid-free paper.

ISBN 13 (hardcover): 978-1-935754-02-2

Library of Congress Cataloging-in-Publication Data

Campanella, Richard.
 Lincoln in New Orleans : the 1828-1831 flatboat voyages and their place in
history / Richard Campanella.
   p. cm.
 Includes bibliographical references and index.
 ISBN 978-1-935754-02-2 (hardcover : alk. paper)
 1. Lincoln, Abraham, 1809-1865--Career in flatboating. 2. Lincoln,
Abraham, 1809-1865--Travel--Louisiana--New Orleans. 3. Lincoln,
Abraham, 1809-1865--Travel--Mississippi River. 4. Lincoln, Abraham,
1809-1865--Childhood and youth. 5. Flatboats--Mississippi River--History--
19th century. I. Title.
 E457.32.C34 2010
 973.7092--dc22
                                    2010034239

Dedicated
to the hoosiers,
the suckers, the pukes,
the huckeyes, the mudheads,
and the corn crackers
of history

Table of Contents

Introduction

On an April morning in 1865, President Abraham Lincoln, rejuvenated by the dawn of peace after four years of unspeakable violence, gathered his cabinet to discuss matters of the day. In a moment of reflection, the president shared with colleagues his previous night's dream. "He seemed to be . . . in a singular and indescribable vessel," recalled one attendee, "moving with great rapidity towards a dark and indefinite shore." It was a recurring vision, Lincoln pointed out, and one that seemed to precede stunning news—battles, for example, at "Antietam . . . Gettysburg, and Vicksburg."[1]

That evening, he was assassinated.

Thirty-seven Aprils earlier, a teenaged Abraham Lincoln floated in a singular vessel down the indefinite banks of the Mississippi River. The voyage culminated in a stunning spectacle—New Orleans, the largest city he would see for decades, the most exotic metropolis in the country, the nation's largest slave marketplace. It also exposed him to a violent and potentially murderous attack. That trip, and a second one in 1831, would form the two longest journeys of Lincoln's life, his only visits to the Deep South, and the closest he ever came to immersing himself in a foreign culture. The two voyages form key experiences in the least-known era of Lincoln's otherwise thoroughly examined adult life.

Perhaps the hypnotic sensation of descending that deceptively placid current, through fog and mist for days and weeks, instilled in the future president's slumbering mind the source imagery from which that recurring riverine dream arose. We can say with greater confidence that the two flatboat voyages to New Orleans informed Lincoln's intellectual and moral development in many ways, some likely profound. We can say with certainty that Lincoln's journeys typified the experience of tens of thousands of Western rivermen who guided cargo down the Ohio and Mississippi during the early nineteenth century, and thus tell an important story about Western river commerce and New Orleans. It is also true that nearly every book ever written about Lincoln, from children's readers to scholarly tomes, briefly recounts the Mississippi flatboat story and ascribes importance to what the man experienced in New Orleans.

---

1. Men in Lincoln's administration, including Gideon Welles, recalled slightly differing versions of the dream. This one comes from John G. Nicolay and John Hay, "Abraham Lincoln: A History—The Fourteenth of April—The Fate of the Assassins—The Mourning Pageant," *Century Illustrated Monthly Magazine*, January 1890, 430.

Shedding new light on these and other aspects of this story, with detailed documentation, contextualization, and critical analysis, is the goal of *Lincoln in New Orleans*. The book begins by tracing two American families—the Lincolns and the Hanks, typical of so many others—over the Appalachian Mountains at the turn of the nineteenth century. We then delve into the childhood and adolescence of one of their progeny, Abraham, and his early exposure to rivers and river commerce. Next we reconstruct in detail Abraham Lincoln's first voyage to New Orleans in 1828, followed by his return to Indiana, his family's move to Illinois, and his second experience in 1831. Much effort is devoted to nailing down the timing of each trip, because that chronology determines the time window in which we may reconstruct the street life in New Orleans to which Lincoln was exposed. We then explore the various interactions Lincoln had with New Orleans after 1831—and particularly after 1862, when the great metropolis that once utterly ignored the poor upcountry boatman fell under his command. We conclude by positing certain influences of the 1828–31 journeys upon Lincoln in his philosophical, moral, and intellectual development. Two detailed appendices situate the story in the broader context of early nineteenth-century Western river commerce and New Orleans as the major Southern node in that system. The appendices' length attests to my conviction that Lincoln's flatboat voyages are important not solely as chapters in the biography of a major historical figure, but also as exemplars of the experiences of thousands of common men who, like Lincoln, worked the Western rivers and ended up, anonymous and marginalized, on New Orleans' flatboat wharves. This is their story too, because, as exceptional as Lincoln later came to be, he was entirely archetypal of the Western rivermen of his youth.

No one has attempted a full-length scholarly study of this topic before, and for good reason: Lincoln did not scribe a journal during the voyages and spoke only fleetingly of them later in life, depriving historians of detailed first-person accounts.[2] There are, however, numerous other fonts of

---

2. Some scholarly journal articles, cited later in this volume, have been written about Lincoln's New Orleans trips. A few fictionalized books have also been published on the topic, generally for juvenile readers. Virginia L. S. Eifert's *Three Rivers South: The Story of Young Abe Lincoln* (New York: Dodd, Mead & Company, 1953), featuring drawings by Thomas Hart Benton, begins with this disclaimer: "The general situation and many of the events described in this book are based upon historical facts. However, the fictional characters are wholly imaginative. . . ." Imaginative indeed were Eifert's accounts—mostly about the 1831 journey—but she nonetheless did her homework in structuring the fiction around a skeleton of historical and geographical facts. A similar book by Meridel

information, ranging from solid primary and reliable secondary sources, to first-person recollections recorded later in life, to family memories and folk knowledge. Reams of geographical data on 1828–31 river conditions, landscapes, and cityscapes, plus scores of journals written by other river travelers and New Orleans visitors, also await investigation. The task of evaluating and synthesizing these myriad sources yields a vast array of facts, contexts, estimations, and clues—as well as fair allotment of the dubious and the apocryphal. Triangulating off the reliable information produces a patchwork of solid facts, likely scenarios, and trajectories of best fit, which may then be carefully quilted into a reconstruction of the journeys. This task entails constant evaluation, weighing of evidence, and calls of judgment, each of which is documented and explained so that readers may critique and challenge my reasoning. The principle of Occam's razor—of embracing the simplest explanation based on the fewest assumptions and supported by the best evidence—guided my reasoning. No literary license is taken; there is zero invented dialogue.

•

I acknowledge the following institutions for access to archival documents, research materials, artifacts, original sites, datasets, and analytical tools used in this volume: Louisiana Collection of the New Orleans Public Library; The Historic New Orleans Collection-Williams Research Center; U.S. Library of Congress; Howard Tilton Library at Tulane University; Louisiana State Museum; U.S. Census Bureau; U.S. Geological Survey; Port of New Orleans; New Orleans Notarial Archives; University of Arkansas Library Special Collections; Lewis Historical Library at Vincennes University; Genealogy Room of the Spencer County Library, Rockport, Indiana; Center for Bioenvironmental Research at Tulane and Xavier Universities; Louisiana Collection and Special Collections of the Earl K. Long Library at the University of New Orleans; U.S. National

Le Sueur aimed at the same readership, *The River Road: A Story of Abraham Lincoln* (New York: Alfred A. Knopf), came out the next year, and has been recently republished. Lavere Anderson's *Abe Lincoln and the River Robbers* (Champaign, IL: Garrard Publishing Company, 1971) and Neil Waldman's *Voyages: Reminiscences of Young Abe Lincoln* (Honesdale, PA: Calkins Creek Books, 2009) also pertain to this genre. In 2009, Rae Katherine Eighmey self-published a book entitled *Abraham Lincoln in New Orleans: A Novel Based on the True Events of March–June 1831*, which, like the aforementioned, embellishes an underlying foundation of facts with fictionalized incidents and dialogue. While not of interest to the historian, these and similar works are nonetheless significant because they help instill lasting popular perceptions about Lincoln's youth and life narrative.

Park Service's Abraham Lincoln Birthplace National Historic Site, Lincoln Boyhood National Memorial, and Lincoln Home National Historic Site; the Abraham Lincoln Presidential Library in Springfield; and the Illinois Department of Natural Resources' Lincoln Trail Homestead State Park, Lincoln's New Salem State Historic Site, and Lincoln-Herndon Law Offices State Historic Site.

Appreciation also goes to the hundreds of informants, diarists, reporters, and researchers cited herein, whose findings and testimonies made this analysis possible. The invaluable work of Lincoln scholar Douglas L. Wilson, particularly his effort (with Rodney O. Davis) to transcribe and edit William H. Herndon's circa-1865 interviews with the people of Lincoln's youth, proved critical to this project.

I am also indebted to Jane Boultinghouse and Barbara Dillon of Rockport, Indiana (both direct descendents of Lincoln's 1828 flatboat captain Allen Gentry), as well as Robert Grose (the only person to participate in two full Lincoln flatboat reenactments, in 1958 and 2008), for sharing their knowledge, family memories, and photographs with me. Melissa Miller of the Spencer County Visitors Bureau kindly provided photographs of the 2008 *Journey of Remembrance*, as did the staff of Lincoln's New Salem State Historic Site for its 2006 flatboat reenactment. Gratitude also goes to Jonathan B. Pritchett and Lawrence Powell of Tulane University; Louisiana National Guard State Historian Lieut. Col. (Ret.) Thomas M. Ryan; Naomi Homison of Pittsburgh, Pennsylvania; Irene Wainwright of the New Orleans Public Library; Norman Vickers of Marion, Arkansas; Thomas Dillard and Andrea Cantrell of the University of Arkansas Library Special Collections; Jill Larson of the Lewis Historical Library at Vincennes, Indiana; Jeff Haller, Lee Goldsmith, and Roger Anderson from the musical *Abe!*; Greg Lambousy of the Louisiana State Museum; Georgia Chadwick of the Louisiana Supreme Court Library; Erin Strobel and colleagues at the Spencer County Public Library in Rockport, Indiana; Sister Mary Pat White and Sister Mary Louise Gavan of the Religious of the Sacred Heart of Jesus; architect Ray Manning and geographer Julie Hernandez for their interest and words of encouragement; Dorothy Ball for her keen editorial review and insightful comments; and others for various ideas and access.

Deep gratitude goes to James D. Wilson Jr., Carl A. Brasseaux, Jessica C. Hornbuckle, Melissa G. Teutsch, and the staff of the University of Louisiana at Lafayette Press, for their steadfast support of my work.

As a six-year-old growing up in Brooklyn, New York, in the early

1970s, I read with my parents' help Barbara Cary's *Meet Abraham Lincoln*. That children's reader represented my first introduction to Lincoln, to slavery, and to New Orleans. Cary's characterization of that city as a remote and exotic place, "at the very end of the Mississippi River," captured my imagination and planted a seed of fascination in my mind that would blossom twenty years later.

I eventually devoted my career to researching the history and geography of New Orleans, an interest that has produced numerous books, articles, lectures, and classes over the past two decades. *Lincoln in New Orleans*, my sixth book, unites all three topics first introduced to me nearly forty years ago. My deepest gratitude goes to my parents, Mario and Rose Campanella, for their tireless efforts in raising and educating me. I still have *Meet Abraham Lincoln* to this day, one of my most cherished possessions.

Finally, my thanks go to my wife, Marina Campanella, brother Thomas J. Campanella, and uncle John Tambasco for their many years of love, support, and guidance.

Origins

~ Lincoln's ancestry ~ Thomas Lincoln in New Orleans ~ Lincoln's Kentucky birth and childhood ~ Indiana boyhood ~ Lincoln and the Ohio River ~ A traumatic end and a new beginning ~

When asked in 1860 to describe his early years, Republican presidential nominee Abraham Lincoln diffidently quoted Thomas Gray's "Elegy Written in a Country Churchyard" by responding, "The short and simple annals of the poor."[1] Extraordinary as Lincoln came to be, the annals of his youth generally typified the experience of many, perhaps most, white American males in the trans-Appalachian West of the early nineteenth century. For most of his life, Lincoln's American experience was not particularly exceptional or unusual. The same may be said of Lincoln's ancestors.

Little more did Lincoln know of his mother's ancestry than she came from "a family of the name of Hanks. . . ."[2] Her clan presents a genealogical challenge because of its intergenerational proclivity to ascribe the same five or so Christian names to its scores of offspring. Her matrilineal progenitor was Adam Shipley, who arrived in Maryland from England in 1668. Shipley's descendents over the next century made their way to Virginia; one, Lucy, married a man named James Hanks. The couple, uneducated farmers of modest means, migrated over the Appalachians to Kentucky around 1780. At least eight girls named Nancy Hanks were born in ensuing years. One, possibly conceived out of wedlock with a Virginia planter and born around 1784, would become the mother of a president.[3]

More is known of Lincoln's paternal side. It traces to Samuel Lincoln,

1. Ward Hill Lamon, *Recollections of Abraham Lincoln, 1847–1865*, ed. Dorothy Lamon Teillard (Chicago, IL: A. C. McClurg and Company, 1895), 9.

2. Abraham Lincoln to Jesse W. Fell, December 20, 1859, in *The Collected Works of Abraham Lincoln*, ed. Roy P. Basler (New Brunswick, NJ: Rutgers University Press, 1953), 3:511.

3. David Herbert Donald, *Lincoln* (New York: Simon & Schuster, 1995), 19–21; Louis A. Warren, *Lincoln's Youth: Indiana Years, Seven to Twenty-One, 1816–1830* (Indianapolis: Indiana Historical Society Press, 1959, reprinted 2002), 6. The story of Nancy Hanks' illegitimate birth allegedly derives from Lincoln himself, as told to his law partner and future biographer William H. Herndon. See Don E. Fehrenbacher and Virginia Fehrenbacher, *Recollected Words of Abraham Lincoln* (Stanford, CA: Stanford University Press, 1996), 240–41.

a seventeen-year-old weaver from Norfolk, England, who immigrated to Hingham, Massachusetts, in 1637. Samuel succeeded as a trader, founded a church, and produced eleven offspring—one named Mordecai, typical of the traditional Christian names favored by the devout family. One of Mordecai's sons, born in 1686 and also christened with that biblical appellation, grew wealthy as an ironmaster and landowner in Pennsylvania. The younger Mordecai Lincoln achieved (in part through marriage) elite status in the political, social, and economic realms of colonial American society. Some family members were Quakers. Mordecai's son John, born in 1716, brought the Lincoln name and impressive wherewithal westward to Virginia's Shenandoah Valley, where in 1768 he established a farm in what later became Rockingham County.

John's son Abraham came to own over two hundred acres, and could have set down Lincoln family roots in that rich Virginia soil. But, as was the case for many ambitious Virginians in this era, the lure of greater fortune in lands to the west proved too tempting to pass up. Reports from distant kin Daniel Boone about fertile soil and lush forest in Kentucky helped convince the Lincolns to uproot and head there. During 1780–81, as the Revolutionary War raged in the East, Abraham Lincoln sold his respectable Virginia holding and led his wife and five children over the Appalachians.[4] Among his sons was Thomas Lincoln, born in 1776 or 1778.

The early 1780s was the prime time for such passage. Daniel Boone's recent blazing of the Wilderness Road enabled American families such as the Lincolns to traverse the Cumberland Gap. Subsequent road expansion invited more emigration. Intensifying pressure on Native Americans and a growing network of frontier forts brought, from the white perspective, some measure of security to the region. New laws supposedly brought some level of stability to Kentucky's notoriously erratic land titles. It is no coincidence that both the Hanks and Lincoln families independently migrated to Kentucky around 1780—the same year that three hundred "large family boats" navigated down the Ohio River to where the Great Falls impeded navigation, thus occasioning the foundation and incorporation of Louisville.[5] Within a few years, the Lincolns owned thousands of acres of fertile Kentucky soil, roughly twenty miles east of Louisville. Their prospects looked bright.

4. Donald, *Lincoln*, 19–21.
5. John G. Nicolay and John Hay, *Abraham Lincoln: A History* (New York: Century Co., 1890), 1:15.

Then, in May 1786, a tragic incident radically altered the family's destiny. In the words of the future president, "My paternal grandfather, Abraham Lincoln . . . was killed by indians, not in battle, but by stealth, when he was laboring to open a farm in the forest"[6] with sons Mordecai, Josiah, and Thomas. The two older boys ran for aid while the bewildered Thomas, eight or ten years old, remained with his slain father. Mordecai returned with a musket just in time to kill the Native American as he attempted to make off with the boy. Josiah soon arrived with reinforcements from a nearby fort to chase off the attackers.[7] The episode reveals the tensions and violence on the Kentucky frontier.

Suddenly without a breadwinner, the Lincolns saw their prospects wither. They were eventually forced to move and disperse. Worse yet, laws of primogeniture in this Virginia-controlled region of Kentucky meant that eldest son Mordecai alone would inherit most of Abraham's estate. Blessed additionally with intelligence and wit, Mordecai Lincoln would become an illustrious citizen, landowner, and racehorse breeder. "Uncle Mord had run off with all the talents of the family," Lincoln once chortled. Added a latter-day historian, "He had also, in effect, run off with all the money."[8]

Mordecai's youngest brother Thomas, lacking a father, an inheritance, and an education, suffered particularly with the family's descent. Working odd jobs with his jack-of-all-trades backwoods skills, he would come to know the proverbial "short and simple annals of the poor." Yet Thomas Lincoln also proved steadfast, reliable, ethical, and amiable to a degree often denied him by history. One acquaintance described Thomas, whose surname was often spelled "Linkhorn," as a

> hale, hearty-looking man, of medium height, heavy and square-built, rather clumsy in his gait, had a kind-looking face, was a moderately good house carpenter . . . quite illiterate . . . regarded as a very honest man.[9]

●

Those qualities helped Thomas gain, by the dawn of the new century,

---

6. Lincoln to Fell, December 20, 1859, in *Collected Works*, 3:511.

7. Nicolay and Hay, *Abraham Lincoln*, 1:21

8. Donald, *Lincoln*, 21–2.

9. Recollection of Capt. Samuel Haycraft, in "Lincoln's Birthplace: Some Incidents and Facts Never before Published," *San Francisco Bulletin* 37, no. 85 (January 16, 1874): 4.

good standing and steady work in the village of Elizabethtown. It also earned him and a man named Isaac Bush the trust of two Elizabethtown storekeepers, Robert Bleakley and William Montgomery, to build and guide a flatboat down to New Orleans to vend produce. Store records show that on February 18, 1806, Thomas Lincoln sold to Bleakley and Montgomery "2400 pounds of pork at 15 pence and 494 pounds of beef at 15 pence," for which his account was credited "21 pounds, 14 shillings and 1½ pence."[10] Bleakley and Montgomery's records also indicate a sale to Thomas of a saw, plane, file, auger, and adze—tools needed for flatboat and house construction—and a credit to Isaac Bush's account for the construction of a flatboat at West Point.[11] From the *embarcadero* (Spanish for boat launch) of that tiny Ohio River settlement, located near the Salt River confluence and so-named because it once (1796) formed the westernmost point of American civilization, Bush and Lincoln commenced their journey to New Orleans. Their exact departure date from West Point is not determinable, nor is the question of whether those 2,894 pounds of meat constituted the cargo. We do know that a Bleakley and Montgomery ledger entry dated May 16, 1806, reads "Thomas Lincoln going to Orleans Ł16.10.0" [16 pounds, 10 shillings], followed by a line reading "gold, Ł13.14.7½" [13 pounds, 14 shillings, 7½ pence], indicating that Thomas was back in Elizabethtown by that date. Based on this documentary evidence, historian Louis A. Warren estimated a departure date around March 1 and a return by May 1.[12]

Does this nine-week period allow enough time to float 1,300 miles downriver, transact business in New Orleans, and return on horseback, foot, or by slow-moving keelboat (this being before the advent of the steamboat)? A typical flatboat launched near West Point took about five days to float down the Ohio, followed by three to four weeks on the Mississippi to New Orleans.[13] A full moon on March 4 would have allowed Lincoln and Bush to travel nocturnally (risky but not impossible) for part

10. Warren, *Lincoln's Youth*, 5, 217.

11. Donald E. McClure, *Two Centuries of Elizabethtown and Hardin County* (Elizabethtown, KY: The Hardin County Historical, 1971), as quoted by Maria Campbell Brent and Joseph E. Brent, *Lincoln, Kentucky & Kentuckians: A Cultural Resource Inventory of Sites in Kentucky Associated with President Abraham Lincoln* (Frankfort, KY: Historical Confederation of Kentucky and the Kentucky Abraham Lincoln Bicentennial Commission, 2005), 4.

12. Warren, *Lincoln's Youth*, 5, 217.

13. Zadok Cramer, *The Navigator, or the Traders' Useful Guide in Navigating the Monongahela, Allegheny, Ohio, and Mississippi Rivers* (Pittsburgh: Zadok Cramer, 1806), 125. See also page 37 of the 1814 edition.

of the downriver journey.[14] Assuming no delays, they might have landed in New Orleans, transacted business, departed immediately, rode by
horse or keelboat back to Natchez (one to two weeks), then continued 600
miles on the Natchez Trace on horseback to Kentucky. Thirty miles being typical daily progress, this leg would have taken around three weeks.[15]
This timeline puts Lincoln and Bush on a tight schedule to fit within
the March-to-May window, although it is not without documented precedent. One Westerner of the same region and era claimed the return trip
took him one month:

> I left New Orleans about the 1st of May, and arrived home
> on the 1st day of June [1810]. . . . In traveling home I passed
> through many Cheyenne and Chickasaw tribes of Indians
> . . . walk[ing] about eight hundred miles, swimming across
> streams, wading through swamps, and sleeping in the open air
> on the ground.[16]

Lincoln and Bush undoubtedly suffered similar conditions. Perhaps they
left immediately after the February 18 ledger transaction and returned just
before the May 16 entry, allowing twelve weeks for the journey. Wharfinger reports in New Orleans, unfortunately, do not clarify the voyage's
timing: the City Council mandated on March 21, 1806, that the Collector of Levee Dues keep records of flatboat arrivals, but the Collector
did not comply with the new rule until April—too late by a few weeks to
capture a Kentucky flatboat crew that was definitely back home on May
16.[17] U.S. Customs Service officials at the Port of New Orleans may have
recorded Thomas' arrival in their manifests (which logged the flatboat's

14. U.S. Naval Observatory Astronomical Applications Department, "Phases of
the Moon," http://aa.usno.navy.mil/data/docs/MoonPhase.php (accessed October 14,
2008).

15. One antebellum visitor reported logging thirty miles per day on horseback through
the wilds of Mississippi. A pedestrian could cover fifteen to twenty-five miles per day
on rural roads and trails, depending on age, cargo, and conditions. As cited by Herman
Freudenberger and Jonathan B. Pritchett, "The Domestic United States Slave Trade:
New Evidence," *Journal of Interdisciplinary History* 21, no. 3 (Winter 1991): 472.

16. Isaac Naylor, "Judge Isaac Naylor, 1790–1873: An Autobiography," *Indiana Magazine of History* 4, no. 3 (September 1908): 136.

17. The Collector of Levee Dues recorded many flatboats not by their captain's surname, but by the names given to their boats. In any case, no Bush or Lincoln appears in
the April 1806 ledger. Wharfinger Reports, Microfilm #75-109 QN420, 1806, New
Orleans Collector of Levee Dues—Registers of Flatboats, Barges, Rafts, and Steamboats
in the Port of New Orleans.

name, captain, crew, and cargo, plus the Marine Hospital tax paid), but those intriguing documents only survive for the month of May 1807.[18] Newspaper reports of the wharfinger's records also fall short: the semi-weekly *Louisiana Gazette*'s "Ship News" column documented numerous "Kentucky boats" or "flats" arriving at New Orleans during late winter and early spring 1806, but none specifically originating from West Point or Elizabethtown, nor affiliated with the surname Lincoln. The newspaper listed a number of flatboats by vessel name and state of origin, rather than owner and city, so perhaps the Bush-Lincoln expedition lies among these entries. More likely, the *Gazette* simply missed it, as its "Ship News" column did not comprehensively cover all flatboat arrivals.[19]

Thomas Lincoln may have made multiple flatboats trip to New Orleans, from Kentucky and later from Indiana, according to reminiscences penned in 1865 by a distant relative named Augustus H. Chapman:

> Thos Lincoln Made Several trips down the River while he lived in Ind taking flat Boats Loaded with Produce, principally Pork, from these trips he realized but little profit simply turning what he raised on his Farm into cash, he sold one entire load on a credit & never realized a cent for the same, he also tooke 2 trips Down the river with flat Boats while he lived in Ky walking all the way from New Orleans to his home in Ky[.][20]

Later in the same letter, Chapman refined his memories. Referring to Thomas Lincoln, he wrote that

> while he resided in Ky he made two trips down the Ohio & Miss Rivers to New Orleans with one Isaac Bush. Th[e] y wa[lked] the entire distance across t[he] country from New Orleans b[ack] to their homes in Ky.[21]

---

18. Survey of Federal Archives in Louisiana, Division of Professional and Service Projects—Works Projects Administration, *Flatboats on the Mississippi in 1807* (Baton Rouge: Louisiana State University Press, 1940).

19. Survey by author of "Ship News" columns, *Louisiana Gazette*, February through May 1806. The February 21 edition listed a pilot named Bush (written "Bufh" in the orthography of the day) arriving from Natchez on a flatboat named *Polly*.

20. A. H. Chapman to William H. Herndon, September 8, 1865, in ed. Douglas L. Wilson and Rodney O. Davis, *Herndon's Informants: Letters, Interviews, and Statements About Abraham Lincoln* (Urbana and Chicago: University of Illinois Press, 1998), 100.

21. Ibid., 102.

Another relative provided additional insights into this question. "Did Ever Thomas Lincoln Send any produce to Neworleans[?]," wrote the relative in response to a written query in 1866; "Not from Indiana," he replied; Thomas "Jest Raised a Nuf for his own use[;] he Did Not Send any produce to any other place. . . ."[22]

Thomas Lincoln's exposure to the untamed lower Mississippi Valley and New Orleans opens up numerous historical questions. What did he experience? What stories—and Thomas Lincoln was a noted storyteller— did he later share with his son? Did he show Abe how to build and guide a flatboat, and tip him off with firsthand knowledge of the journey and destination? And what of slavery?—what did he witness in New Orleans, and did it inform his position on the institution, his later decision to move to Indiana, and what he taught his children? Thomas Lincoln's flatboat trip to New Orleans imparts, at the very least, a cultural dimension—a passing-down of knowledge from father to son—to Abraham Lincoln's journeys decades later.

The revealing Bleakley-Montgomery store ledger shows Thomas making more purchases in late May 1806, this time for domestic items such as cloth and sewing sundries. They were in preparation for his June 12 wedding to an old family acquaintance, twenty-two-year-old Nancy Hanks. Historical characterizations of Nancy lack the range and depth of those ascribed, rightly or wrongly, to her husband. They are also notably contradictory. An 1896 narrative history, perhaps inclined to romanticize the mother of a martyred president, described Nancy Hanks as "a fair and delicate woman, who could read and write, who had ideas of refinement, and a desire to get more from life than fortune allotted her. . . ."[23] A family acquaintance remembered her quite differently, as "rather low-set, heavy-built woman, without education . . . on a par with the ordinary class or circle in which she moved."[24] A contemporary of her youth had yet another recollection, remembering Nancy as "one of the most athletic women in Kentucky, [who] could throw most of the men who ever put her powers to the test."[25] A neighbor who attended Thomas

22. Dennis F. Hanks to William H. Herndon, January 26, 1866, in *Herndon's Informants*, 176.

23. Ida Minerva Tarbell and John McCan Davis, *The Early Life of Abraham Lincoln: Containing Many Unpublished Documents and Unpublished Reminiscences of Lincoln's Early Friends* (New York and London: S. S. McClure, 1896), 37.

24. Recollection of Capt. Samuel Haycraft, in "Lincoln's Birthplace," *San Francisco Bulletin*, 4.

25. Usher Linder, as quoted in Douglas L. Wilson, *Honor's Voice: The Transformation of*

and Nancy's wedding described the bride simply as "a fresh-looking girl, I should say over twenty. . . ." The "infare" (feast) that followed the wedding apparently made a greater impression on him, as he described it with impressive detail:

> We had bear-meat . . . venison; wild turkey and ducks; eggs,
> wild and tame, so common that you could buy them at two bits
> a bushel; maple syrup, swung on a string, to bite off for coffee
> or whiskey; syrup in big gourds; peach-and-honey; a sheep that
> the two families barbecued whole over coals of woods burned
> in a pit, and covered with green boughs to keep the juices in;
> and a race for the whiskey bottle.[26]

•

Thomas and Nancy Lincoln initially settled in Elizabethtown, where their first child, Sarah, arrived on February 10, 1807. Nancy became pregnant again in May 1808. A few months later, Thomas purchased for two hundred dollars a 300-acre farm near Hodgen's Mill (later Hodgenville) in Hardin County. He guided his expectant wife and infant daughter to the new homestead, located along Nolin Creek, fifteen miles southwest of Elizabethtown. A local man later described the area's landscape and explained the origin of the farm's name, Sinking Spring:

> [T]he country round about is rather level, that is no hills of
> note but in many places Small Basins (as they are called here)
> which renders the face of the country uneven & disagreeable to
> work for farming[;] in these little Sinks or basins, ponds [form,]
> which in many cases answer valuable purposes to the farmer
> for Stock. . . . Altogether the place is rather pretty. . . .[27]

The Lincolns' abode on the rocky clay karst topography of Sinking Spring typified that "of the poorer Western pioneer—a one-roomed cabin with a huge outside chimney, no windows, and only a rude floor."[28] There, on Sunday, February 12, 1809, the couple's second child was born. They christened him Abraham, in honor of his murdered grandfather. Infant Abraham and sister Sarah would have scant memories of their Kentucky home, because questionable land titles and poor soils soon forced their

Abraham Lincoln (New York: Alfred A. Knopf, 1998), 27.
   26. Tarbell and Davis, *Early Life of Lincoln*, 40.
   27. E. R. Burba to William H. Herndon, May 25, 1866, in *Herndon's Informants*, 257.
   28. Tarbell and Davis, *Early Life of Lincoln*, 42.

father to look elsewhere to raise his family. In 1811, the family relocated eight miles to the northeast, along Knob Creek.

Knob Creek drained a more rugged landscape than Nolin Creek, one punctuated by a series of wooded "knobs" rising with forty-degree slopes to summits over 200 feet above the streambed. Lincoln's cousin described the countryside as

> knotty—knobby as a piece of land could be . . . tall & peaky hills [that] Stood up against the sky all around . . . with deep hollows—ravines [covered with] cedar trees . . . as thick as trees could grow . . .[29]

Through this narrow valley ran the Old Cumberland Trail, which connected Bardstown, Kentucky, with Nashville, Tennessee.[30] Among these "high hills and deep gorges," as Lincoln described the landscape, lay a slightly broader bottomland—a hollow—in which a nameless stream joined Knob Creek. Upon three fertile fields covering 228 acres near this confluence, the Lincoln family settled.[31]

"My earliest recollection," wrote Lincoln later in life, "is of the Knob Creek place."[32] As a toddler he imbibed Knob Creek's waters, bathed in its pools, caught its creatures, and played in its bed. His grieving mother might have washed in its current the lifeless body of Abe's baby brother Thomas, who lived but days beyond his birth in 1812 and lies today in the Redmon family cemetery on a nearby hillside. Knob Creek once nearly claimed Abe's life: he and playmate Austin Gollaher were chasing partridges when Abe, probably around six, slipped on a log and plunged in the creek's rain-swollen waters. Austin pulled him ashore and shook the gasping child until Knob Creek water spilled from his mouth and breathing resumed. "I would rather see [Austin] that any man living," Lincoln would say during his presidency.[33]

29. Interview, Dennis F. Hanks, by William H. Herndon, June 13, 1865, in *Herndon's Informants*, 38.

30. Lincoln later wrote, "[we] resided on Knob-creek, on the road from Bardstown Ky. to Nashville Tenn. at a point three, or three and a half miles South or South-West of Atherton's ferry on the Rolling Fork." Abraham Lincoln, "Autobiography Written for John L. Scripps," June 1860, *Collected Works*, 4:61.

31. Wayne Whipple, *The Story of Young Abraham Lincoln* (Philadelphia: Henry Altemus Company, 1915), 34.

32. Abraham Lincoln to Samuel Haycraft, June 4, 1860, in *Collected Works*, 4:70; Warren, *Lincoln's Youth*, 11.

33. Recollection of Austin Gollaher, as quoted in Tarbell and Davis, *Early Life of Lincoln*, 43–44. The latter quote appears on the historic sign entitled "Lincoln's Playmate,"

"The place on Knob Creek," wrote Lincoln later in life, "I remember very well. . . ." Here Sarah and Abe learned the alphabet from their mother, and attended a nearby "subscription school" for their first lessons.[34] The region's rugged topography once taught Abe a lesson in hydrology. "Sometimes when there came a big rain in the hills," he reminisced,

> the water would come down through the gorges and spread all over the farm. [Once, we] planted the corn in what we called the big field—it contained seven acres—and I dropped [two] pumpkin seeds [in] every other hill and every other row. The next Sunday morning there came a big rain in the hills. It did not rain a drop in the valley, but the water coming down through the gorges washed ground, corn, pumpkin seeds and all clear off the field.[35]

Past the Lincoln homestead, the creek flowed out of the hills and into the flatlands of the Rolling Fork. Atherton's Ferry, three miles northeast of the homestead, allowed travelers to cross that stream. Its waters thence joined the Salt River, which emptied into the Ohio River; 300 miles downstream, they joined the Mississippi, and 1,300 miles later, intermixed with the sea.[36] Economy, society, and life in whole—among the wooded hollows of the Lincoln homestead and throughout the region—flowed upon those streams and rivers, or arose on account of them. Towns and villages formed where rivers merged, disembogued, or impeded travel. Atherton's Ferry, for example, gained the name Athertonville on account of the people who needed to cross the Rolling Fork there. The confluence of the Salt River with the Ohio River became West Point, where Thomas Lincoln set out on a flatboat for New Orleans. The rocks impeding navigation in the Ohio gave rise to the city of Louisville. Waterways, quite simply, constituted the basic infrastructure of the trans-Appalachian West.

Rivers, roads, towns, ferries, mills, and springs exposed the Lincolns to the new American society constituting itself in the space of displaced natives and felled forests. Peopled disproportionately by Virginians, it was

marking Gollaher's grave in the Pleasant Grove Baptist Church Cemetery near Knob Creek in Kentucky.

34. Abraham Lincoln to Samuel Haycraft, June 4, 1860, in *Collected Works*, 4:70; Warren, *Lincoln's Youth*, 11.

35. As recollected by J. J. Wright in a conversation with Lincoln on June 5, 1864, in Fehrenbacher and Fehrenbacher, *Recollected Words of Lincoln*, 508.

36. Ward H. Lamon, *The Life of Abraham Lincoln, From His Birth to His Inauguration as President* (Boston: James R. Osgood and Company, 1872), 14.

a decidedly Southern society: the four counties surrounding the Lincoln homestead contained more than 41,000 residents in 1810, of whom more than one in six was enslaved. Their own county of Hardin was home to 1,007 slaves, compared to 1,627 adult white males.[37] Travelers, oftentimes with a coffle of slaves in tow, passed regularly in front of the Lincoln cabin trekking the Old Cumberland Trail. The sight troubled Thomas Lincoln and more than a few of his neighbors, for while most were culturally Southern, they generally thought of themselves as Westerners and debated slavery rigorously. In 1808, for example, the South Fork Baptist Church, located two miles from Sinking Spring, saw fifteen members depart "on account of slavery." Ill feelings among the congregants forced the church to close in 1809, when Abe was born. The Lincolns themselves joined the Separate Baptist congregation of the Little Mount Church, in which antislavery sentiment prevailed.[38]

Legal problems added to Thomas' disenchantment with Kentucky. Every additional settler made Kentucky less a frontier and more a structured and regulated society. The land claims of the pioneer era, based on irregular metes-and-bounds surveys in the British tradition, became by the early 1800s increasingly overlapping, confusing, and legally contested. Unclear title to the Sinking Spring farm pushed Thomas to move his family to Knob Creek in 1811, but a lawsuit over the matter persisted in 1813—only to be followed two years later by another legal dispute regarding the Knob Creek property. Eight years struggling with contested land titles had reduced Thomas' total claim of 816 acres to a mere 200 acres, which he later had to sell at a loss for the same reason.[39]

Exasperated, Thomas Lincoln cast his eyes across the Ohio River Valley. Anglo-Americans began arriving into those Indiana Territory lands only recently, following the defeat of the British in the War of 1812 and the forced exile of their Native American allies farther westward. The federal government encouraged the trend: President Madison on May 1, 1816, announced that Indiana Territory lands would be sold to the highest bidder. Better yet, from Thomas Lincoln's perspective, those lands were surveyed systematically according to the Land Ordinance of 1785, and owners were said to be titled clearly. Adding to Indiana's appeal was

37. Computed by author based on county-level populations from the U.S. Census of 1810, as digitized by the National Historical Geographic Information System of the University of Minnesota.

38. Warren, *Lincoln's Youth*, 13.

39. Louis A. Warren, *Lincoln's Parentage and Childhood* (New York and London: Century Company, 1926), 110–21, and *Lincoln's Youth*, 13.

the Ordinance of 1787, which expressly forbade slavery and involuntary servitude in the Northwest Territory. Word that the region would soon join the Union as a free state confirmed the conventional wisdom that slavery would never cross the Ohio. Many other Kentuckians and west-ward-bound Americans eyed the Indiana side of the Ohio River Valley for settlement in the 1810s; the Lincolns' experience, once again, followed larger trends.[40]

•

Setting out in 1816 to investigate Indiana, Thomas Lincoln built a crude flatboat on the Rolling Fork and floated down the Salt and Ohio rivers. The great artery proved too much for the improvised raft, capsizing it and costing him some possessions.[41] Upon landing at Thompson's Ferry (a hundred miles downriver, where Anderson Creek meets the Ohio near present-day Troy), he ventured sixteen miles inland and identified a par-cel of forest at the confluence of Little Pigeon and Big Pigeon creeks, in the Hurricane Township of Perry County near Gentryville. He prompt-ly erected a temporary "half-faced camp" of unhewn logs, fourteen feet square and open on one side. The land demarcated but not yet legally his, Thomas then trekked back to Kentucky to retrieve Nancy, Sarah, and Abe. Given his recent river experience, he decided to lead the family by horse-and-wagon to the new site. Only critical, costly, or dear possessions were packed up; rustic furniture was more easily built anew than trans-ported. The nearly-two-week trip over a hundred terrestrial miles gave young Abe his first view of a great river, the Ohio, and his first trip across it, on Hugh Thompson's ferry.[42] Once in Indiana, the journey became downright arduous, at some points requiring trees to be felled one by one for the party to advance. Finally they arrived at their homestead.

Lincoln later explained his father's decision to leave Kentucky: "[We]

40. Joseph H. Barrett, *Life of Abraham Lincoln, Presenting His Early History, Political Career, and Speeches* (New York: Moore, Wilstach & Baldwin, 1865), 22–24; Warren, *Lincoln's Youth*, 13–15.

41. One historian questioned this generally accepted story and suggested Thomas Lincoln took a land route on this prospecting trip. R. Gerald McMurtry, "The Lincoln Migration from Kentucky to Indiana," *Indiana Magazine of History* 33, no. 4 (December 1937): 388–91.

42. Josiah Gilbert Holland, *The Life of Abraham Lincoln* (Springfield, MA: Gurdon Bill, 1866), 25–26; Whipple, *Story of Young Lincoln*, 37–39; William H. Herndon and Jesse William Weik, *Herndon's Lincoln: The True Story of a Great Life* (Chicago, New York, and San Francisco: Belford, Clarke & Company, 1889), 1:20.

removed to what is now Spencer county Indiana, in the autumn of 1816 . . . partly on account of slavery; but chiefly on account of the difficulty in land titles in Ky."[43] Biographer William Dean Howells offered a more verbose version of Lincoln's characteristically succinct explanation, but because Lincoln hand-edited Howells' work and let his words stand unedited, they are worth quoting:

> Already the evil influences of slavery were beginning to be felt by the poor and the non-slaveholders. But the emigration of Thomas Lincoln is, we believe, to be chiefly attributed to the insecurity of the right by which he held his Kentucky land; for, in those days, land-titles were rather more uncertain than other human affairs.[44]

A twentieth-century historian interpreted three additional factors at work in Thomas Lincoln's decision: the migratory tendencies of his ancestors, the influence of distant kin who previously made the move across the Ohio, and the opportunity presented by the opening of the Indiana Territory.[45]

Indiana's side of the Ohio River Valley exhibited a similar topography, ecology, and climate as the Kentucky side. But it was less populated and more wild, as Lincoln himself recalled poetically years later: "When first my father settled here, 'Twas then the frontier line, The panther's scream, filled the night with fear, And bears preyed on the swine. . . ."[46] Lincoln's less-lyrical cousin Dennis Hanks described circa-1816 southern Indiana in his orthographically rustic vernacular:

> I will jest Say to you that it was the Brushes [brushiest] Cun try that I have Ever Seen . . . all Kinds of undergroth Spice wo[o]d Wild privy Shewmake Dogwood grape vines matted to Geather So that as the old Saying gowes you could Drive a Butcher Knife up to the Handle in it[.] Bares and wile Cats Deer turkeys Squirls Rabits &c[.][47]

43. Lincoln, "Autobiography," June 1860, in *Collected Works*, 4:61–62.

44. William Dean Howells, *Life of Abraham Lincoln*, facsimile edition of campaign biography corrected by the hand of Abraham Lincoln (Bloomington: Indiana University Press, 1960), 21.

45. Louis A. Warren, ed., "Factors Contributing to the 1816 Lincoln Migration," *Lincoln Lore: Bulletin of the Lincoln National Life Foundation*, no. 657 (November 10, 1941).

46. Lincoln, in *Collected Works*, 1:386.

47. Dennis F. Hanks to William H. Herndon, March 22, 1866, in *Herndon's Informants*, 235.

Indiana joined the Union only a few weeks after the Lincolns' autumn 1816 arrival, as a free state despite its decidedly Kentuckian cultural influence, and as the first new state since Louisiana in 1812. The nineteenth state benefitted from the orthogonal American Public Land Survey, a cadastral system far superior to the old English metes-and-bounds method that had long "cursed" eastern and central Kentucky "with defective land titles."[48] Demographically, Indiana counted far fewer blacks than Kentucky: only five African Americans lived in the Lincolns' Spencer County in 1820, compared to 1,877 whites, whereas their old Kentucky county of Hardin contained 1,489 blacks and 9,009 whites.[49] If Thomas Lincoln indeed migrated to Indiana to flee insecure titles and slavery, he acted wisely on both accounts. Indiana's ruling a few years later to declare all substantial waterways as "public highways," and fine those who obstructed them, made the move an even better decision, as it fostered flatboat commerce with New Orleans—a key element to economic development.[50]

Father and son proceeded to clear the landscape of "walnut, beech, oak, elm, maple, and an undergrowth of dog-wood, sumac, and wild grapevine," which abounded in "bear, deer, turkey, and other wild game." Old friends and kin from Kentucky joined the family, assisting with chores and enabling the Lincolns to build a larger cabin of hewn logs. Lincoln later insinuated that the new cabin was finished and occupied "a few days before the completion of [my] eighth year," early February 1817.[51] In October of that year Thomas ventured to the Land Office in Vincennes to begin payment on his quarter-section (160-acre) claim—the southwestern quadrant of Section 32, Township 4, south of Range 5 West—under the so-called two-dollar-an-acre law. On that title-secured land, the extended Lincoln clan would plant corn and wheat; raise hogs, sheep, and cattle; and hunt game at the numerous salt-licks.[52]

Abe would spend the balance of his boyhood at this Indiana home-

48. Holland, *Life of Abraham Lincoln*, 25. The two differing surveying systems affect the landscape to this day, with Indiana exhibiting more orthogonal lines in its county boundaries and land parcels, and Kentucky having more convoluted delineations.

49. Computed by author based on county-level populations from the U.S. Census of 1820, as digitized by the National Historical Geographic Information System of the University of Minnesota.

50. "William P. Dole: Wabash Valley Merchant and Flatboatman," ed. Donald F. Carmony, *Indiana Magazine of History* 67, no. 4 (December 1971): 335.

51. Lincoln, "Autobiography," June 1860, in *Collected Works*, 4:62; Warren, *Lincoln's Youth*, 21–23.

52. Herndon and Weik, *Herndon's Lincoln*, 1:21–22; Carl Sandburg, *Abraham Lincoln: The Prairie Years and The War Years* (New York: Dell Publishing Company, 1954), 32.

stead. "There was an unbroken wilderness there then," he would tell an audience in 1859, "and [there] an axe was put in [my] hand; and with the trees and logs and grubs [I] fought until [my] twentieth year. . . ."[53] A cousin recalled how, in the soils of his father's farm, Abe "and I worked bare footed—grubbed it—plowed—mowed & cradled together—plowed Corn—gathered it & schucked Corn. . . ."[54] Farm work, school, chores, play, and worship filled his boyhood days, while fireside stories rounded out his nights—stories told by Thomas and other elders, usually of Native Americans, of pirates, of hunting exploits and animal attacks, of frontier times.[55] Surely Thomas talked of his 1806 flatboat trip to New Orleans, which marked his only visit to a major city and the apogee of his life's travels.

In Indiana, too, Abe "grew up to his present enormous height" of six feet and four inches, a stature reached by his late teens and manifested disproportionately in his legs.[56] A later account helped establish into American cultural memory the iconic physicality of Lincoln—the ill-fitting cotton osnaburg shirt, the famous ax, the strength, the stoic determination—at this stage of life:

> He learned to use the ax and to hold the plough. He became inured to all the duties of seed-time and harvest. [He drove] his father's team in the field, or from the woods with a heavy draught, or on the rough path to the mill, the store, or the river landing. He was specially . . . adept at felling trees, and acquired a muscular strength in which he was equaled by few. . . .
>
> A vigorous constitution, and a cheerful, unrepining disposition [allowed him] to derive enjoyment from the severest lot. The "dignity of labor," which is with demagogues mere hollow cant, became to him a true and appreciable reality.[57]

Abe in these years began to exhibit an intrinsic intellectual nature set against his rustic backwoods nurturing. Rustic indeed: "There were some schools, so called," he acknowledged, "but no qualification was ever re-

---

53. Abraham Lincoln, "Speech at Indianapolis, Indiana, September 19, 1859," in *Collected Works*, 3:463.

54. Interview, John Hanks, by William H. Herndon, 1865–1866, in *Herndon's Informants*, 455.

55. Warren, *Lincoln's Youth*, 34–41.

56. Lincoln, "Speech at Indianapolis," in *Collected Works*, 3:463.

57. Joseph H. Barrett, *Life of Abraham Lincoln, Presenting His Early History, Political Career, and Speeches* (New York: Moore, Wilstach & Baldwin, 1865), 24–25.

quired of a teacher. . . . There was absolutely nothing to excite ambition for education. . . . If a straggler supposed to understand latin, happened to sojourn in the neighborhood, he was looked upon as a wizzard."[58] Abe himself gained admiration for his early mastery of reading and writing, skills he gained in Kentucky and refined in Indiana. He became the town scribe—"the best penman in the Neighborhood."[59] Wrote one biographer, "[l]etter writing by an adult living on the frontier was an accomplishment, but for a lad of seven years almost unbelievable. . . . [what] psychologists would call a gifted child."[60] The lad also harbored a sensitivity to all living things that defies the stereotype of backwoods Westerners of this era. One might suppose, for example, that his recollection of shooting a wild turkey through a crack in the cabin wall might serve to showcase his cleverness and marksmanship. Quite the opposite: apparently troubled by the creature's violent demise, Abe "never since pulled a finger on any larger game."[61] People close to Abe later recalled how he "preached against Cruelty to animals, Contending that an ants life was to it, as sweet as ours to us. . . ."[62] He was deemed sufficiently responsible at age fourteen to be appointed sexton for the Little Pigeon Church, where his father served as trustee and his family worshipped on the Sabbath.[63]

Inquisitive and thoughtful, Abe hungered for information on the world he did not know and sought explanation for the world he did. He exploited his rudimentary "ABC school" education to the fullest by mastering *"readin, writin, and cipherin, to the Rule of Three,"* and "read Every book he could lay his hands on—Mastered it," as one neighbor put it.[64] His reading formed something of a nightly after-work ritual, as one cousin recalled: "he would go to the Cupboard—Snatch a piece of Corn bread—take down a book—Sit down on a chair—Cock his legs up as high as his head and read. . . ."[65] He read *Robinson Crusoe*, whose themes of long trips,

58. Lincoln to Fell, December 20, 1859, in *Collected Works*, 3:511.

59. Statement, Joseph C. Richardson, for William H. Herndon, 1865–1866, in *Herndon's Informants*, 473.

60. Warren, *Lincoln's Youth*, 25.

61. Lincoln, "Autobiography," June 1860, in *Collected Works*, 4:62.

62. Interview, Matilda Johnston Moore, by William H. Herndon, September 8, 1865, in *Herndon's Informants*, 109.

63. Warren, *Lincoln's Youth*, 121–22.

64. Interview, John S. Hougland, by William H. Herndon, September 17, 1865, in *Herndon's Informants*, 130; Lincoln to Fell, December 20, 1859, in *Collected Works*, 3:511.

65. Interview, John Hanks, by William H. Herndon, 1865–1866, in *Herndon's Informants*, 455.

great rivers, natives, and exotic destinations were not altogether alien to Western experiences. His repeated readings of *Aesop's Fables* may have inculcated in his mind the lesson, "A kingdom divided against itself cannot stand."[66] Another favorite book was *The Arabian Nights*, which Abe "lay on his stummick by the fire, and read out loud" to his kin. (Apparently unfamiliar with the basic premise of literary fiction, one of Abe's listeners dismissed the book as "a pack of lies." "Mighty fine lies," Abe responded.[67]) Reading William Grimshaw's 1821 *History of the United States*, which climaxes with the 1815 American rout of the British at Chalmette, presented Abe with details about New Orleans and Louisiana (probably for the first time), as well as on fellow Westerner and future president Maj. Gen. Andrew Jackson.[68] His reading of M. L. Weems' *Life of George Washington* so impressed the twelve-year-old that, forty years later, he recounted its impact on him passionately to an audience of senators.[69] Indiana would also provide the bulk of Abe's schoolhouse education, which totaled five terms between Kentucky and Indiana (one aggregate year, typical for a boy in that era). "I have not been to school since," wrote Lincoln in 1859; "The little advance I now have [regarding] education, I have picked up from time to time under the pressure of necessity."[70]

Abe's mental acumen by all accounts matched his social and physical vigor, a pairing one admirer described as "a profound correspondence between his peculiar genius and the pioneer culture in which he grew."[71] Every inquisitive moment was matched with an impish one; every thoughtful interlude, a funny one; every display of honesty and ethics, one of mischief and prank. Among the twenty tattered scraps of his Indiana school notebook—the earliest surviving documents penned in Lincoln's own hand—are the playful verses of a daydreaming schoolboy:

> Abraham Lincoln is my nam[e]
> And with my pen I wrote the same

66. As quoted by Donald, *Lincoln*, 31.

67. Warren, *Lincoln's Youth*, 68–70.

68. F. Lauriston Bullard, "Abe Goes Down the River," *Lincoln Herald: A Magazine of Education and Lincolniana* 50, no. 1 (February 1948): 2; William Grimshaw, *History of the United States: From Their First Settlement as Colonies* . . . (Philadelphia: Benjamin Warner, 1821), 255–59.

69. "Story of Lincoln's Struggles as a Boy in Indiana and How He Developed Himself," *Philadelphia Inquirer*, February 28, 1909, p. 11, c. 5.

70. Lincoln to Fell, December 20, 1859, in *Collected Works*, 3:511; Warren, *Lincoln's Youth*, 136.

71. Arnold Gesell, "Introduction," in Warren's *Lincoln's Youth*, xxi.

> I wrote in both hast[e] and speed
> and left it here for fools to read[72]

Many biographers trace Lincoln's later greatness to these seemingly hal-
cyon Indiana years, when the lad first began to rise above (figuratively
and literally) his humble surroundings. But, of course, communities of
all types throughout history have spawned their share of gifted scions
and sent them off into the world. Most end up leading the decent and
productive lives of ordinary people; a precious few, like Lincoln, achieve
immortality. To read future greatness into young Abe's boyhood vignettes
is to ignore the multitudes of similar moments experienced by nameless
counterparts elsewhere. Abe Lincoln indeed started in Indiana to distinguish himself from his cohort, but *normal* would more adequately describe
the individual for many years to come.

    To construe the Indiana years as "halcyon" is also somewhat selec-
tive. They brought nearly as much tragedy as joy. Two kinfolk died in
1818 of milk sickness, the mysterious trans-Appalachian plague caused
by imbibing the milk of cows that ingested the toxin tremetol from white
snakeroot plants. Their deaths left the orphaned teenager Dennis Hanks
in the care of the Lincolns. Shortly thereafter, on October 5, 1818, Abe's
own mother succumbed to the same poisoning. Nine-year-old Abe helped
build her coffin and bury her in the Indiana earth. From a family that
once numbered five, only three Lincolns survived—and that number
nearly dropped to two when, in 1819, Abe himself, in his own words,
"was kicked by a horse, and apparently killed for a time."[73]

    Now a widower with children to raise, Thomas allowed one difficult
year to pass before trekking to Elizabethtown, Kentucky, to approach an
old family friend, Sarah ("Sally") Bush Johnston, about the prospect of
marriage. That Sally was the sister of Isaac Bush, Thomas' crewmate during his 1806 journey to New Orleans, illustrates how flatboat trips served
to forge social bonds. Sally, like Thomas, had also recently lost her spouse,
and found herself alone with three young children. Matrimony in this
era reflecting more pragmatism than romance, it would not have been
viewed as brash or presumptuous for a widower in Thomas' situation to
propose to an old friend's widowed sister in equally dire straits. Realizing
the union was in everyone's best interest, thirty-one-year-old Sally agreed,

---

72. Lincoln, in *Collected Works*, 1:1.
73. Lincoln, "Autobiography," June 1860, in *Collected Works*, 4:62; Warren, *Lincoln's Youth*, 53–55.

on December 2, 1819, to marry Thomas and raise their children together. The five then set out for the Indiana homestead to unite with Sarah and Abe, plus their recently orphaned cousin Dennis Hanks, who was already sharing the cabin.

It must have been a strange experience for Thomas to remarry in the same place and replicate his 1816 Kentucky-to-Indiana migration with an entirely new family. Upon arrival at Pigeon Creek, the Lincoln household, previously numbering three, suddenly grew to eight. Three boys (twenty-one-year-old Dennis Hanks, eleven-year-old Abe, and ten-year-old John D. Johnston), three girls (thirteen-year-old Sarah Elizabeth Johnston, twelve-year-old Sarah Lincoln, and ten-year-old Matilda Johnston), and parents Sally and Thomas, aged thirty-two and forty-two, all squeezed into a tiny one-room log cabin.[74]

So too grew Indiana's side of the Ohio River Valley. The isolated Pigeon Creek area, nearly empty even of Native Americans at the dawn of the century, gained by 1820 fifteen families with eighty-three children living within two miles of the Lincolns. Population density measured around three families per square mile in the 1820s and increased steadily. Near the Lincolns were the Carters, the Gentrys, the Wrights, the Whitmans, the Grigsbys, the Hardins, and the Crawfords, among others. Most, like them, were Anglo-Saxon Baptists recently emigrated from Kentucky and engaged primarily in farming.[75] More people meant more social, economic, and administrative interaction, more visiting and traveling, and better transportation infrastructure. Trails multiplied and widened into roads, one of which connected the Lincoln homestead with the river port of Evansville. Ferries commenced operation wherever roads met rivers, and often spawned spontaneous settlements that grew into towns. Stage lines began operating on main arteries by the 1820s. Presses started cranking out newspapers—sixteen were published in Indiana in the 1820s—and mail flowed to and from a network of post offices.[76] Roads led southward to the river towns of Rockport and Troy, where Anderson Creek discharged into the Ohio and revolutionary new vessels powered by steam occasionally stopped. The seething, smoking contraptions delivered merchandise, carried off cargo, and brought visitors, including prominent men such as the Marquis de Lafayette during his celebrated 1825 tour of

74. Warren, *Lincoln's Youth*, 71.
75. Ibid., 98–102.
76. "Lincoln's Struggles as a Boy," *Philadelphia Inquirer*, February 28, 1909, p. 11; Warren, *Lincoln's Youth*, 168.

the Western states. At the mouth of Anderson Creek "the Lincolns are frequently found during this period," and "on this great highway"—the Ohio River—"Lincoln came in touch with the outside world."[77]

•

There on the banks of the Ohio, Abe began to show the initiative and independence that comes with maturation. Skilled in axing down and splitting trees, and aware that steamboats required a steady diet of cordwood to keep their boilers hot, Abe and two others set out in August 1826 chopping wood and exchanging it for merchandise. The enterprise exposed him to the world of river travel, craft, and culture, and their associated opportunities and characters. Here began Abraham Lincoln's "river years," an era that would last less than a decade but deeply influence the rest of his life. The Ohio River brought to Abe's attention stories and ephemera from what one historian described as that "strange and exotic city at the mouth of the Mississippi." It also brought him to the attention of James Taylor, owner of a packinghouse and ferry in nearby Troy. Taylor hired Abe at six dollars a month to operate a ferry across the Ohio, a job that required the seventeen-year-old to board with the Taylor family. During this employment, which lasted six to nine months, Abe also plowed land, ground corn, and slaughtered hogs.[78] For the first time in Abe's life, home and kin lay behind him and the rest of the world stood in front of him. Wrote Carl Sandburg of Lincoln's Ohio River employ,

> [h]ere Abe saw steamboats, strings of flatboats loaded with farm produce, other boats with cargoes from manufacturing centers[,] [h]ouseboats, arks, sleds, flatboats with small cabins in which families . . . floated toward their new homesteads. . . . Here was the life flow of a main artery of American civilization, at a vivid time of growth.[79]

Taylor's packinghouse stocked pork, beef, venison, bear and other meats for export to New Orleans, and exposed Abe to the flatboat trade.[80] The environment inspired him to try his budding carpentry skills by building

77. John E. Iglehart, "The Coming of the English to Indiana in 1817 and Their Neighbors," *Indiana Magazine of History* 15, no. 2 (June 1919): 142; J. Edward Murr, "Lincoln in Indiana," *Indiana Magazine of History* 14, no. 1 (March 1918): 148.

78. Interview, Green B. Taylor, by William H. Herndon, September 16, 1865, in *Herndon's Informants*, 129–130; Warren, *Lincoln's Youth*, 144–145, 175.

79. Sandburg, *Prairie Years and The War Years*, 45.

80. Warren, *Lincoln's Youth*, 147.

a boat of his own. Lincoln later recounted to his presidential cabinet a memory from these Ohio River days:

> I was standing at the steamboat landing contemplating my new boat, and wondering how I might improve it, when a steamer approached coming down the river. At the same time two passengers . . . wished to be taken out to the packet with their luggage. They looked among the boats, singled out mine, and asked me to scull them to the boat. Sometime prior to this I had constructed a small boat in which I planned to carry some produce South which had been gathered chiefly by my own exertions. We were poor, and in them days people down South who did not own slaves were reckoned as scrubs. When I was requested to scull these men out to the steamer, I gladly did so, and after seeing them and their trunks on board, and the steamer making ready to pass on, I called out to the men: "You have forgotten to pay me." They at once each threw a half dollar in the bottom of the boat in which I was standing.
>
> You gentlemen may think it was a very small matter, and in the light of things now transpiring it was, but I assure you it was one of the most important incidents in my life. I could scarcely believe my eyes. It was difficult for me to realize that I, a poor boy, had earned a dollar in less than a day. The world seemed wider and fairer before me. I was a more hopeful and confident being from that time.[81]

Various versions of the "first dollar" story appear in the literature, because Lincoln told the anecdote to a group and individuals remembered it differently. All relate the same basic story of the money earned, but differ on important river-related details, as shown in this excerpted version:

> . . . I was about eighteen years of age. I belonged, you know, to what they call down South, the 'scrubs;' people who do not own slaves are nobody there. But we had succeeded in raising, chiefly by my labor, sufficient produce, as I thought, to justify me in taking it down the river to sell. After much persuasion, I got the consent of mother to go, and constructed a little flatboat, large enough to take a barrel or two of things, that we had gathered, with myself and little bundle, down to New Orleans. A steamer was coming down the river. . . .[82]

81. As quoted by Murr, "Lincoln in Indiana," 149.
82. Henry J. Raymond, *The Life and Public Services of Abraham Lincoln . . . Together with*

This version later reads, "I was contemplating my new flatboat, and wondering whether I could make it stronger or improve it in any particular way. . . ."

A third version, heard by engineer and Civil War officer Egbert L. Viele during an 1862 outing with Lincoln, has eighteen-year-old Abe hitching a ride on another man's flatboat to sell whiskey and tobacco in New Orleans. While tied up one evening, Lincoln negotiated passage to transport two men on the bank to intercept and board a mid-stream steamboat, thus making his first dollar. While Viele's retelling imparts interesting detail about the flatboat experience (and seems to imply that Lincoln made it all the way to New Orleans), it ranks as the least reliable of the "first dollar" stories because it contradicts Lincoln's own flatboat memories on numerous levels, and erroneously has Lincoln "living in Kentucky" at the time.[83]

At the risk of reading too much into a second-hand account of a nearly-forty-year-old memory, the "first dollar" recollection sheds light on young Lincoln's relationship with rivers. We learn that the teenager engaged in flatboat-building, on a crude and small scale but with a desire to improve his design. He probably learned carpentry at home, having "inherited from his father . . . some skill in the use of tools [to build] a flat-bottomed rowboat. . . ."[84] We also hear for the first time Lincoln's vision to "carry some produce South," specifically to New Orleans, an experience also shared by his father. (Note, however, that Abe, according to the above version, sought approval from his mother for said journey.) Abe's claim that the produce "had been gathered chiefly by my own exertions," or alternately "raised, chiefly by my labor," leaves open whether he himself cultivated such a load—a rather Herculean task—or merely collected it from other farmers. We also hear sensitivity about his family's humble circumstances relative to the ample wherewithal of slave owners. It is curious that Lincoln seemed to cast his environment as the slaveholding South, even though he had lived in free Indiana for eight years by this time. Finally, the weight Lincoln ascribes to the memory of his first

His State Papers . . . (New York: Derby and Miller, 1865), 754.

83. As recollected by Egbert L. Viele, in Fehrenbacher and Fehrenbacher, *Recollected Words of Lincoln*, 453–454. Viele recounted a similar version of this story in a *New York Tribune* editorial picked up by a Massachusetts paper; see "Lincoln Not a Flatboatman: His Trip Down the Mississippi to New Orleans to Sell a Barrel of Whiskey and a Case of Tobacco," *Springfield Republication*, March 12, 1895, p. 12.

84. William E. Barton, "The Girl Across the River: Lincoln's Friend at Court," *Dearborn Independent*, January 8, 1927, 21.

dollar earned ("I assure you it was one of the most important incidents in my life") provides insight as to what he considered to be the formative moments of his youth.

The anecdote also speaks to the important role New Orleans played vicariously in the economies of Ohio River Valley communities. As distant and foreign as it may have been, the great Southern metropolis was nevertheless inextricably linked with places such as bucolic Spencer County, serving as a destination for most exports and a source of many imports and currency. "When [Indiana] pioneers spoke of 'going to town,' they meant to New Orleans," recalled one veteran of the era;

> Not a few of our early statesmen came here from Louisiana, and much early business was transacted at New Orleans. It was our early market, and thereby much Mexican silver was brought to Indiana. Strange as it may seem, the Mexican dollar constituted the larger part of the coin of the pioneers. . . .[85]

Culture traveled with economy, in both directions. Said one aging Hoosier, "I can remember the flatboats that went from here with produce to 'Orleans.'" When one particular flatboatman returned to Indiana, "he brought with him the first oranges and cocoanuts that ever came to Indianapolis. . . . [O]n his return from 'Orleans' he took delight in |showing| little children . . . his stock of tropical fruits and to gladden their child-hearts with presents."[86]

Lincoln's circa-1826 encounters with the world of rivers and flatboats may explain an interesting but almost certainly apocryphal story contending that the seventeen-year-old actually carried out the envisioned voyage down the Mississippi at that time. Indiana researcher J. Edward Murr first heard it from William Forsythe and Jefferson Ray Jr. in an 1892 interview.[87] Forsythe, in his elder years, recalled that Abe, having recently harvested and cured two hogsheads of tobacco, negotiated with a flatboat-builder named Jefferson Ray (father of the 1892 informant) to help him "at the oar" if Ray carried his load to New Orleans and paid Abe the difference. Some residents, including Ray's son and at least one contemporary historian, reported with confidence that the ensuing journey constituted

85. George R. Wilson, "George H. Proffit: His Day and Generation," *Indiana Magazine of History* 18, no. 1 (March 1922): 37.

86. Calvin Fletcher, "Early Indianapolis: The Fletcher Papers—Third Installment," *Indiana Magazine of History* 2, no. 1 (March 1906): 130.

87. Francis Marion Van Natter, *Lincoln's Boyhood: A Chronicle of His Indiana Years* (Washington, D.C.: Public Affairs Press, 1963), 198, footnote #15 to Chapter 4.

Lincoln's first flatboat voyage to New Orleans, two years prior to that which is almost universally accepted.[88] In another version, expounded by Indiana researcher Francis Marion Van Natter, their destination is Memphis.[89] That nascent Tennessee city, however, comprised all of a few dozen houses and a hundred or so residents in 1826, an unlikely target for a long-distance delivery of a crop that could be grown locally. No other evidence corroborates the 1826 story; Forsythe and Ray themselves are the sole sources. Lincoln himself contradicted it when he stated that he was "nineteen [when] he made his first trip upon a flat-boat to New-Orleans," clearly implying it occurred in 1828 and not 1826.[90] Surely Lincoln would have made some reference to an 1826 voyage to Memphis or New Orleans as his "first trip upon a flat-boat," if in fact it happened. Forsythe's recollection may simply reflect an elderly man confusing countless flatboat comings-and-goings with the hazy memories of that one particular summer, when the future president tinkered and toiled at the Troy ferry.

The memory of another river experience in this era, related by distant relative Augustus H. Chapman in 1865, appears at first to be more convincing. "In the year 1827," Chapman wrote,

> A Lincoln & h[is] Step Brother John D Johnston went together to Louisvill Ky to try & get work & earn some money, th[e]y obtained work on their arrivall there on the Louisvill & Portland Canall & when through working there were paid off in silver Dollars. This is the first silver dollars Lincoln ever had or owned of his own & of it he was very proud.[91]

Did Lincoln indeed help dig the Louisville and Portland Canal? What weakens Chapman's otherwise confident recollection is that no other source corroborates this rather major experience for a young country boy on the brink of adulthood. The job would have represented his farthest trip from home (125 river miles), longest time away from family, largest town visited (Louisville), possibly his first lengthy steamboat ride, and first role in a nationally significant project: the circumventing of the Great Falls of the Ohio, which is what the Louisville and Portland Canal even-

---

88. Murr, "Lincoln in Indiana," 18–19.

89. Van Natter, *Lincoln's Boyhood*, 46–48. See also J. Edward Murr, "Life of Abraham Lincoln," as excerpted by Bess V. Ehrmann, *The Missing Chapter in the Life of Abraham Lincoln* (Chicago: Walter M. Hill, 1938), 86. In this source, Murr acknowledges that his hypothesis "has received no credence and has been disallowed. . . ."

90. Lincoln, "Autobiography," June 1860, in *Collected Works*, 62.

91. Chapman to Herndon, September 8, 1865, in *Herndon's Informants*, 100–101.

tually accomplished. So why did Lincoln himself never mention the experience, particularly during the many speeches he would deliver on internal improvements? That the recollection ends on a "first dollar" note invites suspicion that Chapman may have confused parts of Lincoln's own "first dollar" story.

One might surmise that Lincoln's circa-1826–27 river experiences would orient him toward a career as a riverboat clerk or captain.[92] Instead, they gave him his first experience arguing a court case—his own. As recounted earlier, Abraham would occasionally "scull" passengers from the Indiana bank to midstream steamboats. This service earned the reproach of two Kentucky brothers who held licenses to run a ferry service on the other side of the river. One day, they called out to Abe and lured him into paddling over to the Kentucky side, where they confronted him. Barely eschewing fisticuffs, the brothers had Abe arrested and brought to Kentucky court on the charge of operating a ferry without a license. Lincoln argued effectively that while the Kentucky license allowed the Kentuckians to "set passengers across the river" into Indiana, it did not expressly forbid others "to convey a passenger from the Indiana bank to the deck of a passing steamer."[93] Impressed with Abe's honesty and argumentative acumen, the squire dismissed the case.

Lincoln, exhilarated with his newly discovered talent, grew fascinated by legal processes. He attended court in Troy whenever he could and read Indiana legal tomes thoroughly. Troy's post office received a steady stream of regional newspapers, of which "Abe was a Constant reader," recalled his stepmother; "I am sure of this for the years of 1827-28-29-30. The name of the Louisville Journal seems to sound like one. Abe read histories, papers—& other books. . . ."[94] Thus broadened Lincoln's horizons on the banks of the Ohio. Rivers would gainfully employ Abe for the new few years, but the Troy ferry incident would plant in him the seed for a career in law, and later one in politics.

Most accounts of the Lincolns' 1820s domestic life limn an atmosphere of warmth and happiness, despite a houseful of complex and potentially combustible stepfamily relationships. Another Hanks relative, John, added to that mix in 1823, expanding the household to nine members.

92. "When I was a boy," wrote Mark Twain in 1883, "there was but one permanent ambition among my comrades in our village . . . to be a steamboatman." Samuel L. Clemens, *Life on the Mississippi* (New York: Harper & Row, 1958), 28.

93. Barton, "Girl Across the River," *Dearborn Independent,* January 8, 1927, 3–22.

94. Interview, Sarah Bush Lincoln, by William H. Herndon, September 8, 1865, in *Herndon's Informants,* 107.

Villager Aaron Grigsby then joined the family in August 1826 when he married Abe's only surviving full-blood sibling, nineteen-year-old Sarah. The couple moved into their own cabin in anticipation of their firstborn in late 1827.

•

The optimism and hope that came with the new year did not last long. On January 20, 1828, complications at childbirth took the lives of both Sarah and infant. The death of his sister devastated Abraham; the expectant uncle instead became an only child. That Aaron Grigsby, in Lincoln's view, dillydallied instead of seeking medical attention for his wife, spawned a lasting resentment between the two families. A few weeks later Abraham turned nineteen—no longer a child, neither by age nor by the challenges of life. He handled his grief with "periods of depression and despondency," according to one historian.[95] Yet the introspective young man exuded steadfast vigor, trustworthiness, and intelligence. Those qualities brought him to the attention of James Gentry, Pigeon Creek's leading citizen.

James Gentry traced a personal history similar to that of Thomas Lincoln, ten years his senior. Both were born in the South (Lincoln in Virginia, Gentry in North Carolina). Both migrated to Kentucky in their youth and married three years apart (1806 and 1803, respectively). Both moved to Spencer County, Indiana—in 1816 and 1818. Both, like so many young men of the West, had guided flatboats to New Orleans—Thomas at least once, Gentry several times. They differed, however, in matters of finance and ambition. Better off to begin with, James Gentry acquired one thousand acres of land (to Thomas' 160), and soon prospered through farming, a store, and a river landing. The landing operated at the foot of the Ohio River bluffs on which the village of Rockport sat, about seventeen river miles below Troy. Gentry's successes resonated locally, making his clan the community's leading family and inspiring the name of the town. The older children of Gentry's brood of eight, including son Allen, all knew Abe very well; one, Hannah, reputedly had a schoolhouse crush on him.[96] James Gentry is said to have "frequently employed the tall, young Abe to assist him on his farm." Abe, for his part, "was in [the Gentry] home a great part of his youth, [and] could not help but be inspired and helped by the Gentry family, their standards of living, their home comforts and

95. Warren, *Lincoln's Youth*, 174.
96. Ibid., 134, 157.

their conversation."[97] Abe enjoyed lingering at the Gentry Store, which also served as a post office as well as a source of newspapers, political discussion, and civic engagement. The cerebral Abraham found more intellectual stimulation with the Gentrys than the Lincolns—and particularly with James, more so than his father.

Like many storeowners in the region, James Gentry often bartered merchandise in exchange for the agricultural produce of his cash-starved customers. When stockpiles reached a certain level, he arranged a cargo-load to sell in New Orleans for hard currency, usually with the help of his sons. Early in 1828, Gentry decided it was time for such a trip. His son Allen, with one New Orleans voyage already under his belt, would captain the vessel, but he needed a reliable "bow hand—working the foremost oars"[98]—with a hearty constitution and a good head, to join him. Either by his son's suggestion or (more likely) his own judgment, forty-year-old James Gentry offered nineteen-year-old Abraham Lincoln a job to assist twenty-one-year-old Allen Gentry in guiding a flatboat to New Orleans to sell produce, for a salary of "$8.00 per month—from the time of starting to his returning home, [plus the fare for] his way back on a [steam] boat."[99] James might have had a second motive in hiring the level-headed Abe: to keep an eye on Allen.

With the recent memory of his deceased sister and the constant lure of the river, Abe needed little arm twisting to accept. His new job would offer, in the estimation of one historian, "the most exciting and important experience of Abe's Indiana years."[100] The trip, and the destination, would also mark the geographical and cultural apogee of his life, and influence his intellectual fiber in significant ways.

97. Ehrmann, *Missing Chapter*, 6, 20.
98. Interview, Nathaniel Grigsby, by William H. Herndon, September 12, 1865, in *Herndon's Informants*, 114.
99. Ibid., 114.
100. Warren, *Lincoln's Youth*, 175.

The 1828 Experience

~ Warm weather, high water ~ Building the flatboat ~ The launch mystery ~ Initial evidence for a spring launch ~ The case for a fall/winter launch ~ Weaknesses in the fall/winter launch hypothesis ~ Further evidence for a spring launch ~ The likely departure date ~ Launch site, cargo, itinerary, and speed ~ Down the Ohio River ~ Into the Mississippi River ~ Into Louisiana waters ~ Lingering along the Louisiana sugar coast ~ The attack ~ Locating the attack site ~ Recovering and proceeding ~ Arriving in New Orleans ~ Docking at the flatboat wharf ~ Narrowing down the docking site ~ Dispensing of the cargo ~ Life along the flatboat wharf ~ Dismantling the flatboat ~ Footloose in New Orleans ~ Room and board ~ Conspicuous bumpkins ~ "Babel of all Babels . . . Sodom of all Sodoms" ~ Window to the world ~ Slaves on the run, slaves on the block ~ Hewlett's Exchange ~ Sightseeing ~ People-watching ~ Retailing ~ Street life ~ Departure ~ A different view of Indiana ~ Off to Illinois ~ Deep snows, dark times ~

Winter never fully arrived in 1828. Temperatures remained in their autumnal range, often rising to balminess and only occasionally dipping to seasonality or below. Rain fell from persistently cloudy skies, raising the waters of the Ohio and Mississippi. Trees greened prematurely; delighted farmers assumed an early spring and sowed seeds accordingly. Word from Louisiana had it that ears were growing on Indian corn—in February!—while harvestable bolls blossomed on Mississippi cotton plantations. "[E]very thing presents an appearance of June on the banks of the Mississippi," marveled one Louisiana paper, even as it fretted about the river "attain[ing] a height that is truly alarming. . . ."[1] The Ohio had already exceeded its banks and flooded Shawnee Town in Illinois with six feet of water.[2] Bad news for most folks, but good news for boatmen like Allen Gentry and Abraham Lincoln: high water meant swift sailing to New Orleans. First, however, they needed a flatboat.

One account written by a man named C. T. Baker in 1931 holds that the Gentrys purchased a salt boat (a flatboat formerly used to haul salt down from Pittsburgh) in Cincinnati with proceeds from cattle they had

1. *Lafourche Gazette*, as quoted by *The Farmers' Cabinet* (Amherst, NH), March 29, 1828, p. 2; see also Cary J. Mock, Jan Mojzisek, Michele McWaters, Michael Chenoweth, and David W. Stahle, "The Winter of 1827–1828 Over Eastern North America," *Climatic Change* 83, no. 112 (July 2007): 87–115.

2. "High Water," *Village Register and Norfolk County Advertiser* (Dedham, MA), March 13, 1828, p. 2.

sold there. Baker contends that it was this pre-existing flatboat that Gentry, Lincoln, and a third crewmember named Zeb Murphy took to New Orleans.[3] That account, however, is not substantiated by any other source. The fact that Lincoln himself clearly stated that he and Gentry traveled "without other assistance"[4] undermines Baker's credibility. All evidence suggests that Lincoln and Allen Gentry themselves built the flatboat, during which time Lincoln resided in Rockport.

The construction site was probably at Gentry's Landing, a hundred-acre wooded parcel downriver from the Rockport bluff. This area afforded timber, space, and a good spot to launch.[5] Abe certainly possessed the construction skills: he "was thoroughly master of all the phases of frontier life," reported a neighbor, including "woods craft" learned from his father.[6] The procedure for building a flatboat was recorded by John Calvin Gilkeson, who, like Lincoln, was born in Kentucky in 1809 and later moved to Indiana, where he built and piloted flatboats for many years. Gilkeson's instructions are paraphrased here and broken into fourteen steps:

1. Select and fell two straight hardwood trees (poplar and oak if possible) of similar length and at least four feet in diameter. Larger loads require longer trunks.
2. Debark, split, hew, and chisel them down to two massive beams, thirteen inches thick and forty inches wide, with as much length as the trunks allow. (Where available, sawmills powered by water, or by steam after the 1810s, significantly eased this task.)

3. C. T. Baker, "Sandy Creek Landing Greets the Lincolns: An Historical Sketch of Pioneer Days in This Community and County" (1931), self-published monograph stored at Spencer County Library, Ref 977.2 Bak, 24.

4. Francis Marion Van Natter, *Lincoln's Boyhood: A Chronicle of His Indiana Years* (Washington, D.C.: Public Affairs Press, 1963), 57; Abraham Lincoln, "Autobiography Written for John L. Scripps," June 1860, in *The Collected Works of Abraham Lincoln*, ed. Roy P. Basler (New Brunswick, NJ: Rutgers University Press, 1953), 4:62; William Dean Howells, *Life of Abraham Lincoln*, facsimile edition of campaign biography corrected by the hand of Abraham Lincoln (Bloomington: Indiana University Press, 1960), 22.

5. Louis A. Warren, ed., "Lincoln, Miss Roby, and Astronomy," *Lincoln Lore: Bulletin of the Lincoln National Life Foundation*, no. 1349, February 14, 1955. For property maps of Rockport in the late nineteenth century, see B. N. Griffing, *An Illustrated Historical Atlas of Spencer County, Indiana* (Philadelphia: D. J. Lake & Company, 1879), 61, and C. E. Wright, *An Illustrated Historical Atlas of Spencer County, Indiana* (Louisville, KY: John P. Morton & Company, 1896), 46–50.

6. Joseph Gillespie to William H. Herndon, January 31, 1866, in ed. Douglas L. Wilson and Rodney O. Davis, *Herndon's Informants: Letters, Interviews, and Statements About Abraham Lincoln* (Urbana and Chicago: University of Illinois Press, 1998), 181.

3. Taper one end of each beam from forty inches down to about twelve inches.
4. Haul the beams to an appropriate bankside location and lay them parallel, separated by a distance roughly one-third their length. They will form the flatboat's gunwales (pronounced and sometimes spelled "gunnels"), the twin backbones to which all other components fasten.
5. Lay six to eight girders between the parallel gunwales, and join each girder to each gunwale with a dovetail mortise.
6. Lay two end-girders at the bow and stern, and fasten them to the gunwales with dovetail mortises.
7. Lay "streamers" (crossbeams) across the girders, parallel to the gunwales, and join the streamers and girders with wooden pegs. The vessel at this point resembles a giant child's sled laid upside-down, with the tapered gunwales resembling the sled blades.
8. Lay planks across the streamers and fasten them with fourteen wooden pins each, forming the floor.
9. Caulk all seams by hammering in "twisted cords of well broken hemp or flax," then pouring rosin and hot lard into the crevices.[7] The bottom half of the vessel is now complete.

Next came a pivotal moment: the flipping of the frame. Helpers raised one gunwale with levers while holding down the other, then gently lowered the massive frame with ropes into the adjacent water body. The celebratory hoot that arose as the craft splashed and bobbed to life oftentimes fell silent as leaks bubbled up and repairs were made. The next steps added verticality to what, at this point, constituted little more than a sturdy raft:

10. Cut studs (posts) three feet high and insert them vertically into mortises cut every few feet into the gunwales.
11. Panel over the studs to form the walls of the flatboat.
12. Cut slimmer but longer studs and insert them down the middle of the flatboat, in mortises cut into the girders. These posts will uphold the roof. (Some flatboats were entirely roofed like an ark; others were half-roofed. The Gentry-Lincoln vessel, being a small two-man craft,

---

7. John Calvin Gilkeson, "Flatboat Building on Little Raccoon Creek, Parke County, Indiana," ed. Donald F. Carmony and Sam K. Swope, *Indiana Magazine of History* 60, no. 4 (December 1964): 317.

was probably half-roofed.)

13. Fasten short, narrow planks from the tops of the gunwale-mounted studs to the tops of the middle studs. These form the flatboat's roof, which was angled or arched steeply enough to shed water, but flat enough to allow rooftop walking, poling, and oaring.

14. Cover the roof planks perpendicularly with another layer of broader planks, then shingle them over and caulk them to keep out rain, the premier enemy of grain cargo.

Now complete as a vessel, the flatboat required interior work to make it a hold for cargo and a home for crew. A small woodstove and chimney provided for cooking and wintertime calefaction, while specialized storage (shelves, hooks, corrals) maximized capacity. If Gentry and Lincoln transported sacked hominy and smoked ham, floor space and ceiling hooks would have sufficed. A few inches of clay distributed evenly upon the floor helped seal crevices, absorb moisture, and protect the wood-plank floor from cooking fires.[8]

Last came navigational equipment: the steering oar (also called a "streamer," functioning as a rudder) usually measured sixty feet or longer for larger boats, while the side oars ("sweeps") needed to be roughly double the width of the flatboat. A short oar held at the bow, called a "gouger," helped keep the craft in the current. Two long, thin side sweeps protruding from the bulky vessels probably explain why flatboats came to be known as "broadhorns."[9] Because Gentry and Lincoln built their craft to accommodate a minimal crew of two, they probably depended on the steering oar and poling for all navigation, and may have left off the side oars altogether.

No records describe the design of the Gentry-Lincoln flatboat, but a contract for a similar vessel made in Spencer County five years later may shed some light. The $97.50 agreement, found by researcher Louis A. Warren, called for an eighteen-foot-wide, sixty-five-foot-long flatboat with four-and-a-half-feet-high walls, two-foot-wide gunwales, and a two-inch-thick floor. A steering oar and two sweeps protruded from the stern

8. Charles Carleton Coffin, *Abraham Lincoln* (New York: Harper & Brothers, 1893), 42.

9. Gilkeson, "Flatboat Building on Little Raccoon Creek," 309–322; HRA Gray & Pape, LLC, *The Evolution of a Sanctified Landscape: A Historic Resource Study of the Lincoln Boyhood National Memorial, Spencer County, Indiana* (Cincinnati, OH: National Park Service, 2002), 49; "In Flatboat and Keelboat Times On the Mississippi, Over Seventy Years Ago," *Daily Picayune* (New Orleans), March 19, 1896, p. 14, section f, c. 6–7.

and sides, while a cabin covered with a leak-proof roof occupied the rear. While this contract bears no direct relationship to the Gentry-Lincoln case, it is nevertheless informative because its purchaser, William Jones, was affiliated with the Gentry Store and probably had comparable transportation needs.

The size of the Gentry-Lincoln flatboat may be estimated by an 1834 journal describing a flatboat launched from nearby Posey County. It measured eighty feet long and seventeen feet wide (1,360 square feet), manned by five men. A crew of two could typically handle a vessel roughly half that size, 40 or 45 feet long by 15 or so feet wide.[10]

Construction usually took one to two months, depending on the number of helpers and the availability of milled wood. (Hand-hewing significantly slowed down work, but also lowered costs.) Most Indiana men possessed basic carpentry skills and flatboat experience, making workers easy to find. Total costs typically ranged around one dollar per length-foot, but were probably minimal for this two-man homemade enterprise.

•

Exactly when Allen Gentry and Abraham Lincoln launched their flatboat from Rockport is a critical piece of information, because it directs us to the proper time window in which Lincoln would have arrived in New Orleans and thus enables us to reconstruct the daily city life to which he was exposed. While 100 percent of the historical evidence points to *either* an early springtime launch or a late-autumn/early-winter launch in the year 1828, *neither* alternative can be proven by primary historical documentation. There are no registries, no receipts, no contracts, and certainly no journals nailing down the date. But other sources of evidence and clues abound. The following discussion weighs the evidence for the two departure-date hypotheses and posits a judgment.

Contextual evidence accommodates the springtime hypothesis well. Warming temperatures, swiftly flowing rivers, high water levels easing the evasion of sandbars and other navigation obstacles, lengthening daylight, and economic bustle in the destination port all enhance the logic of a springtime launch. Exceptionally warm and wet weather in early 1828 caused extremely high waters in the Ohio and Mississippi, which might have prompted the river-savvy James Gentry to organize a voyage to exploit the swift current. ("The river is rising vary fast and appears to be

10. Asbury C. Jacquess, "The Journals of the Davy Crockett commencing December 20th, 1834," *Indiana Magazine of History* 102, no. 1 (March 2006): 8.

pretty well lined with flatboats," observed one navigator in 1835, indicating that rivermen actively "read" the river and deployed accordingly.[11])
Lincoln himself, as we shall see, set out from Illinois in the month of
April for his 1831 voyage to New Orleans, while his own father had departed in March twenty-five years earlier. Port records show that flatboat
arrivals in general peaked at New Orleans between late March and early
May (when eight to nine flatboats registered daily), implying that upcountry departures peaked proportionately in March and April.[12]

Secondary evidence adds further credence to a springtime launch, the
strongest coming from the research of William H. Herndon. As Lincoln's
longtime Springfield law partner, close friend, and biographer, Herndon
looms large in the literature of Lincoln's early life, so some background on
his work is in order for the purposes of our study.

A few months after the president's assassination in 1865, Herndon set
out for Kentucky, Indiana, and Illinois to interview people with personal
memories of Lincoln, in preparation for a book about his old colleague.
The resultant 250-plus transcripts and letters have been described as "one
of the first extensive oral history projects in American history."[13] Herndon
and collaborator Jesse W. Weik wove the information into narrative form
and published it in 1889 as *Herndon's Lincoln: The True Story of a Great
Life.*

The effort garnered more criticism than praise. Popular audiences
reproached Herndon for the occasionally discomfiting portrayal his findings painted of the immortalized president: his plebeian roots, his apparent secularity, his bouts with depression. Historians criticized Herndon
for sloppy interviewing methods and scoffed at the historiographical legitimacy of unverifiable, decades-old reminiscences. Herndon fueled the
criticism when he mistakenly whipped up Lincoln's relationship with Ann
Rutledge into a life-transforming romantic tragedy and disparaged Mary
Todd's character in ways that influence her unflattering image to this day.
Herndon became viewed by many Lincoln scholars as an opportunistic
writer (note his book's title: *Herndon's Lincoln*) more so than a careful and
reliable historian.

Nevertheless, Herndon's body of material constitutes an unmatched
treasure trove of first-person perspectives on Lincoln's youth. His tireless

11. Ibid., 20.
12. Wharfinger Reports/New Orleans Collector of Levee Dues-Registers of Flatboats,
Barges, Rafts, and Steamboats in the Port of New Orleans, 1818–23 and 1845–49.
13. Charles B. Strozier, as quoted by Wilson and Davis in *Herndon's Informants*, xiii.

fieldwork and well-preserved notes form the source of hundreds of subsequent histories, biographies, and articles, and underlie much of what we think we know about Lincoln before he stepped onto the national stage. Indeed, many, if not most, of Herndon's critics are also Herndon citers. The situation is not unlike that of early decennial censuses, which abound in shortfalls but nevertheless represent valuable datasets. Are Herndon's findings, like the handwritten population schedules of the old censuses, perfectly *precise*? Definitely not. Are most of them generally *accurate*? We have ways to evaluate their accuracy through corroboration, contextual evidence, informant reputation, and other methods. Do they represent the best *available* information on Lincoln's early years, in both depth and breadth? Definitely. Scholars have recently begun to reassess Herndon's unfavorable reputation, and rightfully so.[14]

In 1998, historians Douglas L. Wilson and Rodney O. Davis published Herndon's interview notes and correspondences, granting researchers convenient access to the actual words of Lincoln's aging contemporaries (who, incidentally, have suffered their own share of scholarly dismissal). Although the shortfalls of human memory and interviewing dynamics should always be kept in mind, these first-person recollections offer valuable clues and perspectives for this study. Through these and other "way points," we can reconstruct the chronology, geography, and history of Lincoln's voyage to New Orleans—starting, of course, with the all-important launch date question.

•

Among Herndon's September 1865 inquiries was a valuable interview with fifty-seven-year-old Anna Caroline ("Katie") Gentry, whose now-deceased husband accompanied Lincoln to New Orleans decades earlier.[15] "My name is Mrs. Gentry—wife of Allen Gentry," she declared, "with whom Mr Lincoln went to NO for Ja[me]s Gentry Sen[ior] in April 1828. . . ."[16] Born around the same time as Lincoln and schooled with

14. Douglas L. Wilson, "Herndon's Legacy," in *Lincoln Before Washington: New Perspectives on the Illinois Years,* ed. Douglas L. Wilson (Urbana and Chicago: University of Illinois Press, 1997), 21–34.

15. Allen Gentry died in 1862 when, according to neighbors, he "got drunk and fell off the boat going to Louisville and was drowned." Interview, Nathaniel Grigsby, Silas and Nancy Richardson, and John Romine, by William H. Herndon, September 14, 1865, in *Herndon's Informants,* 116.

16. Interview, Anna Caroline Gentry, by William H. Herndon, September 17, 1865, in *Herndon's Informants,* 131.

him, the widow Gentry continued:

> Speaking about the boat & the trip let me say to you that I saw
> the boat—was on it—saw it start and L[incoln] with it. . . .
> They went down the Ohio & Mississippi . . . they Came back
> in June 1828.[17]

Anna Gentry's clear personal memory forms compelling evidence for a springtime launch, particularly in light of her close relationship to one (indeed both) of the principles. A dangerous weather anomaly made April 1828 particularly memorable: after months of spring-like weather, daytime temperatures suddenly plunged from 60° to 22° F, and dropped lower at night. The hard freeze and light snow killed seedling crops and turned the balmy winter of 1828 into a long-rued "False Spring."[18] Anna's eighty-three-year-old father Absolom Roby, who farmed that year, backed up his daughter's testimony when Herndon interviewed him on the same day in September 1865. Roby affirmed, "[Lincoln] and Gentry did go to N.O. in April 1828. as Said by my daughter . . . I was often at the landing from which Gentry & Abe started to N.O. . . ." But the elderly man later admitted, "my memory is gone & I myself am fast going."[19]

Further substantiation of a spring launch comes from Herndon's interview with neighbors Nathaniel Grigsby, Silas Richardson, Nancy Richardson, and John Romine on September 14, 1865. Romine in particular stated that "Lincoln went to N.O. about '28 or '29. . . . Boat Started out of the Ohio in the Spring—Abe about 20 years of age." A few moments later, Herndon scribbled down the enigmatic phrase, "Give about 2 m," which could mean "around two miles" or "around two months."[20] Luckily, Herndon later clarified his notes of the Romine interview with the phrase, "Gone about two months."[21] Thus we have corroboration of Anna

17. Ibid., 131–132.

18. These temperatures were recorded by William Clark in St. Louis, Missouri, during April 2–5, 1828. Temperatures were probably similar in Rockport, Indiana, offset by half-day or so, as the system moved eastward. William Clark, "William Clark's Diary: May, 1826–February, 1831, Part Two, 1828," ed. Louise Barry, *Kansas Historical Quarterly* 16, no. 2 (May 1948): 143. For vegetative impacts of the April 1828 killing frost, see Mock et al., "Winter of 1827–1828," 87–115.

19. Interview, Absolom Roby, by William H. Herndon, September 17, 1865, in *Herndon's Informants*, 132.

20. Interview, Nathaniel Grigsby, Silas and Nancy Richardson, and John Romine, by William H. Herndon, September 14, 1865, in *Herndon's Informants*, 118.

21. William H. Herndon, citing John Romine, "A Visit to the Lincoln Farm, September 14, 1865," in *The Hidden Lincoln, From the Letters and Papers of William H. Herndon,*

Gentry's stance that the trip began in spring, and that it lasted around two months. Romine, son-in-law of the man (James Gentry) who hired Lincoln to go to New Orleans, makes three Gentry family members (along with Anna and Absolom) who knew Lincoln personally, all concurring on a spring launch.

Armed with this evidence, Herndon reported spring 1828 as the season of the flatboat launch in his 1889 biography. Specifically, he wrote, "In March, 1828, James Gentry . . . fitted out a boat with a stock of grain and meat" for Allen and Abe, but stated no further dates, despite Anna's clear testimony that they departed in April and returned in June. Widely cited, Herndon's March 1828 judgment has since been adopted by numerous tertiary authors.[22]

•

A second hypothesis holds that Gentry and Lincoln launched in late December 1828. Setting out during the cold and brief days of year's end, when the river runs low and slow, might seem risky and counterintuitive. Incessant wind, frost, rain, fog, hail, and snow, for example, slowed one wintertime Indiana-to-New-Orleans flatboat voyage to nearly twice the length of a typical spring trip. The inclement conditions also made the navigator "very unwell . . . with a bad cold [and] Ague [fever].   . The weather is fine for that disease."[23]

But winter travel was not without reason. An end-of-year launch delivered recently harvested agricultural commodities to market before they might go bad. It aligned particularly well with tobacco cultivation, as leaves are cut in August or September, staked on poles in barns to dry for a few months, then braided in November and shipped in December. It coincided with the ideal season for exporting hog meat, as the autumn chill staved off decay in the period between slaughter and curing.[24] Year-end

ed. Emanuel Hertz (New York: The Viking Press, 1938), 360.

22. William H. Herndon and Jesse William Weik, *Herndon's Lincoln: The True Story of a Great Life* (Chicago, New York, and San Francisco: Belford, Clarke & Company, 1889), 1:63.

23. William S. Ward, *Diary* [of Flatboat Trip from New Albany, Indiana to New Orleans, Louisiana, 1839], The Historic New Orleans Collection, Accession Number 2009.0139, p. 1, 27, 33, and 69 (hereafter cited as THNOC). Ward departed New Albany on January 19, 1839, and arrived in New Orleans on March 11, delayed mostly for weather reasons.

24. Interview, Jane Boultinghouse (great-great-great-granddaughter of Allen Gentry and member of an Indiana tobacco-growing and hog-raising family), by Richard Cam-

launches supplied foodstuffs to the New Orleans market just as demand rose with the city's higher wintertime population. Cold-season launches also gave farmers something productive to do in the off-season, and freed up the subsequent spring for planting. In the case of Gentry and Lincoln, a December departure would have allowed them to work the river landing during the subsequent springtime busy season. While temperatures might have indeed plunged below freezing nightly, each southbound mile would have brought slightly warmer temperatures. Low water level surely slowed progress, but it also reduced the risk of losing control of the vessel. These were, after all, two greenhorns at the helm.

The December launch hypothesis stems from Gentry family oral history, as recorded and interpreted by two amateur historians working independently in the early- to mid-twentieth century. Their names were Bess V. Ehrmann and Francis Marion Van Natter.

An enthusiastic and multi-talented curator of the Spencer County Historical Society, Bess V. Ehrmann interviewed numerous Gentry descendents as part of the Southwestern Indiana Historical Society's effort to write the "missing chapter" of Lincoln's life. "Many flatboat men along the Ohio did make their trips in April," Ehrmann acknowledged,

> but the Gentry family was always known to go in the late fall or early winter. There were other men who made their trips in winter, Mr. Louis Gentry[,] the grandson of Allen Gentry[,] told me.
>
> I have known intimately many of the grandchildren and great grandchildren of both James Gentry and Allen Gentry. All members of both families know that their ancestors, three generations of them, made their flatboat trips to New Orleans in the fall or winter, after the hogs were butchered and the summer crops gathered and stored ready for marketing in New Orleans. Ice did not come in the rivers until late in the winter, and as Mr. Louis Gentry told me, "You must remember we were traveling south away from the cold."[25]

Francis Marion Van Natter interviewed Gentry family members around the same time (1936) and wove his findings into a book, *Lincoln's Boyhood: A Chronicle of His Indiana Years*, published posthumously in 1963. Van Natter's work is unusual for a Lincoln book; while it invents dialogue and

panella, December 5, 2008, Rockport, Indiana.
25. Bess V. Ehrmann, *The Missing Chapter in the Life of Abraham Lincoln* (Chicago: Walter M. Hill, 1938), vii, 7.

imbues color into boyhood vignettes, it also contains scholarly apparatus such as footnotes and affidavit-backed interviews with local informants. Indeed, Van Natter worked tirelessly and traveled extensively to understand and reconstruct the flatboat trip, taking scrupulous notes and saving all research materials—which he later donated to the Lewis Library at Vincennes University.

Among Van Natter's archives is an affidavit signed by seventy-two-year-old E. Grant Gentry and notarized on September 5, 1936. Regarding the timing of the flatboat trip, the affidavit states that Allen and Abe left "some time between Christmas day 1828 and New Year's Day 1829," having "delayed leaving on the trip until after the birth of his expected child . . . born on the 18th day of December, 1828. . . ." Revealingly, E. Grant Gentry also stated in the affidavit that his information had been "related to him by his grandmother, Anna Caroline Roby Gentry, more than fifty years ago."[26] What he did not know, or perhaps misremembered, was that, when interviewed by Herndon in 1865, his grandmother pegged the de parture date to April 1828, not December. Based on E. Grant Gentry's testimony, Van Natter, concurring with Bess Ehrmann, judged the launch as taking place "[m]idway between Christmas Day [1828] and New Year [1829]," and proceeded to reconstruct the trip based on that chronology.[27]

What remains unresolved is the chasm between three Gentry family members' *eyewitness* memories of an April launch recorded by Herndon in 1865, versus the passed-down family memories of a December launch recorded by Ehrmann and Van Natter in the 1930s. Interviews in 2008 by this researcher with two direct descendents of Allen Gentry revealed that whatever adamant December-launch memory might have existed in the 1930s did not persist into the 2000s.[28]

One Lincoln family member did vaguely attest to an autumn departure—but dubiously, it turns out. A June 15, 1865, interview with Abraham's earnest but oftentimes unreliable cousin Dennis Hanks recorded that "Mr. Lincoln went to N.O. in the fall. . . ." Hanks then undermined his credibility when he continued, ". . . of [the year] 36 or 37 with Gideon

26. Affidavit, E. Grant Gentry, September 5, 1936, Francis Marion Van Natter Papers–Regional History Collection Number 136, Lewis Historical Library, Vincennes University (hereafter cited as Van Natter Papers).

27. Van Natter, *Lincoln's Boyhood*, 56.

28. Interviews, Jane Boultinghouse and Barbara Dillon (both great-great-great-granddaughters of Allen Gentry), by Richard Campanella, December 5, 2008, Rockport, Indiana.

Romine. . . ."[29] By Lincoln's own words, we know for certain he launched in 1828 and accompanied Allen Gentry, no one else. If Hanks got the year, decade, and companion wrong, his reliability regarding the season is minimal.

Additional clues exist. On the 19th or 20th of March 1828, Allen Gentry wed Anna Caroline Roby, thus confirming at the very least that Gentry and Lincoln were in Indiana on that date.[30] Anna became pregnant within a few days. This information leaves only a week for Herndon's March launch estimate to prove true, although it does no harm to Anna Gentry's April estimate. Nine months later, on December 18, 1828, Anna gave birth to their firstborn, James Junior.[31] The delivery, according to Ehrmann, "had delayed the southern trip as Allen had refused to go until he knew all was well at home. Many years later when Lincoln became famous, the Gentrys were always to remember the date of this particular flatboat trip from the birthdate of the eldest son." A local history buff if ever there was one, Ehrmann wrote and directed a biennial historical pageant, *When Lincoln Went Flatboating From Rockport*, in which the actor who played Allen Gentry was his own great-grandson.[32]

At least one modern-day Gentry family descendent concurred with Ehrmann, sensing that Allen Gentry (her great-great-great-grandfather) would not have parted with his bride once he learned of her pregnancy.[33] If Anna became pregnant around March 21, she would have realized it no later than three weeks hence, based on menstrual cycles. Presuming she told her husband promptly, Allen (and therefore Abraham) would have, under this theory, stayed home until the late-December birth. After a couple of days of assuring the health of both mother and baby, the theory goes, the duo would finally have departed.[34] Van Natter also acknowledged the significance of the birth, although he erroneously dated it to December 28, 1828.

29. Interview, Dennis Hanks, by William H. Herndon, June 15, 1865, in *Herndon's Informants*, 45.

30. The March 20 date comes from *Marriage Records—Spencer County, Indiana 1818–1855*, compiled by Christine Young, Ethel Smith, and Hazel M. Hyde (Thomson, IL: Heritage House, 1974), 8; other sources state March 19.

31. *History of Warrick, Spencer, and Perry Counties, Indiana* (Chicago: Goodspeed, Bros. & Company, 1885), 452

32. Ehrmann, *Missing Chapter*, 8, 128–137.

33. Interview, Barbara Dillon, by Richard Campanella, December 5, 2008, Rockport, Indiana.

34. Ibid.

•

But would Anna *really* have been better off with her husband disappearing into the wintry wilds as she struggled alone with her days-old firstborn? One may reason that the relatively low-risk early months of a pregnancy— balmy April, May, and June, in this case—offered the *ideal* time for a husband to depart on business. This would enable him to be home during the more perilous months of the late term, birth, and first weeks of infancy, when an Indiana winter would only make matters worse. Both mother and child run greater risks in the weeks after birth than in the weeks after conception. Contrary to Ehrmann's reasoning, the Gentry baby issue seems to *buttress* the April launch hypothesis, and *weaken* the case for a December launch. Van Natter dramatically describes "a blizzard threaten[ing] . . . a strong northwest gale . . . the December wind [growing] colder and growl[ing] louder" within hours of the baby's birth.[35] If all this were true meteorologically, such conditions seem to weigh *against* the likelihood of Allen flatboating into the blizzard while leaving an hours-old baby and first-time-mother to fend for themselves. (Perhaps wintry conditions struck as fiercely as Van Natter described. But Western explorer and scientist William Clark, stationed only two hundred miles away in St. Louis, personally recorded very different weather for the last five days of 1828: clear skies, generally calm, and temperatures ranging between 56° and 64° F through morning and afternoon, with December 27 described as a "Beautiful Spring morning [and a] Fine Warm Evening."[36] Van Natter's blizzard diminishes his overall credibility.)

Another weakness in the December hypothesis is the fact that the Ohio and Mississippi rivers ran exceptionally low around that time, quite the opposite of the floodwaters earlier in the year. "The river began to fall in June [1828]," wrote river scientist John W. Monette in the 1850s, and "remained low from August until the last of December"—precisely the time Gentry and Lincoln allegedly departed.[37] William Clark, stationed at St. Louis, recorded the Mississippi "falling" consistently throughout the last ten days of December.[38] The trend continued into the new year: "The Mississippi has fallen eighteen inches," reported the *New Orleans Price*

35. Van Natter, *Lincoln's Boyhood*, 57–58.
36. Clark, "William Clark's Diary," 171–172.
37. John W. Monette, "The Mississippi Floods," in *Publications of the Mississippi Historical Society* 7, ed. Franklin L. Riley (Oxford, MS: Mississippi Historical Society, 1903): 464.
38. Clark, "William Clark's Diary," 172.

Current on January 11, settling at "10½ feet below high water mark, being 7½ feet lower that this time last year." Two weeks later, it had "fallen [another] six inches, [to] 11 feet below high water mark, being 8½ feet lower than at this time last year."[39] Equating to perhaps three to five feet above mean sea level at New Orleans, the current would have flowed around 1.5 to 2.2 miles per hour, peaking at only 2.0 to 2.8 miles per hour—roughly half the speed during springtime high water.[40] Low water in winter could be dangerous as well as tedious, because it was prone to freezing over, particularly along slack-water banks where flatboatmen could get ice-locked overnight. It also brought obstacles closer to the surface: so weakly flowed both the Ohio and Mississippi in November that a snag rose treacherously to the surface, puncturing the hull of the steamboat *Columbus* and sending it and its hundred tons of lead to the bottom.[41] If an experienced riverman like James Gentry witnessed these unfavorable conditions in late December, he might well have cancelled plans for a trip to New Orleans—unless, of course, he already executed that trip the previous spring.

Nevertheless, documents indicate that some flatboats did indeed depart Spencer County in December of other years. A January 22, 1821, letter written by resident C. William Morgan, for example, speaks of launching his flatboats for New Orleans one month earlier, meaning late December. More significant is the aforementioned William Jones flatboat contract of 1833: Jones once worked in Gentry's store and may have owned it by the time he entered into the flatboat contract. If Jones' annual business schedule resembled Gentry's, then Jones' delivery date for the flatboat may shed light on our issue. That date: December 1. Assuming a couple of weeks to load and prepare for the trip, this equates to a mid- or late-December launch. Another example comes from one of the best-documented flatboat voyages of the era, that of the *Davy Crockett*. It launched from Posey County, Indiana, for New Orleans on December 20, 1834—the same day, six years hence, that Gentry and Lincoln supposedly departed under the wintertime hypothesis.[42] None of these cases bear any direct relation to the Lincoln trip; they only show that December launches were not uncommon.

39. *New Orleans Price Current*, January 11 and January 24, 1829, as quoted in *Louisiana Courier*, January 13, 1829, p. 3, c. 1, and January 26, 1829, p. 2, c. 5.

40. U.S. Army Corps of Engineers. "River Velocities at New Orleans, LA. Related to the Carrollton Gage," http://www.mvn.usace.army.mil/eng/edhd/velo_no.asp (visited December 1, 2008).

41. *Daily National Intelligencer* (Washington, D.C.), November 4, 1828, c. F.

42. Jacquess, "Journals of the Davy Crockett," 8–24.

Lincoln himself fell just a few words short of clarifying the departure question. "When [I] was nineteen, still residing in Indiana," he recollected in 1860, "[I] made [my] first trip upon a flat-boat to New-Orleans . . ."[43] His words rule out departures predating his February 12, 1828, birthday and postdating the 1829 birthday, but shed no further light. (Had he departed in December, might he have mentioned reaching his milestone twentieth birthday while on voyage?)

•

Lincoln did, however, serendipitously imply a spring 1828 launch when he hand-edited a short biography entitled *Life of Abraham Lincoln*, written by William Dean Howells during the 1860 presidential campaign. Howells introduced his readers to Lincoln's Indiana boyhood and brought them to the flatboat story:

> The Lincolns continued to live in Spencer county, until 1830, nothing interrupting the even tenor of Abraham's life, except in his nineteenth year, a flat-boat trip to New Orleans.

Howells wrapped up the flatboat story with a few lines of river poetry and a couple of voyage vignettes, then placed Lincoln back in Indiana. He started the next paragraph with the words, "Four years afterward, on the first of March, 1830, his father determined to emigrate once more . . . for Illinois. . . ." When Lincoln edited the draft, the presidential candidate crossed out the word "Four" and wrote in "Two," meaning that the March 1, 1830 emigration date to Illinois postdated the flatboat trip to New Orleans by two years.[44] This corrected chronology aligns neatly with the spring 1828 departure hypothesis, and undermines the late-autumn 1828 hypothesis, which Lincoln presumably would have rounded off to "*One* year afterward. . . ." Because this piece of evidence positions Lincoln personally in the role of clarifying the timing of his flatboat trip as spring 1828, it is weighted heavily in this analysis.

It is greatly disappointing that both Thomas Lincoln's flatboat trip to New Orleans in 1806 and Abraham Lincoln's two trips in 1828 and 1831 all fail to appear in primary documentary evidence in New Orleans today. The city's flatboat records—specifically those of the Collector of Levee Dues and the Wharfinger, stored on microfilm and in the New Orleans Public Library's City Archives—survive only for 1806, 1818–23, and for

---

43. Lincoln, "Autobiography," June 1860, in *Collected Works*, 4:62.
44. Howells, *Life of Abraham Lincoln*, 23.

certain wharves from 1845 through 1852.[45] When we plot out those existing records, we see that late-January and early-February arrivals (boats
that would have left Indiana one month earlier) made mid-winter the second-busiest flatboat season of those years. However, the *busiest* flatboat
season in New Orleans was spring, when arrival rates roughly doubled.
This evidence, albeit contextual and nowhere near the year 1828, adds
some additional support to the springtime hypothesis.

Despite the loss of the original flatboat records, we still have newspaper reports of that information. Perhaps the most compelling piece of
evidence supporting the springtime hypothesis may be found in the daily
"Ship News" ("Marine") columns of the bilingual newspapers *New Orleans Bee* and *New Orleans Argus*. They listed activity at the Port of New
Orleans by vessel type, origin or destination, and load. Flatboats (*chalans*
in French) were listed by their origin, load, and local client. A survey of
the *Bee*'s columns from April 21 through June 24, 1828—a time window
generously spanning all possible Gentry-Lincoln arrival dates under the
springtime hypothesis—uncovered more than 130 flatboats landing at
New Orleans. The *Argus*, meanwhile, recorded around 140. An identical
survey of arrivals in the *Bee* for January 15 through February 20, 1829—
the equivalent time window for the December launch hypothesis—*found
not a single flatboat arriving to New Orleans*. Unfortunately, editions of the
Argus have been lost for early 1829, but we have every reason to believe
they would generally mimic the *Bee*'s reports. The extremely low water in
the river at that time, coupled with freezing temperatures, probably explains why what ordinarily would be the second-busiest flatboat season of
the year saw zero flatboat traffic. ("Water low in Ohio—and ice making,"
warned the *Bee* in mid-February; "Mississippi [is] closed at the mouth of
Ohio; Tennessee and Cumberland [rivers] low."[46]) These data prove that
not only was spring 1828 far busier than winter 1829 in terms of flatboat
arrivals, but that mid-May 1828, as we shall see shortly, ranked as the
busiest flatboat period of the entire year, by a wide margin, while January–
February 1829 turned out to be among the slowest.[47]

45. Searches in all other New Orleans archives, as well as in national databases of
historical documents at other institutions and in private hands, failed to uncover the
missing reports.

46. "Ship News," *New Orleans Bee*, February 16, 1829, p. 3, c. 4.

47. Analysis by author, based on *New Orleans Bee*, April 21–June 24, 1828, and January 15–February 20, 1829. Note: the 1828 editions contain shipping news only in French;
by early 1829, the column appeared in both French and English.

•

Taking stock of the above discussion, we have zero primary documents proving a particular departure date, but ample evidence in support of the spring hypothesis. Anna Gentry said so clearly, and Absolom Roby and John Romine concurred. Lincoln himself left behind clues that buttress the springtime launch, and said or phrased or implied nothing to contradict it. Numerous strands of contextual evidence lend additional support to a spring departure, as do the invitingly high river stages of spring 1828 and the extremely large number of *Bee* and *Argus* flatboat listings. Even Allen and Anna Gentry's situation involving their newborn baby renders a spring voyage more rational than a cold, slow, and potentially dangerous winter trip.

What supports the December hypothesis, on the other hand, is mostly a limited amount of tertiary evidence, reported by two researchers (Bess V. Ehrmann and Francis Marion Van Natter) working one full century after the launch, based on memories that post-date the Lincoln trip by decades. William Jones, the Gentry family associate who contracted for a flatboat to be delivered in the month of December, also lends some weak indirect support. All other strands of December-hypothesis support are contextual and less convincing compared to their counterparts. Most troubling is the utter absence of flatboat arrivals documented in the *Bee* "Ship News" listings during the January–February 1829 time window in which Gentry and Lincoln *should* have arrived, compared to the boom we saw in spring. Nearly all footnoted Lincoln books and articles that report the December hypothesis cite it to Ehrmann and Van Natter, who, with all due respect to their important contributions, may have methodologically leaned too heavily on the century-old memories of family descendents in timing the departure. Van Natter's use of affidavits may have ensured honesty on the part of his informants, but guaranteed nothing in terms of accuracy.

Balancing all of the above, this researcher judges that the springtime 1828 departure hypothesis enjoys a convincing preponderance of evidence. Assigning numerical values and weights to the various levels of evidence—a subjective but nonetheless worthwhile exercise—suggests that the springtime hypothesis is, conservatively speaking, at least four to five times stronger than the wintertime scenario (see graphic, "When in 1828 Did Allen Gentry and Abraham Lincoln Depart by Flatboat for New Orleans?").

We must now attempt to refine exactly *when* in spring 1828 Gentry and Lincoln departed. March is too early: despite Herndon's support, this month has, as previously explained, a demonstrably small time window in which to prove correct. May or June, on the other hand, are too late. This leaves April, as evidenced by Anna Gentry's clear recollection of an April-to-June trip.

When in April? A killer frost on April 5–7 suddenly ended the "False Spring" of 1828, plunging temperatures by forty degrees into the teens (F) "accompanied with a light Snow." Presumably the duo would have waited out that wintry blast. By April 12, afternoon temperatures hit the 80s F.[48] Did they leave then? Anna Gentry drops a clue in her interview with Herndon:

> One Evening Abe & myself were Sitting on the banks of the Ohio or on the [flat]boat Spoken of. I Said to Abe that the Moon was going down. He said, "Thats not so—it don't really go down: it Seems So. The Earth turns from west to East and the revolution of the Earth Carries us under, as it were: we do the sinking . . . The moons sinking is only an appearance.[49]

Only a young crescent moon sets in the evening sky, one to three days after the new moon. In April 1828, the new moon occurred on April 14, thus young crescents would have set in the early evenings of April 15–17.[50] Lacking any further clues and in light of the above evidence, this researcher posits that Allen Gentry and Abraham Lincoln poled out of Rockport, Indiana, around Friday or Saturday, April 18 or 19, 1828.

•

We must address a few other questions before reconstructing the voyage. First, where exactly did Gentry and Lincoln launch? Anna Gentry, who waved goodbye as the men poled away, said Allen and Abe "started from yonder landing—Gentrys Landing . . . say ½ a mile from this house due South & ¾ of a M below Rockport. . . ."[51] Other neighbors initially

48. Clark, "William Clark's Diary," 143; Mock et al., "The Winter of 1827–1828," 95–99.

49. Interview, Anna Caroline Gentry, by William H. Herndon, September 17, 1865, in *Herndon's Informants*, 132.

50. U.S. Naval Observatory Astronomical Applications Department, "Phases of the Moon," http://aa.usno.navy.mil/data/docs/MoonPhase.php (visited December 1, 2008). For further information on this moment, see Louis A. Warren, ed., "Lincoln, Miss Roby, and Astronomy," *Lincoln Lore: Bulletin of the Lincoln National Life Foundation*, no. 1349, February 14, 1955.

51. Interview, Anna Caroline Gentry, by William H. Herndon, September 17, 1865,

reported that the boat "Started from Rockport," but then amended, "a Short distance below rather—at the Gentry landing. . . ."[52] James Gentry originally purchased this hundred-acre riverside tract from a man named Daniel Grass in 1825; a year later, he transferred ownership to son Allen. The wooded parcel offered a convenient source of timber for Allen and Abe's flatboat.[53] Gentry's Landing, intersected by a small stream (Spanker's Branch) and located a few hundred feet downriver from the limestone cliff (Hanging Rock) earning Rockport its name, later became known as the Old Flatboat Landing.[54] The local community has embraced this locale: Bess V. Ehrmann reported in the 1930s that Louis Gentry "pointed out to me the exact spot where his father told him the Gentry flatboat was loaded when Lincoln was Gentry's helper."[55] Ehrmann's biennial historical pageant, *When Lincoln Went Flatboating From Rockport*, took place here in the late 1920s. A limestone monument erected in 1939 marked the spot as "Old Lower Landing" and explained its significance; subsequent ceremonies, including reenactments in 1958 and 2008, launched from here as well. The collective memory of Rockport, Indiana, in every way, shape, and form, holds that this was the spot.

Second, what was their cargo? Amateur flatboat operations in this region carried the standard potpourri of Western produce—corn, oats, beans, pork, beef, venison, livestock, fowl, lumber, hemp, rope, tobacco, whiskey—sacked and barreled and caged and corralled and piled and bottled in organized chaos. Among boatmen, this was known as "mixed cargo," as opposed to the "straight cargo" (single commodity) favored by large professional flatboat enterprises. Informants interviewed in 1865 remembered Lincoln had "[hauled] some of the bacon to the River"—smoked hog meat, in preparation for the voyage.[56] A neighbor recalled buying pigs and corn from the Lincolns, leading one researcher to posit that the cargo probably comprised the two premier agricultural commodities of

in *Herndon's Informants*, 131.

52. Interview, Nathaniel Grigsby, Silas and Nancy Richardson, and John Romine, by William H. Herndon, September 14, 1865, in *Herndon's Informants*, 118.

53. Warren, "Lincoln, Miss Roby, and Astronomy." For property maps of Rockport in the late nineteenth century, see Griffing, *Historical Atlas of Spencer County*, 61, and Wright, *Historical Atlas of Spencer County*, 46–50.

54. Affidavit, E. Grant Gentry, September 5, 1936, Van Natter Papers. Locals once called the Rockport cliff "The Lady Washington;" today it is simply known as "the bluff."

55. Ehrmann, *Missing Chapter*, 108.

56. Interview, Nathaniel Grigsby, Silas and Nancy Richardson, and John Romine, by William H. Herndon, September 14, 1865, in *Herndon's Informants*, 118.

the region, "hogs and hominy."[57] Gentry family memories, recorded in the 1930s, cite "hogs" and typical Indiana "summer crops" as their ancestors' standard flatboat cargo.[58] Another family story, reported by seventy-two-year-old E. Grant Gentry in 1936, claimed the flatboat carried "pork, corn in the ear, potatoes, some hay (was not a regular hay boat), and kraut in the barrel; apparently there were no hoop poles or tobacco. . . ." Lincoln himself dropped a clue: "The nature of part of the cargo-load, as it was called," he wrote in 1860, "made it necessary for [us] to linger and trade along the Sugar coast" of Louisiana.[59] What might have been the nature of their cargo, that it would have traded better at the sugar plantations below Baton Rouge than in New Orleans proper? The aforementioned E. Grant Gentry testified that "the cargo was destined for . . . sugar planters who owned mules and negro slaves, the corn and hay being bought for the mules and the meat and potatoes for the slaves."[60] The cargo may well have included "barrel pork" (as opposed to bulk pork), which Southern planters demanded as a low-cost, high-energy food for slaves.[61] Plantation caretakers constantly required a wide range of Western produce to maintain their village-like operations, and exchanged them for cotton or sugar, which flatboatmen thence carried downriver. One 1824 report, for example, explained that flatboats navigated "from the Ohio, down the Mississippi to New Orleans, *touching at the small towns in their way, and if possible disposing of a part of their multifarious cargo.*"[62] Thus Lincoln's sugar coast clue may not mean too much, except that it rules out straight cargo (by referencing "*part* of the cargo-load"). After "lingering" along the coast, flatboats would then proceed on to New Orleans, where buyers for the standard commodities of cotton and sugar abounded. We know for certain that the cargo belonged to the Gentry family, and by extension to Allen Gentry; Abraham was merely a hired hand earning a set wage.[63]

Third, did they travel at night? Nocturnal navigation could add thirty or more miles to daily progress. It also risked perils, especially given the

57. William E. Bartelt, *"There I Grew Up"—Remembering Lincoln's Indiana Youth* (Indianapolis: Indiana Historical Society Press, 2008), 34.

58. Ehrmann, *Missing Chapter*, 7.

59. Lincoln, "Autobiography," June 1860, in *Collected Works*, 4:62.

60. Affidavit, E. Grant Gentry, September 5, 1936, Van Natter Papers.

61. Jacquess, "Journals of the Davy Crockett," 22.

62. William Newnham Blane, *An Excursion Through the United States and Canada During the Years 1822–23, By An English Gentleman* (London: Baldwin, Cradock, and Joy, 1824), 102 (emphasis added).

63. Interview, Nathaniel Grigsby, by William H. Herndon, September 12, 1865, in *Herndon's Informants*, 114.

high, fast waters of spring 1828. Both men would have needed to be at the
ready with steering oar and pole all night, allowing no time for sleep. We
know for certain no one else helped: "[I] and a son of the owner," wrote
Lincoln in 1860, "without other assistance, made the trip."[64] Given that
neither man ranked as expert pilot—this was Gentry's second trip and
Lincoln's first—the duo probably resigned themselves to tie up at night.
Flatboatmen minimized the lost travel time by launching pre-dawn, landing after sunset, and taking advantage of moonlight whenever possible.

It is worth noting that Francis Marion Van Natter, who hypothesized
Gentry and Lincoln leaving in bitter-cold late December, held that the
men traveled nocturnally to avoid the flatboat icing up along the bank
while tied up. Given the extremely low river stages at that time, this decision would have exposed the greenhorns to unforgiving risk. Another
flatboatman testified to these twin dangers: "The ohio is quite Low and
from the quantity of Sand Bars that Stare us in the face at Every turn we
think it unsafe to run windy days or dark nights."[65] (Van Natter also wrote
that two other flatboatmen, Steve Birch and James H. Cunningham from
Concordia and Stephensport, Kentucky, lashed up their vessel with the
Gentry-Lincoln flatboat and traveled together for hundreds of miles.
While "lashing up" was commonly practiced for safe travel and companionship, no other reliable source backs up this story. Lincoln himself, as
previously noted, specified twice that he and Gentry traveled "without
other assistance."[66])

Fourth, at what velocity did Gentry and Lincoln travel? Flatboats
generally floated at the speed of a brisk walk or jog, depending on river
stage and their navigational trajectory within the channel. High springtime waters meant a steeper gradient to the Gulf and flow rates of five or
six miles per hour or more. When the river ran low (late summer through
early winter), flow rates dropped to half or two-thirds the springtime pace.
Evidence comes from various journals. One flatboatman, for example, reported covering "ninety miles in twenty-four hours" near Natchez, a speed
of 3.75 miles per hour.[67] An English traveler in November–December

64. Lincoln, "Autobiography," June 1860, in *Collected Works*, 4:62.

65. "William P. Dole: Wabash Valley Merchant and Flatboatman," ed. Donald F. Carmony, *Indiana Magazine of History* 67, no. 4 (December 1971): 358.

66. Van Natter, *Lincoln's Boyhood*, 57; Lincoln, "Autobiography," June 1860, in *Collected
Works*, 4:62; Howells, *Life of Abraham Lincoln*, 22.

67. Diary of Micajah Adolphus Clark, as transcribed in "Flatboat Voyage to New Orleans Told Of In a Diary Kept in 1848," *Times-Democrat* (New Orleans), July 9, 1905,
part 3, p. 13, c. 5.

1828 reported that "the current [brings flatboats] down at a rate of four miles an hour."[68] *The Navigator*, an influential western river guide book published from 1801 to 1824, reported that a typical flatboat launched around Rockport, Indiana, took about four or five days to float down the Ohio, followed by three to four weeks down the Mississippi to New Orleans, a voyage totaling approximately 1,300 miles. This equates to 40 miles per day (three to four miles per hour, depending on day length) to 52 miles per day (four to five miles per hour). Pinpointing flatboat speed can be deceptive: one expedition floated from the Ohio/Mississippi confluence to New Orleans (1,023 miles) in two weeks, representing a breakneck pace of 73 miles per day. Careful reading of the journal, however, indicates substantial nighttime travel. When the total hours are tabulated, it averaged a rather normal 3.5 miles per hour.[69] River conditions aside, speed could be maximized by holding the centerline of the current, above the thalweg (the deepest trench in the channel, which leaned to either side when the river meandered), away from the friction and debris of the banks. Thus, the skill of the pilot, as well as the flatboat's design, also affected traveling speed.

As previously mentioned, 1828 water levels ranked exceptionally high and swift for the Mississippi River—and by extension the Ohio, which accounts for the lion's share of the lower Mississippi's water volume. A report field from St. Francisville, Louisiana, on March 8 stated that

> [t]he Mississippi river is now from 2 to 4 inches higher at this place than comes within the memory of man. . . . As the river is still rising, and as the highest flood is rarely ever earlier that the end of April, may we not yet see it this spring as high as it was in 1780 . . . when . . . it was at least three feet higher than it now is . . . ? Two crevasses have [already] been made at Point Coupee. . . .[70]

This level roughly equates, according to modern-day measurements, to surface velocities averaging 5.2 to 6.0 miles per hour, and peaking at 6.7 to

---

68. Frances Milton Trollope, *Domestic Manners of the Americans* (New York: Dodd, Mead, & Company, 1894 republication of 1836 original), 1:22.

69. I estimated 297 hours of daytime and nighttime travel over 1,023 miles, based on the journals of Theodore Armitage, "Flatboating on the Wabash-A Diary of 1847," *Indiana Magazine of History* 9, no. 4 (December 1913): 273–275.

70. As reported in the *Daily National Journal* (Washington, D.C.), April 12, 1828, Issue 1373, column A.

7.9 miles per hour.[71] Friction and occasionally strong headwinds would reduce this speed somewhat, such that we may reasonably assume a 5.5-mile-
per-hour flatboat speed for the springtime launch scenario. These velocity
data, which derive from modern-day Army Corps of Engineers formulae,
corroborate the pioneering work of John W. Monette, whose circa-1850
study *The Mississippi Floods* described scientifically the river system in a
way never done previously. Monette clearly would have concurred with
the above estimate:

> It will be remembered that below the junction of the Ohio,
> the Mississippi, during the floods, presents a deep, wide and
> turbid river; often covered with driftwood and *flowing at the
> rate of five or six miles per hour. . . .*[72]

Did 1828 qualify as a flood year? Indeed it did; Monette described it as
"probably the greatest flood, and the highest water, known in the lower
river within the last fifty years."[73] Thus we settle on the 5.5-mile-per-hour
estimate for the Gentry-Lincoln flatboat. If we assume twelve hours of
travel per day (daylight in this region and season lasts thirteen to fourteen
hours, minus time for launching, docking, problems, and other stops), we
estimate progress at around 66 miles per day.

•

Gentry's Landing at Rockport, lying between river miles 857 and 858
as enumerated from Pittsburgh, marked mile zero for Allen Gentry and
Abraham Lincoln as they poled their flatboat into the gray Ohio River
dawn, around Friday or Saturday, April 18–19, 1828.[74] They launched
carefully into the Ohio's tricky "riffles" (ripples), something that Lincoln would later describe as a key skill for successful navigation.[75] Within

71. U.S. Army Corps of Engineers. "River Velocities at New Orleans, LA. Related
to the Carrollton Gage," http://www.mvn.usace.army.mil/eng/edhd/velo_no.asp (visited
December 1, 2008).

72. Monette, "Mississippi Floods," 7:427 (emphasis added).

73. Ibid., 444.

74. Historical river mileage measurements range widely, depending on the source,
technique, year, and river conditions. Extensive river engineering and rechannelization
has since markedly reduced the distance to the sea. The mileages that follow are based on
those in Zadok Cramer's 1818 guide, *The Navigator* (Pittsburgh: Cramer and Spear).

75. Lincoln once told a group of Sunday school children, "the only assurance of successful navigation of certain 'riffles' depended upon the manner in which [the flatboat]
was started. . . . So it is with you young folks." "As In Years Gone By," *Chicago Daily*,

hours, he expanded his personal geography, laying eyes on terrain he had never seen before. The free North lay to their right; the slave South to their left. Gentry, the veteran, probably took pride in pointing features out to his friend. While the arctic blast two weeks earlier had killed nascent vegetation, forests and fields were now rejuvenating with new life, and it looked beautiful. The landscape into which they floated pleased the eye of a visitor who steamed the same route a few months earlier; she noted its "primaeval forest [hanging] in solemn grandeur from the cliffs . . . broken by frequent settlements [interspersed with] herds and flocks. . . ." Lining the river's edge were "perpendicular rocks; pretty dwellings, with their gay porticos," then more "wild intervals of forest," interrupted by "a mountain torrent . . . pouring its silver tribute to the stream. . . ." Nearly everyone found the undulating Ohio River Valley a scenic delight—*La Belle Riviere*, the French called it.[76]

Danger lay below the beauty. Islands with sandy-bottomed aprons could trap a loaded flatboat beyond the capacity of two men to free it. Experienced boatmen watched for them assiduously—even in high water, which tended to mask and relocate obstacles, more so than eliminate them. Along with large towns, major confluences, prominent topographic features, and distinctive structures, islands served as mile markers and metrics of trip progress. Those flatboatmen who left behind diaries and journals make this abundantly clear.[77]

Gentry and Lincoln would have spied their first impediment about two hours after launch: inundated trees on sandy islands along a slackwater shore. After passing distinctive yellow-tinged banks (site of a now-abandoned eighteenth-century frontier post, at the 12th mile of their journey), islands appeared every few miles. Some were settled; most were wild with dense willows; one stood out for its clusters of mistletoe. They then came upon a curious earthen knob—probably an Indian mound, one of many in the floodplain—known locally as French Camp for an old trading house from colonial times.[78] Somewhere in this vicinity the men tied up the flatboat for their first night's rest.

That evening afforded a first opportunity for Abraham to jot down his experiences. Unfortunately for us, he did not; indeed, the notion prob-

February 13, 1895, p. 5.

76. Trollope, *Domestic Manners*, 1:45–46.

77. See, for example, the 1839 diary of flatboatman William S. Ward, THNOC, Accession Number 2009.0139.

78. *The Navigator* (1818), 114–115.

ably never crossed his mind. Not the diary-keeping type, Lincoln even at the height of his political campaigns never felt comfortable with autobiography. He wrote publicly of himself only when pressed, and even then, veiled personal revelations by using terse syntax and referring to himself in the third person. He left no journals whatsoever of either of his trips to New Orleans.

The first substantial villages Abraham and Allen encountered, around the 80th mile of their trip, occupied an area known as Red Banks: Evansville on the Indiana side of the Ohio, Henderson on the Kentucky side. Ten years earlier, Henderson comprised "30 houses of brick and wood, 2 stores indifferently supplied, 2 long tobacco warehouses, a post office, a jail, and courthouse," an inventory that could describe any number of circa-1820s river communities. A notable navigation hazard awaited them a few hours later: Diamond Island (97th mile), "large and noble," appeared to form "two great and formidable rivers, so suddenly and equally divided is the current here, and so broad, that you scarcely know which to take for the Ohio."[79] That description, written in 1818, reminds us that what appears obvious in a map often presents a far more confusing geography when negotiated from a vessel.

Lincoln and Gentry would have come upon the mouth of the Wabash River, the largest tributary so far in their 135-mile journey, after dawn of their third day. The Wabash/Ohio confluence marked their passage out of Indiana and into Illinois, providing Abraham with his first views of the state that would one day proudly claim him as its greatest citizen. Seven miles downriver appeared a former Shawanee (Shawnee) Native American community, its population of a few hundred (including many free blacks) recently flooded out by the record-breaking spring water. Had they stopped at a low-water time, they might have discovered, as did another visitor, that "[a]rrow-heads of flint, as well as the bones, &c., of these people, are frequently found in the neighbourhood."[80] The men might also have learned of the town's government-owned salt mine, which employed locals and drew flatboat traffic. The aptly named Saline River joined the Ohio shortly downriver.

Battery Rock (156th mile) formed the most prominent topographic landmark since Rockport. The hundred-foot-high cliff extended nearly a

79. Ibid., 116–117.

80. Maximilian, Prince of Wied, *Travels in the Interior of North America*, reprinted in *Early Western Travels, 1748–1846*, ed. Reuben Gold Thwaites (Cleveland, OH: A. H. Clark, 1905), 22:200–201.

half-mile, set among what one flatboatman described as "some of the most stupendious [*sic*] scenes in nature."[81] The feature also marked a "dangerous and conspicuous [sand] bar," and often sent rocks tumbling treacherously into the river.[82] Beyond Battery Rock appeared another noted landmark, dubbed Cave-in-Rock by river travelers. "A most stupendous, curious and solid work of nature," this "House of Nature" came to be as water carved out the base of hundred-foot-high limestone cliffs. The resulting cavern afforded shelter to travelers for generations, many of whom experimented with its echo-chamber acoustics and carved their identities into its soft rock walls. Long associated with bandits and adventurers, Cave-in-Rock also attracted the attention of naturalists, including a German nobleman who visited in 1833. "The rocky wall, in which this well-known opening is situated," wrote Maximilian, Prince of Wied,

> is marked with regular, narrow, yellowish grey or reddish strata of limestone, and is crowned with cedars and other trees. . . . Calcareous petrifactions, or rather impressions [of ancient plants and leaves], are very numerous, [as are] sea shells and animal remains. . . .[83]

Visitors pondered the origin and significance of Cave-in-Rock's ancient enigmas. They also noted the hawks that regularly perched on the red cedars atop the bluff.

The frequency of sand bars, shoals, snags, "sawyers," "planters," logs, and channel-splitting islands, with names like Hurricane Bar and The Three Sisters, increased around their 170th mile.[84] One, near the mouth of the Cumberland River, was identified as where Aaron Burr camped on his flight to Mexico in 1806–7. Another, at the 209th mile, gave Allen and Abraham their first view of Louisiana bald cypress. This distinctive Southern swamp tree, a deciduous conifer with yellow-green springtime needles, would increasingly dominate bankscapes as the men progressed downriver.

81. Jacquess, "Journals of the Davy Crockett," 9.

82. *The Navigator* (1818), 119.

83. Maximilian, *Travels in the Interior of North America*, in *Early Western Travels*, 22:200–201.

84. The terms "snags," "sawyers," and "planters" described "large trees, washed from the shore, which drift down till the roots or branches . . . fasten into the mud and become as firm as when standing in the forest. Should a boat be so unfortunate as to strike one of these, it would in all probability prove fatal." Tilly Buttrick Jr., "Voyages, Travels and Discoveries" (1831), in *Early Western Travels*, 8:59.

Near the Ohio's confluence with the Tennessee (Cherokee) River was Dickey's Elbow, a reminder to flatboatmen of the dangers of their trade. Here in February 1811, five flatboats that tied up in the slack waters of a bankside "elbow" (natural slip) froze in place and had to be rescued. The confluence also spawned sandy obstacles and current shifts, the latter exacerbated on account of swift-flowing high water. Years later, this location would witness the rise of the city of Paducah, Kentucky. Mile 227, a high bank of yellowy soil surrounded by stagnant water and swamp, once hosted the French colonial Fort De L'Ascension, founded in 1757. The Americans replaced it with Fort Massac in 1794, but changing military priorities left it a ruin by the time Gentry and Lincoln passed. Another troop outpost, Wilkinson, met a similar fate a few miles downriver.[85]

•

Toward the end of their fourth day, April 21 or 22, Allen Gentry might have recognized the environs and recommended tying up for the night. Reason: a pilot would not want to tackle the approaching challenge with darkness falling. Just ahead, at mile 264, the Ohio River broadened, grew more turbulent, and doubled in volume as it joined the Father of Waters—which, only 230 miles upstream, had gained the sediment-laden waters of the Missouri River. Lincoln and Gentry must have thrilled at the moment their flatboat dashed into the Mississippi, into waters drained from the unmapped Rockies and now heading straight south to New Orleans and the sea. Years later, Lincoln would marvel, "I don't know anything which has much more power [than] the Mississippi."[86]

Exhilaration would have swiftly yielded to caution, because the rivers' differing water levels scrambled the hydrology in unpredictable ways, particularly during high-water conditions. "[T]he current naturally throws you over towards the Willow Point," a guidebook warned boatmen:

> When the Ohio is the highest, your boat is taken half way across the Mississippi. When the latter is master, you will have to row pretty hard, to reach [the Mississippi's] current, the Ohio, in such cases being backed up for several miles. . . .

85. *The Navigator* (1818), 124–126.
86. Lincoln allegedly made this remark to English war correspondent William H. Russell weeks before the Civil War broke out. Russell would later publish his experiences in secessionist New Orleans and throughout the South during the early years of the conflict. As quoted in Don E. Fehrenbacher and Virginia Fehrenbacher, *Recollected Words of Abraham Lincoln* (Stanford, CA: Stanford University Press, 1996), 388.

> [W]hirls, or swells or boils . . . are so large and strong that a
> boat is thrown half around it in passing over them, and some-
> times shot so rapidly out of them . . . that it takes strong rowing
> to get her under way again.

Heavy, load-bearing flatboats handled the currents better than light vessels bearing passengers. All watercraft needed "a stout, strong, active and
experienced man, and no other [at] the steerage, for in this depends very
much the safety of the boat and cargo." Lincoln by all accounts possessed
the strength for such a task, while Gentry had the experience. The duo
glided through "the union of two of the most noble rivers in the universe" without incident.[87] The "clear and transparent" waters of the Ohio
"remain[ed] separated and distinct, reluctant to unite & struggling for
supremacy" with the "thick and turbid" waters of the Mississippi.[88] Finally, after two or three miles, the twin currents intermixed inextricably,
and Gentry and Lincoln found themselves in a wider, murkier, wilder,
and more curvaceous riverine environment. Surely they breathed a sigh of
relief that their flatboat, built with their own hands, survived the confluence unscathed. Once the navigational excitement died down, another
realization might have struck Abraham: he was now completely immersed
in the slave South.

Ahead lay the main leg of the two-leg journey. Endless hours of tran-
quility, punctuated by occasional moments of alarm and action, awaited
them. To pass the time, flatboatmen often sang songs of the "commin
people," including the folk tune "Barbara Allen," hymns like "Am I a Sol-
ider of Christ," and "what is called carnel songs and love songs [whose
words one] cannot repeat. . . ." A cousin recollected that Lincoln enjoyed
"any thing that was Lively," but "Never would Sing any Religious Songs
it apered to Me that it Did Not souit [suite] him. . . ." A neighbor recalled
"He was always quoting Poetry" and "loved Shakespear. . . ."[89]

Wider and flatter than the Ohio Valley, the Mississippi Valley allowed the river to wend more sinuously, such that the journey ahead measured "1000 miles by water, but only 500 by land."[90] Rookie flatboatmen

---

87. *The Navigator* (1818), 127.

88. William Newton Mercer, "From Louisville to New Orleans in 1816: Diary of William Newton Mercer," ed. Edwin Adams Davis and John C. L. Andreassen, *The Journal
of Southern History* 2, no. 3 (August 1936): 398.

89. Letter, Nathaniel Grigsby, January 21, 1866; letter, Dennis F. Hanks, April 2,
1866; and interview, Caleb Carman, October 12, 1866, all with William H. Herndon, in
Herndon's Informants, 168, 242, and 374.

90. *The Navigator* (1818), 128.

laughed in impatient exasperation when the sun hit them in the face, side, and back within the same hour, as yawning meanders added five to ten extra river miles for every mile of southward progress. *Why not cut off these meanders and save all that time?*, an inquisitive mind might have asked. That the river retained its exceptional level is evidenced by a Louisianan who was undertaking the same journey at the same time as Gentry and Lincoln, reporting that "the Ohio and Mississippi both [flowed] very high . . ."[91]

Sinuosity meant more complicated river currents, more sandy banks and islands, more debris jams, and slower-moving traffic. *The Navigator* warned travelers of these hazards with admonitions like "Must not go too near the Iron Banks, there being an eddy near the shore under them;" "keep pretty close to the right hand point just above the head of the island;" and "one of the most dangerous places in low water between the Ohio and New Orleans." The guide also took time to point out historic sites, namely old forts and frontier posts, as well as the local curiosities that universally appeal to travelers. One island, for example, was home to a "Mr. James Hunter, the only man I ever knew who seemed to take a pride in [being] a professed gambler." Hunter raised hogs, cattle, and geese on the island and kept flatboatmen supplied with meat, butter, and milk.[92]

The 321st mile of the journey, and the 57th on the Mississippi, presented a geological point of interest probably missed by Gentry and Lincoln on account of high water. Here, a bank suddenly dropped off by three to four feet, the trees upon it tilted in a manner that "clearly evince the concussions of the earth" occasioned by the infamous December 1811 New Madrid earthquake. Everyone in the West remembered or heard stories about that tectonic aberration; Lincoln's own cousin referred to it as "the Shaking of Earth" and remembered it as a milestone in his life.[93] By the time Gentry and Lincoln floated by seventeen years later, the visual vestiges of the earthquake had grown obscured, but the stories lived on. Shortly downriver was New Madrid proper, a favorite overnight spot for flatboatmen.[94]

Chickasaw Bluffs, rising at the 175th river mile below the Ohio/Mississippi confluence, formed a series of topographic landmarks reminiscent

---

91. *New Orleans Bee*, May 10, 1828, p. 3, c. 2.

92. *The Navigator* (1818), 155–157 and 161.

93. Dennis F. Hanks, to William H. Herndon, March 7, 1866, in *Herndon's Informants*, 227.

94. See Timothy Flint's colorful 1816 description of flatboatmen overnighting in New Madrid, in "Appendix A: Western River Commerce in the Early 1800s."

of the Ohio River Valley. Tennessee lay to the east; the Arkansas Territory to the west. The bluffs also marked navigational treacheries with names like Devil's Race Ground and Devil's Elbow. The fourth bluff, a long high one of soft silty soil located south of the Wolf River confluence, hosted Fort Pickering. Staffed a decade earlier by "what is called the *half breed . . .* a mixture of the whites and Indians, a race of men too indolent to do any permanent good either for themselves or society,"[95] the fort would soon abut the new city of Memphis. At the time Gentry and Lincoln passed, that nascent Tennessee city counted roughly a few dozen stores, frame houses, and log cabins with one hundred or so residents—"not yet so rich, or so populous, as the ancient capital of Egypt," as one cynic put it.[96] Memphis' riverside landing would have been inundated at this time.

Downriver from Memphis, all topographic references disappeared on both banks. Eastward beneath the rising sun was the wild swampy floodplain of the Mississippi and Yazoo rivers (the so-called Mississippi Delta, Native American territory at the time); westward under the setting sun lay the equally wild Arkansas delta country. Compared to the Ohio River Valley and its bucolic bluff-top towns and pastures, "the only scenery" along this lonely stretch of the Mississippi "was still forest—forest—forest," except where the river receded to form a sand bar or batture, where "a young growth of cane-brake" arose.[97] There was, however, one curious exception: hundred-foot loess (wind-blown silt) bluffs that suddenly appeared to the *west* of the river, unlike most of the topography of the lower Mississippi Valley. Blanketed with hardwood forests, the ridgeline rose and dissipated within ten river miles. Today these hills comprise St. Francis National Forest near Helena, Arkansas.

Mile 659 of the journey (395th on the Mississippi, April 27–28) brought Gentry and Lincoln to their first encounter with a major Western tributary, the Colorado-born Arkansas River. "[F]urs, peltries, buffalo robes, &c., in exchange for goods, whiskey, &c." often passed through here, in large part via flatboats. Had the men stopped at the confluence, it would have provided Lincoln with his closest interaction to date with the far western frontier and its traders. Like the Missouri, the Arkansas changed the Mississippi more so through the injection of sediment than water volume. Muddier water, warmer climes, flatter topography, and more jungle-

95. Ibid., 162–165.
96. J. Orin Oliphant, ed., *Through the South and West with Jeremiah Evarts in 1826* (Lewisburg: Bucknell University Press, 1956), 120.
97. Trollope, *Domestic Manners*, 1:44–45.

like vegetation made real their sense of penetration into the Deep South. So too did extraordinary fauna: "Alligators or crocodiles have been seen as high up as the Arkansas," noted *The Navigator*.

The duo now sailed the least-populated and wildest part of their journey, roughly halfway between the friendly confines of their Indiana home and their exotic destination. Among the few denizens of this wild region were woodcutters and driftwood collectors living with their families in primitive huts along the banks, who made a living by supplying firewood for steamboats or lumber for export. "Great quantities of timber is got here for the Natchez and New Orleans market," explained *The Navigator*, noting that it remained unresolved as to whether the trees constituted a private or public resource. "Louisiana cost the United States 14,000,000 dollars," it marveled, but its "cypress trees [are] worth ten times more than the land they grow on."[98]

•

A few days later, unbeknownst to them, Gentry and Lincoln entered Louisiana waters. The Mississippi by this time finally ceased rising; still extraordinarily high and swift, the river would fall slightly by about eight inches during the remainder of their journey.[99] The scenery remained undistinguished until shortly after the Yazoo River joined the Mississippi from the east, at which point a series of rugged hills and plunging ravines drew close to the river. Atop sat the community known by the Spanish as Nogales and by early Anglos as Walnut Hills (855th mile of the journey, 591st down the Mississippi, around April 30–May 1), until the Vick family and others from the New Jersey region settled there in 1820. By 1828, the well-situated city of Vicksburg commanded that lofty perch over the Mississippi. Conceivably it created a lasting mental image upon which Lincoln could draw thirty-five years later, when the fate of the nation rested in part on military action under his command here. Vicksburg's landing, like most others, lay partially underwater in the spring of 1828.

Subsequent settlements on the Mississippi's rugged eastern bank usually embodied two topographically distinct sections: a residential district "on the hill," and a riverfront landing "under the hill." The former consisted of a domesticated world of families, gardens, stores, and churches, surrounded by farms and plantations. The latter was invariably commercial,

---

98. *The Navigator* (1818), 130–131, 174; Trollope, *Domestic Manners*, 1:28.

99. This is based on a weather report in the *New Orleans Price Current*, as reported in the *New Orleans Argus*, May 19, 1828, p. 2, c. 5.

rough, and raffish—the working end of town, dominated by competitive men "on the make" brusquely tending to river commerce. Connecting the "lower town" were "roads cut into the side of the perpendicular cliffs of earth, communicating with the upper town."[100] The slave trade played out most visibly on the landings, as its shackled victims were marched on those roads like so many head of cattle. One traveler in this era reported, "In all the Towns I have passed [along the Mississippi River] there were crowds of negroes for sale."[101] Interactions between flatboatmen and slaves took various forms, ranging from curious stares, to uncomfortable empathy, to camaraderie, to illicit trade, to violence. One flatboatman in 1830 was arrested by a planter for allegedly selling whiskey to his slaves; the ensuing melee cost the boatman his life.[102] Landings also exhibited "the sound of the fiddle, the roar of debauchery," gambling, drinking, disregard of the Sabbath, "profligacy, assassinations, and all sorts of iniquity."[103] For the rest of their voyage, Gentry and Lincoln would be exposed to an increasingly humanized riverfront, with higher population levels, larger numbers of slaves, frequent landings, more visible displays of wealth and enterprise, extensive plantation agriculture, and an increasingly subtropical ambience. With the wilderness of the inland delta behind him, Abraham Lincoln was now entering the heart of the Slave South for the first time in his life. He witnessed it from a river-landing perspective, and most assuredly saw numerous slaves in transit and in the fields well before arriving at New Orleans.

Those landings that were not inundated bustled with men loading last season's ginned and baled cotton onto New Orleans–bound steamboats. Upcountry flatboats docked at these mini-ports too—places such as Warrington, Grand Gulf, and Rodney ("Petit Gulf"), the latter two "so called from the great number of eddies and whirlpools which are always found here."[104] One flatboatman described Rodney and its topographies a few years after Lincoln's voyages:

This is a small but flourishing place. There is a splendid

100. Joseph Holt Ingraham, "Dots and Lines—No. I; Or, Sketches of Scenes and Incidents in the West," *The Ladies' Companion, A Monthly Magazine, Embracing Every Department of Literature* 11 (New York: William W. Snowden, 1839): 39.

101. James D. Davidson, "A Journey Through the South in 1836: Diary of James D. Davidson," ed. Herbert A. Kellar, *Journal of Southern History* 1, no. 3 (August 1935): 359.

102. "New Orleans, July 19," *New-York Morning Herald*, August 13, 1830, p. 2.

103. Ingraham, "Dots and Lines," 40.

104. Mercer, "Louisville to New Orleans in 1816," 401.

> Church just below town[;] built of brick . . . vary large . . . with pews in the finest style. We then walked on the top of the hill that is at the back of town. It is at least 150 feet higher than the town. Here you can get a beautiful view of the place and of the rivver [*sic*].[105]

All those hilltop towns and plantations generated substantial demand for upcountry produce. Flatboatmen accordingly inquired about prices for their commodities at each stop, and would not turn down a decent deal if offered. Oftentimes they sold items piecemeal: a smoked ham, a bushel of corn, a few chickens ("On almost any terms, Chickens are troublesome things to take on a flat boat," lamented one rueful boat hand; "They were getting sickley & I was glad to get clear of them. . . .)[106] Greater levels of human activity below Vicksburg signaled to flatboatmen that they should now peel their eyes for serious trading opportunities: lots of mouths to feed here, lots of money. Recalled one elder many years later,

> between the years 1823 and 1830 it was a common thing to see, moored at the bank at Rodney between twenty and thirty large flatboats, heavily loaded with western produce. Some were bound to New Orleans, while also peddling their produce along the river, while often the entire cargoes were sold at Rodney.[107]

Itinerant retailing from docked flatboats had a long history throughout the riverine West, particularly the lower Mississippi. Many flatboats were nearly as commodious as the stores of Main Street merchants, and some were almost as well stocked. Low or no rent kept expenses down, and new sources of supply and demand could be exploited with a little poling and floating. Some flatboat merchants had dubious reputations—"chicken thieves," they were called, on account of the suspicion that they stole from one plantation and sold to the next—while others operated as reputably and professionally as town storekeepers.[108]

While professional flatboatmen with clients in New Orleans had no choice but to beeline to their big-city agents, amateur or speculative ex-

105. Jacquess, "Journals of the Davy Crockett," 18.

106. Ibid., 12, 14–15, 17–18, 20. For ample evidence of en route trading, see also "William P. Dole," 335–363.

107. "In Flatboat and Keelboat Times," *Daily Picayune*, March 19, 1896, p. 14, section f, c. 6–7.

108. Lewis E. Atherton, "Itinerant Merchandising in the Ante-Bellum South," *Bulletin of the Business Historical Society* 19, no. 2 (April 1945): 46–47.

peditions often traded en route.[109] Some "worked the river" in methodi-
cal steps—loose cable, float downstream, pole in, drop anchor, tie-up,
haggle, sell, loose cable—repeatedly, from plantation to village and onward. One flatboatman made "some eight trips down the Mississippi . . .
selling produce at all the points from Memphis to New Orleans."[110] Trading
before reaching New Orleans offered certain advantages. It put hard cash
in pockets right away (a bird in the hand . . .). It could also dramatically
shorten the expedition, saving time and expenses while minimizing risk.
But trading en route could also yield lower prices and weaker profits. And
it eliminated the long-awaited chance to "see the elephant" and partake of
New Orleans' delights.[111] Some flatboatmen got the best of both worlds
by selling upcountry produce en route, re-filling the vacated deck space
with locally gathered firewood or Southern commodities such as cotton
and sugar, then proceeding to sell them in New Orleans.

Certain amusements could be found along the river—and not solely
those of liquor, laugh, and lass. Ninety-one-year-old John A. Watkins
remembered one operation that Gentry and Lincoln may well have laid
eyes on, if not experienced. "One of the features of the flatboat system,"
recalled Watkins,

> was that a certain boat was tastily fitted up with a stage, with
> scenery and with other appointments for theatrical exhibitions.
> This floating theatre was tied up for several months at a time at
> the Rodney landing during the seasons from the year 1826 to
> the year 1834, and the company gave performances which were
> highly enjoyed by the country-folk of the vicinity, and along
> the river. 'Hamlet,' 'Othello,' 'Richard III,' the melodrama—
> they hesitated at nothing.[112]

This remarkable flatboat theater, performed by "the accomplished Chapman family—father, mother, children, and grandchildren," illustrates that
Western river trade constituted an economy in-and-of itself, with a host

109. See historian Michael Allen's characterization of professional versus amateur flatboatmen, in "Appendix A: Western River Commerce in the Early 1800s."

110. As cited in "William P. Dole," 336 (emphasis added).

111. The nineteenth-century expression, "to see the elephant," probably traces to the
traveling carnivals of that era, which often held out their most popular exhibit, a live
elephant, as a sort of event climax. The expression came to mean seeing everything there
was to see, to witness the utmost. War gave the phrase darker implications: "seeing the
elephant" meant experiencing combat first-hand.

112. "In Flatboat and Keelboat Times," *Daily Picayune*, March 19, 1896, p. 14, section
f, c. 6–7.

of food vendors, suppliers, bankers, entertainers, innkeepers, prostitutes, and others eager to accommodate the cash-carrying riverman's every need and desire. It also may have presented Lincoln with his first fleeting encounter with theater, a diversion he would come to cherish until his very last moments.

Gentry and Lincoln drew closer to the world of high culture as they approached the unquestioned queen of the Mississippi bluff cities: Natchez. They arrived around May 2–3, two weeks after departure, 959 miles into their journey and 695 miles down the Mississippi. Established as Fort Rosalie in 1716 by the same man (Bienville) who founded New Orleans two years later, Natchez rose by the early nineteenth century to rank among the most important and wealthiest enclaves in the Southwest. By the time Lincoln arrived in 1828, the city had recovered from a series of devastating epidemics, and was poised for an era of economic and urban expansion. Flatboatmen approaching the city would catch sight of a magnificent new lighthouse mounted atop light-colored earthen cliffs "clothed with clouds of foliage," set among the spires and rooftops on the 200-foot-high hill. *Their* world, however, awaited them at the landing— "Natchez Under the Hill," as it has long been called—where, according to a mid-1830s observer,

> several hundred flatboats lined the levee, which was piled for two thirds of a mile with articles of export and import, the stores were crowded with goods and customers, and the throng was as dense as that in the busiest section of New Orleans.[113]

Natchez Under the Hill ranked bigger, busier, and rowdier than all other bluff-country landings. American flatboatmen earned themselves so bad a reputation here as early as the 1790s that Spanish Governor Gayoso prohibited them from climbing the hill and invading the town proper. That prohibition ended with Americanization, but the flatboatmen's reputation did not. Subsequent decades saw the emergence of a veritable industry of vice on the riverside sandbar, with numerous taverns, dance halls, grog shops, boarding houses, and brothels all catering to flatboatmen—"the most infamous place I ever saw," according to one witness.[114] High wa-

113. Ingraham, "Dots and Lines," 39. The lighthouse, completed a year before Lincoln's visit, was described by the *Natchez Ariel* and reported in the *American Advocate* (Hallowell, ME), June 20, 1828, p. 2.

114. As quoted by Michael Allen, *Western Rivermen, 1763–1861: Ohio and Mississippi River Boatmen and the Myth of the Alligator Horse* (Baton Rouge: Louisiana State University Press, 1990), 129–130.

ter flooded much of Under the Hill's honky-tonks at the time of Gentry and Lincoln's visit, but not so much that the men could not tie up for the night. Natchez constituted a major stopover for flatboat traffic, and it is reasonable to believe that Gentry and Lincoln took advantage of the protection against wind and current afforded by the half-moon-shaped harbor. Given Natchez's stature—this would have been the largest and most famous city Lincoln visited to date—flatboatmen often climbed the hill and did some sightseeing, leaving behind one crewmember to guard the cargo. (Those aboard the flatboat *Davy Crockett* a few years later took the time to climb Natchez's hill—to witness the hanging of a black man, and later attend church.[115]) This researcher postulates that Gentry and Lincoln traveled one-third their normal daily mileage on May 2 or 3, so as to allow for some exploration (and possibly trading) here.

Poling out of Natchez set Gentry and Lincoln on the final 300-mile stint of their 1300-mile journey. Pebble-bottomed tributaries such as St. Catherine's Creek and the Homochitto River intercepted their passage on the hilly Mississippi side to the east, while bottomland forest and the occasional cotton plantation dominated the flat Louisiana side to the west. Fort Adams, a military outpost dating to colonial times and now a small settlement, marked roughly the thousandth mile since their Rockport launch. A few miles later they passed the famous 31st Parallel, a former international border that now demarcated the Mississippi/Louisiana state line. They were now entirely in Louisiana. Straight west of that invisible demarcation, muddy water borne in the Rocky Mountains of Mexico (New Mexico today) flowed in from the Natchitoches plantation region. This was the Red River, the last major tributary from the western side of the valley to join the Mississippi. Its waters also flowed "very high and rising," and within a few weeks would flood the town of Alexandria in central Louisiana.[116] When conditions allowed navigating through the Red River's infamous logjams, shipping traffic serving the fertile Natchitoches sugar cane region (one of the oldest in the state and infamous for its brutal brand of bondage) merged onto the Mississippi at this point. Boatmen here would catch sight of the uppermost end of lower Louisiana's 400-mile-long system of manmade levees, lining the Mississippi wherever bluffs or terraces did not.[117]

115. Jacquess, "Journals of the Davy Crockett," 20–21.

116. "Marine Register," *New Orleans Argus*, May 29, 1828, p. 1, c. 5. For more on the serious flooding of Alexandria, see *Louisiana Courier*, June 2, 1828, p. 3, c. 1.

117. "Mississippi Levees: Memorial of Citizens of the State of Louisiana, in Favor of

Immediately below the Red River lay a confusing and potentially dangerous fork. "Be careful that you keep pretty close to the left [eastern] shore from Red river," warned *The Navigator*,

> to avoid being drawn into this current, which runs out on the right shore with great rapidity. This is the first large body of water which leaves the Mississippi, and falls by a regular and separate channel into the Gulf of Mexico.

This was Bayou Chaffalio, today's Atchafalaya River, the first distributary (that is, water flowing out of the main channel) of the lower Mississippi. Steering into the east prong of the fork, the men's attention would have been caught by an "astonishing bridge" of trees, branches, and debris drawn out of the Mississippi by the Atchafalaya's current. So dense and matted was the logjam—at the 1,032nd mile of the trip, 768th on the Mississippi, reached May 3–4—that "cattle and horses are driven over it."[118] The eighty-mile-long Red River Raft wreaked hydrological havoc on the area's ecology under normal conditions, let along during high water. By one 1828 estimate, "the enormous quantity of brush, trunks of trees, &c ... [had] gained at least one mile per annum;" and "back[ed up] the water upon the land for many miles," making "a lake of what was before a prairie. The forests too ... are often killed by the overflow of water, and after standing for a few years with their roots, submersed, the trees become rotten and fall," thus worsening the blockage.[119] The logjam also frustrated economic interests in the Acadian (Cajun) and Red River regions, by limiting direct navigational access to points south. To a problem-solving mind, the situation cried out for intervention.

Navigation interests on the Mississippi were additionally frustrated by the circuitous Old River meander, which lengthened travel time by hours. Rivermen hoped someday to avoid this loop by excavating the so-called Great Cut-Off across a swampy five-mile neck that separated the two yawning meanders (as occurred naturally in 1722 at nearby False River).[120] Over the next decade, the Old River cut-off would be excavated and the Red River logjam would be cleared. Both internal improvements tremendously aided river interests and economic development, but also instigated

Nationalizing the levees of the Mississippi River," U.S. House of Representatives, Mis. Doc. No. 41, January 13, 1873, in reference to H.R. 3419, p. 8.

118. *The Navigator* (1818), 192.

119. "The Raft of Red River," *Baltimore Gazette and Daily Advertiser*, October 17, 1828, p. 2.

120. *The Navigator* (Pittsburgh: Cramer, Spear and Eichbaum, 1814), 218.

a sequence of hydrological processes that would seriously threaten south-eastern Louisiana and New Orleans a century later.

The busy little port of Bayou Sara, named for one of the last significant tributaries draining into the Mississippi, formed another "under-the-hill" landing typical of the east-bank bluffs below Vicksburg. Bayou Sara's higher inland section was actually a separate town, St. Francisville, known for its serene beauty and the prosperity of the surrounding West Feliciana cotton country. This undulating region had changed from French to British to Spanish to independent to American hands within fifty years; by 1828, it deviated from the rest of southern Louisiana in that English-speaking Anglo-American Protestants predominated over Franco-American Creoles and Acadians. The opposite was the case on the flat western side of the river, the Point Coupée region, which represented Gentry's and Lincoln's first encounter with an extensive, century-old Francophone Catholic region in Louisiana. The physical, cultural, and agrarian landscape changed along with the ethnic makeup, as *The Navigator* explained in 1814:

> Here commences the embankment or Levee on the right [western] side of the river, and continues down to New Orleans, and it is here where the beauty of the Mississippi and the delightful prospect of the country open to view. [The banks from here], and from Baton Rouge on the left side down to the city of Orleans, have the appearance of one continued village of handsome and neatly built . . . frame buildings of one story high . . . stand[ing] considerably elevated on piles or pickets from the ground, are well painted and nicely surrounded with orange trees, whose fragrance add much delight to the scenery.[121]

Another observer described the French Louisiana sugar manors as "large square edifices with double piazzas, and surrounded by orange and other evergreen trees [and] the extensive brick 'sucriene' or sugar house." This arrangement differed from the "unpretending cottages [with] the humble wooden 'gin'" of the Anglo-Louisiana cotton landscape on the eastern side of the river. That latter environment petered out at Port Hudson—last of the bluff landings—and at nearby Profit's Island, the penultimate of the pesky atolls. The topography to the east now tapered off from bluffs with white-faced cliffs to low forested terraces, drained by the very last tributary of the Mississippi Valley, Baton Rouge Bayou. Below this stream sat

121. Ibid., 221.

the small city with that circa-1699 name, still years away from becoming the capital of Louisiana. Baton Rouge did, however, host the United States Barracks, a recently erected complex of five two-storied structures arranged in the shape of a pentagon, serving officers and soldiers deployed to the Southwest under the command of Lt. Col. Zachary Taylor. With pearl-white classical columns gleaming on the terrace, the Barracks regularly caught rivermen's attention.

An intriguing legend posits that Lincoln did more than merely gaze at the Barracks from afar. The story seems to have originated with college professor and Confederate veteran Col. David French Boyd, who served as president of Louisiana State University when the institution occupied the decommissioned Barracks in the late 1800s. Boyd perused old garrison papers and recorded the notable military figures listed as visitors, among them the Marquis de Lafayette, Ulysses S. Grant, Robert E. Lee, Thomas J. "Stonewall" Jackson, George A. Custer, and others. Boyd claimed to have identified two other famous names in the papers, each denoted as "civilian" and undated. One was Jefferson Davis; the other was Abraham Lincoln. If true, the record would form the only surviving first-hand vestige of Lincoln in Louisiana. This researcher has been unable to find the "garrison records" that Boyd inspected and thus cannot verify his claim. Intuition, however, works against it. The notion of an anonymous poor young flatboatman visiting a restricted military facility, signing in, and perhaps even spending the night seems highly improbable, not to mention inexplicable. Why would he leave the flatboat? Why would he even approach the barracks, and why would the guards allow the ill-clad youth in? Even if Boyd correctly identified Lincoln's name, it does not follow that Lincoln visited the Baton Rouge Barracks. Both Abraham Lincoln and Jefferson Davis served in the Black Hawk War (1832), as did former barracks commander Zachary Taylor. War records might have gotten mixed up with barracks records.[122]

122. Florence B. Huguet, "The Famous Men Who Passed Through Their Portals," *Baton Rouge Morning Advocate*, June 25, 1961; Walter L. Fleming, *Louisiana State University 1860–1896* (Baton Rouge: Louisiana State University Press, 1936), 440–441; Jonathan Fricker, "United States Barrack (Pentagon Barracks)—Historical and Descriptive Data," Historical American Building Survey Report (HABS No. La-1134), Heritage Conservation and Recreation Service, Departments of the Interior, Washington, D.C., 1978. I searched the papers of David French Boyd, stored in the Special Collections of Hill Memorial Library at Louisiana State University, and found no clues to support Boyd's claim. Further inquiry with the National Archives and Records Administration revealed that its records on the Baton Rouge Barracks (393.7, "Records of U.S. Army Continental Commands, Part 5, Military Installations") almost entirely post-date the era in question.

•

After departing Baton Rouge around May 4, Gentry and Lincoln floated out of the alluvial valley of the Mississippi River and entered its deltaic plain. No longer would "hills (like the oasis of the desert) relieve the eye of the traveller long wearied with the level shores," as one visitor described the topographical transition.[123] The banks—called natural levees—now lay *above* the surrounding landscape, forming the region's highest terrestrial surfaces; cypress swamp, saline marsh, and salt water lay beyond. The Mississippi River in its deltaic plain no longer collected water through tributaries but shed it, through distributaries such as bayous Manchac, Plaquemine, and Lafourche ("the fork"). This was Louisiana's legendary "sugar coast," home to plantation after plantation after plantation, with their manor houses fronting the river and dependencies, slave cabins, and "long lots" of sugar cane stretching toward the backswamp. The sugar coast claimed many of the nation's wealthiest planters, and the region had one of the highest concentrations of slaves (if not *the* highest) in North America. To visitors arriving from upriver, Louisiana seemed more Afro-Caribbean than American, more French than English, more Catholic than Protestant, more tropical than temperate. It certainly grew more sugar cane than cotton (or corn or tobacco or anything else, probably combined). To an upcountry newcomer, the region felt exotic; its society came across as foreign and unknowable. The sense of mystery bred anticipation for the urban culmination that lay ahead.

But Allen Gentry and Abraham Lincoln were here for business, not touring. Like other flatboatmen, they decided—or more likely, had been instructed by James Gentry—to remove their piloting hats at this point of the journey and don their salesmen hats. Lincoln himself stated that, during his "first trip upon a flat-boat to New-Orleans . . . [t]he nature of part of the cargo-load . . . made it necessary for [us] to linger and trade along the Sugar coast." Flatboatmen would pole along the slackwater edge of the river, drop anchor, "cable up" at the plantation landing, inquire for the manager, and offer to trade. "We are now in the sugar belt," wrote one flatboatmen upon reaching the same region; "[t]he river is always dotted with up-country boats, sometimes a score being in sight at once."[124] They

Personal communication, T. Juliette Arai, Textural Archives Services Division, National Archives and Records Administration, February 18, 2009. Gratitude goes to Marc Wellman, John Sykes, Jim Davis, and Judy Smith for assistance on this topic.

    123. Ingraham, "Dots and Lines," 38.

    124. Clark, "Flatboat Voyage to New Orleans," *Times-Democrat*, July 9, 1905, part 3,

shared the banks with washerwomen, water-retrievers, fishermen—and a sight that startled one particular traveler of this same era:

> I was surprised to see the swarms of children of all colours that issued from these [plantation] abodes. In infancy, the progeny of the slave, and that of his master, seem to know no distinction; they mix in their sports, and appear as fond of each other, as the brothers and sisters of one family. . . .[125]

Entrepreneurs also dotted the bank, setting up "tents and board camps" to "catch all the wood and timber floating in the river" and make "rafts which they sell to the sugar mills for fuel."[126] Each cluster of riverfront life, which included riverside towns like Plaquemine, Donaldsonville, and Unionville as well as plantations, offered potential trading opportunities for flatboatmen and other *caboteurs* (coastal peddlers). Some arranged their vessels like riverfront stores during the day, and free boarding houses at night. "Lingering" is how flatboatmen described this itinerant river trading.

For the purposes of our chronology, "lingering" is interpreted here as slowing down from the estimated progress of sixty-six miles per day to half that pace upon entering the deltaic plain, and half again for a few days in the heart of the sugar coast—the busiest, most cultivated, most populated, and most prosperous hundred-mile stretch of the entire Mississippi River system. Some flatboatmen sold everything here and dismantled their vessels before ever reaching New Orleans, selling the lumber to the Flat Boat Wood Yard in Iberville Parish or to similar scrap dealers set up for just that purpose.[127]

In addition to plantations, certain natural features punctuated the journey down the lowermost Mississippi as well. One was a hairpin meander below Baton Rouge that previously sent a plume of river water eastward into lakes Maurepas and Pontchartrain. Called Bayou Manchac, this waterway once hosted the main channel of the Mississippi; later, it

p. 13, c. 6.

125. William Bullock, *Sketch of a Journey through the Western States of North America: from New Orleans . . . to New York, in 1827* (London: J. Miller, 1827), xiii.

126. Clark, "Flatboat Voyage to New Orleans 8," *Times-Democrat*, July 9, 1905, part 3, p. 13, c. 6.

127. Charles J. Pike, *Coast Directory 1847* (ribbon map), THNOC, Accession Number 1953.3; see also Adolphe Henry and Victor Gerodias, *The Louisiana Coast Directory, of the Right and Left Banks of the Mississippi River* (New Orleans: E. C. Wharton, 1857), 16–18.

flowed as a distributary until fellow Westerner Andrew Jackson sealed it off in preparation for his campaign against the British in 1814–15. A similar feature, the Bayou Plaquemine distributary, appeared on the west side eight miles downriver. Such forks were worth avoiding, particularly during high water, because the turbulence caused treacherous currents and sandy shoals. So high flowed the Mississippi that, just below Bayou Plaquemine, a crevasse (breach) opened in the levee while Gentry and Lincoln passed. Reporters documented it a day or so later:

> Baton-Rouge, May 10. The Levee has given way on the plan-
> tation of Joseph Erwin, Esq. two miles below Plaquemine,
> and also on that of Mrs. Wilson next below . . . A gentleman
> . . . informs us that the breech is of considerable width, and
> from ten to fifteen feet deep. It is not expected that it can be
> stopped.[128]

Levee construction ongoing since the 1720s reduced the frequency of cre-vasses in south Louisiana, but by no means terminated them. Major levee failures flooded New Orleans in 1816 and 1849, while smaller breaches like those at the Erwin and Wilson plantations occurred periodically.

Flatboatmen en route to New Orleans expressed relief knowing that Claiborne Island would be their last navigation-impeding isle, and Bayou Lafourche their last shoal-producing distributary. After lingering and trading along the sugar coast for a roughly a week (starting, in this es-timated chronology, around May 5), Gentry and Lincoln tied up for the evening of May 12 or 13 approximately sixty miles above New Orleans. That night would prove to be the most memorable, and dangerous, of Lincoln's entire river career.

•

Using his characteristic brevity and speaking of himself and Gentry in the third person plural, Lincoln recalled many years later what happened next:

> [O]ne night they were attacked by seven negroes with intent
> to kill and rob them. They were hurt some in the melee, but
> succeeded in driving the negroes from the boat, and then "cut
> cable" "weighed anchor" and left.[129]

128. "Baton-Rouge, May 10," *New Orleans Bee*, May 13, 1828, p. 3, c. 2.
129. Lincoln, "Autobiography," June 1860, in *Collected Works*, 4:62.

Biographer William Dean Howells offered a compatible account of the incident, worth quoting because Lincoln personally reviewed Howells' draft and tacitly validated that which he did not edit:

> One night, having tied up their "cumbrous boat," near a solitary plantation on the sugar coast, they were attacked and boarded by seven stalwart negroes; but Lincoln and his comrade, after a severe contest in which both were hurt, succeeded in beating their assailants and driving them from the boat. After which they weighed what anchor they had, as speedily as possible, and gave themselves to the middle current again.[130]

Neighbors interviewed by William Herndon in 1865 readily recalled the incident, suggesting that Gentry and Lincoln featured it in fireside stories about their New Orleans adventure. "Lincoln was attacked by the Negroes," recalled neighbors;

> no doubt of this—Abe told me so—Saw the scar myself.— Suppose at the Wade Hampton farm or near by—probably below at a widow's farm.[131]

Anna Gentry shed more light on the incident, which her spouse Allen experienced firsthand:

> When my husband & L[incoln] went down the river they were attacked by Negroes—Some Say Wade Hamptons Negroes, but I think not: the place was below that called *Mdme Bush-ams Plantation* 6 M below Baton Rouche—Abe fought the Negroes—got them off the boat—pretended to have guns— had none—the Negroes had hickory Clubs—my husband said "Lincoln get the guns and Shoot["]—the Negroes took alarm and left.[132]

John R. Dougherty, an old friend of Allen Gentry whom Herndon interviewed on the same day as Anna, corroborated her details with first-person knowledge of the site:

> Gentry has Shown me the place where the niggers attacked

130. Howells, *Life of Abraham Lincoln*, 23.

131. Interview, Nathaniel Grigsby, Silas and Nancy Richardson, and John Romine, by William H. Herndon, September 14, 1865, in *Herndon's Informants*, 118.

132. Interview, Anna Caroline Gentry, by William H. Herndon, September 17, 1865, in *Herndon's Informants*, 131 (italics in original).

him and Lincoln. The place is not Wade Hamptons—but
was at Mdme Bushans Plantation about 6 M below Baton
Rouche.[133]

Dougherty was not the only Lincoln associate with personal connections
to the site; Lincoln's cousin John Hanks claimed to be in the vicinity when
the attack occurred in 1828. "I was down the River when Negroes tried to
Rob Lincoln's boat," he told Herndon in 1865, but "did not see it."[134]

•

Where exactly did the Louisiana incident occur? We have three waypoints
to triangulate off: (1) a plantation located below Wade Hampton's place,
specifically one (2) affiliated with a woman named "Busham" or "Bushan," (3) located around six miles below Baton Rouge. Wade Hampton's
sugar plantation remains a well-known landmark today, marked by the
magnificent Houmas House in Burnside, which was built twelve years after the incident to replace the antecedent house. Just below the Hampton
place, we seek a woman-affiliated plantation whose surname could only
be remembered as sounding like "Busham" or "Bushan." A parish census
in 1829, the federal census of 1830, and detailed plantation maps made
in 1847 and 1858 record no such surnames, nor a woman-led household
in the specified location.[135] But Herndon apparently gleaned additional
information that did not appear in his interview notes, because when he
published *Herndon's Lincoln* in 1889, he reported "the plantation" belonging not to "Busham" or "Bushan," but to the rhyming "Duchesne"—specifically "Madame Duchesne."[136] That surname, common in France but
not in French Louisiana, also fails to appear in the aforementioned sources.[137] The 1829 St. James Parish Census does list a Dufresne family (with

133. Dougherty's acknowledgement that he "didn't Know Lincoln" grants him an extra level of credibility, in light of the tendency of some informants to write themselves
into history by overstating their interactions with the future president. Interview, John R.
Dougherty, by William H. Herndon, September 17, 1865, in *Herndon's Informants*, 133.
    134. Interview, John Hanks, by William H. Herndon, June 13, 1865, in *Herndon's
Informants*, 45.
    135. Analysis of 1830 Enumeration Census of Ascension Parish by author, using digi-
tal files transcribed by Don Johnson and Deandra Norred Pardue; Pike, *Coast Directory
1847* (ribbon map), THNOC, Accession Number 1953.3; A. Persac, *Norman's Chart of
the Lower Mississippi River* (New Orleans: B. M. Norman, 1858).
    136. Herndon and Weik, *Herndon's Lincoln*, 1:63.
    137. The Historic New Orleans Collection's Louisiana Land Survey—six reels of mi-
crofilm, recording land owners and locations—reveals not a single listing with any of

nineteen slaves), but they do not align with our criteria. The 1830 federal census records only two Duchesne families throughout the entire region, both from New Orleans proper.[138]

Yet there *was* a Duchesne woman affiliated with this area: French-born Rose Philippine Duchesne (1769–1852), who in 1825 founded the Convent of the Sacred Heart (St. Michael's) in present-day Convent, located twelve miles below the Hampton Plantation.[139] Duchesne established Catholic missions, orphanages, convents, and schools for the American branch of the Society of the Sacred Heart, focusing on the Francophone regions of St. Louis and south Louisiana. She became well-known and well-loved in those areas; people called her "Mother Duchesne," and the institutions she founded became known as "Mother Duchesne's convent," "Mother Duchesne's school," etc., even if she did not reside there. (In fact, Duchesne was on assignment in St. Louis when Gentry and Lincoln floated south, and was recorded by the 1830 census as residing in a convent in that Missouri city.[140]) Mother Rose Philippine Duchesne was canonized a saint by the Catholic Church in 1988; a shrine in St. Charles, Missouri, entombs her remains today.

It is plausible that the property affiliated with the woman whose name sounded like "Busham," "Bushan," or "Duchesne" was in fact Mother Duchesne's convent. Gentry and Lincoln may have heard that name from passersby or river traders, and reasonably assumed it was a plantation, notable because it was owned by a woman. The convent itself certainly resembled a large plantation house of the era (see photograph in graphic section). Thus, Mother Duchesne's convent, after thirty-seven years of Indiana storytelling, became "Mdme Bushans Plantation." No other explanation has come to light.

We have one final problem in situating Lincoln's Louisiana melee: Wade Hampton's plantation is not located six miles below Baton Rouge, neither by terrestrial nor riverine measure—but exactly *sixty* river miles.

these three surnames.

138. Their heads of households were Barthe Duchesne and Ferd Duchesne; neither had any apparent connection to an upriver plantation. Population Schedule #273 and #220, Orleans Parish, Louisiana, 1830 U.S. Federal Census. See also Acadian Parish Records, 1806–1829—St. James Parish Census of 1829, MSS 23, Folder 3, Item 1, THNOC.

139. Roger Baudier, *The Catholic Church in Louisiana* (New Orleans: Roger Baudier, 1939), 293, 572.

140. This is evidenced by a letter reproduced in M. Lilliana Owens, "Loretto Foundations in Louisiana and Arkansas," *Louisiana History* 2, no. 2 (Spring, 1961): 212–213. Mother Duchesne appears in the 1830 Census on Population Schedule #328, St. Louis Township, Missouri, 1830 U.S. Federal Census.

Just as Indiana storytelling over many years may have converted "Bushan" to "Duchesne," it also may have shifted "sixty" to "six." It is worth noting that the countryside located six river miles below Baton Rouge lies only slightly beyond the cotton-dominant terraces and bluffs of the Mississippi River's lowermost alluvial valley, and barely onto the sugar-dominant deltaic plain. *Sixty* miles below, however, brings one to the heart of the Louisiana sugar region. Given that Lincoln said he and Gentry "linger[ed] and trad[ed] along the Sugar coast"[141] before the attack occurred, it sounds as though they were deep into sugar country, not recently arrived at its brink.

In sum, then, this researcher posits that Gentry and Lincoln were attacked near, of all things, a convent and girls' school founded by a future American saint. We can say with greater confidence that the melee occurred within St. James Parish, sixty to seventy-two miles downriver from Baton Rouge, on the east bank of the river (as evidenced by all three of our waypoints: Baton Rouge, Hampton's plantation, and Duchesne's convent). Some biographers position the incident as having occurred near Bayou Lafourche and Donaldsonville, but those features sit across the river and a few miles above where all evidence indicates.

Who were the attackers? Numerical probability suggests they were slaves from a nearby plantation. Circumstances, however, imply they might have been runaways. Fugitive slaves were desperate for resources, and (arguably) more inclined to run the risk of stealing to survive. Apparently the attackers spoke English, since they understood Gentry's holler to "get the guns,"[142] and not a single source mentions French words flying. This suggests the men were "American" slaves, as opposed to the French-speaking Creole slaves who predominated on the sugar coast—thus making the fugitive theory slightly more plausible. (Only a few days after the incident, the local sheriff jailed three medium-build "American negro" men, ages 24–32 and speaking English only, who were in St. James Parish "without any free papers."[143])

Legions of Lincoln biographers have imparted dramatic detail into the tussle. Others pondered the irony of the Great Emancipator nearly perishing at the hands of the very people he would later liberate, and won-

141. Lincoln, "Autobiography," June 1860, in *Collected Works*, 4:62.
142. Interview, Anna Caroline Gentry, by William H. Herndon, September 17, 1865, in *Herndon's Informants*, 131.
143. "Notice—Detained in the Jail of the Parish of St. James," posted May 22, *New Orleans Argus*, May 29, 1828, p. 1, c. 5; "Detained in the Jail of the Parish of St. James, on [May] 23," ibid., May 29, 1828, p. 2, c. 6.

dered if some attackers survived long enough to be freed by their victim. Retellings in modern-day articles and travelogues often de-racialize the incident, describing the attackers as "seven men." Others ignore it altogether, perhaps for the inconvenient twist it inflicts upon the traditional black-victimhood narrative associated with Lincoln's New Orleans experience. One writer took another tactic, explaining, with zero evidence, that the thieves were really "half-starved slaves of a no-good plantation owner," and went so far as to fabricate Lincoln saying, "I wish we had fed them instead of fighting them. . . . their owner is really more to blame than they,"[144] despite Lincoln's actual testimony of their lethal intentions.

On a different level, the incident provides insights into the nature of race relations and slavery in this time and place. Blacks attacking whites contradicts standard notions about the rigidity of racial hierarchies in the antebellum South—a hierarchy that, particularly in the New Orleans area, was more rigid *de jure* than *de facto*.[145] On an ethical level, one may view the incident as producing not seven culprits and two victims, nor vice versa, but rather nine victims—victims of the institution of slavery and the violent desperation it engendered. On a practical level, we learn from the incident two details on the flatboat voyage itself: that the men traveled unarmed, and that they indeed avoided nocturnal navigation by tying up at night.

Some say Lincoln received a lasting scar above his right ear from the fight; others say the wound landed above his right eye, although one is not readily apparent in photographs. One informant said Lincoln specifically showed him the scar.[146] The *memory* of the incident certainly lasted a lifetime, and that is perhaps the most significant message we can take away from this episode: according to Lincoln's *public* autobiographical notes, the attack, and not slavery or slave trading, formed the single most salient recollection of both his Louisiana voyages. (Private statements were a different matter; more on this later.) It is no exaggeration to say that Lincoln came very close to being murdered in Louisiana. The incident may also

144. Susan K. Thomas, "A Little Story on the Early Life of Abraham Lincoln, Told by Writer," *Morning Herald* (Hagerstown, MD), February 2, 1954, p. 3, c. 2.

145. See, for example, Roger A. Fischer, "Racial Segregation in Ante Bellum New Orleans," *American Historical Review* 74, no. 3 (February 1969): 930–931.

146. As recollected by Leonard Swett, in *Reminiscences of Abraham Lincoln by Distinguished Men of His Time*, ed. Allen Thorndike Rice (New York: North American Review, 1889), 461–462. Swett misremembered the details of the attack, reporting it as having taken place in Natchez.

underlie an unverified story that Lincoln acquired during his New Orleans trip "a strange fixation—that people were trying to kill him."[147]

•

Nursing their wounds, the shaken and bloodied men made off in the
darkness and continued downriver. The rising sun revealed plantation
houses—some modest, some palatial—fronting both banks at a frequency
of eight or ten per mile and set back by few hundred feet from what one
traveler described as the river's "low and slimy shore."[148] Lacking topographic landmarks, rivermen used planters' houses as milestones: Bayley's,
Arnold's, Forteus', Barange's—"said to be the handsomest on the river."[149]
Surely Gentry and Lincoln saw the ubiquitous lines of whitewashed slave
cabins behind each planter's residence (levee heights were far lower than
they are now), but they may not have seen multitudes of slaves in the cane
fields. At this time in May, Louisiana sugar cane began to develop "joints"
and required little field labor until "October or November, when they cut,
grind and boil the cane. . . ."[150]

Did Gentry and Lincoln continue to stop and trade after the attack?
According to the aforementioned Indiana researcher Francis Marion Van
Natter, Gentry family descendents interviewed in the 1930s contended
that the men not only continued their coastal trading, but sold off all their
cargo, dispensed with their flatboat, and then "caught a cotton boat for
New Orleans."[151] This is not impossible, but it is improbable, particularly
in light of the problems previously identified in Van Natter's research.
First of all, neither Lincoln nor his contemporaries dropped a hint of such
a scenario. Secondly, Gentry and Lincoln were plainly shaken by the attack, and being only a day from New Orleans, would reasonably want to
"linger" no more. Recall that biographer William Dean Howells wrote
(with Lincoln's personal oversight) that Gentry and Lincoln made off "as
speedily as possible, and gave themselves to the middle current again,"[152]
insinuating they bee-lined for their destination after the attack. Thirdly,
selling off everything would have made their trip to New Orleans purely
recreational for the two wounded men—and costly, sans the free trans-

147. Morris B. Higgins, "Seldom-Recalled Lincoln Visit to Orleans on Flatboat
Traced," *Morning Tribune* (New Orleans), February 12, 1940, p. 7, c. 3.
148. Trollope, *Domestic Manners*, 1:7.
149. *The Navigator* (1814), 223.
150. "Cultivation of Sugar," *New Orleans Bee*, May 13, 1828, p. 3, c. 2.
151. Van Natter, *Lincoln's Boyhood*, 144.
152. Howells, *Life of Abraham Lincoln*, 23.

portation and shelter provided by their flatboat. Van Natter's scenario thus seems unlikely.

As Gentry and Lincoln steered downriver, the passing parade of plantation houses occasionally gave way to clusters of humble cottages. Then the parade resumed, in layered sequence: manor house in front of dependencies and sheds, in front of slave cabins, in front of cane fields, with oaks, fruit orchards, and gardens on either side. "The negro quarters are well arranged," wrote one flatboatman; "invariably white and spread in full view of the river, giving the appearance of a continuous settlement."[153] Church steeples punctuated the riverside landscape: Contrell's Church and Bona Cara [Bonnet Carre] Church marked the 942nd and 960th mile down the Mississippi, while the oft-noted Red Church (978th mile) lay halfway between the distinctive West Indian–style double-pitched roofs of the colonial-era Ormond and Destrehan plantations (both of which still stand). Simple wooden cottages appeared in isolation amid fenced gardens—then in greater densities, then merging into contiguous villages, separated by fewer and fewer agrarian expanses. Shipping traffic increased; more and more Gentry and Lincoln found themselves dodging and evading other vessels. Malodorous and noisy operations—steam-powered saw mills, sugar refineries, distilleries, soap factories, tallow chandlers (renderers of animal parts for candle-making)—indicated a proximate metropolis. A cacophony of distant whistles, shouts, bells, horns, hoof beats, and hammer blows carried across the 2,000-foot-wide river, growing ever louder. Long brick warehouses for tobacco and cotton came into view, some pressing cotton lint with horse or steam power.[154]

•

Finally, in the midst of one particularly spectacular meander, a great panoply of rooftops arose on the left horizon. Sunlight glistened off myriad domes and steeples, amid plumes of steam, smoke, and dust. Allen Gentry and Abraham Lincoln had finally reached New Orleans, after 1,009 miles on the Mississippi and a grand total of 1,273 river miles since departing Rockport. The same day that started all too early with the frightening

153. Clark, "Flatboat Voyage to New Orleans," *Times-Democrat*, July 9, 1905, part 3, p. 13, c. 6.

154. Some of these details are drawn from Welcome A. Greene's 1823 journal description of the riverfront activities immediately above New Orleans. They may have changed somewhat by the time Lincoln passed them in 1828. Journal of Welcome A. Greene, reproduced in "Being the Journal of a Quaker Merchant Who Visited N.O. in 1823," *New Orleans Times-Picayune*, October 16, 1921, section 4, pp. 1 and 6.

nighttime attack in St. James Parish, ended with the springtime sunset bathing the Great Southern Emporium in a golden glow.[155]

To what degree can we pinpoint the date Abraham Lincoln first set foot in New Orleans? Because he and Gentry arrived (according to this reconstructed chronology) around dusk on May 13 or 14, it may not have been until the next morning that they paid their six-dollar fee to the Collector of Levee Dues. Those records for the year 1828 have been lost, denying us primary-source confirmation of their arrival. However, as previously explained, the local bilinguals *New Orleans Bee* and *New Orleans Argus* reported the Collector's activities in their daily "Marine Register" and "Marine" ("Ship News") columns, which listed port arrivals and departures. These newspapers mostly survive. Scanning the *Bee* from mid-April through mid-June 1828, we count 158 flatboats arriving to the port, originating from Kentucky, Tennessee, Alabama, Ohio, Virginia (today's West Virginia), and Bayou Lafourche. The *Argus* reported roughly the same number. Many of the flatboats carried cotton; some from Kentucky brought *boucauts* of tobacco, ham, flour, and whiskey. Most freight was already commissioned to local merchants and not owned by the flatboatmen. Only one flatboat is recorded as coming from Indiana, but it definitely was not Lincoln's, because it arrived too early (April 19–20), bore the wrong cargo (tobacco), and belonged to a professional merchant (as opposed to an amateur "owner on board").[156] But then we find a few exceptional listings in the middle of May, each reflecting the previous day's activity. The *Argus* reported in its flatboat section of May 14 the arrival of "Several boats from the western country, with flour, bacon, &c. [with] owners on board."[157] Three days later, the *Bee* reported, "Quinze chalans de divers endroits, avec du produits du pays [Fifteen flatboats from various places, with products from the country]."[158] The *Argus* on May 17 reported those same arrivals as "Fifteen flat boats from the Western country, with flour, whiskey, bacon &c. to owners on board and to order."[159] Tallies

155. Did the attack happen on the same day as the arrival to New Orleans? If the incident occurred somewhere between Burnside and Convent (60 to 72 river miles above New Orleans) and Gentry and Lincoln escaped in pre-dawn darkness at the assumed velocity of 5.5 miles per hour, they would theoretically arrive at New Orleans in about twelve hours—late afternoon or early evening of the same day of the attack.

156. *New Orleans Argus*, April 21, 1828, p. 2, c. 6.

157. Ibid., May 14, 1828, p. 2, c. 6.

158. "Nouvelles Maritimes—Port de la Nlle.-Orleans, *New Orleans Bee*, May 17, 1828, p. 2, c. 4. "Marine" listings appeared only in the French section at this time in 1828.

159. "Marine Register," *New Orleans Argus*, May 17, 1828, p. 2, c. 5.

from both newspapers rank mid-May 1828 as the *busiest flatboat week of the entire year*, by a wide margin, with the *Bee* counting 53 arrivals and the *Argus* enumerating roughly 73 (see graphs, "Flatboat Traffic Arriving to New Orleans, 1828–29 . . ."). Unlike most other flatboat listings in either newspaper, these entries (1) mention miscellaneous farm products rather than standard plantation commodities like cotton and tobacco; (2) indicate that many of the flatboatmen owned their own cargo; (3) describe the flatboats' origins as "various places" in "the Western country"; and (4) lump together more flatboats than any other entry for an entire year. These clues suggest that the arrivals mostly constituted small amateur flatboats from tiny towns with little-known names—places much like Rockport, Indiana. When we consider the overall chronology of the voyage and the exceptionality of these particular listings, we gain confidence that Abraham Lincoln's flatboat was among those reported in the May 14 or May 17 newspapers. Perhaps they arrived on May 13, paid dues immediately, and appeared in the next day's newspaper, or perhaps they arrived on or after May 14, paid dues the next day or so, and appeared in the newspaper a day or so later, meaning May 17. (It is not until the June 3 editions of the *Bee* and *Argus* that we see another entry for small owner-on-board flatboats arriving "from the Western country"—a date nearly three weeks too late to align with all other chronological evidence of the Gentry/Lincoln voyage.[160]) The May 14 listing and the twin May 17 listings may be the closest we every get to documentation of the future president's first arrival in New Orleans.

•

Veteran flatboatmen like Gentry knew where to go and what to do: steer into the current toward the upper end of that long thorny line of poles, masts, rigging, sails, and smokestacks. Silhouette of the great Western fleet, the bristling accoutrements belonged to local vessels like the *bateau à vapeur* (steamboat) *Columbia* departing for Bayou Sara, and to ocean-going sailing ships bound for Liverpool, Havre, and Bordeaux. Those craft crossed paths with the brig *Castillo*, pulling out for New York; the schooner *Triton*, bound for Charleston; and the *Correo*, destined for Tampico, Mexico. Outgoing vessels made room for the Mexican brigs *Doris* and *Orono*, bringing in passengers and Campéche wood from across the Gulf, and the *bateau de remorque* (towboat) *Grampus* coming in from the mouth

160. "Marine Register," ibid., June 3, 1828, p. 2, c. 5.

of the Mississippi.[161] The hypnotic maneuvering—involving ships that Lincoln had previously seen only in drawings, bound for exotic destinations he knew only through books—played out less than a mile downriver from their destination. That stretch, the lowly uptown flatboat wharf, saw none of the spectacular sights and sounds of the downtown steamboat and sailing wharves, but bustled nevertheless with impatient pilots, flailing poles, tossed ropes, and hurled invectives. Gentry and Lincoln, as it turned out, picked a bad time to arrive: mid-May 1828 saw more flatboat arrivals (53) than any other ten-day period during the surrounding year, with the highest single-day total (28) being reported in the *New Orleans Bee* on May 17.[162] Among those *chalans* docking with Gentry and Lincoln were ten from Tennessee and Alabama delivering cotton for local Anglo merchants, three from Kentucky with cotton and tobacco mostly consigned to local dealers, and fourteen small amateur operations like theirs, originating from various upcountry places.[163]

Once at the doorstep of "the grand mart of business, the Alexandria of America," wrote *The Navigator*, the archetypal flatboatman

> leaps upon shore with ecstasy, securing his boat to the bank with a careful tie, mounts the Levee, and with elated heart and joyful countenance, receives the warm and friendly hand of a fellow citizen, in whose integrity he confides, and to whom in confidence he can dispose of his cargo.[164]

That flowery commentary underreported the challenges flatboatmen encountered at the New Orleans levee, which ranked, even in the "warm and friendly" hands of fellow American citizens, as a rough-and-tumble place.

The technical machinations of flatboat docking involved approaching, evading other vessels, negotiating a slot, poling in, and tying up while river currents, surface winds, and impatient competitors formed a shifting obstacle course. One flatboatman described what could go wrong:

161. "Nouvelles Maritimes—Port de la Nlle.-Orleans, *New Orleans Bee*, May 17, 1828, p. 2, c. 4. Illustrating the danger of steam navigation in this era, the *Grampus* wrecked only three months later, when its six boilers exploded while towing four vessels. Seven men were killed, five went missing, and four were wounded. "Items," *Norwich Courier* (Norwich, CT), September 17, 1828, p. 3.

162. Survey of daily "Maritime" columns in the *New Orleans Bee* conducted by author from April 1, 1828, through March 31, 1829.

163. "Nouvelles Maritimes—Port de la Nlle.-Orleans, ibid., May 17, 1828, p. 2, c. 4.

164. *The Navigator* (1814), 225.

> As we were pulling in to make a landing [at New Orleans] one
> of our sweep pins broke, which handicapped us. We pulled with
> all our power for several miles, then ran in below the landing
> and [had to pull] back by ropes. After we got in [we] found we
> had [been dragging] the largest kind of a log all day, which
> explained why our boat was so difficult to manage. . . .[165]

Once a flatboatman jumped ashore and looked around, he would have
noted the same topographical curiosity at which first-time visitors marvel
to this day. Unlike the landings lying *below* the bluff-top cities upriver, the
landing in New Orleans lay *above* its city. "What struck me most," wrote
a visitor from Edinburgh during the same year, "was the [Mississippi's]
surface being six or seven feet higher that the level of the streets of New
Orleans. . . . [I]t seemed as if the smallest shake [would] submerge the
city."[166] The impression would have been even stronger given the high
water of May 1828.

•

While we cannot determine precisely where Gentry and Lincoln docked,
contextual information helps narrow down the possibilities. We know
that in 1828, flatboats, barges, and other small upcountry vessels docked
in a zone starting at the foot of Notre Dame and adjacent Julia streets in
Faubourg St. Mary and extending upriver. How far upriver depended on
overall flatboat activity and docking density, the topics of our next discussion.

A tally of *New Orleans Bee*'s "Maritime" columns for the month leading
up to Lincoln's arrival reveals 104 *chalans* docking at New Orleans.[167] Official reports usually undercount actual figures, so when we adjust for un-
reported arrivals, local traffic, "lingering" flatboats, and other activity not
likely to appear in the newspaper, we can increase that figure by roughly
half. That estimate (of around 150–160) is substantiated by analyzing the
surviving Wharfinger reports from 1819–22 and 1845–49 and interpolat-
ing what sort of activity may have occurred in 1828. Given that an average of 512 dues-paying flatboats (not including barges) arrived annually

165. Clark, "Flatboat Voyage to New Orleans," *Times-Democrat*, July 9, 1905, part 3,
p. 13, c. 7.
166. Basil Hall, *Travels in North America in the Years 1827 and 1828* (Edinburgh and
London, 1830), 3:319–320.
167. Tally of "Maritime" columns of *Bee* conducted by author from April 17, 1828,
through May 17, 1828.

during 1819–22, compared to 1,940 flatboats per year during 1845–49, we calculate that an additional 54 flatboats arrived every year between the early 1820s and the late 1840s.[168] That puts 944 flatboats (512 plus eight years' of the 54-flatboats-per-year increase) arriving to New Orleans during the year of 1828. It also puts 1,188 flatboats arriving to New Orleans during the year 1833—a key year, because that's when visitor Joseph Holt Ingraham estimated "about two hundred of these . . . 'flat-boats' . . . and 'keel-boats'" docked along the uptown flatboat wharves.[169] If Ingraham estimated accurately, this means that 17 percent of the entire year's arrivals could be seen docked simultaneously at any one moment. Applying this percentage to 1828's total arrivals, we corroborate that around 160 flatboats docked at any one time (17 percent of 944) during the busy season.

One-hundred-sixty docked flatboats, each typically measuring 12 to 20 feet in width and requiring about five feet of space on either side, form a 4,160-foot-long flatboat wharf. Density in docking was inconsistent: those lucky enough to tie up closest to the busy Notre Dame/Julia end of the wharf docked two-deep or three-deep, sacrificing the convenience of bankside adjacency in exchange for proximity to inner-city commercial activity. (An 1828 riverfront sketch made by Capt. Basil Hall, one of the best visual depictions of a Lincoln-era flatboat landing, illustrates this practice; see graphic section.[170]) One report noted that flatboats "moored so closely together by the river-side, that one may run along . . . their flat-covered tops with equal facility as upon the deck of a ship," something also evident in Hall's sketch.[171] Flatboatmen who tied up at the quieter, upriver end of the wharf generally spread out and gave themselves elbow room to unload and disassemble their vessels. Adding in occasional open spots (for water, for access, or because of sedimentation or wharf damage) along that line of approximately 160 flatboats, we can safely extend the 4,160-foot-long uptown flatboat wharf by a few blocks.

Based on the above estimations, this analysis views the uptown flatboat wharves in May 1828 as extending roughly one mile upriver from the

168. Statistical analysis by author based on Wharfinger Reports/New Orleans Collector of Levee Dues-Registers of Flatboats, Barges, Rafts, and Steamboats in the Port of New Orleans, 1818–23 and 1845–49, Microfilm #75-109 QN420, New Orleans Public Library, Louisiana Collection.

169. Joseph Holt Ingraham, *The South-West by a Yankee* (New York, 1835), 1:105.

170. Cap. Basil Hall, "The Mississippi at New Orleans," drawn around 1828 and engraved by W. H. Lizars. THNOC, Accession Number 1974.25.30.576 P.C. 30-11-A.

171. "Flat-Boat Commerce," J. D. B. De Bow, *Commercial Review of the South and West* 4, no. 4 (December 1847): 556.

foot of Notre Dame and Julia streets in Faubourg St. Mary, with docking occurring at the highest density at that downriver end and thinning out around Richard and Market streets in the faubourgs La Course and Annunciation. This latter area generally marked the upper edge of urbanization in New Orleans at the time (the adjacent suburb of Lafayette, across Felicity Street in Jefferson Parish, was under development[172]), so it serves to reason that flatboat docking generally correlated to urban density.

Eyewitness confirmation of this one-mile estimate comes from Robert Goodacre, who saw the same sight from the same angle and wrote, "For the first mile along the coast of the Mississippi, flat boats or arks form a continued line. . . . This motley collection is succeeded [below Notre Dame Street] by the steamboats. . . ."[173] Charles Joseph Latrobe corroborated the estimate when he viewed the port from the roof of the Bishop's Hotel on New Year's Day 1834 and estimated "ships and boats of every size [extended] upwards of two miles . . . [h]ighest up the stream lie the flats, arks, and barges. . . ."[174] Given port expansion between 1828 and 1834, and given the location of the Bishop's Hotel at the corner of Camp and Canal, Latrobe's two-mile estimation aligns well with our one-mile estimate. Additional corroboration comes from the detailed journal of the flatboat *Davy Crockett*, which landed "at the upper end of Lafayette New Orleans" in February 1835: seven years of port expansion had by that time extended the flatboat wharf upriver to around Louisiana Avenue, which, at that time, was in the Jefferson Parish city of Lafayette.[175] One final corroboration of the length of the flatboat wharf comes from an 1885 reminiscence of the 1820s, when "hundreds of [flatboats lay] side by side, so that one could walk almost a mile on their curved decks without going ashore."[176]

Another eyewitness account differs markedly from the above. James Stuart, who visited New Orleans during the busy month of March in 1830, wrote that "[t]here are sometimes 1500 flat boats lying at the sides

172. "For Sale, A valuable property, situated in Jefferson parish, Lafayette suburb . . . ," *New Orleans Bee*, May 13, 1828, p. 4, c. 3.

173. "New Orleans—Goodacre's Lecture," *Delaware Weekly Advertiser and Farmer's Journal*, March 27, 1828, vol. 1, no. 28, p. 1, c. 4.

174. Charles Joseph La Trobe, *The Rambler in North America* (New York, 1835), 2:244–245.

175. Jacquess, "Journals of the Davy Crockett," 23.

176. New Orleans Press, *Historical Sketch Book and Guide to New Orleans and Environs* (New York: Will H. Coleman, 1885), p. 201.

of the levee at a time. . . ."[177] This extraordinarily high number does not concord with other evidence. Stuart's use of the word "sometimes" suggests exceptionality or hyperbole. Maybe he included all vessels across the entire port, or perhaps he accidentally added an extra zero to a more likely estimate of 150.

The circa-1828 flatboat wharf occupies today's Warehouse District and Lower Garden District riverfront—but does *not* align with the present-day riverfront. Slight shifts in the channel of the Mississippi River in the early 1800s, coupled with the fact that the flatboat wharf occupied the point-bar side of the river's crescent-shaped meander, allowed an ever-growing sandy beach (batture) to form along the Faubourg St. Mary levee. The question of whether public or private interests owned this valuable new riverfront land spawned a decades-long legal controversy, reflecting differing Creole and American legal philosophies and personally involving at one point President Thomas Jefferson. By the time Lincoln arrived, the so-called St. Mary Batture had formed one to two extra blocks of new land east of Tchoupitoulas Street, which were surveyed with the aptly named New Levee Street (today's South Peters Street) and, where space permitted, Front Levee Street (now Convention Center Boulevard). Further alluvial deposition plus subsequent levee realignments during the nineteenth and twentieth centuries appended another two to four blocks of cityscape to the colonial-era riverfront. This means that the Lincoln-era flatboat wharf is now landlocked hundreds of feet away from the present-day edge of the Mississippi River (see graphic section for photographs and maps). Flatboat remnants have been occasionally uncovered in the soils of today's Warehouse District and Lower Garden District; a newspaper in 1883 reported the "hull of an old [flat]boat, recently dug up on one of our front streets while the men were preparing the foundation of a building."[178]

Probability helps narrow down Gentry and Lincoln's likely landing site. We can be nearly certain that they did *not* dock in the Old City. Some flatboats did land around the foot of Conti Street ("I counted thirty-nine" steamboats docked around Canal Street, stated Robert Goodacre in April 1826, *"Below these is another continued line of flat boats, or arks. . . ."*[179]). But

177. James Stuart, *Three Years in North America* (Edinburgh and London: Robert Cadell and Whittaker and Company, 1833), 2:232.
178. Charles E. Whitney, "Flatboating Days," *Times-Democrat*, June 10, 1883, p. 5, c. 5–6.
179. "New Orleans—Goodacre's Lecture," *Delaware Weekly Advertiser and Farmer's Journal*, March 27, 1828, p. 1, c. 4 (emphasis added).

those flatboats specifically served downtown markets with fresh vegetables, fish, game, firewood, and other retail produce, rather than upcountry bulk produce. Instead, it was the uptown flatboat wharf that almost certainly received Gentry and Lincoln. A coveted slot near Notre Dame/Julia would have been unlikely, because professional merchant navigators running major flatboat operations tended to monopolize that valuable space. Greenhorn amateurs like Gentry and Lincoln probably settled for an easier uptown slot, toward Richard and Market streets. The most probable landing site lies somewhere among the open fields immediately south of the Mississippi River bridges, along South Peters Street near the Henderson intersection. On the bicentennial of Abraham Lincoln's birth, these fields lay vacant, weedy, and eerily silent.

•

Once landed, flatboatmen needed to dispense of their cargo. Lacking any clues on how Gentry and Lincoln handled this critical task, we must look to the experience of other boatmen in this era. Professionals sold their freight in a very different manner than their amateur peers. Merchant navigators and agent flatboatmen, who captained or contracted voyages on a regular basis, generally delivered their order to local clients on a familiar, colleague-to-colleague basis. They carefully marked their cargo with initials and numbers to ensure the right parcels went to the right owners. Evidence from the *New Orleans Bee* indicates that most flatboat cargoes arriving in spring 1828 were already owned by local merchants. Those clients expecting deliveries of cotton usually had Anglo names like Townsely, Christy, Ferguson, Hagan, and Fowler; those awaiting sugar from Bayou Lafourche had Francophone names like Peyroux and Rivarde.[180] Occasionally thieves would exploit the handover and make off with unguarded cargo, as might have been the circumstances behind this announcement a few days prior to Lincoln's arrival:

> Cotton Lost—Any person having received from Obadiah Gordon's flatboats, eight bales of cotton, marked G B, Nos. 1 to 8, shipped at Jackson, Tennessee, will confer a favor by communicating [with] Smith & Hyde, 15 Common-st.[181]

Farmer flatboatmen like Gentry and Lincoln had to figure things out on

180. "Maritime" columns, *New Orleans Bee*, April 15 through June 15, 1828 (analysis by author).
181. *New Orleans Argus*, May 13, 1828, p. 1, c. 1.

their own.[182] The *Bee* described such amateur outfits as *propriétaire à bord*. They lined the wharf and displayed their goods like one long linear market, awaiting customers. According to an 1828 account, "[h]ams, ears of corn, apples, whisky barrels, are strewed upon [each flatboat], or are fixed to poles, to direct the attention of the buyers."[183] Anyone who approached was buttonholed by crewmembers to work out a deal. For a greenhorn country boy, negotiating multiple sales in a brusque and competitive port city could be an intimidating and high-stakes experience. *Who's trustworthy? Who's a crook? Should we hold out for a better price? Is this counterfeit money?* "[A] great degree of rudeness, and a great deal of swearing" flew among the various players on the flatboat wharf.[184] Commodity news during the week of Lincoln's arrival reported cotton doing well, sugar fairly stable, molasses going down, pork selling well at $4 per barrel and rising, bacon selling readily for the past three months but "getting dull," flour getting $4 per barrel, whiskey at 21½ cents per gallon, and sales weakening on bagging and rope.[185] If numerous flatboatmen arrived with similar cargo, those prices could plummet. If buyers colluded, flatboatmen again suffered. If inspectors found fault with the quality of the produce, the entire cargo could be seized and auctioned off as damaged goods, for the benefit of the Port. Every day passing without a buyer meant depreciating cargo, mounting expenses, and further delay before the next paying job. The anxiety got the best of some men, luring them into arson in the hope of an insurance settlement. "Last week," wrote one New Orleanian a few years before Lincoln's visit,

> a poor man, who had a flatboat loaded with 350 to 400 barrels of flour, newly arrived from the upper country, finding no price for his cargo, in a fit of desperation set fire to it at mid day, which communicated to two other flatboats and consumed the whole.[186]

One rare description of a flatboatman's vending experience comes from

182. The term "farmer flatboat" comes from Michael Allen, "The Riverman as Jacksonian Man," *Western Historical Quarterly* 21, no. 3 (August 1990): 312–315.

183. Charles Sealsfield, *The Americans As They Are Described in A Tour Through the Valley of the Mississippi* (London: Hurst, Chance, and Co., 1828), 146.

184. Stuart, *Three Years in North America*, 2:239.

185. "New-York Market" and "From the N. Orleans Price Current of May 17," *New Orleans Argus*, May 19, 1828, p. 2, c. 4–6.

186. "Extract of a Letter from a Gentleman in New-Orleans," *Patron of Industry* (New York), January 24, 1821, p. 2.

Asbury C. Jacquess, who restocked with wood after selling his original cargo on the sugar coast. He and his crew, in February 1835,

> landed at the upper end of Layfayette [sic] New Orleans on 19th at 10 oclock in the morning. Directly after we landed we were offered $1.75 cts for our wood. We tried most of the brick yards & wood yards but the highest offer we have had is $2.00 per cord. The steam boats wont have it, they want Ash. [The next day,] Seeing we can do no better, we have sold out to a French man named De.li.shau at $2.00 per chord. We had to sell our beef at about half its value. I sold 1 lb & 1/2 lb of beef at $5.00 dollars.

There was another option if no wholesaler offered the right price: flatboatmen could retail their cargo piecemeal directly to citizens. Retailing garnered higher prices for smaller quantities, and if it took more time than wholesaling, so be it: flatboatmen slept for free on board their docked vessels, and few complained about extra days in this subtropical Sodom and Gomorrah. "Retailing flat-boats," however, earned the wrath of nearby storekeepers, who paid high rent and taxes and resented the competition from scruffy "Kaintucks." "The owners of the flat-boats no sooner arrive," wrote one business writer, "than they open their floating shops for the sale of their respective cargoes; and as their prices average little more than one-half of those . . . in the stores of the city, there are always numbers of customers thronging the levee and keeping the [flatboat wharf] in a state of remarkable livcliness."[187] Storekeepers battled flatboatmen over this issue throughout the antebellum years, getting the city (in 1823) to fine them five dollars per day if they retailed beyond eight days after landing.[188] Later they succeeded in banishing retailers to the nuisance wharf, over a thousand feet above Notre Dame/Julia, or the retailers would face a severe twenty dollar fine.[189] But this simply pushed the activity upriver.

•

Storekeepers were not alone in hating flatboatmen. The upcountry lads

187. "Flat-Boat Commerce," J. D. B. De Bow, *Commercial Review of the South and West* 4, no. 4 (December 1847): 556.
188. *Conseil de Ville*, Session of March 24, 1823, p. 150 of microfilm #90-222, AB301, New Orleans Public Library Louisiana Collection (hereafter cited as NOPL-LC).
189. *Conseil de Ville*, Session of March 23, 1824, p. 327 of microfilm #90-222, AB301, NOPL-LC; *Louisiana Advertiser*, December 2, 1826, p. 2, c. 3; *New Orleans Bee*, June 22, 1835, p. 2, c. 1.

also earned the reproach of townspeople by fouling the air and polluting the water. Carcasses, debris, and human waste routinely went directly in the Mississippi, and accumulated along the uptown wharf for the same reason that sediment deposited there. Crews using their flatboats as boarding houses produced as much waste as a small family. Those using their vessels as open-fire cooking and smoking operations (to keep meat from spoiling) threatened the highly flammable cotton bales stacked on the wooden wharf. An on-board fire one month before Lincoln's arrival led to an entire flatboat igniting, a spectacle that attracted a crowd of all-too-helpful onlookers. "A number of persons vociferated—*cut her adrift*," recounted a miffed merchant in the newspaper a week later,

> —the most dangerous advice that could have been given, as she must inevitably have drifted among the shipping, [possibly igniting] the steamboats, and part of the city. . . . The practice of smoking bacon in flatboats lying at the Levee, is dangerous and mischievous, and we believe, contrary to law.[190]

Indeed it was: six weeks earlier, the City Council prohibited flatboatmen from smoking meat on board.[191]

Smoking bacon was but one illegal nuisance. Other flatboats "exhale[d] an odor so fetid [from] spoiled corn, and filth of hogs . . . that [a landlord's tenants] have come to notify him, that they were about to leave, not being able any longer to resist those unsanitary exhalations [of] said flatboats. . . ."[192] Nearby homeowners winced at the flatboatmen's "horses, fat and lean cattle, sheep, hogs[,] all sorts of domestic poultry, and various kinds of large and cumbrous materials" dumped in their neighborhood and driven through the streets.[193] The men themselves were deemed, like their livestock, to be nuisances—particularly "Kentucky men, [who] were infinitely the worse of the whole party," as one suffering traveler explained:

> [T]he unheard-of volubility of oaths incessantly uttered, and the delight they appeared to take in cursing and blaspheming,

190. *Louisiana Advertiser*, April 19, 1828.

191. *Conseil de Ville*, Session of March 1, 1828, p. 202 of microfilm #90-223, AB301, NOPL-LC.

192. *Conseil de Ville*, Session of August 21, 1824, p. 54, and Session of March 1, 1828, p. 202, of microfilm #90-223, AB301, NOPL-LC.

193. "New Orleans—Goodacre's Lecture," *Delaware Weekly Advertiser and Farmer's Journal*, March 27, 1828, p. 1, c. 4.

were only equalled by the profligate *novelty* of the execrations
with which their most indifferent observations were interlard-
ed, and which exceeded every thing that I could possibly have
imagined. There were, doubtless, some respectable individuals
[among them; if only they could] have been separated from the
rest. . . .[194]

Uncouth young rascals fouling the city, clogging the wharf, underselling
respectable businessmen, swaggering, swearing, raising Cain: no wonder
agitated "subscribers" denounced the lowly flatboatmen regularly in antebellum newspapers. Decency usually forced the aggrieved parties to use
decorous language in the printed word. *Spoken* word, however, flew more
bluntly, as evidenced by the variety of choice monikers and reputations
ascribed to the upcountry lads. "There's the hoosiers of Indiana, the suckers of Illinoy, the pukes of Missuri," went one characterization of New
Orleans flatboatmen;

> the buckeyes of Ohio, the red horses of Kentucky, the mud-
> heads of Tennessee, the wolverines of Michigan, the eels of
> New England, and the corn crackers of Virginia. . . . It is a
> great caravansary filled with strangers, disperate enough to
> make your hair stand on end, drinkin' all day, gamblin' all
> night, and fightin' all the time.[195]

So widespread grew the flatboatmen's repugnant reputation (deservedly
or not) that it tainted all working-class Anglo-American men and became entrenched in countless historical narratives told many years later.
"[H]undreds of flatboats came down the river, and the city swarmed with
bargemen," went a typical characterization (this one from the *Atlantic
Monthly* in 1901);

> —a rough, disorderly class, which by its boorishness of manner,
> lack of culture, and keen scent for a bargain, gave an evil savor
> to the name "American;" so that to this day many old-fashioned
> residents of the old quarter still look upon the Anglo-Saxon as
> a semi-barbarian . . . and one still hears, occasionally, the negro

194. Henry Tudor, *Narrative of a Tour in North America* (London: James Duncan,
1834), 2:54–55.

195. "Extracts from the Clockmaker," *The Madisonian*, 2, Issue 19, October 20, 1838,
p. 1. Another version of this piece appears as "Sam Slick's Description of New Orleans,"
Barre Gazette (Barre, MA), 5, Issue 37, January 25, 1839, p. 1.

expression *Méricains coquins* ["American rascals"].[196]

Most flatboatmen working the uptown wharf were young Anglo-American males from farming families, poor but hardworking and entrepreneurially motivated, uneducated but savvy, and native to any one of the Western states (although often generalized as "Kaintucks"). Not many locals worked there; those who did tended to be Irish immigrants rather than the Creoles and Frenchmen associated with New Orleans' downtown markets and wharves. Those of African descent seemed to number few, and often walked about unshackled and apparently unmolested. A first-time flatboatman expecting the exotic might have been surprised: New Orleans' uptown flatboat wharf turned out to be much like the various "under-the-hill" landings of Vicksburg, Natchez, Bayou Sara, and other Mississippi River towns, except a hundred times larger and a whole lot flatter. Economically and culturally, the wharf formed the trans-Appalachian West's toehold in New Orleans, populated by a revolving cast of characters floating in and steaming out on a weekly basis. A few blocks away lay the Northeast's *permanent* toehold in New Orleans—Faubourg St. Mary, which, according to one antebellum visitor, reflected "here a little of Boston, there a trifle of New York, and some of Philadelphia, with something of the *rus in urbe* so charmingly common to New England towns. . . ."[197] Gentry and Lincoln would first have to disassemble their flatboat before exploring *that* city, not to mention the *other* city across Canal Street.

•

Disassembling a flatboat went a whole lot faster and easier than building one, but it still took time, space, and brawn. "The weather has been warm, but otherwise favorable for out-door business," reported the *Price Current* when Gentry and Lincoln dismantled their vessel—"until yesterday [May 16], when it became showery."[198] Flatboatmen annoyed port officials when they lingered too long in deconstruction. The city intervened in 1819, 1822, 1827, and 1831 with laws stiffening penalties on the unsanctioned or excessively slow "demolition of Chalans, Barges, Keelboats, Rafts, 'Ca-

196. Albert Phelps, "New Orleans and Reconstruction," *The Atlantic Monthly* 88, no. 525 (July 1901): 123.
197. A. Oakey Hall, *The Manhattaner in New Orleans; or Phases of "Crescent City" Life* (New York: J. S. Redfield, 1851), 35.
198. *New Orleans Price Current*, as reported in the *New Orleans Argus*, May 19, 1828, p. 2, c. 5.

jeaux' and other small craft." At one point, the City Council resolved to "cast adrift" any empty flatboat after twenty-four hours of unloading.[199]

Once deconstructed, flatboat lumber was often purchased by the city to cover the wharf, to construct the city's *banquettes* ("little benches," raised wooden sidewalks along muddy streets), to build sewerage chutes into the river, and for other municipal purposes.[200] Massive gunwales might also see a second life as structural beams, although their tapered ends and mortises rendered them less than ideal. Flatboat boards often became clapboards for the city's thousands of wooden cottages, particularly in the immigrant neighborhoods adjacent to the uptown flatboat wharf (today's Lower Garden District and Irish Channel). Smaller planks ended up in the ubiquitous picket fences lining the muddy streets of outlying faubourgs. Demand for wood ran high; lumber from a dismantled flatboat typically returned one-quarter to one-half its initial construction cost.[201] It is safe to say that some flatboat lumber remains in service today as studs, beams, rafters, and joists in historic New Orleans houses, frozen in place for nearly two centuries after an epic journey from virgin forest, down the Mississippi, to the flatboat wharf.[202]

•

If we postulate Gentry and Lincoln took three or four days after their May 13–14 arrival to vend their cargo, disassemble their flatboat, and sell the lumber, the men would have been released from their duties starting around May 16–18. After this moment of liberation, flatboatmen often treated themselves to a few days or weeks "footloose" in the big city, free from farm toil and nagging kin. Wrote one Hoosier flatboatman after

---

199. *Conseil de Ville*, Session of May 8, 1819, p. 59 of microfilm #90-221, AB301, NOPL-LC. See also June 2, 1819, p. 75 for a later amendment; *Conseil de Ville*, Session of June 1, 1822, pp. 87–88 of microfilm #90-222, AB301, NOPL-LC; "An Ordinance supplementary to the ordinance concerning the police of the Port of New-Orleans," June 23, 1831, *A General Digest of the Ordinances and Resolutions of the Corporation of New-Orleans* (New Orleans: Jerome Bayon, 1831), 339; *Conseil de Ville*, Session of March 10, 1827, pp. 348–351 of microfilm #90-223, AB301, NOPL-LC.

200. *Conseil de Ville*, Session of February 22, 1817, p. 127 of microfilm #90-221, AB301, and Session of October 23, 1823, p. 241 of microfilm #90-222, AB301, NOPL-LC.

201. *The Navigator* (1814), 33; Elias Pym Fordham, *Personal Narrative of Travels in Virginia, Maryland, Pennsylvania, Ohio, Indiana, Kentucky; and of a Residence in the Illinois Territory: 1817–1818*, ed. Frederic Austin Ogg (Cleveland, OH: The Arthur H. Clark Company, 1906), 79.

202. The local term "bargeboard house" denotes such buildings, but is often applied loosely to just about any historic structure finished off with mismatched scrap lumber.

completing his work at the wharf,

> [O]nce more [I] was foot loose to look out for my self now
> about too thousand miles from home [*sic*]. . . . I was in the citty
> [of New Orleans] about 9 days.[203]

Unfortunately, neither Lincoln nor Gentry nor their Indiana acquaintances left behind any waypoints to retrace their steps. The few words Lincoln wrote of his two Louisiana visits pertain mostly to the voyage, not
the destination. We can only gather evidence of what was going on in the
city from primary sources, and reconstruct the urban and social landscape
to which Lincoln was theoretically exposed.

Activities on the land side of the mile-long flatboat wharf gave the Indiana men their first taste of city life. There, rickety wooden "caravanserai" (flop houses) offered four basic services to flatboatmen and other transients: victuals, drink, entertainment, and board. In front on the ground
floor was the saloon; in the back were roulette, faro, and other gambling
tables, all operating in plain sight. (Gambling, legal in private quarters but
prohibited in public spaces, nonetheless abounded throughout the city.)
Upstairs was the boarding house, usually with laundry-festooned balconies. Offensive odors, originating from the fetid riverfront, from kitchens
behind the saloons, from outhouses and from beasts of burden, assaulted
the nose. Cacophonies—hammer blows, hoof beats, hollers, peddler bells,
and roulette calls such as "Twenty-eight on the red" or "Eagle bird by
chance"—assailed the ear.[204]

Once past the flatboat wharf, the cityscape and its attendant humanity upgraded markedly. New Orleans was, after all, the South's greatest
city, and while it might have exhibited an Old World look and *laissez faire*
attitude to visitors from New York or Boston, it struck rural Western-
ers as dazzling, modern, and meticulously managed—at least in the urban core. Sturdy brick storehouses and townhouses, rising three and even
four stories high, exceeded what Lincoln saw in Natchez in size, number,
and style. Roughly half the city, and most of the main commercial areas,
boasted paved streets with curbstones and nighttime illumination from
whale-oil lamps. Additional paving, curbing, and lighting improvements
were the topics of discussion at City Council meetings, particularly for

---

203. John Wilkinson, "'To Do For My Self': Footloose on the Old Northwest Frontier," ed. William C. Wilkinson, *Indiana Magazine of History* 86, no. 4 (December 1990):
415–416.

204. Whitney, "Flatboating Days," *Times-Democrat*, June 10, 1883, p. 5, c. 5.

Faubourg St. Mary (whose Anglo citizens shook their fists at the various municipal slights they perceived emanated from the politically more powerful Creole faction across Canal Street).

Paved streets meant smoother and faster flowing traffic, fostering efficiency but also danger. Horses and mules, often driven by free people of color or hired-out slaves, pulled wagons, trucks, and drays at speeds fast enough to injure or kill unwary pedestrians. For "the Safety and Facility of traffic in the Streets," the city in 1827 prohibited galloping or driving the animals at anything faster than "a stepping pace." Penalties for breaking the ordinance, which was posted on walls and street corners, ran five to fifty dollars for free people and ten lashes for slaves (unless the master paid the fine).[205] Similar ordinances regulated—under penalty of fine or whip—where peddlers and merchants could and could not vend; where smoky forges, foundries, and steam-engine shops could operate; and where rum houses and distilleries could function. Shortly before Lincoln's visit, the City Council even regulated masked balls, limiting them to the period from January 1 through Mardi Gras, requiring a license, and forcing revelers to reveal their identities to policemen upon arriving at the ball.[206] Shortly after Lincoln's visit, the City banned bathing in the river or Carondelet Canal and publically appearing naked or in indecent costume.[207]

New Orleans might have seemed unfettered and carefree to buttoned-up newcomers, but city fathers fought that anti-business image, and endeavored to reverse it through law and order. How well they succeeded is another matter.

•

We can safely presume two issues demanded the men's attention as they set forth into the city. First came food. Clues to what they might have bought come from the previously cited flatboatman Asbury C. Jacquess, who shopped for edibles and sundries after disposing of his cargo and vessel on the uptown wharf:

205. *Conseil de Ville*, Session of February 24, 1827, pp. 339–340 of microfilm #90-223, AB301, NOPL-LC.

206. *Conseil de Ville*, Session of November 22, 1827, pp. 115–120; Session of December 15, 1827, pp. 147–148; and Session of December 29, 1827, p. 158–159 of microfilm #90-223, AB301, NOPL-LC.

207. *Conseil de Ville*, Session of July 19, 1828, p. 285 of microfilm #90-223, AB301, NOPL-LC.

> We today laid in our groceries. I got 1 sack of coffee at 13 cts
> per pound, 1 lb of sugar at 6 1/2 cts per lb, 1 lb of mackeral at
> $7.50 & 1 keg of rice at 4 cts per pound. The whole amounted
> to 49.50$ I also bought 1 pair of half boots at $1.75, The Life
> of William Wallace at $1.00 & The Poetical Works of Pope
> at 4 bits.[208]

Stretching those meager flatboat wages could prove a challenge to a rural
chap in an expensive city. "Nothing can be got done here without a considerable payment in money," complained a traveler shortly after Lincoln's
visit. "I had to pay a quarter of a dollar for sewing the silk part of an um-
brella to one of the whalebones . . . and a dollar per dozen is charged for
washing clothes, no matter what they be. . . . *The object of all seems to be to
make money, and to spend it. . . .*"[209]

The next question involved shelter. New Orleans abounded with high-
end hotels, mid-range inns, boarding houses, and low-end caravanserai.
Residents also opened their homes—cautiously, and for good reason—to
earn a few extra dollars renting an attic or servant's quarters to a stranger.
Where might Gentry and Lincoln have boarded? So many rooms operated off the record that we cannot narrow down the possibilities. Yet one
researcher has offered a startlingly precise answer to that question: 819
St. Ann Street, three blocks behind present-day Jackson Square in the
French Quarter.[210] The house at that address today certainly looks the
part. Built around 1811 for a free family of color named Cazelars, it is
an imposing one-and-a-half-story, two-family brick cottage with a gable
roof and four distinctive attic windows. Twin two-story brick quarters in
the rear accommodated slaves, servants, or boarders.[211] What casts doubt
on this legend is the fact that the house-address system enumerating this
structure as 819 St. Ann Street was not established until 1894; addresses
in the pre-mail-delivery days of 1828 were ad-hoc, highly irregular, and
poorly documented. Without primary documents such as guest registries,
and without the name of the host family or hotel, how could the memory
of Lincoln's 1828 boarding house have been "updated" to the 1894 house-
numbering system? Lincoln would have had to establish a personal relationship that remained in the memory (name and all) of a neighbor or

208. Jacquess, "Journals of the Davy Crockett," 23.
209. Stuart, *Three Years in North America*, 2:235–236 (emphasis added).
210. Van Natter, *Lincoln's Boyhood*, 145, 208. In a footnote, Van Natter identifies the
source of this information simply as "traditional."
211. Vieux Carré Survey, Binder 75, entry for 817–819 St. Ann Street.

landlord until he became famous three decades later. This is unlikely, but not impossible: as we shall see, credible evidence exists from the 1831 flatboat trip that Lincoln indeed established precisely such a relationship, with a man named Ferguson in Arkansas.

The 819 St. Ann Street legend has been repeated by at least one tertiary source. Today the house stands majestically but unmarked for its alleged—and dubious—Lincoln association.

•

Western boatmen were self-aware of their lowly and disdained place in New Orleans society. It was not something they necessarily suffered or resented; in fact, many embraced their rugged, devil-may-care reputation, going so far as to give their vessels names such as *True Poverty, Adventure, Hard Times,* and *Drunkard.*[212] Sometimes urban elites granted the boatmen a begrudging admiration. During Lincoln's visit, for example, a local paper characterized their "western blood" as "half steamboat, half alligator . . . ardent, generous, daring, witty, blunt, and original."[213] More often than not, however, the relationship between the establishment and the boatman was a contentious one, and the characterizations of the latter leaned decisively toward the unflattering, the prejudiced, and the ridiculing.

Attire presented a favorite target, as flatboatmen sported a certain look ambling around town. Lincoln probably donned garments in New Orleans similar to those he wore back home, inventoried by one informant years later:

> flax & tow linnen pantaloons . . . about 5 inches too short in the legs and frequently he had but one Suspender. . . . . he Wore a Calico Shert, [a] coarse Brogans Tan Couler[,] Blue Yarn Socks & straw Hat—old style and without a band[.][214]

Needless to say, such ill-fitting garb drew snickers among the "*fashion-*

212. Survey of Federal Archives in Louisiana, Division of Professional and Service Projects-Works Projects Administration, *Flatboats on the Mississippi in 1807* (Baton Rouge: Louisiana State University, 1940), 57, 65, 85, 126.

213. The article, a review of a New York theatrical production entitled "Lion of the West," appeared during Lincoln's second visit to New Orleans, but reflected sentiments that had existed in 1828 and earlier. "From the *New-York Courier & Enquirer,*" *Louisiana Courier,* May 28, 1831, page indeterminable, c. 1.

214. Statement, Abner Y. Ellis, to William H. Herndon, January 23, 1866, in *Herndon's Informants,* 170.

ables" of this famously vain town.[215] New Orleanians stereotyped upcountry flatboatmen in the same way that residents today poke fun at French Quarter tourists or Ninth Ward hipsters. "The Primitive Hoosier," wrote the *Picayune*, "is as untrammeled by the artifice of fashion and as free from the constraint of foppery as the mighty rivers of the West [or] the buffalo herd over the wild prairie. . . ." A pocketful of cash from "the plunder of his flatboat," plus a city full of soft-goods stores, inspired rag-clad country lads to upgrade their image—all too often, unfortunately, without proper sartorial counsel:

> He has just donned a new blue dress coat with silk linings and flowered gilt buttons. His new pants look rather short for the present fashion, but this is easily account for—they were of stocking fit or French cut at the instep, and thinking they pressed rather close he has curtailed them of some six inches of their fair proportion.

A closer look, wrote the *Picayune*, suggested that you can take the Hoosier out of Indiana, but you can't take Indiana out of the Hoosier:

> He glories in still sporting the same unpolished peg boots, and the woolen, round-topped, wide-leafed hat in which he set out from home.

"A life in the woods for me," the flatboatmen seemed to say to big-city life.[216]

Flatboat crewmates, in groups of two, three, four, five, ambled the streets of New Orleans as young men often do when in a new environment: slowly, hat cocked, hands in pockets, with an affected swagger geared to communicate confidence, hide disorientation and intimidation, and suppress all outward signs of curiosity, surprise, or delight. *Act like you've seen it before; never let 'em see you impressed.* All that changed if individuals found a chance to break free of the group. Ah, anonymity! Nothing liberated a country boy like exploring the big city alone. Solitude "cut the cable" on teasing and gossipy crewmates and severed all channels of communication with the folks back home. New Orleans, then and now, catered to the curious and adventurous single male visitor in just about every way imaginable.

215. Davidson, "Journey Through the South in 1836," 358.

216. *Daily Picayune* (early 1840s), as reproduced in "The Primitive Hoosier," *Indiana Magazine of History* 1, no. 2 (Second Quarter, 1905): 96–97.

Observing the behavior of young men today, sauntering in the French Quarter while on leave from service, ship, school, or business, offers an idea of how flatboatmen acted upon the stage of street life in the circa-1828 city. We can imagine Gentry and Lincoln, twenty and nineteen years old respectively, donning new clothes and a shoulder bag, looking about, inquiring what the other wanted to do and secretly hoping it would align with his own wishes, then shrugging and ambling on in a mutually consensual direction. Lincoln would have attracted extra attention for his striking physiognomy, his bandaged head wound from the attack on the sugar coast, and his six-foot-four height, which towered ten inches over the typical American male of that era and even higher above the many New Orleanians of Mediterranean or Latin descent.

Quite the conspicuous bumpkins were they.

•

One cannot help pondering how teen-aged Lincoln might have behaved in New Orleans. Young single men like him (not to mention older married men) had given this city a notorious reputation throughout the Western world; condemnations of the city's wickedness abound in nineteenth-century literature. A visitor in 1823 wrote,

> New Orleans is of course exposed to greater varieties of human misery, vice, disease, and want, than any other American town. . . . Much has been said about [its] profligacy of manners . . . morals . . . debauchery, and low vice . . . [T]his place has more than once been called the modern Sodom.[217]

An anonymous booklet catalogued the city's stigmas with discourses entitled "Extent of Licentiousness," "Regular Prostitutes," "Prostitution of Wives," "Slave Girls Hired As Bed Companions," "Disregard of the Sabbath," "Bull Fighting," "Drinking Houses," and "Vagrants," among others. The writer held back when he characterized New Orleans as "this Babel of all Babels, this Sodom of all Sodoms . . . this modern Golgotha."[218]

What enticed visitors to indulge in Sodom's various iniquities was the intersection of desire, opportunity, and anonymity. For flatboatmen, distance from home meant a separation from the mothers, wives, sisters,

217. Timothy Flint, *Recollections of the Last Ten Years . . . in the Valley of the Mississippi* (Boston: Cummings, Hillard, and Co.,1826), 305, 309.

218. Anonymous, *New Orleans As It Is: Its Manners and Customs* ("By a Resident, Printed for the Publisher," 1850), 6.

and aunts of their domestic lives. Older flatboatmen often lamented this separation, youths reveled in it, and at least one waxed eloquently on it:

> Men thrown together from all parts of the United States and in deed from the whole world with ther [*sic*] various manners and habits unrestrained by the presence of female influance exhibits a scene of extraordinary novelty and is probably one of the best places for a man to acquire a knowledge of <u>human nature</u>.[219]

That "knowledge" might include gambling, sharping (cheating at gambling), smoking, drinking, fighting, or patronizing the city's sex industry. Citizens fairly or unfairly branded flatboatmen with the worse reputation of any transient group in the city and viewed their uptown landing as both a source and target of criminal activity. "[T]he flat-boats permanently moored [on] the levee . . . are the dens of sharpers by day, and robbers and murderers at night," reported the *Bee* a few years after Lincoln's second visit; "[y]et not the slightest precaution is used."[220] A visitor five years earlier reported seeing flatboats "used as hucksters shops, dwellings, pigpens, museum[s], coopers shops, etc."[221] Others disdained the mile-long "line of gambling-shops" formed by the flatboats on Sundays, not to mention the boatmen themselves, who, by one hyperbolic 1830 account, numbered "5000 or 6000" during the springtime peak (ten percent of the entire city's population).[222] Gentry and Lincoln likely witnessed rowdiness along the wharf—indeed, throughout the city, even on Sundays. "This place is one of the worst I ever witnessed," wrote one newcomer a few years earlier; "the chief amusements are gambling and drinking . . . quarrels and even murders are very frequent here."[223] Another, writing in 1828, observed "the coffee-houses, grog-shops, and the *estaminets* [drinking holes] . . . were open as usual [on Sunday]. . . . A kind of music, accompanied with [singing] resounded in almost every direction. . . . To a new comer . . . this

219. Jacquess, "Journals of the Davy Crockett," 24.

220. *New Orleans Bee*, as quoted by the *Patriot and Eagle* (*Patriot and Democrat*, Hartford, CT), August 8, 1835, p. 2.

221. Journal of Welcome A. Greene, reproduced in "Being the Journal of a Quaker Merchant Who Visited N.O. in 1823," *Times-Picayune*, October 16, 1921, section four, pp. 1 and 6.

222. Stuart, *Three Years in North America*, 2:232.

223. "Extract of a Letter from an Emigrant in New-Orleans," *Newburyport Herald* (Newburyport, MA), October 17, 1817, p. 3, c. 2.

appears very shocking."[224] Another man reported, "drinking establishments are coining money; they monopolize the corners of every square;
whole rows of them may be found in some localities, and new ones are
springing up every day."[225]

While such establishments were scattered citywide, one particular
district catered specifically to boatmen and other transients. Nicknamed
"the Swamp," it was located about a dozen blocks straight inland from
the uptown flatboat wharf, where Julia and Girod streets petered out into
Faubourg St. Mary's cut-over backswamp.[226] This wasteland received all
that civilized New Orleanians did not want in their backyard. The ee-
rie Girod Street Cemetery was laid out here in 1822; the smelly turning
basin of the New Orleans (New Basin) Canal followed in 1832; Charity
Hospital and its yellow fever patients came in 1835. Gas works, garbage
dumps, shantytowns, and stables would later find a home in this "back
of town." So it comes as no surprise that the flatboatmen's den of iniquity ended up here as well, within a stone's throw of the cemetery. Very
few first-person descriptions of this loathsome dive survive; one account
derives from a reminiscence of the 1820s–30s reported in 1883. "The
Swamp," it explained, "was a great rendezvous for the flatboatmen, and
here they reigned supreme, the city police never caring to invade those
precincts. . . ." The Swamp, like Bourbon Street today, repelled some visitors, but enticed others. "The captains or owners of the flatboats were of
the more provident sort" and generally avoided the district, "but the hired
men seldom cared to save their money" and "usually stayed here until they
had spent or gambled the results of their trip away, then left for home by
land." The account described some of the Swamp's characters:

> Old Mother Colby, a dame of about 50 winters and 200 pounds,
> kept a boarding house and caravansary in "The Swamp,"
> known as the "Sure Enuf Hotel," the lower floor of which was
> occupied as a saloon, with a gambling room just behind. The
> old woman was a great favorite with the boys, and she [did
> well] by their patronage. She rented the saloon to two Mexican
> brothers by the name of Contreras, one of whom dealt faro,
> whilst the other attended the bar.[227]

224. Sealsfield, *Americans As They Are*, 147–148.
225. "Life in New Orleans," *Ohio Statesman* (Columbus), May 7, 1847, p. 3, c. 2.
226. Some historians situate "The Swamp" closer to the river, perhaps conflating it
with the generalized gambling and drinking that occurred along the flatboat wharf.
227. Whitney, "Flatboating Days," *Times-Democrat*, June 10, 1883, p. 5, c. 5.

Did Lincoln partake of New Orleans' opportunities for escapism? More than a dozen contemporaries of Lincoln's youth testified that Abraham not only eschewed alcohol, but avoided its affiliated vices as well, even when interviewers pressed for salacious details. Illinois neighbor William G. Greene went out of his way to declare Lincoln "entirely *free* from the vices [of] running after Women[,] Drinking whiskey or playing Cards of Money."[228] Abner Y. Ellis "wondered how [Lincoln] could be so extremely popular and not drink and Carouse with them," illustrating a resistance to peer pressure. "I am certain he Never Drank any intoxicating liquors [nor did he] smoke or chew Tobacco."[229] Others recounted Lincoln's advocacy of total abstention, part of a temperance movement that swept the West in this era. Former Illinois congressman Robert L. Wilson, for example, declared resolutely, "I never Saw Mr. Lincoln drink. [H]e often told me he never drank, had no desire for the drink, nor the companionship of drinking men."[230] Other neighbors, however, allowed that "Sometimes [Lincoln] took his dram as Every body did at that time," but insisted he was always temperate.[231]

Regarding women, most informants pegged Abraham as "a Verry shy Man of Ladies," perhaps, according to one, "on account of his awkward appearance and his wareing apparel." One associate remembered him as "a Man of strong passion for woman—[but] his Conscience Kept him from seduction—this saved many—many a women."[232] The man who interviewed those informants in 1866, former law partner and biographer William H. Herndon, harbored a secret reason for such inquiries. In the 1880s Herndon privately shared a story with a colleague that Lincoln had once confided in him: that around "the year 1835-6 Mr. Lincoln went to Beardstown [Illinois] and during a devilish passion had Connection with a girl and Caught the disease" of syphilis.[233] Herndon never felt entirely

---

228. William G. Greene to William H. Herndon, November 27, 1865, in *Herndon's Informants*, 142 (emphasis in original).

229. Statement, Abner Y. Ellis to William H. Herndon, January 23, 1866, in *Herndon's Informants*, 170.

230. Robert L. Wilson to William H. Herndon, February 10, 1866, in *Herndon's Informants*, 205; see also Louis A. Warren, *Lincoln's Youth: Indiana Years, Seven to Twenty-One, 1816–1830* (Indianapolis: Indiana Historical Society Press, 1959, reprinted 2002), 170–171.

231. Interview, David Turnham, by William H. Herndon, September 15, 1865, in *Herndon's Informants*, 121.

232. Statement, Abner Y. Ellis, January 23, 1866, and Interview, David Davis, September 20, 1866, both with William H. Herndon, in *Herndon's Informants*, 170 and 350.

233. As quoted and interpreted by Douglas L. Wilson, *Honor's Voice: The Transforma-*

confident or comfortable with the story and excluded it from his book, for good reason: Lincoln's future marriage and family life seemly contradict such an allegation. What, if any, dalliances Lincoln may have indulged in at Beardstown or elsewhere is impossible to say, but given that zero contemporaries ever recalled Lincoln drunk, violent, reckless, or lewd, we have every reason to believe he behaved in a far more level-headed manner in New Orleans than most boatmen. The man, throughout his life, famously revered restraint and discipline over pleasure and indulgence.

•

An inquisitive young man like Lincoln, with three weeks at his disposal, would have gravitated toward the many newspapers available in this cosmopolitan port. First-person evidence says he read them voraciously at the Troy Post Office and Gentry Store back home; his own stepmother testified that "Abe was a Constant reader [of newspapers]; I am sure of this for the years of 1827-28-29-30."[234] Unlike Indiana's papers, however, those in New Orleans—the *Bee, Argus, Louisiana Courier, Louisiana Advertiser, Mercantile Advertiser,* and others—ran in French, English, and sometimes Spanish.[235] Competition raged among their Chartres Street offices, the "Newspaper Row" of the mid-antebellum era. Each editor reveled in pointing out the others' errors and inconsistencies, and waxed indignantly whenever their own scoops appeared uncited in competitors' pages.[236] The local dailies shared the newsstands with "European, Northern and Western Papers received regularly," and mined them for their own content.[237] Great reading they were not: the vast majority of every edition comprised commercial advertisements carried over from the previous day. Market reports, shipping news, lottery announcements, runaway slave notices, plagiarized articles, bad poetry, sentimental yarns, patronizing moral les-

tion of Abraham Lincoln (New York: Alfred A. Knopf, 1998), 127–129.

234. Interview, Sarah Bush Lincoln, by William H. Herndon, September 8, 1865, in *Herndon's Informants*, 107.

235. Only partially can we inventory what Lincoln might have read: nearly all editions of the *New Orleans Bee* and *New Orleans Argus* survive for mid-May through early June 1828, but only a few early-June editions of the *Louisiana Courier* remain, and even fewer of the *Louisiana Advertiser.*

236. For examples that appeared during Lincoln's second visit, see "The Argus vs. The Argus," *New Orleans Bee*, June 9, 1831, p. 2, c. 1, and a plagiarizing situation in ibid., May 26, 1831, p. 2, c. 1 and June 4, p. 2, c. 1.

237. "Globe Coffee House," *New-Orleans Directory & Register* (New Orleans: John Adems Paxton, 1830), unpaginated opening section.

sons, freaky anecdotes, and vitriolic political editorials—unchecked by the vaguest notions of journalistic objectivity—filled the rest of a typical four-page, half-French-half-English edition of a circa-1828 New Orleans newspaper.

There was much to editorialize about in the spring of 1828. A concurrence of events made politics particularly polemical that season. Just weeks earlier, Denis Prieur defeated Anathole Peychaud in the New Orleans mayoral race, while ten council seats went before voters. They competed for attention with the U.S. presidential campaign—a mudslinging rematch of the bitterly controversial 1824 election, in which Westerner Andrew Jackson won a plurality of both the popular and electoral vote in a four-candidate, one-party field, but John Quincy Adams attained the presidency after Congress handed down the final selection. Subsequent years saw the emergence of a more manageable two-party system. In 1828, Jackson headed the Democratic Party ticket while Adams represented the National Republican Party (forerunner of the Whig Party, and later the Republican Party). Jackson's heroic defeat of the British at New Orleans in 1815 had made him a national hero with much local support, but did not spare him vociferous enemies. The year 1828 also saw the state's first election in which presidential electors were selected by voters—white males, that is—rather than by the legislature, thus ratcheting up public interest in the contest.[238] Every day in the spring of 1828 the local press featured obsequious encomiums, sarcastic diatribes, vicious rumors, or scandalous allegations spanning multiple columns. The most infamous—the "coffin hand bills," which accused Andrew Jackson of murdering several militiamen executed under his command during the war—circulated throughout the city within days of Lincoln's visit.[239] New Orleans in the red-hot political year of 1828 might well have given Abraham Lincoln his first massive daily dosage of passionate political opinion, via newspapers, broadsides, bills, orations, and overheard conversations.

Newspaper articles published during Lincoln's visit also conveyed the interesting, the curious, the disturbing, and the poignant. Congress, reported the *Bee*, debated funding an expedition to the South Sea, to establish trade routes and explorations to aid the whaling industry. The French prepared for an expedition against the Turks, while the Netherlands negotiated with Guatemala about "cutting a canal to unite the Gulf

---

238. Joseph G. Tregle Jr., *Louisiana in the Age of Jackson: A Clash of Cultures and Personalities* (Baton Rouge: Louisiana State University Press, 1999), 208–228.

239. Ibid., 220.

of Mexico with the Pacific Ocean," a story of particular interest to New Orleans shipping merchants.[240] Of even greater relevance was an article on the recent English "success of combining the steam engine with the rail road," in which "a train of loaded carriages was dragged along by one little steam engine, a distance of 25 miles within two hours." The reporter mused, "[w]ithout in reality changing the distances of places," this invention "would have the effect of bringing all parts nearer to each other."[241]

Indeed, the emerging technology of steam-driven rail conveyance sparked entrepreneurial imaginations on both sides of the Atlantic. Its successful introduction to the trans-Appalachian West would give Lincoln, in due time, the opportunity to rise professionally in both the legal and political realms.

Another issue that would play an important role in Lincoln's future, river navigation, ran regularly in New Orleans papers. Among the stories were the damages of the springtime high water witnessed by Lincoln, and this news:

> A law has been introduced into Congress, and . . . passed the House of Representatives, allowing the Parishes of Iberville, St. Mary, St. Martin, Lafayette and St. Landry . . . to open our navigation with the Mississippi. . . .[242]

That article foretold of the circa-1830s effort to clear out the Red River log jam and open up navigation throughout the Mississippi, Atchafalaya, and Red River regions—a move that would prove, in time, economically beneficial but hydrologically dangerous.

On another topic that would figure prominently in Lincoln's future, there was this story picked up from the London *Courier*:

> [A] small schooner came in [to Bahia] from the coast of Africa, with 400 slaves. . . . [S]he had originally taken on board 600 in all, male and female; but being chased by a ship of war, to prevent capture and to lighten the vessel, the captain had thrown two hundred of them overboard![243]

•

Lincoln did not have to transport himself mentally to Bahia to imagine

240. *New Orleans Bee*, May 12, 1828, p. 3, c. 3–4; May 13, 1828, p. 3, c. 2.
241. "Rail Roads," ibid., May 29, 1828, p. 3, c. 2.
242. Ibid., May 16, 1828, p. 3, c. 2.
243. Ibid., June 2, 1828, p. 3, c. 2.

the machinations of institutionalized slavery. He did not even have to raise his eyes from the newspaper. Practically every page abounded in runaway notices, which appeared day after day in concurrent newspapers, to the point that subscribers almost gained personal familiarity with the fugitives. Only their degrading one-word names and physical scars are known to history, but collectively, those who chose to flee that spring may have reached Lincoln's eye and influenced his conscience in ways we can only guess. Their plight did affect him: "I confess I hate to see the poor creatures hunted down, and caught," Lincoln wrote many years later, "and carried back to their . . . unrewarded toils."[244] Among the slaves on the run during his New Orleans visit was (according to the masters' perspectives) the "Negro wench *Nancy,*" who "had the habit of selling cakes . . . has very black skin, a large breast, a fearful look. . . ."[245] Ten dollars awaited the finder of "Kit," a 39-year-old American negro, "one of his nostrils somewhat larger than the other."[246] The "creole Negress named Celestine," despite her presumed sub-humanity, managed not only to "speak English, French and Spanish," but to outsmart her master, who pointedly warned sailors captains not to "harbour said slave."[247] (Only a few days later, a local court convicted three free black sailors of hiding a runaway on board, punishing them with an impossible-to-pay two-hundred-dollar fine plus a year in prison.[248]) Youths such as the mulatto Buckrit, the mulatto Rueben ("rather slender, but well made . . . very good looking"), and the "creole *Negro Boy by the name of PHILIP,* aged about 9 years, who speaks French only" also took flight.[249] The pursuers were not solely men: Madame Rouquette of St. Claude Street in the Faubourg Tremé offered ten dollars for the return of her "creole Negress named *Catherine*; 5 feet 2 inches in height, french measure, she is of a large face, is a hawker of goods."[250]

Other ads were posted by rural jailers who suspected their prisoners were runaways, and alerted city subscribers in the hope of returning them to their masters. One jail announcement from West Feliciana seemed to describe a typical rural American family of the day—"Jim, and Fanny his

244. Abraham Lincoln to Joshua F. Speed, August 24, 1855, in *Collected Works,* 2:320.

245. *New Orleans Bee,* May 9 and afterwards, 1828, p. 4, c. 2.

246. *New Orleans Argus,* May 13, 1828 and afterwards, p. 1, c. 5.

247. *New Orleans Bee,* May 9 and afterwards, 1828, p. 4, c. 3.

248. Ibid., May 12, 1828, p. 3, c. 2.

249. Ibid., May 9 and afterwards, 1828, p. 4, c. 3; *New Orleans Argus,* May 13 and afterwards, 1828, p. 1, c. 6; *New Orleans Argus,* May 30, 1828, p. 2, c. 6.

250. *New Orleans Bee,* June 3, 1828, p. 3, c. 4.

wife, and their 2 children Margaret and Martha, [who] have on each a calico dress, red grounded; Margaret has on a pair of shoes, and Martha a small head dress of coarse linen; Jim has a good cotton shirt, drab planta-loons, and a very good narrow brimmed hat"[251]—except for the fact that, legally speaking, it constituted an unclaimed-property notice. Another jail ad from Baton Rouge unintentionally impugned the very master it sought to aid, by describing the detained slave as "much scarred with the whip."[252] Sometimes the jailed runaways escaped again: two maroons fled the Jefferson Parish Jail near the uptown flatboat wharf around the time Lincoln and Gentry docked; one was named John, the other Abraham.[253] A sensitive reader like Lincoln, peering into the day-to-day workings of the institution of slavery for the first time, might have appreciated the poignancy of a story published around the day he and Gentry departed New Orleans:

> A negro in Jamaica was tried for theft, and ordered to be flogged. He begged to be heard, which being granted, he asked, ["]if white man buy [s]tolen goods, why he be no flogge[d] too?" "Well," said the Judge, "so he would." "Dare den," replied Mungo, "is my Massa, he buy [s]tollen goods, he knew me [s] toolem, and yet he buy me."[254]

Between the runaway alerts and the jail notices were announcements re-garding the commerce of slaves. New Orleans being the South's busiest slave marketplace, Lincoln would have been exposed to more slave trading here than in any other place in the geography of his life, even more so be-cause springtime marked the peak of the commercial season. Most slaves changed owners via two primary paths: masters privately transacting with individual buyers, and auction houses publicly handling the transaction with a group of buyers. Advertisements for those vended privately by mas-ters read with the same cadence and tone of a modern classified ad: ba-sic specifications, unctuous assurances of quality, potential disadvantages couched as silver linings, and a point of contact, all set within an economy of words. A "good and pretty Negress . . . American by birth, but is per-fectly acclimated to this country, is 18 years of age, and speaks the French language" went on the market directly from the home of her master, just

251. *New Orleans Argus*, May 13 and afterwards, 1828, p. 1, c. 2.
252. Ibid., May 20 and afterwards, 1828, p. 3, c. 1.
253. Ibid., May 13 and afterwards, 1828, p. 1, c. 5.
254. Ibid., June 7, 1828, p. 2, c. 5.

at the time that Lincoln and Gentry landed.[255] A man named Justin was offered "For Sale or to Hire" two weeks later, followed shortly by a deal for a "likely Negro fellow."[256] One ad reads like a contemporary garage sale, except for its human chattel:

> [O]n Wednesday [May] 14th . . . at 4 o'clock in the afternoon, in St. Philippe street, between Royal and Bourbon streets, near the Theatre [will be sold] an assortment of Household Furniture, consisting of Beds, Tables, Sophas, Looking-Glaces [*sic*], Chairs, Silver-plate, &c. ALSO, AT THE SAME PLACE: A Family of Slaves, to wit—the father, mother, and six children. CONDITIONS—the furniture cash down, the family of slaves, to 1, 2, and 3 years, by furnishing endorsed notes bearing mortgage. . . .[257]

Public auction houses engaged in similarly detached and matter-of-fact language in describing slaves, and did so with far greater frequency and a loftier sense of official sanction than individual sellers. It is not coincidental that the city's premier slave-auction house, Hewlett's Exchange, occupied the busiest intersection of the city's most prominent thoroughfare: Chartres Street,

> the "*Broadway*" of New Orleans and the resort of the Fashionable of the City for Shopping and promenading. In Chartres Street I saw the fine people of the City. The Creole population constitute the *Fashionables*. . . . Chartres Street is also the promenade of the fashionable Prostitute, who flaunts along in her gaudy trappings, the subjects of gaze and remark of all who resort to this famous Street.[258]

•

On the downriver/lakeside corner of Chartres Street at the St. Louis intersection stood a two-story brick edifice with arched openings, a tile roof, and a stucco exterior, reflecting typical Spanish colonial and Creole styles. Inside operated famous, notorious Hewlett's Exchange, serving the moneyed white male establishment in all its business and pleasure needs.

255. *New Orleans Bee*, May 10, 1828, p. 4, c. 4.
256. *New Orleans Argus*, May 28 and afterwards, 1828, p. 3, c. 1; ibid., May 30 and afterwards, 1828, p. 2, c. 5.
257. *New Orleans Bee*, May 12, 1828, p. 3, c. 4.
258. Davidson, "Journey Through the South in 1836," 358.

Gaudy décor and ostentatious allusions to greatness, via gigantic paintings of Washington and Napoleon, spoke to the aspirations of owner John
Hewlett's clientele. Here the aristocracy and the upwardly mobile gathered to buy, sell, discuss, plan, socialize, dine, drink, gamble, and board.
Everything that constituted property in antebellum Southern society—
land, houses, vessels, cargo, equipment, wine, furniture, and black people
of both genders and every possible age and background—changed owners
at Hewlett's Exchange. (Horses, mules, and carriages, needing outdoor
space, were by law auctioned on a lot located one block away.[259]) A diary
written a few years after Lincoln's visits attests to the Exchange's importance:

> Hewlett's Exchange is upon Chartres Street. It is here that
> "merchants do most congregate." In it [there are] auctions of
> Slaves. Lots do take place. From 10 AM. 3 P.M. it is a scene
> of tumultuous confusion, in which all the business and profes-
> sional men of the City engage. *It seems to be the Soul of New*
> *Orleans. . . .*[260]

Just as New Orleans ranked as the nation's busiest slave-trading city, so
did Hewlett's Exchange rate as New Orleans' busiest slave mart. Visitors knew about "the Exchange"; it appeared on the antebellum tourism
must-see list along with the levee, market, above-ground cemeteries, and
quadroon balls. "He [who] does not visit it cannot [claim to have] seen all
of New Orleans," wrote the previously quoted sightseer.[261] Many visitors
bravely, if hesitantly, wandered in during the midday auction-block ritu-
als, and some of them documented the spectacle they witnessed. Those
opposing slavery, such as English abolitionist Edward Strutt Abdy, emphasized the degrading banalities of the institution:

> Slaves for sale at New Orleans are publicly exposed at the mart,
> or auction-room; the men ranged on one side, and the wom-
> en on the other. Purchasers are in the habit of examining the
> mouth and the limbs, in the same way that a horse is subjected
> to the scrutinising touch of the buyer. The joints are tried, and
> turned, to see if they are strong and supple. Should the back,

---

259. "An Ordinance concerning the sale of horses, mules, or other animals, carriages,
gigs, carts, drays, &c," February 23, 1829, *General Digest of the Ordinances and Resolutions
of the Corporation of New-Orleans* (New Orleans: Jerome Bayon, 1831), 121.
260. Davidson, "Journey Through the South in 1836," 358 (emphasis added).
261. Ibid., 358.

or shoulders, or any other part of the body, exhibit marks of frequent or severe flogging, the "animal" is set aside, as rebellious and refractory. Twice a week, an exhibition takes place, during the season; and the human cattle are paraded through the streets, decently dressed, and in regular file, to attract customers.[262]

Other disinterested visitors, such as diarist James D. Davidson, drew more ambivalent portrayals:

> I saw a likely negro woman and her three children selling here at public auction. The mother and children wept bitterly during the sale. I pitied them. But the people here are hardened to such things, and they look upon them with indifference. I saw others sold, but they appeared to be cheerful. . . . They were dressed up neatly for the occasion, the women with turbaned handkerchiefs upon their heads, which improve their appearance very much. They are thus marched in a line into the Streets to some public Corner, or Exchange, where they remain from day to day untill sold. I was surprised to find them looking as cheerful and unconcerned as they did. . . .[263]

Victims of the auction-block, denied the education and the opportunity to scribe their perspectives, left precious few recollections for posterity. One, eighty-six-year-old Frank Bell interviewed in 1937, seemed to explain the slaves' apparently "cheerful and unconcerned" demeanor (which surprised Davidson) as a technique to manipulate master-slave relations toward the latter's better treatment. "Yessir, I'se seen several slaves sold," Bell recounted;

> Boy oh boy they would shout and holler and laugh cause they say if [a new] master on the farm bought them they have good master. [But my] master . . . kept me in chains cause I'se didn't do like he want me. . . . Master he stay drunk and he was mean. He shoot several men.[264]

262. Abdy based his description on the reports of another traveler during 1833–34. Edward Strutt Abdy, *Journal of a Residence and Tour in the United States of North America: From April, 1833, to October, 1834* (Cambridge, England: John Murray, 1835), 3:12–13, 387.

263. Davidson, "Journey Through the South in 1836," 359.

264. Interview, Frank Bell, by B. E. Davis, September 22, 1937, *American Slavery: A Composite Autobiography*, Second Supplemental Series, Texas Narratives, vol. 02T, 237–238.

Another slave perspective comes from ninety-three-year-old Sara Ashley, who remembered being bought at age five by an itinerant speculator
named Henry Thomas and removed from her Mississippi home for the
New Orleans auction block. "He buy up lots 'n' niggers 'n' sell 'em," recalled Ashley;

> Us fambly was separate'. My uder two sisters 'n' my fadder was
> sol' t' a man, I neber know he name, in Alabama. I stay wid d'
> spec'lator's gang fo' five 'r' ten year. Den dey put me up on a
> block 'n' bid me off. Dat was in N'Yawlins. I was scare' 'n' cry,
> but dey put me up dere anyway. Dey sol' me 'n' my two sisters.
> Dey tek me t' Georgy [Georgia]. I t'ink dey pay 'bout a t'ousan'
> dollar' fo me.[265]

Super-centenarian Silvia King (who was told by her masters that she was
born in Africa in 1804) told an interviewer in 1937, "De ship . . . come to
dis country to New Orleans an' dar I wuz put on de block an' sold." She
continued,

> Yassum, I knows how dey done on de block. All de blacks wuz
> chained an' all dar close wuz stripped off w'en dey wuz gittin'
> 'em ready fer de block. Dey all, chillun, wimmin an' men had
> ter stan' on a big wooden block, lak de butcher man chops an'
> saws he meat on. . . . De folks [who] wuz gwine ter buy de
> niggers, dey come roun' an' pinch you, an' feel ob your body all
> ober, an' look fer scars an' see you got any broken bones 'fore
> dey buy you. Effen any ob de niggers don' want ter take deir
> close off, de oberseer, he git a long, black whip an' cut 'em up
> hard. . . .[266]

During the weeks of Lincoln's visit, auctioneers J. Le Carpentier, Isaac L.
McCoy, T. Mossy, and others handled the slave bidding, which ran from
late morning through mid-afternoon. Three slaves went on the block—
"all field hands, full guarantee"—as Lincoln and Gentry tied up on the
dock in mid-May.[267] A few days later, "Gabriel, creole, aged 21 years;
Mary, American negro girl, aged 40 years; and Marie, aged 38 years, with
her three children, Nina, Louise, and Bastile" were auctioned via a court

265. Interview, Sarah Ashley, by F. W. Dibble, June 10, 1937, *American Slavery: A Com-*
posite Autobiography, Second Supplemental Series, Texas Narratives, vol. 02T, 87–88.
266. Interview, Silvia King, by P. W. Davis, 1937, *American Slavery: A Composite Auto-*
biography, Second Supplemental Series, Texas Narratives, vol. 06T, 2224.
267. *New Orleans Argus*, May 13 and afterwards, 1828, p. 2, c. 6.

order stemming from a lawsuit by the renowned John McDonogh (later the benefactor of the city's public school system).[268] A probate auction the next day set four black Creoles—Francoise, Marie Rose, Josephine, and Joseph—with new masters.[269] On May 23, another Court of Probate sale involved women who were neither Creole (Louisiana born) nor American (born domestically out-of-state). They were described as

> Nina, an African negress aged about 25 years . . . with her two children . . . Germaine, a Congo negress aged about 60 . . . Marie, a congo negro aged about twenty years.[270]

Born in Africa respectively around 1803, 1768, and 1808, these three women experienced first-hand the Middle Passage of the Atlantic slave trade. International slave trading was banned by the United States in 1808, but it continued *de facto* to varying degrees for years afterward.

Month's end proved to be busy at Hewlett's Exchange. On May 30, twenty-nine-year-old Mary, "a first rate cook, washer and house servant—full guarantee," was sold. The next day, at 11:30 a.m., "A Family of SLAVES," including twenty-one-year-old mulatto Henry, his nineteen-year-old wife Matilda, and their two-year-old child, came up for bids.

> Henry is intelligent, speaks English and French, a first rate house servant; matilda understands housework, nursing, a plain cook, and washing and ironing; they have been brought up in New Orleans, and are consequently acclimated.

Also for sale in the 11:30 a.m. time slot was fifty-year-old bricklayer Fortune and his wife Lydia, plus thirty-five-year-old Byrum, who "has been employed in a Soap Factory." At noon, it was seventeen-year-old Lucinda's turn. All four auctions within that forty-minute window, determining the fate of seven individuals, were handled by the same auctioneer, Isaac L. McCoy.[271] Seventeen-year-old Charles ("free of the vices and maladies prescribed by the law; said negro has been ten years in the country, is very intelligent, and fit for a retail store") and forty-year-old Nace were auctioned on June 2 and 4.[272] Finally, on June 10, three slaves sold at Hewl-

268. Ibid., p. 1, c. 2.
269. Ibid., May 22 and afterwards, 1828, p. 4, c. 2.
270. Ibid., May 15 and afterwards, 1828, p. 1, c. 3.
271. Ibid., May 29 and afterwards, 1828, p. 2, c. 6; ibid., May 19 and afterwards, 1828, p. 1.
272. *New Orleans Argus*, May 24 and afterwards, 1828, p. 2, c. 6; ibid., June 3, 1828, p. 3, c. 1.

ett's, one "with a cancer on [her] nose," another "with her back broken."[273] If we make the conservative assumption that the *Bee* and *Argus* auction ads comprehensively covered the public slave-auctioning scene, then at least thirty-one slaves, named above, were traded at the corner of Chartres and St. Louis during Lincoln's visit.

We cannot place Abraham Lincoln with documentary evidence in the crowded and chaotic auction room of Hewlett's Exchange. Consider, however, the circumstances: (1) Many visitors in this era made a point of seeing famous Chartres Street, whose intersection with St. Louis Street—which Hewlett's Exchange dominated—formed the premier commercial crossroads within the great commercial crossroads that was New Orleans. (2) Visitors knew about Hewlett's, unquestionably the city's foremost slave exchange, and those who left behind journals often documented the proceedings therein, furthering its notoriety. (3) During Lincoln's 1828 visit, the Exchange hosted at least one slave trade per day, and at one point seven slaves changed owners within forty minutes, giving him plenty of opportunity to witness an auction. (4) Lincoln himself wrote in 1860 of having seen "slavery and slave markets [in] New Orleans" (more on this later).[274] A reasonable connecting-of-dots leads this researcher to posit that Lincoln probably visited Hewlett's Exchange, and with equal probability, bore witness to one or some of the aforementioned slaves traded there.

•

Other intrigues—though perhaps none so disturbing—enticed the visitor into New Orleans' narrow streets and anonymous crowds. The most notable sight of all, of course, lay one mile downriver from the flatboat wharf, where belching steamboats docked either side of the foot of Canal Street. May and June 1828 saw a total of 149 steamboats arrive at the Port of New Orleans, a pace of two to three per day. Farther downriver docked the great coastwise and international fleet of fully rigged ocean-going sailing ships (three masts or more), smaller and more maneuverable brigs (two masts), and one-mast schooners, of which a total of 182 arrived during Lincoln's month—over three per day.[275]

273. *New Orleans Argus*, May 14 and afterwards, 1828, p. 1, c. 3.

274. Abraham Lincoln to Alexander Hamilton Stephens, January 19, 1860, in *Some Lincoln Correspondence with Southern Leaders before the Outbreak of the Civil War*, from the Collection of Judd Stewart (New York: J. Stewart, 1909), 8.

275. Computed from *New Orleans Price-Current* compilations, reproduced in "Monthly Arrivals," 1826–29, *New-Orleans Directory & Register* (1830), unpaginated appendix.

Nearly as interesting as the shipping activity was the exotic cargo they unloaded. A Cuban schooner arriving on May 26, for example, unloaded pineapples, plantains, limes, oranges, and mangoes. These delicate tropical fruits, rarely seen upcountry, were all consigned to various local merchants in a city that would dominate the nation's tropical-fruit industry for over a century to come.[276] Many of those merchants operated on Levee and New Levee (now Decatur and North and South Peters) streets, which were lined with scores of dry-goods and equipment stores. Others, particularly fruit vendors, offered a vast array of foodstuffs and curios at the already-famous "Creole" or "French" market on Levee Street, a complex that comprised the butcher's arcade at St. Ann Street and fruit-and-vegetable stalls at St. Philip Street. For retail shops, banks, and professional offices, there were lively Chartres, majestic Royal, and wide-open Canal streets, as well as Common, Gravier, Camp, and St. Charles in the Faubourg St. Mary. For opulent townhouses, there were Bourbon, Royal, Condé, upper Canal, and other streets in both the Old City and St. Mary. The rears of the Old City and St. Mary, and nearly all of faubourgs Tremé and Marigny, were replete with the humble cottages of the working class.

For municipal and religious structures, there were the magnificent but rough-around-the-edges Place d'Armes and its fronting City Hall, St. Louis Church, and rectory. What Lincoln would not have seen is the Jackson Square we know today: the renovated Greek revival–style St. Louis Cathedral, the twin red-brick Pontalba buildings, the mansard roofs and cupolas atop the Cabildo and Presbyteré, and the landscaped square with the Andrew Jackson statue, all postdate Lincoln's visits by over two decades. Nor would Lincoln have seen the iron-lace galleries for which the French Quarter would later gain fame: iron-casting technology appeared in the city around the time he first visited, and did not manifest itself in frilly designs until around 1850. Illustrations in Lincoln books and ephemera commit an anachronism by graphically depicting young Abraham beneath iron-lace galleries in the French Quarter. In fact, at the time of his visits, only narrow Spanish-style balconies with simple wrought-iron cantilevers and railings lined the upper floors of townhouses and storehouses.

Day trips to the adjacent countryside beckoned many visitors. New ferries offered continual service across the Mississippi to Algiers, where

---

276. Cargo Manifest 56, Schooner *Grecian*, from Havana, Cuba, landing in New Orleans May 26, 1828, *Passenger Lists of Vessels Arriving at New Orleans, 1820–1902*, microfilm M259, roll 7, New Orleans Public Library.

boat-building, boiler-making, and other shipping industries operated. That trip might have had particular appeal to Lincoln, recalling his own ferrying experiences on the Ohio River. Back on the east bank, sightseers could stroll the Bayou Road out to the plantations and gardens along Bayou St. John and the adjoining Metairie and Gentilly roads, visit the picturesque (if malodorous) turning basin of the Carondelet Canal, and investigate the famous above-ground cemeteries, which were tourist attractions then as they are now. A day trip to the Lake Pontchartrain shore—five miles straight north—became more accessible in spring 1828, as seen in this invitation, which appeared in the local newspaper when Lincoln and Gentry arrived:

> Notice to Lake Bathers.—The subscriber informs lake bathers, that he has repaired the lake road, and that it may now be travelled night and day without danger.[277]

Awaiting bathers at the lakeshore was Harvey Elkin's public bathhouse, built the previous year at the Bayou St. John outlet to offer "an agreeable Retreat from the City . . . during the scorching heat of our summer sun." Elkin extolled the brackish bay's "salubrity . . . coolness of air . . . beautiful prospect [and] fine fish."[278] The spectacle of Abraham Lincoln frolicking in subtropical salt water under a springtime sun is not a typical one associated with his flatboat trip to New Orleans, but it is a possible one.

So too is the scenario of his exploring the lower *banlieue*—that is, the city's downriver outskirts, comprising present-day neighborhoods of Marigny, Bywater, Lower Ninth Ward, and Arabi—en route to the already-famous Chalmette battlefield, five miles away. There, on January 8, 1815, Maj. Gen. Andrew Jackson and his famously "ragtag" local militia routed professional British troops, decisively ending the War of 1812 and any further English antagonism of its former colony. The enduring national fame of Jackson's victory at the Battle of New Orleans, coupled with his current presidential candidacy and his Western origins, might well have motivated Lincoln and Gentry to visit the battlefield, as so many other visitors did. Jackson himself had campaigned in New Orleans only four months prior, marking the thirteenth anniversary of the battle.[279]

277. *New Orleans Argus*, May 13 and afterwards, 1828, p. 2, c. 6.
278. *Conseil de Ville*, Session of June 23, 1827, p. 11 of microfilm #90-223, AB301, NOPL-LC; "Pontchartrain Retreat," *New-Orleans Directory & Register* (1830), unpaginated opening section.
279. "Gen. Jackson at New Orleans," *Connecticut Herald* (New Haven), February 5, 1828, p. 2.

Years earlier in Indiana, Lincoln had read William Grimshaw's *History of the United States,* which climaxes with the triumph at Chalmette. Years later, Lincoln advocated a resolution in the Illinois state legislature to commemorate "the victory of New-Orleans, and the military fame of Gen. Jackson, though he could never find in his heart to support him as a politician."[280]

•

Lincoln would have seen, heard, smelled, and tasted a level of cultural foreignness in New Orleans that he would experience nowhere else for the balance of his life. Timothy Flint described the diverse humanity a few years earlier, and, quite appropriately, included flatboatmen in the dizzying mosaic:

> This city exhibits the greatest variety of costume, and foreigners; French, Spanish, Portuguese, Irish [and] common people of all the European nations, Creoles, all the intermixtures of Negro and Indian blood, the moody and ruminating Indians, the inhabitants of the Spanish provinces, and a goodly [bunch] of boatmen, "half horse and half alligator". . . . [M]ore languages are spoken here, than in any town in America. There is a sample, in short, of every thing.[281]

"Americans, English, French, Scotch, Spaniards, Swedes, Germans, Irish, Italians, Russians, Creoles, Indians, Negroes, Mexicans, and Brazilians," marveled C. D. Arfwedson of New Orleans' ethnic diversity a few years after Lincoln's visits. He continued:

> This mixture of languages, costumes, and manners, rendered the scene *one of the most singular that I ever witnessed.* . . . [They] formed altogether such a striking contrast, that it was not a little extraordinary to find them united in one single point. If there is a place [representing] the confusion of tongues at the Tower of Babel, it certainly is New Orleans.[282]

Joseph Holt Ingraham, who might have crossed paths with Flint and

---

280. "Remarks [of Abraham Lincoln] in Illinois Legislature Concerning Commemoration of the Battle of New Orleans," *Illinois State Register,* January 15, 1841, in *Collected Works,* 1:226.

281. Flint, *Recollections of the Last Ten Years,* 308.

282. C. D. Arfwedson, *The United States and Canada in 1832, 1833, and 1834* (London: Richard Bentley, 1834), 2:56 (emphasis added).

Arfwedson, bore witness to the same phenomena and came away with similar impressions:

> [T]ruly does New-Orleans represent every other city and nation upon earth. I know of none where is congregated so great a variety of the human species, of every language and colour. Not only natives of the well known European and Asiatic countries are here . . . but occasionally Persians, Turks, Lascars, Maltese, Indian sailors from South America and the Islands of the sea, Hottentots, Laplanders, and, for aught I know to the contrary, Symmezonians.[283]

So too Henry Edward Durell a decade later:

> Jews and Gentiles, the Frenchman, Italian, Spaniard, German, and American, of all conditions and occupations. . . . What a hubbub! what an assemblage of strange faces, of the representatives of distinct people! What a contact of beauty and deformity, of vulgarity and good-breeding! What a collection of costumes . . . ![284]

While nearly all sections of the city exhibited ethnic, racial, linguistic, and religious diversity, the constitutions and proportions of that intermixture varied spatially. Catholics—including white and black Creoles; "foreign French" from France or Haiti; and Spanish, Caribbean, Latin American, Italian, and other immigrants—predominated in the lower half of the Old City and the lower *banlieue*. (Only a few months before Lincoln's arrival, Spanish colonials, who had been "banished from Mexico" after its independence, arrived in significant numbers at the lower city.[285]) Protestant Anglo-Americans and other English speakers, on the other hand, generally gravitated to the upper streets of the Old City, throughout Faubourg St. Mary, and in the new upper-*banlieue* developments of Duplantier, Solet, La Course, and Annunciation. Areas near the flatboat wharves tended to be immigrant-dominated, although the main influxes of Irish and Germans would not arrive and settle here until the 1830s–50s. Enslaved blacks, meanwhile, were "scattered through the city promiscuously," as one newspaper put it, a geography driven by masters' desire to keep their

283. Ingraham, *South-West by a Yankee*, 1:99.

284. Henry Didimus (Henry Edward Durell), *New Orleans As I Found It* (New York: Harper & Brothers, 1845), 29–30.

285. *Conseil de Ville*, Session of March 1, 1828, p. 199 of microfilm #90-223, AB301, NOPL-LC.

domestic slaves handy and controllable.[286] A small number of Jews lived in a dispersed pattern, unaffiliated with a congregation—until 1828, when a leader filed for a state charter to create the city's first permanent Jewish organization. Congregation Shangari Chassed (Gates of Mercy) would also form the first lasting Jewish congregation outside the original thirteen colonies. Its charter request appeared in the local newspapers precisely during Lincoln's visit.

Visitors noticed the city's prevailing downtown-Creole/uptown-Anglo cultural geography and the intermixed patterns therein. This description illustrates the level of foreignness to which Lincoln would have been exposed upon strolling the lower city:

> The number of French and of American inhabitants is [roughly] the same [throughout all of New Orleans]; but the French predominate in the old town, [where] almost all the sign-posts are in the French language, and very many of the store-keepers are unable to speak English.[287]

•

Those Francophone storekeepers filled their window displays Paris-style, with a dazzling array of notions and curiosities from around the world, the likes of which a first-time country visitor could hardly imagine back home. Fine clothing, imported from Britain and quite possibly made from cotton previously shipped through New Orleans, could be bought at 50 Toulouse Street, at Newton's (soon to open at 55 Chartres), or at Theodore Nicholet Co., which also offered sundry European spirits. This being a "wine town" with a taste for fine drink, liquor dealers abounded—at 118 Royal, at 67 Levee, at 182 Royal, and elsewhere. Imports came from Havre, Bordeaux, and elsewhere, demonstrating the continued commercial and cultural relations between France and New Orleans. There was also locally brewed rotgut available at any dram shop, or wholesale from the malt liquor store at 24 Custom House (now Iberville). Pharmacies like Bonnabel's Apothecary—an early drugstore chain with outlets at 33 and 77 Tchoupitoulas—were particularly picturesque, with long marble counters and colorful rows of mysterious remedies, half of which caused more problems than they cured.

Eateries proliferated. Gentry and Lincoln, raised on corn and pork,

---

286. *Daily Picayune*, "A Kaleidoscopic View of New Orleans." September 23, 1843, p. 2, c. 3.

287. Stuart, *Three Years in North America*, 2:235.

might have been amused by the Globe Coffee House announcing that "A fine green turtle will be dressed this day; soup ready at 11 o'clock; turtle steaks." Among those who dined at that fancy restaurant were diplomats from England, France, Spain, Mexico, the Netherlands, Brazil, Sweden, Norway, Sardinia, Sicily, Denmark, Colombia, and Switzerland, all of whom operated consulates within a few blocks of the Globe's upper-Chartres Street locale.[288] Exotic foods like pâté, sardines, sweetmeats, and vermicelli, unloaded recently off the brig *Commerce*, were displayed for sale at 56 Gravier. Stalls in municipal markets abounded with exotic fruits and local specialties such as *gombo*, thick with fresh seafoods all but unknown upcountry.

Other shops specialized in Western products, a bit more familiar to our Indiana men. Beaver hats—all the rage in this era, made from pelts harvested by mountain men in the Rockies—were displayed elegantly at 18 Canal Street and in the new hat store on St. Peter Street by the plaza. Kentucky and Tennessee tobacco ended up in any one of dozens of smoke shops, such as 5 Toulouse, 9 Camp, and 36 Magazine. *Graisse* (lard) and whiskey arriving from Cincinnati could be found at stores such as Charles Byrne's, just off Canal Street, which maintained an enormous rotating inventory of incoming flatboat freight:

> FLOUR, Wiskey [*sic*] . . . first proof New Orleans Rum . . .
> Bacon, comprising Hams, Sides and Shoulders . . . Lard, Bees
> Wax . . . Pork . . . Beef, put up at Cincinnati . . . Gin, Brandy
> . . . Rye Whiskey . . . Sugar . . . Bale Rope, for sale by Chas.
> Byrne, No. 5 Dorsiere-st.[289]

Byrne's competed with scores of other dry-goods stores; their ads filled newspaper columns as much as their shops dominated the streetscapes of Levee, Tchoupitoulas, and other riverfront thoroughfares. The name of one Camp Street store—Lincoln & Green—might have caught Abraham's attention; inside, he could find anything from twine to mackerel.[290] Need a saddle? 30 Levee. Spermaceti oil, carpenter's planes, brimstone, linen bags, paint, glass, or hardware? Visit Martinstein & Hall at 9 Bienville. Glassware? 46 Canal Street. How about reading material, an almanac, or that new book about Columbus by Washington Irving? Benjamin Levy's on Chartres was the city's premier bookseller. Another, William

288. "Foreign Consuls Resident," *New-Orleans Directory & Register* (1830).
289. *New Orleans Bee*, May 29, 1828, p. 3, c. 5.
290. *Louisiana Courier*, November 13, 1828, p. 3, c. 6.

McKean's at 9 Canal Street, advertised Timothy Flint's recently published *Geography and History of the Western States* (quoted above), in which Lincoln could have read about the very flatboating experience he was living.[291] Theater buffs, opera aficionados, and musicians went to John Klemm's at 49 Canal, headquarters for musical instruments and sheet music, including "the admired Overature, Chorus of Highlanders Waltz and Quickstep to the Opera of La Dame Blanche," which had just played at the theater. Klemm also advertises "a collection of New Songs, Variations, Rondos, &c, for the *Piano Forte.*"[292]

Service-oriented businesses ranged from the mundane to the exotic. "Docttor Renou" announced the move of his "Sulphorous baths" from 122 St. Ann to 156 Barracks, assuring prospective clients that "[t]he room for the reception of white people is totally separate from the one fixed for negroes." Renou also charged different prices according to race.[293] If you wanted your hair done, the hairdresser at 182 Chartres offered his services as well as buffalo-horn combs, false hair, beaver gloves, and exotic body lotions. If you needed your dress jacket cleaned, dyed, or "scowered," visit 62 St. Peter. If you sought a license to peddle, hawk, or "exchange merchandize on the great roads and water courses in this State," apply at Conti and Levee, No. 43. Try your luck at a quick fortune? P. V. Barbet's lottery office at 37 St. Louis, opposite Hewlett's Exchange, can arrange a spin of the "Wheel of Fortune." If your timepiece malfunctioned, visit the watchmaker on Chartres Street near Mr. Blanchet's druggist store—a few doors down from Mrs. Herries' Hotel, between St. Louis and Toulouse. Locals seeking to improve their minds were invited to tour the new Jefferson Lyceum, offering language and math classes in Bernard Marigny's old plantation house in the faubourg bearing his name.[294]

•

For every business that advertised in the *Bee* or *Argus*, dozens more lined the streets or operated off the books. Other forms of street life were even less documented by the local papers. Peddlers and hawkers barely ap-

291. "Flint's Geography and History of the Western States," ibid., October 23, 1828, p. 4, c. 3.

292. *New Orleans Argus*, May 28, 1828, p. 1, c. 1 and page 2, c. 6. All other shop information gleaned from editions of the *Bee* and *Argus* from mid-May through early June 1828.

293. *New Orleans Bee*, May 9 and afterwards, 1828, p. 4, c. 4.

294. Shop information gleaned from the *Bee* and *Argus*, mid-May through early June, 1828.

peared; one of the few who posted an advertisement offered a French-made "mechanical theater" (puppet show) for sale at St. Ann and Condé. Real theaters regularly filed ads; the famous Orleans Theater presented *Mr. Good Fortune* plus comedy and vaudeville acts ("The Cat metamorphosed into a Woman") during Lincoln's visit. Later it ran *The White Lady*, an opera in three acts, followed by a two-act farce *The Despair of Jocrisse* and a three-act vaudeville *The Huzzar of Felsheim*.[295] Crime also made the news, including typical urban delinquencies such as a horse stolen on Esplanade Street, a cotton bale lifted from Tchoupitoulas, a gang targeting pedestrians throughout downtown, the post office burglarized of eighty dollars, and a purse snatching.[296]

Two special events brought crowds to the plaza in Faubourg Tremé, situated six blocks behind the Place d'Armes. There, "in the building on the public square of Rampart Street," for admission of fifty cents, ran a "Panoramic picture of the *City of Paris*, the *Capital of the Kingdom of France*." Ads for the traveling exhibit, featuring bird's-eye vistas of Paris' famed palaces and gardens, appeared in English and French for the entire length of Lincoln's visit.[297] Sunday evening, May 25, saw another special event at the same place: a "Grand Exhibition of Fireworks [at] N. Orleans Square, back of the Panorama [Exhibit of Paris]." It cost one dollar (children and people of color, fifty cents) to enjoy a "grand display of Pyratechny."[298] The racial awareness manifested in that pricing policy matched a class-based attempt at segregation, in which mechanics and seamen (including flatboatmen) were encouraged to visit only on weekends so that "*ladies* and *gentlemen*" might enjoy the exhibition on other days without brushing shoulders with the working class. The policy brought an indignant response from one citizen, who declared himself "proud of the appellation of an AMERICAN MECHANIC."[299]

This being Sunday, the exhibit and fireworks would have been joined by another noteworthy spectacle: the weekly convening of slaves enjoying their off day with drumming and dancing. What the newspapers called New Orleans Square was known by everyone else as Circus or Congo Square, another must-see sight on the visitors' circuit and a rare example

295. *New Orleans Argus*, May 13, 1828, p. 2, c. 6; May 19, 1828, p. 3, c. 1; May 23, 1828, p. 2, c. 6.

296. Gleaned from the *Bee* and *Argus*, mid-May through early June, 1828.

297. *New Orleans Bee*, May 9, 1828 and afterwards, p. 3, c. 4.

298. *New Orleans Argus*, May 22, 1828, p. 3, c. 2.

299. "To the editor of the Louisiana Courier," *Louisiana Courier*, May 11, 1831, page undeterminable, c. 1.

of an officially (although reluctantly) tolerated public display of African American cultural expression. The sight horrified and thrilled white visitors unaccustomed to black performance, particularly on the Sabbath, as evinced by this traveler who witnessed the spectacle two decades before Lincoln's visit:

> [A] walk in the rear of the town will . . . astonish [your] bewildered imaginations with the sight of twenty different dancing groups of the wretched Africans, collected together to perform their *worship* after the manner of their country. They have their own national music, consisting . . . of a long kind of narrow drum of various sizes, from two to eight feet in length, three or four of which make a band. The principal dancers or leaders are dressed in a variety of wild and savage fashions, always ornamented with . . . the tails of the smaller wild beasts, and those who appeared most horrible always attracted the largest circle of company. These amusements continue until sunset, when one or two of the city patrole show themselves with their cutlasses, and the crowds immediately disperse.[300]

So popular did Congo Square grow by the time of Lincoln's visit that the City Directory followed its entry for "Circus, Public Square [on] Rampart Street" with the words, "where the Negroes dance on the Sabbath."[301] Combined with the elegant Parisian exhibit and the spectacular pyrotechnics, the "bewildering" and "savage" spectacle of the African slaves must have made Sunday, May 25, 1828, quite a day at Congo Square—smack in the middle of Lincoln's three-week visit. New Orleans' other public parks—the Place d'Armes in the Old City, Washington Square in Faubourg Marigny, Lafayette Square in Faubourg St. Mary, and Coliseum Square and Annunciation Square in the upper faubourgs—regularly hosted circuses, magicians, freak shows, "natural philosophers," bull-fighting, predator-versus-predator animal fights, public floggings, and executions.

Gentry and Lincoln surely spent a fair amount of time promenading the levee, where refreshing breezes rolled off the river and constant shipping activity offered free entertainment. Sixty-eight ocean-going ships, fifty brigs, ten schooners, and six sloops—forming a "forest" of at least

300. Christian Schultz, *Travels on an Inland Voyage Through the States of New-York, Pennsylvania, Virginia, Ohio, Kentucky and Tennessee . . . Performed in the Years 1807 and 1808* (New York: Isaac Riley, 1810), 2:197.

301. Unpaginated section entitled "Streets, &c.—Rues, &c." in *New-Orleans Directory & Register* (1830).

three hundred masts—lined the Old City wharf on May 20. Port calls numbered more that day than on the same date for the two previous years combined, and probably the most up to that point in the history of the rapidly growing city.[302]

Among the brigs was the *United States Bell*, which arrived on May 17 or 18. After tying up and positioning its flying bridges, the *Bell*'s sailors poured ashore and dockworkers began extracting sacks, crates, and parcels. One man dipped in and out of a darkened entrance leading into the hold, as if arranging something. Finally he emerged with someone behind him. It was a black man, chained to another, he to a third, and to a fourth. The coffle comprised men, women, and children, some apparently forming families or fragments thereof. "Norfolk," mumbled some spectators—from Norfolk, Virginia, the latest domestic importation from the slave-supply regions of the Old South to the slave-demanding Southwest and its labor-hungry sugar and cotton plantations. One hundred sixty-nine slaves eventually materialized from the *Bell* and gathered on the levee, rubbing the painful subtropical sun from their eyes and stretching atrophied limbs as much as their chains allowed. The unceremonious arrival of these African Americans, their names lost to history, earned no more than two lines in the local newspaper: "Brick United States, Bell, de Norfolk, avec 169 esclaves."[303] Where they were taken cannot be ascertained, but most likely they spent time at the slave depots in Faubourg St. Mary or Marigny. There, they would have been prepared for the auction block, for delivery to owners already consigned, or for display on sidewalks like furniture. This practice so disturbed residents—more for reasons of neighborhood nuisance than moral degradation—that a "petition, signed by several inhabitants of this City, whose purpose is to ask the Council to take such steps as may be necessary to prevent exposing negroes for sale on the sidewalks" circulated two months before Lincoln's visit. The City Council, prioritizing for commercial interests, rejected the petition and allowed the practice to continue.[304]

If Lincoln caught sight of this coffle, it would have represented the single largest documented public exhibition of slave commerce during his three-week visit. The second largest group arrived toward the end of his

302. *New Orleans Bee*, May 23, 1831, p. 2, c. 2 and page 3, c. 3. The table in this article reports shipping activity for 1825 through 1831.

303. "Nouvelles Maritimes-Port de la Nlle.-Orleans," *New Orleans Bee*, May 19, 1828, p. 2, c. 5.

304. *Conseil de Ville*, Session of March 1, 1828, pp. 201–202 and 222 of microfilm #90-223, AB301, NOPL-LC.

visit, when the Bayou Sara steamboat *Florida* delivered bales of cotton
to various local merchants, along with "17 slaves, 5 horses, 4 oxen to D.
Barrow [and] 17 slaves to J. R. Berford. . . ."[305] These two importations
brought 203 African Americans into the New Orleans slave market. Together with the thirty-one slaves who changed owners at Hewlett's Exchange, the numerous runaways, the hundreds hired out as peddlers and
laborers, and the thousands toiling in courtyards and fields, they formed
a vast cityscape of slavery for Lincoln to see.

•

When Lincoln's father flatboated to New Orleans in 1806, his only options to return home involved keelboats, horses, and his own two feet.
Two decades of technological progress changed all that. Abraham's trip
home from New Orleans would present yet another new experience for
the young man: his first long-distance voyage on a steamboat.

When did Gentry and Lincoln leave New Orleans? We previously
established that the pair left Rockport around April 18 or 19 and returned
in late June. Their departure from New Orleans can thus be estimated by
backing out the typical time a New Orleans steamboat needed to travel
1,273 miles up the Mississippi and Ohio rivers, against the high water
of that year. For reasons that will be explained shortly, this researcher
estimates that Lincoln's northbound steamboat trip took roughly thirteen
to fourteen days. Backing this time span out of a late-June Rockport arrival puts Gentry and Lincoln leaving New Orleans sometime during the
second week of June.

Now we must determine what steamboats left for Ohio River destinations in that time window. Steamboats departed New Orleans most days
of the week, but the lion's share traveled no further than Bayou Sara or
Natchez. Those destined for upcountry cities like Louisville or Nashville
(stopping at selected intermediary landings) numbered only one or two
per week. Scanning the newspapers, we find the 400-ton *Amazon* scheduled to leave for Louisville on Thursday, June 5, at 10 a.m., the 278-ton
Florida (the same steamboat that, days earlier, imported thirty-four slaves)
departing on Sunday, June 8, at the same hour, and the 153-ton *Emerald*
departing Tuesday, June 10.[306] Gentry and Lincoln could have boarded

305. *New Orleans Argus*, June 3, 1828, p. 2, c. 5.
306. *Louisiana Courier*, June 4, 1828, p. 3, c. 4; *New Orleans Argus*, June 6, 1828, p. 2,
c. 1; Ibid., June 7, 1828, p. 2, c. 1. Vessel weights come from "Steam-Boats in the Orleans
Trade," *New-Orleans Directory & Register* (1830), unpaginated rear section.

any of these steamboats—or other "soft-scheduled" vessels that departed whenever their cargo holds and passenger cabins filled. It is also possible the Indiana men hitched a ride on a regional steamboat, and then transferred as they progressed upriver.[307]

Steaming the Mississippi rated far safer than flatboating, but did incur some risk. Just a few weeks earlier, the Louisville-bound *Car of Commerce*—which Gentry and Lincoln would have passed as they floated downriver—"burst her boiler." The fourteen dead, twelve dying, and thirty injured people were mostly crew and deck passengers (as opposed to higher-paying cabin passengers), and undoubtedly included returning flatboatmen.[308] So common had such accidents become that, around the day Gentry and Lincoln left for home, the *Louisiana Courier* published an editorial denouncing negligent engineers and firemen responsible for the fiery disasters.[309]

Few details survive about Lincoln's return trip. In terms of expenses, a neighbor declared that Lincoln was paid "$8.00 per month—from the time of starting to his returning home, [plus James] Gentry paid his way back on a [steam]boat. This I know."[310] Allen Gentry's brother recalled that Abe and Allen returned as "deck passengers,"[311] who traveled with minimal accommodations to keep fares low. Deck passengers often performed onboard services in exchange for heavily discounted passage. "This trade gives employment to hundreds of men," wrote Samuel Judah in 1827:

> These flatboatmen return up the river in steamboats as deck passengers which costs them nothing. Deck passengers are required to help loading & unloading.[312]

Returning flatboatmen made their uncouth presence known to genteel passengers, among them the dainty English traveler Frances Milton Trollope, who steamed upriver around the same time as Gentry and Lincoln.

---

307. Unfortunately, the "Marine Register" columns in local newspapers did not regularly record steamboat departures; the above information comes from advertisements.

308. "Dreadful Catastrophe," *New Orleans Argus*, May 19, 1828, p. 2, c. 3.

309. "Communicated—Engineers," *Louisiana Courier*, June 4, 1828, p. 3, c. 1.

310. Interview, Nathaniel Grigsby, by William H. Herndon, September 12, 1865, in *Herndon's Informants*, 114.

311. Louis A. Warren, ed. "Lincoln's Return Trip from New Orleans," *Lincoln Lore: Bulletin of the Lincoln National Life Foundation*, no. 472, April 25, 1938.

312. Samuel Bernard Judah, "A Journal of Travel from New York to Indiana in 1827," *Indiana Magazine of History* 17, no. 4 (December 1921): 351.

"The deck, as is usual," she wrote,

> was occupied by the Kentucky flat-boat men, returning from
> New Orleans, after having disposed of the boat and cargo
> which they had conveyed thither. . . . We had about two hun-
> dred of these men on board, but [their] part of the vessel . . .
> is so distinct from the cabins, that we never saw them, except
> when we stopped to take in wood; and then they ran, or rather
> sprung and vaulted over each other's heads to the shore, whence
> they all assisted in carrying wood to supply the steam engine;
> the performance of this duty being a stipulated part of the pay-
> ment of their passage.

Mrs. Trollope relied on a secondhand report when she passed judgment
on the lads' behavior: "they are a most disorderly set of persons, constantly
gambling and wrangling, very seldom sober," and sometimes thieving.[313]
Flatboatmen themselves were less inclined to scribe their observations
(much less defend their reputations), although some kept diaries of their
experiences. One described his return trip from New Orleans, using a pho-
netic orthography that captures the accent and enunciation of circa-1832
southern Indiana (see footnote for translation):

> I got pasage on alarge steeme boat for ivens ville on the ohio
> river in the staite of Indiana paid $7.00 on Deck and founde
> my one grube and slep on aborde on ablanket of my one the
> boat that I was on was alarge boat 8—boilars side whees naime
> Ellon Douglas hade on about 300—Deck pasengers whene
> she lefte the Citty of New or-leans. . . . [They] barrid one with
> cilery I lefte the boat in the nite wente up in town saide all
> nite . . .[314]

Approximating Lincoln's return time requires an understanding of steamboat speed. Journals from mid-antebellum travelers hold clues. One comes

---

313. A number of military officers and a judge also on board with Mrs. Trollope met
with greater approval by the judgmental dame—until, that is, she had to suffer their table
manners. Trollope, *Domestic Manners*, 1:22–27.

314. Translated, this passage reads, "I got passage on a large steamboat for Evansville
on the Ohio River in the state of Indiana; I paid $7.00 [to stay on] deck, and found my
[group?] and slept on board on a blanket of mine. The boat that I was on was a large
boat—eight boilers and a side wheel, named Ellen Douglas; had on board about 300 deck
passengers when she left the city of New Orleans. . . . [They] buried one [victim] of cholera [who had become ill in New Orleans]. I left the boat in the night, went up into town
and stayed all night. . . ." Wilkinson, "Footloose on the Northwest Frontier," 414–416.

from Adam Hodgson, who, in 1821, steamed 320 miles upriver from New Orleans against high springtime water in a period of four days, or 80 miles per day.[315] The previously cited circa-1832 account recollected that it took "a bout 7 Days to [reach] Evans ville Indiana [sic]" from New Orleans,[316] a 1,193-mile journey traversed at an impressive (possibly questionable) pace of 170 miles per day. An 1834 traveler wrote that "a journey from New Orleans to [Cincinnati, measuring 1560 river miles] can now be performed in twelve" days, or 130 miles per day.[317] An 1835 voyage from New Orleans to Evansville took sixteen days, or 75 miles per day.[318] Clearly, a number of variables are at play here, including the velocity of the contrary currents, the size and power of the vessel, its load, the number and length of stops, and whether mechanical or navigational problems arose. Had Gentry and Lincoln taken the powerful *Amazon*, which departed June 5, they might have arrived home as early as June 13, because that same vessel a few months earlier traveled from New Orleans to Louisville (fully loaded and against strong current) in only nine days.[319] The *Amazon*, however, was exceptional and possibly expensive. This researcher postulates Lincoln used a mid-range steamboat with a more typical 90- to 100-mile-per-day travel speed, which would have covered the 1,273 miles between New Orleans and Rockport in roughly thirteen days or two weeks.

If Gentry and Lincoln departed on June 8 and steamed upriver at this speed, they would have traversed the sugar coast during the first two days of the voyage. The vessel would have reached Natchez on June 11 and Vicksburg the next day, before entering the bottomland wilderness of the Mississippi-Louisiana-Arkansas upper-delta country, where "the eye of the traveler long wearied with the level shores."[320] Civilization returned at Memphis, after which came the old French towns of Missouri, the Ohio River confluence around June 18, and finally Rockport on June 21. Actual dates could range two or three days on either side of these approximations.

315. Adam Hodgson, *Remarks During a Journey Through North America in the Years 1819, 1820, and 1821* (Samuel Whiting: New York, 1823), 163, 167.

316. Wilkinson, "Footloose on the Northwest Frontier," 415.

317. Abdy, *Journal of a Residence and Tour in the United States*, 3:64.

318. This vessel left New Orleans on Sunday February 22, 1835, at 10 a.m. and arrived in Posey County, Indiana, near Evansville, on March 9 at 10 p.m. Jacquess, "Journals of the Davy Crockett," 24.

319. *Western Sun* (Vincennes, IN), May 24, 1828, as quoted by Warren, *Lincoln's Youth*, 186.

320. Ingraham, "Dots and Lines," 38.

The upriver trip would have given Lincoln a reversed, loftier, and more social perspective of riverine geography. He would have viewed the landscape from a perch at least ten or a dozen feet higher than his surface-hugging flatboat. He also would have interacted with scores of fellow passengers cramped into close quarters, sharing conversation and anecdotes about their travels—quite different from what he and Gentry experienced on the way down. Both men would have brushed shoulders with penny-pinching deck passengers like themselves, and possibly slaves recently purchased at New Orleans. We can only speculate whether this return voyage gave Lincoln his first prolonged, personal interaction with African Americans in the midst of their life-altering transit. Lincoln did describe a similar spectacle on the steamboat *Lebanon* between Louisville and St. Louis in 1841. While not part of Lincoln's New Orleans experience, the 1841 incident provides striking detail on the riverine transport of slaves, and illustrates how the intersection of rivers and slavery informed Lincoln's formative years, in terms of moral outrage and, paradoxically, rationalization:

> A gentleman had purchased twelve negroes in different parts of Kentucky and was taking them to a farm in the South. They were chained six and six together. A small iron clevis was around the left wrist of each, and this fastened to the main chain by a shorter one at a convenient distance from, the others; so that the negroes were strung together precisely like so many fish upon a trot-line. In this condition they were being separated forever from the scenes of their childhood, their friends, their fathers and mothers, and brothers . . . sisters . . . wives and children, and going into perpetual slavery where the lash of the master is . . . ruthless and unrelenting. . . . [Y]et amid all these distressing circumstances . . . they were the most cheerful and apparantly [sic] happy creatures on board. One, whose offence for which he had been sold was an over-fondness for his wife, played the fiddle almost continually; and the others danced, sung, cracked jokes, and played various games with cards from day to day. How true it is that "God tempers the wind to the shorn lamb," or in other words, that He renders the worst of human conditions tolerable, while He permits the best, to be nothing better than tolerable.[321]

Lincoln recalled that searing memory again in 1855, revealing his mental

---

321. Abraham Lincoln to Mary Speed, September 27, 1841, in *Collected Works*, 1:260.

anguish in a poignant discourse about slavery:

> I confess I hate to see the poor creatures hunted down, and
> caught, and carried back to their stripes, and unrewarded toils;
> but I bite my lip and keep quiet. In 1841 you and I had together
> a tedious low-water trip, on a Steam Boat from Louisville to
> St. Louis. You may remember, as I well do, that from Louis-
> ville to the mouth of the Ohio there were, on board, ten or a
> dozen slaves, shackled together with irons. *That sight was a*
> *continual torment to me*; and I see something like it every time I
> touch the Ohio, or any other slave-border."[322]

•

Young men completing their first long-distance journey view the warm
hearth of family differently upon returning home. A place like Spencer
County might suddenly appear quite mundane compared to the now-
expanded universe of the recently returned rookie flatboatman. Spencer
County folks might likewise seem a bit more rustic vis-à-vis the characters of the Mississippi, the nabobs of Natchez, the aristocrats of the sugar
coast, or the Frenchmen of New Orleans. Young globetrotters favored
the company of their worldly fraternity, those who had also "seen the elephant" at New Orleans.

Abraham Lincoln returned home in the opening days of summer 1828,
two months after departure. His payment, at eight dollars per month, represented the largest lump sum he had earned to date. Being below legal
age, however, "law and custom" dictated that he hand the money to his
father.[323] Thomas Lincoln, in turn, did not hesitate to remind his son that
chores beckoned around the Pigeon Creek homestead. It was as if Abraham had never left.

Falling back under father's control was but one of Abraham's increasingly suffocating domestic problems. Two of his stepsisters married within the extended clan—one to distant cousin Dennis Hanks, the other to
Dennis' half-brother Squire Hall. Both couples remained in the cramped
Lincoln household and wasted no time in populating it with offspring.
Then another Kentucky relation moved in: John Hanks, the son of Abraham's biological mother's uncle on her paternal side, who also came to be

---

322. Lincoln to J. F. Speed, August 24, 1855, in *Collected Works*, 2:320 (emphasis added).

323. Sandburg, *Prairie Years and The War Years*, 47.

known as Abraham's "cousin."[324] (John and Dennis Hanks, respectively seven and ten years older than Abraham, would later play important roles in the flatboat story.) The Lincoln cabin grew crowded and contentious; Abraham was outgrowing it, the clan, and all of Pigeon Creek. His rumored teenage crush on Anna Roby—now Allen Gentry's wife for over a year and mother of their infant son—may have further complicated his social terrain.

The mind-expanding trip to New Orleans surely played a role in Lincoln's disenchantment with home. But he could not readily return to that riverine world. The opportunities of the Ohio River lay a full day's walk away; the excitement of New Orleans lay a month away. The possibility of liberation further faded when a neighbor declined to recommend Abraham for a steamboat job until he reached age twenty-one. Lincoln grew estranged from childhood friends, and by some accounts, from his father. He became restless and antagonistic at home. John and Dennis Hanks, for their part, went out on separate trips to investigate opportunities in Macon County, Illinois.[325] At least five members of the Hanks family had settled there by June 1829.[326]

Abraham's only refuge from the banalities of home was the local post office and store, affiliated variously with James Gentry, his kin Gideon Romine, and local merchant William Jones. That enterprise offered the company of other worldly men, with whom Lincoln could swap stories, read newspapers, talk politics, and earn some money. William Jones proved especially interesting to Abraham: nine years his senior, Jones emigrated from North Carolina and had lived in Terre Haute and Louisville before losing his wife and children. He arrived at Pigeon Creek in 1827 with the intention to remain and prosper here. Jones carried a grander vision and lived in a bigger world than most local folk; he knew farming, business, the river, New Orleans—and politics, lots about politics. Abraham admired Jones, who in turn recognized the youth's potential (probably hearing of his successful New Orleans expedition from James Gentry) and hired him at the store. During late 1828 and 1829, Lincoln unpacked boxes, "drove a team[,] cut up Pork . . . chopp[ed] wood [and] clerked for

324. For lineage, see Louis A. Warren, ed., "The Relatives of Lincoln's Mother," *Lincoln Lore: Bulletin of the Lincoln National Life Foundation*, no. 479, June 13, 1938.

325. Interview, William Wood, by William H. Herndon, September 15, 1865, in *Herndon's Informants*, 124; Warren, *Lincoln's Youth*, 204.

326. A petition signed by Charles, James, John, and two men named William Hanks, dated June 25, 1829, is filed in the Hanks Family Papers, Manuscript Collection, SC 644, Abraham Lincoln Presidential Library, Springfield, Illinois.

Jones" in an area immediately west of Gentryville later known as Jones-boro. William Jones, a future colonel, reciprocated with modest financial compensation and intellectual nourishment, in the form of loaned books, conversation, and political mentoring. "Col Jones told me that Lincoln read all his books," recalled one neighbor many years later. Said another, "Col Jones was Lincoln['s] guide & teacher in Politics." This being around the time of Andrew Jackson's presidential election (in which Abe could not yet vote on account of his age), there was plenty of political food for thought, around which Lincoln could formulate his political character. Locals remembered Jones saying "over & over again that Mr Lincoln laid the foundation of his Character in Spencer Co Indiana" and "that Lincoln would make a great man one of these days. . . . Said so as far back as 1828-29. . . ."[327]

An awkward incident one year after the New Orleans trip yanked the maturing but not yet fully mature Abraham back into the petty world of past grievances. How he dealt with it reflected his growing sophistication as well as his lingering adolescence. Two Grigsby brothers—kin of Aaron, the former brother-in-law whom Abraham resented for not having done enough to aid his ailing sister Sarah Lincoln—married their fiancées on the same day and celebrated with a joint "infare." The Grigsbys pointedly did not invite Lincoln. In a mischievous mood, Abraham exacted revenge by penning a ribald satire entitled "The Chronicles of Reuben," in which the two grooms accidentally end up in bed together rather than with their respective brides. Other locals suffered their own indignities within the stinging verses of Abraham's poem, nearly resulting in fisticuffs. The incident both reflected and exacerbated Lincoln's growing rift with all things related to Spencer County.

Harvests and profits on the Lincoln farm served little to brighten prospects. Nor did another outbreak of milk sickness during the winter of 1828–29, which killed villagers and livestock. The only good news seemed to come from neighbors who had migrated to Illinois, namely cousin John Hanks. "I wrote to Thos Lincoln what Kind of a Country it was," recalled Hanks years later, reporting good harvests on rich alluvial soil in the central part of that state.[328] John convinced Dennis Hanks to emigrate, who

---

327. Interviews with John R. Dougherty, Nathaniel Grigsby, and John S. Hougland, September 16–17, 1865, by William H. Herndon, in *Herndon's Informants*, 127, 130, 133; Warren, *Lincoln's Youth*, 188.

328. Interview, John Hanks, by William H. Herndon, 1865–1866, in *Herndon's Informants*, 456.

in turn sold his half-brother Squire Hall on the idea. Because both men had married two of Sally Lincoln's daughters, the notion of family separation arose. Should the extended Lincoln clan go two separate ways, one remaining in the mediocre circumstances of southern Indiana, the other to the promise of a new life westward? Or should they all move together? Sally Lincoln bent her husband's ear.

Reluctantly, Thomas agreed to emigrate, although it is unclear exactly when. We know that Thomas and Sally returned to Elizabethtown, Kentucky, to sell off (on September 8, 1829) their town lot, as if in preparation for a move. We also know that neighbor Charles Grigsby secured a bond toward purchasing Thomas Lincoln's farm on November 26. A few weeks later, on December 12, the Pigeon Creek Baptist Church issued the Lincolns a "letter of Dismission." The subsequent cold months allowed for the selling or packing of possessions and the assemblage of oxen, horses, and wagons. On February 20, 1830, Grigsby closed on the Lincoln land for $125, finally detaching the family from Indiana soil. With the worst winter weather over and planting season still weeks away, it was the perfect time to roll.

While regional- and national-scale issues (irregular land titles and slavery) explain Thomas' decision to move his family from Kentucky to Indiana in 1816, personal matters mostly drove his decision to leave Indiana for Illinois in 1830. Or perhaps we should say his family's decision: historian Louis A. Warren noted that "some pressure must have been brought to bear" (principally by Sally) to convince a fifty-four-year-old man who toiled for fourteen years to carve a homestead out of virgin forest—and earned respect as a family man, farmer, and carpenter—"to start life over again on a new frontier."[329]

•

Much changed for Abraham Lincoln during the month of February 1830. On the twelfth, he reached his "majority"—his twenty-first birthday—officially making him an eligible voter, a keeper of his own wages, and an independent man. On the last day of that month, the Lincolns closed the door on their Pigeon Creek home and boarded with the Gentry family for one final evening. Next day they bade farewell and departed to the northwest. In doing so, Lincoln left behind all he had known since age seven—the friends, the memories, the dreams of working on the Ohio.

329. Warren, *Lincoln's Youth*, 204–208; Sandburg, *Prairie Years and The War Years*, 47–48.

He would also leave behind the graves of his birth mother and full-blood sister. How things had changed since he moved into Indiana: in December 1816, the Lincoln family comprised a nuclear unit of four; by February 1830, it formed an extended clan of thirteen with a confusing array of relatives named Johnston, Hanks, or Hall—sans the two closest women of his life. Years later, Lincoln wrote about the move in the stilted, emotionally detached, and cautiously restrained tone typical of his autobiographical writings:

> March 1st. 1830—[Abraham] having just completed his 21st. year, his father and family, with the families of the two daughters and sons-in-law, of his step-mother, left the old homestead in Indiana, and came to Illinois. Their mode of conveyance was waggons drawn by ox-teams . . . [Abraham] drove one of the teams.[330]

Toward the village of Decatur in Illinois' Macon County, the slow-moving party made its way. Two weeks of grueling passage along half frozen muddy roads and across icy streams brought the emigrants through towns such as Troy, Dale, Jasper, and Petersburg, in a landscape that grew increasingly rural as they distanced themselves from the Ohio River artery. That sense of remoteness changed when they arrived at Vincennes, a century-old former French colonial outpost that had recently served as capital of the Territory of Indiana. The town's position on the Wabash River, a major tributary of the Ohio, connected it with a grander realm and gave it a more worldly air. Many Vincennes residents spoke French, practiced Catholicism, and lived in French Creole–style houses with double-pitched and hipped roofs. Vincennes even boasted a college, founded in 1801. Tradition holds that the Lincoln party stopped here for the night, Abraham taking time to view the printing press at the offices of the Western Sun.

Thomas Lincoln had been to Vincennes before and thus led the way. After the party ferried across the Wabash into Illinois around March 6, Dennis Hanks took the lead. Setting foot on Illinois soil, Abraham ended his fourteen years in Indiana. It would take another fourteen years before he returned, under very different circumstances.

Illinois' landscape comprised intermittent prairie and forest, with a late-winter climate little different from that of southern Indiana. The party bore north into the flat alluvial valley of the Wabash, through settlements that were in some cases larger in 1830 than they are today—

330. Lincoln, "Autobiography," June 1860, in *Collected Works*, 4:63.

Palestine, York, Darwin—and then turned northwestwardly toward the center of the state.[331] Finally, in Lincoln's words,

> [We] reached the county of Macon, and stopped there some time [to meet John Hanks, who provided temporary shelter] within the same month of March. [My] father and family settled a new place on the North side of the Sangamon river, at the junction of the timber-land and prairie, about ten miles Westerly from Decatur.[332]

The 225-mile journey took two weeks. Now came the grueling toil of homesteading. Lincoln continued:

> Here [we] built a log-cabin, into which [we] removed, and made sufficient of rails to fence ten acres of ground, fenced and broke the ground, and raised a crop of sow[n] corn upon it the same year.[333]

John Hanks, proud of his role in enticing the Lincolns into Illinois, re- called the new homestead. It was located

> 10 M west of Decatur--& about 100 Steps from the N[orth] F[ork] of Sangamon River & on the North side of it on a Kind of bluff—The house['s] logs . . . I cut myself in 1829 & gave them to old man Lincoln: The house set East & west—fronted South—chimney as west End. . . .[334]

By summer, that bluff hosted a log cabin, a smokehouse, a barn, fifteen acres of planted corn, split-rail fencing, and thirty nearby acres cleared for John Hanks' brother Charles.[335]

Despite the hard labor, Abraham found time for intellectual engage- ment. One day that summer, a candidate for political office came to town and made a campaign speech on internal improvements. "[I]t was a bad

---

331. Jesse William Weik, *The Real Lincoln: a Portrait* (Boston and New York: Hough- ton Mifflin Company, 1922), 49.

332. Lincoln, "Autobiography," June 1860, in *Collected Works*, 4:63.

333. Lincoln went on to explain that "these are, or are supposed to be, the rails about which so much is being said just now, though they are far from being the first, or only rails ever made by [me]," a reference to his famous campaign image as "the rail-splitter." Lincoln, "Autobiography," June 1860, in *Collected Works*, 4:63.

334. Interview, John Hanks, by William H. Herndon, 1865–1866, in *Herndon's Infor- mants*, 456.

335. Sandburg, *Prairie Years and The War Years*, 49.

one and I Said Abe could beat it," John Hanks recalled.

> I turned down a box or Keg and Abe made his Speech. . . . Abe
> beat [the candidate] to death—his subject being the naviga-
> tion of the Sangamon River. The man . . . took Abe aside and
> asked him where he had learned So much and what he did so
> well. Abe Explained, Stating his manner & method of read-
> ing and what he had read: the man Encouraged Lincoln to
> persevere.[336]

We do not know if Abraham specifically mentioned his 1828 flatboat
voyage to New Orleans, but because that job represented virtually all of
his navigational experience and what he learned on that journey related
directly to internal improvements, it must have at least informed what he
said. Many historians identify this incident as Abraham Lincoln's first
political speech.

•

The progress enjoyed in the summer of 1830 did not last. "In the autumn
all hands were greatly afflicted with augue and fever, to which they had
not been used," remembered Lincoln, "and by which they were greatly
discouraged so much so that they determined on leaving the county."
But weather intervened with a vengeance: it was "the winter of the very
celebrated 'deep snow' of Illinois," recalled Lincoln, with blizzards, sub-
zero temperatures, sickness, and limited food beleaguering the prairie settlers and claiming the lives of new neighbors. Three feet of snow blanked
the region between Christmas and New Year's, followed by freezing rain,
more snow, and two weeks of temperatures in the teens. For employment
Abraham mauled a thousand fence rails for a local landowner who lived
three miles away. During one commute, he nearly suffered permanent
incapacitation, having broken through ice and nearly freezing his feet.[337]

Thomas' reluctance to leave Indiana proved well founded; Illinois had
indeed set the family's circumstances backward. The Lincolns plotted to
relocate again once spring arrived. The wintry confinement, the dreary

336. Interview, John Hanks, with William H. Herndon, 1865–1866, in *Herndon's Informants*, 456.

337. Lincoln, "Autobiography," June 1860, in *Collected Works*, 63; Interview, John
Hanks, by William H. Herndon, 1865–1866, in *Herndon's Informants*, 456; Harry E.
Pratt, *Lincoln: 1809–1839, Being the Day-to-Day Activities of Abraham Lincoln from February 12, 1809 to December 31, 1839* (Springfield, IL: The Abraham Lincoln Association),
9, 220.

prospect of another move, and another cycle of land clearing and cabin building compelled the newly independent Abraham to cast his eyes to the wider world he first experienced two years earlier. His outlet was the little river flowing below their bluff, the Sangamon. Though no Ohio, the wildly sinuous tributary offered (barely) navigable passage into the Illinois River, which joined the Mississippi near the confluence of the Missouri, which lay about two days' travel from the confluence of the Ohio. Unlike the place on Pigeon Creek, this new homestead offered access to the entire riverine West, just a few steps below the bluff. The only thing he lacked was an opportunity.

Abraham's salvation came in the form of a local maverick named Denton Offutt. In some ways, Offutt was to Illinois' Macon and Sangamon counties what James Gentry was to Indiana's Spencer County—farmer, store owner, river merchant, "a brisk and venturesome business man, whose operations extended . . . for many miles."[338] By other accounts, however, Offutt "was a wild—rec[k]less—careless man," not to mention a hard drinker, but nevertheless "Enthusiastic[,] intuitive and prophetic."[339] Nearly all agree he was a perennial dreamer, striving to strike it rich with his next nutty scheme—"the Colonel Sellers of the Lincoln drama," as one historian put it.[340] Offutt crossed paths with John Hanks, who had settled here over two years earlier, and thought Hanks could be of use to his enterprise. "Offutt Came to my house in Feb'y 1831," Hanks recalled, "and wanted to hire me to run a flat boat for him—Saying that he heard that I was quite a flat boatman in Ky: he wanted me to go badly." Hesitant to commit until he recruited boat hands, Hanks returned to the Lincoln homestead and spoke with his two young unmarried relatives, Abraham and his stepbrother John D. Johnston. Both jumped at the opportunity. "We made an Engagement with Offutt at 50 [cents] per day and $60 to make the trip to N Orleans," Hanks remembered.[341] Divided three ways, this compensation amounts to somewhat more than the eight dollars per month plus return fare that James Gentry paid the inexperienced youth three years earlier. Lincoln's own recollection, penned in an 1843 letter, was that his experience "working on a flat boat" paid "ten dollars per

338. Herndon and Weik, *Herndon's Lincoln*, 1:72.

339. Interview, William G. Greene, by William H. Herndon, May 30, 1865, in *Herndon's Informants*, 18.

340. Logan Hay, "Introduction," *Abraham Lincoln Association Papers* (Springfield, IL: Abraham Lincoln Association, 1931), 15.

341. Interview, John Hanks, by William H. Herndon, 1865–1866, in *Herndon's Informants*, 456.

month."[342] Lincoln may have envisioned an additional employment possibility upon landing at New Orleans: according to one hazy recollection, Lincoln had "the intention of staying [in New Orleans] through the winter to Cut Cord Wood."[343] But first came the commitment to Mr. Offutt. Lincoln, writing in the third person years later, filled in the details:

> [Abraham] together with his step-mother's son, John D. Johnston, and John Hanks . . . hired themselves to one Denton Offutt, to take a flat boat from Beardstown Illinois to New-Orleans; and for that purpose, were to join him—Offut—at Springfield, Ills so soon as the snow should go off.[344]

342. Abraham Lincoln to Martin S. Morris, March 26, 1843, in *Collected Works*, 1:319–320.
343. This particular recollection, while not unbelievable, suffers from a number of surrounding factual errors and lacks substantiation in other sources. Letters, J. Rowan Herndon to William H. Herndon, May 28 and June 11, 1865, in *Herndon's Informants*, 6 and 34.
344. Lincoln, "Autobiography," June 1860, in *Collected Works*, 4:63.

The 1831 Experience

Exactly one year after the Lincolns departed for Illinois—Tuesday,
March 1, 1831—John Hanks and Abraham Lincoln set off to meet with
Denton Offutt in Springfield to take charge of their already-loaded flatboat and guide it to New Orleans. The melting of that winter's heavy
snowpack made the roads impassible, so the men "purchased a large canoe," put in directly in front of their home, "and came down the Sangamon river in it." The departure marked the very beginning of the longest
single journey in Abraham Lincoln's life.

Paddling downstream, the men stopped at Judy's Ferry east of Springfield to meet their third crewmember, John D. Johnston, then walked into
town to track down their employer. Recalled Lincoln years later, "This is
the time and the manner of [my] first entrance into Sangamon County,"
where he would later make his home, family, and career.[1]

They found Offutt all right—at the Buckhorn Inn, a favorite Springfield watering hole, utterly negligent of his end of the bargain. Offutt had
cargo for New Orleans, and every intention of paying the men to guide
it there. He just forgot to arrange the flatboat.[2] Regretful and probably
embarrassed, Offutt negotiated on the spot to pay the threesome twelve
dollars per month to build a flatboat from scratch. The unexpected com-
plication wreaked havoc on their springtime plans, throwing off everything by six weeks. But it was paying work, and it got them away from the
family. They took the deal.

A day or so later, Lincoln, Hanks, and Johnston departed for a site

---

1. Abraham Lincoln, "Autobiography Written for John L. Scripps," June 1860, in *The
Collected Works of Abraham Lincoln*, ed. Roy P. Basler (New Brunswick, NJ: Rutgers University Press, 1953), 4:63.

2. Ever respectful of his old friend, Lincoln described Offutt's negligence in this man-
ner: "[We] found Offutt at Springfield, but learned from him that he had failed in get-
ting a boat at Beardstown." Lincoln, "Autobiography," June 1860, in *Collected Works*, 4:63.
See also interview of John Hanks by William H. Herndon, 1865–1866, in ed. Douglas
L. Wilson and Rodney O. Davis, *Herndon's Informants: Letters, Interviews, and Statements
About Abraham Lincoln* (Urbana and Chicago: University of Illinois Press, 1998), 456.

four miles north of Springfield, at the confluence of Spring Creek and the Sangamon River. Here was "Congress land," a patch of old-growth forest "with innumerable flat-boats growing up in their primal timber." The men felled appropriately sized trees, hewed the logs, and floated them downriver where they could be cut into lumber. We know for certain how they cut the wood because Lincoln himself in 1860 crossed out a biographer's presumption that they used "a whip-saw" and corrected it to "a country saw-mill," a reference to Charles Broadwell's steam-driven upright sawmill in the flourishing little river port called Sangamo Town.[3] Timber felling and preparation probably took the men around two weeks, starting the first days of March. (As work progressed—specifically on March 11—Lincoln took time to visit the Sangamon County courthouse and sign his name, as well as those of Hanks and Johnston, on a petition to fill "a vacancy in the office of constable in the Springfield district."[4] Although unrelated to the flatboat, this petition represents the only surviving Lincoln-signed document dating around the time of either flatboat trip. That he took the time to sign the petition, for himself as well as for Hanks and Johnston, reflects his exceptionality within his cohort.)

Once settled at the Sangamo Town construction site, "about 7 miles north west of the City of Springfield" and a few meandering river miles below the timber-cutting site,[5] the threesome erected "a shantee-shed . . . about 90 feet from the River" and "Camped in a Camp on the Sangamon River—done our own Cooking—mending & washing." Lincoln boarded some nights with the members of the Carman family, who operated a nearby sawmill, gristmill, and tavern. Offutt's other employees occasionally lent a hand, among them villagers Walter Carman, John Seaman, a man named Cabanis, and seventeen-year-old John E. Roll.[6] Six decades

3. William Dean Howells, *Life of Abraham Lincoln*, facsimile edition of campaign biography corrected by the hand of Abraham Lincoln (Bloomington: Indiana University Press, 1960), 26; Interviews, Caleb Carman and John Hanks, October 12, 1866 and 1865–1866, by William H. Herndon, in *Herndon's Informants*, 373 and 456–457.

4. Abraham Lincoln, "Petition to Sangamon County Commissions' Court for Appointment of a Constable," March 11, 1831, in *Collected Works*, 1:3.

5. Lincoln campaign biographer John Locke Scripps estimated the location of the construction site as being "near where the Chicago, Alton, and St. Louis Railroad now [1860] crosses the Sangamon River." John Locke Scripps, *Life of Abraham Lincoln*, ed. Roy P. Basler and Lloyd A. Dunlap (Bloomington: Indiana University Press, 1961 reprint of 1860 original), 53.

6. Interviews with William G. Greene (May 29–30, 1865), Caleb Carman (March 1887), and John Hanks (June 13, 1865), by William H. Herndon, in *Herndon's Informants*, 11, 17, 43–44, 607.

later, Roll remembered the sight of Lincoln toiling in Sangamo Town during March–April 1831:

> He had on a suit of blue jeans—if it could be called a suit. It seemed that everything was too short for him. His pantaloons lacked four or five inches of reaching the ground, and when the legs were not stuffed into his rawhide boots they were held down by leather straps which extended under his boots. He wore an old roundabout [that was also] far too short for him, and when he stooped over he showed four or five inches of his suspenders. . . . He wore a drab-colored wool hat, pretty well worn, small-crowned and broad-brimmed. . . . He was the rawest, most primitive looking specimen of humanity I ever saw . . . tall, bony, and as homely as he has ever been pictured.[7]

Roll's 1892 description of Lincoln's appearance complements the recollection of Caleb Carman (recorded in 1866) remarkably well. Carman also remembered Lincoln acting "funny—joky—humorous—full of yarns— stories . . . frequently quoting poetry—reciting prose like orations. . . ." Abe also cooked and "played seven up in the Camp after dark."[8] John E. Roll concurred, saying how local folks would seat themselves on a log bench (which became known as "Abe's log") outside Shepherd's gristmill during morning, noon, and evening breaks, to hear Lincoln's jokes and stories.[9] This being but days before the journey began, we have every reason to believe Abraham looked and acted this way while traveling to and within New Orleans. In a separate interview, Carman offered his impressions of Lincoln just before departure:

> . . . a very inteligent [sic] young man[.] His conversation very often was a bout Books—such as Shakespear & other histories . . . He Talked about politicks Considerable. . . . he was a John Q Adams man. . . . He was opposed to Slavery & said he thougt it a curse to the Land. . . .[10]

Built for a substantial load and an experienced crew of four, the flatboat

---

7. "Lincoln's Flatboat: Story of the Craft Told by One of Its Builders," *Daily Inter-Ocean* (Chicago), May 15, 1892, p. 2.

8. Interview, Caleb Carman, by William H. Herndon, October 12, 1866, in *Herndon's Informants*, 373.

9. "Lincoln's Flatboat," *Daily Inter-Ocean*, May 15, 1892, p. 2.

10. Interview, Caleb Carman, by William H. Herndon, November 30, 1866, in *Herndon's Informants*, 429.

measured larger—"80 feet long & 18 feet wide," recalled Hanks—than the one Lincoln helped Allen Gentry build three years earlier. Otherwise it followed the standard flatboat typology and construction procedure. *Lay down the two gunwales . . . lay girders across and join them . . . lay and join two end-girders at bow and stern . . . lay and join streamers across the girders . . . lay planks across the streamers and pin them down to form the floor . . . caulk all seams. . . .*

While this labor progressed, Lincoln directed some co-workers to excavate a dugout canoe from a sizeable log. Many flatboats carried along such ancillary craft, handy to run small excursions and bank-side errands without committing the entire flatboat. Once the canoe was completed, two workers—John Seaman and Walter Carman—jumped into the unstable craft a bit too enthusiastically, causing it to shoot out from beneath them and sending both into the turbulent early-spring waters of the Sangamon River. Lincoln urged them to swim toward the overhanging branches of an old elm tree—such vegetation encroached the Sangamon—onto which they clung, shivering and straining against the current. The gathering crowd "instinctively conceded [to] Lincoln . . . the leadership in the effort to save the perishing men." Abraham instructed onlookers to seize a log and tie a rope to it. A youth named Jim Dorrell mounted the improvised lifeboat as the group slackened the rope and eased Dorrell and the log into the current. He too fell in, adding another victim to the stretched elm branches. Once the log was retracted, Abraham himself mounted it and drifted out toward the elm tree. His legs submerged in freezing water, Lincoln grasped the men and secured them to the log, then signaled the villagers to haul the foursome to shore. All arrived safely. "The incident," recalled John E. Roll, "made a hero of Abe all along the Sangamon, and the inhabitants never tired of telling of the daring exploit."[11] Oddly, this incident, although recollected by Roll in compelling detail, goes unmentioned in numerous interviews with other people involved in the construction. Whether the dugout canoe ever made it to New Orleans (where it would have been called a "pirogue") is unknown.

Once everyone dried off and warmed up, worked continued on the flatboat. The frame was now ready to be flipped into the water, probably with the same ropes used in the rescue. After the splash into the Sangamon came the detail work: *Cut studs and insert them into the gunwales . . . build walls over the studs . . . insert longer studs into the girders . . . build raf-*

---

11. "Lincoln's Flatboat," *Daily Inter-Ocean*, May 15, 1892, p. 2.

ters atop the studs . . . cover the rafters with roofing planks.[12] One difference between this vessel and Lincoln's Rockport flatboat was the cargo hold: this trip would carry livestock to New Orleans, necessitating corrals and troughs. We also have some design details recollected by John Hanks:

> [We] went down by a Kind of ladder through a scuttle hole [into the sleeping quarters]; We used plank as Sails—& Cloth— Sometimes— . . . people Came out & laughed at us. . . .[13]

"When the boat was completed," recalled John E. Roll, "it was shoved into the river, [which] created something of a stir in the town."[14] The men next loaded sacks of corn, sides of bacon, barrels of pork, and their personal supplies, and possibly Offutt's live hogs, which would be joined by others farther downriver.[15] The men enjoyed one last night in Sangamo Town (either Sunday or Monday), entertained by an itinerant juggler and magician. By Tuesday, April 19, 1831, Offutt, Lincoln, Hanks, Johnston, and some hitchhikers were poling down the wending Sangamon River— "as a sort of flo[a]ting Drift wood," Lincoln later described, "on the great freshit produced in the thawing of that snow."[16] Teen-aged Philip Clark, in the vicinity at the time, recalled many years later that he and his father "were embarking in the business of flat-boating, which was a sort of craze [at the time], when one day in the midst of our work we observed a tall, lank, lean stranger coming . . . toward us. . . . He did not smile; he was so earnest all the while that his very earnestness impressed me. . . . [H]e was the saddest and most earnest man I ever knew. . . . I . . . never have forgotten the impression of sorrow he made on me then."[17]

The first town on their journey was New Salem, about sixteen miles

---

12. John Calvin Gilkeson, "Flatboat Building on Little Raccoon Creek, Parke County, Indiana," ed. Donald F. Carmony and Sam K. Swope, *Indiana Magazine of History* 60, no. 4 (December 1964): 309–322.

13. Interview, John Hanks, with William H. Herndon, 1865–1866, in *Herndon's Informants*, 457.

14. "Lincoln's Flatboat," *Daily Inter-Ocean*, May 15, 1892, p. 2.

15. Interview, John Hanks, by William H. Herndon, June 13, 1865, in *Herndon's Informants*, 43–44.

16. As recollected by William G. Greene from a June 1864 conversation with President Lincoln, in an interview with William H. Herndon, May 29, 1865, in *Herndon's Informants*, 12. A "fresh" (or "freshit," as Lincoln wrote it) referred to the high late-winter or springtime waters that flushed out minor tributaries, often the only time when flatboats could navigate them down to the main channel.

17. "Stories of Lincoln's Youth by Uncle Philip Clarke," *Springfield Republican* (Springfield, MA), April 4, 1897, p. 9, as originally reported by the *Chicago Times-Herald*.

downriver. This tiny bluff-top settlement had been formed only two years prior, when the state legislature granted James Rutledge and John M. Camron permission to build a mill dam there. The dam comprised two elongated wooden trough-like structures built across the Sangamon slightly above normal river height, which were then filled with rocks to withstand the current. The obstacle slowed the water velocity, raised the height (thus partially or completely obscuring the dam), increased the head, and diverted a focused outlet of water off to the side. There Rutledge and Camron positioned their waterwheel, using the energy to run a sawmill and a gristmill. The successful project attracted wood-cutting and corn- and wheat-grinding business from the adjacent countryside, which motivated a storekeeper, a saloonkeeper, a grocer, a cooper, and others to set up shop nearby. Houses followed, and by the time Lincoln and crew approached on April 19, New Salem constituted an identifiable village.[18]

•

Less identifiable were New Salem's navigational hazards. With the winter snowpack entirely melted away and river levels dropping, hidden obstacles such as sandbars, debris, and other impediments drew closer to the surface. Around early afternoon on April 19, Lincoln's flatboat suddenly jolted to a stop with a sickening thud. Bad news: it was the Rutledge-Camron dam. Getting stuck on a soft sandbar brought a flatboat to a dead stop, but at least did not threaten the vessel and freight. Getting lodged on a hard, linear feature could crack the hull, soak the cargo, bankrupt the enterprise, *and* damage the dam.

Bow raised, stern lowered, and gunwales bending dangerously, Lincoln's flatboat resisted initial efforts to pry it off the obstruction. Water, meanwhile, seeped into the lower flanks, and cargo slid toward it. River levels continued to drop, leaving the flatboat "fast on the mill dam and the end over the dam being lowest[,] the water ran to that end."[19] The eighty-foot, multi-ton vessel, six weeks in the making and barely ten miles into its journey, threatened to come to pieces. Boss Denton Offutt did not know what to do. Townspeople came to gawk.

Finally a leader emerged. Villager William G. Greene recalled see-

18. Benjamin P. Thomas, *Lincoln's New Salem* (Carbondale and Edwardsville: Southern Illinois University Press, 1974 reprint of 1954 original), 6–9.

19. Statement, Mentor Graham, as recorded by James Q. Howard, "Biographical Notes," May 1860, Abraham Lincoln Papers at the Library of Congress, Washington, D.C. (hereafter cited as Lincoln Papers).

ing a striking six-foot-four stranger take charge over his well-known but befuddled employer. Lincoln commandeered an empty flatboat and poled it into alignment with the incapacitated vessel. The men then swiftly transferred the cargo, a grueling chore under any circumstances. Once they sufficiently lightened the load, the partially inundated "boat sprang upwards."[20] Water sloshed to the bow end, where Lincoln had augured a hole into the floorboards. The water drained out, the load lightened, and with further prying and coaxing from the crew, the flatboat finally slipped past the dam and safely into the river.[21] The men gingerly poled both vessels a short distance downriver, and after inspecting their craft's river-worthiness, reloaded the cargo.

Lincoln's decisiveness and ingenuity saved the expedition. The incident set the voyage back by one full day, but serendipitously introduced Lincoln to New Salem in a way that would influence the next six years of his life. It also provoked his thinking about how to improve navigation on Illinois' innumerable secondary waterways. Many New Salem residents, for their part, were suitably impressed by the singular young man and his cleverness. Offutt, for one, knew he had found one fine employee. Greene, for another, would develop a lifelong personal and professional friendship with that stranger.[22] Lincoln himself focused on only one thing: getting this thrice-delayed flatboat out of the wretched Sangamon, into the broad Illinois and capacious Mississippi, and on to New Orleans.

One final stop remained, incurring further delay but also comic relief. Offutt, ever scattered in his affairs, "bought thirty odd large fat live hogs, but found difficulty in driving them from where [he] purchased them to the boat." Lincoln himself ruefully recalled what he termed "the ludicrous incident," in which Offutt

> thereupon conceived the whim that he could sew up their eyes and drive them where he pleased. No sooner thought of than decided, he put his [hired] hands, including [me], at the job, which [we] completed—all but the driving. In their blind condition they could not be driven out of the lot or field they were

20. Interview, John Hanks, by William H. Herndon, June 13, 1865, in *Herndon's Informants*, 44.

21. William G. Greene's account of the mill-dam incident differs on one point. "The boreing the hole in the boat," Greene said, "is a story made out of whole cloth—Offutt suggested it and Lincoln said he couldn't see it [working]." Interview, William G. Greene, by William H. Herndon, May 30, 1865, in *Herndon's Informants*, 21.

22. Interview, William G. Greene, by William H. Herndon, May 30, 1865, in *Herndon's Informants*, 17; see also 751.

in. This expedient failing, they were tied and hauled on carts to the boat.[23]

The "hogs Eye affair" demonstrates what can go wrong when a "rattled brained" employer makes zany decisions and level-headed employees are obliged to follow them. Needless to say, Lincoln resisted. He frowned on the unnecessary suffering of animals, and knew all too well how panicky hogs became when frightened. By Hanks' account, "Abe said I Can't sew the Eyes up [but instead] held the head of hogs whilst Offutt did [sew] up their Eyes."[24] By another account, a local offered to spare Lincoln his eye-sewing chore in exchange for plowing his fields.[25] The hog seller seems to have been a man named "Onstott"—presumably Henry Onstott, New Salem's cooper, indicating that the incident happened in town shortly past the mill dam.[26]

The hitchhikers who boated down from Sangamo Town departed at New Salem. This is also the point at which the numerous eyewitness reports of Lincoln's flatboat experience come to an end. From this point on, the 1831 Illinois trip to New Orleans is nearly as poorly documented as the 1828 Indiana trip, in which we had to triangulate off arcane clues and set them against contextual evidence to establish the trip's chronology. Accounting for the various delays and the distance traveled so far, this researcher judges that the crew finally set out from New Salem in earnest for New Orleans on Thursday morning, April 21, 1831. Lincoln himself recollected the departure as occurring "in the last days of April."[27]

•

Unlike the 1828 trip, in which Lincoln clearly stated that he and Allen Gentry journeyed alone to New Orleans, we are less confident about the composition of the 1831 crew. The words in the Lincoln-edited William Dean Howells biography read,

23. Lincoln, "Autobiography," June 1860, in *Collected Works*, 4:64.

24. Interview, John Hanks, by William H. Herndon, June 13, 1865, in *Herndon's Informants*, 44.

25. Coleman Smoot to William H. Herndon, May 7, 1866, in *Herndon's Informants*, 254. Villager Mentor Graham described Denton Offutt as "rattle brained" in a letter to William H. Herndon, May 29, 1865, in *Herndon's Informants*, 9.

26. Interview, Coleman Smoot, by William H. Herndon, May 7, 1866, in *Herndon's Informants*, 254.

27. Abraham Lincoln, "Communication to the People of Sangamo County," *Sangamo Journal*, March 9, 1832, in *Collected Works*, 1:6.

> Denton Offutt . . . took Lincoln into his employment. [Offutt]
> was now about sending another flat-boat to New Orleans, and
> he engaged Lincoln, ~~and the husband of one of Lincoln's step-~~
> ~~sisters,~~ *and his step brother John D. Johnston,* together with their
> comrade, John Hanks, to take charge of his craft. . . .[28]

Lincoln, Hanks, Johnston—but what about Offutt? As owner of the boat
and cargo, did he captain the vessel? Howells' three pages on the subject fall short of confirming whether Offutt joined his employees, but do
suggest that this was *his* operation. For example, the opening paragraph
introduces Offutt as "a backwoods Ulysses . . . ruling the boatmen who
managed his craft, and defying the steamboat captain that swept by the
slow broad-horn. . . ." This imagery positions Offutt as captain of the flatboat, at least figuratively. Later sentences refer to "Denton's ark" and "the
same flatboat for Offutt," and even refers to the dam incident as "his [Of-
futt's] disaster." Lincoln himself confirmed Hanks' and Johnston's participation, but remained ambiguous regarding Offutt's involvement in the
voyage: "During this boat enterprize acquaintance with Offutt, who was
previously an entire stranger, he conceived a liking for [me]. . . ."[29] One
recent secondary history holds that Offutt "traveled south more comfort-
ably on a river steamer [and] met Abe, John Hanks and the Johnston boy
in New Orleans to oversee the sale of his cargo," but does not cite evidence
for this rather illogical arrangement.[30] We do, however, have ample clues
from relatives and villagers along the Sangamon River that suggest Offutt
indeed joined the flatboat crew to New Orleans. New Salem resident John
McNamar hazily recalled that "[Lincoln] went on to New Orleans with
offet [Offutt]."[31] Another New Salemite, James Short, clearly recounted
that Lincoln "went to New Orleans with Denton Offut in a flat boat,
in 1831" and that "Offut came back from N.O. in 1831. . . ."[32] Robert B.
Rutledge, also of New Salem, remembered he first met Lincoln in 1831,
the latter "having just returned with Offatt from New Orleans with whom

28. Howells, *Life of Abraham Lincoln*, 26.
29. Lincoln, "Autobiography," June 1860, in *Collected Works*, 4:64.
30. Thomas Keneally, *Abraham Lincoln* (New York: Lipper/Viking, 2003), 13. What
makes this information dubious, as we shall see later, is the inclusion of John Hanks
among the crewmates in New Orleans.
31. John McNamar to William H. Herndon, June 4, 1866, in *Herndon's Informants*,
259.
32. James Short to William H. Herndon, July 7, 1865, in *Herndon's Informants*, 72–
73.

he had gone on a flat boat as a hand to that city."[33] Biographer William Herndon, who communicated extensively with these and other eyewitnesses, positioned Offutt as a full participant in the trip.[34] This researcher concurs, viewing Denton Offutt, Abraham Lincoln, John Hanks, and John Johnston as the original crewmembers of the 1831 journey. We presume that Offutt, as owner and employer, captained the vessel, and, if experience bore any influence on the pecking order, Hanks probably ranked second, Lincoln third, and Johnston last. Lincoln's actions on the Sangamon, however, may have raised his rank in Offutt's eye, at Hanks' expense. In fact, at least one informant specifically considered Lincoln as "Capt. of Flatboat [that] belonged to Denton Offutt. . . ."[35] We should remember, of course, that rank and pecking order among crewmembers existed mostly in an informal sense on an expedition like this one.

"We then proceeded down the Sangamon," recalled Hanks. The river flowed northward through undulating terrain for about fourteen miles before joining with the Salt Creek—where, according to Hanks, the men loaded one final drove of hogs (presumably with eyes wide open). The Sangamon then veered straight west through a narrow valley, whose flatness allowed the enlarged waterway to meander wildly in a "zig zag course, form[ing] complete peninsulas," as Lincoln described it.[36] In fact, the little river wended for over sixty sinuous miles within its thirty-mile-long valley.[37] Weakening current, logs, and sandbars slowed the expedition to speeds barely faster than a brisk walk. Overhanging canopy made nighttime too dark for safe travel. "[T]he water was lower than it had been since the breaking of winter in February," recalled Lincoln, which made "drifted timber" a constant obstruction.[38] The aforementioned Philip

33. Robert B. Rutledge to William H. Herndon, November 1, 1866, in *Herndon's Informants*, 381.

34. William H. Herndon and Jesse William Weik, *Herndon's Lincoln: The True Story of a Great Life* (Chicago, New York, and San Francisco: Belford, Clarke & Company, 1889), 1:76.

35. Statement, William G. Greene, as recorded by James Q. Howard, "Biographical Notes," May 1860, Lincoln Papers.

36. Lincoln, "People of Sangamo County," *Sangamo Journal*, March 9, 1832, in *Collected Works*, 1:7.

37. Most of the Sangamon's natural meanders were eliminated many years later through channel straightening and levee construction. They are preserved, however, in the Mason, Cass, and Menard county lines, which follow the old channel perfectly. I used these boundaries to map and measure the river as it flowed during Lincoln's day.

38. Lincoln, "People of Sangamo County," *Sangamo Journal*, March 9, 1832, in *Collected Works*, 1:6.

Clark, who flatboated down the Sangamon alongside Lincoln's vessel, recounted interesting details from the shared experience:

> [M]y father, myself and William McLease, with the boat steerer Sam McKee, joined [Lincoln and Offut's operation]. There was danger of the snags and we all tied up at night and built a fire and enjoyed ourselves socially. Lincoln told me he thought he could better his situation, as he had no liking for the flatboat business. He thought seriously of settling in Walnut hills, a place not far from Beardstown. But . . . Lincoln abandoned this idea. . . .
>
> During this trip I became as well acquainted with Lincoln as one young man well could with another. His conversation was such as to draw out information from his companions. He was at all times, even in those cheerless times, aspiring to better knowledge and better position.[39]

Traveling at a tedious pace of about twenty-five miles per day, the crew probably reached the labyrinth of lakes and marshes littering the floodplain of the Illinois River three full travel-days later, in the late afternoon or early evening of Saturday, April 23. Hanks: "[We] got into the Ills"—then, eight miles downstream, "passed Beardstown," a two-year-old but nevertheless bustling river port that served as a popular flatboat stop.[40] Philip Clark claimed the trip to Beardstown took seven days, but he started out farther upriver and included numerous delays in that estimate.[41]

Reconstructing the trip from here requires an estimation of speed. Unlike the memorable river conditions of 1828, the Mississippi in 1831 flowed at rates only somewhat above that of a typical springtime high. Reports at New Orleans on March 26 held that "the Mississippi has risen six inches" but "was yesterday eighteen inches below high water mark" (presumably set in 1828). The river stabilized at that level at least until April 18. By May 14, it had risen only six inches, remaining one foot below the high water mark.[42] These levels equate to roughly 4.2 to 5.2 miles-per-hour surface velocities with peaks in the 5.5 to 6.7 m.p.h. range.[43]

---

39. "Stories of Lincoln's Youth," *Springfield Republican*, April 4, 1897, p. 9.

40. Interview, John Hanks, by William H. Herndon, June 13, 1865, in *Herndon's Informants*, 44.

41. "Stories of Lincoln's Youth," *Springfield Republican*, April 4, 1897, p. 9.

42. *New Orleans Price Current*, as reported in *City Gazette & Commercial Daily Advertiser* (Charleston, SC), April 7, 1831, p. 2 and April 14, 1831, p. 2, and in *Baltimore Patriot*, May 4, 1831, p. 2 and May 27, 1831, p. 2.

43. U.S. Army Corps of Engineers. "River Velocities at New Orleans, LA. Related

Given this information and lacking any clues to the contrary, this study views the flatboat drifting downriver at an average speed of 4.75 m.p.h., compared to 5.5 m.p.h. in 1828. As argued previously, nocturnal flatboat travel presented more risk than reward, and most (though not all) flatboatmen responded accordingly. However, because the crew constituted four veteran navigators, this study assumes an additional two hours of total travel time per day on top of the twelve hours allotted for the two-man rookie expedition of 1828. This is not to suggest that Offutt, Hanks, Lincoln, and Johnston set out regularly at 6 a.m. and docked at 8 p.m.; rather, it accounts for all stops, delays, port calls, pre-dawn starts, late-night stops, and perhaps even an entire day of stoppage or entire night of travel—all averaging out to fourteen hours of 4.75-mile-per-hour movement, totaling to 66.5 river miles daily.

This study also assumes that the 1831 expedition spent less time "lingering" and more time traveling straight to New Orleans than the 1828 voyage. That earlier trip was a small amateur enterprise with two very young men traveling alone; the 1831 trip, on the other hand, constituted a larger and more professional operation, including a captain who owned the cargo and paid the employees. They also had a longer trip ahead of them, and some had families waiting back home. All four had already sunk more time into this job than they originally planned. The fact that squealing hogs were on board meant that every extra day cost extra feed and incurred additional risk. This flatboat expedition had every reason to get to market swiftly.

Setting out from Beardstown on Sunday morning, April 24, Lincoln might have rejoiced at the Illinois' wide and straight channel, compared to the tortuous Sangamon. By next morning, the river's alluvial valley narrowed from about ten miles to under three in width, while the adjacent bluffs rose in elevation. Some towered nearly four hundred feet above the river; others presented dramatic white cliff faces topped with full-canopy hardwood forests. A dozen or so tiny villages, their houses numbering in the single or double digits and their populations barely reaching three digits, lined the scenic banks, each tapping into the riverine lifeline with a dock or landing. In floating down the Illinois River, Lincoln at this point followed the exact route of French Canadian René-Robert Cavelier, sieur de La Salle. One hundred forty-nine years earlier, La Salle confirmed the Mississippi's relationship with the Gulf of Mexico and claimed the river

to the Carrollton Gage," http://www.mvn.usace.army.mil/eng/edhd/velo_no.asp (visited February 14, 2009).

basin in the name of King Louis XIV of France, initiating a colonializa-
tion process that eventually led to the founding of New Orleans in 1718.

Sometime on Monday afternoon, 84 miles downriver from Beardstown and 160 total river miles since New Salem, the crew would have
noticed a particularly spectacular alignment of south-facing cliffs. The
topographic landmark—the most rugged terrain Lincoln had seen to
date—signaled the approaching Mississippi River fork. The confluence
doubled the water volume but did not radically alter the nature of the
river. The valley then broadened, as if in expectation of another tributary.
On their left was the free North and nearby Alton, Illinois; on their right
lay Missouri, Lincoln's first exposure to a slave society in well over a year.
Eighteen miles downriver, that next tributary arrived: the Missouri River,
slightly smaller in volume than the Mississippi but amazingly muddy, almost opaque, bearing the topsoil of the unmapped far-western frontier.
The contrast struck travelers on the river. "The Mississippi is remarkable
for the clearness of its waters, which are of a light blue," went one typical
account of the era;

> The Missouri, on the other hand, is described as being "nearly
> as thick as pea soup," and of a dirty muddy-whitish colour. . . .
> The surface of the Mississippi, above the junction, is generally
> clear of driftwood, while that of the Missouri is all covered
> with half-burnt logs, trees with their branches torn off, and
> great rafts or floating islands of timber . . . sweeping and whirl-
> ing along as a furious rate.[44]

Mud meant sediment, and sediment meant sand bars and islands. Together with logs and debris, the now-enlarged Mississippi grew potentially
dangerous. We have no record of Lincoln's navigation skills from either
the 1828 or 1831 trips, but we do have a recollection of "Captain Abe"
piloting a flatboat down this same stretch of river around 1835. It comes
from an old friend named Stephen W. Garrison of Sullivan, Indiana:

> I went down with him [to St. Louis] twice, and the first time
> we found the Mississippi an angry flood. We tied up for the
> night just after entering the big stream. We had intended to
> float awhile in the evening, but the torrent of waters made us
> land-lubbers feel a little nervous and Mr. Lincoln decided to
> take no chance. He directed us to steer for a certain safe place,

44. "The River Missouri, in North America," citing Basil Hall and others, *Saturday
Magazine* (London) 7, no. 206 (September 19, 1835): 108.

and just as the craft rubbed against the bank, rope in hand, he jumped ashore to make the boat fast. He never would let any-one else do this. When it was necessary to tie up he was always the first ashore. The boat was heavy and he wanted to be the judge of how much slack the cable should have to prevent an accident.[45]

The incident evinces Lincoln's sense of judgment and responsibility.

•

The surrounding landscape at this point—April 24–25, 1831—consti-tuted "prairie land [intermixed with] forest, in which there are numerous plantations. In the midst of it there is a Catholic chapel,"[46] this being a former French colonial region. Another visitor described the scenery as "pretty hilly, [with] green-leaved timber, oaks, and various nut-bearing trees [with] climbing plants mounted over them, wild vines, and ivy." Tiny outposts of French origin, sprinkled with structures with double-pitched hip roofs and airy Louisiana-style galleries, appeared here and there. Chief among the old French towns was nearby St. Charles, with "one thousand inhabitants, who nearly all belong to the Catholic faith."[47] Indian mounds popped up elsewhere along the riverbank. Then plumes of smoke began to appear on the horizon, accompanied by the reverberating din and clat-ter of a big city. It was St. Louis, Missouri, marking their 211th river mile from New Salem. They were halfway to the Ohio River confluence and roughly one-eighth of their way to New Orleans.

St. Louis in this era served the trans-Mississippi frontier in the same manner that Pittsburgh a generation earlier served the trans-Appalachian frontier: as intermediary destination, as supply center, as jumping-off point. With nearly 8,000 residents in a county of more than 14,000 (including 3,000 blacks, mostly enslaved), St. Louis formed the largest population center in the region. Its urban footprint constituted "one long main street, running parallel with the river" for nearly two miles, "from which several side streets run to the heights behind the city." Two-story houses of brick,

45. "Garrison's Prediction: Death of Abraham Lincoln's Friend Recalls a Prophecy Made by the Old Man That Came True," *Omaha World Herald*, September 30, 1899, p. 4.

46. James Stuart, *Three Years in North America*, (Edinburgh and London: Robert Cadell and Whittaker and Company, 1833), 2:356.

47. Bernhard, Duke of Saxe-Weimar-Eisenach, *Travels Through North America, Dur-ing in the Years 1825 and 1826* (Philadelphia: Carey, Lea & Carey, 1828), 2:98–99.

stone, or wood and clay "in the Spanish taste, resembling the old houses of New Orleans," lined the main street, each with terraced gardens extending toward the river.[48] There, along the riverfront, docked a respectable fleet of flatboats and steamboats, transporting standard Western produce as well as iron, lead, and fur coming out of the Missouri backcountry and the Rocky Mountains. *This looks familiar,* Lincoln might have thought. Others would have agreed: St. Louis reminded many visitors of another Mississippi River city. One traveler spelled it out:

> St. Louis is a sort of New Orleans on a smaller scale; in both places are to be found a number of coffeehouses [saloons] and dancing rooms. The French are seen engaged in the same amusements and passions that formerly characterized the creoles of Louisiana. . . . The majority of the inhabitants of [St. Louis] consists of people descended from the French, of Kentuckians, and foreigners of every description—Germans, Spaniards, Italians, Irish, &c.[49]

Whether Lincoln and crew took a few hours to explore this interesting urban environment is unknown. We do know for certain that they stopped at least briefly, but not necessarily to explore. Relating one of the few particulars of the second New Orleans trip, Lincoln himself wrote:

> Hanks had not gone to New-Orleans, but having a family, and being likely to be detained from home longer than at first expected, had turned back from St. Louis.[50]

What happened en route between New Salem and St. Louis that suddenly convinced John Hanks that he should return home to his family? Certainly the entire gambit with Offutt had cost Lincoln, Johnston, and Hanks more time than expected; if Offutt had readied the flatboat on March 1 as originally planned, all four would be well on their way *back* from New Orleans by this time. But each employee had numerous opportunities to quit earlier and closer to home. Lincoln might have treated Hanks generously in the above recollection, perhaps forgiving his cousin a case of workplace envy. Hanks, after all, knew Offutt the longest and personally introduced Lincoln and Johnston to him, positioning himself second in the expedi-

48. Stuart, *Three Years in North America*, 2:342; Bernhard, *Travels Through North America*, 2:97.

49. Charles Sealsfield, *The Americans As They Are Described in A Tour Through the Valley of the Mississippi* (London: Hurst, Chance, and Co., 1828), 94.

50. Lincoln, "Autobiography," June 1860, in *Collected Works*, 4:63–64.

tion's hierarchy. But Lincoln's mill-dam acumen and heroism helping the three men in the Sangamon elevated Abraham in Offutt's eyes, possibly displacing Hanks to a tertiary position in the pecking order. Hanks, in this speculative scenario, may have grown sullen and disenchanted with the expedition, and asked to disembark at the next major steamboat stop under the guise of family matters.

Alternately, perhaps Hanks departed for health reasons. One informant recalled that "Part of the Company got Sick which Caused his and their Riturn Back again," although the garbled memory is tainted by factual errors.[51] Where precisely the crew dropped off Hanks is unknown; if the St. Louis riverfront were anything like other Western river cities, flatboats docked upriver from steamboats, which generally monopolized the wharves in the heart of town. Given the size of St. Louis in 1831, flatboats probably landed in the vicinity of today's Eads and Martin Luther King bridges.

Hanks' St. Louis departure left a crew of three to navigate a fairly large flatboat for another 1,400 miles. His exit adds confidence to our argument that Offutt indeed participated in the expedition, because if he had not, the enterprise would have been left with a skeleton crew of two. More significantly, the departure prevents Hanks—our most loquacious informant about Lincoln's second voyage—from having anything more to experience on the trip, and nothing to remember about it decades later when Lincoln became famous and Herndon arrived in 1865 for his interviews. *Yet Hanks had plenty to say about the remainder of the trip, including some of the most striking and influential statements about what Lincoln saw in New Orleans.* More on this important matter later; for now, we take Lincoln's word that Hanks indeed waved farewell at the St. Louis dock around April 25–26 and never accompanied Lincoln in New Orleans. Hanks headed back to Illinois and would not see Lincoln again for two or three years.

Whatever the reason for Hanks' departure, Lincoln loved his cousin and thought him an honest and good man all his life.[52] He also genuinely liked Denton Offutt, the captain, as evidenced by their lifelong association. Lincoln's relationship with the other crewmember, stepbrother John

---

51. J. Rowan Herndon to William H. Herndon, May 28 and June 11, 1865, in *Herndon's Informants*, 6 and 34.

52. This is Herndon's view on the relationship between Lincoln and Hanks. Phillip Shaw Paludan, "Lincoln and Negro Slavery: I Haven't Got Time for the Pain," *Journal of the Abraham Lincoln Association* 27, no. 2 (2006): 11.

D. Johnston, was less congenial. Twenty years old at the time of the 1831 journey, Johnston first came into Abraham's life in 1820, when Thomas Lincoln guided his new wife Sally Johnston and her three children, including nine-year-old John, from Kentucky to Indiana. The two stepbrothers grew up in close proximity but were never particularly close. By some accounts, Thomas favored his new stepson over his biological son; by other accounts, Johnston demonstrated laziness and unreliability. Lincoln himself later reprimanded him for "uselessly wasting time" and being "an idler;" Johnston accused Abraham of neglecting his aging parents. The two stepbrothers shortly thereafter suffered a fairly serious falling-out.[53] Nevertheless, in their early adulthood, they got along well enough to work together frequently, culminating with this flatboat trip.

•

The Mississippi below St. Louis flowed in a fairly straight channel running through a narrow bluff-lined valley. The sturdy stone edifices of Jefferson Barracks, the premier military outpost in the region, formed the first landmark below the city. Some miles downriver, through an "alluvial bottom, environed by high bluffs," came the town of Herculaneum, known for its nearby lead mines. Veterans of this countryside might have pointed out to a first-timer like Lincoln the odd structures protruding from the summits of the bluffs. They were shot towers, from which molten lead was dropped to form ammunition for artillery. Other protrusions were natural, such as famous Tower Rock, a limestone island long used as a landmark by river travelers. Subsequent towns like Ste. Genevieve and Cape Girardeau might have struck Lincoln as dead-ringers for Louisiana's sugar coast, with their "very singular appearance, from the unusual structure of the houses, they being chiefly of wood, low, and almost surrounded with porches"—typical French Creole gallery houses.[54] People of

53. One relative described Abe and John's relationship in guarded terms. "I think Abe Dun more for John than he desved," he wrote. "John thought that Abe did not Do a Nuff for the old people [and therefore] they Be Cum Enimes for awhile. . . . I Dont want to tell all the thing that I [know;] it would Not Look well in history I Say this Abe treated John well. . . ." Dennis F. Hanks to William H. Herndon, January 26, 1866, in *Herndon's Informants*, 176. See also David Herbert Donald, *Lincoln* (New York: Simon & Schuster, 1995), 33, 152–153, 622, and Louis A. Warren, ed., "A. Lincoln and J. D. Johnston— Step-Brothers," *Lincoln Lore: Bulletin of the Lincoln National Life Foundation*, no. 964, September 29, 1947.

54. Robert Baird, *View of the Valley of the Mississippi, or the Emigrant's and Traveller's Guide to the West* (Philadelphia: H. S. Tanner, 1834), 243.

French Canadian ancestry, as well as German Redemptioners and American emigrants, predominated.

On the fourth day after departing St. Louis, adjacent bluffs briefly drew close to the channel, then suddenly yawned open to a wide alluvial expanse, allowing the Mississippi to meander lazily. Offutt would have recognized the changing terrain: ahead lay the Ohio River confluence. Three years earlier Lincoln negotiated this great fork from the opposite branch; today he sailed on the muddier, lower-volume Mississippi as it joined the clearer, higher-volume Ohio. After the flatboat shot through the torrent and into the greatly enlarged lower Mississippi River, all three crewmembers found themselves in familiar terrain, over 400 miles from home and 1,200 miles from New Orleans. The date was around Friday, April 29, 1831.

Temperatures turned unseasonably cold in May, even as the threesome penetrated deeper into Southern latitudes.[55] Another change materialized subtly, as they cruised silently along the bank. Eddies that normally accumulated treacherous tree trunks were free of debris. Logjams numbered fewer. Less vegetation hung over the banks. What they were witnessing was one of the first major human interventions in the nature and flow of the Mississippi River. Since the previous autumn, Superintendent of Western River Improvements Capt. Henry Miller Shreve, a longtime riverman and navigation advocate, oversaw the specially equipped steamboats *Helopolis* and *Archimedes* in removing 2,000 snags, planters, and sawyers from the 1,000 river miles between the Ohio River confluence and the Louisiana deltaic plain. Along an overlapping 500-mile portion, Shreve's men cut overhanging trees to prevent them from becoming future navigation obstacles. The captain pointed out numerous advantages to his work, among them the following:

> Flatboats navigating the Mississippi river, from the mouth of the Missouri to New Orleans, now float at night with as much safety as they do in the Ohio river, by which means their passage is now made in one half the time it was three years ago.[56]

55. The *New Orleans Price Current* reported on May 14, "The weather has been, for a length of time, very cool, to an unusual degree." *New Orleans Price Current*, as reported in *Baltimore Patriot*, May 27, 1831, p. 2.

56. Henry M. Shreve, "Ohio and Mississippi Rivers: Annual Report of work done in improving the navigation of the Ohio and Mississippi rivers in the present year, ending 30th September 1831," as reproduced in *Daily National Intelligencer* (Washington, D.C.), December 17, 1831, p. 2.

Perhaps Lincoln and crew did exactly that—travel at night—upon encountering Shreve's cleared river below the Ohio confluence. Lacking hard evidence, however, this researcher leans toward a more conservative adjustment, increasing their daily travel time to sixteen hours from the originally presumed fourteen. This equates to 76 miles' progress per day. The remaining reconstructed chronology reflects this velocity adjustment.

Beyond the cleared debris, Lincoln would have experienced only incremental differences between the riverscapes of 1828 and 1831. *April 30: New Madrid, Missouri.* The river flowed at lower levels this spring, opening up more bankside vegetation and sandbars. Landings that were inundated three years ago would have functioned normally now. *May 3: Chickasaw Bluffs north of Memphis, Tennessee.* Populations would have been slightly higher in this region; forests would have been further cleared; new plantations would have sprouted up in their place.

•

An interesting meeting occurred at one of these plantations. As Lincoln and crew tied up near Greenock in the Arkansas Territory, across the river from Memphis, the owner of the adjacent plantation inquired if they would chop some wood. "Abe, the supercargo [the crewmember in charge of the freight], sprang in and helped," earning some extra money and apparently impressing the planter sufficiently to gain his acquaintance. The planter was Col. William D. Ferguson (1800–67), allegedly once a boy-soldier in the Battle of New Orleans, now a sheriff in Crittenden County, and later a state legislator. Years afterward, that same Colonel Ferguson, while in Washington, sought out Congressman Lincoln and later President-elect Lincoln and "renewed the old acquaintance," at which time "they had a chat about old times and the present price of cordwood."[57] This little-known incident, if accurate, sheds light on the nature of social relations Lincoln established with locals during his flatboat voyages. It challenges the general impression that he traveled anonymously through the South, and invites speculation about other relationships and friend-

57. As reported in the *Memphis Appeal* and carried by the *Sun* (Baltimore, MD), March 18, 1861, p. 4; see also Margaret Elizabeth Woolfolk, *A History of Crittenden County, Arkansas* (Marion, AR: Margaret Elizabeth Woolfolk, 1991), 140–141. Embellished versions of the incident appear in two twentieth-century articles, "Abe Lincoln Once Lived in Arkansas," *Arkansas Gazette*, July 4, 1927, and "Lincoln's Visit to Arkansas," *Arkansas Gazette*, Magazine Section, February 7, 1937.

ships he might have formed. What makes the story credible is that Ferguson, a Southern planter who owned forty slaves and presumably did not idolize Lincoln as a presidential candidate, spoke of the encounter *before* Lincoln settled into the presidency (specifically in March 1861) and well before his post-assassination immortalization.[58] That chronology allays suspicions that Ferguson, like other acquaintances of Lincoln's youth, concocted his story to write himself into history. Details on the encounter, however, are murky; it could have occurred during the first trip in 1828, or on the return leg of either trip. This researcher judges that it most likely occurred during this downriver 1831 trip, because an 1861 article relating this story specifically mentions a flatboat (rather than an upriver-bound steamboat) and uses language that implies the flatboat's crew comprised more than two men, with Lincoln, as "supercargo," higher in the crew's pecking order than in the 1828 trip.

The men poled out of Greenock, passed Memphis within an hour, and continued downriver into the wilds of the Mississippi-Yazoo floodplain. *May 5: Arkansas River confluence.* After two days, the topography on the eastern horizon that dissipated after Memphis started to reappear. *May 7: Vicksburg, first of the Mississippi bluff communities.* Cities in this prospering region showed the most marked change since 1828, having spread their hilltop footprints, erected higher structures, and extended their riverine landings by noticeable degrees. The river itself shifted slightly, meandering more broadly in some areas, cutting off meanders in others. "The pilots on our Western rivers steer from *point to point* as they call it," Lincoln explained many years later, "setting the course of the boat no farther than they can see. . . ."[59] So too steered he, arriving to Natchez, Mississippi, around May 8. It was here that, according to Leonard Swett (whose personal recollections of Lincoln were published in 1889), "a negro came very near smashing the head of the future emancipator of his race." Swett explained:

> The boat one night was tied up to the shore and the crew asleep below. A noise being heard Captain Lincoln came up, and just as his head emerged through the hatchway, a negro, who was pilfering, struck him a blow with a heavy stick, but the point of the stick reached over his head, and struck the floor beyond

58. 1850 Federal Census, State of Arkansas, County of Crittenden, Schedule 2—Slave Inhabitants, listed under slave owner William Ferguson.

59. Abraham Lincoln, as quoted by Donald, *Lincoln*, 15. Lincoln used this river analogy to explain his Reconstruction plan to James G. Blaine.

> . . . thus lightening the blow on his head, but making a scar
> which he wore always, and which he showed me at the time of
> telling this story.[60]

This Natchez story, which lacks substantiation in any other source, probably represents a faulty retelling of the Louisiana attack upon Lincoln
and Gentry in 1828. Nevertheless, Swett's first-person memory of Lincoln personally pointing out his scar and explaining its origin is worthy
of note.

The next day found the crew near the confluence of the Red River.
Here the Mississippi wended quite differently than in 1828. Capt. Henry
Shreve, as part of his charge to improve Western river navigation, had but
a few months earlier cut through a meander loop known as Burch's Bend.
"It will be the main channel of the river next spring," Shreve predicted
(meaning spring 1832), "and shorten the distance [by] 24 to 28 miles."[61]
We cannot say whether the cut-off was sufficiently passable in May 1831
for Lincoln and crew to use it, but we do know that complex hydrological processes in the Red, Black, Atchafalaya, and Mississippi rivers were
already being transformed by Shreve's actions. Over the next eight years,
Shreve's meander-cutting and logjam-clearing successes, while greatly
beneficial to navigation interests, would enable the Atchafalaya to gain
gradually more and more of the Mississippi's water volume over the next
century. It would take a Herculean engineering effort, completed a century after Lincoln's presidency, to prevent the Atchafalaya from seizing so
much of the Mississippi's water as to leave New Orleans on an elongated,
useless, undrinkable-brackish-water bay. Lincoln in 1831 would have been
an eyewitness to Shreve's work in progress.

*May 10: past Baton Rouge, the U.S. Barracks, and into the Louisiana sug-
ar coast.* Growth of this season's sugar cane would have lagged about one
month behind what Lincoln witnessed in 1828, on account of the same
severe winter that brought deep snow to his home in Illinois.[62] There is
no direct evidence suggesting that Offutt, Lincoln, and Johnston "lingered" and traded along the sugar coast as Gentry and Lincoln did three
years earlier, although their barrel-pork cargo—which was sold regularly

60. As recollected by Leonard Swett, in *Reminiscences of Abraham Lincoln by Distinguished Men of His Time*, ed. Allen Thorndike Rice (New York: North American Review,
1889), 461–462.

61. Shreve, "Ohio and Mississippi Rivers," in *Daily National Intelligencer*, December 17,
1831, p. 2.

62. "Sugar Crops," *Mercantile Advertiser*, May 5, 1831, p. 2, c. 4.

to planters as food for slaves—raises the possibility. Likewise, some live hogs may have been sold along the rural sugar coast, where they could be husbanded and fattened up more easily than in an urban environment.

A flatboatman's diary scribed later in the 1830s offers an idea of how Lincoln might have demarcated his progress downriver from Baton Rouge: "Patrick's Sugar farm . . . Bayou Placquemine . . . Mr. Laws Sugar Farm . . . Bayou Goula Landing [near present-day White Castle] . . . Bayou La Fourche and Donaldsonville . . . Hamptons Plantation . . ." Shortly below the Hampton property, Lincoln surely would have recalled and perhaps strived to identify his attack site from the 1828 trip with Allen Gentry. Onward: "Bonnet Quarre [Carre] Church . . . Destrehan Point . . . the Red Church . . . Landed at the fair famed City of New Orleans[.] Here at last[!]"[63]

•

We consult flatboat-docking statistics to help narrow down the likely date of Lincoln's second landing at New Orleans. Wharfinger reports, as previously discussed, have been lost for this era. So we must look instead to the Maritime News columns in the only three newspapers fully retrievable today (on microfilm), the *New Orleans Bee, Louisiana Courier,* and *Mercantile Advertiser.* While the competing dailies did not report identical data, all three clearly depicted a surge in flatboat arrivals during the second week in May, specifically May 7–16, with a mutually reported peak of thirty-one flatboats on May 11 (see graph, "Flatboat Arrivals to New Orleans, May 1831").[64] Figures for the first week of May are half the daily rate of the second week, while daily arrivals for the last two weeks of the month drop mostly to zero. In total, the *Bee* reported 123 flatboats and one barge arriving to New Orleans in May 1831, of which 91 percent arrived before May 16. The *Courier* in the same period enumerated 147 flatboats and one barge, with 99 percent arriving before mid-month. The *Advertiser* counted 159 flatboats and one barge, of which 94 percent arrived before mid-month. This good news brings confidence to our hypothesis that Lincoln arrived around May 12, 1831, coincidently close to the third anniversary

63. William S. Ward, *Diary* [of Flatboat Trip from New Albany, Indiana, to New Orleans, Louisiana, 1839], The Historic New Orleans Collection, Accession Number 2009.0139, p. 64–69 (hereafter cited as THNOC).

64. These dates reflect when the information was posted in newspapers; they usually postdate the actual arrival dates by one to two days.

of his initial arrival to New Orleans.[65] Total river distance from New Salem, Illinois, to New Orleans, Louisiana, amounted to at least 1,627 and up to 1,700 river miles, depending on hydrological conditions.

Unfortunately, there is bad news. All three newspapers identified Tennessee, Kentucky, and Alabama as the flatboats' exclusive origins, and listed only cotton and/or tobacco as their freight. The sole exception was that one barge, which came from Opelousas, Louisiana, bearing cotton. We see no arrivals specifically from Illinois or generally from "the Western country," nor any with cargoes of corn, ham, and hogs. This information does not undercut our argument. The very fact that the three newspapers reported differing data suggests that this was not an exact science. The absence of flatboat registrations originating from rapidly developing states such as Ohio, Indiana, Illinois, Missouri, Arkansas, and Mississippi suggests that whoever tabulated these data might have engaged in overly presumptuous or sloppy aggregations. Likewise, it is almost unthinkable that only cotton and tobacco arrived by flatboat this entire month (although it *is* possible that some flatboats traded their Western sundries for those standard commodities while en route to New Orleans).

With abundant and reliable evidence that Lincoln departed New Salem around April 21, this researcher feels confident that the second-week-in-May surge in flatboat arrivals, as reported by three New Orleans newspapers, indeed includes Abraham Lincoln's expedition. The vessel's origin and cargo may have been simply missed or ignored in the brief and generalized maritime reports published in those newspapers.

What went through Lincoln's mind upon landing? Second visits to impressive places generally yield more subdued and sophisticated responses than initial encounters. Familiarity replaces mystery; expectations are already set; mental narratives are established; new stimuli and observations are processed with respect to those antecedents. Giddiness and naïveté give way to nonchalance and savvy; that which surprised and shocked now hardly raises an eyebrow. Lincoln had already "seen the elephant," and, as Offutt was that much more of a regular visitor, the crew knew where to go, how to dock, how to handle the wharfmaster and dockside characters, and what to expect in the streets beyond. Lincoln may well have viewed this experience as the second of many to come, like the Gentrys and Offutts of his world: respectable farmer-merchants who commercially interacted with New Orleans annually.

65. Research by author, "Maritime News" columns, *New Orleans Bee* and *Louisiana Courier*, late April through early June, 1831.

The location and nature of flatboat docking in May 1831 did not differ markedly from Lincoln's 1828 experience. A few minor aspects, however, deviated. The significantly lower river stage would have opened up more sandy beaches along the uptown flatboat wharf. The wharf itself, and the urbanization behind it, would have expanded upriver by a number of blocks, practically fusing with new development in the Jefferson Parish faubourg of Lafayette across Felicity Street. Had the crew unloaded pork, they would have dealt with a meat inspector as well as the dues collector before receiving permission to sell. We do not know the fate of the live hogs (victims of the eye-sewing incident on the Sangamon); either they were sold or exchanged en route, or ended up at any one of New Orleans' numerous *abattoirs*.

Given Offutt's impetuousness, Lincoln's judiciousness, and Johnston's relative obscurity, we can imagine the three manifesting their respective traits in executing wharf-side tasks: Offutt seemingly in command and calling the shots, Lincoln patiently offering counsel and eventually doing the heavy lifting, Johnston quietly lending a hand in unloading, selling, cleaning up, and dismantling the vessel. Apparently other boatmen lingered in cleaning up their wharf space, because that very week, Mayor Prieur announced that anything left unattended on the levee or batture (except iron and stone ballast) would be sold at public auction.[66]

•

During the third week in May, the threesome completed their job and were now footloose in the big city. Temperatures remained unseasonably cool, and strong winds swept in from the north.[67] One crewmate recalled thrilling details of Lincoln's actions "the first time we arrived in New-Orleans:"

> After we had attended to our business the first purchases made by Lincoln were books and surveyors' instruments, and, instead of running around town to see the sights, he would remain at his boarding-house engaged in reading or telling stories to the boarders, who pronounced him to be remarkably gifted in that direction.[68]

66. *Louisiana Courier*, May 12, 1831, p. 4, c. 2.
67. *Mercantile Advertiser*, May 19, 1831, p. 2, c. 4.
68. "Lincoln's Friend, John Hanks: A Garrulous Old Man's Reminiscences," *New York Times*, June 7, 1881, p. 2.

Unfortunately, we must dismiss this interesting information because its source, the verbose John Hanks, was not present to witness it. Hanks' propensity to embellish is addressed in an upcoming discussion.

The same chilly weather that forced Lincoln, Offutt, and Johnston to bundle up at higher latitudes now spared them the discomforting heat and humidity of the subtropics, with "temperatures being nearer that of *March* than May." It was perfect weather for walking. Initial steps toward the heart of the port would have presented the Illinois men with the awesome sight of 67 ocean-going ships of three masts or more, 63 brigs, 43 schooners, 22 steamboats, 4 sloops, and probably around 200 flatboats. During May 20–22 alone, 31 ocean-going vessels arrived, roughly a third of which came from Liverpool; the remainder came from Northeastern, circum-Caribbean, European, and African ports. "[P]robably at any other period," declared a local newspaper, "such a great number of vessels has never been seen in New Orleans."[69]

Banter circulating among boatmen that week told of the underside of port bustle. Last week, for example, the well-known steamboats *Coosa* and *Huntress* collided and exploded upriver; five of the thirteen missing were deck hands—returning flatboatmen.[70] More recently, right here in New Orleans, occurred another violent boating incident. A sheriff positioned at the lighthouse on Lake Pontchartrain spotted a small boat rowing away from the shore. He called out to its crew to return for inspection, but for whatever reason, they continued to sail away. Deputies readied a craft to pursue them, but the sheriff had a different resolution in mind. He leveled a musket at the men and fired, yielding "a very melancholy occurrence."[71] The incident represents the many dangers lurking behind the outward magnificence and seemingly smooth operation of what was, all too often, a rough, tough, violent port city.

Just past the flatboat wharves were two traveling exhibits drawing much attention. On Tchoupitoulas between Poydras and Girod operated a mechanical puppet show of "seventy-five splendid figures which have the motion of life," enacting an event of the recent past relevant to New Orleans: the 1814 signing of the Treaty of Ghent.[72] One block away, at Girod

69. *New Orleans Bee*, May 23, 1831, p. 2, c. 2.

70. "Lamentable Catastrophe!" *Mercantile Advertiser*, May 23, 1831, p. 2, c. 4.

71. *Louisiana Courier*, May 12, 1831, p. 3, c. 1 and May 14, 1831, p. 3, c. 1. The May 14 article indicated that the youth was definitely wounded, possibly mortally.

72. "Mechanism," *Mercantile Advertiser*, May 23, 1831 and afterwards, p. 1, c. 3. The Treaty of Ghent aspired to end the War of 1812, two weeks before the Battle of New Orleans truly ended it.

and Commerce near the steamboat levee, ran a display of a future technology relevant to the city, nation, and Lincoln himself. "EXHIBITION. RAIL ROAD STEAM CARRIAGE," blared a local newspaper:

> This locomotive steam carriage is [built] upon the same principle which will eventually be adopted [on] the numerous rail roads now in progress [across the] country. . . . It has been built for the purpose of dispelling the doubts which have existed as to the practicability of propelling a car by steam. . . .[73]

The steam locomotive exhibit ran throughout spring 1831, increasing the likelihood that an intellectually curious and mechanically inclined visitor like Lincoln would have made the twenty-five-cent investment to inspect the marvel. He would see and learn more of railroads later in his New Orleans sojourn.

•

A walk inland brought visitors to the commercial crossroads of the city, namely the intersection of Chartres and St. Louis streets. Standing prominently on the lakeside/downriver corner was Hewlett's Exchange, busier than ever as the city's premier auction house during an era—the early 1830s—when the reputed "largest slave market in the South . . . was particularly active."[74] Transactions in John Hewlett's gaudy salon, which was also a saloon, brought a steady stream of two valued resources to the attention of bidders: land and human labor, both of which were legally categorized as real estate. Within steps were twelve of the city's fourteen notaries public, ready to notarize whatever deals emerged from the Exchange.[75] One diagonal block away were clustered most of the city's largest banks, eager to offer financing. Around the corner was the office of the influential *New Orleans Bee*, which granted extensive coverage to the proceedings at Hewlett's and profited from the ad revenue. A glance at any May newspaper would have given Lincoln a schedule of auctions slated clear into July—always at Hewlett's, always at noon, never on Sundays.

Slaves imported from the Upper South and West arrived into the

73. "Exhibition. Rail Road Steam Carriage," *Mercantile Advertiser*, May 17, 1831 and afterwards, p. 4, c. 2.

74. Herman Freudenberger and Jonathan B. Pritchett, "The Domestic United States Slave Trade: New Evidence." *Journal of Interdisciplinary History* 21, no. 3 (Winter 1991): 459.

75. "Notaries Public for N. Orleans," *New-Orleans Directory & Register* (New Orleans: John Adems Paxton, 1830), unpaginated.

city's slave market at an average pace of ninety-two per month in 1831 (in addition to local and regional slaves), and at much higher rates during the springtime busy season.[76] Many, if not most, ended up before Hewlett's auctioneers. Around the day Lincoln arrived, thirty-two-year-old Lucy went to the block, her master assuring suspicious bidders that she was being sold "only because her present owner has not use for her services." Retta, "good seamstress, pastry and plain cook," came with similar assurances.[77] Subsequent days saw twenty-six-year-old Charles and twenty-three-year-old Rose and her son, "guaranteed against all vices and diseases provided against by law," endure the ritual.[78] Bidders were assured that the "colored girl Jane . . . can be had on trial before the sale," as if to convince potential masters that she qualified for her own enslavement.[79] The pace of auctions at Hewlett's Exchange picked up right around the time Lincoln commenced to explore the city. *May 17*: "a quarteroon named Adeline . . . a creole, good cook and house servant," with her child Elmira.[80] *May 18*: Louisa, who "has had the small pox."[81] *May 20*: Patsey, her infant Rose, and twenty-five-year-old Mary.[82] *May 21*: Ned and Jane.[83] *May 24*: Mary, on terms of one-fourth cash down and four months credit;[84] *May 25*: Matilda, "a mild and humble disposition," and Juliana, "active, intelligent . . . and fully guaranteed."[85] *May 27*: "[T]he negro wench Julie"; Cecile, a mulatto, with her five-year-old child; Louisa, with her two sons; and teenaged Gabriel.[86] *May 28*: Henry, Louisa, Tom, and Lydia, "first rate American cook."[87] *May 31*: "[L]aundresses and plaiters [braiders], seamstresses, cooks, carpenters, painters and blacksmiths."[88] *June 1*: Dafney and "Aline, an African negro woman, about 30 yrs. of age, with her two

76. A local newspaper reported that 1,011 new slaves arrived between October 17, 1830, and November 17, 1831. The importations undoubtedly were concentrated during the winter and spring months. *New Orleans Bee*, November 18, 1831, p. 2, c. 1.

77. *Mercantile Advertiser*, May 14, 1831, p. 3, c. 6.

78. *Louisiana Courier*, May 11, 1831, p. 3, c. 6–7.

79. Ibid., May 13, 1831, p. 3, c. 6.

80. Ibid., May 14, 1831, p. 4, c. 4.

81. Ibid., May 18, 1831, p. 3, c. 7.

82. Ibid., May 14, 1831, p. 4, c. 4.

83. Ibid., May 19, 1831, p. 3, c. 7 and *Mercantile Advertiser*, May 20, 1831, p. 5, c. 6.

84. *Louisiana Courier*, May 21, 1831, p. 3, c. 4.

85. Ibid., May 23, 1831, p. 3, c. 7 and *Mercantile Advertiser*, May 24, 1831, p. 3, c. 6.

86. *Louisiana Courier*, May 11, 1831, p. 3, c. 6.

87. Ibid., May 26, 1831, p. 3, c. 7 and *Mercantile Advertiser*, May 28, 1831, p. 3, c. 6.

88. *New Orleans Bee*, May 31, 1831, p. 2, c. 4. These skilled slaves were not offered at Hewlett's but at the operation of "R. Salaun, Broker and Exchange Broker," located on "Royale, between Hospital and Barracks streets."

children Juliette 9 years of age, and Matilda 2 years of age. . . ."[89] *Also on June 1*: Nelly and her one-year-old child;[90] a "black girl called Aimeé, 24 years of age, a cook and laundress. She has been 7 years in the country.— Another black wench, Louisa, 16 years of age, Houseservant and somewhat of a washerwoman."[91] *June 2*: George, Abram, Carey, Sarah, Horton, Emily, and her two toddlers Claricy and Mary.[92] *June 3*: a mulatto named Hammond and a cook named Celia.[93] *June 3*: Francoise, Jacques, Philip, Auguste, Venus, Heloise, another Heloise, Caroline, Polly, and Bellony ("not honest"). "Almost all these slaves are creoles," explained the master, "and are, with the exception of [Bellony], good negroes. . . ."[94] *June 4*: Honoré, Aimée, and Louise. *June 6*: "negro wench named LOUISE, aged about 50 years" and "Another negress named Mary."[95] *June 6*: "For Sale— two valuable female servants, aged 18 and 24 years . . . sold in consequence of the owner having no use for them this summer. . . ."[96] *June 7*: "Sophie, a Congo negress, aged about 37 yrs.; Fine, a creole negress . . . Pognon, a creole negress . . . with her two children" and "Paul, a negro, aged about 76 years."[97] Also auctioned on this day were Micah, Julien, Zenon, Charlot, Pauline, Desiree, Manon, and Tempe, ranging in age from fifteen to thirty-five and described variously as "an american negro," "a mulatto," a "creole negro," "a creole girl," "a black boy," "a black girl," "an African negress," and "an american wench";[98] Harriett, Albany, and the "African negro woman" Aline with her children Juliette and Matilda (who apparently had not drawn an acceptable bid when they were initially offered on June 1).[99] *Also on June 7*: Fifty-five slaves from a St. Charles Parish plantation, ages two to sixty, described in the same taxonomy as above but with the additional categories of "a creole mulatto," "an african negro," "a creole sambo," "a sambo creole (inferior)." They included Tom, Louis, Jesse, Ned, Azie, Maximin, Robert, Bob, Azic, James, George, Dick, Sam, William

89. *Louisiana Courier*, May 31, 1831, p. 3, c. 6.

90. Ibid., May 28, 1831, p. 3, c. 7.

91. *New Orleans Bee*, May 31, 1831, p. 2, c. 6.

92. *Mercantile Advertiser*, May 31, 1831, p. 3, c. 6.

93. *Louisiana Courier*, May 24, 1831, p. 3, c. 7 and *Mercantile Advertiser*, May 31, 1831, p. 3, c. 6.

94. *Louisiana Courier*, May 18, 1831, p. 3, c. 7.

95. Ibid., June 3, 1831, p. 3, c. 7.

96. Ibid., June 6, 1831, p. 3, c. 4. This ad represented a for-sale-by-owner offer rather than an auction at Hewlett's Exchange.

97. Ibid., May 20, 1831, p. 4, c. 6.

98. *New Orleans Bee*, May 13, 1831, p. 1, c. 2.

99. Ibid., June 6, 1831, p. 2, c. 6 and *Mercantile Advertiser*, June 1, 1831, p. 3, c. 6.

Chicot, Laurince, Henry, Gros John, Joe, Baptiste, Prosper, John, Raphael, Jean Baptiste, John Trot, Victorin, William Johnson, Daniel, Valentine, Alexander, Peter Hall, Pierre, Yoke, Prudent, Gautier, George, Gabriel, Nina, Cecila, Helene, Rose, Azelin, Michel, Jean Baptiste, Carisse, Hannah, Nancy, Henriette, Caroline, Josephine, Georgette, Adamine, Marie, Sophie, Francoise, Old Sophie, and Ester. Most were field hands and cart drivers, reflecting their plantation (rather than urban) origin, and presumably their destiny.[100] *June 8*: Charles and "About 10 SERVANTS, amongst whom are house servants and field hands. . . ."[101] *June 9*: Sally and child Peter,[102] along with Julien, Tom, Fon ("well acquainted with the business of a [sugar] refinery"), Pierre, Tom, Gregoire, Solomon, Thomas, Daniel, and Francois. "All of the above slaves are very intelligent and handy at all sorts of work."[103] *June 11*: Henny.[104] *June 14*: "A negress named Sophia, aged about 50 years, sickly and vicious."[105]

In all, more than 170 people—seven per day, six days a week—were sold at Hewlett's Exchange during the span of Lincoln's visit. Others were vended privately in nearby commercial offices. Brokers Doyle & Brown, for example, offered (along with land and lottery tickets) three women and two children for sale from their Conti Street office. A few steps away, P. F. Duconge's firm retailed a teenager, while James Saul of the Bank of the United States offered a man and two women along with furniture, horses, and a riding harness. Slaves who failed to sell in such private venues usually ended up on the public auction block at Hewlett's.[106]

For every six unique auction advertisements that ran in local newspapers, one runaway-slave notice appeared—and reappeared, day after day, for weeks. While auction ads boasted slaves' physical strengths and capabilities, runaway notices emphasized their irregularities and abnormalities. Irritated masters yoked together anatomical and behavioral descriptions in unexpected, oftentimes jarring, and consistently dehumanizing ways. What results is a lexicon of degradation, a parlance that rejects black membership in humanity (in terms of deformity, disability, ugliness,

100. *New Orleans Bee*, May 13, 1831, p. 1, c. 2–3.

101. *Louisiana Courier*, June 6–7, 1831, p. 3, c. 7.

102. Ibid., June 7, 1831, p. 3, c. 7.

103. *New Orleans Bee*, May 16, 1831, p. 1, c. 2.

104. *Louisiana Courier*, June 9, 1831, p. 3, c. 7.

105. Ibid., May 20, 1831, p. 4, c. 6.

106. "For Sale—A black girl," *Mercantile Advertiser*, May 19, 1831, p. 3, c. 3; "Negroes for Sale," *Mercantile Advertiser*, May 14, 1831, p. 3, c. 1; "Servants, Furniture, Horses & Gig," ibid., May 23, 1831, p. 3, c. 5.

misogyny) while paradoxically betraying the writers' observations to the contrary (acknowledging slaves' intelligence, attractiveness, even beauty). One woman, for example, was described as

> an American [bl]ack wench, called GRACE or GRACEY. . . .
> She is google-eyed; has a scar behind her neck, another on her
> left ear, and a deformity of the thumb nail . . . She is very intel-
> ligent and may probably pass herself off as free. . . .[107]

Another, a "mulatto wench," had, according to her master, a "light complexion, [a] good looking countenance, [and] a burn on her breast."[108] Usley, something of a free spirit, was described as "a good looking young woman . . . light complexion . . . a little inclined to be fleshy . . . wears ear rings . . . is fond of dress and has many fine clothes . . ."[109] George was "a light mulatto, rather a decent appearance [except for] a piece of skin lately off his nose."[110] Sally was "good looking" but "lost one of her upper front teeth . . ."[111] Thurington "talks a great deal and stutters a little."[112] Celestine, who ran away from a Chartres Street hairdresser, was only "13 years of age."[113] Narcisse, who was considered by her owner to bear "a sambo complexion," measured only "4 feet six inches," presumably pre-adolescent.[114] The master seeking "Bill or William" described his runaway in terms that hinted at the sexual: "a good looking fellow [with] beautiful eye-brows [who] wore a fine cloth roundabout and cottonmade pantaloons. . . ."[115] Owners of the Planters & Merchants Hotel described their twenty-one-year-old slave-waiter Wesley as "a light mulatto . . . very handsome . . . genteel in his appearance" (adding, with audacious naïveté, that the misguided youth "disappeared without any cause or reason whatever.")[116] Dick, on the other hand, was nothing more than "jet black";[117] Caroline had "an ugly face," spoke "bad," "absconded . . . and is lurking about town. . . ."[118] Readers were asked to keep an eye out for other

107. *New Orleans Bee*, May 28, 1831, p. 2, c. 4.
108. *Louisiana Courier*, May 12, 1831, p. 3, c. 5.
109. *Mercantile Advertiser*, May 13, 1831 and afterwards, p. 4, c. 6.
110. *Louisiana Courier*, May 12, 1831, p. 4, c. 7.
111. *Mercantile Advertiser*, May 13, 1831, p. 4, c. 6.
112. *Louisiana Courier*, May 13, 1831, p. 4, c. 7.
113. *New Orleans Bee*, May 26, 1831, p. 2, c. 3.
114. *Louisiana Courier*, May 30, 1831, p. 3, c. 5.
115. *New Orleans Bee*, May 13, 1831, p. 2, c. 3.
116. *Mercantile Advertiser*, June 6, 1831, p. 3, c. 4.
117. *Louisiana Courier*, May 12, 1831, p. 4, c. 7.
118. Ibid., June 10, 1831, p. 3, c. 3.

runaways' "high cheek bones. . . . pug nose . . . scar on the right breast . . .
two smallest toes of each foot a great deal shorter than the rest . . . flat
nose, and a little turned up . . . pretty thick lips, lively look . . . black, thick
lips . . . very black complexion . . . thick red lips . . . very wild look."[119]
    Other runaways were distinguished by their broken shackles. Frank
had "a small chain round his neck, fastened with a padlock"; Jerry "had
an iron ring around his neck."[120] One especially tragic case involved John,
who escaped while Lincoln was in town. Around sixty years old, John
"stoops considerably when walking, feet somewhat swelled from having
been frost bitten, *has every appearance of being worn down by years.*" A victim of the Middle Passage, the old man was "a native of Africa, has the
Congo dialect, speaks French and English. . . ." John's master died, and
one might have expected that the executors of his estate would have freed
the elderly man to live out his tortured life in peace. No such luck: John
was publically auctioned in April by U.S. Marshals. His new master S.
Blossman suspected the elderly disabled runaway was "lurking about the
upper faubourgs."[121] A more oppressed life can hardly be imagined, but
they in fact abounded. During Lincoln's visit, white New Orleanians were
also asked to look out for Bill, Kelsy, Chloe, Sanket, Beauchamps, Nelson,
Louis, Sally, Celestine, Grace, Surprise, Ellin, Sophie, Madison, Melin-
da, Ben, Mary, George, Dick, Nathan, George Smith, Maryann, Henry
Bell, Benjamin, Narcisse, Caroline, and Louisa.
    Evidence of the commodification of humanity extended beyond auc-
tion and runaway notices. Some ads offered to the marketplace the very
breast milk of nursing black women, to nourish white infants for the financial benefit of white masters or mistresses. "To be hired," stated one
such ad during Lincoln's visit,

> A nurse, a black young girl, has a child about 15 days old; she
> is very sound, and has a great quantity of milk. Apply. Bourbon
> street, no. 276."[122]

Another wet nurse for hire was described as a " mulatto woman, very
healthy . . . very handy . . . faithful slave. . . ."[123] Similar ads ran on the

119. These descriptions are culled from *Louisiana Courier*, May 30, 1831, p. 3, c. 5 and
Mercantile Advertiser, June 10, 1831, p. 4, c. 5.
120. *Mercantile Advertiser*, May 13, 1831 and afterwards, p. 4, c. 5 and June 10, 1831,
p. 4, c. 5.
121. Ibid., May 25, 1831, p. 3, c. 1 (emphasis added).
122. *New Orleans Bee*, May 13, 1831, p. 2, c. 4.
123. Ibid., May 20, 1831, p. 2, c. 5.

demand side:

> Wet nurse wanted—A young woman with a new breast of milk
> is wanted immediately to nurse a young child. Apply at 119,
> Royal street, corner of St. Louis street.[124]

•

The eternal threat of violence in maintaining the institution of slavery occasionally met with resistance. One day while Lincoln explored the city,
a trader sold two slave boys to a local master. The youths established a
friendship and, five days later, escaped together. A neighbor helped capture one boy, named Elisha, and guarded him while the master pursued
the other. In the meantime, Elisha stabbed the neighbor eleven times,
nearly killing him. Police arrested Elisha and brought him to court. Noteworthy names presided in the case: Hon. J. Pitot served as judge, G. Eastis
and Charles Gayarré as prosecutors, and A. Pichot as attorney for the
defense. A "jury of six freeholders" needed only a "short deliberation" before returning a verdict of "*guilty*; and sentence of death."[125] Four days
later, Elisha was brought before the gallows, most likely at the Parish
Prison in the Faubourg Tremé. Word spread; a crowd of morbid spectators
assembled in late afternoon. Among them was the same slave boy who
befriended and escaped with Elisha, who himself had been recaptured
but nevertheless managed to arrive at the scene. As the trap door sent
Elisha to his death, the friend "fell into sudden convulsions" and shortly
thereafter "died in violent spasms." The newspaper acknowledged that the
simultaneous demise of two friends at society's bottom rung "almost bears
the stamp of romance," but guided readers away from such sentimentality.
"This occurrence would seem very singular," pontificated the *Bee*,

> were not its causes to be traced to another source than that of
> sympathy in the fate of the culprit. It appears that the boy had
> been sick for a few weeks previous; his physical debility, the
> oppressive heat of the weather, added, perhaps, to the impres-
> sion of the awful scene, brought on fatal convulsions.[126]

Another newspaper saw the story as an opportunity to protest "these
wretches imported into our state by wanton men . . . who seek and ransack

124. *Louisiana Courier*, May 12, 1831, p. 4, c. 7.
125. *New Orleans Bee*, May 31, 1831, p. 2, c. 1.
126. Ibid., June 7, 1831, p. 2, c. 1.

for the vilest of slaves, and then place them among us, either to run away to be repurchased, or knowing them capable of murder, and guaranteeing them against vices."[127] The incident encapsulated the tense framework of greed, exploitation, oppression, and violence that wired masters, traders, and slaves together in New Orleans society.

Did Lincoln learn of the incident? The verdict was announced in the newspapers on May 31 and the execution occurred on June 4, while Lincoln was most likely still in the city. Public executions in this era occurred occasionally in the rural West, but were a fairly common event in vice-ridden New Orleans. Rural rivermen visiting the city, with time on their hands and curiosity in their veins, would have gravitated to such a spectacle. A flatboatman visiting Natchez a few years later wrote matter-of-factly of going out of his way to witness the hanging of a black man.[128] Perhaps Lincoln heard about the incident from fellow boatmen, or read the *Bee* article—in which the journalist, with unintentional poignancy, spelled the slave's name not as *Elisha*, but *Elijah*.[129]

•

Hearing, watching, and reading about daily life in New Orleans in the late spring of 1831 would have informed a visitor like Lincoln of a much bigger talk-of-the-town topic. Conversations at a popular exhibit at Girod and Commerce streets would have dropped additional hints. More subtle clues abounded at Hewlett's Exchange, where, between the auctions for slaves and steamboats and sugar mills were biddings for "114 Valuable Lots . . . 250 lots[,] delightfully situated. . . . 19 VALUABLE LOTS. . . ." They signaled a veritable real estate boom in an otherwise déclassé Creole-and-immigrant neighborhood.[130] Fueling the chatter and the speculation was an exciting new transportation technology, coming out of England via the Northeast and executed successfully for the first time west of the Appalachians right here in New Orleans' own Faubourg Marigny. It was the railroad.

Plans for this revolutionary development commenced a month after Lincoln's first visit to New Orleans, when, on July 28, 1828, "friends of

127. "Trial of Slave Elijah," *Mercantile Advertiser*, May 31, 1831, p. 2, c. 4; "Execution of Slave Elijah," ibid., June 6, 1831, p. 2, c. 5.

128. Asbury C. Jacquess, "The Journals of the Davy Crockett commencing December 20th, 1834," *Indiana Magazine of History* 102, no. 1 (March 2006): 20–21.

129. *New Orleans Bee*, June 7, 1831, p. 2, c. 1.

130. Ibid., May 13 and 14, 1831, p. 2, c. 6; May 26, 1831, p. 2, c. 1.

internal improvements" met at Hewlett's Exchange and resolved to research "the construction of a RAIL ROAD, from the Mississippi to
Lake Pontchartrain."[131] Among the attendees was a Baltimorian named
Maurice W. Hoffman, an enthusiastic protégé of the Baltimore and Ohio
Railroad who sought to launch similar projects in new markets. The next
three years saw the chartering of the enterprise, the surveying of the route,
the purchasing of supplies, the hiring (and buying) of labor, the preparation of the bed, and the construction of the straight-as-an-arrow five-
mile track from riverfront to lakeshore (today's Elysian Fields Avenue).
On April 23, 1831—just as Lincoln left Illinois on his second trip to New
Orleans—the horse-drawn Pontchartrain Railroad made its inaugural
run. Six stagecoach-like cars bearing state and local dignitaries, a band,
and company stockholders

> moved in the most imposing manner to the sound of music
> amidst a large concourse of admiring spectators, who lined
> each side of the road, and reached the lake by happy coinci-
> dence at the moment the Mobile steamboat arrived for the
> first time at Port Pontchartrain with the mail. The mail and
> passengers were immediately forwarded to the city . . . and
> reached the head of the road in half an hour.[132]

Efficient transportation to the lake meant new business opportunities
with the resource-rich "Florida parishes" as well as the passenger-rich cities of Biloxi, Mobile, Pensacola, and points east. The tiny rail depot on
the lake won designation as Port Pontchartrain, an official port-of-entry
into the United States. "That the system of Rail-roads now clearly demonstrated to the public, will be of exceeding advantage to the mercantile
community, is beyond a doubt," proclaimed one newspaper a month after
the inauguration, while Lincoln explored the city.[133]

Indeed, the project proved to be an immediate success, and occasioned
a real estate boom at the railroad's riverside and lakeside termini. Every advertisement boasted of its respective land's proximity to the artery,
with phrases like "fronting the rail road," "NEAR THE RAILROAD,"
"[SHORT] DISTANCE from the Rail Road," and "most agreeably situated . . . on the east side of the Rail Road."[134] The most dramatic conse-

131. "Rail Road," *Louisiana Courier*, July 17, 1828, p. 3, c. 3; July 31, 1828, p. 3, c. 1.
132. *Louisiana Advertiser*, "Opening of the Rail Road." April 25, 1831, p. 2, c. 4.
133. "Rail Road," *Mercantile Advertiser*, May 20, 1831, p. 2, c. 4.
134. *New Orleans Bee*, May 13, 1831, p. 2, c. 6; ibid., May 14, 1831, p. 2, c. 6; ibid.,
May 19, 1831, p. 2, c. 6.

quence, in terms of urban development, was the subdivision of lots along the Lake Pontchartrain shore. Dubbed Milneburg for landowner Alexander Milne, the subdivision represented New Orleans' first effort to develop this tidally influenced saline marsh, a process that would not come to completion for well over a century. Milne's advertisement extolled the area's amenities:

> This town delightfully situated on the border of Lake Pontchartrain, (lately become a port of entry by a law of the United States, under the denomination of port Pontchartrain,) the rail road from the city of New Orleans passing through the centre of it, (. . . only a ten minutes ride on a locomotive carriage . . .). The site of this town is beautiful in the extreme, and it possesses many and great advantages, as the whole of the commerce of the lakes with a great part of the coasting trade, must [soon] center there . . . [It is also] a watering place for health and recreation. . . .[135]

Milneburg lots sold well, yielding $259,247 at the May 20 auction at Hewlett's (at which three slaves were sold as well).[136] A lakeside hotel opened in Milneburg right on schedule, eager to accommodate day-trippers and passengers in transit:

> To the Visitors of the Lake: [The] Pontchartrain Hotel, will be opened on Sunday the 29th [of May] and visitors will find every species of refection and refreshments, at all hours of the day and evening. . . .[137]

Land parcels in the Faubourg Marigny along the railroad sold even better, due to their proximity to the urban core and the fact that "[t]hese lots are among the most elevated in that part of the city."[138]

Behind the local real estate boom was an international fever among the business class for railroads, railroads, railroads. The *Bee* on May 17

---

135. *New Orleans Bee*, May 13, 1831, p. 2, c. 6. What Milne failed to mention was that his lots lay practically at sea level, supremely vulnerable to gulf storms. Only twelve weeks after this ad ran and ten weeks after Lincoln departed, a hurricane struck New Orleans, causing great damage to the ships in port, "literally carr[ying] away" the new lakefront structures, and damaging many of the adjacent "Rail-Road establishments." *New Orleans Bee*, August 18, 1831, p. 2, c. 1–2.

136. *New Orleans Bee*, May 21, 1831, p. 2, c. 1.

137. Ibid., May 26, 1831, p. 2, c. 3.

138. Ibid., May 14, 1831, p. 2, c. 6.

published railroad news from New Orleans, Mobile, and England.[139] The next day, a Baltimore railcar salesman lauded the superiority of horse-drawn trains over newfangled steam locomotives. In the same column ran this story:

> [A] project is on foot to make a rail-way across the isthmus of Suez, and carrying over it vessels of the heaviest burden from the Mediterranean to the Red Sea. . . . *Thus the rail-way mania—for we cannot yet bring ourselves to look at it in any other light—is diffusing itself all over the world, and seems likely to spread until it shall have cured itself by some sudden and irreparable explosion.*[140]

"Rail-way mania" indeed: the same newspaper contained railroad-related news in English, French, and—a rarity—Spanish, in which the technology was introduced as "Camino de Corredera llamado *Rail Road.*" Local businessmen caught the mania as well. On May 21, stockholders of the New Orleans Locomotive Steam Engine Company met in the Globe Coffee House on Chartres Street. "Punctual attendance is required," ordered the president, "as business of importance is to be laid before the meeting."[141] A block away, the previously mentioned Conti Street brokers Doyle & Brown (who also traded slaves) offered for sale "a beautiful little Locomotive Carriage and Railroad, suitable for exhibition . . . the purchaser will be instructed gratis how to put it in operation."[142]

By this time, entrepreneur Maurice Hoffman was off evangelizing on railroads in the cotton country near Woodville, Mississippi. Leaders in that area, which was slated to be connected with Bayou Sara by a railroad chartered by the Louisiana Legislature just two months earlier, eagerly sought advice on the new infrastructure.[143] To the *Woodville Republican* Hoffman released his trade secrets—everything potential investors needed to know to bring railroads to their region, from the purchasing of cedar logs for ties and iron for rails, to grading the soil and laying the track.[144] The editors of the *Louisiana Courier* acquired the piece and ran it in their New Orleans paper on Monday, May 30. Five days earlier a similar article

139. Ibid., May 17, 1831, p. 2, c. 2.
140. Ibid., May 18, 1831, p. 2, c. 1 (emphasis added).
141. "Notice," *Mercantile Advertiser*, May 21, 1831, p. 3, c. 2.
142. "For Sale," ibid., May 30, 1831, p. 3, c. 3.
143. Exhibit, "West Feliciana Railroad," Ferdinand Street, St. Francisville, Louisiana.
144. *Louisiana Courier*, May 30, 1831, p. 3, c. 1–2.

ran in the *Mercantile Advertiser*, in which a South Carolina railroad company detailed all its experiences and expenditures.[145]

That all this activity coincided perfectly with Lincoln's visit raises interesting historical possibilities. Did he read about, witness, visit, or ride the railroad while in town? If so, did the experience inspire him? In light of Lincoln's intellect, curiosity, mechanical skills, and appreciation of Western transportation needs, it seems highly plausible that he took special note of New Orleans' spring 1831 bout with "rail-way mania." Evidence for his inquisitive mind regarding all things mechanical comes from various sources, including an 1850s traveling companion who recollected how Lincoln would find

> some farming implement, machine or tool, and . . . carefully examine it all over, first generally and then critically; he would "sight" it to determine if it was straight or warped: if he could make a practical test of it, he would do that; he would turn it over or around and stoop down . . . to look under it. . . . [H]e would shake it, lift it, roll it about, up-end it, overset it, and thus ascertain every quality and utility which inhered in it, so far as acute and patient investigation could do it.[146]

As we shall see, only ten months after this trip, railroads would figure into Lincoln's first run for public office. He later rose to professional prominence as a railroad lawyer, and came to national attention in part for his advocacy of the nation's railway system.[147] We will contemplate the influence of the New Orleans visit on Lincoln's railroading career later; for now, we can say with confidence that the brand-new Pontchartrain Railroad (departing from its easy-to-find Elysian Fields Avenue station only two blocks below the already-famous French Market) formed something of a must-see attraction for visitors, many of whom rode it out to the lake. Likewise, the well-advertised, long-running locomotive exhibit at Girod and Commerce streets, just blocks from the flatboat wharf, must have garnered the attention of nearly everyone circulating in that area.

•

145. "Annual Report of the Rail-Road," *Mercantile Advertiser*, May 25, 1831, p. 2, c. 4–5.

146. Henry C. Whitney, *Life on the Circuit with Lincoln* (Boston: Estes and Lauriat, 1892), 109.

147. Legal issues involving landowners versus railroads appeared at least once in the local press during May 1831. *New Orleans Bee*, May 16, 1831, p. 2, c. 1.

We can estimate when Lincoln ended his visit to New Orleans by working off his return time, as remembered by Illinois villagers. James Short, for example, recalled "fresh in his memory" meeting his future friend Abraham for the first time "in May or June 1831 at New Salem."[148] Another villager, Royal Clary, remembered knowing "Abe Lincoln in June 1831."[149] Lincoln himself stated that he had settled into New Salem during July.[150] County records indicate that Denton Offutt received a retailing license on July 8, which later enabled him to open a store and hire Lincoln to clerk.[151] From these insights we may surmise that Lincoln, Offutt, and Johnston returned to New Salem in late June or early July.

When they left New Orleans, then, may be hindcasted by assuming the same 90- to 100-mile-per-day steamboat travel speed we estimated for the 1828 return trip over the 1,588-mile trip up the lower Mississippi, the upper Mississippi, and the Illinois River to Beardstown. This amounts to sixteen to seventeen days of travel. Because a change of boats would have been required at least at St. Louis, we extend this time span to eighteen days. Next came the 138-river-mile trip up the wending Sangamon, impassable by steamboats and barely navigable by keelboats. Lincoln and company may well have traversed the much-shorter terrestrial distance between Beardstown and New Salem on foot, requiring about three to four days. The entire return trip thus consuming approximately three weeks and ending in late June or early July, we estimate Lincoln departing New Orleans sometime between June 4 and June 13. The *Mercantile Advertiser* announced around ten upcoming steamboat departures per day during that week. Some were destined for Southern river cities; others were slated to veer eastward to Ohio River cities; any one of them could have taken the men partway home. It would have been more logical, however, for them to choose a steamboat heading up the upper Mississippi, closer to their central Illinois home. That narrowed the options down to the few steamboats destined for St. Louis. They included the *Walter Scott* (departing June 4–6), the *North America* (June 13) and the *Oregon* (June 14). Lincoln's last view of New Orleans, from the steamboat deck, would have been a spectacular one: 160 vessels docked at the levee, "more

148. Short to Herndon, July 7, 1865, in *Herndon's Informants*, 72.

149. Interview, Royal Clary, by William H. Herndon, October 1866, in *Herndon's Informants*, 370.

150. Lincoln, "Autobiography," June 1860, in *Collected Works*, 4:64.

151. Sangamon County Commissioners' Record C, 256, as cited in *The Lincoln Log: A Daily Chronology of the Life of Abraham Lincoln*, entry for April 8, 1831 – July 8, 1831. Available http://www.thelincolnlog.org/view/1831/4, visited February 26, 2009.

... than there has been ... at any former period."[152]

John Hanks, whose testimony for events occurring after April 25–26 must be handled judiciously because Lincoln stated Hanks was not present to observe them, nevertheless managed to provide details about the return trip. They are worth reporting here because they may contain some kernels of truth. "Offutt—Johnson [*sic*]—Abe & myself left NO in June 1831," Hanks claimed.

> We Came to St. Louis on the Steam boat together walked to Edwardsville 25 [miles] N.E. of St Louis—Abe, Johnson & Myself, [and then] Abe & Johnson went to Coles Co. & I to Springfield.[153]

Herndon built his return-from-New-Orleans narrative around Hanks' testimony, and many subsequent biographers and historians based their accounts upon Herndon's. We cannot verify Hanks' story, but we can say confidently that the month of June began with Lincoln in New Orleans and ended with him in or approaching New Salem, Illinois.

We have some secondary accounts of Lincoln's 1831 return trip. One entails the alternate version of the previously recounted incident with Col. William D. Ferguson in Arkansas. Readers will recall that Ferguson, owner of a plantation across the river from Memphis, claimed to have employed Lincoln to chop wood, and remembered the tall youth well enough to reunite with him during his congressional and presidential years. That primary version, reported in 1861, placed Lincoln on a flatboat and thus implied that the employment occurred on the downriver leg of the journey. The alternate version, described in an 1873 history of Memphis, holds that it occurred on the return trip, as Lincoln's steamboat stopped at Wappanocha "to wood" at Ferguson's landing. Lincoln disembarked to help load the wood, a task regularly performed by returning flatboatmen to defray the cost of their passage. He struck up a conversation with Ferguson and revealed that he had been robbed on board and left penniless. Ferguson responded by employing Lincoln for a few days to cut firewood and allowing him to stay at his house until he earned enough money to board another northbound steamer.[154] While this 1873

---

152. *Mercantile Advertiser*, June 3–June 13, 1831, p. 2, c. 1; "The Shipping," ibid., June 13, 1831, p. 2, c. 4. Many steamboats did not depart at specific times, but rather when they were fully loaded.

153. Interview, John Hanks, by William H. Herndon, 1865–1866, in *Herndon's Informants*, 458.

154. James D. Davis, *The History of the City of Memphis* (Memphis, TN: Hite, Crump-

version fails to identify a primary source, it succeeds in explaining how Ferguson might have remembered Lincoln so many years later because it situates Lincoln as Ferguson's houseguest, during which time the two might have become well acquainted. If true, this scenario would add a few days to Lincoln's return time to New Salem, add a second criminal attack to Lincoln's Southern experience (the first in Louisiana in 1828), and position Lincoln as traveling home alone for the remainder of the trip. This researcher views the 1873 version as problematic: Lincoln, who made ample reference to the 1828 Louisiana attack, never once mentioned being attacked a second time. Besides, the 1861 version (explained earlier) was recorded directly from Ferguson's account while both he and Lincoln were alive. The 1873 version is secondary, appearing in a book about Memphis history.

Another story of Lincoln's return trip comes from an 1899 narrative history of Illinois' early years. Without citing a source, author Harvey Lee Ross contends that

> instead of paying $40 for a passage and spending his time drinking, smoking and playing cards as the other young men did, [Lincoln] went to the captain and asked him if he wanted another hand on the boat. The captain [obliged], so he got his passage free and made a nice little sum of money besides. When he got to St. Louis he found the Illinois river steamboat had just left and that there would not be another one going for several days. He left his baggage with his partner and went across the country to Coles county to visit his parents, but did not stay long, as he was anxious to return to New Salem and turn over the money to the man who had shipped the produce.[155]

This anecdote, incompatible with the Ferguson story, suggests—contrary to other sources—that Denton Offutt remained in Illinois, leaving Lincoln to travel to New Orleans with only one partner. Ross also erroneously states that Lincoln was twenty-one at the time.

ton & Kelly, 1873), 176–177; *Sun*, March 18, 1861, p. 4. Louis A. Warren heard a third variation of this story from an informant in 1939, who held that the Ferguson employment occurred on the 1828 return trip and lasted for weeks. Warren could not verify that version. Warren, *Lincoln's Youth: Indiana Years, Seven to Twenty-One, 1816–1830* (Indianapolis: Indiana Historical Society Press, 1959, reprinted 2002), 261, endnote #53.

155. Harvey Lee Ross, *The Early Pioneers and Pioneer Events of the State of Illinois: Including Personal Recollections of the Writer; of Abraham Lincoln, Andrew Jackson, and Peter Cartwright . . .* (Chicago: Eastman Brothers, 1899), 110–111.

One final story of the return trip, traced to Lincoln himself, ranks as the most plausible. The *New York Daily Tribune*, reporting the candidate's autobiographical details for the upcoming 1860 presidential election, wrote that "[o]n this trip up the river [from New Orleans], Mr. Lincoln states that he first met the Hon. Jesse R. Du Bois, the present State Auditor of Illinois and candidate on the Republican ticket for re-election, who was also discharging the duties of deckhand."[156] Despite some factual errors elsewhere in the article and a lack of substantiating sources, this information seems credible. Jesse Kilgore Dubois, a descendent of French colonials who settled in Vincennes in the eighteenth century, was born in Illinois in 1811 and, by his own account, knew Lincoln since "the two were young men."[157] He would have been twenty years old—prime flatboating age—at the time of the alleged meeting on the Mississippi. Dubois later became "Uncle Jesse" to the Lincoln family, and enjoyed a close (but occasionally contentious) friendship with Lincoln from his earliest political years through the presidency. If the two indeed first met as deckhands on the same New Orleans steamboat in 1831, the encounter further demonstrates that Lincoln established lasting social relationships during his New Orleans trips. One problem exists: Lincoln once wrote that his "acquaintance first began with [Dubois] in 1836," during their state legislature terms.[158] This does not necessarily rule out an initial introduction in 1831.

Lincoln would call the tiny village of New Salem, site of the mill dam incident, his home for the next six years. Effective immediately upon returning from New Orleans, he permanently moved away from his family and commenced living on his own. Lincoln during 1831–32 clerked for Offutt, served in the Black Hawk War, and ran (unsuccessfully) for state legislature. He also continued captaining flatboats, guiding cargo to St. Louis at least twice in 1834–35 and probably to numerous local destinations.[159] Also during the New Salem years Lincoln surveyed new towns, studied law, and won a seat in the state legislature, before moving

156. "Lincoln's Early Days," *New York Daily Tribune* (*New York Herald-Tribune*), July 9, 1860, p. 6.

157. Jesse K. Dubois, interview with William H. Herndon (written down December 1, 1888, but carried out years earlier, Dubois having died in 1876), in *Herndon's Informants*, 719; Helen L. Allen, "A Sketch of the Dubois Family, Pioneers of Indiana and Illinois," *Journal of the Illinois Historical Society* 5, no. 1 (April 1912): 61–62.

158. Abraham Lincoln, undated letter of recommendation for Jesse K. Dubois, *Collected Works*, 8:422.

159. "Garrison's Prediction," *Omaha World Herald*, September 30, 1899, p. 4.

to Springfield to practice law and politics.

Lincoln came to travel routinely on steamboats and, later, railroads, expanding his personal geography until it spanned longitudinally from Boston to Council Bluffs, and latitudinally from Niagara Falls in Canada to Hampton Roads in Virginia. But never again would he sail down the lower Mississippi, never again would he set foot in the Deep South, and never again would he see New Orleans.

Left: This earliest-known daguerreotype of Abraham Lincoln, attributed to Nicholas H. Shepherd and taken around 1846–47, is the closest we can come to picturing how Lincoln looked during his flatboat years. His massive hands were ideal for the steering oar. *Image courtesy Library of Congress, LC-USZ6-299.*

Below: Mapping Lincoln's life illustrates the exceptional nature of his two flatboat voyages to New Orleans. They formed the longest journeys of his life, his first experiences in a major city, his only visits to the Deep South, his sole exposure to the region's brand of slavery and slave trading, his only time in the subtropics, and the closest he ever came to immersing himself in a foreign culture. They highlight the least-known era of Lincoln's otherwise thoroughly examined adult life. *Map by Richard Campanella.*

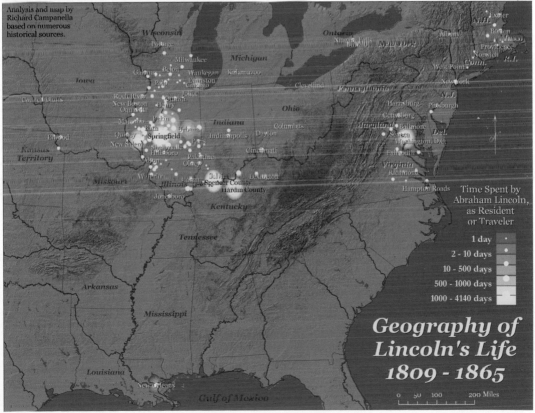

Analysis and map by Richard Campanella based on numerous historical sources.

Time Spent by Abraham Lincoln, as Resident or Traveler

1 day
2 - 10 days
10 - 500 days
500 - 1000 days
1000 - 4140 days

Geography of Lincoln's Life 1809 - 1865

0   50   100   200 Miles

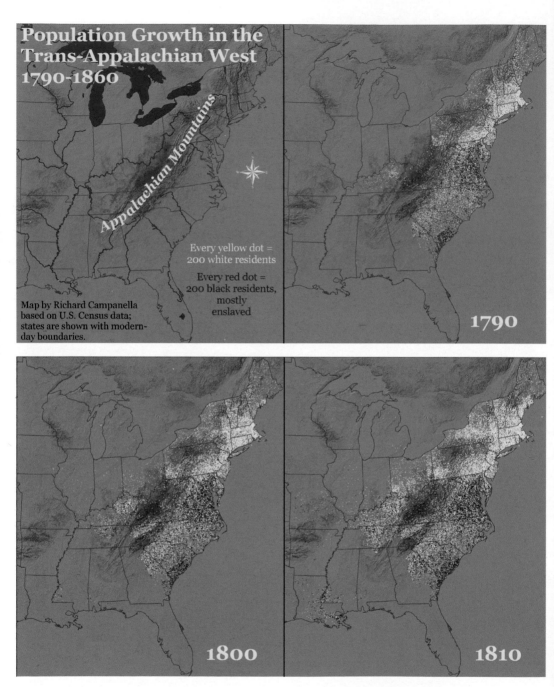

Population Growth in the Trans-Appalachian West 1790-1860

Appalachian Mountains

Map by Richard Campanella based on U.S. Census data; states are shown with modern-day boundaries.

Every yellow dot = 200 white residents

Every red dot = 200 black residents, mostly enslaved

1790

1800

1810

Lincoln's ancestors emulated thousands of other Americans who, between the 1780s and 1810s, migrated westward over the Appalachian Mountains and into the Ohio and Mississippi river valleys. In a remarkably short period, Western-ers produced far more agricultural commodities—corn, wheat, hogs, tobacco—than they could consume or trade locally. They exported surpluses via flatboats to New Orleans and the lower Mississippi Valley plantation country, in exchange for much-needed hard currency. *Maps by Richard Campanella.*

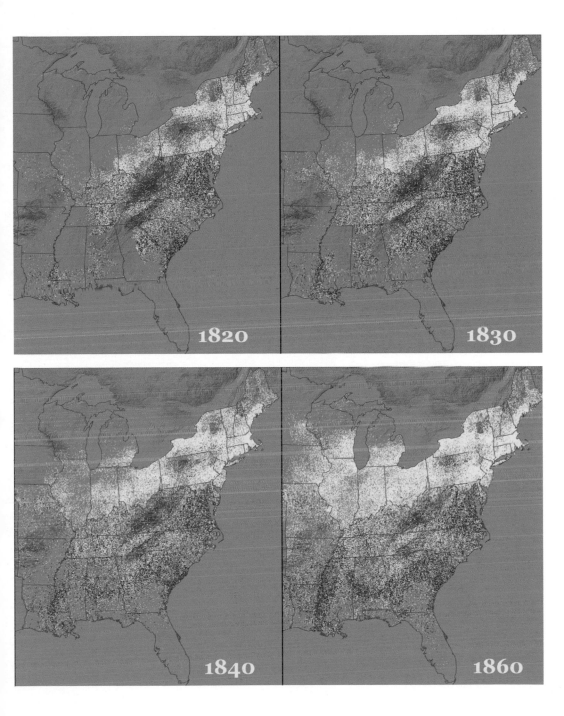

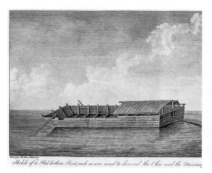

Above: A typical flatboat of the Western rivers, ca. 1820s. These vernacular vessels of oak, poplar, or pine typically measured twelve to twenty feet in width, twenty-five to forty feet in length, and capable of bearing well over thirty tons. An on-deck cabin sheltered cargo and crew. From the 1780s to the 1860s, men by the thousands guided flatboats downriver to the New Orleans market. *Image from Victor Collot,* A Journey in North America *(Paris, France: Arthur Bertrand, 1826).*

Top right: George Caleb Bingham's *The Jolly Flatboatmen* (1846) captures how most Americans came to perceive Mississippi boatmen. Flatboats were commonly called "broad horns," for the two long oars ("sweeps") protruding from the sides, as depicted in Bingham's painting.

Middle and bottom right: The advent of steamboats in the 1810s effectively ended the problem of contra-current navigation, and made sail- and oar-powered keelboats all but obsolete on the main arteries of the West. Flatboats, however, were so cost-effective—cheap to build and mobilized gratis by the current—that they coexisted with steamboats for nearly half a century, as depicted in these illustrations. After selling their cargo in New Orleans, crews dismantled their flatboats, sold the scrap lumber, and rode steamboats home, reducing their overall time investment and making flatboat commerce more economical. They performed on-board tasks for steamboat captains, such as loading firewood, to reduce or eliminate their fares. *Details of "Bound Down the River" by Currier & Ives (1870) and "A Steamboat Race on the Mississippi" by George F. Fuller (1859) courtesy Library of Congress, LC-USZ62-5 and LC-DIG-pga-03028.*

Above: The uppermost sign on this flood marker (just below the spotlights) dramatically illustrates how high the Ohio River used to rise before the advent of dams and flood control. Flatboatmen loved high water because it meant swift river velocities. **Below**: City Hall bulletin board in West Point, Kentucky. River towns along the Ohio and Mississippi exude a poignant sense of past grandeur. Once strategically located, they now sit on backwaters, as the nation and world have advanced to new forms of transportation. *Photos by Richard Campanella, 2008.*

Above scenes: Thomas Lincoln launched a flatboat from the embarcadero of the tiny Ohio River outpost of West Point, Kentucky, in March 1806, guiding it to New Orleans and returning by early May. Flatboating to New Orleans formed something of a rite of passage for young Western men; Thomas' neighbors, son, neighbors' sons, and many others in his world performed the ritual multiple times. *Photos by Richard Campanella, 2008.*

Top: Downtown Elizabethtown, Kentucky, where Thomas Lincoln and Nancy Hanks married, settled, produced a daughter, and conceived a son. The Lincolns then moved to Hodgen's Mill (later Hodgenville, **second from top**) in Hardin County, specifically to a place known as Sinking Spring (which still flows at the bottom of this rock staircase, **right**) near Nolin Creek. There, Abraham Lincoln was born on February 12, 1809, in a log cabin now commemorated by a massive Classical monument (**below**). Lincoln's memory dominates the modern-day landscape of this region; allusions to his name, image, and narrative are ubiquitous. *Photos by Richard Campanella, 2008.*

Above, left, and right: Questionable Kentucky land titles and poor soils forced Thomas Lincoln in 1811 to relocate his family to a rugged region eight miles northeast of Sinking Spring. The Knob Creek farm, named for the adjacent hills rising two hundred feet in elevation, saw Abraham grow from a toddler to an active youth of seven. "My earliest recollection," wrote Lincoln later in life "is of the Knob Creek place." The site today is the most peaceful and pristine of the Lincoln landscapes. *Photos by Richard Campanella, 2008.*

"[We] removed to what is now Spencer county Indiana, in the autumn of 1816," Lincoln explained. "partly on account of slavery; but chiefly on account of the difficulty in land titles in K[entuck]y." The family settled near what is now Gentryville (**top left**), in the dense hardwood forests and gently undulating terrain of Pigeon Creek (**middle left**). The footprint of the Lincolns' one-room cabin is marked today by this bronzed frame (**bottom left**), which incorporates what are probably the original hearthstones. One of the many hardships endured in this region was the mysterious affliction known as milk sickness. Lincoln's own mother Nancy succumbed to it in the autumn of 1818; she lies today in this grave (**bottom right**). *Photos by Richard Campanella, 2008.*

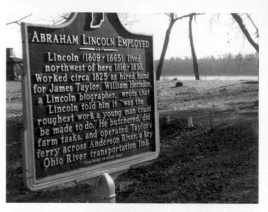

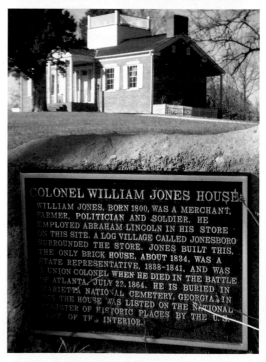

Southern Indiana saw Lincoln grow from a boy of seven to a man of twenty-one. His first experience with rivers, vessels, and riverine commerce came in 1828 at the busy Anderson Creek confluence (**top left**), where he gained employment on Indiana's side of the Ohio River (**top right**). Among his most influential neighbors was the Gentry family, whose patriarch, James, owned extensive landholdings, a river launch, and a store (**middle left**), where Abraham enjoyed newspapers and conversation. In 1828, James Gentry hired Abraham to assist his son Allen in guiding a flatboat to New Orleans. Gentry family members remain in southern Indiana in large numbers. Buried in the same Pigeon Creek Baptist Church Cemetery as these Gentry kin (**middle right**) is Lincoln's older sister Sarah (**bottom left**), who died during childbirth in 1828. Closer to Gentryville stands the home of William Jones (**bottom right**), another influential flatboating figure from Lincoln's Indiana years. *Photos by Richard Campanella, 2008.*

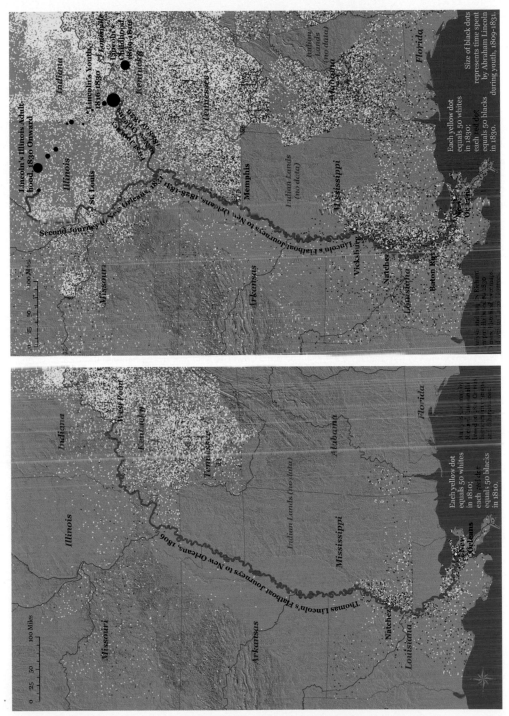

These maps show Thomas Lincoln's flatboat route from West Point, Kentucky, in 1806 (**left**) and his son Abraham's route from Rockport, Indiana, in 1828 (**right**), overlaid with the racial demographics as enumerated by the U.S. Census closest to those dates. Although both men saw slavery up-close in Kentucky, their respective trips to New Orleans exposed them to large-scale plantation slavery and slave trading for the first time. *Maps by Richard Campanella.*

Each yellow dot equals 50 whites in 1810; each red dot equals 50 blacks in 1810.

Each yellow dot equals 50 whites in 1830; each red dot equals 50 blacks in 1830.

Size of black dots represents time spent by Abraham Lincoln during youth, 1809-1831.

Top two scenes: View of the Ohio River and Main Street in downtown Rockport. The name of this Indiana town comes from the white limestone bluff (**middle left**) along its riverfront, a landmark for navigators and a landing for steamboats, as seen in this image (**middle right**) from around 1900. *Steamboat photograph by John M. Killian, courtesy Spencer County Public Library, Box 1, Picture B-030; other photos by Richard Campanella, 2008.*

Above and right: A few hundred feet downriver from the bluff lies the Old Lower Landing (Gentry's Landing), where Allen Gentry and Abraham Lincoln built and launched their flatboat for New Orleans in the spring of 1828. A limestone monument marks the spot today, inscribed with the notoriously dubious but oft-quoted line, "If I ever get a chance to hit that thing [slavery], I'll hit it hard." *Photos by Richard Campanella, 2008.*

MARKING OLD LOWER LANDING
WHERE IN 1828 – AGE 19 –
ABRAHAM LINCOLN
WITH ALLEN GENTRY MADE HIS FIRST
FLATBOAT TRIP TO NEW ORLEANS. HE SAW
SLAVES SOLD AND SAID, "IF I EVER GET A
CHANCE TO HIT THAT THING, I'LL HIT IT HARD."
IN A VERY REAL SENSE OF THE WORD IT MIGHT BE SAID THAT
THE EMANCIPATION PROCLAMATION WHICH LINCOLN
ISSUED IN 1863 OWES IT'S ORIGIN TO THIS FLATBOAT TRIP
THIS MARKER ERECTED BY THE SPENCER COUNTY HISTORICAL
SOCIETY AND THE ROCKPORT CITY PARK BOARD IN 1938

When in 1828 Did Allen Gentry and Abraham Lincoln Depart by Flatboat for New Orleans?

Evidence for Springtime Departure

Evidence	Primary	Secondary	Tertiary	Contextual
Maritime reports confirming very high number of flatboat arrivals to N.O. during time we expect Lincoln to land according to spring departure hypothesis, and very low number for corresponging autumn/winter hypothesis	1.0			
Lincoln's statement, "When[I] was nineteen...[I] made [my] first trip upon a flat-boat to New-Orleans..."	0.2			
Lincoln's hand-editing of Howell biography, in which he corrected spring-1830 departure date for Illinois as being two years after New Orleans trip	0.5			
Anna Gentry's personal recollection of an April-to-June trip		0.9		
Absolom Roby's concurrence of Anna Gentry's recollection		0.2		
Grigsby's, Richardson's, and Romine's recollection of spring departure		0.5		
High, swift rivers in spring 1828 versus low, slow waters in December				0.4
Warmer temperatures, safer climate				0.3
Busiest flatboat season in general				0.5
Gentry family baby situation				0.5
Weight factor (importance)	3.0	2.0	1.0	1.0
Sum of evidence strength multiplied by weight	5.1	3.2	0.0	1.7
Total strength of springtime hypothesis	10.0			

Evidence for Autumn/Winter Departure

Evidence	Primary	Secondary	Tertiary	Contextual
Gentry family asscoiate William Jones contracts for flatboat to be delivered in December 1833	0.2			
Bess Ehrmann's circa-1920s interviews with numerous Gentry descendents, followed by Francis Marion Van Natter's affadavits in the 1960s.			1.0	
Fairly busy flatboat season in general				0.25
Convenient alignment with harvest and planting schedules				0.3
Weight factor (importance)	3.0	2.0	1.0	1.0
Sum of evidence strength multiplied by weight	0.6	0.0	1.0	0.55
Total strength of autumn/winter hypothesis	2.15			

Above: The mystery of Lincoln's first trip to New Orleans concerns whether he launched in the spring of 1828, or in the late fall and early winter of that year. What he experienced on the Mississippi and in New Orleans is contingent on resolving this key question. Evidence presented in this book, and weighed numerically in this chart, leans decisively to an April 1828 launch. *Analysis and chart by Richard Campanella, see text for details.*

Left: This bankside view near Mt. Vernon, Indiana, represents what Lincoln and Gentry would have seen while drifting down the Ohio River shortly after launch. **Right**: This riverside bluff may appear to be as pristine and wild as it was in 1828; in fact, vast hydrological, topographical, and ecological changes have been wrought by man upon the Mississippi River Valley since Lincoln's time. *Photos courtesy Spencer County Visitors Bureau, September 2008.*

Above: Mrs. Jane Boultinghouse views the Rockport riverfront monument marking where her great-great-great-grandfather Allen Gentry and his assistant Abraham Lincoln launched for New Orleans 180 years earlier. **Above right**: Mr. Robert Grose, the only man to complete two full formal reenactments of Lincoln's Rockport-to-New Orleans journey, shows photos of his 2008 trip (including a visit to Bourbon Street) to Mrs. Barbara Dillon, who is also a great-great-great-granddaughter of Allen Gentry. **Right**: The Spencer County Library holds a treasure trove of local historical material and flatboat memorabilia. Lincoln's connection with the town and county, and the significance of his flatboat trip, are major sources of local pride, as evidenced by Victor Kupcek's art work on display at the library. His paintings (**below**) depict Lincoln and Gentry launching at Rockport and witnessing a slave auction at New Orleans. *Photos by Richard Campanella, 2008.*

Top: This drawing depicts the river landing in front of a prototypical cotton plantation, where flatboats and riverboats commercially interacted with plantation life. The topography (which is exaggerated in this illustration) represents the Mississippi's bluff-lined eastern bank from Vicksburg to Baton Rouge. River towns here embodied two topographically distinct sections: a residential district "on the hill," and a rough commercial boat landing "under the hill." Natchez, Mississippi, which Lincoln passed in 1828 and 1831, best preserves this two-tiered geography today: Natchez Under the Hill is shown in the **middle and bottom left** photos; Natchez proper, "on the hill," appears at **bottom right**. This Mississippi city ranked second only to New Orleans in terms of flatboat traffic. U.S. Custom Service manifests show that some flatboats operated in a sort of triangular trade, carrying Western produce from the upcountry to Natchez, exchanging it there for cotton and other Southern produce, then transporting their new cargo to New Orleans to complete their enterprise and return upcountry with cash. *Drawing by Adrien Persac, detail,* Norman's Chart of the Lower Mississippi River *(1858), courtesy Library of Congress; photos by Richard Campanella, 2004–07.*

Top left: The Old River Control Structure, which regulates the amount of water flowing between the Atchafalaya and Mississippi rivers, traces its origins to navigation improvements starting around the time of Lincoln's second trip to New Orleans. **Top right**: A resident of the remote village of Fort Adams in extreme southwestern Mississippi, once a prominent flatboat landing, points to the bluff on which the fortification (1783–1810) once stood. **Second from top**: Cypress trees grow along the unleveed, slack-water banks of the Mississippi River in remote Wilkinson County near Fort Adams. **Above pair**: Continuing downriver, the next major stop for flatboatmen was Bayou Sara, a bustling river landing ranking third in commerce behind Natchez and New Orleans. Bayou Sara fell victim to floods and changing times, but its hilltop corollary, St. Francisville, remains today one of Louisiana's most beautiful towns. **Right**: Next stop downriver was Port Hudson, last of the bluff towns and, in 1863, site of a key battle and siege that eventually cost the Confederacy control of the Mississippi River. Port Hudson's landing, too, has been lost to the river; only a few old houses on the bluff survive. *Photos by Richard Campanella, 2004–08.*

Top left: Rivermen in Lincoln's time knew Baton Rouge (population 3,000) for its landmark U.S. Barracks, a recently erected complex of five two-storied structures with pearl-white classical columns arranged in the shape of a pentagon. The Barracks served officers and soldiers deployed to the Southwest under the command of Lt. Col. Zachary Taylor. An intriguing legend holds that Lincoln visited, signed-in, and perhaps even spent the night at the Barracks. No one, however, has been able to produce the garrison records to prove it, and the story is probably mistaken. Lincoln undoubtedly saw the structures—four of which still stand (**top right**)—and he later served under Taylor in the Black Hawk War. **Second from top**: This 1858 depiction of the Baton Rouge riverfront by Adrien Persac shows the U.S. Barracks at top left (note flagpole), with a flatboat similar to Lincoln's floating in front of it. **Left**: Once past Baton Rouge, flatboatmen entered the sugar coast, known for its opulent sugar cane plantations and plentiful trading opportunities, including at Donaldsonville (shown here) at the Bayou LaFourche distributary. The decline in traditional river traffic by the end of the nineteenth century led to the disappearance of many riverfront boat landings, including the term "landing" as a place name. Caire's Landing in Edgard (**bottom left**) is an exception. *Photos by Richard Campanella, 2004–09; drawing by Adrien Persac, detail,* Norman's Chart of the Lower Mississippi River *(1858), courtesy Library of Congress.*

Right: Drawing of a prototypical sugar plantation (1858); note cane fields to the right, mill behind mansion, and slave cabins in rear. Flatboatmen, including Lincoln, often "lingered" along Louisiana's prosperous and highly enslaved sugar coast, trading from plantation to plantation en route to New Orleans. Most vestiges of this antebellum civilization have vanished; shown here are among the last survivors in Ascension, St. James, St. John the Baptist, and St. Charles parishes. *Drawing by Adrien Persac, detail,* Norman's Chart of the Lower Mississippi River *(1858), courtesy Library of Congress; photos by Richard Campanella, 2003–09.*

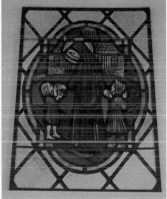

Around May 12–13, 1828, Lincoln and Gentry were, in Lincoln's words, "attacked by seven negroes with intent to kill and rob. . . ." The historical record offers a number of clues that help narrow down the attack site. Acquaintances recalled it occurred below Baton Rouge, near Wade Hampton's plantation (today's Houmas House, **top left**), close to a place associated with a woman named "Busham," "Bushan," or "Duchesne," and remembered as "Madame Duchesne." Documents record no such woman—except for French-born Rose Philippine Duchesne (1769–1852), who in 1825 founded the Convent of the Sacred Heart (St. Michael's, **top right**) twelve miles below the Hampton Plantation, in the present-day town of Convent. These and other clues suggest the attack occurred near the site of the now-demolished Sacred Heart Convent, a few hundred feet upriver from the present-day St. Michael's Church (**middle left**), along this Mississippi River bank (**middle right**). The Catholic Church canonized Mother Duchesne as a saint in 1988; a shrine in St. Charles, Missouri, (**bottom left**) entombs her remains today. Note the depiction of a Creole-style hip-roof house, typical of Louisiana, in the shrine's stained glass window (**bottom right**). *Photo of original convent courtesy Archives of the Society of the Sacred Heart, Sister Mary Louise Gavan, and Sister Mary Pat White; other photos by Richard Campanella, 2008–09.*

Above left: This 1820 map of the lower Mississippi River (with New Orleans appearing at lower right) depicts the location of the Hampton Plantation and the "Church" (St. Michael's) where the Convent of the Sacred Heart would be founded five years later. **Above right**: Detail of map to the left, focusing on St. James Parish. Somewhere between "Hampton" and "Church" on the east (upper) bank of the Mississippi lies the spot where Lincoln and Gentry were nearly murdered in 1828. **Below**: This researcher identifies the area mapped in green tones, on the east bank of the Mississippi near the present-day town of Convent, as the most likely attack site. *"Map of Mississippi" by John Melish (1820), courtesy Library of Congress; analytical map by Richard Campanella.*

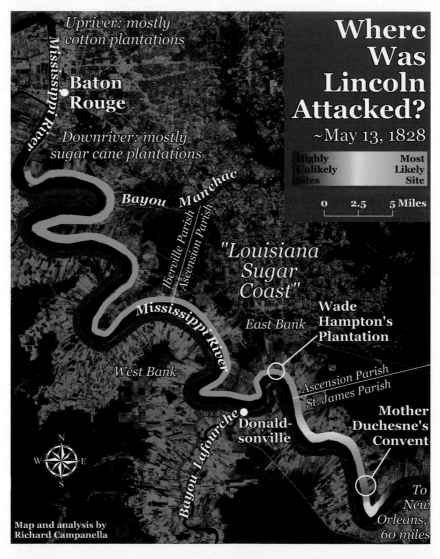

Upriver: mostly cotton plantations

Mississippi River

Baton Rouge

Downriver: mostly sugar cane plantations

Bayou Manchac

Iberville Parish
Ascension Parish

"Louisiana Sugar Coast"

Mississippi River

East Bank

West Bank

Wade Hampton's Plantation

Ascension Parish
St. James Parish

Bayou Lafourche

Donald-sonville

Mother Duchesne's Convent

To New Orleans, 60 miles

Map and analysis by Richard Campanella

Where Was Lincoln Attacked?
~May 13, 1828

Highly Unlikely Sites — Most Likely Site

0   2.5   5 Miles

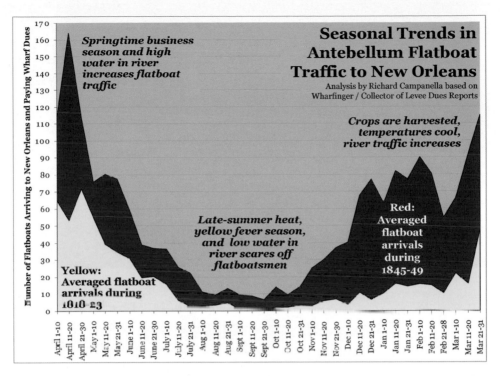

Above: Annual flatboat traffic at New Orleans peaked in early spring and bottomed out in late summer. This graph shows seasonal arrival patterns of dues-paying flatboats averaged over the years 1818–23 (yellow curve) and 1845–49 (red curve). All other comprehensive wharf reports for the interceding years have been lost, including those from Lincoln's years of 1828 and 1831, although newspaper reports of those missing data survive.

Below: This pair of graphs shows absolute (top) and relative (bottom) numbers of rafts, barges, steamboats, and flatboats arriving to the Port of New Orleans during 1818–23, based on records of the Collector of the Levee Dues. Not shown are sailing vessels arriving from the Gulf of Mexico. *Graphs and analysis by Richard Campanella based on Wharfinger Reports / New Orleans Collector of Levee Dues-Registers of Flatboats, Barges, Rafts, and Steamboats in the Port of New Orleans, 1818–23 and 1845–49. Note: 1840s data represent Second Municipality only, where most flatboats landed.*

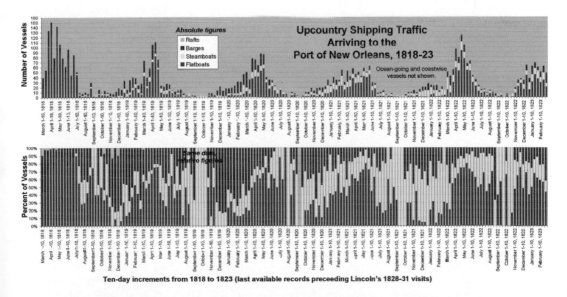

Top: When Lincoln flatboated down these last few miles of the Mississippi River before reaching New Orleans, nearly all areas visible in this aerial view comprised sugar cane plantations. Today they host the residential districts of uptown New Orleans and the container wharves of the Port of New Orleans. **Middle**: This drawing of the late-antebellum Port of New Orleans shows the plank-covered levee and docks where ocean-going vessels moored, in front of the French Quarter and Faubourg Marigny (right). Flatboats docked at the opposite end of the city and, lacking the picturesqueness of sailing ships and drama of smoke-spewing steamboats, rarely earned their way into drawings, paintings, or photographs. **Bottom**: Contemporary view of downtown New Orleans from river level. Flatboatmen of the 1820s–30s would have seen a skyline composed of church spires, domes, steep-pitched rooftops, and storehouses no more than three to four floors high, punctuated with plumes of smoke and dust. *Drawing by Adrien Persac, detail,* Norman's Chart of the Lower Mississippi River *(1858), courtesy Library of Congress; photos by Jaap van der Salm and Richard Campanella, 2008–09.*

Top: One of the best illustrations of flatboats moored at New Orleans dates from shortly before Lincoln's 1828 arrival. It does not show the main uptown flatboat wharf where Lincoln most likely landed, but rather the smaller downtown station around Conti Street (note St. Louis Church in extreme left). Sketched by Capt. Basil Hall using a *camera lucida*, this drawing may be the closest thing we have to a photograph of the antebellum flatboat wharves. **Middle**: Lincoln most likely tied up his flatboat somewhere along a line running diagonally from the upper right to lower left of this photograph. Aligning with South Peters Street, this corridor traces the circa-1830 flatboat wharf. Sediment deposition has since shifted the riverfront outward by a few blocks. **Bottom**: This photograph situates Lincoln's flatboat experience in the context of modern-day downtown New Orleans. Flatboatmen landed at the area at the center-right of the photo, and, after selling their goods and dismantling their vessels, walked into the heart of the city (extreme left). The foreground of this photo, by the Superdome, is where the ca. 1830 city petered out into backswamp. *Hall drawing courtesy Louisiana State Museum; photos by Richard Campanella and Jaap van der Salm, 2004–09.*

1500 feet

French Quarter (Old City)

Conti St.

Canal Street

Faubourg St. Mary

Notre Dame St.
Julia St.

Faubourgs Duplantier, Solet, La Course, and Annunciation

Tchoupitoulas Street

South Peters Street

Orleans Parish
Jefferson Parish

Sailing Ships

Flatboats

Steamboats

Flatboat Docking Area

Circa-1830 docking stations of the Port of New Orleans, overlaid upon 2006 satellite image

Modern-day Mississippi riverfront, shifted eastward by years of sediment deposition

Map and analysis by Richard Campanella; satellite image courtesy DigitalGlobe

Where Did Lincoln Land?

Highly Unlikely — Most Likely

Left scenes: These photos show what the location of the old flatboat wharf looks like today, well inland from its former position along the now-shifted riverfront. The hip-roof cottage (**bottom left**, now a restaurant) on Religious Street at the Orange intersection is the oldest surviving structure closest to Lincoln's landing site, about four blocks away. Dating probably to the 1810s, it represents typical working-class multi-family common-wall housing of this area and era. **Right**: This map shows how different vessels (ocean-going sailing ships, river steamboats, and flatboats) were assigned their respective docking stations at the time of Lincoln's voyages. The multi-colored line marks the location of the riverfront in that era. We cannot pinpoint exactly where Lincoln landed, but, working off ancillary information, can identify the most likely area, shown here in yellow-to-green shades. *Map and photos by Richard Campanella, 2004–09.*

When did Lincoln first set foot in New Orleans? Documents from the Collector of Levee Dues and the Wharfinger (such as the excerpt at **top left**), which recorded flatboat arrivals, do not survive for 1828–31. However, two local newspapers reported this information

in their "Maritime News" columns. When plotted from April 1, 1828, through March 31, 1829, (graph **below** represents the *Bee*'s reports; graph at **bottom** shows the *Argus* tally) we see that large numbers of flatboats arrived in spring 1828, but very few in early 1829. This, together with other evidence explained in this book, strongly suggests that Lincoln first set foot in New Orleans in mid-May 1828, and not in winter 1829 as many suggest. Further evidence indicates that Lincoln's vessel was among the fifteen flatboats from "the country" (green color in graphs) arriving around May 13–14, 1828. The *Bee* reported these fifteen arrivals on May 17 (**at right, marked by arrow**) with the words, "Quinze chalans de divers endroits, avec du produits du pays"—"fifteen flatboats from various places, with products from the country." The author contends that Lincoln's vessel was in that cohort. **Second from bottom right**: Once dismantled, flatboat lumber was sold and used for scrap purposes around town. Here, the author inspects old boards containing pairs of peg holes and mortise-and-tenon

joints typical of flatboat construction. These pieces may have originally served as a plank and girder on a flatboat-like vessel. They remain today in the attic of St. Mary Church (built in 1845) in the French Quarter. **Bottom right**: Shown here is a flatboat board found in an uptown house dating from 1850, on display in the Louisiana State Museum in Baton Rouge. Note the flat nail, peg holes, and white striping from where lathing was applied when mounted into the wall. *Analysis by Richard Campanella based on daily tally of "chalans" (flatboats), plus a small number of barges and keelboats, listed in the "Maritime" reports in the* Bee *and* Argus; *photos by Richard Campanella and Greg Lambousy of the Louisiana State Museum.*

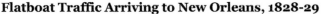

Flatboat Traffic Arriving to New Orleans, 1828-29

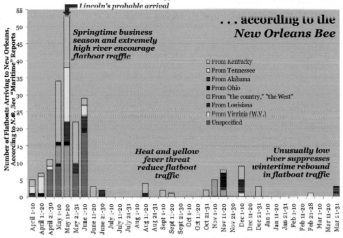

Lincoln's probable arrival

... according to the New Orleans Bee

Springtime business season and extremely high river encourage flatboat traffic

☐ From Kentucky
☐ From Tennessee
■ From Alabama
■ From Ohio
☐ From "the country," "the West"
■ From Louisiana
☐ From Virginia (W.V.)
▣ Unspecified

Heat and yellow fever threat reduce flatboat traffic

Unusually low river suppresses wintertime rebound in flatboat traffic

Number of Flatboats Arriving to New Orleans, According to N.O. *Bee* "Maritime" Reports

Arrival Dates, Spring 1828 through Winter 1829

Analysis by Richard Campanella based on "Maritime" reports in *New Orleans Bee*

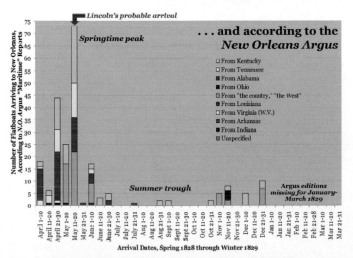

Lincoln's probable arrival

Springtime peak

... and according to the New Orleans Argus

☐ From Kentucky
☐ From Tennessee
■ From Alabama
■ From Ohio
■ From "the country," "the West"
■ From Louisiana
☐ From Virginia (W.V.)
▣ From Arkansas
☐ From Indiana
▣ Unspecified

Summer trough

Argus editions missing for January–March 1829

Number of Flatboats Arriving to New Orleans, According to N.O. *Argus* "Maritime" Reports

Arrival Dates, Spring 1828 through Winter 1829

Analysis by Richard Campanella based on "Maritime" reports in *New Orleans Argus*; special thanks to Naomi Homison for assistance.

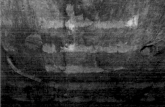

Two premier intersections in the New Orleans that Lincoln visited in 1828–31 remain busy today—and retain five of the eight corner structures from that era. **Above**: Chartres Street at the St. Louis intersection hosted some of the most important commercial houses of the city; Chartres itself was widely viewed as "the 'Broadway' of New Orleans." The city's number-one slave auctioning venue, Hewlett's Exchange, was located on the corner at left (now occupied by the Omni Royal Orleans Hotel). The Girod House (now home to the famous Napoleon House Bar) appears at center. At right is an edifice built around the same time and in the same style as Hewlett's, known today (erroneously) as Maspero's Slave Exchange. Visitors in the 1820s–30s made a point of seeing Chartres Street, particularly this bustling intersection, and oftentimes stepped into Hewlett's Exchange to witness the daily slave-auctioning ritual. "It seems to be the Soul of New Orleans," one visitor said of Hewlett's in 1836; "He [who] does not visit it cannot [claim to have] seen all of New Orleans." **Below**: The Royal Street intersection with Conti formed the heart of the banking and financial district. The three corner buildings seen here date from the 1790s–1820s. Benjamin Latrobe, architect of the pastel-yellow bank at right, also designed the U.S. Capitol, which was not completed until Lincoln's administration. *Photos by Richard Campanella, 2009; special thanks to Georgia Chadwick and Greg Lambousy for access to the roof of the Louisiana Supreme Court Building.*

Top left: Illustrations of Lincoln in New Orleans often depict streets lined with the city's famous iron-lace galleries. While simple narrow balconies of wrought iron abounded, ornate cast-iron galleries did not arrive until around 1850. Buildings along lower Conti Street, with arched openings on the ground floor and no galleries, would have been more typical of the inner-city streetscapes Lincoln saw. **Top center**: Hewlett's Exchange, where thousands of slaves changed owners, occupied this corner until a few years after Lincoln's second visit, when it was replaced with the grand St. Louis Exchange Hotel (1840), also the site of slave auctions. Damage inflicted by the 1915 hurricane led to its razing. The lot remained empty until 1960, when the present-day Omni Royal Orleans Hotel was erected in a style similar to the old St. Louis Exchange. Architects preserved a fragment of the 1840 structure: note the palimpsest of the word "EXCHANGE" above the man's head at right. **Top right**: An obscure legend posits that Lincoln boarded at this house on St. Ann Street. While this particular cottage did exist during his visit, and many such residences did take in boarders, no evidence corroborates the story. *Photos by Richard Campanella, 2008–09.*

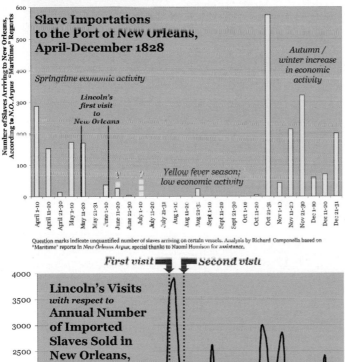

Slave Importations to the Port of New Orleans, April–December 1828

Number of Slaves Arriving to New Orleans, According to N.O. Argus "Maritime" Reports

Springtime economic activity

Lincoln's first visit to New Orleans

Autumn / winter increase in economic activity

Yellow fever season; low economic activity

Question marks indicate unquantified number of slaves arriving on certain vessels. Analysis by Richard Campanella based on "Maritime" reports in *New Orleans Argus*, special thanks to Naomi Humison for assistance.

First visit ▬ Second visit

Lincoln's Visits with respect to **Annual Number of Imported Slaves Sold in New Orleans, 1804–1860**

Left: In terms of season and era, Lincoln visited New Orleans when it engaged in the importation and trading of slaves with great vigor. New Orleans not only boasted the nation's busiest slave market, but its trafficking of human beings, wrote historian Frederic Bancroft, "had a peculiar dash: it rejoiced in its display and prosperity; it felt unashamed, almost proud." *Graphs by Richard Campanella based on "Maritime" reports in* New Orleans Argus, *and Notarial Archives records researched by Fogel and Engerman (1974) and tabulated by Jonathon B. Pritchett (1991).*

Graph based on Notarial Archives records researched by Fogel and Engerman (1974) and tabulated by Jonathon B. Pritchett (1991). Figures reflect only those slaves imported from out-of-state and sold in New Orleans, with records in the Notarial Archives.

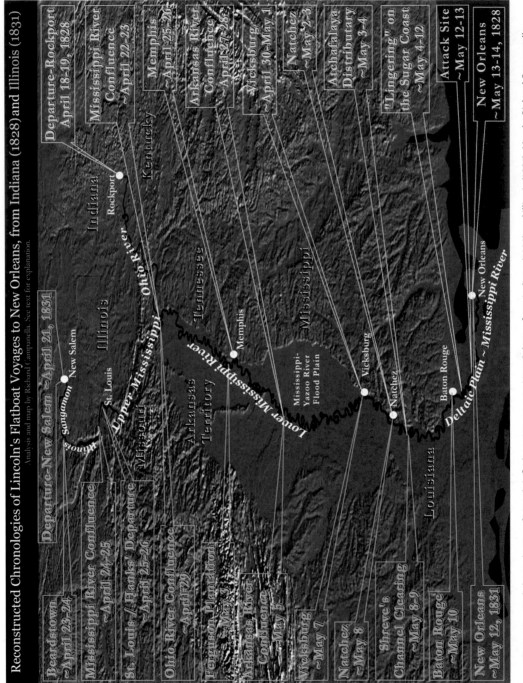

Reconstructed Chronologies of Lincoln's Flatboat Voyages to New Orleans, from Indiana (1828) and Illinois (1831)

Analysis and map by Richard Campanella. See text for explanation.

Departure-Rockport April 18-19, 1828

Mississippi River Confluence ~April 22-23

Memphis ~April 25-26

Arkansas River Confluence ~April 27-28

Vicksburg ~April 30-May 1

Natchez ~May 2-3

Atchafalaya Distributary ~May 3-4

"Lingering" on the Sugar Coast ~May 4-12

Attack Site ~May 12-13

New Orleans ~May 13-14, 1828

Departure-New Salem ~April 21, 1831

Beardstown ~April 23-24

Mississippi River Confluence ~April 24-25

St. Louis / Hanks' Departure ~April 25-26

Ohio River Confluence ~April 29

Ferguson Plantation ~May 3

Arkansas River Confluence ~May 5

Vicksburg ~May 7

Natchez ~May 8

Shreve's Channel Clearing ~May 8-9

Baton Rouge ~May 10

New Orleans ~May 12, 1831

Indiana

Illinois

Kentucky

Tennessee

Mississippi

Arkansas Territory

Missouri

Louisiana

New Salem

Sangamon

St. Louis

Memphis

Vicksburg

Natchez

Baton Rouge

New Orleans

Rockport

Mississippi-Yazoo River Flood Plain

Ohio River

Upper Mississippi

Lower Mississippi River

Deltaic Plain ~ Mississippi River

Reconstructed chronologies of Lincoln's flatboat journeys to New Orleans, from Indiana (1828) and Illinois (1831). *Map by Richard Campanella.*

Left: Vincennes, strategically located on the Wabash River, formed the most important settlement in Indiana during its French colonial and early American era. When Thomas Lincoln came here in 1817 to finalize his Pigeon Creek property purchase, the influence of the town's French-speaking Catholic population predominated in the streetscape. It may be seen to this day in "The Old French House" (**middle left**), built around 1806 in a style similar to that of Louisiana. It was at Vincennes that the Lincoln family, in March 1830, crossed the Wabash (**middle right**) and first set foot on Illinois soil. The migration occurred two years after Abraham's first flatboat trip to New Orleans and one year before the second. The state of Illinois commemorates the arrival of its most famous son with this monument (**bottom**). *Photos by Richard Campanella, 2009.*

IN THE LATE WINTER OF 1830 A FEW WEEKS AFTER HIS 21ST BIRTHDAY
ABRAHAM LINCOLN PASSED THIS WAY WITH HIS FATHERS FAMILY
ENTERING THE STATE OF ILLINOIS FOR THE FIRST TIME

PRESENTED TO THE STATE OF ILLINOIS BY THE ILLINOIS ORGANIZATION
DAUGHTERS OF THE AMERICAN REVOLUTION JUNE 14 1938

Above: In early spring 1830, the Lincolns settled on this bluff overlooking the Sangamon River, near Decatur in Illinois' Macon County. They built a cabin at the spot in the distant right marked with a boulder (plaque on boulder appears in **right**). Here, Lincoln and his cousin John Hanks launched their canoe to commence the first leg of their spring 1831 journey to New Orleans. The pair picked up Lincoln's stepbrother John D. Johnston outside Springfield and then found Denton Offutt, their boss, who was supposed to have prepared a flatboat for the crew to guide to New Orleans. Failing to acquire the vessel, Offutt instead hired the three men to build a flatboat. *Photos by Richard Campanella, 2009.*

FIRST HOME OF ABRAHAM LINCOLN IN ILLINOIS
IN MARCH, 1830 ABRAHAM LINCOLN CAME
FROM INDIANA WITH HIS FAMILY TO SETTLE
HERE IN MACON COUNTY AT A PLACE ON THE
NORTH SIDE OF THE SANGAMON RIVER TEN
MILES WESTERLY FROM DECATUR. THE
LINCOLNS BUILT A LOG CABIN AND
BROKE THE SOD TO RAISE A CROP OF
CORN. ON THIS SITE THE FAMILY ENDURED
THE FAMOUS TERRIBLE WINTER OF
DEEP SNOW UNTIL MARCH OF 1831 WHEN
ABRAHAM LEFT TO TAKE A FLATBOAT
DOWN THE MISSISSIPPI AND THOMAS
LINCOLN MOVED TO COLES COUNTY.

Above: This bank on the Sangamon River, seen here with swollen waters in May 2009, is within earshot of where Lincoln and colleagues built their rustic craft. The construction and launch were filled with mishaps, including, most influentially, getting hung up on the mill dam at New Salem (**left**, showing a detail of an idealized 1909 depiction of the incident, with the mill enumerated as "1," Lincoln's flatboat as "2," and the mill dam as "3"). Lincoln's ingenious method of freeing the vessel impressed many villagers. New Salem apparently impressed Lincoln, because, immediately after his return from New Orleans, he spent the next six years of his life there. *Photo by Richard Campanella, 2009; drawing by Arthur L. Brown, "New Salem: Home of Abraham Lincoln 1831 to 1837" (Peoria, Illinois: R. J. Onstott, 1909), courtesy Library of Congress.*

Bypassed by railroads and dependent on the unreliably navigable Sangamon, New Salem withered away and disappeared by 1840, three years after Lincoln departed for Springfield. A twentieth-century reconstruction of New Salem's shops, cabins, and the mill dam (**left**) that nearly destroyed Lincoln's flatboat, receives thousands of visitors annually. **Below**: In the halls of the Illinois State Capitol in Springfield hang murals of New Salem painted around 1885, including one depicting Lincoln's mill-dam incident. *Photos by Richard Campanella, 2009.*

Top: Once beyond the wending Sangamon in late April 1831, Lincoln, Offutt, Hanks, and Johnston floated down the wider, straighter Illinois River, through scenery just as bucolic today as during the flatboat era. After the Illinois joined the Mississippi River (**second from top**), the terrain on the eastern bank presented the most rugged topography (**second from bottom, left**) Lincoln had seen to date—including one limestone cliff famous for an indigenous painting of a winged monster first described by Marquette and Joliet in 1673. A modern mural of the beast recalls the "Legend of the Piasa" today (**second from bottom, middle**). Next came Lincoln's first view of Alton, Illinois, whose historic riverfront downtown (**second from bottom, right**) includes the Franklin House Hotel, where Lincoln would, many years later, debate Stephen A. Douglas. Finally, around April 25–26, the party arrived at St. Louis. Flatboats usually docked upriver from steamboats, making these areas near the foot of the Eads Bridge (**bottom**), north of the Gateway Arch, the likely spot where the Lincoln flatboat stopped to deposit crewmember John Hanks. His departure marked a significant moment in Lincoln's second trip to New Orleans—and ended up, in a strange way, twisting the way that trip would be interpreted by history. *Photos by Richard Campanella, 2009.*

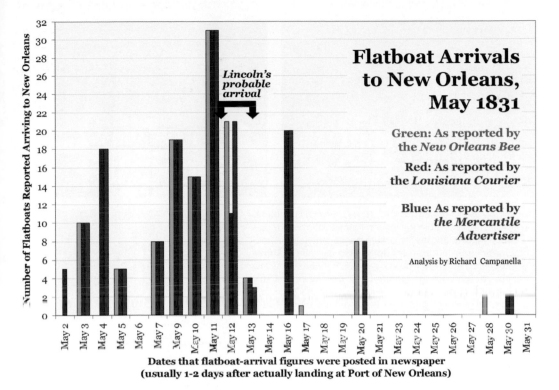

Flatboat Arrivals to New Orleans, May 1831

Number of Flatboats Reported Arriving to New Orleans

Lincoln's probable arrival

Green: As reported by the *New Orleans Bee*

Red: As reported by the *Louisiana Courier*

Blue: As reported by *the Mercantile Advertiser*

Analysis by Richard Campanella

**Dates that flatboat-arrival figures were posted in newspaper
(usually 1-2 days after actually landing at Port of New Orleans)**

Above: This graph plots Lincoln's probable arrival window against the frequency of other flatboats arriving to New Orleans, as recorded by three local newspapers. **Below left**: When Lincoln arrived in May 1831, New Orleans was abuzz about a new infrastructure technology, railroads. At this intersection of Girod and Commerce streets (now occupied by this edifice built later in the 1800s), a few blocks from his landing site, a special exhibit gave New Orleanians their first demonstration of a steam-powered locomotive. Two miles downriver, the first railroad west of the Appalachians, a horse-drawn line inaugurated only weeks earlier, connected the Old City with Lake Pontchartrain on what is now Elysian Fields Avenue. Internal improvements in general, and railroads in particular, would play a major role in Lincoln's future legal and political career. **Below right**: This photograph, taken in 1922, shows the same Pontchartrain Railroad line a decade before it was finally removed. *Photo and graph by Richard Campanella, 2009; 1922 photo courtesy Southeastern Architectural Archive, Tulane University.*

On a few occasions during 1831–61, New Orleans factored into Lincoln's life. In 1857, a black Illinoisan named John Shelby was imprisoned in New Orleans for lacking papers proving his freedom. Lincoln, working from his Springfield law office (**above left**), negotiated with New Orleans lawyer B. F. Jonas (whose law office, **above right**, operated in this St. Charles Avenue / Canal Street building, formerly Crescent Hall) to pay Shelby's fine and spare him enslavement. Shelby ranks as among the first African Americans (if not the first) ever freed by Abraham Lincoln. **Right**: At this spot in downtown Springfield, William de Fleurville ("Billy" Florville) worked as a barber and befriended his customer, Abraham Lincoln. Born in Haiti of mixed Franco-African ancestry, Florville spent some time in New Orleans in the 1820s, and like Shelby three decades later, found it a risky place for a free black man. In 1863, "Billy the Barber" wrote President Lincoln a warm letter of gratitude for issuing the Emancipation Proclamation. **Below left**: Stories of New Orleans' treatment of slaves circulated throughout the West. One, in April 1834, involved an incident of slave torturing in the Royal Street mansion of a wealthy Creole woman named Madame Lalaurie. Lurid news stories of the abuse reached a young Kentucky girl who would later marry Lincoln, and helped her form her anti-slavery position. The Lalaurie story is well known locally to this day; tourists taking French Quarter

"ghost tours" hear the (greatly embellished) story nightly. **Below right**: Three frontier symbols helped sell Lincoln the presidential candidate to skeptical voters: rail-splitting, the log cabin, and the flatboat. Thousands of supporters marched in front of Lincoln's home (distant left) in Springfield in August 1860, pulling along "a mammoth flatboat on wheels" in their procession. Seen here is a recreation of one of the log cabin floats from that campaign procession. Other rallies featured a float depicting "a flatboat on which smoke exuded from a stove pipe and roosters crowed in their coops." *Photos by Richard Campanella, 2009.*

Frontier symbolism figured heavily in Lincoln's 1860 campaign. **Left:** This broadside featured a color wood engraving of Lincoln poling a flatboat down the Mississippi, surrounded by a border of split-railed fences anchored by illustrations of log cabins and flatboats. Its caption read, "Abraham Lincoln has served an apprenticeship to flatboating, and may he yet guide the Ship of State with his own inherent honesty of purpose." One editorialist would have none of it. "Make Linkin Capting of the Ship of State," he wrote, exaggerating a rustic dialect, "and in less than a year she'll be without rudder, compass, or anchor. Who wants to see the Ship of State degenerate into a rickety old flat-boat?" **Right:** Composer Charles Grobe parlayed Lincoln's campaign symbols into song and dance. Lyrics to his 1860 "Lincoln Quick Step" (featuring a flatboat, rail-splitting, and a log cabin on the cover) went, "HONEST OLD ABE' has split many a rail / He is up to his work, and he'll surely, not fail, / He has guided his FLAT-BOAT thro' many a strait, / And watchful he'll prove at the HELM of the State." Courtesy Library of Congress.

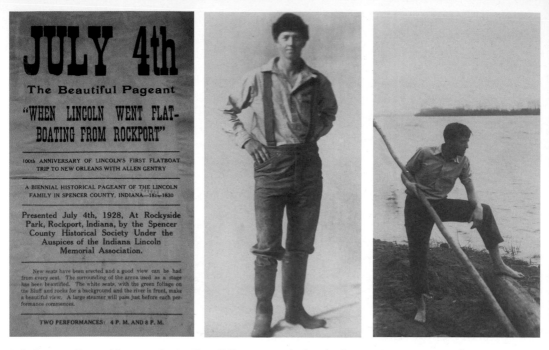

Left: Spencer County history enthusiast Bess V. Ehrmann worked tirelessly to commemorate Lincoln's Indiana roots. Her biennial riverfront pageant, "When Lincoln Went Flatboating from Rockport", ran on July 4 from 1926 through 1930 and involved five hundred actors, including descendants of Lincoln family, friends, and neighbors. Among them were Roby Gentry (**center**), who played his own great-grandfather Allen Gentry, and Roby's friend Millard Huffman (**right**, who portrayed Allen's friend Abraham Lincoln. *Spencer County Public Library, Box 7, Picture E-049, E-026, E-003, and E-048; special thanks to the library staff for access to these and other materials.*

Above: The 1928 pageant began with the reenactment (note film crew at right) of the Lincolns' 1816 ferry crossing of the Ohio River from Kentucky into Indiana. Later, the Gentry and Lincoln characters reenacted their launch for New Orleans using a flat-boat-like river barge (**right**). Rockport's biennial pageants are a thing of the past, but Lincoln's trip to New Orleans would inspire future reenactments in 1958 and 2008. *Spencer County Public Library, Box 7, Picture E-049, E-026, E-003, and E-048; special thanks to the library staff for access to these and other materials.*

To commemorate the sesquicentennial of Lincoln's birth, Duane Walter and the Rockport Jaycees in 1958 built a flatboat and reenacted the 1828 trip to New Orleans. Their boatbuilding skills falling short of their enthusiasm, crewmembers constructed a rather rickety ropa wall raft. The *Pride of Indiana*—propelled by two donated Evinrudes powerful enough only to keep the craft in the current. The journey commenced in July with a big parade on Main Street (**top left**—that's Robert Grose in the wheelbarrow, who also journeyed exactly fifty years later), then launched in front of a large crowd on the Rockport bluff (**top right**) and crossed the Ohio River to greet neighbors in Owensboro, Kentucky (**middle**). After various adventures—getting stuck on a sand bar, narrowly evading a deep-draft vessel, and receiving warm welcomes in Mississippi—the crew arrived safely in Louisiana (**bottom**), where they were treated to a meal by Louisiana Gov. Earl K. Long. *Photos courtesy crewmember Robert Grose and Spencer County Public Library; used with permission.*

Lincoln Movie Films to Be Taken in Orleans

New Orleans Times-Picayune
December 3, 1918

Henry Belmar, director of a moving picture corporation, is in New Orleans to make a movie of the entire life of Abraham Lincoln, with Laurel Love playing the role of Nancy Hanks.

"I have worked for seven years getting the ideas together for this picture," said Mr. Belmar at the St. Charles Hotel Monday, "and I figure that it will take fully nine months to finish the entire film.

"We came here because we understood that a studio was available, but were much disappointed when we found that this was not so. But we shall construct one, as all we need is the four walls of some large empty building. For the proper wooded effects to simulate Kentucky scenes we shall probably have to go to Alabama.

"Here in New Orleans we will show levee scenes, the French Market, and other places of interest at the time Lincoln came to this city, as he did, you know, on a flatboat with wares for sale. We intend to reproduce the Capitol at Washington with the approach to it as it was in Lincoln's day, the White House, Ford's Theater and many other historic structures. These will all be set up in New Orleans."

Top: A movie of Lincoln's life, to be filmed entirely in New Orleans in 1919, might have influenced popular perceptions of the former president's relationship with the city, but the plan never came to fruition. *Excerpt from* New Orleans Times-Picayune, *December 3, 1918, p. 7.* **Above scenes**: Flatboat scenes appear prominently in Robert E. Sherwood's *Abe Lincoln in Illinois* (1940), which depicts the 1831 trip down the Sangamon River and the mill-dam incident but not New Orleans proper. *Courtesy RKO Radio Pictures.*

Above: Illinois reenactors built and launched a flatboat into the Sangamon River on the 175th anniversary (1831–2006) of Lincoln's New Salem departure. Measuring thirty feet by twelve feet and constructed of tulip and poplar, the realistic vessel was designed according to nineteenth-century documents and built using wood-joining techniques of that era. **Right**: New Orleans slave-auction scenes lend themselves to dramatic depictions of the Lincoln story; theatrical productions have featured them at least since 1891 and probably earlier. The 2009 musical *Abe!*, by Lee Goldsmith and Roger Anderson, opens with this auction scene below a projected image of the dome of the St. Louis Hotel. A thoughtful Lincoln subsequently contemplates what he had just witnessed. *Scenes from* Abe! *used with permission; special thanks to Jeff Haller, Lee Goldsmith, and Roger Anderson; photos courtesy Lincoln's New Salem State Historic Site.*

Above: In 2008, the Spencer County Visitors Bureau and partner organizations sponsored a full-length reenactment of the 1828 New Orleans trip to mark the upcoming bicentennial of Lincoln's birth. Using a well-built sixty-foot flatboat made by local farmer and Washington lawyer Ron Drake (a descendent of flatboatmen affiliated with the Lincolns' Little Pigeon Primitive Baptist Church), the *Journey of Remembrance* launched with fanfare on September 9, 2008. Slow river currents, storms, seven foot swells, and the remnants of Hurricane Ike did not prevent the crew from making over twenty event-filled stops educating thousands of townsfolk about the significance of the voyage. The bearded gentleman seated by the model flatboat is Robert Grose, a veteran of the 1958 trip. He is the only person to complete two full-scale reenactments of Lincoln's voyage. **Below**: The *Journey of Remembrance* entered Louisiana waters in early October and arrived to New Orleans a few days later. The city, unfortunately, proved to be as aloof to the flatboat crew as it was to Lincoln 180 years earlier: officials at the Port of New Orleans ignored organizers' repeated requests to dock downtown, forcing them instead to tie up at a private Harvey Canal dock on the West Bank. Undaunted, the crew piled in a car and, like so many flatboatmen before them, enjoyed a night in the French Quarter. *Photos courtesy* Journey of Remembrance *crewmembers and the Spencer County Visitors Bureau; special thanks to Melissa Miller.*

While Illinois, Indiana, and Kentucky poured millions of dollars into commemorating Lincoln's bicentennial in 2009, Louisiana conducted a broad range of innovative activities with dedicated volunteers and a shoestring budget of $3,000. **Below**: Chaired by David Madden and themed "Lincoln Chose Louisiana" (a reference to the president's vision to use the state as a model for swift and non-vengeful reconstruction), the Louisiana Abraham Lincoln Bicentennial Commission held poetry readings, lectures, symposia, art showings, plays, exhibits, and a February 12 ceremony on the steps of the State Capitol in Baton Rouge (**right**). The newfound appreciation for Lincoln's Louisiana connection contrasts with the historical scorn once directed at the man. Lincoln place names, for example, remain rare in greater New Orleans; most—a few streets, a school, an abandoned park—are affiliated with the African American population. Perhaps the most famous is the now-defunct Lincoln Beach (**middle right**), the blacks-only lakefront recreational facility that operated during the last two decades of Jim Crow. Only its weathered entrance signs remain. The Lincoln toponym located closest to the area traversed by the flatboatman is Lincoln Court (**bottom right**), a tiny street in a working-class section of the Seventh Ward. It measures one block long, hosts a single street-fronting home, and suffered five feet of flooding during Hurricane Katrina. *Commission images courtesy Louisiana Abraham Lincoln Bicentennial Commission; photos by Richard Campanella, 2009.*

LINCOLN'S
UNIQUE LOUISIANA
CONNECTION

A LECTURE BY DAVID MADDEN

Left: Allen Gentry (1806–62), captain of the 1828 journey, rests under this leaning tombstone in Rockport Cemetery, Spencer County, Indiana. **Below left**: His assistant, greenhorn boatman Abraham Lincoln (1809–65), two years his junior, lies beneath this tomb in Springfield, Illinois. *Photos by Richard Campanella, 2008–09.*

Bottom left: The irrepressible John Hanks (1802–89), source of many colorful details (reliable and otherwise) about Lincoln's flatboat journeys, lies in this simple grave in the Hickory Point Township Cemetery in Decatur, Illinois. **Bottom right**: His distant cousin—fellow rail-splitter and flatboatman, seven years Hanks' junior and the target of much good-natured ribbing—is remembered today by the Lincoln Memorial in Washington, D.C. *Photos by Richard Campanella, 2009.*

Voyage of Life: Youth, second in a series of four paintings (*Birth*, *Youth*, *Manhood*, and *Old Age*) by Thomas Cole, 1840. The New Orleans flatboat journeys resonate in Lincoln's biography in part because they invoke many key elements of classic mythology: a youth mired in the most ordinary of circumstances receives a call to adventure and embarks on a long trip to an exotic destination. There he encounters danger, crosses a moral threshold, and returns enlightened—and eventually saves his people. The basic form of the monomyth recurs in countless stories, from Greek mythology and the Bible to classic literature and recent cinema. Lincoln throughout life reflected on the river years of his youth and drew lessons from them; the New Orleans trips in particular punctuated his four-year (1828–32) transformation from adolescence to manhood. Perhaps this explains why Lincoln owned a print of Cole's riverine painting *Youth*, and displayed it prominently in the dining room of his Springfield home. It hangs there to this day. *Image courtesy National Gallery of Art, 1971.16.2; special thanks to Marina Campanella.*

Lincoln and New Orleans, 1831–1865

~The Lalaurie incident~William de Fleurville~The John Shelby inci-
dent~Presidency and war~Fall of New Orleans~Emancipation~A spy in New
Orleans~The Louisiana experiment~Roudanez and Bertonneau~A dark and
indefinite shore~

Lincoln's direct interaction with New Orleans ceased in June 1831 and
would not resume until his presidency commenced in March 1861. On a
few occasions during those three intervening decades, however, the city
factored into Lincoln's life. This was typical: New Orleans' vast commercial hinterland, nourished by a relentless flow of waterborne traffic,
made the metropolis relevant to most inhabitants of the riverine West,
even if they never set foot in the city. Many items in Lincoln's New Salem store, for example, transshipped at New Orleans. Any time Lincoln
and his neighbors drank coffee, sweetened with sugar, enjoyed tropical
fruit, or partook of numerous other imports, they became consumers in
the greater New Orleans economic system. News, too, diffused upriver
from the Crescent City (a nickname coined in a popular 1835 publication,
which subsequently spread nationwide[1]), and, given the city's reputation
for the lascivious, the shocking, and the wicked, certain stories traveled as
fast as the swiftest steamboat.

One such news item may have brought New Orleans' sordid character—and its brand of human enslavement—directly into the Lincoln par-
lor. One evening in April 1834, a blaze damaged a French Quarter mansion, revealing that owner Madame Delphine Lalaurie had been torturing
her live-in slaves in the attic. A riot ensued among outraged neighbors on
Royal Street. Sensationalized newspaper articles about the incident propelled the story up the Mississippi and Ohio rivers in subsequent weeks,
landing it in the hands of, among many others, two young ladies in the
Todd family of Lexington, Kentucky. The teenagers "shivered with hor-
ror" over the lurid details reported in the *New Orleans Bee*:[2]

---

1. The publication was Joseph Holt Ingraham's, *The South-West by a Yankee* (New York,
1835), 1:91. See "The Lexicon of Place: Deconstructing New Orleans' Names, Nick-
names, and Slogans," in Richard Campanella, *Bienville's Dilemma: A Historical Geography
of New Orleans* (Lafayette: University of Louisiana Press, 2008), 279–287.
2. Katherine Helm, *The True Story of Mary, Wife of Lincoln, Containing the Recollection of Mary Lincoln's Sister Emilie, Extracts from Her War-Time Diary, Numerous Letters*

> [S]laves . . . horribly mutilated, were seen suspended by the
> neck, with their limbs apparently stretched and torn from one
> extremity to the other. Language is powerless . . . to give a
> proper conception of the horror. . . . These slaves were the
> property of the demon, in the shape of a woman. . . .[3]

"We were horrified and talked of nothing else for days," remembered one of the Kentucky girls; "If one such case could happen, it damned the whole institution [of slavery]." The other girl, her niece and best friend Mary, would later marry Abraham Lincoln. We do not know if Mary Todd Lincoln shared the gruesome story and its New Orleans connection with her husband, but we do know that the Lalaurie story directly inspired Mary to question the morality of the institution of slavery and her family's affiliation with it. It also moved Mary to aid her beloved "Mammy" in assisting runaways.[4] Mary Todd Lincoln would come to abhor slavery and push her husband to take increasingly radical stances against it. In a larger sense, the Lalaurie story illustrates how New Orleans unintentionally produced and exported countless narratives about the brutality of human bondage to an American nation growing increasingly uncomfortable with the whole beastly business. To this day, the story of Madame Lalaurie and her tortured slaves remains a mainstay of local history, told to scores of visitors taking nightly "ghost tours" of the French Quarter.

New Orleans factored into Mary Todd's life economically as well. Her father interacted commercially with the city regularly, via flatboat and steamboat, helping elevate his family's status to that of the Lexington elite. He regularly brought back embroidered French swisses, muslins, lace, dolls, and other luxury items for Mary, who spoke French fluently and kept abreast of the latest political news. According to one (somewhat romanticized) recollection by her niece Katherine Helm, Mary sported elegant New Orleans fashions when she first met Abraham.[5]

•

If Mary thought Abraham well-groomed, she might have thanked his

and Other Documents Now First Published (New York and London: Harper and Brothers Publishers, 1928), 38–40.

   3. *New Orleans Bee*, April 11, 1834, p. 2, c. 1.
   4. Helm, *Story of Mary*, 38–40.
   5. Ibid., 30, 44–45, 73–74. The Todd family would later remember Louisiana as where one of their own, Confederate Lt. Alexander H. Todd (Mary's half-brother) met his fate, in fighting near Baton Rouge.

barber, William "Billy" Florville. Born of mixed Franco-African ancestry at Cape Haytien in Haiti around 1806, the teenaged William de Fleurville escaped a revolution in 1821–22 and made his way to Baltimore with his godmother. There, while at St. Mary's Convent, he apprenticed in barbering. After his godmother died, he decided, for reasons unclear, to leave for New Orleans. We do not know the timing or circumstances of his New Orleans experience, but we do know it proved to be a bad decision. New Orleans in the late 1820s grew increasingly hostile to free people of color, curtailing their rights, proscribing their moving into the city, and expelling those recently arrived. Fearing kidnapping and enslavement, Fleurville departed for St. Louis and found his way up the Illinois and Sangamon rivers in 1831. A county history picks up the story from there:

> While approaching the village of New Salem, he overtook a tall man wearing a red flannel shirt, and carrying an axe on his shoulder. They fell into a conversation, and walked to a little grocery store together. The tall man was Abraham Lincoln, who soon learned that the stranger was a barber out of money. Mr. Lincoln took him to his boarding house, and told the people his business and situation. That opened the way for an evening's work among the boarders. . . .[6]

Lincoln later convinced Fleurville—who anglicized his name to Florville—to settle in Springfield. There he married, raised a family, and prospered as the haircutter for hundreds of Springfield men and children, including Lincoln, who knew him endearingly as "Billy the Barber." It was Florville who groomed Lincoln's iconic mustacheless beard prior to his departure for the White House. We can only imagine the conversations the future president shared with his bilingual, Catholic, Franco-African-Haitian-American friend—conversations about the Caribbean, the Mississippi, New Orleans, slavery—at the barber shop on East Adams Street. They seem to have been of substance, and the foundation of a genuine friendship, because in late 1863, Florville wrote Lincoln a warm letter of gratitude for the emancipation that was steadily sweeping the South. It read in part,

> I . . . thought it might not be improper for one so humble in life and occupation, to address the President of the United States—

6. *History of Sangamon County, Illinois, Together with Sketches of its Cities, Villages, and Townships* (Chicago: Inter-state Publishing Company, 1881), 736–737.

Yet, I do so, feeling that if it is received by you . . . it will be read with pleasure as a communication from Billy the Barber. . . .

I and my people feel greatful to you for . . . your Proclamation. . . . The Shackels have fallen, and Bondmen have become freeman to Some extent already. . . . And I hope ere long, it may be universal in all the Slave States. That your Authority May Soon extend over them all, to all the oppressed, releiving [*sic*] them from their Bondage, and cruel Masters; Who make them work, and fight, against the Goverment [*sic*]. . . . May God grant you health, and Strength, and wisdom . . . your [obedient] Servant, William Florville the Barber[7]

In all likelihood Lincoln first learned of Haiti and its conditions from Florville when the two men first met in 1831. Three decades later, President Lincoln officially established diplomatic relations with that independent Caribbean nation.[8]

•

Florville was one of seven black barbers in Springfield, which had an African American population of twenty-seven families in 1850. News spread rapidly within that tight-knit community about a member who committed the same mistake Florville once made: traveling to New Orleans. The story began some years earlier, when a white Kentuckian named Hinkle (or Henkle) moved into Illinois, whereupon he freed his accompanying slaves. Among them were a woman named Polly Mack and her son, John Shelby. In late 1856, Shelby, by then a young man, ventured to St. Louis and took a deckhand job aboard a Mississippi steamboat bound for New Orleans. Upon arriving at the Crescent City, Shelby, like Lincoln or any other young chap, eagerly stepped ashore to explore the enticing metrop-

7. William Florville to Abraham Lincoln, December 27, 1863, Abraham Lincoln Papers at the Library of Congress, Washington, D.C. (hereafter cited as Lincoln Papers).

8. In this case, however, Lincoln failed to demonstrate the wisdom Florville would later wish him. Lincoln's recognition of Haiti aimed to enable an uncharacteristically impractical scheme: to deport freed slaves to L'Ile à Vache, based on the notion that free blacks would be better off among their own. Despite the abysmal failure of the L'Ile à Vache project, Lincoln obsessively dabbled in deportation plans—to Panama, to the Caribbean, to Liberia—up to the last days of his life. One of the men who stonewalled the Commander in Chief's attempts to further these schemes was none other than Lincoln's commanding office in the occupation of New Orleans, Benjamin Butler. James D. Lockett, "Abraham Lincoln and Colonization: An Episode That Ends in Tragedy at L'Ile à Vache, Haiti, 1863–1864," *Journal of Black Studies* 21, no. 4 (June 1991): 428–444.

olis. What Shelby did not realize was that New Orleans, finding itself increasingly on the defensive regarding slavery, aggressively limited the rights of free blacks in this era. The establishment viewed out-of-state free black males in particular as potential subversives whose very existence threatened the institution. A contemporaneous *Picayune* editorial, for example, angrily described "free negroes" as an "evil," a "plague and a pest" responsible for "mischief to the slave population," and recommended deporting them to Liberia and cracking down on further emancipations.[9] Authorities generally felt the same way, and mandated that unsupervised blacks without papers be jailed.

Shelby, who neglected to procure a pass from his captain before setting out into the streets, suffered exactly that fate at the hands of the police. The imprisoned youth was later "brought out[,] tried, [and] fined," but because his steamboat by then had left, he had no way to pay his penalty.[10] Shelby was "thrown [back] into prison," and,

> as no one was especially interested in him, he was forgotten. After a certain length of time, established by law, he would inevitably have been sold into slavery to defray prison expenses.[11]

Shelby somehow established contact with a sympathetic young Springfield-raised New Orleans attorney named Benjamin F. Jonas, and suggested to him that another lawyer back home, by the name of Abraham Lincoln, might adopt his case and arrange for his liberation. Jonas recognized the name: Lincoln was a close friend of his father Abraham Jonas, a leading citizen of Springfield and one of the first Jewish settlers in the region. Word was sent upriver to Shelby's mother and to Lincoln. A later history narrated Lincoln's response:

> Mr. Lincoln was very much moved, and requested [his law partner] Mr. Herndon to . . . inquire of Governor Bissell if there was not something that he could do to obtain possession of the negro. Mr. Herndon . . . returned with the report that the Governor regretted to say that he had no legal or constitutional right to [act]. Mr. Lincoln rose to his feet in great excite-

9. "Freed Negroes," *Daily Picayune* (New Orleans), March 8, 1856, p. 3, c. 2.

10. Josiah Gilbert Holland, *Life of Abraham Lincoln* (Springfield, MA: Gurdon Bill, 1866), 127–128.

11. Annie E. Jonas to William H. Herndon, October 28, 1866, in ed. Douglas L. Wilson and Rodney O. Davis, *Herndon's Informants: Letters, Interviews, and Statements About Abraham Lincoln* (Urbana and Chicago: University of Illinois Press, 1998), 379–380.

ment, and exclaimed, "By the Almighty, I'll have that negro back soon, or I'll have a twenty years' agitation in Illinois, until the Governor *does* have a legal and constitutional right to do something. . . ."[12]

Lacking further recourse and all too aware that New Orleans had the law on its side, Lincoln and Herndon drafted $69.30 out of the Metropolitan Bank of New York and, on May 27, sent the funds from their law office at South 6th and East Adams streets in Springfield to Benjamin Jonas at his 3 St. Charles Street law office in New Orleans. Jonas paid the fine and, by early June, won Shelby's release and returned him safely to Springfield. "[S]hould he come south again," Jonas warned Lincoln, "be sure [he has] his papers with him—and he must also be careful not to be away from the boat at night—without a pass [from] the captain. . . ."[13]

We may justly view John Shelby as among the first African Americans (if not *the* first) ever freed by Abraham Lincoln—from a New Orleans imprisonment that would have led to forced labor, and quite possibly to permanent enslavement. What makes the case even more remarkable is the situation in which the Jonases would find themselves when war broke out in 1861. The Illinois-based Jonas family had many relatives in New Orleans, some of whom secretly informed Abraham Jonas of Confederate activities, who in turn passed the intelligence directly to President Lincoln.[14] Others, however, sided with the Confederacy—including, paradoxically, the same Benjamin Jonas who helped liberate Shelby in 1857. Despite the divided loyalties, President Lincoln maintained his affection for the Jonas family, unionists and rebels alike; Benjamin once recalled that "Mr. Lincoln always asked after us when he saw any one from New Orleans during the war." The president even granted a three-week parole to Benjamin's imprisoned Confederate brother Charles so he could visit his dying father (and Lincoln's longtime friend and informant), Abraham Jonas. Benjamin F. Jonas would later serve as Senator for the State of Louisiana.[15]

Lincoln's rise from regional to national prominence during the 1860 presidential campaign introduced his biographical details into popular culture for the first time. The publication of Lincoln's brief autobiography

---

12. Holland, *Life of Abraham Lincoln*, 127–128 (emphasis added).
13. B. F. Jonas to Abraham Lincoln, June 4, 1857, Lincoln Papers.
14. Abraham Jonas to Abraham Lincoln, December 30, 1860, Lincoln Papers.
15. Isaac Markens, *Abraham Lincoln and the Jews* (New York: Isaac Markens, 1909), 19–21.

in June 1860, followed by newspaper articles reporting the details therein, informed many New Orleanians for the first time about their least-favorite candidate's surprising connection to their city.

That connection would intensify over the next five years.

•

Abraham Lincoln's election to the presidency in November 1860 triggered the secession of seven Southern states, of which Louisiana (on January 26, 1861) numbered sixth. Each eventually ratified the Confederate constitution; Louisiana did so after a two-month period of proclaimed sovereignty, complete with its own national flag. A season of mounting tension followed, in which the United States of America denied the existence of the Confederate States of America even as the latter boldly seized U.S. assets, formed a government, and organized a military. All-out conflict lay but one violent act away. "In *your* hands, my dissatisfied fellow countrymen, and not in *mine*," warned a solemn President Lincoln in his March 4 inaugural address, "is the momentous issue of civil war."[16]

One night the following month, Lincoln dreamed strangely. He felt "a vague sense of floating—floating away on some vast and indistinct expanse toward an unknown shore."[17] The recurring vision, similar to the sensation experienced by flatboatmen navigating through darkness or mist, never failed to arrest him.

The next day brought stunning news. Confederate Brig. Gen. Pierre Gustave Toutant Beauregard—a white Creole from the New Orleans area—had bombarded Fort Sumter in Charleston Harbor, one of only two U.S. military garrisons that resisted Confederate seizure. Here was the first strike everyone had long anticipated. Four additional states seceded in the following weeks, as Southerners *en masse* took up arms for the rebellion—some in support of states' rights or to preserve slavery, others to defend their homeland, and the rest simply because they were forced to. President Lincoln responded with equal determination to suppress the rebellion and recruited thousands of Northerners to fight for that cause.

16. Abraham Lincoln, "First Inaugural Address—Final Text," March 4, 1861, in *The Collected Works of Abraham Lincoln*, ed. Roy P. Basler (New Brunswick, NJ: Rutgers University Press, 1953), 4:271 (emphasis in original).

17. As recollected by Frederick W. Seward, in Don E. Fehrenbacher and Virginia Fehrenbacher, *Recollected Words of Abraham Lincoln* (Stanford, CA: Stanford University Press, 1996), 398. This particular recollection of the dream dates to April 14, 1865, but Lincoln specifically explained that he had the same dream numerous times throughout his presidency.

In time, conscription would replace volunteerism, creating the two largest militaries on earth.

Lincoln's goal to preserve the Union at all costs inspired a strategy of seeking and battling armed rebels, more so than capturing population centers. The Confederacy, in Lincoln's mind, did not exist as a government, and the South held no status as a nation; the *rebellion* was the enemy. Riverine and railroad cities, however, were the exceptions. They strategically controlled critical supply lines and could not remain in rebel hands. The Mississippi River ranked as the premier Western supply line and thus the top Union priority. New Orleans, gatekeeper of the lower Mississippi, became the priority's priority.

Secession defied federal authority most flagrantly at lucrative Southern ports. From Washington's perspective, these municipalities were effectively stealing U.S. tax revenue generated by enormous shipments of cotton, tobacco, sugar, rice, and other cargo. Worse yet, those revenues now flowed into Confederate munitions. Secession emboldened the insurgents to attack and seize vessels deemed threatening to Confederate interests, even as they sailed in waters that the United States quite pointedly viewed to be in its domain. Secession also left Southern ports in a position to interact with foreign agents in a manner that further affronted U.S. authority. With these crises in mind, Lincoln, one week after Fort Sumter, officially blocked all Southern ports.[18] The blockade would form a critical component of Gen. Winfield Scott's proposed Anaconda Plan: to encircle and strangle the Confederacy by controlling its coastal and riverine periphery.

The blockade proclamation, however, meant more on paper than in reality. So thinly was the U.S. Navy dispersed along Southern coasts that its vessels either failed to barricade ships or succumbed to Confederate forces. London war correspondent William Howard Russell, for example, had no problem traveling "coastwise" one month after Fort Sumter (and six weeks after meeting personally with President Lincoln). Tensions, however, were apparent as Russell steamed from Mobile into New Orleans: rumors flew about armed U.S. cruisers threatening coastal positions; armed rebels in uniform eyed the boat as it steamed past Biloxi-area beaches; some military men on board nearly came to blows over politics. Russell also noted "a thin, fiery-eyed little woman . . . express[ing] a fervid desire for bits of 'Old Abe'—his ear, his hair; [either] for the purpose of eating or as curi-

18. Abraham Lincoln, "Proclamation of a Blockade," April 19, 1861, in *Collected Works*, 4:338–339.

ous relics. . . ."[19] Upon arriving in New Orleans, Russell found life in the streets throbbing with "a whirl of secession and politics:"

> The Confederate flag was flying from the public buildings and from many private houses. Military companies paraded through the streets, and a large proportion of men were in uniform . . .
> The streets are full of Turcos, Zouaves, Chasseurs [French infantry units and other foreign soldiers who wore distinctive uniforms]; walls are covered with placards of volunteer companies; there are Pickwick rifles, La Fayette, Beauregard, MacMahon guards, Irish, German, Italian and Spanish and native volunteers. . . . Tailors are busy night and day making uniforms. . . .

Sentiment behind closed doors was another matter. Many members of the merchant and planter class, particularly Anglo-Americans with Northern ties, remained skeptical of secession or privately loyal to the Union. Poor whites and immigrants suspected they would be the ones shedding the blood. Free people of color feared secession would further erode their dwindling rights, and slaves could only guess how their fate might change. Only the most optimistic viewed the new order as a peaceful ending to the ever-escalating sectional discord:

> There are some who maintain there will be no war after all. . . . No one imagines the South will ever go back to the Union voluntarily, or that the North has power to thrust it back at the point of the bayonet.[20]

Shortly thereafter, news arrived at New Orleans that federal troops had "invaded" Virginia. The subsequent battle at Manassas produced a surprise Confederate victory (led again by Brig. Gen. Beauregard), shocking the North, inspiring the South, and motivating both sides to conscript hundreds of thousands of men to prepare for a long and violent conflict.

With every passing day in 1861–2, more and more New Orleanians marched off to the front. Military preparations dominated the cityscape. Fewer steamboats arrived from upriver, bearing less cargo. Fewer sailing ships arrived from the sea. Commodity trading slackened, and slave commerce froze. A "free market" of foodstuffs donated by regional planters

19. William Howard Russell, *My Diary North and South* (Boston and New York, 1863), 230–31.
20. Ibid., 230–31.

kept city dwellers fed, but with steadily diminishing quantity and quality.[21] New Orleanians who had utterly ignored the nameless flatboatman strolling their streets thirty years earlier, now shook their fists at the hated new president of the enemy nation to the north.

Lincoln acted on his blockade by divvying up Southern coasts and deploying naval squadrons to each section. New Orleans fell within the charge of the West Gulf Blockading Squadron, commanded by Capt. David Glasgow Farragut. "[G]et into New Orleans if you can," Lincoln instructed his military, "and the backbone of the rebellion will be broken."[22] Farragut's four ships, escorted by nearly two score gun- and mortar-boats, convened in the Gulf of Mexico in the spring of 1862. Their presence scared off most commercial traffic.

Preparations in and around New Orleans, meanwhile, floundered. An inquiry later conducted by the Confederate States of America revealed that the region "was almost entirely defenceless," unable to "make an hour's fight." Soldiers were "badly armed and had very little ammunition." "A line of entrenchments around the city itself had been planned [and] commenced [but lay] entirely unfinished, not a gun was mounted, a magazine built, nor a platform laid." The city relied almost entirely on its regional fortification system, whose citadels dated to post–War of 1812 or colonial times. Their general condition: "dilapidated . . . crumbling . . . [with] neither shot nor shell" for their guns, which were mounted on carriages that were "old[,] defective from long exposure [and] so decayed that [one] could insert a pen-knife with ease into the wood." Of absolute criticality were forts St. Philip and Jackson, positioned on either side of the lowermost Mississippi River in Plaquemines Parish. The dual bastions "were in a better state of preparation than the other works, but still sadly deficient. . . ." Perhaps the most innovative defense constituted a boom of cypress-log rafts and de-masted schooners blocking the lower Mississippi River, strung together by cables and chains and held in place by anchors. Designed to impede Union vessels in direct line of cannon fire from the forts, the boom itself proved a challenge, as the shifting sands of the deep river jostled its anchorages, and accumulating flotsam stressed the cables

21. Julia LeGrand, *The Journal of Julia LeGrand: New Orleans—1862–1863*, ed. Kate Mason Rowland and Mrs. Morris L. Croxall (Richmond, VA: Everett Waddey Company, 1911), 37–38.

22. As recollected by Benjamin F. Butler, in *Reminiscences of Abraham Lincoln by Distinguished Men of His Time*, ed. Allen Thorndike Rice (New York: North American Review, 1889), 142. Lincoln later added to the above directive, "but don't interfere with the slavery question."

and chains.[23] Upriver from the boom lingered a small but fierce flotilla of Confederate steamers and ironclads.

•

On April 16, Farragut's fleet entered the mouth of the Mississippi River. Two days later it arrived within mortar range of the forts. Each side proceeded to lob shells at the other, with occasional strikes but little consequence. Farragut grew impatient and prepared to escalate. He could not attempt to run the gauntlet, however, without first severing the boom. At 10 p.m. on the drizzly moonless night of April 20, he deployed two explosives-laden gunboats toward the floating iron-and-wood hulk. Amid drifting rafts set ablaze by upstream Confederates, specialists boarded the tangled apparatus and, with surprising ease, unraveled its cables and chains. Being only as strong as its weakest link, the severed boom swung open with the river's current [24] Now only two forts and two dozen gunboats separated Lincoln's warships from Confederate New Orleans.

In the wee hours of April 24, the Union fleet fired up its engines, weighed anchor, and ploughed into the darkness. Confederates discovered the advance and responded with thunderous fire. Broadside cannons roared in return. Exploding shells turned night into day, clouded by the suffocating smoke and coal exhaust enveloping every vessel. Blazing rafts released upstream drifted treacherously among maneuvering warships. "[T]he sublimity of the scene can never be exceeded," Maj. Gen. Benjamin F. Butler later reported to Lincoln. Nor could the confusion and uncertainty, amid darkness, smoke, toppled masts, tangled rigging, damaged hulls, and mounting casualties.

Then, as dawn approached, the lethal cacophony subsided, and the armadas began to disassociate. Fourteen of the seventeen Union vessels pulled away upriver, leaving their stunned and weary foes behind in swampy isolation. "Of the gallantry, courage, and conduct of this heroic action, unprecedented in naval warfare," wrote Butler of the Union's effort, "too much cannot be said."[25] The gauntlet had been run. After re-

23. War Department, Confederate States of America, *Proceedings of the Court of Inquiry Relative to the Fall of New Orleans* (Richmond, VA: R. M. Smith, 1864), 10–12, 20-22.

24. Chester G. Hearn, *The Capture of New Orleans 1862* (Baton Rouge and London: Louisiana State University Press, 1995), 201.

25. Report of Maj. Gen. Benjamin F. Butler, Headquarters-Department of the Gulf, April 29, 1862, United States War Department, *The War of the Rebellion: A Compilation of the Official Records of the Union and Confederate Armies*, Series 1 (Washington, D.C.: Government Printing Office, 1882), 6:503–505.

grouping in the safety of the Quarantine Station to tend to wounds and repairs, the U.S. Navy advanced to Confederate New Orleans.[26]

Telegrams alerted city authorities of the terrible news. Bells tolled to rouse citizens. Yet no vast militia took positions along the riverfront, no massive fortifications readied their artillery, and no great fleet of iron-clads raced downriver. Having invested most of their soldiers and fire-power at forts Jackson and St. Philip, Confederate commanders decided to evacuate the remainder northward to fight another day. Aside from a brief exchange of fire at Chalmette and a steady stream of burning cotton bales and smoldering wreckage drifting downriver, the U.S. Navy advanced into Confederate Louisiana largely unmolested. According to one Union eyewitness, a scant few white civilians came out on the levee and glared silently at the fleet. Blacks, on the other hand, were more numerous, "more communicative and more friendly." When out of their master's sight, the slaves

> gave enthusiastic evidence of good will, dancing at us, waving hats or branches and shouting welcome. One old mauma . . . capered vigorously on the levee, screaming, "Bress de Lawd! I knows dat ar flag. I knew it would come. Praise de Lawd!"[27]

They were the first enslaved Louisianans to see emancipation—*de facto*, if not quite yet *de jure*—on the horizon.

As the fleet approached New Orleans, sailors witnessed an apocalypse of flame and smoke, the handiwork of rebels determined to deprive the enemy of spoils by igniting wharves, cargo, and watercraft. The city it-self remained intact, but given the belligerent mob and uncooperative au-thorities confronting the federals upon landing, that situation could have changed in a flash. Tensions were such during the next five days that a single unexpected discharge of arms could have set off a full-scale metro-politan obliteration. Beyond the bravado, however, were poverty, hunger, and desperation. "The town is fairly and squarely on the point of starva-tion," wrote one Union eyewitness of the "poor Germans, poorer French Creoles and ragged slaves. . . . No one denies now that our blockage has been effective. . . ."[28] Those conditions forced reluctant city authorities finally to succumb peacefully, and on May 1, 1862, federal troops entered

---

26. Hearn, *Capture of New Orleans 1862*, 209–236.
27. John William De Forest, *A Volunteer's Adventures: A Union Captain's Record of the Civil War*, ed. James H. Croushore (New Haven, CT: Yale University Press, 1946), 17.
28. Ibid., 21.

en masse. One week later, Major General Butler wrote the flatboatman-turned-president, "New Orleans . . . is at your command."[29]

"Poor New Orleans! What has become of all your promised greatness!" lamented one New Orleanian in her journal; "Never can I forget the day that the alarm bell rang."[30] Shockwaves reverberated nationwide: the sudden loss of their largest city and most lucrative region confounded Southerners, who until then thrilled to a steady stream of military successes. It gave President Lincoln and Northerners, on the other hand, a much-needed dose of encouraging news. Subsequent battles on other fronts soon diverted attention, but Lincoln continued to contemplate New Orleans, because the city presented him with an array of enormous policy decisions. This was, after all, the first major section of the rebellious South to return to federal control; policies enacted here for rejoining the Union might establish a model to be refined and replicated elsewhere. New Orleans' size and importance, its substantial population of educated free blacks, and its numerous Union sympathizers (some of them forming organizations such as the Pioneer Lincoln Club, which audaciously applauded the U.S. commander in chief) made the city and region that much more attractive as a laboratory for what would later be termed "re-construction."[31] So too did its extensive international affiliations: "If Louisiana could be made a showcase of reconstruction," wrote historian David Herbert Donald, "Europeans would receive an inescapable signal of the inevitable collapse of the Confederacy."[32] At stake in the Louisiana experiment were fundamental questions regarding slavery, freedom, suffrage, national allegiance, the fate of former rebels, and the reestablishment of state government and congressional representation.

•

Two schools formed on reconstruction. One side favored leniency to Louisiana and a "soft" re-assimilation into the Union, even if it meant the continued domination of the planter elite and the subordination of blacks. Others sought to punish the rebels via emancipation, full black suffrage, and the exclusion of former Confederates from state government. Up for grabs was not only the future of Louisiana society and potentially other

29. Benjamin F. Butler to Abraham Lincoln, May 8, 1862, Lincoln Papers.
30. LeGrand, *Journal of Julia LeGrand*, 40.
31. "Meeting of the Pioneer Lincoln Club," *Daily True Delta* (New Orleans), February 23, 1864, p. 1, c. 5.
32. David Herbert Donald, *Lincoln* (New York: Simon & Schuster, 1995), 484–485.

Southern states, but valuable political turf for warring Democrat and Republican partisans, each with their own spectrum of conservatives, moderates, and radicals. White New Orleans society, for its part, exhibited similar schisms. Merchants and Union sympathizers advocated for conciliation and tolerated black rights, while hard-core secessionists insisted on vindicating wounded Southern honor and rejecting any level of black equality in the new racial order. Free men of color, meanwhile, organized among themselves to seize this long-awaited opportunity toward gaining full civil rights. Their newspaper, *L'Union*, founded in 1862 and published in French at the corner of Chartres and St. Louis (ironically near the old Hewlett's Exchange) kept their people informed.

President Lincoln initially assumed a moderate Republican stance in the debate, reflecting his clearly stated prioritization for Union preservation above all. His position frustrated hard-liners who sought punitive action. One wealthy pro-Union New Orleans planter complained of Lincoln's indecision and "vacillating policy" on reconstruction; Lincoln personally responded by taking exception to the suggestion that he had "no policy," and patiently explained that he had been advocating for national reconciliation ever since his inauguration. "Broken eggs cannot be mended," wrote Lincoln, "Louisiana has nothing to do now but to take her place in the Union. . . ."[33] Increasingly, however, Lincoln fretted that his desire for reconciliation might fast-track Louisiana toward rejoining the Union without outlawing slavery, thus setting a worrisome precedent.

When Northern popular support wavered for the increasingly bloody toll required for Union-saving, Lincoln reconsidered his priorities. Southern military successes, he realized, derived in part from the Confederacy's reliance on four million slaves to produce food and income-generating commodities. The North enjoyed no such advantage: every man in uniform was one out of economic production. Emancipating slaves, then, would handicap the South economically and militarily, while affronting its social order. Emancipation might also deliver to Northern lines thousands of freedmen to take up arms against their former masters. In a larger sense, emancipation would redefine a conflict currently being fought over political abstractions (states' rights and secession) into a struggle for freedom, a more compelling cause for many Northerners growing disgusted with both the South and the war. Freeing slaves, the commander in chief

33. Abraham Lincoln to August Belmont, July 31, 1862, in *Collected Works*, 5:350–351. This communication with Belmont responds to a letter written to Lincoln by an unnamed New Orleanian; Belmont himself was a wealthy New York financier.

appreciated, now melded conveniently with his ultimate goal of preserving the Union.

Lincoln worked on his emancipation plan secretly during the summer of 1862. He withheld announcing the bombshell, waiting for a Union military victory that would boost a sense of momentum and inevitability, or at least make the move seem less like an act of desperation. None came. Then, one night in mid-September, Lincoln dreamed that strange riverine vision again, of sailing swiftly in a strange vessel toward an indefinite shore—the same dream he had the night before Fort Sumter.[34] Once again, he learned shortly thereafter of dramatic news: his troops had successfully held off major Confederate advances in Maryland, in a terribly costly strategic victory that ranks today as the bloodiest day in American military history. The Battle of Antietam provided just enough impetus for Lincoln to announce his own stunning news. On September 22, 1862, he issued the Emancipation Proclamation.

Lincoln's proclamation emancipated no one until its January 1, 1863, effective date. Even then, it liberated few slaves, targeting only those where the U.S. government had no power to enforce it. Slaves in loyal border states or areas under federal control, including "the [Louisiana] Parishes of St. Bernard, Plaquemines, Jefferson, St. Johns, St. Charles, St. James[,] Ascension, Assumption, Terrebonne, Lafourche, St. Mary, St. Martin, and Orleans, including the City of New-Orleans,"[35] would remain enslaved. Lincoln thus specifically refrained from emancipating slaves in the very city whose practice of the institution so affected him decades earlier. The Emancipation Proclamation was initially conceived only as a military strategy aimed at rebellious areas.

But the effects of the proclamation went far beyond military strategy. It transformed federal troops from rebellion-suppressers into liberation forces. Every territorial gain exacted by the bluecoats left freedom in their wake. Many slaves in Union-held Louisiana, while technically excluded from the proclamation, proceeded to liberate themselves by walking off the plantation, their masters powerless to stop them. Others in nearby graycoat-held areas escaped to join their brethren. In droves the freed-

---

34. Details of Lincoln's dream, here and later in this chapter, are drawn from Fehrenbacher and Fehrenbacher, *Recollected Words of Lincoln*, 398, and from John G. Nicolay and John Hay, "Abraham Lincoln: A History—The Fourteenth of April—The Fate of the Assassins—The Mourning Pageant," *Century Illustrated Monthly Magazine*, January 1890, 430.

35. Abraham Lincoln, "Emancipation Proclamation," January 1, 1863, in *Collected Works*, 6:28–30.

men—hungry, penniless, and homeless—beelined for Camp Parapet and other federal encampments, presenting Union officers with humanitarian and policy crises even as they had a war on their hands. Slavery in the New Orleans region, the law of the land every day since 1719, unraveled piecemeal throughout the months and years following Lincoln's colossal decision.[36] While the president crafted the Emancipation Proclamation with an eye toward pragmatism, the reality of total war now liberated Lincoln from his own cautious instincts to seek Solomonic compromise with slaveholders, and motivated him to take more aggressive steps toward finally and totally destroying the ancient institution.

As he worked on the Emancipation Proclamation, Lincoln concurrently directed General Butler and military commander George F. Shepley to conduct fair and legal elections in which Louisianans—and not Northern soldiers or carpetbaggers—could elect representatives. Union loyalists came out in relatively high numbers to vote on December 3, 1862, resulting in the election of Benjamin Flanders and Michael Hahn. Upon arriving in Washington, however, Flanders and Hahn found themselves less than welcome—and subjects of the same continuing debate over how, exactly, to reconstruct defeated Southern regions.[37] Behind those arguments loomed even more polemical matters: what shall be the fate of slavery as the war progressed? And as the ranks of freedmen expanded, what shall be their rights, particularly in regard to suffrage? New Orleans' free people of color—many of whom were well-educated, moneyed, organized, and increasingly vocal—pushed for Louisiana to rejoin as a free state, with full citizenship and rights for their people.

•

Lincoln during his presidency occasionally solicited secret insights about affairs in occupied New Orleans. His premier informant was Isachar Zacharie, an English-born American of Jewish ancestry whose skills as a chiropodist matched his relentless ambition and opportunism. In November 1862, Zacharie, working as Lincoln's foot doctor, convinced his presidential patient to send him to New Orleans as the commander in

---

36. Self-liberation in fact commenced shortly after the Union arrival in late spring 1862. One Union captain in July of that year remembered slaves "continually quitting the plantations and swarming to us for protection and support. . . . They are mainly a burden." De Forest, *Volunteer's Adventures*, 31.

37. Peyton McCrary, *Abraham Lincoln and Reconstruction* (Princeton, NJ: Princeton University Press, 1978), 100–101.

chief's "correspondent."[38] Lincoln obliged. Once there, the doctor used his social and professional connections to supply Lincoln with intelligence on troop movements, public sentiment, political sympathies, commercial activity, race relations, and the behavior of the president's generals. At one point he served directly under Gen. Nathanial Banks; at another, he organized a team of spies disguised as peddlers and sent them across the region collecting data. Evidence suggests Zacharie also attempted to enrich himself from his arrangements.[39] Throughout the occupation, Zacharie (in addition to performing medical services) communicated extensively with Union authorities and the president, forming a link not only between Lincoln and New Orleans, but between the White House and American Jews. When a Zionist advocate discussed with the president a possible state in Palestine, Lincoln is said to have responded, "I myself have a regard for the Jews. My chiropodist is a Jew, and he has so many times 'put me on my feet,' that I would have no objection to giving his countrymen 'a leg up.'"[40]

Spring and summer 1863 brought new action to the theaters of war, denying Lincoln the luxury of focusing on Louisiana or other matters. One early-summer evening, the mysterious riverine dream returned to Lincoln's slumbering mind—and, once again, it foretold astonishing news. On July 3–4, Union forces repelled a major Confederate northward foray at a town called Gettysburg, engaging the world's two greatest armies in a battle that would rank as the largest ever in the Western Hemisphere. At the same time a thousand miles to the southwest, the key Mississippi River stronghold of Vicksburg finally relented to a forty-day Union siege. Within a single summer weekend, the course of the conflict shifted to Northern favor. The fall of Vicksburg left the tiny bluff-top town of Port Hudson, Louisiana, as the last remaining Confederate hold on the Mississippi River. It too fell later in July, in a battle and siege that involved Louisianians of both races. "The signs look better," proclaimed Lincoln

38. Charles M. Segal, "Notes And Documents Isachar Zacharie: Lincoln's Chiropodist," *Publications of the American Jewish Historical Society* 44, no. 1–4 (September 1954–June 1955).

39. Ibid.

40. Letters between Isachar Zacharie and Abraham Lincoln, dating between January 14, 1863, and December 26, 1864, Lincoln Papers; Charles M. Segal, "Isachar Zacharie: Lincoln's Chiropodist," *Publications of the American Jewish Historical Society* 43, no. 1–4 (September 1953), 71–126.

toward the end of that breathtaking season; "The Father of Waters again goes unvexed to the sea."[41]

•

With military matters progressing, the Mississippi River in federal hands, Arkansas and Tennessee falling to Union control, and the Emancipation Proclamation in place, Lincoln returned to reconstruction policy in Louisiana. On December 8, 1863, he presented a plan: If 10 percent of Louisiana's 1860 voter turnout swore allegiance to the United States and abided by the Emancipation Proclamation, the state would be allowed to elect a government and draft a constitution—so long as it outlawed slavery. Louisiana would then be recognized and readmitted to the Union. Inserting the slavery-ban condition reflected the rising prioritization Lincoln ascribed to black freedom, although he hoped that the state would do the outlawing itself without his personal intervention. Setting the allegiance bar so low as 10 percent reflected Lincoln's desire to reconcile swiftly with defeated states and lure still-rebellious states back into the Union, perhaps precipitating an end to a war growing increasingly unpopular with Northern Democrats. He probably also had political motivations, with the 1864 reelection campaign on the horizon. The lenient plan paralleled his decision earlier in the year to replace the hard-line Gen. Benjamin Butler—loathed by white New Orleanians, loved by blacks, and admired by radical Republicans—with the conservative-moderate Gen. Nathanial Banks.[42]

Lincoln's Ten Percent Plan prompted a response from the radical Republicans in the form of the Wade Davis Bill, which, among other things, hardened the allegiance criteria and upped the bar from 10 to 50 percent. Lincoln refused to sign it. The Ten Percent Plan motivated pro-Union delegates in Louisiana to set to work electing a governor and drafting a new state constitution.

Both tasks focused attention on one major issue: what to do with the ever-increasing ranks of freedmen. Immediate concerns regarding food and shelter proved challenging enough, to say nothing of long-term matters involving land, housing, employment, and education. Most pressing of all, from a constitutional perspective, was the question of suffrage. The sugar coast and New Orleans being home to the largest major concentration of African Americans nationwide, the question of voting rights would

41. Abraham Lincoln to James C. Conkling, August 26, 1863, in *Collected Works*, 6:409.

42. McCrary, *Lincoln and Reconstruction*, 124–125.

determine the political future of Louisiana. Lincoln's position echoed his earlier stance on slavery: it originally reflected cautious conciliatory accommodation, but moved steadily toward progressive social change.

•

Two prominent New Orleanians, *L'Union* newspaper co-founder Jean-Baptiste Roudanez and merchant-turned-Union-captain Arnold Bertonneau, helped further that transformation. Both free black Francophone Creoles, Roudanez and Bertonneau were selected by their peers to travel to Washington, under risky wartime conditions, to promote black suffrage to Union authorities. They brought with them (according to their liaison Thomas J. Durant, in his letter to the president), "a petition numerously signed by respectable persons of [New Orleans] in favor of the extension of political privileges to the citizens of African descent,"[13]

On March 12, 1864, Roudanez and Bertonneau arrived at the White House. That African-descended people were received in the highest office of the land demonstrated President Lincoln's respect for them as men. Their message apparently won his sympathy because, the very next day, Lincoln transmitted to the newly elected Louisiana governor an encapsulation of the New Orleanians' message. After congratulating Michael Hahn for becoming "the first free-state Governor of Louisiana" about to oversee a Constitutional Convention to "define the elective franchise" in Louisiana, Lincoln, with characteristic caution, wrote:

> I barely suggest for your private consideration whether some of the colored people may not be let in [to the Convention]—as, for instance, the very intelligent, and especially those who have fought gallantly in our ranks. They would probably help, in some trying time to come, to keep the jewel of liberty within the family of freedom. But this is only a suggestion, not to the public, but to you alone.[44]

•

One eventful year later, General Lee surrendered to General Grant at Appomattox, essentially ending the catastrophic four-year conflict. President Lincoln addressed the breathless nation two evening later, in a tone that muted jubilation with forewarning about the challenge of national reuni-

43. Thomas J. Durant to Abraham Lincoln, February 10, 1864, Lincoln Papers.
44. Abraham Lincoln to Michael Hahn, March 13, 1864, in *Collected Works*, 7:243.

fication that lay ahead. Having broached the term "re-construction" to describe that task, Lincoln then presented his Louisiana experiment of the last three years as a blueprint for the future. "Some twelve thousand voters in the heretofore slave-state of Louisiana," Lincoln proudly proclaimed,

> have sworn allegiance to the Union, assumed to be the rightful political power of the State, held elections, organized a State government, adopted a free-state constitution, giving the benefit of public schools equally to black and white, and empowering the Legislature to confer the elective franchise upon the colored man.[45]

Spurning all this progress by adopting a vindictive and radical approach to reconstruction, Lincoln warned, would

> in effect say to the white men, "You are worthless, or worse—we will neither help you, nor be helped by you." To the blacks we say "This cup of liberty which these, your old masters, hold to your lips, we will dash from you, and leave you to the chances of gathering the spilled and scattered contents in some vague and undefined when, where, and how."[46]

It was the most Louisiana-focused speech of Lincoln's career. The message set a tone for the postbellum era that was both progressive and magnanimous. It grated, however, on radicals at both extremes—among them a man in Lincoln's audience that evening, the well-known actor John Wilkes Booth.

Two nights later, Lincoln envisaged his river dream again—the strange and indescribable vessel, the swift glide across the dark expanse, the vague and indefinite shore. Next morning, Good Friday, the president shared the reoccurring vision with his Cabinet members, pointing out the curious way it foretold Fort Sumter, Bull Run, Antietam, Gettysburg, Stones River, Vicksburg, and other startling news. Now, with peace breaking out all over, Lincoln could only suppose to hear from Sherman, and surely the triumphant general would bear good news.[47]

Louisiana remained on President Lincoln's mind that day. At one point, he commended the state's effort to present "one of the best con-

45. Abraham Lincoln, Last Public Address, April 11, 1865, in *Collected Works*, 8:399–405.
46. Ibid., 399-405.
47. As recollected by Gideon Welles, in Fehrenbacher and Fehrenbacher, *Recollected Words of Lincoln*, 486–487.

stitutions that has ever been formed." At another, he appointed William P. Kellogg as Collector for the Port of New Orleans, allegedly directing him, "I want you to make love to those people down there." Amid sundry ministerial tasks, he also recounted an old boating anecdote about the Sangamon River, origin of his second flatboat trip to New Orleans.[48]

The First Lady in the meantime kept the president apprised of their plans to join guests at a play that evening. The invitation, extended by the theater's management, reached the ears of the thespian John Wilkes Booth. Here, finally, was an opportunity to act on a rancorous scheme Booth had been mulling for months.

Weary but rejuvenated, President Lincoln seemed to enjoy himself at the Ford's Theater production of the comedy *Our American Cousin*. Booth, meanwhile, cowered in the stairwell awaiting a certain moment in the play. Timing his entry into the presidential box to coincide with audience laughter, Booth cracked open the door, slinked up behind the president, leveled a derringer behind his ear, and pulled the trigger.

At 7:22 a.m. Saturday, April 15, 1865, the old flatboatman was dead.

48. Recollections of what Lincoln said and did during the last days of his life vary among sources; according to John W. Starr, those mentioned here occurred on April 14, 1865. John W. Starr, Jr., *Lincoln's Last Day* (New York: Frederick A. Stokes Company, 1922), 12–15, 19–20, 29–30.

Conclusions

What shall we make of Lincoln's flatboat journeys to New Orleans?

Set in the context of Western river commerce and antebellum New Orleans, the two expeditions constitute worthwhile history regardless of the Lincoln connection. They warrant attention today for no other reason than having formed part of the human adventure. That the early life of Abraham Lincoln ranks among the best documented of that era and region, and generally represents the lives of thousands of others who flatboated to New Orleans, further justifies historical interest. It's a Mississippi River story, a New Orleans story, an American story.

But Lincoln, of course, was no ordinary individual. He would later lead a nation, fight to save it, and emancipate millions of its people. Researchers ever since have scoured Lincoln's earlier life for insights and clues toward understanding how such a towering figure could emerge from such ordinary circumstances. The flatboat journeys to New Orleans thus rise to (potentially) greater significance, on *biographical* grounds. This chapter explores how those experiences affected the man so readily identified by Americans as their greatest president, by positing five specific influences: on the matter of slavery, on the issue of internal improvements, on Lincoln's political image during the 1860 presidential campaign, on his personal worldview, and as a folk rite of passage from boyhood to manhood. We conclude with reflections on how the historical narratives of the flatboat journeys have influenced Americans' interpretations of that president.

•

Innumerable histories and biographies have deduced one core narrative from Lincoln's flatboat journeys: that the sight of slavery in New Orleans—specifically slave trading, on a large scale and in all its brutal vulgarity—helped convince the young man of the institution's moral bankruptcy, and planted in him the seeds of opposition that would eventually lead into its destruction. So prevalent is that narrative, it is literally written into stone. Proclaims the plaque on the limestone monument at the Rockport launch spot,

> IN A VERY REAL SENSE OF THE WORD, IT MIGHT
> BE SAID THAT THE EMANCIPATION PROCLAMA-
> TION, WHICH LINCOLN ISSUED IN 1863, OWES ITS
> ORIGINS TO THIS FLATBOAT TRIP.

That interpretation owes *its* origins to a quotation recited further down on the plaque:

> [HERE] IN 1828 . . . ABRAHAM LINCOLN WITH AL-
> LEN GENTRY MADE HIS FIRST FLATBOAT TRIP
> TO NEW ORLEANS. HE SAW SLAVES SOLD AND
> SAID, "IF I EVER GET A CHANCE TO HIT THAT
> THING, I'LL HIT IT HARD."

Because that oft-cited "hit it hard" quotation plays such a fundamental role in interpretations, it warrants thorough investigation here.

The quote arrived to the historical record courtesy John Hanks, the cousin of Lincoln's biological mother who joined Lincoln on the second trip departing from Illinois in 1831. Hanks claimed he heard Lincoln say it at a New Orleans slave market, and reported it to William H. Herndon during a circa-1865 interview. Strangely, Herndon did not jot down that specific quote in his notes, despite its striking cadence and incredible pre-science. Here is what Herndon scribed as Hanks spoke:

> [I]n May [1831] we landed in N.O. There it was we Saw Ne-
> groes Chained—maltreated—whipt & scourged. Lincoln
> Saw it—his heart bled—Said nothing much—was silent from
> feeling—was Sad—looked bad—felt bad—was thoughtful &
> abstracted—I Can say Knowingly that it was on this trip that
> he formed his opinions of Slavery: it ran its iron in him then &
> there—May 1831. I have heard him say—often & often. . . .[1]

Herndon generously shared his notes with Ward H. Lamon, whose 1872 book *The Life of Abraham Lincoln* repeated the above notes of Hanks' interview, with cleaned-up syntax.[2] Lamon did not, however, mention the "hit it hard" line. Those words would not come to public attention until

---

1. Interview, John Hanks, by William H. Herndon, 1865–1866, in ed. Douglas L. Wilson and Rodney O. Davis, *Herndon's Informants: Letters, Interviews, and Statements About Abraham Lincoln* (Urbana and Chicago: University of Illinois Press, 1998), 457.
2. Ward H. Lamon, *The Life of Abraham Lincoln; from His Birth to His Inauguration as President* (Boston: James R. Osgood and Company, 1872), iii–iv and 82–83.

a decade later, when former Lincoln advisor and friend Isaac N. Arnold, while researching his own book about Lincoln, wrote to Herndon about a rumor alleging that Lincoln had visited in New Orleans "an old fortune teller, a Voudou negress" who "became very much excited" and predicted "You will be President, and all the negroes will be free." Herndon, again displaying exceptional generosity to a competing author, wrote back on October 21, 1882, answering the fortune-teller question and offering additional information on slavery (italicized emphases appear in the original):

> It *seems* to me *just now* that I once heard of the fortune-telling story, but can not state when I heard it, nor from whom I got it. It *seems* that John Hanks, who was with Lincoln at New Orleans in 1831, told me the story. At that time and place, Lincoln was made an anti-slavery man. He saw a slave, a beautiful mulatto girl, sold at auction. She was *felt over*, *pinched*, *trotted* around to show to bidders that said article was sound, etc. Lincoln walked away from the sad, inhumane scene with a deep feeling of *unsmotherable* hate. He said to John Hanks this: "By God! If I ever get a chance to hit that institution, I'll hit it hard, John." He got his chance, and *did hit it hard*. John Hanks, who was two or three times examined by me, told me the above facts about the negro girl and Lincoln's declaration. There is no doubt about this. As to the fortune-telling story, I do not affirm anything or deny anything.[3]

Arnold reproduced Herndon's words verbatim in a footnote to his *Life of Abraham Lincoln*, published posthumously in 1885. Apparently either Arnold or Herndon shared the letter's content with another author, William D. Kelley, because Kelley quoted it in his 1885 book, *Lincoln and Stanton*. A few other writers picked up the line from these sources over the next few years.[4]

It was not until 1889, however, that the "hit it hard" quote became culturally entrenched, when Herndon himself finally released his decades-in-the-making *Herndon's Lincoln*. The section on New Orleans construed Hanks' original recollections into this narration:

---

3. Isaac N. Arnold, *The Life of Abraham Lincoln* (Chicago: Jansen, McClurg, & Company, 1885), 31.

4. William Darrah Kelley, *Lincoln and Stanton: A Study of the War Administration of 1861 and 1862* (New York and London: G. P. Putnam's Sons, 1885), 86–87.

In New Orleans, for the first time Lincoln beheld the true horrors of human slavery. He saw "negroes in chains—whipped and scourged." Against this inhumanity his sense of right and justice rebelled, and his mind and conscience were awakened to a realization of what he had often heard and read. No doubt, as one of his companions has said, "Slavery ran the iron into him then and there." One morning in their rambles over the city the trio passed a slave auction. A vigorous and comely mulatto girl was being sold. She underwent a thorough examination at the hands of the bidders; they pinched her flesh and made her trot up and down the room like a horse, to show how she moved, and in order, as the auctioneer said, that "bidders might satisfy themselves" whether the article they were offering to buy was sound or not. The whole thing was so revolting that Lincoln moved away from the scene with a deep feeling of "unconquerable hate." Bidding his companions follow him he said, "By God, boys, let's get away from this. If ever I get a chance to hit that thing [meaning slavery], I'll hit it hard." This incident was furnished me in 1865, by John Hanks. . . .[5]

Herndon's Lincoln came to be highly influential, cited in countless subsequent books, articles, plaques, performances, and documentaries. Writers consistently exploited the dramatically pithy "hit it hard" line (often tweaking its exact wordage for effect) as the encapsulation of everything people needed to take away from the Lincoln-in–New Orleans episode. In 1891, for example, a Chicago theater company staged a play in which an outraged Lincoln in a New Orleans auction house stammers, "If I ever get an opportunity to hit that institution of slavery, I will hit it, and hit it hard."[6] In 1893, author Charles Carleton Coffin attributed the line to Herndon's 1889 book, but nonetheless took liberties as he described the scene in the breathless present:

> The boatman turns away with something rising in his throat, and goes out with John Hanks into the sunshine. His lips are quivering, for his soul is on fire. *"John, if I ever get a chance to hit that institution, I'll hit it hard, by the Eternal God!"*

5. William H. Herndon and Jesse William Weik, *Herndon's Lincoln: The True Story of a Great Life* (Chicago, New York, and San Francisco: Belford, Clarke & Company, 1889), 1:76.

6. "Is It In Good Taste? Public Opinion Divided as to the Play 'Abraham Lincoln,'" *Chicago Daily*, September 13, 1891, p. 32.

Coffin concluded, "certainly no words ever spoken by the prophets of Israel have had a larger fulfillment than those uttered by Abraham Lincoln in the streets of New Orleans."[7]

Other authors constructed, with increasing levels of literary license, melodramatic scenes of auction-block indignities unfurling before the silently outraged young sage. More often that not, the one-paragraph chronicles climax with an angry Abraham storming off, with "hit it hard" tumbling from his lips. Authors John George Nicolay and John Hay (1905) worked the quote into an alliterative drumbeat worthy of "The Battle Hymn of the Republic":

> It is recorded how [Lincoln's] soul burned with indignation . . . in the slave shambles of New Orleans . . . and that he then exclaimed, "If I ever get a chance to hit that thing, I'll hit it hard." He "hit it hard" when as a member of the Illinois Legislature he protested that "the institution of slavery is founded on both injustice and bad policy. He "hit it hard" when as a member of Congress he 'voted for the Wilmot Proviso as good as forty times.' He "hit it hard" when he stumped his state against the Kansas-Nebraska bill. . . . He "hit it hard" when he approved the law abolishing slavery in the District of Columbia. . . . He "hit it hard" when he signed the acts abolishing slavery in all the Territories. . . .[8]

An 1895 article entitled "God in Lincoln" rode the quote into the theological realm, rhetorically pounding on the words "thing" and "it" (slavery) until climaxing,

> [T]he very same hand that was lifted in solemn oath before God in the New Orleans slave mart took up the God-inspired pen of liberty, and dashed off the Emancipation Proclamation. . . . That was an act worthy of Jesus Christ. It was the act of Jesus Christ; for it was the spirit of Jesus Christ that filled [Lincoln] with power. . . .[9]

7. Charles Carleton Coffin, *Abraham Lincoln* (New York: Harper & Brothers, 1893), 59 (italics in original).

8. John George Nicolay and John Hay, eds., *Complete Works of Abraham Lincoln* (New York, Francis D. Tandy Company, 1905), 5:xix–xx.

9. David Gregg, "God In Lincoln," *The Independent, Devoted to the Consideration of Politics, Social and Economic Tendencies, History, Literature, and the Arts*, April 4, 1895, p. 15.

T: "hit it hard" quote, however, suffers from one fatal flaw: Lincoln took
ns to explain in his 1860 campaign autobiography that John Hanks
ver accompanied him to New Orleans in 1831. Hanks disembarked in St.
:uis and returned to Illinois on his own.[10] Given that Lincoln had abso-
tely nothing to gain in pointing out Hanks' departure, and that Hanks
heoretically had everything to gain by writing himself into history after
the assassination, we are inclined to take Lincoln's word over Hanks' by a
wide margin.

Some historians have cast John Hanks in unfavorable light because
' this inconsistency, questioning not only his memory and reliability but
:o his honesty. Evidence suggests that John Hanks himself felt some
comfort with his "hit it hard" claim: in an 1887 letter written to Jesse
'k in response to a now-lost list of questions, the eighty-five-year-
Hanks cryptically answered, "It was his step Brother he mad[e] that
ark to. his name was John Johson [*sic*] I was not at the sail at the
e[.]"[11] We cannot be certain what question Hanks addressed with that
ponse; historians Douglas L. Wilson and Rodney O. Davis suggest
at Weik had in fact asked Hanks about the "hit it hard" quote. Clues
i the sentence certainly point in that direction. If so, then Hanks, with
hose words, seems to acknowledge finally that he did not accompany
Lincoln to New Orleans, and that perhaps it was John D. Johnston who
heard the future emancipator's bold proclamation. In any case, Weik did
not act on Hanks' clarification, and when *Herndon's Lincoln* came out in
1889, the "hit it hard" quote made its way into history.

(Incidentally, Weik later inquired about that far zanier rumor, unsur-
prisingly also traced to John Hanks: that a "Voodoo negress" in New Orleans predicted Lincoln would one day become president and emancipate
the slaves. An irritated Hanks disassociated himself with that story too,
saying, "I Don't [k]Now whether he got his fortune told or Not."[12] Weik
and Herndon omitted the Voodoo story from *Herndon's Lincoln*.)

Two twentieth-century Indiana researchers, Bess V. Ehrmann and
Francis Marion Van Natter, claimed that the "hit it hard" line was not
overheard by John Hanks in 1831, but rather by Allen Gentry during Lincoln's first trip in 1828 (or 1829, as Ehrmann and Van Natter surmised).

10. Abraham Lincoln, "Autobiography Written for John L. Scripps," June 1860, in
Collected Works, 4:64.

11. John Hanks to Jesse William Weik, June 12, 1887, in *Herndon's Informants*, 615
and footnote.

12. Hanks to Weik, April 19, 1888, in *Herndon's Informants*, 656. See also Arnold, *Life
of Abraham Lincoln*, 31.

Ehrmann obtained her information in a 1930s interview she conducted with Absolom Gentry, who recalled that his father Allen said years after the experience, "We stood and watched the slaves sold in New Orleans and Abraham was very angry. . . [.]"[13] Ehrmann obtained additional details from Absolom Gentry and built them into this narrative of that moment:

> One day as [Lincoln and Gentry] were walking along the street a crowd attracted their attention, and they drew near to see what was going on. A man was making a speech and offering for sale a young negro woman standing on a huge block used for the slave market. The two men were horrified, and as the girl, with tears streaming down her face, was given to the highest bidder, young Abe, in a frenzy of anger, turned to his friend and said, "If I ever get a chance to hit that thing, I'll hit it hard."[14]

Van Natter obtained similar information when he interviewed another Gentry family descendent. Seventy-two-year-old E. Grant Gentry recalled his grandmother Anna Gentry remembering her husband Allen speaking of his experiences with Abraham in New Orleans in February 1829, and testified to those thrice-passed-down memories in a sworn affidavit notarized on September 5, 1936:

> [A]s Gentry and Lincoln went up on the levee, their attention was attracted by a sale of negro slaves, naked except for hip-clouts, being sold on a raised platform on the levee; that the "yaller" girls, after being pinched by prospective buyers, brought a lot higher price than the black men and women slaves; that the actions of the buyers and auctioneers towards the "yaller" girls were disgusting to Allen Gentry and Abraham Lincoln, and that Lincoln said to Gentry: "Allen, that's a disgrace. If I ever get a lick at that thing, I will hit it hard."[15]

13. Louis A. Warren, *Lincoln's Youth: Indiana Years, Seven to Twenty-One, 1816–1830* (Indianapolis: Indiana Historical Society Press, 1959, reprinted 2002), 185 and 261, endnote #48.

14. Bess V. Ehrmann, *The Missing Chapter in the Life of Abraham Lincoln* (Chicago: Walter M. Hill, 1938), 9.

15. Affidavit, E. Grant Gentry, September 5, 1936, Francis Marion Van Natter Papers-Regional History Collection Number 136, Lewis Historical Library, Vincennes University (hereafter cited as Van Natter Papers). While E. Grant Gentry certainly felt this information accurately represented family tradition, it is replete with dubious details. Slaves were rarely auctioned directly on the flatboat docks, and "yaller" (mixed-race)

Van Natter wove those recollections (plus other information gleaned in interviews with Joe, Wayne, Anna, Hannah, Rose, and Absalom Gentry) into his book *Lincoln's Boyhood: A Chronicle of His Indiana Years*, published posthumously in 1963. Wrote Van Natter,

> Due to his height Lincoln could see over the crowd and what he saw angered him. For probably the first time in his life he was witnessing the scene he had heard discussed so often— people selling people. He doubled his fists tightly; his knuckles went white. He watched men wearing big white hats and long black coats buy field hands and house servants. Black and ugly, such Negroes sold for $500 to $800 each. The sale of "fancy girls" began. Bids started at $1500 or almost twice the top sale price for field hands. Bidding continued until some of the girls were knocked off at $2500 apiece. Unable to stand it any longer, Lincoln muttered to Gentry: "Allen, that's a disgrace! If I ever get a lick at that thing I'll hit it hard." Gentry: "We'd better get out of here, Abe."[16]

What to make of these 1828–29 versions? Given the nearly identical phraseology and the fact that the Hanks/Herndon 1831 version had been circulating for nearly half a century before the Gentry 1828–29 version started to surface, we may hypothesize that *Gentry family descendents interviewed in the 1930s had unknowingly—over the course of two generations—internalized the Hanks/Herndon version and mistakenly credited it to their own ancestor.* Van Natter and Ehrmann, who worked tirelessly in researching Lincoln's Indiana boyhood and deserve ample credit for their contributions, may have erred in their methodology by over-relying on the testimony of people over a century removed from the fact, with no primary sources at their disposal.[17] Van Natter may have also blundered methodologically when, according to his own notes, he asked what might be called a "binary leading question." Informants are vulnerable to being "led" toward answering in a certain way, a risk that increases when the question is posed to yield a binary (yes or no) response. So when Van

girls, who were often employed as domestics, would rarely sell for more money than a productive young male field hand.

16. Van Natter, *Lincoln's Boyhood: A Chronicle of His Indiana Years* (Washington, D.C.: Public Affairs Press, 1963), 145.

17. It should be noted that Ehrmann and Van Natter strove to shine light on Lincoln's *Indiana* heritage. They were partisans in the battle with Illinois (and to a lesser degree Kentucky) regarding which state lays claim to "forming" the Great Emancipator. By dating the "hit it hard" line to 1828–29 rather than 1831, it becomes an Indiana story.

Natter asked a Gentry descendent, "At New Orleans slave market did Lincoln say to Allen Gentry, 'If I ever get a chance to lick that thing, I'll lick it hard?,'" he unintentionally fed the old Hanks/Herndon quote to his informant, who eagerly validated it.[18] Not all informants, however, answered affirmatively: When Van Natter asked the same question to granddaughters Anna, Hannah, and Rose Gentry on January 21, 1936, they responded, "Never heard it said."[19] That inconvenient testimony did not make it into the book.

Ironically, Van Natter knew about Hanks' claim that Lincoln said the "hit it hard" line in 1831, but he dismissed it because he realized Hanks did not accompany Lincoln to New Orleans.[20] What Van Natter failed to see was that the relationship between Hanks' 1831 allegation and his informants' 1828–29 recollection was not merely coincidental; in fact, the former spawned the latter. Despite the Gentry family descendents' honest intentions and heartfelt testimonies, they simply passed on old stories gleaned unknowingly from multiple sources, including Hanks. In that manner, the "hit it hard"/"lick it hard" quotation spread virally throughout Lincoln literature and public perception.

The historical record nearly suffered a far more insidious infection in the 1920s, when a journalist named Wilma Frances Minor stunned the editors of the venerated *Atlantic Monthly* with a treasure trove of newly discovered Lincoln documents. Minor's interpretation of the material, serialized by the magazine in 1928–29, validated long-held Lincoln theories and popular perceptions in a manner that seemed almost too good to be true. In contextualizing one particular document—a letter by Lincoln to county surveyor John Calhoun—Minor set up Lincoln's visit to New Orleans with the obligatory local color ("lacy parasols . . . quaint cemeteries"), and reminded readers of the "familiar record" of the "hit it hard" line. Then she unveiled Lincoln's amazing letter:

> I never have forgotten a single instance of my memorable stay in New Orleans which was so marked by the atrocious cruelty practiced by many slave holders. . . . [Once] I had stopped to question an old slave who appeared dejected at his task. I questioned him, are you happy in slavery? the old fellow un-

18. Note Card #1 of interview of Wayne Gentry by Francis Marion Van Natter, December 30, 1935, Van Natter Papers.

19. Note Card #1 of interview of Anna, Hannah, and Rose Gentry by Francis Marion Van Natter, January 21, 1936, Van Natter Papers.

20. Van Natter, *Lincoln's Boyhood*, 186.

bent his back as much as possible and raising a face of hopeless resignation answered—'No—no Marse I nevah is happy no mo. whippins is things that black folks nevah can stop remembrin about—they hurt so. . . .' I am not a 'nigger lover' by any [means, but] I shall pursue my wonted course [against slavery] though half the world disagrees with me. . . .[21]

Minor's discoveries seemingly elevated the New Orleans trips to lofty historical significance. But shortly after publication, they were shown to be utterly fraudulent. The mendacious forger had concocted the whole collection, after doing ample background research, cleverly capturing Lincoln's halting syntax, and replicating his penmanship upon dog-eared nineteenth-century paper stock. The incident is remembered today mostly for the misinformation it spread about Lincoln's relationship with Ann Rutledge in New Salem, but it did no favors for those seeking the truth about his relationship with New Orleans.

The dubious provenance of the "hit it hard" quote and the additional distraction of Minor's fraud weaken the larger case for finding historical importance in Lincoln's visits to New Orleans. One senses that modern scholars tend to shy away from ascribing as high a level of significance to the trips as their predecessors did, once they realize that the most famous piece of evidence upon which those predecessors relied is, in fact, tainted. The case suffers additionally from the fact that Lincoln remained silent regarding impressions or lessons learned from New Orleans when he penned his autobiographical notes. The fleeting recollections he wrote in the Scripps autobiography mostly cover mundane who-what-when-where-why trip details, yet still managed to leave many basic questions unanswered, not to mention deeper philosophical inquiries. Of greatest irony is the fact that Lincoln devoted over one-third of his account of the first trip—39 out of 102 words—to the attack of the "seven negroes," an emphasis inconveniently contrary to the black-victimhood narrative favored in the historiography.

But perhaps we ask for too much in expecting this famously private man to spell out such revelations publically. One of Lincoln's defining traits was his solemn reverence for discipline and rationality over emotion.[22] Painful personal memories he expressed only privately, if at all.

21. Wilma Frances Minor, "Lincoln the Lover: I. The Setting—New Salem," *Atlantic Monthly*, December 1928, 844–846.

22. David Herbert Donald, *Lincoln* (New York: Simon & Schuster, 1995), 66–67, 80–83, 118.

It should also be remembered that Lincoln was running for president in a turbulent nation divided over slavery when he penned those flatboat memories. Waxing emotionally on the horrors he witnessed in the Queen City of the South would have needlessly exacerbated estrangement with Southerners in general, and with that important city in particular. Lincoln's emotional introversion, coupled with his political savvy, may explain why the Scripps autobiographical accounts in general are replete with inconsequential minutiae and frustratingly devoid of insight and substance—almost as if Lincoln was hiding something.

Lincoln may have alluded to that "something" in a private letter addressed to former Whig congressman and future Confederate vice-president Alexander Hamilton Stephens (with a similar version sent to Senator J. J. Crittenden). While the original letter has not been found, a duplicate made shortly after Lincoln first dictated its contents on January 19, 1860, found its way into the collection of Judd Steward, who published it and associated missives in a 1909 booklet. The letter includes a heartfelt paragraph imploring Stephens to recognize the emerging national reassessment of human enslavement and embrace the preservation of the Union, in which Lincoln said,

> [Y]ou say that slavery is the corner stone of the south and if separated, would be that of a new Republic; God forbid. *When a boy I went to New Orleans on a flat boat and there I saw slavery and slave markets as I have never seen them in Kentucky, and I heard worse of the Red River plantations.* I hoped and prayed that the gradual emancipation plan . . . or the Liberian colonization [plan] might lead to its extinction in the United States. . . .[23]

Here, finally, we have in Lincoln's own words, a reliable citation of what he saw in New Orleans and how they impressed him, as well as an explicit yoking of that influence with his personal desire—through *hope* and *prayer*—to bring the troubling institution to some sort of peaceful end. That he "heard worse of the Red River plantations" corroborates the reputation of that central-Louisiana region in its treatment of slaves, a reputation dramatized in the wildly popular *Uncle Tom's Cabin* (1852) by Harriet Beecher Stowe and the subsequent autobiography *Twelve Years a Slave* by Solomon Northup. What Lincoln seemingly restrained him-

---

23. Abraham Lincoln to Alexander Hamilton Stephens, January 19, 1860, in *Some Lincoln Correspondence with Southern Leaders before the Outbreak of the Civil War*, from the Collection of Judd Stewart (New York: J. Stewart, 1909), 8 (emphasis added).

self from saying publically in the Scripps autobiography and elsewhere, he said privately to Stephens—briefly, but clearly and passionately. Stephens himself later "certified as correct" the version that Judd Steward published in 1909, a confirmation that, combined with the letter's perfectly credible content and context, leads Lincoln scholars to accept Steward's letter collection as authentic Lincoln communiqués.[24] Their authenticity is further corroborated by the fact that the original version of another letter appearing in Judd Steward's booklet, from Stephens to Lincoln dated December 14, 1860, fortuitously turned up in the Lincoln Papers released to the public by the Library of Congress in 1947—and matched Steward's version word for word.[25] Because of the late arrival of the January 19 letter to scholarly attention, the New Orleans information contained therein evaded many early Lincoln histories, and remains infrequently cited today. How unfortunate that the unreliable but dramatic Hanks quote dominates the literature, while the reliable but somber Lincoln quote goes all but forgotten.[26]

The Lincoln quote, coupled with the empirical evidence presented in this book that a veritable cityscape of bondage greeted Lincoln in New Orleans, invites us to revisit Hanks' "hit it hard" quote. We should not overcompensate for its *imprecise* wording by tossing aside its overall *accurate* implication: that Lincoln witnessed in New Orleans the brutal realities of the slave trade and internalized them in his intellectual development. (*Precision* and *accuracy* are not synonymous; the former implies level of detail, while the latter means overall correctness. Accuracy with precision is optimal; accuracy without precision is still acceptable if no better information exists. But *in*accuracy is worthless, *regardless* of precision. What we have in the "hit it hard" quote may be regarded as a case of accuracy without precision.)

Support of that accuracy comes not only from the Stephens letter, but from the recollection of Illinois office boy Robert H. Browne, who clerked for Lincoln in the early 1850s and remembered him saying, "I saw [slavery] all myself when I was only a little older than you are now, and the horrid pictures are in my mind yet." Lincoln apparently meant that he saw

24. Stephen's certification is cited in *Some Lincoln Correspondence*, 3, 9, and 16.

25. Letter, Alexander H. Stephens to Abraham Lincoln, December 14, 1860, Abraham Lincoln Papers at the Library of Congress, Washington, D.C., and *Some Lincoln Correspondence*, 18.

26. State of Georgia—Executive Department, certification signed by Alexander H. Stephens, January 19, 1883, confirming authenticity of Lincoln's letter to Stephens, in *Some Lincoln Correspondence*, 16.

those horrors in New Orleans, because Browne, born in 1835, would have been slightly younger in the early 1850s than Lincoln was during the 1828 New Orleans experience.[27] Support also comes from Lincoln's long-time friend and law partner William H. Herndon—"Billy," as Lincoln affectionately called him—who backed up the implications of the "hit it hard" quote by solemnly affirming, "I have also heard Mr. Lincoln refer to it himself."[28] Herndon's margin notes, scrawled next to where he documented his interviews, reiterate his conviction: "I can say that this testimony can be implicitly relied on. Mr. Lincoln loved this man [Hanks]—thought him truthful—honest and noble. Lincoln has stated this to me over and over again."[29]

John Hanks himself also warrants reconsideration. His countrified way of communicating history—through embellished storytelling—clashed with the sophisticated standards of the educated upper-class men who took it upon themselves to scribe history. Because of those social-class differences, Hanks has suffered in the historical record. This researcher suggests we reconsider Hanks' contributions in their cultural context, and appreciate him for what he has brought to historical attention—in his earnest and endearing manner. Rather than dismissing him as a yarn-spinner, we should listen more closely to the man: *"I have heard [Lincoln] say—often & often,"* that slavery in New Orleans seared his memory.[30] Granted, we know Hanks did not hear Lincoln state that sentiment *in* New Orleans, but that is not the only place Lincoln could have said it. It is possible, as a *New York Times* article suggested in 1929, that while Hanks "did not go as far as New Orleans," the two men "talked afterward [and] Lincoln told him of seeing in that city human beings sold on the auction block." Out of this Illinois conversation may have come the famous line, or, more importantly, the implication behind it.[31]

Beset as Lincoln might have been, however, the experience in New Orleans did not suddenly make the future president an abolitionist, nor

27. As recollected by Robert E. Browne, in Don E. Fehrenbacher and Virginia Fehrenbacher, *Recollected Words of Abraham Lincoln* (Stanford, CA: Stanford University Press, 1996), 61.

28. Herndon and Weik, *Herndon's Lincoln*, 1:76.

29. As quoted by Phillip Shaw Paludan, "Lincoln and Negro Slavery: I Haven't Got Time for the Pain," *Journal of the Abraham Lincoln Association* 27, no. 2 (2006), 11. Paludan found this marginal note to be overly defensive on the part of Herndon.

30. Interview, John Hanks, by William H. Herndon, 1865–1866, in *Herndon's Informants*, 457 (emphasis added).

31. William E. Barton, "Lincoln's Two Cousins Who Swayed His Life," *New York Times*, September 22, 1929, p. 17, c. 4.

even a racial egalitarian. Recent scholarship has shed refreshing light on Lincoln's views on slavery, race, and black Americans. The mythological Lincoln—the deified icon, assassinated for America's racial sins on Good Friday and resurrected on Easter Sunday as the Great Emancipator—now appears more complicated, flawed, savvy, compromising, and paradoxical. Lincoln, it turns out, was human, and thus a product of his times. He used the same brusque and degrading language as those around him when speaking of black people. He believed those of African descent to be generally inferior to whites, if not biologically. He opposed slavery as an institution offensive to American ideals of liberty and contrary to economic progress, more so than as a force of suffering imposed daily on millions of individual human beings (whose personal anguish he rarely spoke of).[32] "He came into the Presidential chair upon one principle alone," wrote Frederick Douglass, "namely, opposition to the extension of slavery," not the *end* of slavery.[33] Lincoln envisioned sending African Americans back to Africa more so than emancipating them domestically, and generally favored a gradual fading-out of the institution rather than its swift and immediate destruction. His Emancipation Proclamation, which freed slaves in the Confederacy but not in the loyal border states nor in federally controlled areas such as New Orleans, revealed his prioritization for military strategy over human liberation. Lincoln, in short, opposed slavery as a hypocritical and counterproductive blight on his land, his nation, and what Douglass famously called Lincoln's "children," white Americans. He did not end slavery for the sake of his "step-children," black Americans.[34]

We would be naïve, then, to over-interpret the New Orleans experience as Lincoln's life-pivoting racial epiphany, as the "hit it hard" line suggests. We would be guilty of oversimplification if we viewed the experience as the origin of the Emancipation Proclamation, as the Rockport plaque declares. Rather, the New Orleans trips implanted in the budding young intellectual unforgettable eyewitness memories that would serve, subtly and episodically for a lifetime, to spark ethical contemplation, elucidate personal conviction, and embolden moral courage on the issue of slavery. Whatever his political expediencies, whatever his visceral feelings about race, whatever his "true" motivations might have been, the fact remains that Abraham Lincoln ended slavery in the United States of

32. Paludan, "Lincoln and Negro Slavery," 1–23.
33. Frederick Douglass, *The Life and Times of Frederick Douglass: From 1817–1882*, edited by John Lobb (London, England: Christian Age Office, 1882), 372.
34. Ibid., 373.

America, all the while drawing from the wellspring of signature mental imagery witnessed in New Orleans.

•

The two flatboat journeys exposed Lincoln, for weeks on end, to the vastness of the American landscape. No subsequent life travels would ever match the length of those journeys. They inculcated in him the relationship between transportation and economic development in the West, demonstrating personally just how much time, effort, and risk went into delivering hard-earned crops to market.

Efforts to reduce that risk, and speed that access to market, pulsated throughout the West of Abraham Lincoln's youth. He built his first flatboat at a time when circumventing the Great Falls at Louisville with a manmade canal was the talk of the Ohio Valley. (One informant claimed Lincoln even helped excavate that ditch—the Louisville and Portland Canal—together with John D. Johnston, in 1827.[35]) He navigated the Father of Waters at a time when Capt. Henry Shreve's channel improvements were the talk of the Mississippi Valley. He cursed the Sangamon River's shallow water, wrestled with its obstacles, and hacked its overhanging vegetation. In the Illinois, Ohio, and Mississippi rivers he dodged sawyers, poled around sandbars, evaded logjams, witnessed crevasses, and suffered hours drifting around yawning meanders that could have been eliminated with short cut-offs. He traversed the Mississippi Valley at a time when railroad fever first swept the region, and visited New Orleans precisely as the first complete rail line west of the Appalachians commenced service there. The river experiences of 1826–32, and particularly the New Orleans trips of 1828 and 1831, introduced Abraham Lincoln to the promise of long-distance commerce and the problems of existing transportation. The solution was what Americans at the time called "internal improvements," and what we now call "infrastructure": navigable rivers, canals, railroads, roads, bridges, ferries, locks, and dams.

It comes as no surprise, then, that Lincoln's first public-affairs speech, delivered extemporaneously two years after the first New Orleans trip, promoted internal improvements for central Illinois. Nor should it seem unusual that, while running for Illinois state legislature nine months after his second New Orleans trip, Lincoln featured the improved navigability of the Sangamon River as his platform. He drew liberally from his

35. A. H. Chapman to William H. Herndon, September 8, 1865, in *Herndon's Informants*, 100–101.

flatboating experience when announcing his candidacy, even citing the incident at the mill dam:

> [F]or the last twelve months I have given as particular atten-
> tion to the stage of the water in this river, as any other per-
> son in the country. In the month of March, 1831, in company
> with others, I commenced the building of a flat boat on the
> Sangamo [*sic*], and finished and took her out in the course of
> the spring. Since that time, I have been concerned in the mill
> at New Salem.[36]

Cutting out "drifted timber," "removing the turf," "damming up the old channel," "increasing the velocity of the current": Lincoln unveiled a litany of proposals demonstrating both his economic vision and boatman's savvy toward making the Sangamon wide, deep, and straight enough for steamboat traffic. In a passage seemingly gleaned from Capt. Henry Shreve's channel-improvements advocacy on the lower Mississippi, Lincoln proposed excavating cut-offs on the Sangamon's meander loops:

> There are also many places above this where the river, in its zig
> zag course, forms such complete peninsulas, as to be easier cut
> through at the necks than to remove the obstructions from the
> bends—which if done, would also lessen the distance.[37]

Lincoln also paid homage to the other internal improvement ongoing in New Orleans: railroads. "A meeting has been held [regarding] constructing a rail road from . . . the Illinois river [through] Jacksonville [to] Springfield," Lincoln reported during his 1832 political campaign. He then opined:

> This is, indeed, a very desirable object. No other improvement
> . . . can equal in utility the rail road. It is a never failing source
> of communication, between places of business remotely situ-
> ated from each other. Upon the rail road the regular progress of
> commercial intercourse is not interrupted by either high or low
> water, or freezing weather, which . . . render our future hopes
> of water communication precarious and uncertain.[38]

Clearly Lincoln recognized the revolutionary promise of railroads. But the

---

36. Abraham Lincoln, "Communication to the People of Sangamo County," *Sangamo Journal*, March 9, 1832, in *Collected Works*, 1:6.
37. Ibid., 7.
38. Ibid., 5–6.

budding politician had his priorities straight: a railroad connecting Jacksonville and Springfield with the Illinois River would bypass New Salem, regardless of improvements on the Sangamon. His primary constituents were not the people of Jacksonville or Springfield, but of New Salem. Bemoaning the "heart appalling shock accompanying [the railroad's] cost," which he estimated at $290,000, Lincoln offered no further support for the railroad in the campaign.[39]

Shortly after announcing his candidacy, Lincoln demonstrated his commitment to navigation by successfully piloting the steamboat *Talisman* up the Sangamon for the first time. Dropping water levels, however, made the return trip hasty and risky, and the *Talisman* nearly ended up stranded on the same mill dam that bedeviled Lincoln's flatboat the year prior. Lincoln proved two points with his dramatic demonstration: he was indeed a skilled river man, and the Sangamon River desperately needed state-funded improvement.

Lincoln lost that first election (despite overwhelming support in New Salem), in part because his April-through-July-1832 service in the Black Hawk War interrupted the campaign. The political experience nevertheless reinforced in him that internal improvements ranked utterly fundamental for Illinois, a message he carried to the state legislature when he ran again and won in 1834. Unfortunately, those improvements never arrived to the Sangamon River, and, as if to prove once again Lincoln's point, New Salem accordingly withered away and disappeared by 1840. Lincoln himself departed for Springfield in 1837. Except for his Washington years, he would call Springfield home for the rest of his life.

Drawing from his personal river experience, realizing the triumph of New York's Erie Canal, and knowing firsthand the Louisville and Portland Canal's success in bypassing the Great Falls of the Ohio River, Lincoln championed internal improvements throughout his 1830s–40s legislative career. By no means married to waterways, he also recognized the power of the iron horse to rework the economic geographies of a region hitherto tethered to the patterns of natural hydrology. He enthusiastically supported state subsidies for internal improvements and helped design Illinois' ambitious plans for a network of canals, roads, bridges, and tracks, even after the Panic of 1837 derailed them. He cast the winning vote for funding the Illinois and Michigan Canal, which, when finally excavated, replaced the terrestrial Chicago Portage with a commercial waterway connecting the Great Lakes and Gulf of Mexico watersheds (setting the stage

39. Ibid., 6.

for the twentieth-century ascendancy of Chicago).[40] In Lincoln's mind, such modernization—what we would call "infrastructure investment" or "capital improvement" today—delivered the promise of the America Dream to the common farmer and working man. Wrote historian G. S. Boritt, Lincoln "understood and preached that a better transportation system would quicken the pulse of Illinois economic life, raise living standards for all, enhance property values, and attract immigrants."[41] Lincoln expressed little interest in core Whig social and cultural philosophies on matters such as temperance, religion, morality, and foreign immigration, which very much leaned toward the conservative. Rather, his Whig impulses expressed themselves mostly in the economic realm, and in this he was passionate, supporting protective tariffs, a national bank, and, most of all, federal and state investment in transportation modernization.[42] Reflected long-time Lincoln friend Joshua Speed, "Mr Lincoln [viewed] Internal improvements [as] the best interest and advancement of this State. . . . [H]is highest ambition was to become the De Witt Clinton of Ill[inoi]s."[43]

Ever the tinkerer, Lincoln engaged personally in solving the nation's transportation problems. Inspired by a steamboat trip across Lake Erie as well as his flatboat experiences, Lincoln designed a device to levitate steamboats lodged on sand bars. It involved air chambers that were lowered by vertical poles into the water on both sides of the vessel, like giant buoyant crutches. Once inflated, the bellows would then lift up the hull enough to slip the entire operation off the obstacle and into safer waters. In 1849 Lincoln secured Patent No. 6469 for his invention, the only American president to be so distinguished. "Although I regarded the thing as impractical I said nothing," confided William Herndon to his readers, "probably out of respect for Lincoln's well-known reputation as a boatman." The *Scientific American* was a bit kinder when it pointed out in 1860, "there are thousands of mechanics who would devise a better apparatus for buoying steamboats over bars, but how many of them would be able to compete successfully in the race for the Presidency?" "A. Lincoln's Improved Manner of Buoying Vessels," as Abraham called his

40. Donald, *Lincoln*, 58–59.

41. G. S. Boritt, *Lincoln and the Economics of the American Dream* (Memphis, TN: Memphis State University Press, 1978), 9.

42. Ibid.; Eric Froner, "A New Abraham Lincoln?," *Reviews in American History* 7, no. 3 (September 1979): 375–379.

43. Interview, Joshua F. Speed, by William H. Herndon, 1865–1866, in *Herndon's Informants*, 476.

contraption, never went into production, but did demonstrate a creative mind grappling constantly with ways to improve the nation's transportation system.[44]

Amid years as a clerk, postman, surveyor, and country lawyer on central Illinois' Fourteenth Circuit (dubbed "the mud circuit" for its bad roads), Lincoln also served four terms in the Illinois state legislature and one term in the U.S. House of Representatives between 1834 and 1849. By the early 1850s he shifted professionally from making law to practicing law. With new tracks now crisscrossing the state, railroads became a mainstay of Lincoln's increasingly successful legal practice, in cases involving rights-of-way, eminent domain, and tax liability. Perhaps his most influential case, involving the Rock Island Railroad, legally cleared the way for the construction of railroad bridges over navigable waterways—a flash point in the war between boatmen and railroad men, and a turning point for the latter's enormous progress in the late nineteenth century.[45] Lincoln in this era also represented clients *suing* railroad companies: like most lawyers, he "accepted whatever promising cases came his way" and did not "pursue some political or philosophical agenda through litigation."[46]

Lincoln's rising stature in the legal profession, based largely on railroad cases, enabled him to return to national-level politics by decade's end. Less than a year separated Lincoln the railroad attorney from Lincoln the president. As chief executive, he signed into law the Pacific Railway Act of 1862, for the construction of a railroad and telegraph line from the Missouri River to the Pacific Ocean. By decade's end, iron tracks and iron horses united the nation.

Circumstantial evidence and explicit words connect Lincoln's Whig commitment to internal improvements with the river experiences of his early adulthood, most prominently his flatboat journeys to New Orleans. The voyages offered firsthand justification for his brand of economic Whiggery. Volumes have been written on the emergence of Lincoln's political philosophies, but at least one informant who was present at their

44. Louis A. Warren, ed., "A. Lincoln Manner of Buoying Vessels," *Lincoln Lore: Bulletin of the Lincoln National Life Foundation*, no. 1439, January 1958. Quotations are from "Abraham Lincoln: An Extraordinary Life," exhibition at National Museum of American History, Smithsonian Institution, visited April 14, 2009.

45. Louis A. Warren, ed., "The Railsplitter and the Railroads," *Lincoln Lore: Bulletin of the Lincoln National Life Foundation*, no. 484, July 18, 1938.

46. James W. Ely Jr., "Abraham Lincoln as a Railroad Attorney," 2005 Railroad Symposium Essays, Indiana Historical Society Press, available http://www.indianahistory. org.

birth specifically recalled Lincoln switching allegiances from that of a "Jackson Democrat" to "whig—or whiggish"—around 1828, the year of his first New Orleans trip.[47] In the same way that slavery in New Orleans instilled in Lincoln's mind signature imagery demonstrating the evils of that institution, the transportation trials and tribulations of his flatboat journeys, and possibly the demonstrative experiences of Shreve's channel improvements, the New Orleans steam locomotive exhibit, and the Pontchartrain Railroad, provided evidence and rationale for Lincoln's lifelong advocacy of internal improvements.

•

"I am not ashamed to confess," presidential candidate Abraham Lincoln told a New Haven audience in 1860, "that twenty five years ago I was a hired laborer, mauling rails, at work on a flat-boat."[48] In doing so, Lincoln yoked his flatboating to what would soon become his most famous symbolic image, that of the rail-splitter.

Illinois state politician and Lincoln advocate Richard James Oglesby gets credit for shaping that triumph of political iconography. Aware of the power of folksy slogans—"Old Hickory," "Tippecanoe and Tyler Too," etc.—that were *de rigueur* in nineteenth-century American politics, Oglesby sought an accessible symbol that would portray Abraham Lincoln as a frontier commoner with mythical properties of strength and moral fiber. At the 1860 Republican Party state nominating convention, Oglesby erected an enormous temporary meetinghouse in downtown Decatur and dubbed it a "wigwam" as a metaphor (widely recognized at the time) of citizen participation in the political arena.[49] A faux wigwam, however, spoke nothing of Lincoln himself. Seeking better ideas from those who knew the candidate well, Oglesby asked a garrulous curmudgeon whom he had known for years what sort of work Lincoln excelled at in his youth. "Well, not much of any kind but dreaming," the informant

47. This information comes from Dennis Hanks, who at one point recalled "1828–9" as the time when Lincoln changed his politics, and later revised it to "1827–8." Others disagreed; John Hanks claimed Abe "was never a Democrat, he was always a Whig; so was his father before him." Interview, Dennis Hanks, by William H. Herndon, September 8, 1865, in *Herndon's Informants*, 103–105; Louis A. Warren, *Lincoln's Youth*, 189.

48. Abraham Lincoln, "Speech at New Haven, Connecticut," March 6, 1860, in *Collected Works*, 4:24.

49. A drawing of the Republican Wigwam appears in "The Republican Standard," broadside published by Rufus Blanchard, Chicago, Illinois, 1860. Alfred Whital Stern Collection of Lincolniana, Library of Congress (hereafter cited as Stern Collection).

responded, "but he did help me split a lot of rails when we made a clearing twelve miles west of here." Next day the two men rode out to the spot and retrieved two weathered fence rails deemed to be ones Lincoln mauled thirty years earlier.[50] They hauled them back to Decatur, and at the right moment during the convention inside the wigwam, Oglesby's informant dramatically marched in bearing the wooden rails with an affixed sign reading, "Abraham Lincoln, the Rail Candidate, For President in 1860. Two rails from a lot of 3000 made in 1830. . . ." The informant's name: John Hanks, the same irrepressible spirit who gave us the "hit it hard" quote, the Voodoo tale, and so many other colorful details (reliable and otherwise) about Lincoln's youth. Newspapers picked up on "Lincoln the Rail Splitter," the campaign encouraged it with words and images, supporters responded enthusiastically, and political history was made.[51] So effective was the symbol that farmers in the Northeast complained that souvenir-hunters were making off with their fence rails.[52]

Hanks could have just as easily mentioned to Oglesby Lincoln's flat-boating experience. Had he done so, "Lincoln the Boatman" might have emerged as the candidate's premier symbol of rustic appeal. At least one deferential article dubbed Lincoln "The Flatboat Man."[53] That image, however, had problems. Piloting a flatboat—a group activity involving a bulky vessel—did not pictographically hold a candle to the individualized heroism of a tall, powerful frontiersman swinging an axe in a wilderness forest. Additionally, flatboatmen in general suffered bad reputations. The politically savvy Oglesby might have thumbed-down "Lincoln the Boatman" had Hanks or others suggested it.[54]

50. A document dated June 1, 1860, signed by John Hanks with an X and attested by R. J. Oglesby, certifies that the rails were "from a lot of 30,000 made by Abraham Lincoln and myself thirty years ago in this county. . . ." The figure was later reduced to a more reasonable 3000. Hanks Family Papers, Manuscript Collection, SC 644, Abraham Lincoln Presidential Library, Springfield, Illinois.

51. J. McCan Davis, "Origin of the Lincoln Rail, As Related by Governor Oglesby," *Century Illustrated Magazine* 60, no. 2 (June 1900): 271; Mark A. Plummer, *Lincoln's Rail-Splitter: Governor Richard J. Oglesby* (Urbana and Chicago: University of Illinois Press, 2001), 11–13.

52. "Political Intelligence—Complaint Among the Farmers," *New York Herald*, June 25, 1860, p. 5, c. C.

53. "The Republican Nominees," article originally appearing in the *Boston Journal*, picked up by the *St. Albans Daily Messenger* (St. Albans, VT), May 31, 1860, p. 1.

54. Lincoln himself gave equal weight to rail-mauling and flatboating in his speech at New Haven—which, incidentally, occurred two months before the Decatur convention and the birth of the Rail-Splitter.

Flatboating instead assumed a secondary but nonetheless significant role in symbolizing Lincoln the candidate. A famous campaign painting by an unknown artist, for example, prominently featured the Rail-Splitter mauling logs in a bankside forest overlooking an Ohio-like river in the distance—and a tiny flatboat drifts downriver behind Lincoln's figure. Envelopes used to mail campaign fliers featured the famous split-rail fences, but also graphically incorporated "Old Abe in his flatboat" or "Honest Abe Lincoln and His Flat Boat" into the design.[55] One campaign item deployed flatboating as its primary iconography: a broadside entitled *The Republican Standard* featured a colored wood engraving of Lincoln poling a flatboat down the Mississippi, surrounded by a border of split-rail fences anchored by two log cabins and two flatboats. Its caption read,

LINCOLN AS A FLATBOATMAN ON THE
MISSISSIPPI RIVER
QUINCY IN THE DISTANCE
Peter the Great, to whose genius Russia owes her fame, served an apprenticeship to ship building. Abraham Lincoln has served an apprenticeship to flatboating, and may he yet guide the Ship of State with his own inherent honesty of purpose.[56]

No documented evidence indicates that Lincoln flatboated past Quincy, Illinois, which abuts the Mississippi well *upriver* from its confluence with the Illinois River. (Flatboats could not navigate against the current). The broadside's biographical text read,

At twenty-one he removed to Illinois, and passed the first year . . . in active labor on a farm, where he and a fellow laborer (named Hanks) SPLIT THREE THOUSAND RAILS, in the year 1830. It will be interesting to the millions before whom he is now placed as a candidate for the highest office in the gift of a free people, to know that he once *managed a flatboat* on the Ohio River. The anecdotes which he sometimes related to his friends of his maritime experience before the introduction of steam on the western rivers, are indescribably laughable.[57]

Note that New Orleans and the entire southern leg of his journeys go unmentioned. Quincy, on the other hand, gets prominent treatment. Would shining light on Lincoln's experiences in the South's premier slave mart

55. "Winnowings," *New York Times*, November 5, 1888, p. 4.
56. "Republican Standard," Stern Collection.
57. Ibid. (emphasis in original)

invite potentially distracting questions, at a time when any further national divisiveness might prompt secession? Or might it add to the suspicions of ardent abolitionists that Kentucky-born Lincoln dabbled all too much in the South and its slave-holding economy—his in-laws were prominent slave-owners—and lacked the passion to destroy the institution? The omission corresponds with Lincoln's own 1860 autobiographical notes, which, as pointed out earlier, remain conspicuously silent on slave trading in New Orleans compared to what he wrote and said in private. The campaign, like Lincoln, seemed to be hiding something.

In another example of political symbolism, composer Charles Grobe parlayed the candidate's metaphors into song and dance. His 1860 "Lincoln Quick Step" featured frontier drawings on the cover, matched with lyrics inside:

> "HONEST OLD ABE" has split many a rail
> He is up to his work, and he'll surely not fail,
> He has guided his FLAT-BOAT thro' many a strait,
> And watchful he'll prove at the HELM of the State.[58]

Musically inclined Lincoln supporters also published *The Wide-Awake Vocalist or, Rail Splitters' Song Book*, which invoked flatboat themes in ditties such as "Lincoln Boat Horn":

> I shall go for Abraham Lincoln, the Farm-hand, the Flat-boat-
> man . . .
> Lincoln, [the] Boatman of the Sangamo!
> Lincoln, the Boatman, is the people's Friend!
> Lincoln, the Boatman, lead to victory![59]

Supporters also used the flatboat icon in material culture. Republicans in Cassopolis, Michigan, built "a Lincoln Flat-Boat Cabin, or Wigwam, for their use during the campaign."[60] The tens of thousands of wildly enthusiastic supporters who descended on Springfield in August 1860 pulled along "a mammoth flatboat on wheels" in their mile-and-a-half-long procession.[61] Other rallies later that month featured floats depicting all three

58. Charles Grobe, "Lincoln Quick Step, Dedicated to the Hon. Abraham Lincoln," sheet music (Philadelphia: Lee & Walker, 1860), 2. Stern Collection.

59. *The Wide-Awake Vocalist or, Rail Splitters' Song Book* (New York: E. A. Daggett, 1860), 29, 58.

60. "Summary of News," *The Constitution* (Washington, D.C.), June 2, 1860, p. 3.

61. "Lincoln at Home: Seventy-Five Thousand Republications Call on Him—Imposing Demonstration," *Chicago Press and Tribune*, August 9, 1860, p. 1.

symbols: the splitting of rails, the log cabin, and "a flatboat on which smoke exuded from a stove pipe and roosters crowed in their coops."[62] Some supporters saw deeper symbolism in the flatboat—of the poverty imposed on good Americans like Lincoln via the evils of slavery, from which Lincoln sought personal liberation:

> Slavery, by depriving [Lincoln's] youth of all advantages, launched and left him on a flat boat. But that flat boat, bearing him across the Ohio to free soil, freedom supplied what slavery denied, and bore him steadily upward to the Presidency. . . . Abraham Lincoln . . .—*from the flat-boat to the Presidential Chair.* . . .[63]

Skeptics and enemies saw through the manipulative political imagery, emphasizing instead Lincoln's not-so-bucolic ascendancy into the comfortable professional class. Others disdained the man on *account* of his rustic riverine roots. "They hate Lincoln," wrote a Lincoln sympathizer in reference to this group; "They are refined and educated men; he a vulgar jester, *redolent of the flat-boat and the backwoods.*"[64] One elite New York newspaper, suspicious of the rural Western "Goths and Vandals" whom the president-elect might appoint to federal positions, turned the imagery into insults by describing Lincoln's men as "rail splitters" who "have been on board the same flatboat, and taken whiskey out of the same tin cup with [Lincoln]."[65] A Cleveland editorialist poked fun at candidate Lincoln by cackling in an exaggerated rural Western dialect, "He split some rails in Illinoy and bossed a roarin' flat-boat. Them is his only qualifications, aside frum [*sic*] his personal beauty, for President of the United States." The editorialist also derided the aforementioned *Republican Standard* broadside heralding the former flatboat captain rising to guide the Ship of State:

> Make Linkin Capting of the Ship of State, and in less than a year she'll be without rudder, compass, or anchor. Who

---

62. *Canton Regular*, August 28, 1860, as interpreted by H. Preston James, "Political Pageantry in the Campaign of 1860 in Illinois," *Abraham Lincoln Quarterly* 4, no. 7 (September 1947): 332.

63. "Our Representative Men," *Chicago Tribune*, June 11, 1864, p. 2 (emphasis added).

64. "The Light-Haired to the Front," *Daily Ohio Statesman* (Columbus), 31, no. 291, June 2, 1864, p. 2 (emphasis added).

65. "A Raid Upon Washington," *New York Herald*, March 2, 1861, p. 6, c. C.

wants to see the Ship of State degenerate into a rickety old flat-boat?[66]

Other opponents threw in the hapless John Hanks, disdained as an inarticulate yokel, as they lampooned Lincoln's provincial biography:

> Old Abe is born. He suffers from teething and a bad "nuss." He deserts . . . his home with an axe on his shoulder for Illinois [and] becomes midshipman on a flatboat. . . . He deserts the service, flings his commission to the wind, again shoulders his axe, and commences his career as a rail splitter. He cast his lot with one as celebrated as himself, named Hanks. He feels the inspiration of his talent, spits upon rail splitting, tears himself from Hanks, and turns lawyer. . . . An extraordinary convulsion of nature casts him into the State Legislature. A still more extraordinary convulsion lands him in Congress, where he denounces the Mexican War, opposes the American soldiers and gets his mileage. He goes home and is driven into obscurity by an indignant constituency. He is picked out to run at the head of the abolition machine for President, and anxiously awaits the result.[67]

A particularly scurrilous satirical pamphlet released in 1864 by the Copperheads (Northern and Western anti-war Democrats who viewed Lincoln as a despot) mocked the images and questioned their veracity. "Now gentlemen," says the Lincoln figure in one vignette, "people are very fond of calling me a flat boatman, a rail splitter, and so forth. I assure you I never made but one voyage on a flat boat and never split but one rail and that's the *rail* truth." "*Really*, Lincoln," responded a disgusted citizen, "you are the meanest li—," only to stop in mid-sentence as he watched Lincoln guzzle cheap whiskey.[68]

Republicans used the attacks on Lincoln's rusticity to their advantage—and deftly so, for they knew that the log cabin, the split rails, and the flatboat not only humanized their candidate but successfully undercut Democrats' depiction of Whigs and the new Republicans as the party

66. "A Political Sermon—by the Rev. Hardshell Pike," originally published in the *Cleveland Plaindealer* and picked up by the *Wisconsin Patriot* (Madison, WI), August 18, 1860, p. 7.

67. "Life of Lincoln" pamphlet circulating at Chicago nominating convention, as reported by *Weekly Wisconsin Patriot* (Madison, WI), June 30, 1860, p. 6.

68. *Abraham Africanus I: His Secret Life, as Revealed Under the Mesmeric Influence* (New York: J. F. Feeks, 1864), 31 (emphasis in original).

of the entrenched wealthy aristocracy. Members of the passionately pro-Lincoln "Wide Awakes" explicitly co-opted their opponents' tactics by singing,

> Let them prate about rail-splitting, splitting, splitting, Flat-boating, too;
> We'll swing the maul, and drive the wedge, For Lincoln, the true. . . .[69]

Later, those same appealing symbols helped endear the assassinated president to the ages.[70] Most Americans to this day can recite at least one of them; the U.S. Mint featured two of them (the log cabin and the rail-splitter) on its Lincoln Bicentennial redesigns of the penny. All three icons share a common theme: the rendering of the wilderness (represented by timber) into domesticity (log cabins), agriculture, pasture (split-rail fences), and commerce (flatboats), through individual strength, determination, and hard work. While the flatboat lagged in press references and popular imagination, it may well be the case that of the three symbols, flatboating proved to be the most genuinely influential in Lincoln's life.

•

Weltanschauung refers to an individual's comprehensive conceptualization of humanity and life on earth. Its loan translation from German in the late nineteenth century produced the convenient and self-defining English word "worldview." Flatboatmen saw their worldviews change as a result of their journeys, and they broadened the perspectives of folks back home in recounting their experiences. "These river-men . . . brought us strange accounts of the countries in the far South," recalled one old Hoosier;

> They told us of the magnolia, the cypress, the live-oak, of the fields of cane and cotton, and of the large and populous

---

69. *The Wide-Awake Vocalist or, Rail Splitters' Song Book* (New York: E. A. Daggett, 1860), 27.

70. The flatboat symbol, however, retained a certain stigma for decades. One admirer of the former president declared in 1895 that, although Lincoln had guided flatboats, "Lincoln was never in any sense of the word a 'flatboatman.'" Viele defined that word not as an occupation, but as a character: flatboatmen were "a distinct class of men . . . rough and lawless, [and] a terror to [steamboat] passengers by their wild orgies. . . . To say, or suppose, that Abraham Lincoln was ever one of these men is simply absurd." Gen. Egbert L. Viele, "Lincoln Not a Flatboatman: His Trip Down the Mississippi to New Orleans to Sell a Barrel of Whiskey and a Case of Tobacco," *Springfield Republication* (Springfield, MA), March 12, 1895, p. 12.

plantations . . . where the overseer would buy almost a whole boat-load of supplies. They had seen also the negro slaves, men and women, working on the plantations, and the guards armed with guns and whips. . . . They told us, in an undertone, that this was very hard to look at; that is was all wrong, but that the law allowed these things.[71]

"The tremendous part the river life played in developing the ambitions and intelligence of the western settlers can never be estimated," contended a journalist later in the nineteenth century. "*To them it brought all they knew of the civilized world. By it alone they touched men and progress.*"[72] Lincoln himself alluded to the notion of *Weltanschauung* when recalling his first dollar earned on the Ohio River: "The *world seemed wider* and fairer before me. I was a more *hopeful and confident being* from that time."[73] The experience broadened his worldview.

Geographically, environmentally, culturally, racially, religiously, linguistically, and economically, Lincoln's trips to New Orleans informed and expanded his worldview.

The trips placed Lincoln in a subtropical zone for the first and only time in his life. Magnolias and a few palms he would have seen during his Washington years, but the luxuriant flora and distinctive fauna associated with a nine-month growing season and five to six feet of annual rainfall met his eyes only during the trips to New Orleans. Portions of the voyages, particularly through the floodplain of the Mississippi and Yazoo rivers between Memphis and Vicksburg, exposed Lincoln to one of the last vast bottomland wildernesses of the eastern half of the continent. Had he visited Lake Pontchartrain while in New Orleans—and with a new road in 1828 and a new railroad in 1831, he certainly could have—Lincoln would have gained his one and only view of gulf waters. According to one recollection, the trips to New Orleans also impressed upon Lincoln the dynamism of the untamed Mississippi River. "Examining a large military map hanging against the wall," remembered Kentucky Congressman George Yeaman after a visit to the Lincoln White House, the president

pointed out where the Mississippi river once made a horse-

71. As quoted by Richard Lawrence Miller, *Lincoln and his World: The Early Years, Birth to Illinois Legislature* (Mechanicsburg, PA: Stackpole Books, 2006), 83.

72. "The Mississippi Valley Fleet," *Salt Lake Herald*, July 12, 1896, p. 10, c. 3 (emphasis added).

73. As quoted by J. Edward Murr, "Lincoln in Indiana," *Indiana Magazine of History* 14, no. 1 (March 1918): 149 (emphasis added).

shoe bend, nearly a complete circuit, around which he went
on a flatboat in descending the river, and pointed out where
the river broke through the narrow peninsula, while he was at
New Orleans, making a new channel through which the pilot,
on the up journey, guided the steamer, where it was dry land
on the down trip.[74]

That geographical education informed Lincoln's advocacy for improved
navigation, and conceivably his role as military commander in chief.

Floating into the subtropics, Lincoln would have seen for the first time
extensive cultivations of two non-native species upon which the South's
economy rested: cotton and sugar cane. By no means would the field slaves
working those plantations have been the first Lincoln ever saw; he spent
one-third of his youth in the South, and often witnessed enslaved men,
women, and children in transit or toil. The trips to New Orleans did,
however, represent his first and only penetration deep into the slave South
(indeed, across the entire region) and into places where enslaved African
Americans not only abounded, but predominated overwhelmingly.

New Orleans ranked as the largest city the young Lincoln had ever
seen, and would remain so until he stepped upon the national stage as a
newly elected congressman in 1848. It also formed the most ethnically
diverse and culturally foreign city in the United States. We cannot say that
Lincoln's visits to the Southern entrepôt were the closest the future president ever came to setting foot in another country, because he day-tripped
into Niagara Falls, Canada, in 1857. Nor can we say the city first exposed
Lincoln to French- or Spanish-speakers, immigrants, or Catholics and
Catholicism, as he occasionally encountered such peoples and their cultural ways in Indiana, Illinois, or on the Ohio River.[75] But we can say
that Lincoln immersed himself in a different culture—in terms of ethnicity, ancestry, religion, language, race, caste, class, foodways, architecture,
and sheer urban magnitude—more so in New Orleans than in any other
place or time of his life. "New Orleans," stated scholar Louis A. Warren, "gave [Lincoln] an opportunity to visualize a typical foreign city."[76] It
would also expose him to the nation's largest concentration of free people

74. As quoted in Louis A. Warren, ed., "Lincoln's Return Trip from New Orleans,"
Lincoln Lore: Bulletin of the Lincoln National Life Foundation, no. 472, April 25, 1938.

75. For a discussion on Lincoln and Catholicism, see Louis A. Warren, ed., "President
Lincoln's Interest in Catholic Institutions," *Lincoln Lore: Bulletin of the Lincoln National
Life Foundation*, no. 790, May 29, 1944.

76. Louis A. Warren, ed., "Lincoln in New Orleans," *Lincoln Lore: Bulletin of the Lincoln National Life Foundation*, no. 333, August 26, 1935.

of color, among them some of the wealthiest and best-educated people of African ancestry anywhere. Lincoln never specifically commented on the city's diversity, but came close when he personally hand-edited biographical words on that topic penned by W. D. Howells in 1860. After marveling at "the many-negroed planter of the sugar-coast, and the patriarchal creole of Louisiana," without edits from Lincoln, Howells saluted

> that cosmopolitan port, where the French voyageur and the rude hunter that trapped the beaver on the Osage and Missouri, met the polished old-world exile, and the tongues of France, Spain, and England made babel in the streets. . . .[77]

Lincoln explicitly embraced the sort of pluralism he first witnessed in the large Catholic and foreign-born population of New Orleans. In an 1855 letter to friend Joshua Speed, he wrote forcefully against the nativist political movement gaining popularity at that time. "I am not a Know-Nothing," he declared.

> That is certain. How could I be? How can any one who abhors the oppression of negroes, be in favor of degrading classes of white people? . . . As a nation, we began by declaring that *"all men are created equal."* We now practically read it "all men are created equal, *except negroes.*" When the Know-Nothings get control, it will read "all men are created equal, except negroes, and foreigners, and catholics." When it comes to this I should prefer emigrating to some country where they make no pretence of loving liberty—to Russia, for instance, where despotism can be taken pure, and without the base alloy of hypocracy [*sic*].[78]

One other worldview influence warrants mention, one that parlayed conveniently into military strategizing. Lincoln later in life regularly traveled Western rivers while on legal and political circuits. But only during the New Orleans voyages did he ever traverse the main lower trunk channel of the Mississippi River system. During the Civil War, that artery became vital to the Union's strategy to—as the commander in chief put it—"bisect

---

77. William Dean Howells, *Life of Abraham Lincoln*, facsimile edition of campaign biography corrected by the hand of Abraham Lincoln (Bloomington: Indiana University Press, 1960), 25.

78. Abraham Lincoln to Joshua F. Speed, August 24, 1855, in *Collected Works*, 2:323 (emphasis in original).

the Confederacy and have the Mississippi flow unvexed to the sea."[79] The bluff-top cities that Lincoln looked up to in 1828 and 1831 now, in 1861, aimed artillery down on his troops. As Lincoln met with his generals and devised strategy, the only personal mental imagery he could possibly have drawn upon in envisioning places like Memphis, Vicksburg, Grand Gulf, Natchez, Port Hudson, Baton Rouge, and New Orleans all traced back to his decades-old flatboat memories. When, after each of those places fell to Union troops, Lincoln beamed optimistically, "The signs look better. The Father of Waters again goes unvexed to the sea."[80]

•

Nearly all cultures commemorate milestones in the cycle of life. Passage from childhood to adulthood gets special treatment, marked in the Western world through religious rites such as Christianity's confirmation and Judaism's Bar and Bat Mitzvah, and in modern secular culture with graduations, debuts, sweet sixteens, and *quinceañeras*. Such formal rites are usually pegged to a certain age, in the expectation that adulthood is forthcoming.

Demonstrating adulthood, rather than declaring it, occurs more informally and variously. In rural America, a boy's first hunt is often viewed as a coming-of-age experience. Service in the armed forces is a passage expected of young men growing up in families with military traditions. Proselytizing missions are a prerequisite for nineteen-year-olds before they gain full standing in the Mormon Church. Studying a semester abroad, working a summer in the Rockies, or joining the Peace Corps are regularly pitched to college students as personal-development opportunities of special significance. What each example has in common is a long trip, taken alone or without parents (usually for the first time), requiring responsibility and resourcefulness, involving discomfort and risk, and promising a transformative experience. Figuratively speaking, they may be thought of as "rites of passage." Accepting the "rite" and "passing" satisfactorily earns social approval and professional advancement for the youth; declining or failing it garners disappointment and consternation, particularly from elders, who may view it as a rejection of their tutelage and way of life.

For young white males in the trans-Appalachian West of the early

79. As recollected by James F. Rusling, in Fehrenbacher and Fehrenbacher, *Recollected Words of Lincoln*, 388.

80. Abraham Lincoln to James C. Conkling, August 26, 1863, in *Collected Works*, 6:409.

1800s, flatboating to New Orleans informally validated the passage from boyhood to manhood. Farming families, merchants, and those who made a living off river transportation expected such service from their sons. In return, local society viewed what might be called "flatboat credentials"—piloting skills, commercial savvy, knowledge of the Mississippi River and New Orleans—as a litmus test for who could opine about certain topics, who could be trusted with certain tasks, who might make a good hire, who can tell a good story—who, in sum, had proven his manhood. "No young man could count himself among the elite young bucks of the community," stated one Indiana county history, "without having made at least one [flatboat] trip."[81] Even if the youth earned no profit in the venture, "What matter! He had been to 'Orleans' and ever after life meant a thousand new things."[82] Lincoln's father Thomas performed his flatboat rite of passage in 1806 and perhaps afterward; his close friend Peter Sibert Jr. would later become a famous Mississippi River navigator.[83] Thomas' son Abraham followed his father's path to New Orleans two decades later, as did Abraham's relatives on both his mother's and stepmother's sides (John Hanks, Dennis Hanks, and John D. Johnston), all of whom came of age under Thomas' custody. Abraham's paternal-side cousin Elijah Lincoln also performed the rite—and had a similar experience in New Orleans, as reported in this 1907 interview:

> I was like "Abe" [when he went to New Orleans on a flatboat].
> I could not stand that infernal slavery. I saw "niggers" killed by
> their masters. I jes' couldn't stand it.[84]

Lincoln's employers flatboated to New Orleans and directed the young men under their charge to do the same. One, James Gentry of Spencer County, performed the rite regularly, as did his son Allen, his brothers, and their sons. Another, Denton Offutt, tested Lincoln with a flatboat job before hiring him to run his New Salem store. The rite dominated the business of the Todd family of Lexington, Kentucky, whose daughter

81. As quoted in Michael Allen, *Western Rivermen, 1763–1861: Ohio and Mississippi Boatmen and the Myth of the Alligator Horse* (Baton Rouge and London: Louisiana State University Press, 1990), 172.

82. "The Mississippi Valley Fleet," *Salt Lake Herald*, July 12, 1896, p. 10, c. 3.

83. Louis A. Warren, ed., "A Riverside Lincoln Memorial," *Lincoln Lore: Bulletin of the Lincoln National Life Foundation*, no. 553, November 13, 1939.

84. "Abraham Lincoln's First Cousin Still Living, Gives Recollections of the Great Emancipator." *Chicago Daily Tribune*, February 10, 1907, p. F6.

Mary would one day marry Abraham.[85] "I had resolved when a small boy," declared one Hoosier, "to go to New Orleans on a flatboat. . . ."[86] Lincoln and his peers would have expressed the same sentiment.[87]

The flatboat journeys do not stand alone in making Lincoln a man, but rather punctuate a four-year passage (1828–32) from the impetuousness and semi-dependence of late adolescence, to the responsibilities and independence of adulthood.[88] That journey began, as readers will recall, with the unexpected death of his beloved sister during childbirth in January 1828, a tragedy that also deprived Lincoln of ever being a blood uncle. Three months later, and partly because of that trauma, came the first flatboat trip and all its influences. After returning, the already-changing Abraham started finding more and more fault with his sincere but simple father. He also alienated village peers and burned social bridges in a manner that revealed he was outgrowing the people of his childhood. Menial farm work, bloody hog-slaughtering, and wearisome rail-splitting convinced him that the life of those around him would not be the one for him. Then, on February 12, 1830, Lincoln turned twenty-one and gained legal independence from his father, including the right to vote and keep his own wages. A few weeks later, the Lincoln family left Indiana, ending for Abraham fourteen years of familiarity and community affiliations. Settling into Illinois in summer 1830 meant more manual labor—but also new associations, opportunities, and challenges, from which spawned the second flatboat trip in spring 1831. Upon returning that summer, Lincoln for the first time established permanent residency apart from his parents,

85. Jean H. Baker, *Mary Todd Lincoln: A Biography* (New York and London: W. W. Norton & Company, 1987), 25, 33–34.

86. Isaac Naylor, "Judge Isaac Naylor, 1790–1873: An Autobiography," *Indiana Magazine of History* 4, no. 3 (September 1908): 136.

87. It is interesting to note that Robert T. Lincoln (1843–1926), Abraham's only child to reach adulthood, also visited New Orleans, in 1893. Unlike his father, this Lincoln was welcomed by local leaders and given a private sight-seeing tour of the city, including forays to Metairie Cemetery, the Soldiers' Home, and the French Opera House on Bourbon Street. Whether the party toured the site of the old flatboat wharf, or discussed his father's famous visit, is unknown. "I . . . am pleased with my visit to New Orleans," Robert told a reporter, "which I have found to be a hospitable city full of intelligent and progressive people." He felt that New Orleanians "had now fully realized the uselessness and absurdity of doting on the unpleasantness of the past." "Pleased with New Orleans: Hon. Robert T. Lincoln Visits the Soldiers' Home and the Opera," *Daily Picayune*, November 8, 1893, p. 8, c. E

88. See Joseph Kett's discussion of semi-dependence as a stage of life in nineteenth-century America. Joseph Kett, *Rites of Passage: Adolescence in America, 1790 to Present* (New York: Basic Books, Inc. Publishers, 1977), 29–36.

and earned his own wages clerking in Offutt's New Salem store. The following spring he served in the Black Hawk War, an experience that, while not involving combat, posed danger, required leadership and responsibility, and involved long trips into new regions.[89] Upon returning from military service in summer 1832, Lincoln campaigned for a seat in the state legislature. He would eventually lose, but by then he was a man by any measure, tested by four years of tragedy, travel, responsibility, independence—and two lengthy flatboat journeys.

Belgian anthropologist Arnold Van Gennep's seminal work *The Rites of Passage* (1960) identified three interconnected stages commemorated by such practices worldwide. First comes separation from the familiar world of one's youth, followed by a liminal era of transition, ordeal, and ambiguity. Finally, after the passage, the youth re-incorporates into society and assumes his or her newly earned higher status. Lincoln's flatboat years map out well to Van Gennep's stages: the 1828 trip marks the initial separation; the alienation and discord of 1828–31 represent the ambiguous transitional era, which culminates with the second trip to New Orleans and subsequent Black Hawk War experience. Afterward—indeed, immediately upon returning from New Orleans—Lincoln re-incorporates into New Salem society with full manhood status, living alone, supporting himself, and aspiring to lead by running for office.

Evidence of this passage into adulthood comes from a rare personal recollection of Lincoln as a flatboat captain guiding cargo from New Salem to St. Louis around 1835. "One noticeable trait about Lincoln was that he never intrusted [*sic*] to anybody what he considered his work," recalled crewmate Stephen W. Garrison; "The boat was in his charge and we addressed him as 'Cap' or 'Captain.'" Accompanying Lincoln's deeply held sense of responsibility and seriousness of purpose was "a sad look" on his face, as if he was "in a deep study" or "had lost a friend or relative." Introversion and thoughtfulness occupied whatever moments navigation did not: "When the boat was on smooth water and needed but little attention, he read some and talked some. . . . He never had anything to say about himself." The crewmates took no offense at Lincoln's emotional distance,

89. Fighting Indians, like flatboating to New Orleans, also formed something of a rite of passage for young white males of this time and place, as evidenced by the previously cited Isaac Naylor (quoted here in full): "I had resolved when a small boy to accomplish two objects if I had the opportunity to do so. I had determined to go to New Orleans on a flatboat, and to go on a campaign against the Indians. Having accomplished the former object, I had an opportunity of accomplishing the latter." Naylor, "Judge Isaac Naylor," 136.

regarding him instead as "a good, kind master and we all liked him." That was in 1835. In 1861, Garrison saw Lincoln again in Cincinnati en route to Washington to assume the presidency. "I could still detect the same expression of sadness on his face that I first saw a quarter of a century previously when we floated down the Illinois together."[90]

A related life-passage phenomenon relevant to Lincoln's flatboat experience is that of the "sea change." Today this overused expression implies any significant shift in thinking caused by nearly any agency. The original expression, traceable to Shakespeare's The Tempest, suggests that sailing across open ocean profoundly transformed first-time travelers. Passengers, the theory went, forged new survival strategies, created social alliances, and formulated spiritual awareness as they sailed across the threatening unknown, and disembarked at their destination with new perspectives and outlooks on life. No doubt there is truth in the "sea change;" human beings transform slightly every day, thus it seems reasonable that significant shifts occur over the course of lengthy, risky, first-time trans-oceanic travel.

But what about rivers? Travel on rivers, with the visible safety of their nearby banks, imparts less mystery and risk than open seas. Yet Lincoln's flatboating experience arguably may be viewed as forming a "river change" of sorts. Evidence presented in this book shows that Lincoln the flatboatman saw new conditions and geographies, experienced peril, witnessed poignant spectacles, gained skills, built confidence, and came home changed. Others saw the change in Lincoln, even prior to the intense microanalysis Lincoln's life received after the assassination. An admiring congressman, speaking in 1864, traced Lincoln's intellectual, social, and moral development to his river journeys:

> [T]hat one trading trip on his flatboat to New-Orleans was worth a whole college course. The youth . . . passed, day after day, down the mighty Father of Waters, saw its tributaries, and thought of the vast continent it drained, observed and took advantage of its currents and shores, conversed and traded with its people, and fought with midnight robbers, gained an enlargement of soul and intellect, a variety of information, a tact and independence of character that no learned professors could have imparted. He did even the lowest duties he undertook

90. "Garrison's Prediction: Death of Abraham Lincoln's Friend Recalls a Prophecy Made by the Old Man That Came True," *Omaha World Herald*, September 30, 1899, p. 4.

honestly and well, yet his ever-expanding mind called him to
higher duties in life . . .[91]

Four years later, an aging Horace Greeley drew a similar interpretation of
the river trips as intrinsically life-changing, going so far as to analogize
them to a college diploma inscribed on sheepskin:

> How far his two flatboat voyages to New Orleans are to be
> classed as educational exercises [like] a freshman's year in col-
> lege, I will not say. . . . [Lincoln's] first introduction to the
> outside world from the deck of a "broad-horn" must have been
> wonderfully interesting and suggestive. To one whose utmost
> experience of civilization had been a county town[,] that must
> have been a marvelous spectacle which glowed in his face from
> the banks of the Ohio and the lower Mississippi. Though Cairo
> was then but a desolate swamp, Memphis a wood-landing and
> Vicksburgh [sic] a timbered ridge with a few stores at its base,
> even these were in striking contrast to the somber monotony of
> the great woods. The rivers were enlivened by countless swift-
> speeding steamboats, dispensing smoke by day and flame by
> night; while New Orleans, though scarcely one-fourth the city
> she now is, was the focus of a vast commerce, and of a civiliza-
> tion which (for America) might be deemed antique. I doubt
> not that our tall and green young backwoodsman needed only
> a piece of well-tanned sheepskin suitably . . . inscribed to have
> rendered those two boat trips memorable as his degrees in ca-
> pacity to act well his part on that stage which has mankind for
> its audience.[92]

We should be skeptical, however, of ascribing agency to inanimate natural forces. The Mississippi did nothing but flow to the Gulf; it was the
human constructs exploiting its current and lining its banks—the toil of
navigation, the commerce, the plantations, the people, the metropolis, the
bondage—that influenced travelers like Lincoln.

Lincoln himself alluded to the role that his flatboat experiences played
in personal development. According to one recollection, he referenced his
river days while lecturing a group of Sunday school students, explain-

91. "Character of President Lincoln—Remarks by Hon. A. Wakeman," *New York Times*, November 27, 1864, p. 5.

92. Horace Greeley, "Greeley's Estimate of Lincoln: An Unpublished Address," *Century Illustrated Magazine* 42, no. 3 (July 1891): 372. Greeley originally wrote this address circa 1868.

ing that "the only assurance of successful navigation . . . on the Mississippi . . . depended upon the manner in which [the flatboat] was started." Concluded Lincoln, "So it is with you young folks. . . . Be sure you get started right as you begin life, and you'll make a good voyage to a happy harbour."[93] While on the campaign trail in 1843, Lincoln cast his 1831 flatboat voyage as an authenticating, dues-paying experience, assuring his political supporters that his presently rising stature made him no less a man of the people:

> It would astonish . . . the older citizens of [Menard] County who twelve years ago knew me a strange[r], *friendless, uneducated, penniless boy, working on a flat boat—at ten dollars per month* to learn that I have been put down here as the candidate of pride, wealth, and arristocratic family distinction [*sic*].[94]

In 1860, while speaking in New Haven on the presidential campaign trail, Lincoln invoked his flatboat toils as evidence of his personal passage out of the poverty of his youth—a passage, he went on to say, that could be replicated by the free black man:

> [F]ree society is such that [a poor man] knows he can better his condition; he knows that there is no fixed condition of labor, for his whole life. *I am not ashamed to confess that twenty five years ago I was a hired laborer, mauling rails, at work on a flat-boat—just what might happen to any poor man's son!* I want every man to have the chance—and I believe a black man is entitled to it—in which he can better his condition—when he may look forward and hope to be a hired laborer this year and the next, work for himself afterward, and finally to hire men to work for him![95]

Observers noticed how the river experiences affected Lincoln's way of communicating. A journalist writing in January 1865 detected "flat-boat lingo" in the president's diction, such as in his promise upon attaining the presidency to "run the machine as he found it."[96] After the assassination,

93. "As In Years Gone By," *Chicago Daily*, February 13, 1895, p. 5.
94. Abraham Lincoln to Martin S. Morris, March 26, 1843, in *Collected Works*, 1:319–320 (emphasis added).
95. Lincoln, "Speech at New Haven," March 6, 1860, in *Collected Works*, 4:24–25 (emphasis added).
96. "Latest News from the South," *Sun* (Baltimore, MD) January 21, 1865, p. 1, citing other Southern newspapers.

a New York City politician, reflecting on the late president's mannerisms, wrote:

> [T]he young man who was to become President . . . made several voyages as a boat-hand, and apparently, not without impressing some of the peculiarities of that vocation upon his character; for, with the thoughtful and somewhat reticent nature of Mr. Lincoln's mind, was always blended the free and open manners of the voyageur. The sallies of wit and aptness of anecdote, with which the tedium of the boatman's life was varied, remained a characteristic of Mr. Lincoln's conversation. . . . A distinguished statesman and intimate friend of the deceased President [stated that] many of the most important discussions . . . of State policy received point and illustration from the application of an apt anecdote, drawn from the stores of a memory which seemed fully supplied with them.[97]

Lincoln explicitly found inspiration in the boatman's patient ability to focus on the challenges of the moment. "The pilots on our Western rivers steer from *point to point*," he remarked, "setting the course of the boat no farther than they can see. . . ."[98] Indeed, the notion of river travel as a metaphor for life occupied a special place in Lincoln's world—literally. On the wall of his Springfield dining room hung a framed print of the second of Thomas Cole's four famous *Voyage of Life* paintings, respectively subtitled *Birth*, *Youth*, *Manhood*, and *Old Age*. It features a robust lad departing on a gilded vessel down a lush river, toward a sublime landscape of majestic mountains and celestial clouds.

Voyage of Life: Youth hangs in the Lincoln home to this day.[99]

•

This study finds that Lincoln's flatboat journeys to New Orleans influenced the man in meaningful ways. We conclude by contemplating how the historical narrative of those journeys has influenced our never-ending quest to understand the enigmatic man we so readily identify as our greatest president. For better or worse, rightly or wrongly, we have mytholo-

97. David Thomas Valentine, *Obsequies of Abraham Lincoln, in the City of New York, Under the Auspices of the Common Council* (New York: E. Jones & Company, 1866), xvi–xvii.

98. Abraham Lincoln, as quoted by Donald, *Lincoln*, 15 (emphasis added). Lincoln used this river analogy to explain his Reconstruction plan to James G. Blaine.

99. A U.S. Park Service ranger attested to the author that the Cole print indeed belonged to the Lincolns and hung in their dining room at the time of their occupancy.

gized Lincoln, and therein lies a clue in understanding the role the flat-boat journeys play in Lincoln literature.

In his revolutionary 1948 book *The Hero With a Thousand Faces*, my-thologist Joseph Campbell analyzed myriad legends across human history and found consistencies among their storylines, characters, and lessons. From these patterns Campbell extracted what he termed the "mono-myth," the core stages through which the mythological hero passes. First, the hero toils anonymously in ordinary circumstances. He then receives a call to adventure. Reluctant at first, he is encouraged by wise elders and eventually submits. The hero then embarks on his adventure, which usually takes the form of a long trip into the unknown. He encounters tests and battles and finally crosses the threshold into a dangerous and exotic place. There, he engages in an epic ordeal and suffers brushes with mortality—only to battle back heroically, "seize the sword," and emerge victorious. The return trip confronts additional threats, but the hero, now enlightened, thrillingly overcomes adversaries with ever-mounting ease. He finally returns to his ordinary world, but no longer is he ordinary, for he has brought back an elixir—a power, a treasure, or a lesson learned—from the great adventure. It has transformed him, and, so empowered, the hero is now destined for greatness: the saving of his people. The basic form of the monomyth recurs in countless stories, from Greek mythology and the Bible to *Robinson Crusoe*, *Moby Dick*, *Alice in Wonderland*, *The Wizard of Oz*, *Star Wars*, and *Harry Potter*.

Lincoln's New Orleans trips, as depicted in historical literature over the past 150 years, align well with the elements of Campbell's monomyth. A man emerges from the most ordinary of circumstances. Like most of his peers, he hears the call for adventure to set sail down the Mississippi, something encouraged and expected by his elders. Off he goes on the long trip to a dangerous and exotic destination, New Orleans. He encounters risk (in river navigation, as all flatboatmen did), engages in battles (with the seven black men in Louisiana) and struggles with an ordeal (witness-ing slavery and slave trading). He triumphs in each case, evading naviga-tional hazards, resisting bandits, and exacting a lesson of moral outrage—*If I ever get a chance to hit that thing, I'll hit it hard*—from what he saw at the slave auction. He returns transformed; the seeds of greatness are planted. One day he will use them to save his people.

Problems emerge, of course, when we investigate the New Orleans trips critically. The seemingly seamless alignment of traditional Lincoln literature with the monomyth starts to show some gaps. For example, the trips did not stand alone in Lincoln's passage to adulthood, but rather punctuated a four-year-long maturation. He probably never said the "hit it hard" line, although he certainly gained moral edification in witnessing New Orleans–style slavery. Even then, the experience did not make him a racial egalitarian, nor even an abolitionist. And, resisting supernatural impulses, we may rationally maintain that Lincoln was never "destined" for greatness, as the hero myth projects; he was merely a good man who arrived, rather serendipitously, at the right time and place in American history to achieve greatness, and did.

Nevertheless, the New Orleans flatboat journeys retain remarkable parallels with the monomyth. This is especially the case when we remember that we are contemplating a true story with documented details, and not an imaginary construct implied by the word "myth." The parallel may explain the appeal of the flatboat story, and why it features prominently in nearly every book written about Abraham Lincoln, from children's readers to scholarly tomes. It speaks to a storyline we have heard before—one that profoundly resonates in the human mind, given that, as Joseph Campbell discovered, we have been telling it since time immemorial.

Appendix A: Western River Commerce in the Early 1800s

~ Americans in the Ohio and Mississippi river valleys ~ Routes to market ~ Western river craft ~ The flatboat ~ "Cutting loose" ~ Life on board ~ Flatboat travel ~ Flatboat cargo ~ The keelboat ~ The steamboat ~ Voyage of the *New Orleans* ~ The new West ~ Western river trade in Lincoln's era ~ The flatboatman in Lincoln's era ~

Only three out of every hundred U.S. citizens lived in the Mississippi Valley in 1790, a time when most of that vast basin belonged to Spain. Those emigrants—numbering 117,572, plus 14,338 people of African ancestry, mostly enslaved—generally used Fort Pitt (Pittsburgh) or the Cumberland Gap as their gateway into the trans-Appalachian region. The first wave settled in the uppermost Ohio River Valley, nearest to the young nation's hearth. Those who ventured farther west into Kentucky could justly be described as pioneers, living independently on the frontier and exchanging locally to survive. Rates of westward migration increased in the 1790s with the establishment of the Lancaster Turnpike across the Alleghany Mountains and the defeat of Indian resistance in the Ohio Valley. Pittsburgh, Cincinnati, and Louisville emerged as the premier urban nodes along the Ohio River gateway to the West.[1]

The stroke of a pen in 1803 expanded the United States' western border from the Mississippi River to the Continental Divide. Settlers subsequently headed into the lands of the Louisiana Purchase at a rate of tens of thousands per year, pushing out Indian occupants via deals, deception, disease, vice, and violence. An intricate system of navigable waterways extending maximally 16,000 miles fostered the diffusion. By 1810, nearly one million whites and more than 156,000 blacks populated the Mississippi Valley, representing about one in six Americans. In response to the relentless flow, Pittsburgh bookbinder Zadok Cramer published *The Navigator, Containing Directions for Navigating the Monongahela, Allegheny, Ohio, and Mississippi Rivers*, replete with geographical descriptions, navigation maps, and advice. Revised twelve times from 1801 to 1824, *The Navigator* guided thousands of Americans west of the Appalachians.

---

1. Archer B. Hulbert, *The Paths of Inland Commerce: A Chronicle of Trail, Road, and Waterway* (New Haven, CT: Yale University Press, 1920), 53–55, 67–68.

By 1820, that population numbered over two million, one in every five Americans.[2]

Bearing traits of individualism, risk-taking, and wayfaring, emigrants brought their personal aspirations and cultural baggage over the mountains. A new archetypal American emerged: the Westerner. A New England preacher described the father of one such family floating down the Ohio in the 1820s:

> . . . a fine, healthy-looking Kentuckian, with a young and pretty wife, two or three negro-servants, and two small children. He was a fair specimen of the rough and frank Kentucky character . . . an independent farmer, who had swarmed from the old homestead hive in Kentucky [where] [l]and . . . had already become too scarce and dear. He wanted elbow-room, did not wish to have a neighbour within three miles of him, and was moving to the upper Mississippi, for range. . . . He proved . . . a kind and friendly, if not pleasant companion [and] generally concluded [his stories] with a song. . . .[3]

Americans like that Kentuckian fought and displaced natives, hunted game, felled trees, built cabins, planted crops, formed governments, imposed laws, and granted land titles. Natural landscapes once altered subtly by indigenous peoples over millennia transformed swiftly in the hands of European Americans and their African American slaves. Maps once filled with the squiggly hachures of unknown physical geography were redrawn with the straight lines of political geography: new territories, new settlements, new states, new counties, new cadasters. Of the trans-Appalachian territories, Kentucky, Tennessee, and Ohio gained statehood first (1792–1802); Louisiana followed in 1812, then Indiana, Mississippi, and Illinois during 1816–8. Missouri joined the Union in 1821, the first state entirely west of the Mississippi.

Settlers coaxed impressive harvests from the valley's fertile soils in a remarkably short time. Once agricultural yields exceeded their person-

2. *The Navigator, Containing Directions for Navigating the Monongahela, Allegheny, Ohio, and Mississippi Rivers* (Pittsburgh: Cramer, Spear and Eichbaum, 1814), iii; Pamela D. Arceneaux, "The Navigator," *The Historic New Orleans Collection Quarterly* 25, no. 3 (Summer 2008): 6–8. Population figures computed by Richard Campanella based on county-level data from the U.S. Census of 1790, 1810, and 1820, as digitized by the National Historical Geographic Information System of the University of Minnesota.

3. Timothy Flint, *Recollections of the Last Ten Years . . . in the Valley of the Mississippi* (Boston: Cummings, Hillard, and Co., 1826), 34–36.

al and community trading needs, farmers sought to export surpluses to distant population centers for cash. The frontier-exchange economy of the pioneer era expanded into an increasingly sophisticated market-based economy, stretching from Canada to Louisiana and linked by three transportation alternatives.

•

One alternative was to ship cargo up the Ohio River—against the current and around the impeding Great Falls at Louisville—to Wheeling or Pittsburgh, then haul it over the Appalachians to rivers like the Potomac, to reach, finally, the Eastern Seaboard. Although many settlers traveled this route, the numerous break-of-bulk junctions and extensive overland treks made it woefully inadequate for handling heavy freight, even after completion of the National Road in 1817. Not until canals and railways were built in the 1830s 50s would this route attract substantial freight traffic.

The second alternative ranked even less efficient. ship northward (against the current and over numerous portages) through the Great Lakes, out the St. Lawrence River, then south along the Eastern Seaboard. Only a few hundred tons per year traveled this circuitous and seasonally icebound route.[4]

In contrast, the third alternative—the Southern route, shipping down the Ohio and Mississippi to New Orleans—offered the cheapest, easiest, fastest, and climatologically most congenial way to get Western shipments to market. Used since prehistoric times, this route hosted increased traffic with the French colonization of the Mississippi Valley. By the 1730s, shipments mostly of furs from upper Louisiana flowed downriver to New Orleans at rates of 80,000 pounds sterling per year, and increased in Spanish colonial times to around $4 million annually.[5] The attractiveness of the Southern route increased substantially after regular steamboat service commenced on the Mississippi in the late 1810s, giving rivermen a way to return home swiftly. It grew again after new packet (passenger) lines began running coastwise between New Orleans and New York in the 1820s, opening the great Eastern markets to Western exports. Sixty

4. Traffic on a portion of this route increased dramatically after 1825, when the newly opened Erie Canal connected the Great Lakes with the Hudson River and New York City.

5. Harry A. Mitchell, "The Development of New Orleans as a Wholesale Trading Center," *Louisiana Historical Quarterly* 27, no. 4 (October 1944): 934–939.

thousand tons of commodities from the trans-Appalachian West arrived in New Orleans in 1810; by 1820, that figure rose to 106,700; by 1830, it more than doubled to 260,900. For the first third of the nineteenth century, shipping down the Mississippi through New Orleans accounted for the overwhelming majority—between 99 and 100 percent—of freight shipments out of the Mississippi Valley. (This route also dominated importations, including non-standardized manufactured goods, though to a lesser degree than exports.) The Southern route, quite simply, formed *the* economic artery between the West and the East from late colonial times to the mid-antebellum years.[6] Reverence for the great river, and grandiose visions for the strategically situated city of New Orleans, became axiomatic. Charles Sealsfield echoed the sentiments of many when he wrote in 1828,

> Standing on the extreme point of the longest river in the world, New Orleans commands all the commerce of the immense territory. . . . You may [sail for] 1000 miles from New Orleans up the Red river...up the Arkansas river; . . . up the Missouri and its branches . . . to the falls of St. Anthony; [and] the same distance from New Orleans up the Illinois . . . the big Wabash . . . the Tennessee . . . the Cumberland, and . . . the Ohio up to Pittsburgh. Thus New Orleans has in its rear this immense territory, [plus] the coast of Mexico, the West India islands, and the half of America to the south, the rest of America on its left, and the continent of Europe beyond the Atlantic. *New Orleans is beyond a doubt the most important commercial point on the face of the earth.*[7]

•

An ever-evolving progression of watercraft accompanied the river-based economic development of the trans-Appalachian West. The earliest white explorers adopted lightweight birch-bark or bison-skin canoe designs directly from natives. Cheap to construct, maneuverable, and easily portaged, canoes satisfied the explorers' requirement to travel lightly and efficiently. Those needing to haul bulky pelts built larger canoes or replaced

6. Erik F. Haites, James Mak, and Gary M. Walton, *Western River Transportation The Era of Early Internal Development, 1810–1860* (Baltimore and London: Johns Hopkins University Press, 1975), 5–9, 124–126, drawing upon the terminology of Albert Kohlmeier.

7. Charles Sealsfield, *The Americans As They Are; Described in A Tour Through the Valley of the Mississippi* (London: Hurst, Chance, and Co., 1828), 165–66 (emphasis added).

them with sturdier "pirogues" or "dugout canoes" of varying sizes. Jonathan Carver, traveling in North America in the 1760s, observed that

> French traders who go into . . . the head branches of the Mississippi . . . to purchase furs[,] make of [the yellow ash tree] periaguays [pirogues] . . . by excavating them with fire, and when they are completed, convey in them the produce of their trade to New Orleans, where they find a good market for both their vessels and cargoes.[8]

Frenchman François Marie Perrin Du Lac described in 1807 a pirogue as

> a sort of boat made of a hollow tree, which many savage nations employed at the time of the discovery of America. The sycamore which grows . . . to an extraordinary size, is the tree most frequently used. When dried, it is extremely light . . . Some of these pirogues are so small, that a man . . . cannot stand upright in them, without fear of falling, others on the contrary carry besides a number of men, provisions sufficient for a voyage of many months.[9]

Frontiersmen modified these indigenous designs according to need. Splitting a hollowed log and inserting planks in between, for example, broadened a pirogue into a "skiff," capable of carrying crew and light cargo in a more stable manner. Tapering a skiff's blunt ends produced a more maneuverable "bateau." The improvements meant less risk, more space, more power, more oars and poles in the water (perhaps even a sail), and an ability to carry heavier cargo over longer distances at faster speeds.[10]

River craft construction advanced as hand-hewn lumber came to replace dug-out logs, as water powered sawmills supplanted axes and saws, and as pegs and iron nails phased out sinew and cord. Key design elements—bow, hull, stern, storage space, and on-board shelter—were tweaked according to materials and requirements. Experimentation flourished: "The first thing that strikes a stranger from the Atlantic," wrote an

8. Jonathon Carver, *Travels Through the Interior Parts of North-America, in the Years 1766, 1767, and 1768* (London, England: Jonathon Carver, 1778), 497.

9. M. Perrin Du Lac, *Travels Through the Two Louisianas . . . in 1801, 1802, & 1803* (London, England: Richard Phillips, 1807), 40.

10. H. E. Hoagland, "Early Transportation on the Mississippi," *Journal of Political Economy* 19, no. 2 (February 1911): 111–112; Haites, Mak, and Walton, *Western River Transportation*, 13–14.

Easterner in the 1820s,

> is the singular, whimsical, and amusing spectacle, of the vari-
> eties of water-craft, of all shapes and structures. . . . [I]n this
> land of freedom and invention . . . there are [specimens] re-
> ducible to no specific class of boats . . . whimsical archetypes
> of things [created by] inventive men, who reject the slavery of
> being obliged to build in any received form. You can scarcely
> imagine an abstract form in which a boat can be built, that in
> some part of the Ohio or Mississippi you will not see, actually
> in motion.[11]

Wrote a later observer, "no accurate classification can be made of the various kinds of craft engaged in this vast traffic. Everything that would
float . . . was commandeered into service, and what was found unsuitable
for the strenuous purposes of commercial transportation was palmed off
whenever possible on unsuspecting emigrants. . . ."[12] Yet from this decen-
tralized creative chaos of frontier experimentation, certain forms proved
more effective than others, and a broad taxonomy of Western river craft
typologies emerged.

•

For much downriver traffic in the eighteenth century, a simple raft of
strapped-together logs had to suffice. Advances in woodworking enabled
the addition of walls and roofs by the 1780s, turning two-dimensional
rafts into three-dimensional "flatboats." One early documented American flatboat voyage to the foreign city of New Orleans occurred in May
1782, piloted by a Revolutionary War veteran named Jacob Yoder of the
Monongahela River, near future Pittsburgh.[13] The southward flow of
Western produce increased after 1787, when Gen. James Wilkinson established a secret alliance with the Spanish in New Orleans to accept
Western exports. Flatboats bearing raw materials and foodstuffs for the
New Orleans market would thence prove to be a key force fueling Western development.[14] The rustic vessels of oak, poplar, or pine—"clumsy

11. Flint, *Recollections of the Last Ten Years*, 13–14.
12. Hulbert, *Paths of Inland Commerce*, 65.
13. "The First Flat Boat on the Mississippi," *Hazard's Register of Pennsylvania*, ed.
Samuel Hazard (Philadelphia: William F. Geddes, 1834), 295. For an earlier documented journey, see "Down the Mississippi in 1767: The Journey of George Morgan," *Times-
Democrat* (New Orleans), October 23, 1905, p. 10, c. 5–7.
14. Harry G. Enoch. *Original Journal of John Halley of His Trips to New Orleans Per-*

construction," observed one traveler, "but very burthensome"—typically measured twelve to twenty feet in width and two to four times that in length, capable of carrying thirty tons in the early years and nearly ten times that amount later on.[15] Further enhancement introduced on-deck cabins—sometimes no more than a canopy—to shelter the crew and protect cargo. If the cabin (sometimes called a *tendelet*, caboose, or wigwam) covered the entire deck, the craft was called an "ark," for its resemblance to Noah's biblical vessel. In other sources, flatboats are referred to loosely as "flat-bottomed boats," "barges" (a term also applied to skiffs and rafts), or "boxes." Others dubbed them by their origin or destination ("New Orleans," "Kentucky," or "Arkansas boats") or their cargo ("tobacco," "horse," or "cattle boats"). The French called them *voitures* (carts, carriages) or *chalans* (rafts). Most famously flatboats were called "broad horns," reputedly for the long oars or "sweeps" protruding on each side, or, alternately, for the cattle horns traditionally mounted on the prow.[16]

Captains often christened their flatboats with dramatic or whimsical names, to inspire *espirit de corps* or simply for insurance and record-keeping purposes. Wharfinger reports and U.S. Customs Service manifests list numerous flatboats with names referencing sweethearts back home (*Nancy, Sally, Elizabeth*), while others reflected patriotism (*Republican, Thomas Jefferson, Fair American, Sovereign*), regional pride (*Kentucky, Cincinnati*), drama (*Alligator, Gallant, Adventure, Thunder, Hurricane*), irony (*Queen Mary, Dolphin, Flying Mary, Mayflower*), and self-deprecation (*True Poverty, Hard Times, Fearnought, Drunkard, Escape*).[17] Whatever their name or nickname, flatboats were viewed by the barons of commerce as the

formed in the Years 1789 & 1791 (Winchester, KY: Bluegrass Heritage Museum, 2004), 2–3.

15. Estwick Evans, "A Pedestrious Tour, of Four Thousand Miles, Through the Western States and Territories," in *Early Western Travels 1748–1846*, ed. Reuben Gold Thwaites (Cleveland, OH: The Arthur H. Clark Company, 1904), 8:257; Haites, Mak, and Walton, *Western River Transportation*, 15.

16. "In Flatboat and Keelboat Times On the Mississippi, Over Seventy Years Ago," *Daily Picayune* (New Orleans), March 19, 1896, section F, p. 14, c. 6–7; Hoagland, "Transportation on the Mississippi," 119; Hulbert, *Paths of Inland Commerce*, 64–66; Thomas Ashe, *Travels in America Performed in the Year 1806* (London: Richard Phillips, 1809), 59.

17. Names culled from Wharfinger Reports, Microfilm #75-109 QN420, 1806, New Orleans Collector of Levee Dues-Registers of Flatboats, Barges, Rafts, and Steamboats in the Port of New Orleans, and Survey of Federal Archives in Louisiana, Division of Professional and Service Projects-Works Projects Administration, *Flatboats on the Mississippi in 1807* (Baton Rouge: Louisiana State University, 1940).

lowest form of river transportation, as made clear by this antebellum business writer:

> A flat-boat is nothing more than a quadrangular floating box—a wooden dripping tin—a capacious washing tub, composed of rough sawn planks, and provided with a crude kind of cabin, made sufficiently water-tight to [reach] its destination, and no more.[18]

At Pittsburgh and other major jumping-off points, flatboats could be purchased from a number of professional workshops.[19] Elsewhere, overwhelmingly, they were homemade. Expenses varied depending on timber, labor, and other inputs; one 1818 source estimated that a typical flatboat cost one dollar per foot in length to construct.[20] Flatboats represented a folk technology, so simple in design amid abundant timber that ordinary farmers and their hands could build and deploy them without hiring specialized labor. They constructed them according to received knowledge—via father, uncle, neighbor, friend—and modified the designs according to available resources, tools, needs, and the environment. Flatboats on the upper Ohio River, for example, were built no wider than fourteen feet, "so they might pass through the chute on the Indiana side at the falls of the Ohio near Louisville."[21] Efficiency and maneuverability were afterthoughts, because the river's current powered flatboats gratis. A steering oar mounted at the stern and two sweeps protruding from each side usually sufficed to keep the vessel in deep current, while poling skills and sheer muscle were needed to negotiate the shallows.

•

A number of factors influenced when flatboatmen "cut loose" and launched. Most rivermen avoided departure dates that would land them in New Orleans during its dreaded epidemic-plagued slack season of August through October. An autumn or early-winter departure, on the other hand, put them in New Orleans just as temperatures cooled, scourges

18. "Flat-Boat Commerce," J. D. B. De Bow, *Commercial Review of the South and West* 4, no. 4 (December 1847): 556.

19. Ashe, *Travels Performed in 1806*, 60.

20. Elias Pym Fordham, *Personal Narrative of Travels in Virginia, Maryland, Pennsylvania, Ohio, Indiana, Kentucky; and of a Residence in the Illinois Territory: 1817–1818*, ed. Frederic Austin Ogg (Cleveland, OH: The Arthur H. Clark Company, 1906), 79.

21. Rolla M. Hogue, "Life in Indiana, 1800–1820," *Indiana Magazine of History* 9, no. 2 (June 1913): 88.

abated, and demand for their goods increased. Departing at year's end also gave Western farmers something to do after the harvest, while freeing up the subsequent spring for planting. But it also meant frigid temperatures and possibly ice on the river upon returning. Alternately, late winter and early spring departures clashed with agricultural cycles, but meant warmer temperatures, melting snow, and higher river stages—thus a steeper gradient to the Gulf and swifter flow velocities. The 1814 *Navigator* travelers' guide pointed out that "the labour of navigating the Ohio in times of high water is very inconsiderable, [compared] to what it is when it is low, when continual rowing is necessary." On many smaller tributaries, high late-winter and springtime water (called "freshes") were absolutely essential to reach the main channel ("going out with the fresh"); such rivulets were otherwise unnavigable.[22] High water also allowed vessels to glide over obstacles such as the Great Falls of the Ohio, not to mention the ubiquitous snags and sandbars. Certain agricultural products, depending on their harvest time and durability, also determined departure dates, although most flatboat cargo—grain, flour, whiskey, livestock, lumber, hemp, lard, and smoked or salted meat—could travel anytime. Concluded *The Navigator*,

> The best seasons for navigating the Ohio, are in spring and autumn. The spring season commences at the breaking of the ice, which generally happens about the middle of February, and continues good for about three months and sometimes four. The fall season generally commences in October, and continues good until the first of December, and sometimes all through that month; when the ice begins to form and the river close.[23]

Upon cutting loose, flatboatmen did their best to exploit every river advantage and dodge every hindrance. Crews avoided the friction-inducing, debris-strewn, shoal-choked banks, preferring instead the river's deep and brisk thalweg. Maintaining the current (whose trajectory leaned left or right depending on the meander) was more difficult than it seems, requiring significant human force against crosscurrents, strong winds, and oncoming obstacles. Launching, docking, and dislodging from sandbars required special brawn and teamwork. Veterans handled these challenges

---

22. Louis A. Warren, "A Riverside Lincoln Memorial," *Lincoln Lore: Bulletin of the Lincoln National Life Foundation*, no. 553, November 13, 1939.

23. *The Navigator*, (1814), 36–37.

skillfully; greenhorns were a different matter. "[W]hen merchants are young[,] inexperienced [and] flushed with the idea of a fortune before them," admonished *The Navigator*, they "hastily buy a boat, load, jump into it themselves, fly to the steering oar, and halloo to the hands to *pull out*."[24] Only too soon would they find themselves spiraling uncontrollably at the mercy of a complex and unforgiving force. It got worse downriver, according to this 1808 account:

> A voyage down the Mississippi is very different from one on the Ohio, where the numberless improvements arrest the attention, and the gentleness of the current affords time to . . . admire the thousand beauties of that delightful stream. But on the Mississippi you are descending through an immense unimproved wilderness, [dealing with] the rapidity of the stream, obstructed with endless islands, sandbars, snags, sawyers, and planters. . . .[25]

•

From the perspective of a flatboat captain, a trip to New Orleans constituted a litany of decisions and worries for which he bore full responsibility. From the perspective of a new hand barely beyond his mother's care, the voyage represented hard work, on-the-job learning, occasional danger, boredom, fun, peer competition, persistent discomfort, risqué indulgence, and eye-opening adventure.

Life on board meant tedious hours of exposure to sun, wind, rain, and cold, as crewmembers stumbled across the jostling floor cramped with barrels, sacks, stacks, and sometimes live animals. Boatmen might eat heartily, though by no means delectably, if their cargo consisted of edibles. Typical fare included "the usual western staples of corn, potatoes, hardtack, and meat," cooked in the most functional of ways.[26] A crew of five, traveling on December 25, 1834, enjoyed an on-board Yuletide feast of "the shank of a shoulder, some dried pumpkins, corn dodger & coffee," prepared by a full-time cook.[27]

24. Ibid., 38–39.
25. Christian Schultz, *Travels on an Inland Voyage Through the States of New-York, Pennsylvania, Virginia, Ohio, Kentucky and Tennessee . . . Performed in the Years 1807 and 1808* (New York: Isaac Riley, 1810), 2:164.
26. Leland D. Baldwin, *The Keelboat Age on Western Waters* (Pittsburgh: Western Pennsylvania Historical Survey, 1941), 87.
27. Asbury C. Jacquess, "The Journals of the Davy Crockett commencing December 20th, 1834," *Indiana Magazine of History* 102, no. 1 (March 2006): 10.

Fish and game offered both fresh victuals and amusing sport. Catfish, buffalo fish, pike, sturgeon, perch, suckers, herring, shad, eels, and soft-shell turtles could be hooked, netted, or trapped. "Turkies, pheasant and partridges, are numerous on [the Ohio's] banks," reported a guide; "these, with the opportunity of sometimes shooting bears and deer swimming across the river, afford much pleasure to the navigator, and form sumptu-ous meals to the boat's crew."[28] Bankside peddlers and townspeople ea-gerly vended snacks and meals. Boatmen drank from the river "as it is; and some suppose it . . . conducive to health. It must not, however, be taken from the eddies," where impurities accumulated.[29]

Flatboats would sometimes launch *en masse* from a single town, crewed by men who all knew each other and worked the same fields. Thirty or forty flatboats, for example, departed Chillicothe, Ohio, in mid-February 1820, "loaded with the produce of the country, [bound] for New Orleans."[30] Convoys offered protection from marauders who target-ed lone flatboats for their cash and cargo. Floating downriver at roughly the same speed, some crews would "lash" their flatboats together, forming a "floating town" nearly an acre in size. Camaraderie and entertainment seem to explain this arrangement more so than navigational safety or effi-ciency: the union enabled socializing, retailing, bartering, and butchering livestock for a group meal—not to mention setting up a "dram shop" for the vending of spirits. A decent meal was a powerful incentive: the *Davy Crockett* "lashed up" with "some of our hoosier friends" while floating past Memphis in 1835, motivated primarily by the culinary expertise of Mike, the other boat's steward.[31] Lashing up might lead to a "frolic" and inevita-bly a "quarrel, in which case the aggrieved party dissolves the partnership by unlashing, and managing his own boat, in his own way."[32] (Mike the steward proved to be a fine cook and a trustworthy crewmember. But he had enemies, a dark past, and a price on his head. He was murdered four days after the lash-up.)

•

Barring disasters, a flatboat trip from Pittsburgh to New Orleans usually took five to seven weeks. Ten days was typical from Pittsburgh to the

28. *The Navigator* (1814), 27–28.
29. Evans, "Pedestrious Tour," in *Early Western Travels*, 8:344.
30. "Chilicothe," *Indiana Centinel* (Vincennes, IN), March 4, 1820, p. 3.
31. Jacquess, "Journals of the Davy Crockett," 14–15.
32. Flint, *Recollections of the Last Ten Years*, 105.

Great Falls of the Ohio at Louisville, five days thence to the confluence with the Mississippi, and three to four weeks from there to New Orleans.[33] Such was the experience of George Hunter, who departed Pittsburgh on June 15, 1804, arrived in Natchez on July 24 and remained until July 31, and arrived in New Orleans on August 7. Total travel time: over six weeks.[34] Voyage length, however, varied greatly depending on current, wind, weather, troubles, stops, nighttime navigation, and the era in which the expedition occurred. One voyage in 1800 "reached Natchez in fifty-seven days after leaving Pittsburgh, and New-Orleans city in thirteen days thereafter"—ten full weeks, replete with numerous "adventures and escapes from great peril by land and water."[35] Each passing year saw new navigational improvements, more obstacles removed, and further developments in shipping infrastructure, all of which reduced trip time.

Nocturnal navigation rewarded boatmen with doubled daily mileage, but jeopardized them with increased risk of entanglements and crashes. *The Navigator* advised its readers on this important matter differently depending on hydrological conditions. For the Ohio, the guide noted that rest stops not only squandered time but increased exposure to bankside hazards, and recommended

> you should contrive to land as seldom as possible; you need not even lie by at night, provided you trust to the current, and keep a good look out: If you have moon light so much the better.[36]

But for the main channel of the Mississippi, fraught with driftwood, sandbars, and treacherous currents, "it must be evident how imprudent it is attempting to go after night, even when assisted by a clear moon. . . ." That advice changed again for the well-traversed lowermost three hundred miles, where the Mississippi River leaves its alluvial valley and enters the deltaic plain: "[O]nce arrived at Natchez you may safely proceed day and night, the river from that place to its mouth being clear, and opposing

33. *The Navigator, or the Traders' Useful Guide in Navigating the Monongahela, Allegheny, Ohio, and Mississippi Rivers* (Pittsburgh: Zadok Cramer, 1806), 125. See also page 37 of 1814 edition.

34. John Francis McDermott, "The Western Journals of Dr. George Hunter, 1796–1805," *Transactions of the American Philosophical Society* New Series, 53, no. 4 (1963): 59–62.

35. S. De Witt Bloodgood, *A Treatise on Roads, Their History, Character and Utility* (Albany, NY: Oliver Steele, 1838), 171.

36. *The Navigator* (1806), 21.

nothing to your progress but a few eddies. . . ."[37] George Hunter apparently concurred with that advice, having floated "night & day" in slow water from Natchez to New Orleans in seven days.[38] Theodore Armitage boated from the Ohio/Mississippi confluence to New Orleans (1,023 miles) in only thirteen days, a trip that would have taken over three weeks had he not "run all night."[39] Lanterns, torches, and deck fires were used to spot floating obstacles and warn oncoming vessels.

Other rivermen warned against nighttime travel absolutely. "[I]t is a rule," wrote Vincent Nolte recollecting his 1811–2 journey, "never to trust your craft in the night to the force of the current, for the surface of the water is so frequently broken by trees. . . ."[40] Still others—probably the majority—navigated opportunistically, floating into the night if they thought favorable conditions mitigated the danger, and docking in daytime if conditions fouled. William Ward's January 1839 flatboat diary, for example, abounds with statements such as "a fine night for floating, clear and no wind," or "high winds . . . still blowing hard" during the day.[41]

Navigation practices changed after 1830–31, when Capt. Henry Shreve deployed two special steamboats to remove bankside trees and excavate meander loops. By Shreve's account, flatboats could now float nocturnally on the Mississippi "with as much safety as they do in the Ohio river," and thus cut their travel time in half.[42] But darkness veiled threats beyond mere floating debris, and prudent flatboatmen continued to tie up at night. Journals of the Indiana flatboat *Davey Crockett*, which carried an enormous cargo to New Orleans in winter 1834–35, stopped regularly every sundown for the night and "loosed cable" between 4 a.m. and sunrise next day.[43]

37. *The Navigator* (1814), 165–166.

38. McDermott, "Journals of Dr. George Hunter," 62.

39. Theodore Armitage, "Flatboating on the Wabash-A Diary of 1847," *Indiana Magazine of History* 9, no. 4 (December 1913): 273–275.

40. Vincent Nolte, *Fifty Years in Both Hemispheres* (New York: Redfield, 1854), 181.

41. Ward calculated that the voyage from New Albany, Indiana, to the mouth of the Ohio River spanned nine days: 123 hours for traveling and the remainder (93 hours) to tying-up and waiting. William S. Ward, *Diary* [of Flatboat Trip from New Albany, Indiana, to New Orleans, Louisiana, 1839], The Historic New Orleans Collection, Accession Number 2009.0139, p. 12 (hereafter cited as THNOC).

42. Henry M. Shreve, "Ohio and Mississippi Rivers: Annual Report of work done in improving the navigation of the Ohio and Mississippi rivers in the present year, ending 30th September 1831," as reproduced in *Daily National Intelligencer* (Washington, D.C.), December 17, 1831, p. 2.

43. Jacquess, "Journals of the Davy Crockett," 8–24.

   Whether moving or moored, crews usually slept upon sacks or pal-
lets on deck. Nightly mooring fueled the development of tiny river towns,
which sprouted every so often to serve the improvised fleet with victuals,
accoutrements, entertainment, rest, and trading opportunities. Other
towns founded during French or Spanish colonial times grew markedly
when the new American river traffic arrived. Timothy Flint described the
atmosphere at one such harbor in Missouri on a spring evening around
1816:

> [O]ne hundred boats . . . arriving in fleets . . . landed in one day
> at the mouth of the Bayan, at New Madrid. . . . You can name
> no point from the numerous rivers of the Ohio and the Missis-
> sippi, from which some of these boats have not come.

•

Some of the flatboats seen by Flint carried pine planks from western New
York forests; others, manufactured merchandise from Ohio, or cattle and
horses from Illinois and Missouri. Kentucky vessels bore "pork, flour,
whiskey, hemp, tobacco, bagging, and bale-rope," while the Tennesseans
carried "great quantities of cotton." Foodstuffs such as corn, apples, potatoes, cider, dried fruits, lard, beef, venison, and whiskey joined raw materials such as firewood, coal, and peltries, derived "from regions, thousands of miles apart . . . floated to a common point of union."[44] In other
cases, "[s]alt, iron, cider and peach brandy" flowed south, while "molasses,
sugar, coffee, lead, and hides" headed north.[45] Miscellaneous items such as
hickory nuts, walnuts, pumpkins, beeswax, butter, soap, tallow, cordage,
staves and hoop-poles used to make barrels, "shook" lumber (wood cut to
make boxes and crates), "biscuit" (unglazed pottery), and furniture also
shipped on the homemade vessels.[46] The *Davy Crockett*, which departed
Posey County, Indiana, in late 1834, provides an idea of the relationship
between flatboat size and cargo capacity. On its 1,360-square-foot deck,
the *Crockett* carried "1700 bushels of corn[,] 11,000 weight of pork, 3
thousand weight of beef in barrels, 6 large steers, 15 bushels of oats, 40

---

44. Flint, *Recollections of the Last Ten Years*, 103–104.
45. Hulbert, *Paths of Inland Commerce*, 65.
46. Anonymous, "River Navigation in Indiana," *The Indiana Magazine of History* 2,
no. 2 (June 1906): 92; Survey of Federal Archives in Louisiana, Division of Professional
and Service Projects-Works Projects Administration, *Flatboats on the Mississippi in 1807*
(Baton Rouge: Louisiana State University, 1940), 184–188.

kegs of lard, 30 dozen of chickens & 40 Turkeys."[47]

When heading into Southern plantation country, flatboats delivered "barrel pork" to planters for feeding their slaves.[48] Others carried slaves themselves. The *Mary*, for example, bore "40 barrels whiskey, 6 barrels potatoes, 13 barrels & kegs lard, 2 casks spun yarn, and 2 negroes" to New Orleans according to an 1807 manifest. A few miles behind came the *Charlotte*, with "8 negroes" among its tobacco, flour, butter, pork, and saddles.[49]

Then there were the live animals: squealing swine, gobbling turkeys, clucking chickens, mooing cows, neighing horses. The nervous and confused beasts—"almost as great a medley . . . as ever Noah could have stored"[50]—created only half the cacophony at the various river landings; flatboatmen provided the rest:

> The boisterous gaiety of the hands, the congratulations, the moving picture of life on board the boats. . . . The hands travel about from boat to boat, make inquiries, and acquaintances, and form alliances to yield mutual assistance to each other, on their descent . . . to New Orleans. . . . After an hour or two passed in this way, they spring on shore to raise the wind in town. It [benefits] the people of the village, if [the hands] do not become riotous in the course of the evening; in which case I have often seen the most summary and strong measures taken.
>
> About midnight the uproar is all hushed. . . . Next morning at the first dawn, the bugles sound. Every thing in and about the boats . . . is in motion, [and] in half an hour, are all under way.
>
> The fleet unites once more at Natchez, or New Orleans, and, although they live on the same river, they may, perhaps, never meet each other again on the earth.[51]

•

47. Jacquess, "Journals of the Davy Crockett," 8–9.

48. Ibid., 22.

49. Survey of Federal Archives in Louisiana, Division of Professional and Service Projects-Works Projects Administration, *Flatboats on the Mississippi in 1807* (Baton Rouge: Louisiana State University, 1940), 51 and 58.

50. William Newnham Blane, *An Excursion Through the United States and Canada During the Years 1822–23, By An English Gentleman* (London: Baldwin, Cradock, and Joy, 1824), 102.

51. Flint, *Recollections of the Last Ten Years*, 103–104.

Some flatboats docked for extended periods, serving as waterborne work-shops for tinners, blacksmiths, and toolmakers, or as dry-goods stores complete with "handsomely arranged . . . shelves."[52] Others tied up near towns and functioned as free housing for the crew or warehousing for their cargo—oftentimes to the displeasure of local inn-keepers and merchants. An entire economy and culture revolved around flatboats.

Incapable of navigating against the current, flatboats never returned upriver. The crude vessels were almost always disassembled at their des-tination and sold as scrap lumber or firewood, "for half [their] first cost" by one account, or, by another, one-quarter their initial dollar-per-foot construction cost.[53] Flatboats thus not only transported cargo; they *comprised* cargo. They represented a simple technological solution to a high-stakes economic challenge: how to get surplus agricultural commodities to distant sources of demand at minimum cost. So well did the flatboat solve this problem that it remained in service for an extraordinarily long period of time—into the 1860s, outliving other frontier-era river craft by decades.

•

Prior to the mid-1810s, travelers had two options in returning upriver. The first was to go by foot or horse the entire distance. The second, for a higher fee but less effort, greater storage capacity, and some savings of time, was to take a "keelboat" as far upstream as possible, then continue by land.

A keelboat may be considered a descendent of the aforementioned canoe-skiff-bateau lineage, or, in terms of form, a hybrid of a (very large) canoe and a flatboat. Like a canoe, a keelboat had a ribbed hull with rounded edges (to which was added a bottom board, hence the name), a pointed bow and stern, and an elongated overall shape. Like a flatboat, it was large, made of wood, had a flat bottom, drew minimal water, and accommodated storage space and shelter (for passengers as well as cargo). Unlike canoes and flatboats, however, keelboats usually required special-ized labor to construct and pilot, and were not scrapped for lumber until they were otherwise unprofitable. Completely covered keelboats formed the first packet services in the West, ferrying passengers along certain routes on a regular schedule. Keelboats were equipped with a single mast on which the crew rigged up a simple sail whenever winds favored their

52. Ibid., 104–105.
53. *The Navigator* (1814), 33; Fordham, *Personal Narrative of Travels*, 79.

assault against the current. With their upturned ends, multiple oarsmen, and single sail, keelboats on Western rivers bore an anachronistic Meso-potamian or Asian look. (One explorer in 1804 described his keelboat as built in the "Chinese stile" [sic].[54]) Their crews battled the same conditions as their ancient forbears with precisely the same resources: wind, current, and manpower.

A typical Mississippi River keelboat weighed twenty to sixty tons, measured forty to eighty feet long and ten to fifteen feet wide, and drew about two feet of water. Larger keelboats, sometimes dubbed "barges," sported two sails and more manpower. What they sacrificed in sturdiness and carrying capacity, keelboats gained in maneuverability: the narrow, streamlined design permitted crewmembers to row, pole, pull, "warp," or sail their way upriver. The trick was to avoid the middle and the cutbank portions of the river (above the thalweg, where the water ran fast and downriver traffic predominated) in favor of the point bar or batture side, where the current flowed slow and shallow. "It is beside the question," wrote Flint in 1816, "to think of forcing the boat up against the main cur-rent. . . . [A]ny impediments near the shore, must either be surmounted, or the river crossed to avoid them. . . ."[55] Once they crossed the thalweg, the crew was able to row against the slower current, while shallow depths meant they could "set poles" into the mud and, pole pressed to shoul-der, walk them bow-to-stern along narrow running-boards. Sails were set whenever winds blew favorably. If all else failed, a "cordelle" (towline) was thrown to shore (or swum there by a crewmember with the rope held tight in his teeth), looped around a distant tree, and used as a pulley to "warp" the vessel upriver. Lacking trees, crewmembers "bush-wacked" by grabbing the branches of overhanging vegetation and heaving the ves-sel upriver. Lacking bushes, men or beasts on the bank would haul the craft upriver by cordelle. Occasionally, the shape of the river fortuitously reversed the bankside current, thrilling the crew with a welcome burst of speed. Sticking near the banks also ensured a certain measure of safety in the event of capsizing, particularly if passengers were involved.[56]

Boatman culture gave rise to a peculiar folklore and lexicon. A "Ken-tuck" was said to be "the best man at a pole," while Frenchmen proved

54. As quoted by McDermott, "Western Journals of Dr. George Hunter," 10.
55. Flint, *Recollections of the Last Ten Years*, 91–92.
56. Hoagland, "Transportation on the Mississippi," 113; Haites, Mak, and Walton, *Western River Transportation*, 15–17; Flint, *Recollections of the Last Ten Years*, 87, 91, and 94.

more adroit with the oar. Poling off a fixed log, called a "reverend set," propelled the keelboat fastest, and allowed it to evade dangers such as "'riffles" (ripples), "planters," "points," "bends," "wreck-heaps," and "shoots, a corruption . . . of the French 'chute.'" A boat "swinging" out of control and exposing its flanks to the current could end up entangled or punctured by dangerous "snags," "planters," and "sawyers," which collectively were

> large trees, washed from the shore, which drift down till the roots or branches . . . fasten into the mud and become as firm as when standing in the forest. Should a boat be so unfortunate as to strike one of these, it would in all probability prove fatal.[57]

A bobbing motion, cutting the surface of the water, earned sawyers their name. When planters and sawyers broke lose *en masse* and matted together, they formed "wooden-islands . . . more dangerous than real ones," because of the unpredictability of the surrounding flow. Those currents could produce "whirls, or swells, or boils . . . so large and strong that a boat is thrown half around in passing over them, and sometimes shot so rapidly out of them. . . ."[58] Foggy conditions forced crewmen to call out blindly to other vessels or to the bank to gauge their whereabouts, a tense exchange that often denigrated into "obscenity, abuse, and blasphemy . . . sometimes to the length of exchanging musket shots." Flint continued,

> The manners of the boatmen are as strange as their language. Their peculiar way of life has given origin not only to an appropriate dialect, but to new modes of enjoyment, riot, and fighting. Almost every boat, while it lies in the harbour has one or more fiddles scraping continually aboard, to which you often see the boatmen dancing.[59]

Fifteen miles a day was considered a fair clip for an upriver-bound keelboat. A voyage from New Orleans up to St. Louis could easily take three months. Every passing mile grew more challenging, as the gradient steepened and current strengthened. Keelboats needed larger and more skilled crew than flatboats and, with less carrying capacity and longer voyages, charged much higher fees. Many New Orleans–based keelboats ventured no farther than Natchez, where passengers disembarked and trekked by

57. Tilly Buttrick Jr., "Voyages, Travels and Discoveries" (1831), in *Early Western Travels*, 8:59.

58. *The Navigator* (1814), 144, 164–165.

59. Flint, *Recollections of the Last Ten Years*, 15; see also 31, 91–92.

horse or foot the equally dangerous Natchez Trace (or the Unicoy Road, across eastern Mississippi) back to the Ohio River Valley.[60] Given the ease of flatboating downriver versus keelboating upriver, it comes as no surprise that flatboats outnumbered keelboats by a twenty-to-one ratio.

All vessels dealt with myriad riverine dangers. High winds produced swells that frustrated navigational control. Lightening storms could prove fatal.[61] "Shears," errant currents that swiped across the river with no apparent warning, could wrench a steering oar from a pilot's hands and send a vessel spiraling. Wrecks abounded; broken-up vessels littered the banks, and bodies frequently floated by. "Upon the western rivers a great many boatmen die, and their graves upon the banks are numerous," wrote one observer in 1818; "[f]loating barrels of flour are often seen in the Mississippi; and hundreds of barrels of wheat, and hogsheads of tobacco, lie on its shores in a state of ruin."[62] Occasionally, fully loaded vessels would lodge in the bank, its crew inexplicably disappeared. An unmanned flatboat "loaded with timber" was found drifting along the New Orleans riverfront during the week of Lincoln's arrival, its crew probably the victims of crime or accident.[63] One expedition approaching New Orleans found a dead man drifting among their flatboats, spotted another corpse under the tree the next day, and saw a third moments later.[64] Among the greatest dangers were thieves and bandits, who preyed on boatmen tied up at night along remote riverbanks.

Keelboats offered the best available solution to the upriver problem, but fell woefully short of solving it. Entrepreneurs competed to offer a better one. Some tried sailing ships, but they struggled to make it so far as Natchez, as sharp meanders reversed favorable winds, narrow river widths precluded tacking, and shallow banks endangered deep-draft hulls.[65] Oth-

---

60. See map of routes in Seymour Dunbar's *A History of Travel in America* (Indianapolis: The Bobbs-Merrill Company, 1915), 1:152–153.

61. "Notice—A Flatboat loaded with Stone Coal . . . ," *Louisiana State Gazette* (New Orleans), June 23, 1826, "Auctions" column; Maj. Stephen H. Long, *Account of an Expedition from Pittsburgh to the Rocky Mountains, Performed in the Years 1819, 1820*, ed. Edwin James (London: Longman, Hurst, Rees, Orme, and Brown, 1823), 1:15.

62. Evans, "Pedestrious Tour," in *Early Western Travels*, 8:260 and 301.

63. "Notice," *New Orleans Argus*, May 22, 1828, p. 2, c. 5.

64. Diary of Micajah Adolphus Clark, as transcribed in "Flatboat Voyage to New Orleans Told Of In a Diary Kept in 1848," *Times-Democrat*, July 9, 1905, part 3, p. 13, c. 7.

65. Schultz, *Travels on an Inland Voyage*, 2:137. Some sailing ships were built in the upper Ohio River Valley in the early nineteenth century, but were simply floated like flatboats down the river for service on the seas. Frank Haigh Dixon, "A Traffic History of the Mississippi River System," Document No. 11, National Waterways Commission

ers rigged keelboats with horses, tethering the unfortunate beasts to poles geared to paddles, or trotting them awkwardly on deck-based treadmills. The results were comical for a spectator, costly for the entrepreneur, and sometimes fatal for the horses.

•

The solution to the upriver problem emerged from the increasingly successful British and American efforts of the late eighteenth century to harness the pressure released by boiling water. Mechanics competed to adapt steam engine technology to watercraft, with some of the most promising work coming out of Philadelphia. In 1786, John Fitch attached a three-inch-cylinder steam engine to a side-mounted screw and successfully propelled a large skiff on the Delaware River. Another prototype utilized what might be described as mechanical oarsmen to move the vessel. Other inventors demonstrated a subsequent model to the framers of the Constitution as they convened in 1787—a noteworthy historical moment if ever there was one. Further experimentation led to better designs and new models during the 1790s.[66] Meanwhile, terrestrially based steam engines, promising to outwork man and beast in everything from the sawing of logs to the spinning of cotton, diffused rapidly from Philadelphia workshops to the southwestern frontier. By one account, Capt. James McKeever and M. Louis Valcour were the first to introduce the emerging technology to the Mississippi River in 1803, building a steamboat for service between New Orleans and Natchez. But the craft ran into shallow water, and the men ran out of capital, before the concept could be demonstrated.[67] It soon became clear that existing craft designs could not be simply retrofitted with steam engines; they had to be redesigned entirely with broad, flat bottoms to minimize draft and maximize carrying capacity.

What also became clear was that lucrative business opportunities awaited whoever came up with an optimal design *and* monopolized legal rights to serve the busiest waterways. Pennsylvania-born inventor Robert Fulton brought to bear the design skills, improving both engine and craft in the U.S. and France during the 1790s–1800s. While in Paris, Fulton befriended the American diplomat and steam-engine investor Robert R. Livingston, who provided the legal prowess and financial wherewithal.

(Washington, D.C.: Government Printing Office, December 1909), 11.

66. E. W. Gould, *Fifty Years on the Mississippi; or, Gould's History of River Navigation* (St. Louis: Nixon-Jones Printing Company, 1889), 3–6.

67. Haites, Mak, and Walton, *Western River Transportation*, 17.

Together Fulton and Livingston obtained patents and secured exclusive legal rights for steam shipping on key waterways. While most jurisdictions bordering the Ohio and Mississippi rivers resisted granting steamboat monopolies, Louisiana—the most important because it received the most traffic—agreed to the arrangement. Fulton and Livingston's Ohio Steam Boat Company then contracted Nicholas J. Roosevelt to conduct research on river hydrology and assist in vessel design. Working out of Pittsburgh on the banks of the Monongahela River, the company brought in a team of New York mechanics to construct a 116-by-20-foot vessel with a 34-inch cylinder and boiler driving a stern-wheel, with sails to assist when the winds blew favorably. Costs totaled $38,000.[68] Christened the *New Orleans*, the craft launched in September 1811 amid great throngs seeing it off down the Ohio destined for its namesake city. "'Your boat may go down the river,'" wrote one observer, giving voice to the skeptical crowd, "'but as to coming up, the idea is an absurd one.'" Perhaps wary that the contraption might just perform as promised, "[t]he keel-boat men crowded around the strange visitor and shook their head[s]."

•

The maiden voyage of the *New Orleans* proved extraordinary. That autumn saw a spectacular astronomical event, the Great Comet of 1811, which passengers witnessed nightly; at one point they feared that it might plunge nearby. River levels at the Great Falls of the Ohio—the navigation obstacle whose circumventing portage led to the foundation of Louisville—flowed too low to allow passage. The *New Orleans* had to return upriver, taking advantage of the delay by demonstrating to onlookers its ability to navigate against the current. When water levels rose, the *New Orleans* embarked downriver once again and gingerly made its way over the falls.

Soon after, a fire broke out on board. Then, while anchored below Louisville, the passengers felt an odd shock wave. They later discovered, upon reaching Missouri, that what came to be recognized as the most powerful earthquake ever recorded in North America had altered the channel of the Mississippi and brought devastation to the river town of New Madrid. There, "terror-stricken people begged to be taken on

68. Another source holds that the *New Orleans* measured 138 feet by 30 feet, weighed 200 tons, cost $40,000, and departed Pittsburgh in October 1811, with nine crewmembers plus Roosevelt's family aboard. Robert H. Thurston, *A History of the Growth of the Steam-Engine* (New York: D. Appleton and Company, 1903), 284.

board, while others, dreading the steamboat more than the earthquake, hid themselves as she approached." Tremors, felt as far away as New Orleans, continued for weeks. Continuing downriver, the vessel contended with "shoals, snags and sawyers," some of which had become mobilized by the quake.[69] Passengers pondered if the coincident celestial and tectonic oddities bore any spiritual significance. In fact, the newfangled conveyance beneath their feet would prove far more historically significant than the comet or the quake.

The remainder of the trip went smoothly, and on Friday evening, January 10, 1812, the steamboat *New Orleans* docked at its namesake city. Travel time, excluding numerous stops, totaled 259 hours. "She is intended as a regular trader between [here] and Natchez," explained the *Louisiana Gazette* to its readers Monday morning, "and will, it is generally believed, meet the most sanguine expectations of [Fulton and Livingston's] company." Another demonstration occurred a week later, when the *New Orleans* "left [here] at 11 o'clock, went five leagues down, and returned at 4 o'clock," proving to skeptical bankers and investors its contra-current capabilities.[70] Ever the entrepreneurs, the operators also ran excursions to English Turn for the hefty price of two to three dollars per passenger, and commenced freight and passenger service to Natchez a few days later.[71] The *New Orleans* served for three years until a snag pierced its hull and sunk it. By then, the technology had proven its worth.

Subsequent years saw new steamboats demonstrate increasing capacity, speed, and power, promising to transform dramatically traditional river travel. "There is now on foot a new mode of navigating our western waters," declared one river guide in 1814; "[t]his is with boats propelled by the power of steam."[72] Capt. Henry Shreve's record twenty-five-day journey of the 400-ton *Washington*, from New Orleans all the way to Louisville in 1817, convinced the last doubters that the power of steam solved the upriver problem.

After a few years of resolving technological, logistical, and legal barriers (namely the monopoly granted to Fulton and Livingston, overruled by the Supreme Court in 1824), steamboats proceeded to revolutionize

---

69. As quoted from passenger journals by Gould, *Fifty Years on the Mississippi*, 84–87.

70. Not easily impressed, the *Gazette* sarcastically opined, "Had Mr. Fulton's Torpedoes succeeded equal to his Steam Boats, we might now laugh at the thunder of the British Navy."

71. *Louisiana Gazette and New-Orleans Daily Advertiser*, January 13, 1812, p. 2; January 17, 1812, p. 3; January 18, 1812, p. 2, and January 21, 1812, p. 5.

72. *The Navigator* (1814), 30.

western river travel and communities. Increased competition meant larger numbers of bigger and better boats charging lower rates for swifter service. A decade after the maiden voyage of the *New Orleans*, 73 steamboats averaging 200 tons apiece plied western rivers. Roughly a dozen new vessels joined the western fleet annually until the end of the Fulton-Livingston monopoly, after which two to three dozen were built each year. Twenty years after the *New Orleans*, 183 steamboats traveled the western rivers; that number would more than triple by the fortieth anniversary, when New Orleans alone tallied 3,566 steamboat arrivals in a year—a pace of one every 147 minutes round-the-clock. Steam technology also aided ocean-going shipping arriving to New Orleans, as brigs and schooners once dependent entirely on wind now added steam-driven side wheels to their power supply. They benefited additionally from the new steam-powered towboats (tugs) that could rescue them from navigational obstacles at the mouth of the river, or guide them into their narrow berths along the crowded riverfront.[73]

No wonder elders would later view "the year 1811 [as] the *annus mirabilis* of the West."[74]

•

Steamboat transportation raised the value of exports and thus stoked the economic development and population growth of the Western river region. Government attention and federal dollars for navigation improvements followed, fueling more growth. Steamboats also diminished the cost, time, and discomfort associated with traveling to the former frontier. Getting from New York to New Orleans via the Ohio and Mississippi, for example, took twelve weeks in 1800, including a grueling overland trek and a wild river journey. The same trip in 1839, via rail, stage, and steamer, took under thirteen days, cost less money, posed fewer risks, and offered greater comfort.[75] Americans poured west: for every one citizen living beyond the Appalachians in 1810, more than twelve resided there in 1860, totaling 12,984,100 (over 41 percent of the national population). For every one acre of improved Western land in 1810, more than eighteen acres were under cultivation in 1860, totaling 80,631,934 acres from Michigan to Louisiana. The blossoming society and its agrarian export

73. Haites, Mak, and Walton, *Western River Transportation*, 18, 130–131; Dixon, "Traffic History of the Mississippi," 15.
74. As quoted from passenger journals by Gould, *Fifty Years on the Mississippi*, 89.
75. Bloodgood, *Treatise on Roads*, 171–172.

economy soon spawned a manufacturing sector; imprecisely measured in the early years, it earned $84 million in 1840, $188 million in 1850, and $419 million in 1860. For every ton exported by the trans-Appalachian West in 1810, nearly *eighty* tons shipped in 1860.[76] The Mississippi River and its tributaries served as the vital arteries for this explosive economic growth, and steamboats rendered them efficient.

Steamboat transportation also transformed life on the river. Horse-powered boats and other impracticalities became campfire stories. Keelboats held on for a few years but soon declined and mostly disappeared on trunk routes; only two specimens, the last of their breed, officially docked at New Orleans during 1828–29.[77] Keelboatmen found other jobs, often becoming (as Samuel Clemens explained) "a deck-hand or a mate or a pilot on the steamer."[78] Others continued to row, warp, and pole their antiquated vessels up remote tributaries—until progress replaced them there too.

Flatboat traffic, however, actually increased with the rise of steamboats, because they provided a swift way for boatmen to return home. "Ten years ago the flatboatmen returned on foot & experienced great hardships," wrote Samuel Judah in 1827. "Case is now altered."[79] Flatboatmen also benefited from zero fuel expenses, minimal labor costs, low wharfage fees, and from the fact that the overall boon to agriculture provided by steamboats sent a certain share of the resultant commodities-shipping business onto their rustic vessels. So while steamboats killed keelboats, they had a symbiotic relationship with flatboats; both craft types increased in usage for nearly four decades. Flatboat arrivals at New Orleans increased from 455 in 1806 to 2,792 during the peak season of 1846–47, an era in which flatboats helped make downriver shipping anywhere from two to five times cheaper than upriver shipping. As steamboats became more common, larger, and more efficient, that ratio evened out, implying that flatboats were no longer the bargain they once were. Flatboat traffic to New Orleans accordingly declined to between 540 and 700 per year in the mid-1850s.[80] They continued to form a part of the picturesque

76. Haites, Mak, and Walton, *Western River Transportation*, 112, 115, 117, 124–125.

77. "Marine—Port de la Nouvelle Orleans," *New Orleans Bee*, February 24, 1829, p. 3, c. 4 and March 22, 1829, p. 2, c. 3. Survey of "Maritime" columns of *Bee* conducted by author from April 1, 1828, through March 31, 1829.

78. Samuel L. Clemens, *Life on the Mississippi* (New York: Harper & Row), 14.

79. Samuel Bernard Judah, "A Journal of Travel from New York to Indiana in 1827," *Indiana Magazine of History* 17, no. 4 (December 1921): 351.

80. These figures reflect official records for years in which they are available. Actual

New Orleans riverfront for another few years before they, too, would go the way of the keelboat, the skiff, the bateau, and the birch-bark canoe. The interruption of the Civil War helped seal the fate of the Mississippi flatboat, but its root cause was technological progress. After the war, new docking facilities for powered barges replaced the old flatboat landing; coal continued to be shipped downriver on flatboat-like barges, but little else. "Probably we will never again see the old days of flatboats revived," wrote one local journalist in 1866. In fact, a small number of rustic craft continued to arrive for the remainder of the nineteenth century, usually guided by poor independent farmers and traders who squatted along the uptown batture like "tramps," as one observer put it. About two hundred such vessels arrived annually to New Orleans into the late 1880s—the last "Surviv[ors] of the Old Flat-Boating Days."[81]

•

Placing Abraham Lincoln's 1828–31 river experiences in the context of antebellum Western commerce requires addressing some popular perceptions drawn from the ample lore of that era. Words such as "wilderness," "frontier," and "pioneer" come to mind, not to mention "alligator horses," "ruffians," and "Kaintocks." We also conjure up figures like Mike Fink, the hard-living boatman who was later mythologized into a Paul Bunyan–like "big man" character of the Western rivers after his violent death in 1823.[82] These images should not be dismissed merely because they are popular; indeed, folklore and traditional knowledge reveal much about history and how we go about making it. The images should, however, be viewed in the light of whatever hard historical data do exist, and either refined, conditioned, balanced, or debunked accordingly.

If the word "wilderness" implies nature touched minimally by "modern" (European?) man, the circa-1830 trans-Appalachian West had not been wilderness for two to three generations. French and French Canadian settlers arrived at what they called upper Louisiana (from Missouri to Michigan) a full century earlier, clearing land and exploiting resources

numbers of flatboat arrivals were probably significantly higher. Haites, Mak, and Walton, *Western River Transportation*, 21.

81. *New Orleans Times*, November 23, 1866, p. 7, c. 1; "Mississippi Shanty Boats— A Survival of the Old Flat-Boating Days," *Springfield Republican* (Springfield, MA), July 27, 1899, p. 10.

82. Michael Allen, *Western Rivermen, 1763–1861: Ohio and Mississippi River Boatmen and the Myth of the Alligator Horse* (Baton Rouge: Louisiana State University Press, 1990), 9–11.

as much as their numbers and technology allowed. Indigenous peoples, of course, did the same for millennia prior, and probably in larger numbers and with greater environmental impact than the popular harmony-with-nature myth implies.[83] Indeed, the very notion of the New World as primeval and virgin wilderness is a somewhat naïve and Eurocentric construct. The lands of Lincoln's youth were certainly rural and largely wild, but did not constitute wilderness—lest one softens the superlative condition of that word's meaning.

If the word "frontier" connotes those lands at the fringes of a society's knowledge and control, then the trans-Appalachian West of the 1820s–30s was at least one full generation removed from that state. If the word "pioneer" applies to the initial representatives of a group settling in a frontier, then Lincoln's ancestors qualified for that status, but most of his contemporaries probably did not. By the time Lincoln reached adulthood, more than a million Americans populated his home states of Kentucky, Indiana, and Illinois, and over one-quarter of all Americans lived west of the Appalachians. Most of their settlements had entered the Union by 1821 and enjoyed increasingly strong representation in Congress. In the words of Maj. Stephen Long, the era of the "buck-eye" (that is, the "indigenous backwoodsmen" nicknamed for the Ohio forest nut shaped like a deer's eye) had given way by 1819 to that of the "Yankee"—"the numerous emigrants who are introducing themselves from the eastern states."[84] Southerners also migrated into the Ohio River region, adding another cultural dimension to the trans-Appalachian West. Manifestations of a civilization—the formation of towns and cities linked by transportation routes; the creation of political, legal, economic, and social structures; the delineation and titling of land; the planting of crops—took shape as that population grew. Settlers altered natural landscapes to accommodate their needs and constantly demanded federal funds to improve river navigation, construct roads, excavate canals, and build railroads.[85] In the twenty years between Lincoln's birth and his flatboat voyages, the trans-Appalachian West's population tripled, cultivated acreage quadrupled, export tonnage quintupled, and the number of steamboats plying the region's waterways

83. See, for example, William M. Denevan, "The Pristine Myth: The Landscape of the Americas in 1492," *Annals of the Association of American Geographers* 82, no. 3 (September 1992): 369–385, and Charles C. Mann, *1491: New Revelations of the Americas Before Columbus* (New York: Knopf, 2006).

84. Long, *Expedition from Pittsburgh*, 1:20.

85. Curtis Nettels, "The Mississippi Valley and the Constitution, 1813–29," *The Mississippi Valley Historical Review* 11, no. 3 (December 1924): 332–357.

grew from zero to 150.[86] The Mississippi Valley that young Abraham cast his eyes upon in 1828 and 1831 hosted a small agrarian American society expanding steadfastly along navigable waterways at the expense of hardwood forests and the remnants of indigenous society. Members of that new society raised impressive quantities of crops through both free and enslaved labor and interacted economically and culturally with the rest of the nation and world as extensively as transportation and communication networks permitted. Wilderness, frontier, and pioneers had all shifted, by this time, hundreds of miles westward.

Lincoln traveled the Mississippi in an era when Western river traffic had become dominated by steamboats and flatboats. Freed from the constraints of the legally overruled Fulton-Livingston monopoly, steamers experienced their greatest surge in productivity in those years; 118 plied western waters in 1828, and 183 did so in 1831. They weighed on average 300 tons each and carried around 270 tons of cargo downriver (half that capacity when heading upriver). Keelboats, unable to compete with steam power, retreated to wherever steamers could not go; perhaps a few hundred operated in waters traversed by Lincoln, usually in shallow tributaries.

Flatboats, on the other hand, remained competitive. Costing about $9.60 per ton of cargo in 1830 compared to $11.25 for steamboats, flatboats increased in number for over a quarter-century after the rise of steamers, although they ferried decreasing percentages of total cargo. A typical professional flatboat operation traveling from Louisville to New Orleans in 1830 cost $324 in total expenses: $73 to build the vessel, $235 to employ a crew of usually five men ($75 for the captain and $40 for the hands) plus $7.50 to feed them, and $8 in wharfage fees. The fifty or so tons of cargo plus the sale of the vessel's wood yielded total revenue of around $464 and a net profit of $140. In an era when a dollar-a-day wage was considered decent pay, a single successful flatboat expedition could compensate a farmer for most of his growing-season toils. The crew would earn fairly well for four weeks of potentially risky but not particularly grueling labor, laced with adventure and enticement. More than one thousand flatboats registered at New Orleans annually during the era of Lincoln's voyages.[87]

Visualizing the extent of Mississippi River activity experienced by Lincoln entails a few gross assumptions. If a thousand flatboats per year paid dues at New Orleans and the vast majority voyaged during the six-month

86. Haites, Mak, and Walton, *Western River Transportation*, 112, 115, 117, 124–131.
87. Ibid., 21, 36, 62, 83, 124, 130, 158, 166, 168.

winter-spring peak season, then approximately 150 flatboats passed any given point during a typical peak-season month. This rate equates to five New Orleans–bound flatboats per day, or about one every two daylight hours, not including vessels bound for intermediary destinations such as Memphis, Natchez, and the sugar coast. Accounting for those other flatboats might increase that pace to a few vessels per hour or higher.

The above estimates may be conservative. In busier stretches during peak season, vessels of various typologies often traveled within shouting distance, and had to dodge each other at major stop-off points. By one remarkably precise count in 1818, "Six hundred and forty-three flatboats were counted descending the Mississippi and Ohio, by a person in a steam boat in his passage up." If that trip took about thirty days, then roughly twenty flatboats passed daily—a pace corroborated by a boatman who recalled the river in late January 1835 "pretty well lined with flat boats . . . well on to 20 passed us to day."[88] Estimates go much higher: an observer in 1816 counted two *thousand* flatboats during the twenty-five-day trip between Natchez and Louisville, an enumeration that probably lumped itinerate peddlers circulating locally together with those vessels engaged in long-distance trade.[89] Elders recollected that between the mouth of the Ohio and New Orleans, the Mississippi

> was constantly dotted with flatboats. Nearly all the time [during winter-spring peaks] a flatboat was in sight, often several could be seen at the same time in a single coup d'oell [glance]. The number of flatboats thus passing [any one point on the lower river] may be estimated at more than 1000 annually.[90]

An account made at the time of Lincoln's 1831 voyage reported fifty-four steamboat arrivals and departures, plus more than one thousand flatboats, solely on the Wabash tributary of the Ohio River. Another source reported forty ocean-going ships, thirty-three steamboats, and thirty-nine

88. *Niles' Weekly Register*, July 11, 1818, as cited by Donald F. Carmony and Sam K. Swope, eds., "Flatboat Building on Little Raccoon Creek, Parke County, Indiana," *Indiana Magazine of History* 60, no. 4 (December 1964): 306; Jacquess, "Journals of the Davy Crockett," 20.

89. As quoted by F. Lauriston Bullard, "Abe Goes Down the River," *Lincoln Herald: A Magazine of Education and Lincolniana* 50, no. 1 (February 1948): 5. See also Lewis E. Atherton, "Itinerant Merchandising in the Ante-Bellum South, *Bulletin of the Business Historical Society* 19, no. 2 (April 1945): 46.

90. "In Flatboat and Keelboat Times," *Daily Picayune*, March 19, 1896, p. 14, section f, c. 6–7.

flatboats arriving to New Orleans during a single week in late November 1835, a daytime pace of one vessel every thirty or forty minutes, not including departures or local traffic.[91] Still another account estimated "upwards of four hundred ships of all nations . . . moored three deep along the Leveé" in 1806, an estimate that excluded the lowly flatboats.[92]

Rarely was traffic distributed evenly along the river. Rather, it clumped in diurnal waves, concentrating nightly at certain stop-over points and launching simultaneously at sunrise. Riverine and atmospheric conditions also clustered the flow: flatboatman William Ward, for example, joined a fleet of "about 60 Flat Boats . . . 71 counted" waiting out "wind blowing like Thunder" at the confluence of the Ohio and Mississippi rivers. He later "remained at Natchez [three days] on account of Rain & Fog."[93] And when rivers flowed very low, traffic all but disappeared because of slow currents and exposed obstacles. As the "Mississippi [fell] fifteen feet below the mouth of the Ohio" in spring 1826, for example, "scarcely any flatboats" traveled between Louisville and Natchez.[94]

This much is clear: the Mississippi River of Lincoln's era hosted an irregularly pulsating stream of traffic bearing the fruit of the ever-growing trans-Appalachian West. To New Orleans went the biggest and best share. Over 99.8 percent—307,300 tons in 1831 alone—arrived at that city's wharves, guided there by an estimated 90,000 men who worked the Western rivers.[95] New Orleans formed a special part of their lives, a place where money was made, business associations were established, social networks were woven, cultural traits were imported and exported, and fun was had. As early as 1796, a traveler noted that people in what is now Indiana spoke of New Orleans "as if it were a walk of half an hour [away], though it is fifteen hundred miles down the river."[96] So connected was New Orleans with its steadily developing hinterland that the first volume of verse ever published about Illinois featured the Louisiana city prominently:

91. "The Wabash," *Daily National Journal* (Washington, D.C.), May 12, 1831, p. 3; "New-Orleans, Dec. 1," *Macon Weekly Telegraph* (*Georgia Telegraph*), December 17, 1835, p. 2.

92. Ashe, *Travels Performed in 1806*, 309.

93. Ward, *Diary*, THNOC, Accession Number 2009.0139, p. 14, 53.

94. *Louisiana State Gazette*, June 27, 1826, p. 2.

95. Haites, Mak, and Walton, *Western River Transportation*, 124–125; Bullard, "Abe Goes Down the River," 6.

96. As quoted by Andrew R. L. Cayton, *Frontier Indiana* (Bloomington: Indiana University Press, 1996), 56.

Let commerce next unfold her various store
Conveying it with speed from shore to shore:
Diffusing what may benefit mankind,
To serve the body or regale the mind: . . .
What merchants here collect with studious pains,
The *Mississippi* wafts to *New Orleans*: . . .
If men would cultivate a friendly trade,
And each to other lend their social aid:
Thus knowledge would increase, and arts abound,
The blessed fruits of peace, thro' nations round: . . .[97]

•

What of the flatboatman? His role in Mississippi Valley economic development, from late colonial times to the Civil War, may be described as fundamental. "Only by means of his brawn and his genius for navigation," wrote historian Archer B. Hulbert, "could these innumerable tons of flour, tobacco, and bacon have been kept from rotting on the shores."[98] Rivermen cycling between the upcountry and New Orleans served as unsuspecting agents of cultural diffusion. At the most basic level, they brought down surplus raw materials and agricultural products unavailable in the subtropics, and returned with highly needed capital. The men themselves exchanged perspectives, language, and knowledge—and sometimes their genes—to both ends of the river and all points between. Many Northern youths first witnessed the institution of slavery, particularly large-scale slave trading, on their maiden voyages to New Orleans, and formed opinions accordingly. They shared stories and spread perceptions about the river, the city, and the South; some even brought home exotic mementos, such as tropical fruits or sugary treats. One hypothesis traces the South's nickname "Dixie" to boatmen and their cycle of riverine trade, which entailed the circulation of a ten-dollar New Orleans banknote emblazoned with the French word *dix*.[99]

This role of economic and cultural exchange, however, jars with the

97. "Mount Carmel: A Poem," written by "a gentleman in London," as reproduced in "First Volume of Verse About Illinois," Historical Notes, *Journal of the Illinois State Historical Society* 48, no. 4 (Winter 1955): 470 (emphasis in original).

98. Hulbert, *Paths of Inland Commerce*, 70.

99. Another hypothesis views the term *Dixie* as a derivative of the Mason-Dixon Line, while a third theory traces it to an earlier New York slave owner by the name of Dixy. Most researchers agree that *Dixie* did not gain widespread popularity until Northern composer Daniel Emmett published "I Wish I Was in Dixie" in 1859. President Lincoln enjoyed the song.

popular image of the flatboatman. "[T]he man himself," continued Archer B. Hulbert, "remains a legend grotesque and mysterious, one of the shadowy figures of a time when history was being made too rapidly to be written." Hulbert illustrated how legends reduced flatboatmen's all-too-real challenges to folksy caricature:

> If we ask how he loaded his flatboat . . . we are told that "one squint of his eye would blister a bull's heel." When we inquire how he found the channel amid the shifting bars and floating islands of that tortuous two-thousand-mile journey to New Orleans, we are informed that he was "the very infant that turned from his mother's breast and called out for a bottle of old rye." When we ask how he overcame the natural difficulties of trade—lack of commission houses, varying standards of money, want of systems of credit and low prices due to the glutting of the market when hundreds of flatboats arrived in the South simultaneously . . . we are informed that "Billy Earthquake is the geniwine, double-acting engine, and can out-run, out-swim, chaw more tobacco and spit less, drink more whiskey and keep soberer than any other man in these localities."[100]

The popular imagery of the puckish "Kaintuck" ruffian derives in part from our tendency to observe, record, and remember that which deviates from the norm. Left out, all too often, is what *constitutes* the norm. The bell-shaped curve of actual experiences—that is, the statistical distribution plotting the predomination of that which is typical and the paucity of that which is exceptional—thus becomes inverted in their documentation and recollection. The typical becomes the exceptional, and the exceptional becomes the typical. First-person narratives of nineteenth-century New Orleans are replete with this sort of reversed reality: we have ample anecdotes of transgressions, debaucheries, and curiosities, but surprisingly little information on how plain folk lived their everyday lives.

So too are those sources describing flatboatmen: diary-keepers with an eye for the peculiar, not to mention travel writers enamored with local color and reporters with a taste for the sensational, were more likely to ignore the numerous ordinary, diligent, quiet young men and their long, uneventful days on the river, in favor of the swaggering hero, the brawling hooligan, the tall tale, and the occasional *bona fide* adventure. Louis Fitzgerald Tasistro's circa-1840 description is prototypical:

---

100. Hulbert, *Paths of Inland Commerce*, 70–71.

> The crew of a flat-boat is generally composed of five or six
> daredevils, armed to the teeth with bowie-knives and pistols;
> the sworn foes of [drinking] unadulterated water; equally alive
> to the attractions of a fight as of a mint-julep; the loudest in
> their applause of a theatrical performance, and invariably noisy
> everywhere: they are, in short, a concentrated essence of good
> and evil, and may truly be said to constitute, not the cream, but
> the cayenne and mustard of ordinary life in New-Orleans.[101]

Flatboatmen themselves, usually little-schooled and preoccupied with
their work, rarely recorded their own experiences. Thus, their legacy has
mostly been documented by others, whose eyes and ears sought out deviancy and drama rather than monotonous normalcy. Collective memory,
transmitted through folk tales, bedtime stories, dime novels, and Disney
movies, reinforces this disproportionate coverage, oftentimes tainting (or
exalting) an entire group with the reputation of numerical exception.

Historian Michael Allen, inspired by William H. Goetzmann's
groundbreaking research on Rocky Mountain fur trappers, studied more
than seventy accounts written by flatboatmen themselves, with the goal
of characterizing the *heart* of the statistical bell-shaped curve rather than
its exceptional fringes. Allen found that most flatboatmen, from the
steamboat age to the Civil War, were white men of Anglo or Celtic heritage; common hands ranged in age from late teens to early twenties, and
captains from late twenties to forties, or older. The former were usually
bachelors; the latter, married men with children (a status that steamboats
helped foster by dramatically speeding return trips). Some flatboat operations employed foreign immigrants, pure- or mixed-blood Indians, or
blacks (both free and enslaved). Women sometimes rode as passengers or
worked as cooks on larger commercial operations.[102]

The fraternity of antebellum flatboatmen, Allen discovered, broke
down into various levels of commitment, or "castes." At the top were the
"merchant navigators" and the "agent flatboatmen," who captained or contracted expeditions to deliver clients' cargo to New Orleans on a regular
basis. They were professionals who carefully managed their enterprises,
insured their trips, hired and fired help, and maintained business relationships with New Orleans merchants. Usually husbands and fathers and

101. Louis Fitzgerald Tasistro, *Random Shots and Southern Breezes* (New York: Harper
& Brothers, 1842), 1:58.
102. Michael Allen, "The Riverman as Jacksonian Man," *The Western Historical Quarterly* 21, no. 3 (August 1990): 305–320; Allen, *Western Rivermen*.

often pillars of the community, these merchant navigators and agents took no unnecessary risks and wanted nothing to do with those who did.

These river capitalists shared the waters with "farmer flatboatmen," family farmers who supplemented their main occupation with an occasional marketing trip to convert surplus harvests into cash. (The etymologically mysterious term "hoosier" came to describe such amateur flatboatmen of the Ohio River region. Perhaps because so many farmer-boatmen came from Indiana, "hoosier," by the early 1830s, came to mean a native of that state.[103]) Like their professional peers, these amateurs had much to lose if trips were viewed as opportunities for escapism, if interactions turned violent, or if alcohol or indulgence compromised judgment.

Working under each flatboat captain were anywhere from one to a dozen helpers. Crew roles and skills varied; the captain of the Indiana-based *Davy Crockett* (1834) employed a "steersman & pilot," a bowsman, a cook, and a "Clerk & Journalist."[104] Usually, crews simply comprised "common boatmen," or "hands." They were oftentimes teenagers or twenty-somethings on their first paying job (and first long-distance trip), helping deliver their fathers', uncles', or neighbors' produce to market. Other hands were hired by agents or merchant navigators and had no relationship with the cargo owner. Still others were transients or men from other trades looking to fill employment gaps. "[I]nexperienced, but motivated," the common flatboatman, wrote Allen, sought "adventure and a few dollars to get his start in life."[105] The opportunity also provided the lad with a shot at doing something risky and important—to accomplish something that his peers and elders had done, and expected him to do. The voyage to New Orleans served as a rite of passage between boyhood and manhood, between dependence and independence, between the familiar and the foreign. Once that rite had been secured, once or twice or a handful of times, common flatboatmen usually made their living in other endeavors.

Beyond mastering river navigation, a boatman also had to be knowledgeable, resourceful, and savvy. Captains bore responsibility for bringing these attributes to bear, but common hands also had a stake in the voyage's success and played a critical role in it. Boats had to be constructed properly without the benefit of official guidelines or inspections; according to

103. Jonathan Clark Smith, "Not Southern Scorn But Local Pride: The Origins of the Word *Hoosier* and Indiana's River Culture," *Indiana Magazine of History* 103, no. 2 (June 2007): 183–189.

104. Jacquess, "Journals of the Davy Crockett," 8–9.

105. Allen, "Riverman as Jacksonian Man," 317.

one observer in 1806, "many of the accidents that happen in navigating the Ohio and Mississippi [owe] to the unpardonable carelessness and penuriousness of the boat builder."[106] Once afloat, cargo had to be handled properly and protected from rain, rot, mold, infestations, and pirates. Barrels leaked, got wet, popped their heads, or cracked open; contents spilled or developed dreaded mildew growth; "flour turn[ed] sour."[107] Fowl lay vulnerable to predators: in one case, minks infested a docked flatboat and killed numerous chickens on multiple nights.[108] Livestock had to arrive healthy and calm. The sustenance and well-being of the crew were paramount; afflictions such as sunburn, dysentery, pneumonia, and yellow fever (not to mention hypothermia and drowning) made the flatboat trade a major health risk. Tying up at night prevented exposure to the dangers of nocturnal travel, but increased vulnerability to thieves and marauders; crews regularly slept with hand on club or gun. When things went wrong, captains had to be quick thinkers in mitigating damages and recovering losses. For example, one three-boat, sixteen-man expedition carrying lumber from Wheeling in 1807 shipwrecked disastrously, forcing the captains to reconstitute their cargo in smaller form. Their solution: break their lumber into staves and proceed to New Orleans to sell them to coopers.[109] Even when sailing went smoothly, captains had to decide whether miscellaneous upcountry produce should be traded en route for standard commodities such as cotton, sugar, bricks, and firewood, for which buyers in New Orleans could always be found.

Approaching the wharf at New Orleans brought the challenges of claiming a berth and safely poling into place amid swirling river traffic. Once docked, finding a trustworthy, cash-carrying buyer at the right time, place, and price presented a tense challenge, given that hundreds of other captains vying to do the same thing created a buyer's market. Money changers, banks, credit lines, and other financial players had to be evaluated judiciously. Prices could plummet between loading upstream and unloading in New Orleans, a possibility to which wise captains responded by diversifying their cargo. Currency being so sundry and crude in this era, river traders had to keep an eye out for counterfeit money, a huge problem

106. Ashe, *Travels Performed in 1806*, 60.

107. Adam Hodgson, *Remarks During a Journey Through North America in the Years 1819, 1820, and 1821* (Samuel Whiting: New York, 1823), 32.

108. Jacquess, "Journals of the Davy Crockett," 16.

109. Survey of Federal Archives in Louisiana, Division of Professional and Service Projects-Works Projects Administration, *Flatboats on the Mississippi in 1807* (Baton Rouge: Louisiana State University, 1940), 101.

up and down the river.[110]

Bureaucracy also demanded attention: docking required the payment of a wharfage fee, and if the voyage encountered losses, the captain had to register a "Ship Captain's Protest" with the one of New Orleans' fourteen notaries public. This notarized record documented what happened (vessel problems, wreckage, pirate attack, etc.), usually for insurance purposes. Some flatboat captains hired clerks to handle all inventory, money, and paperwork matters, indicating how professionalized the Western flatboat trade had grown by the mid-antebellum era.[111]

New Orleans itself presented additional risks. The city's criminal element targeted certain flatboatmen as naïve bumpkins flush with cash, while its mosquito-borne yellow fever virus disproportionately afflicted newcomers and led to quarantines of returning crews that might have been infected in the epidemic-plagued city.[112] If all went well, getting one's money and one's self safely home presented the next trial, and many a crewmember failed in either or both. For a successful flatboat captain and crew to evade this minefield of tribulations required not just physical brawn and navigational acumen but also a keen business sense, jack-of-all-trades mechanical skills, personal discipline, leadership, fatherly wisdom, and a bearing of cautious responsibility.

Estwick Evans, who traveled the river in the 1810s, sensed that the popular perception of the brash brawler did not match his observations. "The boatmen of the west," he acknowledged,

> are conspicuous for their habits of . . . swearing[;] my ears were shocked by their oaths and curses. . . . [But] I witnessed much less intemperance than information previously obtained had led me to anticipate. . . . I may add, that I have often heard of the low conversation, which is said to prevail among the boatmen of the west; and also of their quarrelsome and fighting habits. All these practices are much less than they are represented to be.[113]

110. William O. Stoddard, *Abraham Lincoln: A True Story of a Great Life* (New York: Fords, Howard, & Hulbert, 1884), 54.

111. One example is Jacquess, "Journals of the Davy Crockett," 8–24; "Notaries Public for N. Orleans," *New-Orleans Directory & Register* (New Orleans: John Adems Paxton, 1830), unpaginated.

112. "New-Orleans, Sept. 4," *Pittsfield Sun* (Pittsfield, MA), October 2, 1823, p. 2; "Extract of a Letter to the Editors of the National Advocate," *Baltimore Patriot*, June 19, 1826, p. 2.

113. Evans, "Pedestrious Tour," in *Early Western Travels*, 8:260–261.

> The numerous stories, which have so often been circulated, and believed, respecting the cruel modes of fighting . . . among the boatmen of the west, are, generally speaking, untrue. During the whole of my tour, I did not witness one engagement, or see a single person, who bore those marks of violence which proceed from the inhuman mode of fighting, said to exist in the west, particularly in Kentucky and Tennessee. The society of this part of the world is becoming less savage, and more refined.[114]

Historian Michael Allen found that most flatboatmen were not the "swashbuckling 'Alligator Horses,'—hard-drinking, fighting, gambling, promiscuous frontier adventurers"—of popular legend. The typical riverman, by contrast, could be described as "a Jacksonian man—an expectant entrepreneur who worked tirelessly for the main chance and reveled in the promise of capitalism, the industrial revolution, and modern America." Working the western rivers simply offered a way to make a living to more than 200,000 Americans over half a century. Flatboatmen thus resembled other working Americans of the era more than their colorful folk counterparts. "[R]ivermen were very much a part of the Jacksonian society they supposedly sought to escape." Allen continued:

> Boatmen were modern men. They had traveled and seen something of the world. They had visited large cities, seen urban squalor, and experienced ethnic diversity. They commuted home on the decks of steam-powered riverboats. They attended church and some even signed temperance pledges. They read newspapers, talked of politics, and became involved in the hotly contested elections of that era.[115]

Authors of *The Navigator*, the western river guide book published in the 1810s, would have concurred with Allen's assessment:

> This voyage [down the Ohio to New Orleans and back] performed[,] the trader returns doubly invigorated, and enabled to enlarge his vessel and cargo, he sets out again; this is repeated, until . . . he sets himself down in some town or village as a wholesale merchant, druggist or apothecary, practicing physi-

---

114. Ibid., 344.
115. Allen, "Riverman as Jacksonian Man," 305–306, 319–320.

cian or lawyer. . . .render[ing] him respectable in the eyes of his neighbors. . . .[116]

This characterization would accurately foretell Abraham Lincoln's post-flatboat career.

116. *The Navigator* (1814), 33.

Appendix B: New Orleans in the 1820s–1830s

~ Rough start in a place apart ~ A dramatic change of destiny ~ Creoles in a new American city ~ Americans in an old Creole city ~ Cotton and sugar commerce ~ Risk, ruin, and reward ~ A growing and diversifying population ~ Ethnic tensions ~ Slavery and race relations ~ Geography of slavery ~ A cityscape of bondage ~ Slave trading ~ The city from afar ~ The port up close ~ Port management ~ Port controversies ~ Urban growth and internal improvements ~ The Great Southern Emporium ~

As Anglo-Americans migrated westward and southward into the lands of the Louisiana Purchase, they contacted, fought, and displaced indigenous populations whose ranks had been previously thinned by European disease. The emigrants also encountered occasional trading posts and settlements left behind by recently departed French and Spanish colonial regimes. The contact positioned Anglo-Americans, often for the first time, in the backyards of Franco-, Hispano-, Caribbean- and African Americans: different language, law, government, religion, architecture, and foodways. Chief among those culturally divergent places was New Orleans.

Isolated from the hearth of North American colonial activity by over a thousand terrestrial miles and two thousand nautical miles, the French colonial port city of Nouvelle Orleans and its adjacent Gulf Coast enclaves marched to a markedly different beat for two generations before the American nation even formed. While societies of the Eastern Seaboard looked primarily to Protestant England to inform their culture, Nouvelle Orleans looked to Catholic France and its New World colonies. Denizens came from the geographic and economic fringes of the Francophone world: some from the lower strata of French society, others from French Canada, still others from Saint-Domingue and the West Indies via the nascent coastal outposts of Pensacola, Mobile, and Biloxi. Nearly half the city's population was forcibly removed from the Senegambia region of Africa throughout the 1720s for enslavement in Louisiana. As in the Caribbean, a small mixed-race caste emerged from the intermingling, one that enjoyed more rights than the enslaved but far less than the white ruling caste. A few miles upriver from Nouvelle Orleans settled German and Swiss farmers who immigrated a few years after the city's founding in 1718; beyond this "German Coast" lay the "Acadian Coast," where French

Canadian exiles settled after the British victors of the French and Indian War expelled them from Acadie between 1755 and 1785.

Crushing defeat in that conflict forced France to relinquish most of its North American empire to the detested English. King Louis XV, however, foreseeing the loss in 1762, secretly ceded areas west the Mississippi to his Spanish cousin King Carlos III. Cleverly included in the treaty was Nouvelle Orleans, which, on account of Bayou Manchac and the lakes, formed something of an "isle," cartographically detachable from the east-of-the-Mississippi mainland destined for British hands. Louisiana thus became Luisiana, and Nouvelle Orleans became Nueva Orleans. While dominion fully transferred by 1769 to the hands and standards of the Spanish colonials, the populace generally retained its Francophone culture and viewed its new governors with thinly veiled disdain.

So too did Spain view Nueva Orleans, perceiving it as an unpromising distraction from its vast and valuable (but increasingly restless) New World empire. Distant and disappointing, the city came to be something of a colonial afterthought in the late 1700s, even more so as revolution and insurgency rocked the Atlantic world. Violence to the north ousted British colonials and launched a new American nation; violence across the ocean overthrew the French monarchy and spawned a shaky new republic; violence in the Caribbean fueled a slave insurrection in France's most valued colony, Saint-Domingue. Agitation for independence bubbled up throughout New Spain, further threatening the imperial *status quo*.

•

As political tumult transpired internationally around the turn of the nineteenth century, technological breakthroughs began to alter the lower Louisiana landscape. Eli Whitney's 1793 patent for the "cotton engine," which efficiently separated lint from seed, made cotton cultivation lucrative and fostered its dramatic spread into newly cleared lands in the lower Mississippi Valley. Two years later, Jean Etienne de Boré of New Orleans succeeded in granulating Louisiana sugar cane (a process practiced for centuries in the tropical West Indies but elusive in this subtropical clime), and replicated the process commercially. Sugar cane cultivation swiftly replaced fading colonial-era crops such as indigo, rice, and tobacco throughout the deltaic region. Cotton and sugar shipments had only one economical way to reach sources of demand: down the Mississippi for deposit at Nueva Orleans and transshipment to world markets—where new steam-engine technology revolutionized the processing of cotton lint into fabric and garments.

Dramatic political news punctuated these advancements. Spain, declining in power and apprehensive about the United States' mounting interest in Nueva Orleans, secretly retroceded (1800) its Louisiana colony to Napoleon's militarily mighty France and prohibited Americans from depositing goods (1802) there. Upon learning of these provocations, an alarmed President Thomas Jefferson aspired to gain control of the once-marginalized, now-treasured port city, as France shockingly returned to the North American stage. But where Jefferson saw strategic advantage, Napoleon saw subservience: the future emperor viewed his regained Nouvelle Orleans and its adjoining Louisiana colony as little more than a breadbasket to feed the astonishingly lucrative sugar colony of Saint-Domingue—once, of course, its insurgent slaves were crushed.

Instead, Napoleon's 20,000 troops, sent to Saint-Domingue in 1802 to restore order, were vanquished through bloody battles and lethal yellow fever outbreaks. Loss of the keystone colony undermined whatever passive interest Napoleon had in Louisiana. Wary of overextending his colonial empire, in need of money, and in light of impending war, Napoleon decided to sell the entire colony to the United States, which had bargained previously only for Nouvelle Orleans. "A vast and unlimited territory [became American] without the loss of a drop of blood," marveled one sanguine Westerner[1] The eighty-five-year-old port once envisioned to command that territory for France instead became the new American city of New Orleans.

Colonial authorities lowered the French tri-color for the last time during the Louisiana Purchase ceremony in the Place d'Armes on December 20, 1803. In only a few years, New Orleans' fortunes had dramatically reversed. For decades the colonial orphan of two distracted Old World monarchies, the city now found itself strategically positioned under the dominion of an ascendant, expanding, unabashedly capitalistic New World democracy. Westward-bound Americans received the news "with elated heart and joyful countenance," enthused that they could now do business with the "friendly hand of a fellow citizen" rather than the foreign "tyrants . . . whose every glance was dire jealousy and suspicion . . . bombastic pride and ostentation . . . bribery, fraud, and chicanery."[2] Prominent observers routinely predicted that this new American city would, as one put it, "doubtless one day become the greatest [on the] continent, per-

---

1. *The Navigator, or the Traders' Useful Guide in Navigating the Monongahela, Allegheny, Ohio, and Mississippi Rivers* (Pittsburgh, Pennsylvania: Zadok Cramer, 1806), 128.
2. Ibid., 128.

haps even in the world."[3] Another went further, foreseeing New Orleans as "one of the greatest commercial cities in the universe."[4]

•

Yet New Orleanians, who numbered roughly 8,000 in 1803, found themselves woefully unprepared for such radical change in dominion and destiny. Compared to their new compatriots, they spoke a different language, practiced a different religion, and followed distinct legal philosophies. They perceived race and managed slavery differently. They surveyed land and built houses in their own way. They ate different foods, celebrated different festivals, and idolized different heroes. They even entombed their dead differently. Their leaders for the previous eighty-five years had been appointed to them, not elected amongst them. New Orleanians were *told*, not polled; decisions and policies flowed from the top down, with little feedback tolerated from the bottom up. River commerce was controlled not by entrepreneurs serving market forces, but by "individuals purchasing the rights of monopoly from the king," through which "wealth circulated in a very partial manner," as one outsider disapprovingly huffed.[5] Provincial, culturally conservative, resistant to change, oftentimes unlettered, naïve to the ways of republican government, and ill-equipped for the fiercely competitive world of free-market capitalism, New Orleanians fretted, then resented, then resisted the onslaught of *les Américains*.

In the face of this impending threat, New Orleans' mostly Catholic Francophone population came to view its shared colonial-era heritage and deep-rooted Louisiana nativity as a unifying bond—a pan-racial, place-based sort of ethnicity—that distinguished them from the incoming English-speaking, Protestant, Anglo-Americans. In certain contexts, the natives described themselves as the *ancienne population*; in others, including vernacular speech, they became known far and wide as "the Creoles"—a modification of the old Spanish and Portuguese word *criollo*, which originally meant New World–born offspring of Old World–born parents. Other appellations loosely dropped upon this ethnic group by

3. Hugh Murray, *Historical Account of Discoveries and Travels in North America* (London: Longman, Rees, Orme, Brown, & Green, 1829), 426.
4. Daniel Blowe, *A Geographical, Historical, Commercial, and Agricultural View of the United States of America* (London: Edwards & Knibb, 1820), 64–65.
5. Thomas Ashe, *Travels in America Performed in the Year 1806* (London: Richard Phillips, 1809), 309–10.

contemporary Anglophones included "the French," "the Gallics," "the Gauls,"or "the Latins."

New Orleans' physical environment differed, too. It occupied a dynamic, fluid, and youthful deltaic plain rather than the ancient hardened lithosphere of the rest of North America. Its meager topography provided not a single visual landmark or vantage point beyond the slightly upraised natural levee. The region enjoyed a subtropical rather than a temperate climate, nurtured crops that tolerated those temperatures, and suffered diseases and disasters associated with those environs.

New Orleans, in sum, formed the expanding American nation's first major encounter with a large, complex, subtropical urban society that, from the Americans' perspective, seemed exotic and foreign in just about every way imaginable.

•

"There is in fact no part of the world where a fortune may be made more speedily and certainly," wrote one commentator about New Orleans; "there is more employment in every trade than there are hands to execute: even a good tailor may make a little fortune in a few years."[6] That sense of opportunity trumped aversion to the alien, motivating waves of outsiders to cast their lot with this peculiar place. "The Americans [are] swarming in from the northern states," recollected Pierre Clément de Laussat, the last French official to oversee Louisiana. "Each one turned over in his mind a little plan of speculation[;] they were invading Louisiana as the holy tribes invaded the land of Canaan."[7] Their arrival rapidly affected the city's economy. "The influx of American speculators was so great" after the Louisiana Purchase, wrote one observer a few years later, "that the character of commerce instantaneously changed, and violence and competition, which in America means contention, reigned triumphantly. . . ." The number of merchants in New Orleans, he continued, increased fifty-fold within six years.[8] Similarly did the numbers grow for bankers, factors, agents, lawyers, and planters—all eagerly "on the make," laying claim to as much opportunity, power, and influence as the city could offer.[9] The

6. Murray, *Account of Discoveries and Travels*, 427.
7. Pierre Clément de Laussat, *Memoirs of My Life* (Baton Rouge and New Orleans, 1978 translation of 1831 memoir), 103.
8. Ashe, *Travels Performed in 1806*, 309–10.
9. Joseph G. Tregle Jr., *Louisiana in the Age of Jackson: A Clash of Cultures and Personalities* (Baton Rouge: Louisiana State University Press, 1999), 43.

Americans also changed the city's ethnic geography, as they generally settled in the upper streets of the original city and then upriver into the Faubourg Ste. Marie (which became anglicized as "St. Mary"). American emigration increased after statehood in 1812, and again following the resounding defeat of the British at the Battle of New Orleans in 1815. That victory launched Maj. Gen. Andrew Jackson to national fame, and further introduced curious Americans to the exotic city now within their country.

Anglo-Americans were not the only *arrivistes*: more than 9,000 refugees—roughly equally divided among whites, free people of color, and the enslaved—arrived in 1809 from former Saint-Domingue, now the independent nation of Haiti. The Francophone refugees breathed new life into the city's Franco-Afro-Caribbean culture, and complicated the process of Americanization. They also complicated the position of the Creoles, who now had to share power, resources, and living space with a third faction. Such also was the Creoles' relationship with immigrants arriving directly from France, who like the Americans tended to be more worldly, erudite, competitive, and ambitious—but like the Creoles spoke French, practiced Catholicism, and exhibited Latin cultural ways. Immigrants from the Spanish-speaking world further diversified New Orleans' ethnic landscape, arriving since the 1770s from Mexico, Cuba, Central and South America, the Canary Islands, and Spain itself. At least a few representatives of nearly every society of the greater Atlantic Basin, and many beyond, circulated in New Orleans in the early 1800s. They came for countless proximate reasons, but the ultimate reason usually involved the myriad commercial opportunities generated by the city's supreme geographical advantage. Topping the list were all things related to cotton and sugar.

•

[P]lantations . . . from Natchez to New Orleans and still lower down, were formerly appropriated to the culture of indigo and rice, but the demand for these articles...being on the decline, the attention of the planters is now turned to that of sugar and cotton, both of which [make] excellent shipments. . . .[10]

—Fortescue Cuming, 1810

10. Fortescue Cuming, *Sketches of a Tour to the Western Country through the States of Ohio and Kentucky* (Pittsburgh, 1810), 338.

Following Whitney's invention of the "gin," cotton production in Louisiana rose to 2 million pounds by 1811, grown mostly in the Anglo-dominated regions north of Baton Rouge. That figure quintupled in ten years, quadrupled again to 38 million pounds in 1826, then rose to 62 million by 1834. Production in the state of Mississippi (the vast majority from the southwestern corner) rose from 10 million pounds in 1821 to 85 million pounds in 1834.[11] Louisiana and Mississippi contributed nearly two-thirds of the cotton arriving to New Orleans' wharves; Alabama and Tennessee sent down most of the remainder, with places as far away as Illinois and Florida contributing as well.[12] Bales arrived first on flatboats and later on steamboats, in such quantities that the city began to develop a sophisticated cotton marketing and services industry. In the seven years leading up to Lincoln's first visit, cotton handled at New Orleans doubled from 156,030 to 304,848 bales, and was shipped to Great Britain (47 percent, principally to Liverpool), cities of the northeastern United States (28 percent, mainly New York), France (22 percent), and a host of smaller international ports.[13]

Sugar cane boomed commensurately, although it was raised on a more local scale compared to cotton, and shipped mostly to domestic markets. Southeastern Louisiana produced 2,500 tons of sugar in 1802, just seven seasons after Boré's granulation breakthrough. A year later, sixty to seventy sugar plantations lined both banks of the river from present-day Kenner to English Turn.[14] While Anglos generally dominated cotton production, Creoles and Acadians controlled most sugar production. By 1816, with over $40 million invested regionally in the sugar industry, "the great impetus thus given to the trade was felt in every direction and the

11. *The Southern States, Embracing a Series of Papers Condensed from the Earlier Volumes of De Bow's Review* (1856), 1:123; *New-Orleans Price-Current and Commercial Intelligencer* (October 10, 1835); and J. D. B. De Bow, *The Commercial Review of the South and West* (1848), 6:434.

12. These figures are from 1828. John Wilie, "Exports of cotton and tobacco from the port of New Orleans during the last seven years . . . [1821–28] Imports from the interior . . . Exports of sugar and molasses . . ." (New Orleans: Benjamin Levy, 1828), broadside stored at Tulane University, Louisiana Collection, 976.31 (380) E96.

13. Wilie, "Exports from New Orleans," broadside stored at Tulane University, Louisiana Collection, 976.31 (380) E96.

14. John G. Clark, *New Orleans, 1718–1812: An Economic History* (Baton Rouge: Louisiana State University Press, 1970), 219. By another count, Louisiana's sugar-related production in 1802 included 5,000 hogheads of sugar, 5,000 barrels of molasses, and 5,000 casks of rum. "The Sugar Exchange: Formal Opening of the Beautiful Building," *Times-Democrat* (New Orleans), June 4, 1884, address by J. Dymond, p. 3, c. 3–5.

city of New Orleans rapidly increased in wealth and population, tripling the same within twenty years after the opening of the sugar industry."[15] Between 1824 and 1830, the number of sugar plantations grew from under 200 to nearly 700.[16] Of the 39,063 hogsheads of sugar handled at New Orleans in the year preceding Lincoln's first trip, nearly half went to New York, a quarter to Philadelphia, and the rest to fourteen other large American cities.[17]

These two commodities, not to mention tobacco and numerous other crops from the rapidly populating trans-Appalachian West, spectacularly increased port traffic at New Orleans. "The exportation commerce of Louisiana, fifteen years ago, was carried on with thirty ships of moderate size," wrote a Frenchman in 1807 after visiting the region in 1801–03; "Since the cultivation of sugar and cotton, it has so increased, that above two hundred are employed."[18] The freight arrived in New Orleans at first via a fleet of flatboats originating from numerous lower Mississippi River villages, joined after the 1810s by a new fleet of steamboats. "The flatboat coast trade and the fortunes of the flatboatmen . . . were entirely dependent on the success of the cotton and sugar planters of Mississippi and Louisiana," explained one elder who knew firsthand; "When crops were bad[,] it was 'hard times' among the flatboatmen."[19]

Vast quantities of capital, largely from Northeastern and European financial hubs, poured into the city's banks to fund agricultural enterprises, as well as internal improvements, buildings, facilities, and land development. New Orleans emerged as a key Southern node in the Atlantic Basin economic system. The city's banking system as a whole expanded markedly in the 1830s; at least fourteen banks operated around the time of Lincoln's visits. Clustering primarily on upper Chartres and Royal streets, they included the venerable Citizens, the Union, the Orleans, Consolidated, the State, the Louisiana, the Gaslight, and the Commercial; even the Orleans Theater Company got into the financial scene. Bankers interacted with commission merchants, who advanced funds speculatively

15. "The Sugar Exchange," *Times-Democrat*, June 4, 1884, p. 3, c. 3–5.

16. J. H. Galloway, *The Sugar Cane Industry: An Historical Geography from its Origins to 1914* (Cambridge, England: Cambridge University Press, 1989), 190.

17. Wilie, "Exports from New Orleans," broadside stored at Tulane University, Louisiana Collection, 976.31 (380) E96.

18. M. Perrin Du Lac, *Travels Through the Two Louisianas . . . in 1801, 1802, & 1803* (London: Richard Phillips, 1807), 92.

19. "In Flatboat and Keelboat Times On the Mississippi, Over Seventy Years Ago," *Daily Picayune*, March 19, 1896, p. 14, section f, c. 6–7.

to plantation owners, oftentimes driving up commodity prices. Cotton and sugar factors allied themselves with planters and represented their interests in urban affairs, while lawyers oversaw their legal matters and sued relentlessly over every imaginable dispute. Merchants, brokers, and commercial agents added to the professional class: the 1822 city directory listed 265 merchants, 66 commission merchants, 24 brokers or exchange brokers, 7 cotton brokers, and 2 commercial agents.[20] By the mid-1830s, the city was home to 323 wholesale merchants, 786 retailers, 83 brokers, 16 auctioneers, and 17 notary publics (not to mention over 1,300 taverns, cabarets, and hotels).[21] Countering the speculative risks encouraged by liberal capital was a parallel rise in insurance companies, each with their teams of agents, bookkeepers, and lawyers.

New Orleans' vast class of professional middlemen prospered enormously on the risks taken by planters, who in turn profited on the forced labor of slaves—the foundation upon which the entire system rested. The early-nineteenth-century cotton and sugar cane boom in fact breathed new life into the institution of slavery; importations from Africa into the porous underbelly of the Louisiana coast continued even after the United States prohibited international slave trading in 1808. Domestic slave trading from Virginia and the Upper South filled its place, delivering thousands of "surplus" bondmen into the brutal, high-priced Deep South slave market. Yet another professional class tended to the handling of human chattel, making New Orleans the nation's premier slave-trading post. New Orleans in the antebellum era served as the South's financial nerve center in just about every way imaginable. No surprise, then, that the lower Mississippi River region boasted the nation's highest concentration of millionaires.[22]

This is not to say that every ambitious free white male became rich, or that the economy did nothing but hum. Many entrepreneurs strived doggedly and lost everything. Prices for many Louisiana commodities actually declined for much of the 1820s, earning investors less return for greater risk or toil. Markets crashed infamously in the Panic of 1837 and

20. *New-Orleans Directory and Register* (New Orleans: John Adems Paxton, 1822), unpaginated section entitled "List of Names."

21. James E. Winston, "Notes on the Economic History of New Orleans, 1803–1836," *The Mississippi Valley Historical Review* 11, no. 2 (September 1924): 216–218; Gavin Wrigh, *The Political Economy of the Cotton South* (New York: W. W. Norton & Company, 1978), 223.

22. Winston, "Economic History of New Orleans," 223; Wright, *Economy of the Cotton South*, 13.

struggled for six years thence, costing many a New Orleans aristocrat his family's fortune.[23] Even the very lifeblood of the city's success—the monopoly on Western traffic afforded by the Mississippi River—came under assault in this era, with the completion of the Erie Canal (1825) and subsequent waterways and railroads connecting the eastern metropolises directly with the trans-Appalachian West. But because the "pie" represented by that region's agricultural bounty grew so dramatically in absolute terms, it disguised the fact that New Orleans' relative slice of that pie was shrinking. Likewise, the magnificent wealth accumulated by those who *did* succeed drew more far attention, and inspired more emulation, than did the money lost quietly by those who failed.

•

So enticingly did the allure of riches beckon, ambitious entrepreneurs willingly exposed themselves to the risks of a hazardous physical environment. Those further down on the social pyramid had no choice but to suffer even greater exposure to those hazards. New Orleans became known as the Necropolis of the South—the Wet Grave—a filthy, flood-prone, storm-battered, disease-infested city that suffered forty to seventy deaths annually per thousand people (and well over double that rate during epidemics).[24] Crime and vice took additional tolls on health and welfare. Many people sensed a causative relationship between the city's physical mortality and moral depravity. An 1812 article in a New York paper, for example, viewed the city's recent bouts with hurricanes and fires as divine retribution for being "a second Sodom . . . exhibiting . . . scenes of the most licentious wickedness."[25] An 1815 editorial characterized the city "as a place that has disgraced America by its worthlessness and vice... very little better than old Sodom and Gomorrah."[26] A missionary minister visiting in 1823 reminded his readers that "New Orleans is of course exposed to greater varieties of human misery, vice, disease, and want, than any other American town. . . . Much has been said about [its] profligacy of manners . . . morals . . . debauchery, and low vice. . . ."[27] A travel descrip-

23. Thomas E. Redard, "The Port of New Orleans: An Economic History, 1821–1860" (Ph.D. dissertation, Louisiana State University, 1985), 1:18–21.

24. The City Planning and Zoning Commission, *Major Street Report* (New Orleans, 1927), 75.

25. *New-York Gazette & General Advertiser*, October 12, 1812, p. 2, c. 3.

26. *Independent Chronicle* (Boston), September 25, 1815, p. 1, c. 4.

27. Timothy Flint, *Recollections of the Last Ten Years . . . in the Valley of the Mississippi* (Boston: Cummings, Hillard, and Co., 1826), 305 and 309.

tion written by Hugh Murray at the time of Lincoln's first visit assessed the city's "moral aspect" as "the most sinister [of] any city of America," a by-product of the city's ability to attract "adventurers" and "refuse":

> [T]he sound of music and dancing echo[es] from the ball-rooms [even] on a Sunday. . . . Gaming-houses abound in every quarter; and nothing prevents the inhabitants from plunging into the utmost excesses of dissipation except the avidity for making a fortune. . . . Masked balls, bull-fights, and sensual indulgencies, form almost the exclusive enjoyments of the greater part of the inhabitants.[28]

An Englishman visiting the next year corroborated those observations. "The number of billiard-rooms, gambling-houses, and lottery-offices is immense," wrote James Stuart after his 1830 tour of New Orleans. "In the old city every second house seems to be [so] occupied. . . ."

Pious? Hardly, Murray went on to say, pointing out that decades-old Pittsburgh had four churches for its 10,000 citizens, while century-old New Orleans counted only five for 40,000. Stuart concurred, "There are fewer churches here in relation to the population than in any other of the American cities," noting also that even some houses of worship got into the gambling business. "There is the French Evangelical Church Lottery, the Baton Rouge Church Lottery, the Natchitoche's Catholic Church Lottery, &c." Both visitors shuddered at the rampant disregard of the Sabbath, a local cultural distinction at which nearly all judgmental visitors shook their heads.[29]

And literate? Even less so. The city's only free library in 1830, sponsored by an out-of-state Jew, had to beg space from a church owned by out-of-state Presbyterians.[30] A small college had recently shut down for want of students, and "all attempts have failed to form even a reading-room, though there is not in other parts of the Union a town of 2000 inhabitants without one."[31] The state's exploding population, which increased nine-fold between 1810 and 1830, could not prevent the number of Louisiana newspapers during those years from declining, ten to nine.[32] Such judg-

28. Murray, *Account of Discoveries and Travels*, 428–429.

29. James Stuart, *Three Years in North America*, (Edinburgh and London: Robert Cadell and Whittaker and Company, 1833), 2:236–239.

30. *New-Orleans Directory & Register* (New Orleans: John Adems Paxton, 1830), unpaginated entry for Touro Free Library.

31. Murray, *Account of Discoveries and Travels*, 428–429.

32. Stuart, *Three Years in North America*, 2:245–246.

ments of New Orleans' moral, civic, religious, and intellectual decadence were by no means exceptional in this era; they were the rule—so much so that writers grappled with words and built upon others' denunciations to express the sheer magnitude of the city's perceived iniquity. Murray himself quoted another visitor, Henry Bradshaw Fearon, who wrote in 1819,

> to all men whose desire only is to be rich, and to live a short life but a merry one, I have no hesitation in recommending New Orleans.[33]

"[B]ut the merriment appears at least not to be of a very refined nature," snorted Murray before moving on to a chapter on American industry—in which, incidentally, New Orleans earns not a single mention.[34]

Despite these universally recognized city stigmas (or perhaps because of them), New Orleans witnessed during the 1820s and 1830s the most dramatic sustained population growth of its entire history. The 1820 census enumerated 27,276 people in the city proper, more than triple the population at the time of the Louisiana Purchase. That figure increased by 83 percent over the next decade, and by another 105 percent between 1830 and 1840. When Lincoln visited in 1828 and 1831, at least 45,000 and 55,000 people, respectively, resided in the city—not including thousands of "strangers" (part-time residents, visitors, and transients) nor uncounted indigents, many of whom circulated in the same riverfront sections traversed by visiting flatboatmen. One journalist estimated the city's permanent population "near 60,000" at the time of Lincoln's second visit, and reported that "there are frequently from 25 to 50,000 strangers in the place" during winter.[35]

Indeed, seasonal activity waxed and waned so dramatically that a wintertime visitor and his summertime counterpart (few that there were) might come away with divergent impressions of the Southern metropolis. Shipping activity of all types began to increase in mid-autumn, as farmers harvested crops and sent them to market. It peaked in late winter and early spring, then declined and bottomed out in late summer and early autumn, when only one-quarter to one-sixth of the peak traffic called at the port.[36] Traffic from upcountry (as opposed to the sea) ranged particularly

33. Henry Bradshaw Fearon, *Sketches of America: A Narrative of a Journey of Five Thousand Miles Through The Eastern and Western States of America* (London, 1819), 278.

34. Murray, *Account of Discoveries and Travels*, 429–430.

35. "New-Orleans," *New-Bedford Courier* (New Bedford, MA), August 16, 1831, p. 1.

36. Estimated from Collector of Levee Dues records of 1818–23 and from monthly shipping arrival records from 1826–29, as summarized on the last page of the *New-*

widely with the seasons: a typical April saw two hundred to four hundred flatboats, steamboats, barges, and rafts arrive at New Orleans' wharves, while the month of September might see as few as five.[37] That shipping cycle fueled the economy, and thus the number of visiting businessmen, sailors, boat hands, and itinerants, plus all those locals in the secondary and tertiary economies who fed, clothed, sheltered, and served the cash-carrying transients. One observer in the late 1840s estimated that while the city's official population exceeded 100,000, "a transient population of thirty or forty thousand [departs] in swarms . . . as soon as the warm season commences, [and returns] as wild geese do from the North, on the first appearance of a flake of snow."[38] The seasonal visitors found accommodations according to their means: sailors would sleep aboard their ships; laborers crowded into notoriously rowdy "caravanserai"[39] (flop houses for poor transients); and professionals stayed at exchange hotels, found apartments, or boarded with affluent residents. "A few gentlemen can be accommodated with boarding in a genteel French family, in a central part of a city," read one *Courier* notice at the outset of the 1828–29 busy season. To screen out undesirables—and there were many—the family directed prospective tenants to apply not at their house, but "at the Office of *The Courier.*"[40]

Oppressive heat, humidity, and a slack economy gave sufficient cause for people to avoid a New Orleans summer. But the premier reason for the annual exodus was to minimize the chances of a lonely and excruciating death by the scourge of "the sickly season," yellow fever.[41] The dreaded late-summer plague scared off vessels calling at the port and drove away visiting businessmen as well as wealthy residents. Their departure stifled economic activity, which only intensified the pressure to flee. "In summer it becomes intensely hot, and the resident is cruelly annoyed by the musquitoes [*sic*]," reported one traveler in 1828. Unaware of the relationship between certain mosquitoes (namely the invasive African *Aedes aegypti*)

Orleans Directory & Register (1830).

37. Wharfinger Reports, Microfilm #75-109 QN420, 1818–23, New Orleans Collector of Levee Dues-Registers of Flatboats, Barges, Rafts, and Steamboats in the Port of New Orleans.

38. Anonymous, *New Orleans As It Is: Its Manners and Customs* ("By a Resident, Printed for the Publisher," 1850), 23.

39. A. Oakey Hall, *The Manhattaner in New Orleans; or Phases of "Crescent City" Life* (New York: J. S. Redfield, 1851), 178.

40. "Private Boarding," *Louisiana Courier*, November 13, 1828, p. 3, c. 4.

41. Henry Tudor, *Narrative of a Tour in North America* (London: James Duncan, 1834), 2:380.

and the "terrible malady," he went on to say that yellow fever

> makes it first appearance in the early days of August, and con-
> tinues till October. During that era New Orleans appears like
> a deserted city; all who possibly can, fly to the north or the up-
> per country, most of the shops are shut, and the silence of the
> streets is only interrupted by the sound of the hearse passing
> through them.[42]

   Those of African ancestry, as well as those born in the city (Creoles,
who were "acclimated" to the virus through childhood exposure) seemed
to be more resistant to yellow fever, although this may have been more
perception than reality. Newcomers, on the other hand, suffered disproportionately, especially if they lived near swamps or stagnant water. The
poor suffered more than the rich, for reasons of inequitable residential-
settlement geographies, inferior domestic environs, and the lack of financial wherewithal to depart. Summertime New Orleans in the antebellum
era thus constituted a markedly quieter, riskier, poorer, less cosmopolitan,
more Creole, more black, more gender-balanced, more Catholic, and more
Francophone urban environment than wintertime New Orleans—not to
mention hotter, more humid, and more prone to hurricanes. (Ten weeks
after Lincoln's 1831 departure, a powerful hurricane struck New Orleans,
destroying, among other things, a number of flatboats and killing their
crews.[43]) Even slave commerce quieted down, as traders reduced the prices
of their human chattel in the face of weak demand and threat of illness.[44]
"I am now at the head-quarters of Death!" bemoaned one visitor in 1831,
"and were it the month of August or September[,] I should scarcely expect
to be alive this day [next] week."[45] Winter and springtime populations,
however, had Mississippi River flood threats to worry about, while Asiatic
cholera, smallpox, and other diseases struck with little regard to season.
(A year after Lincoln's second visit, the city's worst-ever cholera epidemic
claimed 4,340 lives and scared away another 11,000.[46]) Risks to public
health, in sum, were not evenly distributed in antebellum New Orleans,

   42. Murray, *Account of Discoveries and Travels*, 427.
   43. *New Orleans Bee*, August 18, 1831, p. 2, c. 1. The hurricane struck on August 16–
17.
   44. Frederic Bancroft, *Slave Trading in the Old South* (Baltimore: J. H. Furst Company,
1931), 317.
   45. Tudor, *Narrative of a Tour in North America*, 2:64.
   46. John Wilds, *Collectors of Customs at the Port of New Orleans* (United States Customs
Service, 1991), 14.

not spatially nor demographically nor temporally. Neither were they ever particularly low—anyplace, for anyone, at any time. Risk of death was the cost of opportunity.

•

Opportunity prevailed; population data attest to it. The early antebellum era—up to 1840—proved to be the only sustained period in which New Orleans' permanent population rose in absolute numbers *and* relative to other American cities. Not only was the city growing, it was gaining on other cities. New Orleans ranked as the tenth-largest American city at the time of its first U.S. Census in 1810; when Lincoln visited, it ranked fifth and rising; by 1840, it peaked at number three. The city's total population would continue to rise for another 120 years, but not for a century would it ever rise in relative rank again (and then only slightly and briefly, at fifteenth). Abraham Lincoln visited New Orleans when it was the largest and most important urban center in the South, and *the* ascendant city in the nation.[47]

New Orleans in the early 1800s also presented the most diverse society in the nation, in terms of ethnicity, nativity, race, religion, language, and culture. Even unobservant visitors noted, upon circulating throughout the bustling entrepôt, strikingly high ratios of immigrants to those born locally; of African-descended peoples to those of European stock; of free people of color to slaves; of Gallics and Latins to Anglos and Germanics; and of Francophones to Anglophones. Curious visitors came in droves, and recorded their impressions emphatically in the travel narratives popular in that era. "No city perhaps on the globe," wrote William Darby in 1817, "presents a greater contrast of national manners, language, and complexion, than does New Orleans"—an assessment that precedes by decades the arrival of the major waves of European immigration.[48] Locals, too, extolled their city's cosmopolitan nature. "The population is much mixed," wrote John Adems Paxton in the 1822 City Directory; "there is a great *'confusion of tongues,'* and on the Levée, during a busy day, can be seen people of every grade, colour and condition: *in short it is a world in miniature.*"[49] Alexis de Tocqueville, who visited New Orleans a year after

47. Decennial census figures derived from compendium volumes of the U.S. Census; interpolations computed by author.

48. William Darby, *Geographical Description of the State of Louisiana* (New York: James Olmstead, 1817), 75.

49. *New-Orleans Directory and Register* (1822), 45-46 (emphasis in original).

Lincoln's second trip, learned of the city's ethnic mosaic through an interview with the prominent local lawyer Etienne Mazureau:

> Q. They say that in New Orleans is to be found a mixture of all the nations?
>
> A. That's true; you see here a mingling of all races. Not a country in America or Europe but has sent us some representatives. New Orleans is a patch-work of peoples.[50]

Testimonies to New Orleans' superlative diversity, often expressed in a similar lexicon and cadence, augmented during the peak immigration decades of the 1830s–50s. Numerical records substantiate the eyewitness exhortations. The limited demographic data offered by the 1820 census (white, non-naturalized foreigners, free people of color, and slaves) places New Orleans alongside Charleston, South Carolina, as the most diverse city in the nation. Over the next four decades, far more immigrants arrived at the United States through New Orleans—more than 550,000 from 1820 to 1860, with 300,000 in the 1850s alone—than through any other Southern city. For most of the late antebellum era, New Orleans ranked as the nation's number-two immigrant port, ahead of Boston and behind only New York.[51] An analysis of the 1850 census, the first to record birthplace, shows that New Orleans was home to more significantly sized ethnic groups (measured by ancestry, nativity, race, and enslavement status) than any other American city. That is, when we break urban populations into the sub-groups tabulated by the 1850 census, fully seven groups in New Orleans each constituted at least 5 percent of the city's total population. No other major American city had more than five such groups.[52]

All this went without saying to an editorialist for the *Daily Picayune*, who wrote:

> When we state that in no city in the New or in the Old World

50. As quoted by George Wilson Pierson, *Tocqueville in America* (Baltimore: The Johns Hopkins University Press, 1996), 627–628.

51. Treasury Department, Bureau of Statistics, *Tables Showing Arrivals of Alien Passengers and Immigrants in the United States from 1820 to 1888* (Washington, D.C.: Government Printing Office, 1889), 108–109.

52. The subgroups were aggregated as (1) locally born; (2) born elsewhere in U.S.; (3) born in England, Wales, or Scotland; (4) born in Ireland; (5) born in Germany, Prussia, or Austria; (6) born in France; (7) born in Spain; (8) born in Italy; (9) free people of color; and (10) enslaved blacks. Analysis by Richard Campanella based on J. D. B. De Bow, *Statistical View of the United States—Compendium of the Seventh Census* (Washington, D.C., 1854), 395–99.

is there a greater variety of nations represented than in [New Orleans], we are but asserting an established truism. New Orleans is a world in miniature, subdivided into smaller commonwealths, [in which] distinctive traits of national character are to be seen, and the peculiar language of its people is to be heard spoken.[53]

•

The *Picayune*'s subtly ambivalent editorial hints at the discord beneath New Orleans' colorful social diversity. What amazed visitors, more often than not, bred angst and antagonism among residents. Competition among Creoles, Anglos, and immigrants underscored all matters of social, political, and economic life. Exacerbating the tension were deeper hostilities between slave and master and between free people of color and whites—not to mention between free blacks and bondmen and between domestic slaves and field slaves. The slow and painful absorption of postcolonial Creole New Orleans into the Anglo-American United States, which on occasion came "perilously close to armed violence,"[54] peaked around the time of Lincoln's visits.

On one side was an uneasy alliance between Francophone Creoles, foreign French (that is, immigrants from France and refugees from Haiti), and Mediterranean, Caribbean, and Latin American immigrants. Possessing the numerical majority, this Catholic, Latin alliance maintained political and cultural control. On the other side were Anglophone Protestants of Anglo-American ethnicity, who enjoyed commercial dominance and padded their numbers by establishing alliances with Germanic and Irish immigrants. Each side criticized the other's wielding of influence, cultural habits, and idiosyncrasies. "There is, as everyone knows," wrote the English sociologist-philosopher Harriet Martineau,

a mutual jealousy between the French and American creoles in Louisiana. . . . The division between the American and French factions is visible even in the drawing-room. The French complain that the Americans will not speak French; will not meet their neighbors even half way in accommodation of speech.

53. "A Kaleidoscopic View of New Orleans," *Daily Picayune*, September 23, 1843, p. 2, c. 3.

54. Joseph G. Tregle Jr., "Creoles and Americans," in *Creole New Orleans: Race and Americanization*, ed. Arnold R. Hirsch and Joseph Logsdon (Baton Rouge and London: Louisiana State University Press, 1992), 153.

The Americans ridicule the toilet practices of the French ladies; their liberal use of rouge and pearl powder. . . . Till lately,
the French creoles have carried everything their own way, from
their superior numbers.[55]

Because Americans generally settled in upriver neighborhoods of "Faubourg St. Mary, Delor, Saulet, and La Course" (known as the *banlieue su-
périeure*, or upper outskirts) while Creoles and Latin immigrants predominated in "the City District and the lower Faubourgs" (*banlieue inférieure*),
some viewed the manipulation of political geography as the solution to
the ethnic "differences of opinion." On December 2, 1826, City Council
members called for what one journalist termed the "dismemberment" of
New Orleans, cleaving the city down the center of Canal Street.[56] A bill
circulated in the state legislature in subsequent months for "converting the
whole [of New Orleans] into two cities, to be called the Upper and Lower
City . . . arising from the opposing influence of American (as they are
called) and French interests." The proposal passed the House of Representatives but failed the Senate by a narrow margin. Seeing the writing on
the wall, French (Creole) interests countered with a conciliatory proposal
"re-organizing the city government [such that] measures objected to by
the Americans were removed, and their influence on the city councils
greatly increased." Concluded an "impartial spectator" in 1828,

> This measure has restored harmony for the present, but it is
> easy . . . to perceive that Gallic influence must at no distant day
> succumb under the weight of talent, enterprise, and population
> annually rolling in from the northern states. . . .[57]

Into the midst of this complex and contentious social, economic, and political landscape walked a young Abraham Lincoln in 1828 and 1831. Evidence of ethnic tension would have abounded to an observant visitor—in

55. Harriet Martineau, *Retrospect of Western Travel* (London and New York: Saunders
and Otley, 1838), 1:263 and 271

56. *Conseil de Ville*, Session of December 2, 1826, pp. 294–295 of microfilm #90-223,
AB301, NOPL-LC.

57. Robert Goodacre, "New Orleans—Goodacre's Lecture," *Baltimore Gazette and
Daily Advertise*, January 30, 1828, p. 1. Those divisive forces eventually prevailed in 1836,
when the Americans won legislative consent to divide New Orleans into three semiautonomous units, essentially to free themselves of Creole predomination. The inefficient
"municipality system" was abandoned in 1852, but only after the Americans established
alliances with uptown German and Irish immigrants to ensure numerical superiority over
the Creoles.

the streets, in conversation, and in the press. One Anglo editorial, for example, complained of a new Supreme Court decision that City Council ordinances be published in French, despite that "most of those whose mother tongue is [French] speak [English], and a majority of those whose native language is English, do not speak anything else. . . ."[58] In another paper, the *New-Orleans American* (note the name) announced its intention to establish a publishing operation in "the fauxbourg St. Marie" ("the location is considered advantageous," on account of its Anglo-American population, "to whose interests and gratification [the newspaper] will be especially, almost exclusively devoted."). The editors promised that their "views and principles . . . shall be *purely American*," even as they assured potential subscribers that they "will be shackled by no party. . . ."[59] Both pieces ran in newspapers while Lincoln visited the city in May 1831.

Ethnic discord eventually did "dismember" New Orleans. In 1836, the American contingent finally won legislative consent to divide the city into three semiautonomous municipalities, essentially to free themselves of Creole political predomination. For sixteen years, New Orleans operated under one mayor but three separate systems of governance in everything from policing to education to port management. Municipalities even issued their own treasury notes. The terribly inefficient "municipality system" further poisoned social relations, pitting the populations of the First, Second, and Third municipalities against each other in fierce competition. "Had the Legislature sought, by the most careful efforts," wrote the Third Municipality's *Daily Orleanian* in 1849, "to create a war of races, to make distinction between Creole and American, they could not have chosen a better means for these objects, than the present division operates."[60] The city reunified in 1852, but only after the Americans established alliances with German and Irish immigrants to ensure numerical superiority over the Creoles.

The cultural distinction between Anglo and Creole would blur over time. The distinction between white and black, however, was subjected to the legally regimented institution of chattel slavery.

•

The presence, experience, and treatment of people of African ancestry

58. *Mercantile Advertiser*, May 26, 1831, p. 2, c. 4.
59. "New-Orleans American," *New Orleans Bee*, May 13, 1831, p. 2, c. 4. The paper never got off the ground.
60. *Daily Orleanian*, February 19, 1849, p. 2, c. 3.

figured prominently in forming the impression cast by New Orleans upon first-time visitors like Lincoln. That impression may be assessed from three angles: via the population's magnitude and characteristics in local society, via its residential settlement patterns, and, perhaps most importantly, via the ubiquity and nature of the institution of slavery in the cityscape.

By the time of Lincoln's visits, many New Orleanians of African blood traced roots over a century deep into Louisiana soil, their ancestors having been forcibly removed from Africa's Senegambia region by French colonials starting in 1719. Two main waves of African importations followed, the first under French rule in the 1720s and a larger one under Spanish dominion in the 1780s. Coupled with the New World slave trade and natural increases, New Orleans claimed an African-ancestry population of 4,108 (compared to 3,948 whites) by the time of the Louisiana Purchase. Unlike most North American cities, New Orleans maintained the Caribbean notion of a "gradient" between free white and enslaved black, manifested by the somewhat privileged mixed-race middle caste known as the *gens de couleur libre* (free people of color). Slaves outnumbered free people of color by a 2.1-to-1 ratio in circa-1803 New Orleans, a ratio that would equalize in upcoming decades. Despite increasingly oppressive laws, more free people of color would call New Orleans home than any other Southern city (and occasionally more than any American city, in both relative and absolute terms) throughout most of the antebellum era. According to the decennial census, their populations in New Orleans totaled 6,237 in 1820, 8,041 in 1830, a suspiciously high 19,226 in 1840 (probably a mistake), 9,905 in 1850, and 10,689 a year before the Civil War.[61] Most free people of color belonged to the working or lower-middle class, but a significant number gained middle- or upper-class status through skilled trades, real estate, and business investments. By one count, nine of the twenty-one richest blacks in antebellum America were New Orleanians, while an additional eight came from nearby parishes. By another estimate, free people of color in New Orleans lived, worked, and earned better than their counterparts in New York City—indeed better than some whites.[62]

61. Figures differ somewhat in various aggregations of census data. Richard Wade, *Slavery in the Cities: The South 1820–1860* (London, Oxford, New York: Oxford University Press, 1964), 326.
62. Juliet E. K. Walker, "Racism, Slavery, and Free Enterprise: Black Entrepreneurship in the United States before the Civil War," *Business History Review* 60, no. 3 (Autumn, 1986): 350; Robert William Fogel and Stanley L. Engerman, *Time On The Cross: The Economics of American Negro Slavery* (Boston and Toronto: Little, Brown and Com-

Free people of color could not vote, but they could legally earn money, own property, sue in court, and bequeath wealth to the next generation. Some even owned slaves, who themselves might possess significant amounts of white blood. The racial complexity of Louisiana-style slavery is evident in an announcement that ran during Lincoln's 1831 visit, which listed the slaves belonging to "f.w.c." (free woman of color) Marie Cordeviola of the Faubourg Tremé:

> Sally, a negress . . . with her two children named Louis a negro [and] Daniel a mulatto . . . Henriette, a negress . . . with her child named Louis a mulatto . . . Marianne, a negress . . . now with child. . . .[63]

The presence of the free people of color as a distinct and legally recognized caste helped distinguish New Orleans and Louisiana society from the American two-caste norm—that is, pure white on one side, and black to any degree on the other. ("The French in Louisiana," geographer Friedrich Ratzel later commented, "never set themselves off so strictly from their slaves and freed men as the Anglo-Americans did in the other slave states."[64]) That sense of cultural deviation traced also to 1809, when more than 9,000 refugees from Haiti doubled the population of New Orleans, augmenting each of its three castes (white, free people of color, and enslaved black), and breathing new life into its Francophone Caribbean culture.

The city's African American population further reconfigured when the U.S. banned international slave trading in 1808. The law shifted the movement of slaves into the hands of illegal international smugglers and legal domestic traders, the latter sending "surplus" slaves from the Upper South into the Deep South plantation economy to satisfy its insatiable demand for labor. More than 750,000 slaves were forcibly shipped southward during the antebellum era, a shift in the geography of people of African descent so significant that one historian described it the "Second Middle Passage."[65]

pany, 1974), 244.

63. *Louisiana Courier,* June 4, 1831, p. 4, c. 4.

64. Friedrich Ratzel, *Sketches of Urban and Cultural Life in North America,* trans. and ed. Stewart A. Stehlin (New Brunswick and London, 1988 translation of 1873 treatise), 214.

65. Ira Berlin, *Generations of Captivity: A History of African-American Slaves* (Cambridge: Harvard University Press, 2003), 161–163.

Disproportionately, the victims of this domestic slave trade landed in New Orleans. "I have understood that from Maryland and Virginia alone," wrote one visitor in the early 1820s, "from 4000 to 5000 [slaves] per annum are occasionally sent down to New-Orleans; a place, the very name of which seems to strike terror into the slaves and free Negroes of the Middle States."[66] In addition to the "coastwise" trade along the Eastern Seaboard, slave importations came to New Orleans from the West (that is, down the Mississippi), sometimes on the same flatboats that transported corn, flour, and hogs. The Pittsburgh-published river guide *The Navigator* listed 286 slaves among the 64,750 pounds of lard, 216 bushels of potatoes, 155 horses, and dozens of other loads from the Ohio River in 1810–11.[67] Henry Bradshaw Fearon witnessed fourteen flatboats docked at Natchez loaded with "a great many coloured people, particularly females" from Louisville, destined for market.[68] In a single month shortly after Lincoln's 1831 trip, more than one thousand slaves disembarked at the New Orleans levee, with 180 arriving aboard a Louisville steamer in a single day.[69] Roughly 50,000 enslaved African Americans were imported into Louisiana between 1810 and 1830, a period in which the state's total slave population more than tripled. From the Louisiana Purchase to the Civil War, no era saw more imported slave sales in New Orleans than 1828 through 1831, when 2,000–4,000 were sold annually.[70] Abraham Lincoln visited New Orleans in 1828 and 1831.

The enslaved population did not constitute a monolithic group. Masters, keen to exploit cultural similarities and differences, pointed out slaves' birthplaces, ethnicities, and racial mixtures (as well as their ages, skills, and, reluctantly, their defects) when preparing them for the auction block. One typical advertisement for an 1828 plantation auction listed "*Lubin*, from Senegal . . . *Joe*, mulatto . . . Abraham, American . . . *Tom*, a griff American . . . *Honore*, a mulattoe creole . . . *Achilles*, a Spaniard . . . *Jacques*, Congo . . . *Jean Giles* . . . from St. Domingo," and Charlat and Zenon,

66. Adam Hodgson, *Remarks During a Journey Through North America in the Years 1819, 1820, and 1821* (Samuel Whiting: New York, 1823), 178–179.

67. *The Navigator, Containing Directions for Navigating the Monongahela, Allegheny, Ohio, and Mississippi Rivers* (Pittsburgh, Pennsylvania: Cramer, Spear, and Eichbaum, 1814), 360.

68. Fearon, *Sketches of America*, 267–268.

69. *New Orleans Bee*, November 18, 1831, p. 2, c. 1.

70. Jonathan B. Pritchett, "Forced Migration and the Interregional Slave Trade," paper presented to the 1991 Annual Meeting of the Social Science History Association, p. 8 and Figure 3. This information is based on Notarial Records originally collected by Robert W. Fogel and Stanley L. Engerman and analyzed by Jonathan B. Pritchett.

both creoles, among others.[71] Linguistic, religious, and other cultural differences among these African-born or Virginia-born or Caribbean-born or Louisiana-born people were as broad and complex as those of any immigrant group of this era. New Orleans' slave markets were, in their own way, as diverse and multicultural as the city's famed food markets.

Whites with a stake in the game reveled in the booming interstate commerce of human beings. Traders profited in handling the banalities of the business; planters relied on the growing labor force; investors sunk wealth into the human chattel. Yet much of the white population was vexed by the constant importations, not out of concern for the victims, but for fear of being racially overwhelmed and possibly overthrown. State government in the late 1820s curtailed the flow when it became apparent—or suspected—that Upper South masters were unloading "undesirable" slaves—sickly, lazy, violent, or rebellious, from the white perspective—into the Louisiana market, thus benefiting doubly in the process. The state legislature banned domestically imported slave sales altogether in 1826, but strong demand forced the repeal of the act in 1828. Importations resumed immediately: around the time of Lincoln's first visit, "three vessels from Norfolk, having on board nearly six hundred slaves [arrived] at New Orleans."[72] White concerns resurfaced, as evidenced by this alarmed message in the *Louisiana Courier* in January 1829:

> There has been *TWO THOUSAND SIX HUNDRED & SEV-ENTY* **SLAVES** brought to this place [since October 1, 1828] by way of the Balize![73]

A compromise act in 1829 allowed the imports to continue so long as a Certificate of Good Character accompanied all slaves over the age of twelve, signed by two or more non-vendor whites from the exporting county who swore to the slave's obedience and "moral character."[74] Enforcement of this law, too, faded after two years, despite widespread consternation among whites about growing black numerical superiority. Those worries heightened after Nat Turner launched his August 1831

71. "State of Louisiana—Parish of St. Charles—County of German Coast—Court of Probate: A Sugar Plantation," *Louisiana Courier*, October 4, 1828, p. 3, c. 5 (emphasis in original).

72. *New York Gazette*, as quoted by the *Baltimore Patriot*, November 28, 1828, p. 2.

73. *Louisiana Courier*, January 13, 1829, p. 3, c. 1 (emphasis in original).

74. Herman Freudenberger and Jonathan B. Pritchett, "The Domestic United States Slave Trade: New Evidence." *Journal of Interdisciplinary History* 21, no. 3 (Winter 1991): 447–49.

rebellion in Virginia (the source region for many Deep South–destined slaves), frightening the Louisiana slave-owning class that they might be importing future insurgents.[75] The disturbed editors of the *New Orleans Bee*, noting the "clashing interests" in the state legislature on this controversial issue, reported on November 18, 1831, that "[o]ne hundred and eighty slaves" arrived just yesterday from Louisville, bringing the total from the past eleven months to "ONE THOUSAND AND ELEVEN."[76] The state again banned the importations in 1832, diverting business to Natchez (the second busiest slave mart)—then lifted the ban yet again two years later.[77]

Racial fear was not only directed at imported slaves. Incoming free people of color—occupants of that curious middle caste in New Orleans society with whom Anglo Louisianans in particular never felt comfortable—also came under increasing scrutiny in the 1820s. Many whites saw "f.p.c.'s" as potential subversives fomenting racial rebellion and spreading abolitionism. A state law in 1817 prohibited the entry of free blacks convicted of crimes; two additional pieces of legislation in 1827–28 proposed to keep out "free colored persons and negroes" altogether, but fell short of passage. Two years later—amid rumors of insurgency, arson, and an incident in which four free men of color were apprehended for circulating a "diabolical Boston pamphlet" urging running away—a new law passed to prohibit *all* free blacks from moving into Louisiana, to expel those who arrived after 1825, and to require all those arriving before 1825 to register with the mayor or face a fine.[78] Lincoln arrived in New Orleans when discourse on these charged topics raged in local coffee houses and exchanges—so much so that they spilled into the streets and the ears of first-time visitors. Englishman James Stuart devoted three pages of his book to express his moral outrage at the new racial-oppression laws passed during his March 1830 visit.[79]

Despite attempts to restrict interstate slave trading, Louisiana's slave population increased dramatically in the 1830s. That decade, by one assessment, would prove to be "the beginning of the heyday of the profes-

75. Joe Gray Taylor, *Negro Slavery in Louisiana* (New York: Negro Universities Press, 1963), 37–45

76. *New Orleans Bee*, November 18, 1831, p. 2, c. 1 (emphasis in original).

77. Michael Tadman, *Speculators and Slaves: Masters, Traders, and Slaves in the Old South* (Madison: University of Wisconsin Press, 1989), 96.

78. Donald Edward Everett, "Free Persons of Color in New Orleans, 1803–1865" (Ph.D. dissertation, Tulane University, 1952), 89–96.

79. Stuart, *Three Years in North America*, 2:242–244.

sional slave trader."[80] Some slaves arrived at the city's auction blocks via speculative sales, others through successions, still others through tax-related seizures or foreclosures—of which there were many, so dependent on credit was the plantation economy. Most slave transactions—nearly nine in ten, by one count—occurred at public auctions, held at well-advertised times and places by professional auctioneers following ritualized protocols. The remaining transactions were private sales, carried out for a negotiated price on the street, in pens, or at masters' houses. Sometimes slaves were even raffled off, "by authority of the state," in intricate lottery schemes complete with legal disclaimers, like modern-day contests. One such lottery offered, a few months after Lincoln's first visit, eighteen people as Prize Nos. 1, 4, 5, and 7, along with twenty other prizes of land, horses, oxen, ploughs, and a carriage.[81]

With every transaction, the institution of slavery grew increasingly entrenched economically, protected legally, sacred politically, and unquestioned socially. "[T]he people of the south are so extremely sensitive [about] *slavery*," remonstrated one Northerner, "that they will hardly allow you to hold or express an opinion respecting it. . . ."[82] By the time of Lincoln's arrival into Louisiana, slavery in the region had, according to historian Kenneth M. Stampp, "crystallized" from its relatively malleable colonial-era form into a "hardened" and "fixed" institution on which Southern agriculture depended utterly, and in which Southern society had invested intrinsically. "In 1860," wrote Stampp, "the peculiar institution was almost precisely what it had been thirty years before. If anything, the chains of bondage were strengthened, not weakened. . . . [S]laves . . . were to labor diligently and breed prolifically for the comfort of their white masters."[83] To the slave-holding establishment, the enslaved Negro represented the promise of future wealth and a vessel for past profit; slavery itself symbolized a proper moral order, a paternalistic favor granted to an

80. Taylor, *Slavery in Louisiana*, 45–46; Robert H. Gudmestad, *A Troublesome Commerce: The Transformation of the Interstate Slave Trade* (Baton Rouge: Louisiana State University Press, 2003), 25. At times during the antebellum era, Charleston's market exceeded that of New Orleans.

81. Taylor, *Slavery in Louisiana*, 25–26; Judith Kelleher Schafer, "New Orleans Slavery in 1850 as Seen in Advertisements," *Journal of Southern History* 47, no.1 (February 1981): 41; "Plan of a Lottery of Property of William Wikoff, Senior," *Louisiana Courier*, October 3, 1828, p. 4, c. 4–5.

82. "Slavery in New Orleans," *Jamestown Journal* (Jamestown, NY), November 10, 1830, p. 4 (emphasis in original).

83. Kenneth M. Stampp, *The Peculiar Institution: Slavery in the Ante-Bellum South* (New York: Vintage Books, 1956), 27–29.

inferior race incapable of self-sufficiency and governance. White Southern society married itself to the institution of black slavery by continually buying into it and constructing wealth upon it.

New Orleans' strident urban expansion increased internal demand for domestic, artisan, and chain-gang labor, and occasioned a commensurate increase in the city's African-ancestry population. By 1830, New Orleans enumerated 28,545 blacks (both enslaved and free) and 21,281 whites, with the slave-to-free-colored ratio declining to 1.4-to-1. The next ten years witnessed a remarkable demographic shift, as Irish, German, and other immigrants made New Orleans a majority-white city for the first time since early colonial times. Greater numbers of working-class whites meant domestic, port, municipal, and other menial tasks could be performed by low-paid white immigrants, rather than by valuable slaves requiring food and housing. The racial breakpoint occurred around 1835; by the time of the 1840 census, the city had dropped to 42 percent black (42,674 blacks and 59,519 whites, with a slave-to-free-colored ratio of 1.2-to-1.) That figure diminished to 23 percent black in 1850 and 15 percent in 1860. Replaced largely by white immigrant laborers and domestic servants, urban slaves had, in the late antebellum years, been sold off by the thousands to rural plantations. Ironically, the resident slave population of New Orleans decreased even as the *commerce* of slaves increased in the city's auction houses and slave pens. When war broke out in 1861, slaves comprised only one out of every twelve New Orleanians.[84] Lincoln thus witnessed New Orleans in the waning years of its status as a majority-black city. It would not regain that status until the late 1970s.

•

Where did African American New Orleanians reside? Urban slaves who labored as domestics usually resided in the distinctive slant-roof quarters appended behind townhouses and cottages. Others, ranging from skilled craftsmen and artisans to hired-out laborers, lived in detached group quarters on back streets, close to the abodes of their masters. A city ordinance in 1817 prohibited slaves from living "in any house, out-house, building, or enclosure" not owned by their master or representative (except with documented permission), else the slave face jail time and twenty lashes,

84. These statistics represent only the city's permanent population. Inclusion of the thousands of seasonal visitors renders the city's *de facto* demographics more white and male for seven or eight months out of any given antebellum year.

and the master a five-dollar fine.[85] The following real estate advertisement, which ran during Lincoln's second visit, exemplifies the residential
adjacency arranged by masters for slaves:

> To Let, a good brick house, No. 113 Casa Calvo [Royal Street],
> faubourg Marigny, consisting of 4 rooms, 2 closets and gallery,
> a kitchen, stable, coach house, and 2 wells; *also a large frame
> house on the adjoining lot, calculated to lodge 200 negroes.*[86]

Most masters needed no legislative prodding to keep their slaves close by;
it abetted their financial interest and personal comfort to do so. Proximity enabled monitoring of movement and promptness of service. This so-
called back-alley settlement pattern imparted an ironic spatial integration
into New Orleans' antebellum racial geography, despite the severe and oppressive social segregation of chattel slavery. Master and slave, white and
black, lived steps away from each other. Dempsey Jordan, born a slave in
New Orleans in 1836, described just that arrangement when interviewed
a century later: "Our quarters was small, one room house built in the
back yard of Maser's home . . . built out of rough lumber like [a] smoke
house. . . ."[87] Not unique to New Orleans, the intermixed pattern has been
documented in Charleston, Washington, and Baltimore.[88]

Free people of color, who unlike their enslaved brethren *chose* their
residences, clustered in the lower French Quarter, Bayou Road, the faubourgs Tremé, Marigny, New Marigny, Franklin, and those making up
the present-day neighborhood of Bywater. This was the older, Francophone, Catholic side of town, a social environment rendered by Creole
culture and more conducive to their interests. The mostly Anglo-American Protestant world on the upper side of town was not only culturally
foreign terrain, but its English-speaking inhabitants were generally more
hostile to the very notion of a free person having African blood.

The geography of black New Orleans, then, consisted of slaves intri-

85. "An ordinance in relation to slaves in the city and suburbs of New-Orleans," October 15, 1817, *A General Digest of the Ordinances and Resolutions of the Corporation of New-
Orleans* (New Orleans: Jerome Bayon, 1831), 133.

86. *Louisiana Courier*, May 28, 1831, p. 4, c. 3 (emphasis added).

87. Interview, Demsey Jordan, by B. E. Davis, 1937, *American Slavery: A Composite
Autobiography*, Second Supplemental Series, Texas Narratives, Vol. 06T, 2156.

88. Larry Ford and Ernst Griffin, "The Ghettoization of Paradise," *Geographical Review* 69, no. 2 (April 1979): 156–57. See also David T. Herbert and Colin J. Thomas,
Urban Geography: A First Approach (Chichester, New York, Brisbane, Toronto and Singapore, 1982), 312–314.

cately intermixed citywide and free people of color predominating in the lower neighborhoods. Anecdotal evidence of these patterns comes from an 1843 article in the *Daily Picayune*:

> The Negroes are scattered through the city promiscuously; those of mixed blood, such as Griffes, Quarteroons, &c., [Creoles of color] showing a preference for the back streets of the First [French Quarter, Faubourg Tremé] and part of the Third Municipality [Faubourg Marigny and adjacent areas].[89]

With the exception of the backswamp edge, where very poor manumitted or hired-out blacks and other indigents lived in squatter-like conditions, there were no expansive, exclusively black neighborhoods in antebellum New Orleans. An observant first-time visitor like Lincoln thus might see slaves residing on (or behind) nearly any street on which lived people of the middle or upper class. But he would see a predomination of lighted-skinned blacks—free, often landed, and sometimes slaveholding—only in the Old City and the lower faubourgs. Here too he would hear French, cast his eyes on older and more unusual buildings, smell more exotic aromas, and sense a more foreign ambience.

•

How was slavery inscribed into the cityscape, visible to a visitor like Lincoln? Its ministerial ephemera were ubiquitous. Broadsides for slave auctions paneled walls and posts. Signs for slave dealers, pens, and bondage accoutrements protruded into city streets. Any newspaper on any given day listed numerous auction notices and runaway announcements, accompanied by a terse clinical description of the slave and, for runaways, an unintentionally sympathetic drawing of a frightened fugitive in flight. The ads' brutally banal lexis offers insights into the ethnicity, linguistics, dress, and circumstances of the slave (viewed, of course, from the slaveholders' perspective). In the following ad, which appeared during Lincoln's first visit, we see the youthful age at which some ran away, as well as clues to ethnicity, garb, and physicality:

> Notice—The creole *Negro Boy by the name of PHILIP*, aged about 9 years, who speaks French only, disappeared. . . . He

---

89. *Daily Picayune*, "A Kaleidoscopic View of New Orleans," September 23, 1843, p. 2, c. 3. "Griffe" or "quarteroon" implied a black person with one white grandparent; that is, the offspring of a mulatto and a negro.

was clothed in a jacket and pantaloons . . . of blue-striped printanniere; he is very black, bowlegged, and has a scar on the right side, below the lower lip. He is the son of a creole negro woman named Rose, who belonged for a great while to mr David Urquhart. Ten Dollars reward. . . .[90]

By one count, at least 3,500 slave-sale ads and 475 runaway-slave notices appeared locally in a single year.[91] Additionally, sheriffs and jailers throughout the sugar coast, from Baton Rouge to Plaquemines Parish, regularly posted in New Orleans newspapers descriptions of the suspected runaways they caught and imprisoned.[92]

Urban slave labor assumed myriad forms, ranging from the surprisingly unsupervised, to the carefully regulated, to the violently oppressive. Domestic slaves drew little attention from outsiders, if they could be seen at all. Skilled artisans hired out by their masters might work alone or side-by-side with whites, making the institution appear benevolent to naïve newcomers—until they noticed the brass badges pinned to the blacks' shirts, indicating their caste.[93] One ad "For Sale or to Hire" that ran during Lincoln's first visit extolled the mattress-making skills of "[t]he creole mulatto JUSTIN," apparently learned from his former owner, an upholsterer. The current owner, J. B. Cajus, "requests the person employing said mulatto to pay the amount . . . to [me]."[94] Other slaves peddling merchandise or running errands freely in the streets—activities that might give a softer impression of the reality of bondage—were in fact, like Justin the mattress-maker, toiling for their owner's profit.[95] Slaves working as drivers of drays, coaches, cabriolets, and other vehicles might appear well-employed—until they broke a traffic law, in which case they were whipped twenty-five times.[96] Other bondmen hired out as dockworkers, loaders, screwmen, or to do other riverfront jobs requiring physical liberty could easily be confused with free people, particularly since free blacks

90. "Notice," *New Orleans Argus*, May 30, 1828, p. 2, c. 6 (emphasis in original).

91. Schafer, "Slavery as Seen in Advertisements," 35 and 42.

92. See, for example, *New Orleans Argus*, Tuesday, June 3, 1828, p. 1, c. 2–3, which dates to Lincoln's first visit.

93. "An Ordinance concerning slaves employed as hirelings by the day," November 10, 1817, *Ordinances and Resolutions of New-Orleans*, 139.

94. "For Sale or to Hire," *New Orleans Argus*, May 28, 1828, p. 3, c. 1.

95. See, for example, *Conseil de Ville*, Session of July 10, 1824, p. 22 of microfilm #90-223, AB301, NOPL-LC.

96. *Conseil de Ville*, Session of August 18, 1824, p. 49 of microfilm #90-223, AB301, NOPL-LC.

worked among them. (One slave named Jacques made the best of this confusion. While working on the levee a few weeks before Lincoln's first arrival and only a few blocks from where he landed, Jacques changed his name to William, claimed freedom, and escaped. His flustered owner offered ten dollars to whomever returned his admittedly "very inteligent" [*sic*] property.[97]) Still other slaves worked as hotel staff, waiters, and store clerks, imparting even more incongruity to the outward appearance of the institution. An auction ad that ran during Lincoln's 1828 visit proclaimed that "Charles, aged about 17 years . . . is very intelligent, and fit for a retail store."[98] A guest at the Planters and Merchants Hotel in spring 1830 observed that

> the waiters [were] all slaves, hired from their masters,—many of them very fine-looking men. Their masters receive from twenty to twenty-five dollars a month for their work, and board and washing are all furnished [by] the hotel. The value of a slave is prodigiously increased when he is instructed as a waiter[;] his value rises from 500 dollars to 1800 dollars [and sometimes to] 3000 dollars. The highest value attaches to such slaves . . . who can read and write. But a slave is not now allowed to be *taught* to read or to write in the State of Louisiana. . . .[99]

Slaves were often hired out to private or public projects and assembled into work groups. Such "chain gangs" were less likely to garner the institution of slavery a generous judgment from visitors. "The cleaning of the streets," wrote the same 1830 visitor quoted above, "is performed . . . by slaves . . . [e]ven females . . . chained together, and with hardly any clothes on their backs, sent [by] their masters, as a punishment for some delinquency, [for] about one shilling Sterling per day."[100] Jailed slaves—the fate of any undocumented bondman unable to account for his owner—were by law "put to the chain [and] employed in the works of the city," else whipped.[101] City-controlled chain gangs were led by two white overseers, who, six days a week, marched the bondmen to the work site at dawn and worked them until sunset, save for a two-hour noon break. Bondwomen cleaned gut-

---

97. "Runaway," *Louisiana Courier*, November 13, 1828, p. 3, c. 5.
98. "By Bauduc & Domingo," *New Orleans Argus*, May 24, 1828, p. 2, c. 6.
99. Stuart, *Three Years in North America*, 2:228–229 (emphasis added).
100. Ibid., 235.
101. "An Ordinance Concerning the Police Jail for the Detention of Slaves," October 8, 1817, *Ordinances and Resolutions of New Orleans*, 127–129.

ters, streets, and *banquettes*.[102] Council proceedings from the antebellum era are replete with official city actions deploying enslaved chain gangs for every conceivable municipal project: building levees, repairing wharves, paving streets, digging graves, fighting fires, and constructing Charity Hospital.[103] Corporate ownership of slaves was unusual but not rare: the firms behind New Orleans' two biggest internal improvements around the time of Lincoln's visits—the New Orleans Canal and Banking Company and the Pontchartrain Railroad Company—both counted scores of slaves among their corporate assets.[104]

Field hands, who accounted for the vast majority of enslaved persons in Louisiana, toiled beyond the view of most city visitors, lest they ventured to the sugar fields (some within an hour walk from downtown New Orleans). Most visitors did, however, gain antiseptic long-distance views of plantation slavery as they steamed on the Mississippi. From the comfort of the upper deck of a steamboat, they viewed the "pleasing" and "quiet" landscape of the sugar coast, where

> plantations, orange groves, white slave villages [lay] amid the green fields [and] extensive views beneath the mild heavens. . . .[105]

The public assemblage of slaves commanded particular attention from visitors. Enslaved persons gathered every Sunday at such rendezvous as Congo (Circus) Square for music, dance, and social interaction. The exotic spectacle endured for decades and grew popular with tourists, ranking alongside the French Market, quadroon balls, and aboveground cemeteries as must-see sights. Convening slaves always made whites nervous, but because the outright banning of assemblage might inadvertently instigate the very insurrection whites feared, a compromise emerged. Authorities in 1817 prohibited slaves from meeting together "in any street, public square, the meat-market, or in any house, building, tavern, or lot," but allowed assemblage for divine services, funerals, sports, dances, and "merriment"—on Sundays only, before sunset, and at approved sites. Any

102. "An Ordinance to regulate the service of slaves employed in the works of the city," November 10, 1817, *Ordinances and Resolutions of New-Orleans*, 141–145.

103. *Conseil de Ville*, Session of December 31, 1824, p. 160; Session of March 22, 1825, p. 211; Session of July 6, 1825, p. 317; Session of November 4, 1826, p. 279; Session of July 14, 1827, p. 27 of microfilm #90-223, AB301, NOPL-LC.

104. Wade, *Slavery in the Cities*, 23, 37.

105. Fredrika Bremer, *The Homes of the New World: Impressions of America* (New York: Harper & Brothers, 1853), 2:193–194.

white person was legally deputized to apprehend violators, who thence faced the standard punishment of jail, lash, and fine. "[W]hopping," "hallooing," or "singing aloud any indecent song"—even walking with a cane or stick, which could be construed as a weapon—earned slaves that same legal response. And should they "be guilty of disrespect towards any white person" or "insult any free person," more lashes awaited them.[106] "A friend told me," wrote one visitor around 1820, "that while walking on the Levée at New-Orleans, he has distinctly heard the successive lashes on the back of a poor slave on the other side of the Mississippi, which is half a-mile across."[107]

Black numerical superiority stoked the omnipresent white fear of slave insurrection, which motivated the formation of a ubiquitous police presence. "There is a corps of mounted *gens d'armes*," reported one visitor around the time of Lincoln's visits. "In this respect . . . Charleston and New Orleans do not resemble the free cities of America; but the great number of the black population, and the way in which they are treated by the whites, render this precaution . . . indispensably necessary."[108] Police also regularly patrolled the levee in two nightly shifts.[109] For its enslaved residents, New Orleans in this era was nothing short of an oppressive police state, and it looked the part.

While slaves assembling in the city vexed the white establishment, so did those traveling alone in the swamps behind the city. Bondmen who ventured off to fish in Lake Pontchartrain were suspected of attempting to escape, or considered vulnerable to be "carried off" by white abductors. An 1813 city law curtailed swamp and lake visits for all African Americans, including free people of color.[110] The backswamp indeed provided immediate refuge for slaves fleeing New Orleans; most other terrestrial areas were either cultivated or populated. One master suspected his escaped slave was "no doubt *lurking*"—a favorite verb—"in the *rear of the city*."[111] During Lincoln's 1828 visit, the *Louisiana Courier* alerted its readers to watch for its "young negro named Charles, who carries the *Courier . . .*

---

106. "An ordinance in relation to slaves in the city and suburbs of New-Orleans," October 15, 1817, *Ordinances and Resolutions of New-Orleans*, 135–137.

107. Hodgson, *Journey Through North America*, 174–175.

108. Stuart, *Three Years in North America*, 2:236.

109. *Conseil de Ville*, Session of March 1, 1817, p. 129 of microfilm #90-221, AB301, NOPL-LC.

110. "An Ordinance concerning persons navigating to lake Pontchartrain," August 20, 1813, *Ordinances and Resolutions of New-Orleans*, 247–249.

111. As quoted by Schafer, "Slavery as Seen in Advertisements," 49 (emphasis added).

seen yesterday morning at the Lake, leading some horses. . . ."[112] A large maroon enclave is said to have existed in the swamps behind Algiers.

The backswamp was but one refuge for the runaway. Urbanized New Orleans, replete with sanctuaries and daily waterborne intercourse with the rest of the world, also attracted runaways in "great numbers." As the mayor lamented in 1834, they "crowd in the city, hide, and make of our City a den."[113] Announcements of runaway slaves in the newspapers often warned visiting ship captains not to "harbour" on board or hire the slave in question.[114]

•

It is in the trading of slaves—their shipping, escorting, jailing, preparing, marketing, presenting, auctioning, and purchasing—that the "peculiar institution" made the greatest impression on visitors. Antebellum travel narratives abound in detailed descriptions of the city's human chattel industry. Those written by Europeans or Northerners (the lion's share) usually expressed compassion for the slave, dismay at the institution, and outright loathing for the trader. Southern sympathizers, ever fond of pointing out paternalistic master–slave relations and anecdotes of slave contentedness, either remained silent on the grim spectacle of the auction block, or effusively scapegoated the trader so as to exonerate the master and institution.

In fact, traders formed but one cog in slave commerce. They interacted (and oftentimes blurred roles) with shippers, brokers, lawyers, auctioneers, pen-keepers, and others who profited in transferring the ownership of a slave. Such players proliferated; new ones entered the market constantly, proclaiming their openings with collegial solemnity. "Newman & Mortimer," read one such announcement in 1828, "have formed a partnership [of] Brokers, offer[ing] their services to their friends and public [in the] buying and selling of real property, slaves and all kinds of produce. . . ." Located in the Creole side of town, Newman and Mortimer accommodated their multilingual clientele by promising that "translations in the French, English and Spanish languages will be done at [our] office, No. 7, Conti Street."[115] Nearly all New Orleans' professional firms, banks, and

112. *Louisiana Courier*, June 2, 1828, p. 3, c. 3.
113. As quoted in Wade, *Slavery in the Cities*, 214–215.
114. See, for example, announcements in the *New Orleans Bee*, May 9, 1828, p. 4, c. 3.
115. "Notice—The undersigned having formed a partnership . . . ," *Louisiana Courier*, October 20, 1828, p. 3, c. 6.

insurance companies had their hands in the slave trade to one degree or another.

Despite the grotesque public image of the commerce of slavery, city leaders in both the public and private sectors made little attempt to hide or disguise it. The two major slave-commerce environments—private pens run by dealers, brokers, or traders, who bought and displayed numerous slaves and sold them to walk-in customers, and public auctions, in which auctioneers coordinated transactions between current and prospective masters—were located in prominent places, open to all free classes, and advertised aggressively. Because of their public nature and ritualistic spectacle, auctions attracted much more attention from visitors than the private one-on-one retail transactions that occurred at the pens.

Since the early American years, auctions usually occurred in "exchanges," meeting houses that offered a variety of business and social functions. Among the first, the Exchange Coffee House on Conti Street (1806), so grew in popularity as a saloon that it attracted commercial functions, including the auctioning of ships, houses, land, and, inevitably, slaves. It soon earned competition from a new operation erected in 1810–11 at the corner of Chartres and St. Louis streets. Originally called Tremoulet's Commercial (or New Exchange) Coffee House, this business became Maspero's Exchange in 1814, Elkin's Exchange after Pierre Maspero's death in 1822, and by 1826, Hewlett's Exchange, named for new owner John Hewlett. Because of the place's popularity and frequent management changes, newspapers and directories ascribed a variety of names to the business at 129 (now 501) Chartres: the "Exchange Coffee House," "New Exchange Coffee House," "Hewlett's Coffee House," or "La Bourse de Hewlett."[116]

To call Hewlett's enterprise a coffee house is an understatement bordering on the ironic. "Coffee house" was a euphemism for saloon, and "exchange," by the 1820s, implied a full-service business-networking center, where white men could convene, discuss, negotiate, socialize, recreate, gamble, dine, drink, and board. The two-story, fifty-five-by-sixty-two-foot edifice boasted behind its gaudy Venetian screens a nineteen-foot-high ceiling, four twelve-lamp glass chandeliers, framed maps and oil paintings

---

116. Unpaginated entry for John Hewlett in *New-Orleans Directory & Register* (New Orleans: John Adems Paxton, 1830); Samuel Wilson, Jr., "Maspero's Exchange: Its Predecessors and Successors," *Louisiana History* 30, no. 2 (Spring 1989): 192–219. Some secondary sources claim Hewlett's first name was James, but city directories of the era consistently list him as John.

(described by one Northerner as "licentious"), wood-and-marble finishing, and an enormous bar with French glassware. Like many of New Orleans' "coffee houses," the upper floor contained billiards and gambling tables. Throughout the mid-antebellum years, Hewlett's Exchange buzzed with trilingual auctioning activity, in which everything from ships to houses to land to horses to sugar kettles to people legally changed hands.[117] The city's seven auctioneers worked the block on a rotating schedule, every day except Sunday, oftentimes maintaining other jobs elsewhere. Joseph Le Carpentier handled Mondays, Wednesdays, and Saturdays; Toussaint Mossy (president of the New Orleans Architect Company) worked Tuesdays and Fridays; H. J. Domingon, George Boyd, and Joseph Baudue got Tuesdays, Thursdays, and Saturdays; and the busy Isaac McCoy and Francois Dutillet worked six days a week.[118] At the time of Lincoln's visit Hewlett's Exchange was the New Orleans business community's single most important public meeting site for networking, news-gathering, and dealing.

In the decades after Lincoln's visits, slave auctioning added two illustrious new venues to the New Orleans business scene. In 1837 the magnificent St. Charles Exchange arose in Faubourg St. Mary, followed the next year by the imposing City Exchange on St. Louis Street in the Old City (for which Hewlett's Exchange and adjacent structures were demolished). Both edifices, occupying entire city blocks, rising over four stories, and topped with landmark domes, ranked among the nation's most splendid hotels. Both became famous, and infamous, for their auction blocks.

Not all slave owners subjected their human property to the slave pens and auction houses. Some masters, particularly residents of the city proper, opted to handle sales themselves by inviting prospective buyers to their houses. Urban domestic slaves, with whom white families frequently developed ostensibly warm relations, often changed hands in this manner. For-sale-by-owner ads appeared in local newspapers at a rate around one or two per day:

> For Sale—*A NEGRO WOMAN* 18 years of age: guaranteed against the diseases and vices proscribed by law . . . speaks English and French—understands cooking either in the French or English stile [*sic*], something of a washer, and a good nurse.

---

117. Gleaned from the "Sales at Auction" sections of the *Louisiana Courier*, 1828–29; Henry C. Castellanos, *New Orleans as It Was: Episodes of Louisiana Life* (Baton Rouge: Louisiana State University Press, 2006 republication of 1895 original), 148–149.

118. "Auctioneers," *New-Orleans Directory & Register*, unpaginated.

Prospective buyers of this teenager were directed to visit master J. Montamat at his house on Elysian Fields Avenue. Another announcement, posted during Lincoln's 1828 visit, advertised "a young and likely Negro fellow [and] several others of both sexes, for sale by the subscriber [David C. McClure] at No. 116, Bienville street." (One of McClure's slaves escaped, prompting the perturbed master to post a ten dollar reward for thirty-three-year-old "John . . . very stout built, black complected, [with] rather a frown on his countenance.")[119]

Comparative measurements of the nation's various urban slave marketplaces are difficult to make, because each Southern city documented the trafficking in differing and erratic ways. Yet nearly all qualified observers, in both historical times and today, agree that New Orleans' slave-trading enterprise trumped that of all other American cities for most of the antebellum era, usually by a wide margin. The reason stemmed from same economic-geographical factors driving New Orleans' overall commercial success: the metropolis was positioned perfectly as a transshipment point along the watery intercourse between the slave-supply regions of the Upper South and the labor-demanding plantations of the Mississippi Valley. As the largest city in the South, serving the nation's highest regional concentration of millionaires, New Orleans also demanded thousands of slaves for its own needs, and eagerly developed the physical, financial, and administrative infrastructure to handle the commerce.

The size of that commerce may be estimated through various metrics. City directories from the era of Lincoln's visits did not enumerate traders specifically, but evidence from the 1840s indicates that two to three hundred professionals dealt directly in the city's slave trade, handling at least a few thousand sales per year. Journal accounts provide some idea of the ever-rotating population of the city's slave-holding pens. Wrote one visitor, "There were about 1000 slaves for sale at New Orleans while I was there" in March 1830.[120] "I cannot say as to the number of negroes in the [New Orleans] market," wrote a trader in 1834, "though am of the opinion there is 12-1500 and upwards, and small lots constantly coming in." Other eyewitnesses estimated 3,000 slaves for sale at a particular moment later in the antebellum era, equating to roughly one marketed slave for every

119. "For Sale—A Negro Woman," *Louisiana Courier*, November 13, 1828, p. 3, c. 6; "For Sale," *New Orleans Argus*, May 30, 1828, p. 2, c. 5; "$10 Reward," *New Orleans Argus*, June 2, 1828, p. 2, c. 6.

120. Stuart, *Three Years in North America*, 2:241.

five resident slaves in the city.[121]

Official documents provide further insights into the size of New Orleans' slave trade. Conveyance records of real property transactions (Louisiana's civil law tradition viewed slaves as real estate, thus requiring title) show that 4,435 slave purchases occurred in the city in 1830.[122] That same cohort was also tracked through the Notarial Archives' collection of Certificates of Good Character, the document required by law from 1829 to 1831 to prevent "undesirable" Upper South slaves from entering Louisiana. Economic historians Herman Freudenberger and Jonathan B. Pritchett tabulated 2,289 such slaves arriving into the New Orleans market in 1830. Their findings show that this group came mostly from the Old South states along the Eastern Seaboard. They were disproportionately male by roughly a sixty-forty ratio, probably reflecting the needs of the sugar cane plantations. Over 93 percent ranged from eleven to thirty years old, with healthy young adult males typically selling for around five hundred dollars. Those who embarked at the major export cities of Richmond, Norfolk, and Charleston endured coastwise journeys lasting about three weeks. Those who were marched overland in coffles suffered awkward and tortuous experiences that could easily take two months. Whether delivered by sea, river, or land, Virginia supplied the largest share (44 percent) of slaves to the Deep South, followed by North Carolina (19 percent) and Maryland (15 percent), with other Southern states ranging between .02 and 5 percent. The buyers, on the other hand, were mostly from Louisiana (71 percent). Scores of Virginians, Tennesseans, Georgians, and others also bought members of this cohort of 2,289, but it is likely these out-of-state planters had Louisiana ties.[123]

Slave sales were not evenly distributed throughout the year. They rose steadily in late autumn and peaked in the winter and early spring with the approaching planting season, then declined as temperatures rose and bottomed-out with the high heat of the epidemic months of late summer and early fall. First-person accounts as well as numerical data point to January, February, and March as being particularly busy times in the New Orleans

---

121. As quoted by Tadman, *Speculators and Slaves*, 95–96. The estimate of three thousand slaves on the market dates from 1859; a year later, the census enumerated 14,484 slaves residing in the city.

122. Everett, "Free Persons of Color in New Orleans," 209. Five percent of those slave purchases were made by free people of color. Special thanks to Jonathan B. Pritchett of Tulane University for his insights on this topic.

123. Freudenberger and Pritchett, "Domestic Slave Trade," 450–472.

slave trade[124]—the same period when shipping activity, flatboat arrivals, and most other economic and social activity peaked. Slaves were thus imported and traded here in greater frequency and in wider view precisely as visitors circulated throughout the city in greater numbers. Because slaves typically endured an average of forty days in limbo—that is, after arriving but before being sold[125]—they accumulated in various holding pens and camps in downtown New Orleans, creating yet another jaw-dropping spectacle for the uninitiated. New Orleans not only boasted the nation's busiest slave market, but its trafficking of human beings, wrote one historian, "had a peculiar dash: it rejoiced in its display and prosperity; it felt unashamed, almost proud."[126] A typical newcomer like Lincoln, strolling the levee or peeking into a coffee house, would thus encounter the crass realities of human chattel business constantly, unavoidably.

Citizens sometimes launched efforts to curtail the flagrancy of the commerce, perhaps because its unsettling appearance played into the hands of visiting abolitionists, but more likely because concentrations of slaves in transit were thought to constitute a public health nuisance. During the time of Lincoln's first visit, "several inhabitants of this City" signed a petition "to ask the Council . . . to prevent exposing negroes for sale on the sidewalks." Leery officials wavered on the request, procrastinated, read a report on the matter, and finally rejected it.[127] The issue came up a few months later, when citizens asked "if it would not be proper to fix places for storing negroes for sale outside the body of the city,"[128] fearing the risk of an epidemic. Others complained of the odors emanating from the unsanitary conditions in the pens, or from the cooking of cheap barrel pork used to feed the captives. Finally, in the year between Lincoln's visits, the City Council passed laws prohibiting public exposition of slaves for sale, as well as their nighttime lodging, in the area bounded by Girod Street, Esplanade Avenue, Levee Street along the riverfront, and Tremé Street behind the city. Even then, the law did little to conceal the spectacle. Protests from slave traders below Esplanade Avenue led the

124. Tadman, *Speculators and Slaves*, 70.

125. Freudenberger and Pritchett, "Domestic Slave Trade," 463–472.

126. Bancroft, *Slave Trading in the Old South*, 312. A survey of newspaper ads revealed that at least 3,500 slave sales occurred in the year 1850 alone, not including unadvertised transactions. Schafer, "Slavery as Seen in Advertisements," 35.

127. *Conseil de Ville*, Session of March 1, 1828, pp. 201–202, 212, 222 of microfilm #90-223, AB301, NOPL-LC.

128. *Conseil de Ville*, Session of May 24, 1828, p. 252 of microfilm #90-223, AB301, NOPL-LC.

Council to clarify, in 1830, that "all negroe traders may keep and expose for sale their negroes within the whole extent of the limits of the suburb Marigny, all resolutions to the contrary notwithstanding."[129] At least one trader above Esplanade Avenue, where public exposition was supposedly banned, nevertheless openly inaugurated a private slave-trading operation during Lincoln's second visit:

> R. Salaun, Broker and Exchange Broker, Royale, between Hospital and Barracks streets, has the honor of informing his friends and the public, that he attends to the sales and purchases of slaves and real estate. Persons, who may feel inclined to leave their slaves with him, for sale, can be assured that no exertion will be neglected to have them disposed of on the best terms and shortest delay. He offers for sale, at present, laundresses and plaiters [braiders], seamstresses, cooks, carpenters, painters and blacksmiths.[130]

In 1835, the law against public exposure of "negroes for sale" was expanded to the entire city, but once again was promptly amended to permit such activity in the faubourgs above Gaiennié Street and anywhere in the Faubourg Marigny, provided the slaves were lodged in brick buildings at least two stories high.[131]

These and later laws show that city officials actively grappled with slave dealing, but mostly out of concern for their own health, comfort, profit, and public image. (Other Southern cities did the same for similar reasons: Natchez, for example, passed laws in 1833 relocating its downtown slave pens to the infamous "Forks in the Road" beyond city limits.[132]) Rarely did authorities fret over the slaves' trauma or degradation, and never did they question the underlying institution. Lincoln arrived while this debate raged, and if the laws were enforced as they were written, he may have witnessed slave trading in the cityscape to a greater extent during his 1828 visit than in 1831. Had he returned twenty-five years later, he would have seen an even broader and deeper manifestation of the controversial commerce: in the late 1850s, around twenty-five slave depots, yards, pens, or

---

129. Resolutions of March 30, April 15, and April 21, 1829, and November 12, 1830, *Ordinances and Resolutions of New Orleans*, 147–149.

130. *New Orleans Bee*, May 31, 1831, p. 2, c. 4.

131. Resolutions of November 29, 1834, and January 27 and April 10, 1835, *Digeste des Ordonnances, Resolutions et Reglemens de la Corporation de la Nouvelle-Orleans* (New Orleans: Gaston Brusle, 1836), 139–141.

132. Gudmestad, *Troublesome Commerce*, 24–25.

booths operated in the heart of Faubourg St. Mary, with a dozen on Gravier Street, a half dozen on Baronne, and others on Common and Magazine. Another dozen functioned in the Old City, on Exchange Place, St. Louis Street, Esplanade at Chartres, and elsewhere.[133]

A visitor to New Orleans arriving anytime prior to the Civil War could not help but witness an entire cityscape of slavery. If the written record is any indication, the sight left searing impressions.

•

On the unseasonably warm afternoon of February 25, 1827, two thousand New Orleanians gathered by the levee to witness a breathtaking aeronautical spectacle. A "hardy aeronaut" named Mr. Robinson mounted a basket attached to a balloon, and, tethered to the ground, floated above the gasping spectators. Waving a flag dedicated to the Marquis de Lafayette and George Washington—a Frenchman and an American—Mr. Robinson then cut loose and soared high over the Franco-American city, to a hundred feet, then a thousand, then six thousand. Southwesterly winds swept him "into the regions of the upper air" and out of sight. The anxious crowd remained in the streets for hours, pondering the daredevil's fate. Rumors of his demise circulated. Then, early that evening, "shouts from a thousand voices proclaimed his arrival in the city." The hero landed safely, if awkwardly, waist-deep in mud and water on Madame Coriocourt's Gentilly Road plantation eight miles away. A newspaper described the day's events as "wonderful, glorious and sublime beyond expression."[134]

Wonderful indeed might have been the spectacle of manned flight. An equally sublime sight awaited Mr. Robinson as he peered down from his lofty perch onto the largest city of the South, astride the greatest river on the continent. Below him lay eight thousand houses, four thousand commercial buildings, and sixty public edifices squeezed into roughly three square miles—a panoply of jagged rooftops, steep and double-pitched in that West Indian style, complicated by chimneys and dormers, punctuated by domes and spires, enveloped in smoke and dust.[135] Structural density

133. Bancroft, *Slave Trading in the Old South*, 319–320.

134. *Louisiana Advertiser*, February 26, 1827.

135. These figures are interpolated from the 1822 *New-Orleans Directory and Register* (page 13), which stated that the city and suburbs contained "1436 brick, and 4401 wooden dwellings; 1258 brick and 1567 wooden warehouses, workshops, &c.; 28 brick and 15 wooden public buildings, making in the whole 8,705 buildings of every description." Population having increased by about 35 percent between 1822 and 1827, I increased the above figures accordingly.

peaked in the crux of the arc-shaped metropolis (the nickname "Crescent City" would not be coined until eight years later), while adjacent faubourgs had a more village-like appearance. They gave way to an agrarian landscape of sugar cane plantations, laid out in elongated parcels radiating from the river like the ribs of a sinuous snake.

To Mr. Robinson's north extended a vast swamp, "level as the ocean, with the dark woods growing gray in the distance, then blue, and fainter blue, as they vanish over the rim of the world."[136] To his south swept grandly the graceful meanders of the Mississippi, "gray, turbid, and broad,"[137] with villages, forest, and coastal marsh disappearing into the curvature of the earth. An occasional navigation canal, drainage ditch, road, or bayou branched outwardly from the metropolis and splayed into distant bays.

The most riveting spectacle of all, however, lay directly below Mr. Robinson's feet. There, hundreds of different vessels—"the most extraordinary medley of . . . [c]raft of every possible variety"—lined up along the riverfront.[138] Port authorities employed a specialized nautical lexicon, some of it borrowed from their French predecessors, to classify vessel typology: Ships. Barks. Brigs. Hermaprodite Brigs. Schooners. Sloops. Barges. Keelboats. Flatboats. Feluccas. Galliots. Ketchers. Luggers. Pettiauger. Brigantines. Batteau. Steamboats. Steamships. Steamers. Steam Ferries. Steam Propellers. Steam Tugs. Steam Schooners. Schooner Yachts. Yachts.[139] Masts, stacks, spider-web-like rigging, and plumes of smoke and steam darkened the riverfront around its Canal Street focal point, while smaller craft clustered along the upper and lower fringes. The great fleet fronted sundry cargo and ant-like "bustle and confusion"[140] circulating upon the spacious wood-planked levee. What Mr. Robinson saw, by one estimation, would soon be "rated . . . as the fourth port in point of commerce in the world, exceeded only by London, Liverpool, and New York." By another, it represented "the leading export city of the United

136. "John Mitchell in New Orleans," *Sunday Delta* (New Orleans), April 18, 1858, p. 7, c. 1. These words are Mitchell's, not Robinson's.

137. Bremer, *Homes of the New World*, 2:181.

138. S. A. Ferrall, *A Ramble of Six Thousand Miles Through the United States of America* (London: Effingham Wilson, Royal Exchange, 1832), 190.

139. This nomenclature is gleaned from the records of vessels officially registered or enrolled at the Port of New Orleans from 1804 to 1870. Survey of Federal Archives in Louisiana, Division of Community Service Programs-Works Projects Administration, *Ship Registers and Enrollments of New Orleans, Louisiana*, 2 vols. (Baton Rouge: Louisiana State University, 1941).

140. Ferrall, *Ramble of Six Thousand Miles*, 190.

States and one of the leading ports of the world."[141] Only from such a remote standpoint as Mr. Robinson's balloon could human eyes truly appreciate the existential relationship between antebellum New Orleans and its riverfront port.

•

Maps of the era show scores of docks protruding into the river every hundred feet or so, spaced evenly from the lower reaches of Faubourg Marigny to around Felicity Street three miles upriver. The docks perpendicularly adjoined the wharf, a plank-covered platform "40 yards wide generally," thousands of feet long and open to the sky. The wharf overlaid the artificial levee, the earthen riverfront dike erected in colonial times and reinforced constantly to keep out springtime floods. The artificial levee, in turn, topped the crest of the natural levee, the deposition of coarse alluvium deposited by the river over the past five to seven millennia, forming the highest natural land on the deltaic plain. On the city side of the wharf ran a road—Levee and New Levee streets, now Decatur and North and South Peters streets, among others. Its river side

> serves not only for a wharf where vast quantities of merchandise and *up country* productions are landed from ships and boats, but also for a market, and a sort of exchange, or place where extensive sales, transfers, &c. of commodities are constantly taking place.[142]

The entire feature, known variously as "the levee," "the quay," "the wharf," "the landing," or "the riverfront," formed the busiest and most important place in New Orleans, indeed in the entire Southwest. Here, the Queen City of the South commercially interacted with its vast hinterland and foreland. Nearly every educated person in the Western world knew about the New Orleans levee; it ranked as famous, and as notorious, as the city's ethnic diversity and moral depravity.

Crews moored vessels to the docks and arranged "flying bridges" against their flanks to discharge cargo. Additional ships tied up to already-docked vessels in parallel "rows" or "tiers," two, four, sometimes six

141. Winston, "Economic History of New Orleans," 203; Frank Haigh Dixon, "A Traffic History of the Mississippi River System," Document No. 11, National Waterways Commission (Washington, D.C.: Government Printing Office, December 1909), 15.
142. "New-Orleans," *New-Bedford Courier*, August 16, 1831, p. 1 (emphasis in original).

deep. Awaiting vessels anchored sixty fathoms (360 feet) away, fighting currents and evading traffic.[143] Dock length, wharf width, facility quality, and vessel congestion generally increased with proximity to the urban core—the Old City and St. Mary riverfront—and diminished toward the lower and upper *banlieues*. The curving river dealt different hydrological challenges to various sections of the riverfront: those above the Place d'Armes grappled with alluvial deposition and batture formation on account of the slack river velocity there; those below the city, being in a cutbank, constantly battled bank erosion. The expanding batture along the Faubourg St. Mary riverfront, the subject of constant legal discord throughout the antebellum era, created such a shallow-water beach that the city in 1819 had to invest in "flying-bridges [for] unloading of commodities aboard the flat-boats."[144] Riverfront problems, accidents, and conflicts of one sort or another occurred almost daily; policing, managing, and maintaining the facility formed a constant source of citizen griping and fist-shaking against local authorities. Why were some agents allowed to hog wharf space with sloppily arranged deposits? Why were certain captains permitted to impede others by mooring inconveniently? Why were some wharves rotting, unplanked, insufficiently extended, or not properly numbered? How can those flatboats get away with "remain[ing] permanently on the beach as fruit stores and haunts for villains of every cast and color[?]" Why doesn't the city impose a *per diem* wharfage fee, to motivate vessels to do their business and scram? "The committee of the city council on levees," solemnly concluded one editorialist in 1835, "appear[s] to be very negligent."[145]

•

Everyday grievances aside, port activity—a chief source of government revenue—was carefully regulated by federal and local officials.[146] The Collector of Customs, a prestigious presidential appointment confirmed by the Senate, represented the federal government in all port matters. He oversaw the duties owed by foreign importers, controlled outbound ves-

143. *Conseil de Ville*, Session of April 8, 1817, p. 138 of microfilm #90-221, AB301, and Session of March 23, 1824, p. 330 of microfilm #90-222, AB301, NOPL-LC.

144. *Conseil de Ville*, Session of May 15, 1819, p. 63 of microfilm #90-221, AB301, NOPL-LC.

145. "The Levee," *New Orleans Bee*, June 22, 1835, p. 2, c. 1.

146. New Orleans surpassed New York as the nation's chief exporter in 1836. Its imports, however, lagged by at best one-half its exports. Tregle, *Louisiana in the Age of Jackson*, 17–18.

sels, and policed against smugglers, pirates, filibusters, illegal slave traders, rumrunners, and other lawbreakers.[147] Locally, the City Council and the Governor of Louisiana (who was based in New Orleans, this being the state's capital for all but two years between statehood and 1849, when Baton Rouge gained the honor) enacted regulations and appointed officials. The governor-appointed Harbor Master and his subordinates enforced those regulations and oversaw day-to-day operations. Among their charges were skilled ship pilots who boarded incoming sea vessels at Pilot Town and guided them up the navigationally challenging lower Mississippi—a practice that continues today.[148] Also beneath the Harbor Master were the Wharfinger, who collected duties from ocean-going sailing ships, and a Wharfmaster, who did the same for steamboats, keelboats, and flatboats. Both officials had to submit "a list of all ships, barges and other craft subject to levee tax which [enter] the port of New Orleans" weekly to the mayor and thence to the City Council.[149] The Master Warden and his assistants enforced rules and ensured duties were paid.

Abundant regulations, and a rotating horde of transient sailors willing to test them, kept the wardens busy. Every ship had to have at least one capable hand—by law, a white man—on board at all times. No ballast, wastewater, pitch, or tar could be discharged along the riverfront. Onboard kitchen fires were closely regulated for fear of a riverfront blaze, as were cargoes of hay, gunpowder, and other flammables and combustibles. Excessively heavy cargo like granite pillars or lead bars could not be piled upon the wooden wharf, lest they "break down the same" and damage the levee. Discharging of cannons and firearms was forbidden. The Master Warden, cognizant that time meant money, also ensured that port calls were quick and efficient. *Moor, unload, load, and depart. No dillydallying. No vending. No upkeep, repairs, or tinkering. Dismantle and remove broken-down craft immediately. Unload merchandise swiftly and arrange it neatly and unobtrusively, and carry it off after no more than five days. Abandoned craft become city property after twenty-four hours, to be auctioned off with no recompense.* Penalties included steep fines, seizure, or banishment of the offending vessel to the rural fringes.[150]

147. Wilds, *Collectors of Customs*, 5.

148. Redard, "Port of New Orleans," 1:32–33.

149. *Conseil de Ville*, Session of April 26, 1817, p. 147 of microfilm #90-221, AB301, NOPL-LC.

150. *Conseil de Ville*, Session of March 23, 1824, pp. 327-336 of microfilm #90-222, AB301, NOPL-LC; "An Ordinance supplementary to the ordinance concerning the police of the Port of New-Orleans," June 23, 1831, *Ordinances and Resolutions of New-*

Behind the wardens were teams of inspectors for flour, beef and pork, tobacco, and other perishables. Inspectors seized damaged goods to prevent them from entering the market unlabeled, and then auctioned them off identified as such. "By order and under the inspection of the port wardens," read one ad around the time of Lincoln's first visit, "will be sold ... 375 barrels of superior flour, damaged on board of a flatboat ... from Louisville, Kentucky."[151] Inspectors also examined vessels and verified weights and measures—important, because duties were based on tonnage. Around the time of Lincoln's visits, a sea vessel would pay a twelve-dollar wharfage fee for a hundred tons of cargo, and up to sixty dollars for over 450 tons. Steamboats owed six to twelve dollars for eighty to 160 tons. A loaded flatboat, regardless of weight, paid six dollars.[152]

Beyond this cadre of port officials toiled a much larger professional workforce of agents, factors, brokers, slave traders, merchants, lawyers, bankers, and others stewarding (and skimming their share of) the wealth transshipping at their doorstep. When things went awry—when vessels sunk, crews were robbed, cargo went bad, or livestock died—shippers trekked over to any one of the city's fourteen notaries public to document their loss by filing a Ship Captain's Protest.[153] This document evidenced the legitimacy of the loss to the captain's clients, insulating him from legal action and empowering the client to file a claim from his insurance agent. Thousands of Ship Captain's Protests remain filed in the New Orleans Notarial Archives, each written in the graceful cursive and staid boilerplate of nineteenth-century bureaucracy.

The port never closed. While late summer and early autumn activity paled in comparison to winter and spring, vessels nevertheless arrived year-round, seven days a week. Wharf action slowed down on Sundays to about one-third normal levels.[154] Nightfall precluded much activity, but lanterns, torches, gaslights, and moonlight allowed shipmen to squeeze additional hours out of their port call.

Bustling traffic, limited space, and cargo of varying value meant officials had to regulate where certain vessels were allowed to dock. "A par-

151. *New Orleans Argus*, May 13, 1828, p. 2, c. 6.

152. "Port Officers" and "Wharfage or Levee Duty" *New-Orleans Directory & Register*, unpaginated.

153. Fourteen notaries served in 1829; their offices were mostly on Chartres Street, with some on St. Louis and Royal. "Notaries Public for N. Orleans," *New-Orleans Directory & Register*, unpaginated.

154. Hodgson, *Journey Through North America*, 79.

ticular part of the quay is appropriated to each description of craft," wrote one visitor, "and a penalty is enforced for any deviation from port regulations." Each vessel zone along the quay was referred to as a "station."[155] Ocean-going sailing ships arriving from the Gulf were assigned to the downriver stations, while interior vessels exporting bulk commodities from upcountry docked in upriver stations. Gov. William C. C. Claiborne codified this hydrologically sensible colonial-era rule within days of the American takeover, as one of his twelve articles regulating the Port of New Orleans:

> All rafts or flatboats descending the river and destined for this port, shall [dock along] the levee, above the upper gate [present-day Tchoupitoulas/Common intersection], as the harbor master shall appoint.[156]

The advent of the steamboat brought a major new player to the riverfront stage, starting with the celebrated arrival of the *New Orleans* in January 1812. Only six steamboats had called in 1816 (compared to 594 barges and 1,287 flatboats), but two years later the City Council found it necessary to "enlarge the space reserved in the upper part of the Port of New Orleans, for the use of the steamboats, [whose numbers] increase daily. . . ." They rose high enough by July 1818 for the Collector of Levee Dues to start enumerating their arrivals, which the next year totaled 287. By early spring 1830, steamboats arrived at a pace of one per hour, with fifty docked at the levee at one time. Throughout the antebellum era, steamboat calls would run into the low thousands annually. Their numbers matched those of flatboats during the busy winter-spring season and outdid them during the low-water autumn months, when the weak current handicapped flatboat navigability.[157]

Where should the steamboats dock? Piecemeal adjustments in traffic management proved inadequate vis-à-vis increasing numbers and varieties of craft, arriving from all directions and bearing a broader array of

155. Joseph Holt Ingraham, *The South-West by a Yankee* (New York, 1835), 1:105.

156. William C. C. Claiborne, "Port Regulations," decreed on January 1, 1804, and published in numerous documents, including *The Reporter* (Brattleboro, VT); February 18, 1804, p. 2.

157. Stuart, *Three Years in North America*, 2:232; Wharfinger Reports, Microfilm #75-109 QN420 New Orleans Collector of Levee Dues-Registers of Flatboats, Barges, Rafts, and Steamboats in the Port of New Orleans, 1818; *Conseil de Ville*, Session of June 16, 1818, p. 185 of microfilm #90-221, AB301, NOPL-LC. See also Winston, "Economic History of New Orleans," 202.

cargo. The City Council debated at length what to do, and on March 23, 1824, adopted a sweeping new ordinance "concerning the Port and the Levee of New Orleans." First came clear declaration of jurisdiction: the Port officially spanned from Faubourg Declouet to the Rousseau plantation (present-day Desire Street in Bywater to Felicity Street in the Lower Garden District) on the "left [east] bank," and from the Duverger plantation to the McDonogh plantation on the right bank (present-day Verret to Hamilton/Stumpf on the West Bank). Jurisdiction also included "the whole width of the said river between."[158] The vast majority of activity, of course, occurred on the left bank. Divvying up stations for various vessels, and thus laying claim to the attendant jobs and economic activity, drew upon ethnic settlement patterns and political tensions. The American element, predominating in Faubourg St. Mary and upriver faubourgs, and the Creoles of the Old City and Faubourg Marigny each wanted a share of each type of vessel traffic, even though hydrology dictated that upcountry rivercraft ought to dock uptown and sea vessels downtown.

The resultant ordinance represents something of a compromise between a contested human geography and an uncontestable physical geography. On the American side, ocean-going vessels were stationed at and below the foot of Common Street, while steamboats controlled the docks from Common up to Poydras Street. "Flatboats, barges, keel-boats, and other smaller vessels" came next, from Poydras up to St. Joseph Street.[159] On the Creole side, steamboats controlled from Elysian Fields Avenue down to Mandeville Street, but, with permission, could also dock along the flatboat landing measuring 460 feet above Conti Street. Usually, however, only flatboats docked here. A stretch of 200 feet along the Meat Market (St. Ann downriver) allowed for "smaller vessels doing the coasting trade" to deliver foodstuffs to the stalls, while an 80-foot stretch at the foot of Conti Street was reserved for the landing of the Ferry Steamboat. Ocean-going sailing ships controlled most other sections of the Old City riverfront, creating an amazing sight visitors often described as a "forest of masts."[160] They also docked along the semi-rural stretch below Enghien Street (present-day Franklin Avenue).[161] Another source from 1834 placed

158. *Conseil de Ville*, Session of March 23, 1824, pp. 327–336 of microfilm #90-222, AB301, NOPL-LC.

159. Joseph Holt Ingraham estimated about two hundred flatboats in this area during his December 1833 visit. Ingraham, *South-West by a Yankee*, 1:105.

160. Stuart, *Three Years in North America*, 2:231.

161. *Conseil de Ville*, Session of March 23, 1824, pp. 327–336 of microfilm #90-222, AB301, NOPL-LC.

the official "Lower line of the Port of Orleans" at present-day Alabo Street in the Lower Ninth Ward.[162]

One of the best sketches of moored flatboats dates from a few months before Lincoln's first arrival. Its foreground depicts the Conti Street flatboat landing, where hulking, low-profile vessels with slightly domed cabin roofs docked two deep, so close that a network of planks unified their roofs into a contiguous unloading surface. The provincial vessels and their ant-like crew contrast dramatically with the spectacular "forest of masts" marking the ocean-going sailing ships immediately downriver, which disappear into the Faubourg Marigny background. Sketched by Capt. Basil Hall through the *camera lucida* process (in which the artist peers down into an optical device that imposes a reflection of the subject over the canvas, allowing him to trace out true dimensions and details), this drawing may be the closest thing we have to a photograph of the Lincoln-era flatboat wharves. Unfortunately, it does not show the main uptown flatboat wharf where Lincoln likely landed, but rather the smaller downtown station around Conti Street. We know this because of the appearance of St. Louis Church in the extreme left of the drawing, the tell-tale angle in the levee between St. Louis and Conti streets, and the absence of steamboats between the flatboat zone and the sailing-ship zone.[163] Other reliable illustrations of the flatboat wharves are few and far between. Artists apparently found little reason to capture the lowly and lumbering flatboat, particularly when the majestic verticality of the great sailing ships and seething emanations of the raucous steamboats commanded so much more attention.

Flatboats, the notorious bearers of nuisance-emitting cargo, required special handling from port managers. Those carrying "horses, hogs, oxen, or other animals" or rotting or damaged cargo "emitting disagreeable odors, or vapors injurious to the salubrity of the air," were exiled beyond St. Joseph Street up to the De Hart property uptown, or below Enghien Street downtown.[164] Offensive odors could indeed overwhelm a newcomer to the New Orleans wharf. Citizens regularly dumped "filth in the current . . . of the [Mississippi] in front of the City" using ramps built of flatboat

162. Charles F. Zimpel, *Topographical Map of New Orleans and Its Vicinity, 1834*, Southeastern Architectural Archive, Tulane University Special Collections.

163. Capt. Basil Hall, "The Mississippi at New Orleans" (1828), engraved by W. H. Lizars, The Historic New Orleans Collection, Accession Number 1974.25.30.576 P.C. 30-11-A.

164. *Conseil de Ville*, Session of March 23, 1824, p. 329 of microfilm #90-222, AB301, NOPL-LC.

timber. The city acknowledged that "the banks of the river from Faubourg Ste. Marie to the lower boundary of Faubourg Marigny are in a most unsanitary condition," replete with "dead animals and an accumulation of filth whose pestilential effluvia may be prejudicial to public health." Its solution: task "the negroes of the city work shop to empty and clean said river bank. . . ."[165]

Other changing conditions warranted constant modifications in laws and regulations. In 1826, for example, increasing flatboat traffic forced the relocation of the upper edge of the St. Mary flatboat station up to the lower line of the De Hart property. In 1827, the Mayor gained authorization to charge the Wharfinger to redirect flatboats to new stations "on account of the fall and rise of the River."[166] Later that year, increasing steamboat traffic motivated the rezoning of Canal Street up to Notre Dame, and subsequently Canal down to Conti, as exclusively for steamboats.[167] A few years later, the City Council further allocated wharf space by cargo: flatboats bearing wood and bricks could only land at the foot of Elysian Fields and Julia, while those hauling corn, oats, hay, and other fodder had to tie up between Girod and Julia.[168] Levee repairs, sediment deposition, river conditions, and dock damage also reshuffled the wharfscape. This dynamism, not to mention widespread non-compliance with the law, complicates attempts to try to identify precisely where a particular vessel, like Lincoln's, might have landed in a particular year.

Eyewitness descriptions bring some level of order to the seemingly convoluted zoning. "The upper part is occupied with flat-boats, arks, peerogues, rafts, keel-boats, canoes, and steam-boats," wrote one circa-1830 visitor of the riverfront roughly from Felicity Street to Common Street—"and below these are stationed schooners, cutters, brigs, ships, &c, in regular succession," meaning along the riverfront of the Old City.[169] Charles Joseph Latrobe, viewing the spectacle from the roof of the Bishop's Hotel on New Year's 1834, estimated "ships and boats of every size [extending] upwards of two miles . . ."

165. *Conseil de Ville*, Session of February 22, 1817, p. 127 and Session of June 19, 1819, p. 85 of microfilm #90-221, AB301, NOPL-LC.

166. *Conseil de Ville*, Session of April 17, 1826, pp. 142–143, and Session of April 14, 1827, pp. 372–373, of microfilm #90-223, AB301, NOPL-LC.

167. *Conseil de Ville*, Session of August 11, 1827, p. 39, and January 12, 1828, p. 167, of microfilm #90-223, AB301, NOPL-LC.

168. Resolutions of November 24 and December 11, 1835, *Ordonnances, Resolutions et Reglemens de la Nouvelle-Orleans*, 215–217.

169. Ferrall, *Ramble of Six Thousand Miles*, 190.

> Highest up the stream lie the flats, arks, and barges, and below
> them the tier of steam-boats, fifty . . . at one time. Then come
> the brigs ranged in rows, with their bows against the breast of
> the levee; these are succeeded by the three-masters, lying in
> tiers of two or three deep, with their broadside to the shore. . . .
> [W]hen the sails of the whole are exposed to the air, and their
> signals or national flags abroad, [it] is one of the most singu-
> larly beautiful [sights] you can conceive.[170]

Another visitor described the distribution of vessels as he approached New
Orleans from upstream. First he cast his eyes along the riverfront of what
is today called the Lower Garden District:

> The first object that presents itself is the dirty and uncouth
> backwoods flat boat. . . . Close by are the rather more decent
> keel-boats, with cotton, furs, whiskey, flour. . . .

Around Julia Street the sights and sounds changed:

> [N]ext the elegant steam-boat, which by its hissing and re-
> peated sounds, announces either its arrival or departure, and
> sends forth immense columns of black smoke, that form into
> long clouds above the city.

After around Toulouse Street came the coastwise and international traffic:

> Farther on are the smaller merchant vessels, the sloops and
> schooners from the Havannah, Vera Cruz, Tampico; then the
> brigs; and lastly the elegant ships, appearing like a forest of
> masts.[171]

Hydrology and port management caused a cultural and linguistic sort-
ing of incoming watercraft that serendipitously aligned with, and perhaps
reinforced, the ethnic geography of the city. Upcountry craft bringing in
cotton, tobacco, corn, flour, pork, and other interior commodities usually bore English-speaking Anglo-American crews, who landed in the
predominately English-speaking Anglo-American Faubourg St. Mary
(dubbed "the American quarter" or "the American sector"). Sea vessels

170. Charles Joseph La Trobe, *The Rambler in North America* (New York, 1835),
2:244–245.
171. Charles Sealsfield, *The Americans As They Are; Described in A Tour Through the Valley of the Mississippi* (London: Hurst, Chance, and Co., 1828), 146.

importing goods and merchandise from Europe, the West Indies, Mexico, and Latin America generally moored in the predominantly Francophone Creole lower city (the "French" or "Creole quarter"), which looked, sounded, and smelled much like the ports of origin of its callers. Slaves imported domestically disembarked into the vast New Orleans humanity market depending on their point of origin and vessel of arrival: the roughly 10 percent who came downriver from Kentucky, Missouri, Arkansas, Tennessee, upper Louisiana, and Mississippi arrived at the uptown steamboat or flatboat wharves. The 90 percent who came from Virginia, Maryland, the Carolinas, or Gulf Coast landed at the downtown wharves reserved for coastwise or ocean-going vessels. They arrived not on the specially designed slave ships associated with the trans-Atlantic slave trade (prohibited in the U.S. since 1808 but still occurring illegally off Louisiana's coast), but rather on the same fleet of vessels bringing in merchandise to New Orleans' levee. Local traders met the human cargo on the wharf and marched the coffle unceremoniously to the holding pens to be readied for sale. The importer by law had to report the number and demographics of the shipment to the mayor.[172] "[S]eventy three *Virginia Slaves*, selected principally for the Planters," proclaimed one 1828 announcement, are "now at the Levee . . . and will be for sale as soon as they are landed."[173]

•

Activity along the riverfront played out through daily dynamics among buyers and sellers, transients and locals, shipmen of various vessels and sponsors, competing laborer castes and classes, and between all of the above and the dues-collecting, rules-enforcing officials.

The interactions sometimes yielded inefficiencies. Faubourg St. Mary businessmen in 1820, for example, built their own wharf and donated their riverfront rights to the city, in the hope of luring steamboats and their attendant business. But the facility silted up when the city failed to maintain it, allowing only lowly flatboats to monopolize the wharf. Even where steamboats could dock physically, regulations prevented them from doing so.

The interactions also produced conflicts and tensions. One ongoing

---

172. "Additional Ordinances—Slaves," October 20, 1831, *Ordinances and Resolutions of New-Orleans*, 410–411. The figures for states of origin of slaves arriving to the New Orleans market in 1830 are based on the research of Freudenberger and Pritchett, "Domestic Slave Trade," 460.

173. "Slaves," *Louisiana Courier*, October 20, 1828, p. 3, c. 4 (emphasis in original).

discord involved "retailing flat-boats," in which boatmen exploited their port call by vending their cargo like floating shopkeepers.

The practice enraged local merchants, who paid high rent and taxes only to lose business to the lowly short-timing squatters.[174] City officials responded by imposing a five-dollar-a-day fine on boatmen retailing eight days after their initial landing; the next year, they banished retailing flat-boats to the De Hart property, the same zone reserved for the nuisance flatboats, or face a steep twenty-dollar fine.[175] The practice nevertheless persisted, because it was lucrative: retailing boatmen minimized costs by paying no rent, no taxes, and no board (they slept on board), while gaining a competitive advantage by cutting out the middlemen and selling directly to consumers (who benefited from wholesale prices). A decade after the laws went into effect, flatboats brazenly operated as fruit storehouses supplying illegal food stands in the nearby Place d'Armes, while others sold directly to city dwellers. Just a week's worth of incoming flatboats bore enough cargo to affect commodity supply, demand, and prices citywide. One 1835 report inventoried 28,671 barrels of coal; 5,246 of flour; 3,762 of corn; 1,912 of oats; 400 of pork; 153 of whiskey; 175 of molasses; 22 of beef; and 14 of potatoes. Additionally there were 2,500 gallon-sized stoneware jugs; 1,380 kegs of lard; and 42 casks of ham. Piled near the barrels and jars were 2,563 sacks of oats and 171 of corn; 489 bales of hay and 64 bales of cotton. More than 1,800 pumpkins, plus cider, apples, apple brandy, and kraut, filled every remaining nook. All this arrived on only thirty-nine flatboats during a single week in late November—hardly the busiest time of year.[176]

After flatboatmen sold the last of their cargo, they proceeded to dismantle their vessels. This noisy task cluttered valuable wharf space for extensive periods of time, at the expense of incoming dues-paying vessels. It represented yet another flashpoint between local businessmen and boatmen. So annoyed did councilman Bernard Marigny get over this activity in the Faubourg Marigny that he led the City Council in 1819 to prohibit "the demolishing of flat boats, [subject to] a fine of twenty dollars."[177]

174. *Louisiana Advertiser*, December 2, 1826, p. 2, c. 3; *New Orleans Bee*, June 22, 1835, p. 2, c. 1.

175. *Conseil de Ville*, Session of March 24, 1823, p. 150 of microfilm #90-222, AB301 and Session of March 23, 1824, p. 327 of microfilm #90-222, AB301, NOPL-LC.

176. "New-Orleans, Dec. 1," *Macon Weekly Telegraph* (*Georgia Telegraph*), December 17, 1835, p. 2.

177. *Conseil de Ville*, Session of May 8, 1819, p. 59 of microfilm #90-221, AB301, NOPL-LC. See also June 2, 1819, p. 75 for a later amendment.

Upriver, where far more flatboats docked, the problem forced the City Council to intervene again in 1822. It decreed,

> Whereas the number of the flatboats . . . augments daily, on account of the great increase of produce from the Western Country, and as it is necessary to facilitate the unloading of the same, which cannot be accomplished without taking effectual measures to prevent the breaking up of flatboats in [those wharves] destined for the unloading of the said produce. . . . It is [thus] forbidden . . . to break up any flatboat, barge, keelboat, or other rivercraft between Enghien Street in the lower section of the City and the Steammill of Mr. Weathers in the upper part of the City; no flatboat, keelboat, or other craft shall remain the limits above prescribed more than 48 hours after having effected its discharge.[178]

Such odious practices continued, in part because flatboatmen (particularly amateurs) were often ill-informed of local law, but mostly because they were inclined to make the most of their trip to New Orleans. Multiply this inclination by the thousands of other transients "on the make" in the Great Southern Emporium, and a portrait of one contentious place emerges.

For the most part, however, order prevailed on the riverfront; there was too much money at stake to allow chaos to reign. Challenges abounded, not the least of which was the sheer technical difficulty of sailing safely into the port. Negotiating the Mississippi's tricky currents amid heavy traffic, shifting winds, sandy bottoms, and primitive steam engines tested the very best captains as they identified their berth, waited their turn, docked and tied up, paid their dues, unloaded, conducted their business, serviced their vessel, loaded, and departed—all while avoiding danger, vice, and virus. Vessel overcrowding presented another problem: on the very week that Lincoln departed New Orleans for the last time, an editorialist called on authorities "to look to widening the . . . wharfage and the landing of articles, both from the shipping and steamboats, [to handle] immense additional tonnage. . . . The evil, of want of room and convenience, is felt sufficiently at this moment." Flatboats were pointedly excluded from the recommendation. They usually ended up sacrificing space to the steamboats.[179]

178. *Conseil de Ville*, Session of June 1, 1822, pp. 87–88 of microfilm #90-222, AB301, NOPL-LC.
179. "The Shipping," *Mercantile Advertiser*, June 13, 1831, p. 2, c. 4.

When New Orleans separated into three semi-autonomous municipalities (1836 to 1852), port management and nearly all other city functions grew more complicated. The quantity of officials, records, rates, and
bureaucracy in general all tripled. Each municipality sought its piece of
the riverfront action, and renegotiated the geography of vessel stations
accordingly. One of the best maps of this era, Hirt's *Plan of New Orleans*
(1841), shows that each municipality numbered its riverfront docks and
assigned vessels to them differently. The First Municipality (the Old City,
or French Quarter) hosted steamboats from Canal Street to Toulouse,
schooners to St. Ann, flatboats and "planters' pirogues" to Dumaine, and
ships to its lowermost limit at Esplanade Avenue. The Second Municipality (Faubourg St. Mary) directed steamboats from Canal Street upriver
to Julia, flatboats up to Delord (present-day Howard Avenue), ships to
Robin, flatboats again to Orange, and ships to the city limit at Felicity Street. The Third Municipality—Faubourg Marigny, the poorest and
farthest downriver—reserved most of its space for ships, as it was too inconvenient for upcountry steamboats and flatboats. Not shown in Hirt's
map are wharves in adjacent Jefferson Parish (established in 1825), which
at this time lay above Felicity Street; there, flatboats docked almost exclusively, and in large numbers.[180] An 1850 map of the Jefferson Parish
city of Lafayette shows that wharves—presumably mostly for flatboats—
extended well upriver by that year, almost to Louisiana Avenue.[181] Other
communities above and below New Orleans, plus hundreds of plantations
(many of which effectively operated as self-sufficient villages), hosted their
own riverfront landings and docking vessels.

•

For all its strategic advantages, the New Orleans riverfront was ironically ill positioned to handle certain resources needed by city dwellers for
everyday life. Firewood, lumber, pitch, tar, and wild game abounded in
the piney woods of the Florida Parishes across Lake Pontchartrain, while
the lake itself, plus the adjacent tidal lagoons that communicated with
the Mississippi Sound and productive saline marshes, yielded seemingly

180. L. Hirt, *Plan of New Orleans with perspective and geometrical Views of the principal
Buildings of the City*, The Historic New Orleans Collection, Accession Number 1952.4.
See also Winston, "Economic History of New Orleans," 204.
   181. J. T. Hammond, *Map of New Orleans and Environs, Engraved Expressly for
Cohen's Directory-1850*, The Historic New Orleans Collection, Accession Number
1974.25.18.111.

limitless finfish, shellfish, and fowl. But suppliers from these regions required multiple days and considerable risk to reach New Orleans via the
Mississippi River. The alterative, practiced since prehistoric times, was to
ship across Lake Pontchartrain and up Bayou St. John, then discharge at
Bayou Road and walk the remaining two miles to the "back door" of the
city. Spanish colonials supplanted the terrestrial leg of that awkward journey in 1794 by excavating the Carondelet Canal, but even after the canal's
widening and the addition of a shell road, the back-door route left much
to be desired. A visitor from Mobile in 1828 made this clear:

> We landed at a place called, I think, the Piquets [probably
> Spanish Fort, where Bayou St. John adjoins Lake Pontchar-
> train], about six or seven miles from New Orleans. . . . This
> short distance we passed over on a road skirting a sluggish
> Creek [Bayou St. John] running in the midst of a swamp
> overgrown with cypress and other thirsty trees, rising out of a
> thick, rank underwood.[182]

Increasing demand for swift passenger and freight service to coastwise
cities motivated entrepreneurs to propose additional city-to-lake connections. The two projects that succeeded both coalesced around the time of
Lincoln's visits.

During the year of Lincoln's first trip, businessmen in the predominantly Creole lower city endeavored to solve the lake-access problem with
an exciting new transportation technology imported from the Northeast: the railroad. They formed a company in 1829, won a state charter
in 1830, gained rights to an unobstructed five-mile beeline connecting
river and lake, and commenced clearing the bed and building the track.
Noting how the "loudly expressed . . . doubts of many [had] vanished,"
the company proudly inaugurated its horse-drawn Pontchartrain Railroad
on April 23, 1831, the first railroad west of the Appalachians and first
in the nation with a completed track system.[183] Seventeen months later,
the company introduced steam rail locomotion to the city, taking to the
lake twelve cars and four hundred passengers, "accompanied by a band
of music, moving off in a gallant style beneath streaming banners and an
admiring multitude."[184] By early 1835, more than ninety vessels (nearly

182. Basil Hall, *Travels in North America in the Years 1827 and 1828* (Edinburgh and
London, 1830), 3:318.
183. *Mercantile Advertiser*, April 20, 1831, p. 2, c. 4 and "Railroad," April 26, 1831, p.
2, c. 4.
184. *Louisiana Advertiser*, September 18, 1832, p. 2, c. 4.

one-third of them steamboats) called monthly at the railroad's lakefront Port Pontchartrain, bearing approximately 500 passengers, 2,200 bales of cotton, and voluminous coastwise cargo.[185] Thousands of subsequent visitors to New Orleans sailed not up the Mississippi to the city's world-famous riverfront, but instead through the Rigolets channel and across the lake to Port Pontchartrain, where, sometimes confused and disoriented, they boarded the Pontchartrain Railroad and rode down Elysian Fields Avenue to the city.

The Pontchartrain Railroad proved a success. It fueled a real estate boom in the Faubourg Marigny and in the Milneburg community that arose around Port Pontchartrain. It also piqued the interest of Anglo-American businessmen, who envisioned an even better city-to-lake connection for their upper part of town. Word of the impending competition from uptown inspired lower-city businessmen to propose yet another canal to connect their neighborhood with Lake Borgne, the same water body their peers in nearby St. Bernard Parish planned to access with a new railroad.[186]

Lofty visions, however, outpaced action on the ground, and of the three projects, only the uptown canal came to fruition—in 1831, when the New Orleans Canal and Banking Company invested four million dollars to excavate a waterway directly connecting the Faubourg St. Mary with Lake Pontchartrain. Designed to outperform the extant Carondelet Canal, the waterway would measure sixty feet wide, accommodate six-foot-draft vessels, adjoin a paved toll road, and terminate in a spacious turning basin (located near the present-day intersection of Howard and Loyola avenues). The Company recruited unskilled Irish laborers locally, nationally, and internationally to serve as "ditchers" for the six-mile-long excavation. The grueling toil commenced in 1832, a few months after Lincoln's final departure, and immediately took a terrible toll on the immigrants. Many died in a cholera and yellow fever epidemic that claimed one of every six New Orleanians that year. Thousands more would perish by the time the New Orleans Canal was completed in 1838. Nicknamed the New Basin Canal to distinguish it from the Carondelet ("Old Basin") Canal, the waterway succeeded commercially, bringing to the American sector a steady stream of sand, gravel, and shell for fill; lumber, firewood, and charcoal; fruits, vegetables, cotton, and seafood; and other cargo from

---

185. Merl E. Reed, *New Orleans and the Railroads: The Struggle for Commercial Empire, 1830–1860* (Baton Rouge: Louisiana State University Press, 1966), 33–36.
    186. Ibid., 33–38.

the lake and Gulf. The navigation canals, their adjacent shells roads, and the Pontchartrain Railroad all circumvented the tedious and difficult river route, and helped connect New Orleans more efficiently with its neighbors. "The citizens seem *determined* to avoid the one hundred and ten miles of river navigation," wrote one visitor in 1832 regarding the new infrastructure.[187]

The next year, uptown investors, aiming to create valuable real estate between New Orleans and Carrollton, won a charter for the city's second railroad. Gaining access to a 120-foot-wide easement, they set to work in 1834 laying 4.5 miles of track through a number of sugar cane plantations, running parallel to the river and halfway between the riverfront and backswamp. The New Orleans and Carrolton Rail Road commenced full scheduled service on September 26, 1835. "The route passes through a level and beautiful country," reported the *Bee* on opening day,

> very high, dry and arable land; and affording one of the most pleasant drives in the southern states. It passes through the limits of an ancient forest of live oaks . . . one of the very few of its kind now remaining in the south.[188]

The railroad's right-of-way aligned with Nyades Street and formed a corridor that would later be renamed St. Charles Avenue. In short time, the new conveyance affected the city's human geography, allowing wealthy city dwellers to establish domiciles in the bucolic upper suburbs, helping form today's Garden District and positioning St. Charles Avenue to become the city's grand uptown avenue. The very term "uptown" started to be heard (1820s-30s) in the local English vernacular, coined in Manhattan and brought down by transplanted New Yorkers. The city grew in the shape of an arc, inspiring Northern visitor Joseph Holt Ingraham to nickname it, in 1835, "the crescent city[,] from its being built around . . . a graceful curve of the river. . . ."[189] Most former sugar plantations along the St. Charles Rail Road were subdivided by 1855; subsequent decades saw those lots built up with houses, those streets lined with oaks, and their addresses change to Orleans Parish, as the City of New Orleans annexed the former Jefferson Parish cities of Lafayette in 1852, Jefferson in 1870,

---

187. J. E. Alexander, *Transatlantic Sketches, Comprising Visits to the Most Interesting Scenes in North and South America, and the West Indies* (London, 1833), 2:32 (emphasis added).

188. *New Orleans Bee*, September 25 and September 28, 1835, p. 2, c. 1.

189. Ingraham, *South-West by a Yankee*, 1:91.

and Carrollton in 1874. The municipal expansion traced its provenance to the investments of the 1820s–30s—an era that also saw extensive street paving and illumination, the construction of the nationally famous St. Charles and St. Louis exchange hotels, the formation of private gas and water companies, the extension of Esplanade Avenue to Bayou St. John, the quadrupling of the municipal market system, the erection of the New Orleans Barracks (later Jackson Barracks), the launch of three ferry lines crossing the river, and the modernization of the city's architectural aesthetic from colonial-era French Creole and Spanish styles to imposing new Greek Revival fashions.

•

New Orleans around the time of Lincoln's visits increasingly wove itself into regional, national, and world economic systems by manipulating its environment, building infrastructure, peopling its neighborhoods, and handling its shipping traffic to the utmost commercial advantage. The Great Southern Emporium in the 1820s–30s approached the zenith of its geo-economic significance, dominating Mississippi Valley commerce, growing dramatically in population, and developing a distinctive and spectacular urban character. New Orleans' aristocracy reveled in comfort and leisure to the extent that their wherewithal allowed—and for many, that was a lot. New Orleans' Latin Catholic peoples rendered the city more foreign; its black population, more Afro-Caribbean; its immigrant population, more multicultural; and its transient population, more rowdy and raffish than most if not all other American cities. The city's environmental hazards, public-health atrocities, vice, crime, and rampant bondage also made this place an object of dread and denouncement. To a wide-eyed young flatboat hand arriving from the rural upcountry, New Orleans in 1828–31 must have formed one dazzling, dangerous, colorful, contentious, splendid, polluted, liberating, oppressive, promising, and utterly exciting place.

References

Abbreviations

Collected
Works   *The Collected Works of Abraham Lincoln*. Edited by Roy P.
                 Basler. New Brunswick, NJ: Rutgers University Press, 1953.

Herndon's
Informants   *Herndon's Informants: Letters, Interviews, and Statements About
                 Abraham Lincoln*. Edited by Douglas L. Wilson and Rodney O.
                 Davis. Urbana and Chicago: University of Illinois Press, 1998

Lincoln
Lore   *Lincoln Lore: Bulletin of the Lincoln National Life Foundation*

NOPL–LC   New Orleans Public Library—Louisiana Collection

~Letters, Statements, Interviews, Speeches, Manuscripts, and Affidavits~

Ashley, Sarah. Interview with F. W. Dibble, June 10, 1937. In *American Slavery: A Composite Autobiography*, Second Supplemental Series, Texas Narratives, vol. 02T.

Bell, Frank. Interview with B. E. Davis, September 22, 1937. In *American Slavery: A Composite Autobiography*, Second Supplemental Series, Texas Narratives, vol. 02T.

Boultinghouse, Jane. Interview with Richard Campanella, December 5, 2008, Rockport, Indiana.

Burba, E. R. Letter to William H. Herndon, May 25, 1866. In *Herndon's Informants*.

Butler, Benjamin F. Letter to Abraham Lincoln, May 8, 1862. Abraham Lincoln Papers at the Library of Congress, Washington, D.C.

Carman, Caleb. Interview with William H. Herndon, October 12, 1866. In *Herndon's Informants*.

———. Interview with William H. Herndon, March 1887. In *Herndon's Informants*.

———. Interview with William H. Herndon, November 30, 1866. In *Herndon's Informants*.

Chapman, A. H. Letter to William H. Herndon, September 8, 1865. In *Herndon's Informants*.

Clary, Royal. Interview with William H. Herndon, October 1866. In *Herndon's Informants*.

Dillon, Barbara. Interview with Richard Campanella, December 5, 2008, Rockport, Indiana.

Dougherty, John R. Interview with William H. Herndon, September 17, 1865. In *Herndon's Informants.*

Dougherty, John R., Nathaniel Grigsby, and John S. Hougland, September 16–17, 1865, Interviews with William H. Herndon. In *Herndon's Informants.*

Dubois, Jesse K. Interview with William H. Herndon, date unknown, transcribed December 1, 1888. In *Herndon's Informants.*

Durant, Thomas J. Letter to Abraham Lincoln, February 10, 1864. Abraham Lincoln Papers at the Library of Congress, Washington, D.C.

Ellis, Abner Y. Statement to William H. Herndon, January 23, 1866. In *Herndon's Informants.*

Florville, William. Letter to Abraham Lincoln, December 27, 1863. Abraham Lincoln Papers at the Library of Congress, Washington, D.C.

Gentry, Anna Caroline. Interview with William H. Herndon, September 17, 1865. In *Herndon's Informants.*

Gentry, Anna, Hannah, and Rose. Interview with Francis Marion Van Natter, January 21, 1936. Francis Marion Van Natter Papers-Regional History Collection No. 136, note card #1, Lewis Historical Library, Vincennes University.

Gentry, E. Grant. Affidavit dated September 5, 1936. Francis Marion Van Natter Papers-Regional History Collection No. 136, Lewis Historical Library, Vincennes University.

Gentry, Wayne. Interview with Francis Marion Van Natter, December 30, 1935. Francis Marion Van Natter Papers-Regional History Collection No. 136, note card #1, Lewis Historical Library, Vincennes University.

Gillespie, Joseph. Letter to William H. Herndon, January 31, 1866. In *Herndon's Informants.*

Graham, Mentor. Letter to William H. Herndon, May 29, 1865. In *Herndon's Informants.*

———. Statement recorded by James Q. Howard, "Biographical Notes," May 1860. Abraham Lincoln Papers at the Library of Congress, Washington, D.C.

Greene, William G. Interview with William H. Herndon, May 29, 1865. In *Herndon's Informants.*

———. Letter to William H. Herndon, November 27, 1865. In *Herndon's Informants.*

———. Interview with William H. Herndon, May 29, 1865. In *Herndon's Informants.*

———. Interview with William H. Herndon, May 30, 1865. In *Herndon's Informants.*

———. Statement recorded by James Q. Howard, "Biographical Notes," May 1860. Abraham Lincoln Papers at the Library of Congress, Washington, D.C.

Grigsby, Nathaniel. Interview with William H. Herndon, September 12, 1865. In *Herndon's Informants.*

———. Letter to William H. Herndon, January 21, 1866. In *Herndon's Informants.*

————, Silas and Nancy Richardson, and John Romine. Interviews with William H. Herndon, September 14, 1865. In *Herndon's Informants*.

Hanks Family Papers, Manuscript Collection, SC 644, Abraham Lincoln Presidential Library, Springfield, Illinois.

Hanks, Dennis F. Letter to William H. Herndon, April 2, 1866. In *Herndon's Informants*.

————. Letter to William H. Herndon, January 26, 1866. In *Herndon's Informants*.

————. Letter to William H. Herndon, March 22, 1866. In *Herndon's Informants*.

————. Letter to William H. Herndon, March 7, 1866. In *Herndon's Informants*.

————. Interview with William H. Herndon, June 13, 1865. In *Herndon's Informants*.

————. Interview with William H. Herndon, June 15, 1865. In *Herndon's Informants*.

————. Interview with William H. Herndon, September 8, 1865. In *Herndon's Informants*.

Hanks, John. Interview with William H. Herndon, 1865–1866. In *Herndon's Informants*.

————. Interview with William H. Herndon, June 13, 1865. In *Herndon's Informants*.

————. Letter to Jesse W. Weik, April 19, 1888. In *Herndon's Informants*.

————. Letter to Jesse W. Weik, June 12, 1887. In *Herndon's Informants*.

Herndon, J. Rowan. Letters to William H. Herndon, May 28 and June 11, 1865. In *Herndon's Informants*.

Hougland, John S. Interview with William H. Herndon, September 17, 1865. In *Herndon's Informants*.

Jonas, Abraham. Letter to Abraham Lincoln, December 30, 1860. Abraham Lincoln Papers at the Library of Congress, Washington, D.C.

Jonas, Annie E. Letter to William H. Herndon, October 28, 1866. Abraham Lincoln Papers at the Urbana and Chicago: University of Illinois Press, 1998.

Jonas, B. F. Letter to Abraham Lincoln, June 4, 1857. Abraham Lincoln Papers at the Library of Congress, Washington, D.C.

King, Silvia. Interview with P. W. Davis, 1937. In *American Slavery: A Composite Autobiography*, Second Supplemental Series, Texas Narratives, vol. 06T.

Lincoln, Abraham. "Autobiography Written for John L. Scripps," June 1860. In *Collected Works*, vol. 4.

————. "Communication to the People of Sangamo County," *Sangamo Journal*, March 9, 1832. In *Collected Works*, vol. 1.

————. "First Inaugural Address—Final Text," March 4, 1861. In *Collected Works*, vol. 4.

————. "Last Public Address," April 11, 1865. In *Collected Works*, vol. 8.

————. Letter of Recommendation for Jesse K. Dubois, undated. In *Collected Works*, vol. 8.

————. Letter to Alexander Hamilton Stephens, January 19, 1860. In *Some Lincoln Correspondence with Southern Leaders before the Outbreak of the Civil War*, from the Collection of Judd Stewart. New York: J. Stewart, 1909.

————. Letter to August Belmont, July 31, 1862. In *Collected Works*, vol. 5.

————. Letter to James C. Conkling, August 26, 1863. In *Collected Works*, vol. 6.

————. Letter to Jesse W. Fell, December 20, 1859. In *Collected Works*, vol. 3.

————. Letter to Joshua F. Speed, August 24, 1855. In *Collected Works*, vol. 2.

————. Letter to Martin S. Morris, March 26, 1843. In *Collected Works*, vol. 1.

————. Letter to Mary Speed, September 27, 1841. In *Collected Works*, vol. 1.

————. Letter to Michael Hahn, March 13, 1864. *Collected Works*, vol. 7.

————. "Petition to Sangamon County Commissions' Court for Appointment of a Constable," March 11, 1831. In *Collected Works*, vol. 1.

————. "Speech at Indianapolis, Indiana, September 19, 1859." In *Collected Works*, vol. 3.

————. "Speech at New Haven, Connecticut," March 6, 1860. In *Collected Works*, vol. 4.

Lincoln, Sarah Bush. Interview with William H. Herndon, September 8, 1865. In *Herndon's Informants*.

McNamar, John. Letter to William H. Herndon, June 4, 1866. In *Herndon's Informants*.

Moore, Matilda Johnston. Interview with William H. Herndon, September 8, 1865. In *Herndon's Informants*.

Richardson, Joseph C. Statement to William H. Herndon, 1865–1866. In *Herndon's Informants*.

Roby, Absolom. Interview with William H. Herndon, September 17, 1865. In *Herndon's Informants*.

Rutledge, Robert B. Letter to William H. Herndon, November 1, 1866. In *Herndon's Informants*.

Short, James. Letter to William H. Herndon, July 7, 1865. In *Herndon's Informants*.

Smoot, Coleman. Letter to William H. Herndon, May 7, 1866. In *Herndon's Informants*.

Speed, Joshua F. Interview with William H. Herndon, 1865–1866. In *Herndon's Informants*.

Stephens, Alexander H. Letter to Abraham Lincoln, December 14, 1860. Abraham Lincoln Papers at the Library of Congress, Washington, D.C., and in *Some Lincoln Correspondence with Southern Leaders before the Outbreak of the Civil War*, from the Collection of Judd Stewart. New York: J. Stewart, 1909.

————. State of Georgia—Executive Department, certification signed by Stephens, January 19, 1883, confirming authenticity of Lincoln's letter to Stephens. In *Some Lincoln Correspondence with Southern Leaders before the Outbreak of the Civil War*, from the Collection of Judd Stewart. New York: J. Stewart, 1909.

Taylor, Green B. Interview with William H. Herndon, September 16, 1865. In

Herndon's Informants.

Turnham, David. Interview with William H. Herndon, September 15, 1865. In *Herndon's Informants.*

Van Natter, Francis Marion. Papers and Research Materials, Regional History Collection No. 136, Lewis Historical Library, Vincennes University.

William S. Ward, *Diary* [of Flatboat Trip from New Albany, Indiana to New Orleans, Louisiana, 1839], The Historic New Orleans Collection, Accession Number 2009.0139.

Wilson, Robert L. Letter to William H. Herndon, February 10, 1866. In *Herndon's Informants.*

Wood, William. Interview with William H. Herndon, September 15, 1865. In *Herndon's Informants.*

Zacharie, Isachar. Letters exchanged with Abraham Lincoln, from January 14, 1863 through December 26, 1864. Abraham Lincoln Papers at the Library of Congress, Washington, D.C.

~Official Documents, Laws, and Ordinances~

Acadian Parish Records, 1806–1829—St. James Parish Census of 1829, MSS 23, folder 3, item 1. The Historic New Orleans Collection.

Butler, Maj. Gen. Benjamin F. Report, Headquarters-Department of the Gulf, April 29, 1862, United States War Department, *The War of the Rebellion: A Compilation of the Official Records of the Union and Confederate Armies*, series 1, vol. 6. Washington, D.C.: Government Printing Office, 1882.

Census of Ascension Parish, 1830 Enumeration, transcribed by Don Johnson and Deandra Norred Parduc.

Claiborne, William C. C. "Port Regulations," decreed on January 1, 1804 and published in numerous documents, including *The Reporter* (Brattleboro, VT) 2, no. 1, February 18, 1804, p. 2.

Confederate States of America, War Department. *Proceedings of the Court of Inquiry Relative to the Fall of New Orleans.* Richmond, VA: R. M. Smith, 1864.

Conseil de Ville, Official Proceedings, AB301, NOPL–LC.

    February 22, 1817, WPA microfilm #90–221.
    April 8, 1817, WPA microfilm #90–221.
    April 26, 1817, WPA microfilm #90–221.
    June 16, 1818, WPA microfilm #90–221.
    May 8, 1819, WPA microfilm #90–221.
    May 15, 1819, WPA microfilm #90–221.
    June 2, 1819, WPA microfilm #90–221.
    June 19, 1819, WPA microfilm #90–221.
    June 1, 1822, WPA microfilm #90–222.
    March 24, 1823, WPA microfilm #90–222.
    October 23, 1823, WPA microfilm #90–222.
    March 23, 1824, WPA microfilm #90–222.
    July 10, 1824, WPA microfilm #90–223.

August 18, 1824, WPA microfilm #90–223.

August 21, 1824, WPA microfilm #90–223.

December 31, 1824, WPA microfilm #90–223.

March 22, 1825, WPA microfilm #90–223.

July 6, 1825, WPA microfilm #90–223.

April 17, 1826, WPA microfilm #90–223.

November 4, 1826, WPA microfilm #90–223.

December 2, 1826, WPA microfilm #90–223.

February 24, 1827, WPA microfilm #90–223.

March 10, 1827, WPA microfilm #90–223.

April 14, 1827, WPA translations-microfilm #90-223.

June 23, 1827, WPA microfilm #90–223.

July 14, 1827, WPA microfilm #90–223.

August 11, 1827, WPA microfilm #90–223.

November 22, 1827, WPA microfilm #90–223.

December 15, 1827, WPA microfilm #90–223.

December 29, 1827, WPA microfilm #90–223.

January 12, 1828, WPA microfilm #90–223.

March 1, 1828, WPA microfilm #90–223.

May 24, 1828, WPA microfilm #90–223.

July 19, 1828, WPA microfilm #90–223.

General Digest of the Ordinances and Resolutions of the Corporation of New Orleans. New Orleans: Jerome Bayon, 1831.

"Additional Ordinances—Slaves," October 20, 1831.

"An Ordinance concerning persons navigating to lake Pontchartrain," August 20, 1813.

"An Ordinance concerning slaves employed as hirelings by the day," November 10, 1817.

"An Ordinance Concerning the Police Jail for the Detention of Slaves," October 8, 1817.

"An Ordinance concerning the sale of horses, mules, or other animals, carriages, gigs, carts, drays, &c," February 23, 1829.

"An ordinance in relation to slaves in the city and suburbs of New-Orleans," October 15, 1817.

"An Ordinance supplementary to the ordinance concerning the police of the Port of New-Orleans," June 23, 1831.

"An Ordinance to regulate the service of slaves employed in the works of the city," November 10, 1817.

Resolutions of March 30, April 15, and April 21, 1829, and November 12, 1830.

Digeste des Ordonnances, Resolutions et Reglemens de la Corporation de la Nouvelle-Orleans. New Orleans: Gaston Brusle, 1836.

Resolutions of November 24 and December 11, 1835.

Resolutions of November 29, 1834 and January 27 and April 10, 1835.

Lincoln, Abraham. "Emancipation Proclamation," January 1, 1863. In *Collected Works*, vol. 4.

———. "Proclamation of a Blockade," April 19, 1861. In *Collected Works*, vol. 4.

National Archives and Records Administration, Baton Rouge Barracks, 393.7, "Records of U.S. Army Continental Commands, Part 5, Military Installations."

Passenger Lists of Vessels Arriving at New Orleans, 1820–1902, microfilm #M259, roll 7, New Orleans Public Library.

Sangamon County Commissioners' Record C, 256, as cited in *The Lincoln Log: A Daily Chronology of the Life of Abraham Lincoln*, entry for April 8, 1831 – July 8, 1831. Available http://www.thelincolnlog.org/view/1831/4, visited February 26, 2009.

Shreve, Henry M. "Ohio and Mississippi Rivers: Annual Report of work done in improving the navigation of the Ohio and Mississippi rivers in the present year, ending 30th September 1831." Reproduced in *Daily National Intelligencer* (Washington, D.C.), 19, no. 5886, December 17, 1831, p. 2

Survey of Federal Archives in Louisiana, Division of Community Service Programs-Works Projects Administration. *Ship Registers and Enrollments of New Orleans, Louisiana*. 2 vols. Baton Rouge: Louisiana State University, 1941.

Survey of Federal Archives in Louisiana, Division of Professional and Service Projects-Works Projects Administration, *Flatboats on the Mississippi in 1807*. Baton Rouge: Louisiana State University, 1940.

Textural Archives Services Division, National Archives and Records Administration, Personal Communication, February 18, 2009.

U.S. Army Corps of Engineers. "River Velocities at New Orleans, LA. Related to the Carrollton Gage," http://www.mvn.usace.army.mil/eng/edhd/velo_no.asp.

U.S. Census of 1790, 1800, 1810, and 1820, as digitized by the National Historical Geographic Information System of the University of Minnesota.

U.S. Census Bureau, Population Schedule #328, St. Louis Township, Missouri, 1830.

U.S. Census Bureau. "Aggregate Amount of Persons Within the United States in the Year 1810: Aggregate Amount of Each Description of Persons Within the Territory of Orleans," 1810.

U.S. Census Bureau. *Census for 1820*. Washington, D.C.: Gales & Seaton, 1821.

U.S. Census, State of Arkansas, County of Crittenden, Schedule 2—Slave Inhabitants, William Ferguson, 1850.

U.S. Federal Census, Orleans Parish, Louisiana, 1830, Population Schedule #273 and #220.

U.S. House of Representatives. "Mississippi Levees: Memorial of Citizens of the State of Louisiana, in Favor of Nationalizing the levees of the Mississippi River." Mis. Doc. No. 41, January 13, 1873, in reference to H.R. 3419, p. 8.

U.S. Naval Observatory Astronomical Applications Department, "Phases of the Moon," http://aa.usno.navy.mil/data/docs/MoonPhase.php.

Wharfinger Reports/New Orleans Collector of Levee Dues-Registers of Flat-
    boats, Barges, Rafts, and Steamboats in the Port of New Orleans, 1818–1823
    and 1845–1849, Microfilm #75-109 QN420, NOPL–LC.
Wharfinger Reports, Microfilm #75-109 QN420 New Orleans Collector of Le-
    vee Dues-Registers of Flatboats, Barges, Rafts, and Steamboats in the Port of
    New Orleans, 1806 and 1818, NOPL–LC.
Wharfinger Reports, Microfilm #75-109 QN420, New Orleans Collector of Le-
    vee Dues-Registers of Flatboats, Barges, Rafts, and Steamboats in the Port of
    New Orleans, 1818–1823, NOPL–LC.
Young, Christine, Ethel Smith, and Hazel M. Hyde. *Marriage Records—Spencer
    County, Indiana 1818–1855*. Thomson, IL: Heritage House, 1974.

~Newspapers~
American Advocate (Hallowell, ME), June 20, 1828, p. 2.
Arkansas Gazette, "Abe Lincoln Once Lived in Arkansas," July 4, 1927.
    "Lincoln's Visit to Arkansas," Magazine Section, February 7, 1937.
Baltimore Gazette and Daily Advertiser, "The Raft of Red River," October 17, 1828,
    p. 2.
Baltimore Patriot
    "Extract of a Letter to the Editors of the National Advocate," June 19, 1826,
        p. 2.
    November 28, 1828, p. 2.
    May 4, 1831, p. 2.
    May 27, 1831, p. 2.
Barre Gazette (Barre, Massachusetts), "Sam Slick's Description of New Orleans,"
    January 25, 1839, p. 1.
Chicago Daily
    "As In Years Gone By," February 13, 1895, p. 5.
    "Is It In Good Taste? Public Opinion Divided as to the Play 'Abraham Lin-
        coln,'" September 13, 1891, p. 32.
Chicago Daily Tribune, "Abraham Lincoln's First Cousin Still Living, Gives Recol-
    lections of the Great Emancipator," February 10, 1907, p. F6.
Chicago Press and Tribune, "Lincoln at Home: Seventy-Five Thousand Replica-
    tions Call on Him—Imposing Demonstration," August 9, 1860, p. 1.
Chicago Tribune, "Our Representative Men," June 11, 1864, p. 2.
City Gazette & Commercial Daily Advertiser (Charleston, SC), April 7, 1831, p. 2.
Connecticut Herald (New Haven), "Gen. Jackson at New Orleans," February 5,
    1828, p. 2.
Constitution (Washington, D.C.), "Summary of News," June 2, 1860, p. 3.
Daily Inter-Ocean (Chicago), "Lincoln's Flatboat: Story of the Craft Told by One of
    Its Builders," May 15, 1892, p. 2.
Daily National Intelligencer (Washington, D.C.), November 4, 1828, c. F.
Daily National Journal (Washington, D.C.)
    April 12, 1828, c. A.

"The Wabash," May 12, 1831, p. 3.

Daily Ohio Statesman (Columbus, OH), "The Light-Haired to the Front," June 2, 1864, p. 2.

Daily Orleanian, February 19, 1849, p. 2, c. 3.

Daily Picayune (New Orleans)

"In Flatboat and Keelboat Times On the Mississippi, Over Seventy Years Ago," March 19, 1896, section F, p. 14, c. 6–7.

"Freed Negroes," March 8, 1856, p. 3, c. 2.

"A Kaleidoscopic View of New Orleans," September 23, 1843, p. 2, c. 3.

"Pleased with New Orleans: Hon. Robert T. Lincoln Visits the Soldiers' Home and the Opera," November 8, 1893, p. 8, c. E.

Daily True Delta (New Orleans), "Meeting of the Pioneer Lincoln Club," February 23, 1864, p. 1, c. 5.

Delaware Weekly Advertiser and Farmer's Journal, "New Orleans—Goodacre's Lecture," March 27, 1828, p. 1, c. 4.

Farmers' Cabinet (Amherst, NH), March 29, 1828, p. 2.

Independent Chronicle (Boston, MA), September 25, 1815, p. 1, c. 4.

Indiana Centinel (Vincennes, IN), "Chilicothe," March 4, 1820, p. 3.

Jamestown Journal (Jamestown, NY), "Slavery in New Orleans," November 10, 1830, p. 4.

Louisiana Advertiser

"Opening of the Rail Road." April 25, 1831, p. 2, c. 4.

December 2, 1826, p. 2, c. 3.

February 26, 1827.

April 19, 1828.

September 18, 1832, p. 2, c. 4.

Louisiana Courier

"Communicated—Engineers," June 4, 1828, p. 3, c. 1.

"Flint's Geography and History of the Western States," October 23, 1828, p. 4, c. 3.

"For Sale—A Negro Woman," November 13, 1828, p. 3, c. 6.

"From the *New-York Courier & Enquirer*," May 28, 1831, page indeterminable, c. 1.

"Maritime News" columns, April through June, 1831

"Notice—The undersigned having formed a partnership . . .," October 20, 1828, p. 3, c. 6.

"Plan of a Lottery of Property of William Wikoff, Senior," October 3, 1828, p. 4, c. 4–5.

"Private Boarding," November 13, 1828, p. 3, c. 4.

"Rail Road," July 17, 1828, p. 3, c. 3.

"Rail Road," July 31, 1828, p. 3, c. 1.

"Runaway," November 13, 1828, p. 3, c. 5.

"Slaves," October 20, 1828, p. 3, c. 4.

"State of Louisiana—Parish of St. Charles—County of German Coast—
    Court of Probate: A Sugar Plantation," October 4, 1828, p. 3, c. 5.
"To the editor of the Louisiana Courier," May 11, 1831.
June 2–9, 1828.
November 13, 1828.
January 13, 1829.
January 26, 1829.
May 11–31, 1831.
June 10, 1831.
Louisiana Gazette
    February–May 1806.
    June 27, 1826.
Louisiana Gazette and New-Orleans Daily Advertiser
    January 13, 1812.
    January 17, 1812.
    January 18, 1812.
    January 21, 1812.
Louisiana State Gazette, "Notice—A Flatboat loaded with Stone Coal . . .," June 23,
    1826, "Auctions" column.
Macon Weekly Telegraph (*Georgia Telegraph*), "New-Orleans, Dec. 1," December 17,
    1835, p. 2.
Madisonian, "Extracts from the Clockmaker," October 20, 1838, p. 1.
Memphis Appeal as carried by *The Sun* (Baltimore, Maryland), March 18, 1861, p.
    4.
Mercantile Advertiser
    "Annual Report of the Rail-Road," May 25, 1831, p. 2, c. 4–5.
    "Execution of Slave Elijah," June 6, 1831, p. 2, c. 5.
    "Exhibition. Rail Road Steam Carriage," May 17, 1831, p. 4, c. 2.
    "For Sale," May 30, 1831, p. 3, c. 3.
    "For Sale—A black girl," May 19, 1831, p. 3, c. 3.
    "Lamentable Catastrophe!," May 23, 1831, p. 2, c. 4.
    "Mechanism," May 23, 1831, p. 1, c. 3.
    "Negroes for Sale," May 14, 1831, p. 3, c. 1.
    "Notice," May 21, 1831, p. 3, c. 2.
    "Rail Road," May 20, 1831, p. 2, c. 4.
    "Railroad," April 26, 1831, p. 2, c. 4.
    "Servants, Furniture, Horses & Gig," May 23, 1831, p. 3, c. 5.
    "The Shipping," June 13, 1831, p. 2, c. 4.
    "Sugar Crops," May 5, 1831, p. 2, c. 4.
    "Trial of Slave Elijah," May 31, 1831, p. 2, c. 4.
    April 20, 1831.
    May 13–14, 1831.
    May 19–20, 1831.
    May 24–28, 1831.

June 1, 1831.

June 3–13, 1831.

Morning Tribute (New Orleans), "Seldom-Recalled Lincoln Visit to Orleans on Flatboat Traced," by Morris B. Higgins, February 12, 1940, p. 7, c. 3.

New Orleans Argus

"$10 Reward," June 2, 1828, p. 2, c. 6.

"By Bauduc & Domingo," May 24, 1828, p. 2, c. 6.

"Detained in the Jail of the Parish of St. James, on [May] 23," May 29, 1828, p. 2, c. 6.

"Dreadful Catastrophe," May 19, 1828, p. 2, c. 3.

"For Sale," May 30, 1828, p. 2, c. 5.

"For Sale or to Hire," May 28, 1828, p. 3, c. 1.

"Marine Register," June 3, 1828, p. 2, c. 5.

"Marine Register," May 17, 1828, p. 2, c. 5.

"Marine Register," May 29, 1828, p. 1, c. 5.

"New-York Market;" "From the N. Orleans Price Current of May 17," May 19, 1828, p. 2, c. 4–6.

"Notice," May 22, 1828, p. 2, c. 5.

"Notice," May 30, 1828, p. 2, c. 6.

"Notice—Detained in the Jail of the Parish of St. James," May 29, 1828, p. 1, c. 5.

April 21, 1828, p. 2, c. 6.

May 13–15, 1828.

May 19–30, 1828.

June 3, 1828.

June 6–7, 1828.

New Orleans Bee

"The Argus vs. The Argus," June 9, 1831, p. 2, c. 1.

"Baton-Rouge, May 10," May 13, 1828, p. 3, c. 2.

"Cultivation of Sugar," May 13, 1828, p. 3, c. 2.

"For Sale, A valuable property, situated in Jefferson parish, Lafayette suburb . . . ," May 13, 1828, p 4, c 3

"The Levee," June 22, 1835, p. 2, c. 1.

"Marine—Port de la Nouvelle Orleans," February 24, 1829, p. 3, c. 4.

"Marine—Port de la Nouvelle Orleans," March 22, 1829, p. 2, c. 3.

"Maritime News" columns, April through June, 1831.

"Maritime" columns, April 1, 1828 through March 31, 1829.

"Maritime" columns, April 15 through June 15, 1828.

"New-Orleans American," May 13, 1831, p. 2, c. 4.

"Nouvelles Maritimes—Port de la Nlle.-Orleans," May 19, 1828, p. 2, c. 5.

"Nouvelles Maritimes—Port de la Nlle.-Orleans," May 17, 1828, p. 2, c. 4.

"Rail Roads," May 29, 1828, p. 3, c. 2.

"Rail-Road establishments." August 18, 1831, p. 2, c. 1–2.

"Ship News," February 16, 1829, p. 3, c. 4.

April 21–June 24, 1828.

January 15–February 20, 1829.

August 18, 1831, p. 2, c. 1.

November 18, 1831, p. 2, c. 1.

April 11, 1834, p. 2, c. 1.

June 22, 1835, p. 2, c. 1.

September 25–28, 1835, p. 2, c. 1.

New Orleans Times, November 23, 1866, p. 7, c. 1.

New Orleans Times-Picayune, "Lincoln Movie Films to be Taken in Orleans," December 3, 1918, p. 7.

New York Daily Tribune (*New York Herald-Tribune*), "Lincoln's Early Days," July 9, 1860.

New York Herald

"A Raid Upon Washington," March 2, 1861, p. 6, c. C.

"Political Intelligence—Complaint Among the Farmers," June 25, 1860, p. 5.

New York Times

"Character of President Lincoln—Remarks by Hon. A. Wakeman," November 27, 1864, p. 5.

"Lincoln's Friend, John Hanks: A Garrulous Old Man's Reminiscences," June 7, 1881, p. 2.

"Lincoln's Two Cousins Who Swayed His Life," September 22, 1929, p. 17, c. 4.

"Winnowings," November 5, 1888, p. 4.

September 22, 1929, p. 17, c. 4.

New-Bedford Courier (New Bedford, MA), "New-Orleans," August 16, 1831, p. 1.

Newburyport Herald (Newburyport, MA), "Extract of a Letter from an Emigrant in New-Orleans," October 17, 1817, p. 3, c. 2.

New-Orleans Directory & Register. New Orleans: John Adems Paxton, 1830.

New-Orleans Price-Current and Commercial Intelligencer, October 10, 1835.

New-York Gazette & General Advertiser, October 12, 1812, p. 2, c. 3.

New-York Morning Herald, "New Orleans, July 19," August 13, 1830, p. 2.

Niles' Weekly Register, July 11, 1818.

Norwich Courier (Norwich, CT), "Items," September 17, 1828, p. 3.

Ohio Statesman (Columbus), "Life in New Orleans," May 7, 1847, p. 3, c. 2.

Omaha World Herald, "Garrison's Prediction: Death of Abraham Lincoln's Friend Recalls a Prophecy Made by the Old Man That Came True," September 30, 1899, p. 4.

Patriot and Eagle (*Patriot and Democrat*, Hartford, CT), August 8, 1835, 2.

Patron of Industry (New York), "Extract of a Letter from a Gentleman in New-Orleans," January 24, 1821, p. 2.

Philadelphia Inquirer, "Story of Lincoln's Struggles as a Boy in Indiana and How He Developed Himself," February 28, 1909, p. 11, c. 5.

Pittsfield Sun (Pittsfield, MA), "New-Orleans, Sept. 4," October 2, 1823, p. 2.

Reporter (Brattleboro, VT), February 18, 1804, p. 2.

St. Albans Daily Messenger (St. Albans, VT), "The Republican Nominees," May 31, 1860, p. 1.

Salt Lake Herald

"The Mississippi Valley Fleet," July 12, 1896, p. 10, c. 3.

"The Western Flatboatmen: They Were As Lawless as Literature Has Painted Them," May 26, 1895, unpaginated.

San Francisco Bulletin, "Lincoln's Birthplace. Some Incidents and Facts Never before Published," January 16, 1874, p. 4.

Saturday Magazine (London), "The River Missouri, in North America," September 19, 1835.

Springfield Republican (Springfield, MA)

"Mississippi Shanty Boats—A Survival of the Old Flat-Boating Days," July 27, 1899, p. 10.

"Stories of Lincoln's Youth by Uncle Philip Clarke," April 4, 1897, p. 9.

Springfield Republication (Springfield, MA), "Lincoln Not a Flatboatman: His Trip Down the Mississippi to New Orleans to Sell a Barrel of Whiskey and a Case of Tobacco," March 12, 1895, p. 12.

Sun (Baltimore, MD)

"Latest News from the South," January 21, 1865, p. 1.

March 18, 1861, p. 4.

Sunday Delta (New Orleans), "John Mitchell in New Orleans," April 18, 1858, p. 7, c. 1.

Times-Democrat (New Orleans)

"Down the Mississippi in 1767: The Journey of George Morgan," October 23, 1905, p. 10, c. 5–7.

"Flatboating Days," by Charles E. Whitney, June 10, 1883, p. 5, c. 5.

"The Sugar Exchange: Formal Opening of the Beautiful Building," June 4, 1884, address by J. Dymond, p. 3, c. 3–5.

Village Register and Norfolk County Advertiser (Dedham, MA), "High Water," March 13, 1828, p. 2.

Weekly Wisconsin Patriot (Madison), June 30, 1860, p. 6.

Western Sun (Vincennes, IN), May 24, 1828.

Wisconsin Patriot (Madison), "A Political Sermon—by the Rev. Hardshell Pike," August 18, 1860, p. 7.

~Historical Publications~

Abdy, Edward Strutt. *Journal of a Residence and Tour in the United States of North America: From April, 1833, to October, 1834*, vol. 3. Cambridge, England: John Murray, 1835.

Alexander, J. E. *Transatlantic Sketches, Comprising Visits to the Most Interesting Scenes in North and South America, and the West Indies*, vol. 3. London, 1833.

Anonymous. *Abraham Africanus I: His Secret Life, as Revealed Under the Mesmeric Influence*. New York: J. F. Feeks, 1864.

Anonymous. *New Orleans As It Is: Its Manners and Customs*. "By a Resident, Printed for the Publisher," 1850.

Anonymous. *Southern States, Embracing a Series of Papers Condensed from the Earlier Volumes of De Bow's Review*, vol. 1 (1856).

Anonymous. "The Primitive Hoosier." *Indiana Magazine of History* 1, no. 2 (Second Quarter, 1905).

Arfwedson, C. D. *The United States and Canada in 1832, 1833, and 1834*, vol. 2. London: Richard Bentley, 1834.

Armitage, Theodore. "Flatboating on the Wabash-A Diary of 1847." *Indiana Magazine of History* 9, no. 4 (December 1913): 272–275.

Ashe, Thomas. *Travels in America Performed in the Year 1806*. London: Richard Phillips, 1809.

Baird, Robert. *View of the Valley of the Mississippi, or the Emigrant's and Traveller's Guide to the West*. Philadelphia: H. S. Tanner, 1834.

Barrett, Joseph H. *Life of Abraham Lincoln, Presenting His Early History, Political Career, and Speeches*. New York: Moore, Wilstach & Baldwin, 1865.

Bernhard, Duke of Saxe-Weimar-Eisenach. *Travels Through North America, During in the Years 1825 and 1826*, vol. 2. Philadelphia: Carey, Lea & Carey, 1828.

Blane, William Newnham. *An Excursion Through the United States and Canada During the Years 1822–23, By An English Gentleman*. London: Baldwin, Cradock, and Joy, 1824.

Bloodgood, S. De Witt. *A Treatise on Roads, Their History, Character and Utility*. Albany, NY: Oliver Steele, 1838.

Blowe, Daniel. *A Geographical, Historical, Commercial, and Agricultural View of the United States of America*. London: Edwards & Knibb, 1820.

Bremer, Fredrika. *The Homes of the New World: Impressions of America*, vol. 2. New York: Harper & Brothers, 1853.

Bullock, William. *Sketch of a Journey through the Western States of North America: from New Orleans . . . to New York, in 1827*. London: J. Miller, 1827.

Buttrick, Tilly Jr. "Voyages, Travels and Discoveries." In *Early Western Travels 1748–1846*, vol. 8, edited by Reuben Gold Thwaites. Cleveland, OH: The Arthur H. Clarke Company, 1904.

Carmony, Donald F. "William P. Dole: Wabash Valley Merchant and Flatboatman." *Indiana Magazine of History* 67, no. 4 (December 1971): 335–363.

———— and Sam K. Swope, eds., "Flatboat Building on Little Raccoon Creek, Parke County, Indiana." *Indiana Magazine of History* 60, no. 4 (December 1964): 305–322.

Carver, Jonathon. *Travels Through the Interior Parts of North-America, in the Years 1766, 1767, and 1768*. London: Jonathon Carver, 1778.

Castellanos, Henry C. *New Orleans as It Was: Episodes of Louisiana Life*. Baton Rouge: Louisiana State University Press, 2006 republication of 1895 original.

Clark, Micajah Adolphus. Diary transcribed in "Flatboat Voyage to New Orleans Told Of In a Diary Kept in 1848." *Times-Democrat* (New Orleans), July 9, 1905, part 3, p. 13, c. 7.

Clark, William. "William Clark's Diary: May, 1826–February, 1831, Part Two,

1828." Edited by Louise Barry. *Kansas Historical Quarterly* 16, no. 2 (May 1948).

Cramer, Zadok. *The Navigator, or the Traders' Useful Guide in Navigating the Monongahela, Allegheny, Ohio, and Mississippi Rivers*. Pittsburgh: Zadok Cramer, 1806.

———. *The Navigator, or the Traders' Useful Guide in Navigating the Monongahela, Allegheny, Ohio, and Mississippi Rivers*. Pittsburgh: Cramer and Spear, 1818.

———, Spear and Eichbaum. *The Navigator, Containing Directions for Navigating the Monongahela, Allegheny, Ohio, and Mississippi Rivers*. Pittsburgh: Cramer, Spear and Eichbaum, 1814.

Cuming, Fortescue. *Sketches of a Tour to the Western Country through the States of Ohio and Kentucky*. Pittsburgh, 1810.

Darby, William. *Geographical Description of the State of Louisiana*. New York: James Olmstead, 1817.

Davidson, James D. "A Journey Through the South in 1836: Diary of James D. Davidson." Edited by Herbert A. Kellar. *The Journal of Southern History* 1, no. 3 (August 1935): 345–377.

De Bow, J. D. B. "Flat Boat Commerce." *The Commercial Review of the South and West* 4, no. 4 (December 1847).

———. *Statistical View of the United States—Compendium of the Seventh Census*. Washington, D.C.: A.O.P. Nicholson, Printer, 1854.

———. *The Commercial Review of the South and West*, 8 vols. New Orleans: J.D.B. De Bow, 1846–1850.

Didimus, Henry (Henry Edward Durell). *New Orleans As I Found It*. New York: Harper & Brothers, 1845.

Douglass, Frederick. *The Life and Times of Frederick Douglass: From 1817–1882*, edited by John Lobb. London: Christian Age Office, 1882.

Du Lac, M. Perrin. *Travels Through the Two Louisianas . . . in 1801, 1802, & 1803*. London: Richard Phillips, 1807.

Durell, Henry Edward (Henry Didimus). *New Orleans As I Found It*. New York: Harper & Brothers, 1845.

Enoch, Harry G. *Original Journal of John Halley of His Trips to New Orleans Performed in the Years 1789 & 1791*. Winchester, KY: Bluegrass Heritage Museum, 2004.

Evans, Estwick. "A Pedestrious Tour, of Four Thousand Miles, Through the Western States and Territories." In *Early Western Travels 1748–1846*, vol. 8, edited by Reuben Gold Thwaites. Cleveland, OH: The Arthur H. Clark Company, 1904.

Fearon, Henry Bradshaw. *Sketches of America: A Narrative of a Journey of Five Thousand Miles Through The Eastern and Western States of America*. London, 1819.

Ferrall, S. A. *A Rumble of Six Thousand Miles Through the United States of America*. London: Effingham Wilson, Royal Exchange, 1832.

Flint, Timothy. *Recollections of the Last Ten Years . . . in the Valley of the Mississippi*. Boston: Cummings, Hilliard, and Company, 1826.

Fordham, Elias Pym. *Personal Narrative of Travels in Virginia, Maryland, Pennsylvania, Ohio, Indiana, Kentucky; and of a Residence in the Illinois Territory: 1817–1818.* Edited by Frederic Austin Ogg. Cleveland, OH: The Arthur H. Clark Company, 1906.

Gilkeson, John Calvin. "Flatboat Building on Little Raccoon Creek, Parke County, Indiana." Edited by Donald F. Carmony and Sam K. Swope, *Indiana Magazine of History* 60, no. 4 (December 1964): 305–322.

Goodacre, Robert. "New Orleans—Goodacre's Lecture." *Baltimore Gazette and Daily Advertise,* January 30, 1828, p. 1.

Gould, E. W. *Fifty Years on the Mississippi; or, Gould's History of River Navigation.* St. Louis: Nixon-Jones Printing Company, 1889.

Greeley, Horace. "Greeley's Estimate of Lincoln: An Unpublished Address." *The Century Illustrated Magazine* 42, no. 3 (July 1891): 371–382.

Greene, Welcome A. "Being the Journal of a Quaker Merchant Who Visited N.O. in 1823." *New Orleans Times-Picayune,* October 16, 1921, section four, pages 1 and 6.

Gregg, David. "God In Lincoln." *The Independent, Devoted to the Consideration of Politics, Social and Economic Tendencies, History, Literature, and the Arts,* April 4, 1895, p. 15.

Griffing, B. N. *An Illustrated Historical Atlas of Spencer County, Indiana.* Philadelphia: D. J. Lake & Company, 1879.

Grimshaw, William. *History of the United States: From Their First Settlement as Colonies. . . .* Philadelphia: Benjamin Warner, 1821.

Hall, A. Oakey. *The Manhattaner in New Orleans; or Phases of "Crescent City" Life.* New York: J. S. Redfield, 1851.

Hall, Basil. *Travels in North America in the Years 1827 and 1828,* vol. 3. Edinburgh and London, 1830.

Harriet Martineau. *Retrospect of Western Travel,* vol. 1. London and New York: Saunders and Otley, 1838.

Hazard, Samuel. "The First Flat Boat on the Mississippi." *Hazard's Register of Pennsylvania.* Philadelphia: William F. Geddes, 1834.

Henry, Adolphe and Victor Gerodias. *The Louisiana Coast Directory, of the Right and Left Banks of the Mississippi River.* New Orleans: E. C. Wharton, 1857.

Hodgson, Adam. *Remarks During a Journey Through North America in the Years 1819, 1820, and 1821.* New York: Samuel Whiting, 1823.

Howells, William Dean. *Life of Abraham Lincoln,* facsimile edition of campaign biography corrected by the hand of Abraham Lincoln. Bloomington: Indiana University Press, 1960.

Illinois State Register. "Remarks [of Abraham Lincoln] in Illinois Legislature Concerning Commemoration of the Battle of New Orleans," January 15, 1841. In *Collected Works,* vol. 1.

Ingraham, Joseph Holt. "Dots and Lines—No. I; Or, Sketches of Scenes and Incidents in the West." *The Ladies' Companion, A Monthly Magazine, Embracing Every Department of Literature,* vol. 11. New York: William W. Snowden,

1839.

Ingraham, Joseph Holt. *The South-West by a Yankee*, 2 vols. New York, 1835.

Jacquess, Asbury C. "The Journals of the Davy Crockett commencing December 20th, 1834." *Indiana Magazine of History* 102, no. 1 (March 2006): 8–24.

Judah, Samuel Bernard. "A Journal of Travel from New York to Indiana in 1827." *Indiana Magazine of History* 17, no. 4 (December 1921): 338–352.

Kelley, William Darrah. *Lincoln and Stanton: A Study of the War Administration of 1861 and 1862*. New York and London: G. P. Putnam's Sons, 1885.

La Trobe, Charles Joseph. *The Rambler in North America*, vol. 2. New York, 1835.

Laussat, Pierre Clément de. *Memoirs of My Life*. Baton Rouge and New Orleans, 1978 translation of 1831 memoir.

LeGrand, Julia. *The Journal of Julia LeGrand: New Orleans—1862–1863*. Richmond, VA: Everett Waddey Company, 1911.

Long, Maj. Stephen H. *Account of an Expedition from Pittsburgh to the Rocky Mountains, Performed in the Years 1819, 1820*, vol. I. Edited by Edwin James. London: Longman, Hurst, Rees, Orme, and Brown, 1823.

Maximilian, Prince of Wied. *Travels in the Interior of North America*, reprinted in *Early Western Travels, 1748–1846*, vol. 22, edited by Reuben Gold Thwaites. Cleveland, OH: A. H. Clark, 1905.

McDermott, John Francis. "The Western Journals of Dr. George Hunter, 1796–1805." *Transactions of the American Philosophical Society*, New Series, 53, no. 4 (1963): 1–133.

Mercer, William Newton. "From Louisville to New Orleans in 1816: Diary of William Newton Mercer." Edited by Edwin Adams Davis and John C. L. Andreassen. *The Journal of Southern History* 2, no. 3 (August 1936): 390–402.

Monette, John W. "The Mississippi Floods (1850)." *Publications of the Mississippi Historical Society*, vol. 7, edited by Franklin L. Riley. Oxford, MS: Mississippi Historical Society, 1903.

Murray, Hugh. *Historical Account of Discoveries and Travels in North America*. London: Longman, Rees, Orme, Brown, & Green, 1829.

Nolte, Vincent. *Fifty Years in Both Hemispheres*. New York: Redfield, 1854.

Paxton, John Adems. *The New-Orleans Directory and Register*. New Orleans: Benjamin Levy & Co., 1822.

———. *The New-Orleans Directory & Register*. New Orleans: John Adems Paxton, 1830.

Raymond, Henry J. *The Life and Public Services of Abraham Lincoln . . . Together with His State Papers. . . .* New York: Derby and Miller, 1865.

Russell, William Howard. *My Diary North and South*. Boston and New York, 1863.

Schultz, Christian. *Travels on an Inland Voyage Through the States of New-York, Pennsylvania, Virginia, Ohio, Kentucky and Tennessee . . . Performed in the Years 1807 and 1808*, vol. 2. New York: Isaac Riley, 1810.

Scripps, John Locke. *Life of Abraham Lincoln*. Edited by Roy P. Basler and Lloyd A. Dunlap. Bloomington: Indiana University Press, 1961 reprint of 1860 original.

Sealsfield, Charles. *The Americans As They Are; Described in A Tour Through the Valley of the Mississippi.* London: Hurst, Chance, and Co., 1828.

Stuart, James. *Three Years in North America*, vol. 2. Edinburgh and London: Robert Cadell and Whittaker and Company, 1833.

Tasistro, Louis Fitzgerald. *Random Shots and Southern Breezes*, vol. 1. New York: Harper & Brothers, 1842.

Trollope, Frances Milton. *Domestic Manners of the Americans*, vol. 1. New York: Dodd, Mead, & Company, 1894 republication of 1836 original.

Tudor, Henry. *Narrative of a Tour in North America*, vol. 2. London: James Duncan, 1834.

Valentine, David Thomas. *Obsequies of Abraham Lincoln, in the City of New York, Under the Auspices of the Common Council.* New York: E. Jones & Company, 1866.

Wilkinson, John. "'To Do For My Self': Footloose on the Old Northwest Frontier." Edited by William C. Wilkinson. *Indiana Magazine of History* 86, no. 4 (December 1990): 399–420.

Wilson, George R. "George H. Proffit: His Day and Generation." *Indiana Magazine of History* 18, no. 1 (March 1922): 1–46.

~Modern Publications~

Allen, Helen L. "A Sketch of the Dubois Family, Pioneers of Indiana and Illinois." *Journal of the Illinois Historical Society* 5, no. 1 (April 1912): 50–65.

Allen, Michael. "The Riverman as Jacksonian Man." *The Western Historical Quarterly* 21, no. 3 (August 1990): 305–320.

Allen, Michael. *Western Rivermen, 1763–1861: Ohio and Mississippi River Boatmen and the Myth of the Alligator Horse.* Baton Rouge: Louisiana State University Press, 1990.

Anonymous. "River Navigation in Indiana." *The Indiana Magazine of History* 2, no. 2 (June 1906): 89–95.

Anonymous. "First Volume of Verse About Illinois." Historical Notes, *Journal of the Illinois State Historical Society* 48, no. 4 (Winter 1955): 469–470.

Arceneaux, Pamela D. "The Navigator." *The Historic New Orleans Collection Quarterly* 25, no. 3 (Summer 2008).

Arnold, Isaac N. *The Life of Abraham Lincoln.* Chicago: Jansen, McClurg, & Company, 1885.

Atherton, Lewis E. "Itinerant Merchandising in the Ante-Bellum South." *Bulletin of the Business Historical Society* 19, no. 2 (April 1945).

Baker, C. T. *Sandy Creek Landing Greets the Lincolns: An Historical Sketch of Pioneer Days in This Community and County.* Self-published monograph: Spencer County Library, 1931, Ref 977.2 Bak.

Baker, Jean H. *Mary Todd Lincoln: A Biography.* New York and London: W. W. Norton & Company, 1987.

Bancroft, Frederic. *Slave Trading in the Old South.* Baltimore, MD: J. H. Furst

Company, 1931.

Bartelt, William E. *There I Grew Up"—Remembering Lincoln's Indiana Youth*. Indianapolis: Indiana Historical Society Press, 2008.

Barton, William E. "The Girl Across the River: Lincoln's Friend at Court." *Dearborn Independent*, vol. 27, no. 12 (January 8, 1927): 3–23.

Basler, Roy P. *The Collected Works of Abraham Lincoln*, 8 vols., New Brunswick, NJ: Rutgers University Press, 1953.

Baudier, Roger. *The Catholic Church in Louisiana*. New Orleans: Roger Baudier, 1939.

Berlin, Ira. *Generations of Captivity: A History of African-American Slaves*. Cambridge: Harvard University Press, 2003.

Boritt, G. S. *Lincoln and the Economics of the American Dream*. Memphis, TN: Memphis State University Press, 1978.

Brent, Maria Campbell and Joseph E. Brent. *Lincoln, Kentucky & Kentuckians: A Cultural Resource Inventory of Sites in Kentucky Associated with President Abraham Lincoln*. Frankfort, KY: Historical Confederation of Kentucky and the Kentucky Abraham Lincoln Bicentennial Commission, 2005.

Bullard, F. Lauriston. "Abe Goes Down the River." *Lincoln Herald: A Magazine of Education and Lincolniana* 50, no. 1 (February 1948): 2–14.

Campanella, Richard. *Bienville's Dilemma: A Historical Geography of New Orleans*. Lafayette: University of Louisiana at Lafayette Press, 2008.

———. *Geographies of New Orleans: Urban Fabrics Before the Storm*. Lafayette, LA: Center for Louisiana Studies, 2006.

———. *Time and Place in New Orleans: Past Geographies in the Present Day*. Gretna, LA: Pelican Publishing Company, 2002.

Campbell, Joseph. *The Hero with a Thousand Faces*. Princeton, NJ: Princeton University Press, 1968.

Cayton, Andrew R. L. *Frontier Indiana*. Bloomington: Indiana University Press, 1996.

City Planning and Zoning Commission. *Major Street Report*. New Orleans, 1927.

Clark, John G. *New Orleans, 1718–1812: An Economic History*. Baton Rouge: Louisiana State University Press, 1970.

Clemens, Samuel L. *Life on the Mississippi*. New York: Harper & Row, 1958 republication of 1883 original.

Coffin, Charles Carleton. *Abraham Lincoln*. New York: Harper & Brothers, 1893.

Davis, James D. *The History of the City of Memphis*. Memphis, TN: Hite, Crumpton & Kelly, 1873.

Davis, John McCan. "Origin of the Lincoln Rail, As Related by Governor Oglesby." *Century Illustrated Magazine* 40, no. 2 (June 1900).

De Forest, John William. *A Volunteer's Adventures: A Union Captain's Record of the Civil War*. Edited by James H. Croushore. New Haven, CT: Yale University Press, 1946.

Denevan, William M. "The Pristine Myth: The Landscape of the Americas in 1492." *Annals of the Association of American Geographers* 82, no. 3 (September

1992): 369–385.

Dixon, Frank Haigh. "A Traffic History of the Mississippi River System." Document No. 11, National Waterways Commission. Washington, D.C.: Government Printing Office, December 1909.

Donald, David Herbert. *Lincoln*. New York: Simon & Schuster, 1995.

Dunbar, Seymour. *A History of Travel in America*, vol. 1. Indianapolis, IN: The Bobbs-Merrill Company, 1915.

Ehrmann, Bess V. *The Missing Chapter in the Life of Abraham Lincoln: A Number of Articles, Episodes, Photographs . . . of Abraham Lincoln in Spencer County, Indiana, between 1816–1830 and 1844*. Chicago: Walter M. Hill, 1938.

Ely, James W. Jr. "Abraham Lincoln as a Railroad Attorney." 2005 Railroad Symposium Essays, Indiana Historical Society Press, available http://www.indianahistory.org.

Everett, Donald Edward. "Free Persons of Color in New Orleans, 1803–1865." Ph.D. dissertation, Tulane University, 1952.

Fehrenbacher, Don E. and Virginia Fehrenbacher. *Recollected Words of Abraham Lincoln*. Stanford, CA: Stanford University Press, 1996.

Fischer, Roger A. "Racial Segregation in Ante Bellum New Orleans." *American Historical Review* 74, no. 3 (February 1969): 926–937.

Fleming, Walter L. *Louisiana State University 1860–1896*. Baton Rouge: Louisiana State University Press, 1936.

Fletcher, Calvin. "Early Indianapolis: The Fletcher Papers—Third Installment." *Indiana Magazine of History* 2, no. 1 (March 1906): 127–130.

Fogel, Robert William and Stanley L. Engerman. *Time On The Cross: The Economics of American Negro Slavery*. Boston and Toronto: Little, Brown and Company, 1974.

Ford, Larry and Ernst Griffin. "The Ghettoization of Paradise." *Geographical Review* 69, no. 2 (April 1979): 140–158.

Freudenberger, Herman and Jonathan B. Pritchett. "The Domestic United States Slave Trade: New Evidence." *Journal of Interdisciplinary History* , no.3 (Winter 1991): 447–477.

Fricker, Jonathan. "United States Barrack (Pentagon Barracks)—Historical and Descriptive Data." Historical American Building Survey Report (HABS No. La-1134). Heritage Conservation and Recreation Service, Departments of the Interior, Washington, D.C., 1978.

Froner, Eric. "A New Abraham Lincoln?," *Reviews in American History* 7, no. 3 (September 1979): 375–379.

Galloway, J. H. *The Sugar Cane Industry: An Historical Geography from its Origins to 1914*. Cambridge, New York, New Rochelle, Melbourne, and Sydney: Cambridge University Press, 1989.

Gudmestad, Robert H. *A Troublesome Commerce: The Transformation of the Interstate Slave Trade*. Baton Rouge: Louisiana State University Press, 2003.

Haites, Erik F., James Mak, and Gary M. Walton. *Western River Transportation: The Era of Early Internal Development, 1810–1860*. Baltimore and London:

Johns Hopkins University Press, 1975.

Hay, Logan. "Introduction." *Abraham Lincoln Association Papers.* Springfield, IL: Abraham Lincoln Association, 1931.

Hearn, Chester G. *The Capture of New Orleans 1862.* Baton Rouge and London: Louisiana State University Press, 1995.

Helm, Katherine. *The True Story of Mary, Wife of Lincoln, Containing the Recollection of Mary Lincoln's Sister Emilie, Extracts from Her War-Time Diary, Numerous Letters and Other Documents Now First Published.* New York and London: Harper and Brothers Publishers, 1928.

Herbert, David T. and Colin J. Thomas. *Urban Geography: A First Approach.* Chichester, New York, Brisbane, Toronto and Singapore, 1982.

Herndon, William H. "A Visit to the Lincoln Farm, September 14, 1865." In *The Hidden Lincoln, From the Letters and Papers of William H. Herndon,* edited by Emanuel Hertz. New York: The Viking Press, 1938.

Herndon, William H. and Jesse William Weik. *Herndon's Lincoln: The True Story of a Great Life,* vol. 1. Chicago, New York, and San Francisco: Belford, Clarke & Company, 1889.

Hertz, Emanuel, ed. *The Hidden Lincoln, From the Letters and Papers of William H. Herndon.* New York: The Viking Press, 1938.

History of Sangamon County, Illinois, Together with Sketches of its Cities, Villages, and Townships. Chicago: Inter-state Publishing Company, 1881

History of Warrick, Spencer, and Perry Counties, Indiana. Chicago: Goodspeed, Bros. & Company, 1885.

Hoagland, H. E. "Early Transportation on the Mississippi." *Journal of Political Economy* 19, no. 2 (February 1911).

Hogue, Rolla M. "Life in Indiana, 1800–1820." *Indiana Magazine of History* 9, no. 2 (June 1913): 83–92.

Holland, Josiah Gilbert. *The Life of Abraham Lincoln.* Springfield, MA: Gurdon Bill, 1866.

HRA Gray & Pape, LLC. *The Evolution of a Sanctified Landscape: A Historic Resource Study of the Lincoln Boyhood National Memorial, Spencer County, Indiana.* Cincinnati, OH: National Park Service, 2002.

Huguet, Florence B. "The Famous Men Who Passed Through Their Portals." *Baton Rouge Morning Advocate,* June 25, 1961.

Hulbert, Archer B. *The Paths of Inland Commerce: A Chronicle of Trail, Road, and Waterway.* New Haven, CT: Yale University Press, 1920.

Iglehart, John E. "The Coming of the English to Indiana in 1817 and Their Neighbors." *Indiana Magazine of History* 15, no. 2 (June 1919): 89–178.

Keneally, Thomas. *Abraham Lincoln.* New York: Lipper/Viking, 2003.

Kett, Joseph. *Rites of Passage: Adolescence in America, 1790 to Present.* New York: Basic Books, Inc. Publishers, 1977.

Lamon, Ward H. *The Life of Abraham Lincoln; from His Birth to His Inauguration as President.* Boston: James R. Osgood and Company, 1872.

Leland D. Baldwin. *The Keelboat Age on Western Waters.* Pittsburgh: Western Pennsylvania Historical Survey, 1941.

Lockett, James D. "Abraham Lincoln and Colonization: An Episode That Ends in Tragedy at L'Ile à Vache, Haiti, 1863–1864." *Journal of Black Studies* 21, no. 4 (June, 1991): 428–444.

Mac Donald, James. "'If Ever I Get A Chance to Hit That Thing, I'll Hit It Hard:' Abraham Lincoln in New Orleans," presented at the Fifty-First Annual Meeting of the Louisiana Historical Association, March 19–21, 2009, Monroe, Louisiana.

Mann, Charles C. *1491: New Revelations of the Americas Before Columbus.* New York: Knopf, 2006.

Markens, Isaac. *Abraham Lincoln and the Jews.* New York: Isaac Markens, 1909.

McClure, Donald E. *Two Centuries of Elizabethtown and Hardin County.* Elizabethtown, KY: The Hardin County Historical, 1971.

McCrary, Peyton. *Abraham Lincoln and Reconstruction.* Princeton, NJ: Princeton University Press, 1978.

McMurtry, R. Gerald. "The Lincoln Migration from Kentucky to Indiana." *Indiana Magazine of History* 33, no. 4 (December 1937): 385–421.

Miller, Richard Lawrence. *Lincoln and his World: The Early Years, Birth to Illinois Legislature.* Mechanicsburg, Pennsylvania: Stackpole Books, 2006.

Minor, Wilma Frances. "Lincoln the Lover: I. The Setting—New Salem." *Atlantic Monthly*, December 1928, 844–846 (later shown to be fraudulent).

Mitchell, Harry A. "The Development of New Orleans as a Wholesale Trading Center." *Louisiana Historical Quarterly* 27, no. 4 (October 1944): 934–939.

Mock, Cary J., Jan Mojzisek, Michele McWaters, Michael Chenoweth, and David W. Stahle. "The Winter of 1827–1828 Over Eastern North America: A Season of Extraordinary Climatic Anomalies, Societal Impacts, and False Spring." *Climatic Change* 83, no. 1-2 (July 2007): 87–115

Murr, J. Edward. "Lincoln in Indiana." *Indiana Magazine of History* 14, no. 1 (March 1918): 148–183.

Naylor, Isaac. "Judge Isaac Naylor, 1790–1873: An Autobiography." *Indiana Magazine of History* 4, no. 3 (September 1908): 134–140.

Nettels, Curtis, "The Mississippi Valley and the Constitution, 1813–29." *Mississippi Valley Historical Review* 11, no. 3 (December 1924): 332–357.

New Orleans Press. *Historical Sketch Book and Guide to New Orleans and Environs.* New York: Will H. Coleman, 1885.

Nicolay, John G. and John Hay. "Abraham Lincoln: A History—The Fourteenth of April—The Fate of the Assassins—The Mourning Pageant." *The Century Illustrated Monthly Magazine* 39, no. 3 (January 1890): 428–443.

———. *Abraham Lincoln: A History*, vol. 1. New York: The Century Co., 1890.

———, eds., *Complete Works of Abraham Lincoln*, vol. 5. New York, Francis D. Tandy Company, 1905.

Oliphant, J. Orin, ed. *Through the South and West with Jeremiah Evarts in 1826.* Lewisburg: Bucknell University Press, 1956

Owens, M. Lilliana. "Loretto Foundations in Louisiana and Arkansas." *Louisiana*

History 2, no. 2 (Spring, 1961): 202–229.

Paludan, Phillip Shaw. "Lincoln and Negro Slavery: I Haven't Got Time for the Pain." *Journal of the Abraham Lincoln Association* 27, no. 2, (2006): 1–23.

Phelps, Albert. "New Orleans and Reconstruction." *The Atlantic Monthly* 88, no. 525 (July 1901): 121–131.

Picard, George H. "Lincoln and the Question of Slavery." *The Iron Era* (Dover, NJ), February 10, 1905, p. 12, c. 2.

Pierson, George Wilson. *Tocqueville in America*. Baltimore, MD: The Johns Hopkins University Press, 1996.

Plummer, Mark A. *Lincoln's Rail-Splitter: Governor Richard J. Oglesby*. Urbana and Chicago: University of Illinois Press, 2001.

Pratt, Harry E. *Lincoln: 1809–1839, Being the Day-to-Day Activities of Abraham Lincoln from February 12, 1809 to December 31, 1839*. Springfield, IL: The Abraham Lincoln Association.

Preston, James H. "Political Pageantry in the Campaign of 1860 in Illinois." *Abraham Lincoln Quarterly* 4, no. 7 (September 1947): 313–364.

Pritchett, Jonathan B. "Forced Migration and the Interregional Slave Trade," paper presented to the 1991 Annual Meeting of the Social Science History Association.

Ratzel, Friedrich. *Sketches of Urban and Cultural Life in North America*. Translated and edited by Stewart A. Stehlin. New Brunswick and London, 1988 translation of 1873 treatise.

Redard, Thomas E. "The Port of New Orleans: An Economic History, 1821–1860." Ph.D. dissertation, Louisiana State University, 1985.

Reed, Merl E. *New Orleans and the Railroads: The Struggle for Commercial Empire, 1830–1860*. Baton Rouge: Louisiana State University Press, 1966.

Rice, Allen Thorndike, editor. *Reminiscences of Abraham Lincoln by Distinguished Men of His Time*. New York: North American Review, 1889.

Ross, Harvey Lee. *The Early Pioneers and Pioneer Events of the State of Illinois: Including Personal Recollections of the Writer; of Abraham Lincoln, Andrew Jackson, and Peter Cartwright. . . .* Chicago: Eastman Brothers, 1899.

Schafer, Judith Kelleher. "New Orleans Slavery in 1850 as Seen in Advertisements." *Journal of Southern History* 47, no.1, (February 1981).

Segal, Charles M. "Isachar Zacharie: Lincoln's Chiropodist." *Publications of the American Jewish Historical Society* 43, no. 1–4 (September 1953): 71–126.

———. "Notes and Documents: Isachar Zacharie: Lincoln's Chiropodist." *Publications of the American Jewish Historical Society* 44, no. 1–4 (September 1954–June 1955): 106–113.

Smith, Jonathan Clark. "Not Southern Scorn But Local Pride: The Origins of the Word *Hoosier* and Indiana's River Culture." *Indiana Magazine of History* 103, no. 2 (June 2007): 183–194.

Stampp, Kenneth M. *The Peculiar Institution: Slavery in the Ante-Bellum South*. New York: Vintage Books, 1956.

Starr, John W. Jr. *Lincoln's Last Day*. New York: Frederick Stokes Company, 1922.

Stewart, Judd, ed. *Some Lincoln Correspondence with Southern Leaders before the Outbreak of the Civil War*, New York: J. Stewart, 1909.

Stoddard, William O. *Abraham Lincoln: A True Story of a Great Life*. New York: Fords, Howard, & Hulbert, 1884.

Tadman, Michael. *Speculators and Slaves: Masters, Traders, and Slaves in the Old South*. Madison: The University of Wisconsin Press, 1989.

Tarbell, Ida Minerva and John McCan Davis. *The Early Life of Abraham Lincoln: Containing Many Unpublished Documents and Unpublished Reminiscences of Lincoln's Early Friends*. New York and London: S. S. McClure, 1896.

Taylor, Joe Gray. *Negro Slavery in Louisiana*. New York: Negro Universities Press, 1963.

Teillard, Dorothy Lamon, ed. *Recollections of Abraham Lincoln, 1847–1865*. Chicago: A. C. McClurg and Company, 1895.

Thomas, Benjamin P. *Lincoln's New Salem*. Carbondale and Edwardsville: Southern Illinois University Press, 1974.

Thomas, Susan K., "A Little Story on the Early Life of Abraham Lincoln, Told by Writer." *The Morning Herald* (Hagerstown, MD), February 2, 1954, p. 3, c. 2.

Thurston, Robert H. *A History of the Growth of the Steam-Engine*. New York: D. Appleton and Company, 1903.

Treasury Department, Bureau of Statistics, *Tables Showing Arrivals of Alien Passengers and Immigrants in the United States from 1820 to 1888*. Washington, D.C.: Government Printing Office, 1889.

Tregle Joseph G. Jr. *Louisiana in the Age of Jackson: A Clash of Cultures and Personalities*. Baton Rouge: Louisiana State University Press, 1999.

Tregle, Joseph G. Jr. "Creoles and Americans." In *Creole New Orleans: Race and Americanization*, edited by Arnold R. Hirsch and Joseph Logsdon. Baton Rouge and London: Louisiana State University Press, 1992.

Van Gennep, Arnold. *The Rites of Passage*. Chicago: University of Chicago Press, 1960.

Van Natter, Francis Marion. *Lincoln's Boyhood: A Chronicle of His Indiana Years*. Washington, D.C.: Public Affairs Press, 1963.

Vieux Carré Survey, Binder 75, entry for 817–819 St. Ann Street (stored at The Historic New Orleans Collection).

Wade, Richard. *Slavery in the Cities: The South 1820–1860*. London, Oxford, New York: Oxford University Press, 1964.

Walker, Juliet E. K. "Racism, Slavery, and Free Enterprise: Black Entrepreneurship in the United States before the Civil War." *The Business History Review* 60, no. 3 (Autumn 1986): 343–382.

Warren, Louis A. *Lincoln's Youth: Indiana Years, Seven to Twenty-One, 1816–1830*. Indianapolis: Indiana Historical Society Press, 1959, reprinted 2002,

———. *Lincoln's Parentage and Childhood*. New York and London: The Century Company, 1926,

———, ed. "President Lincoln's Interest in Catholic Institutions." *Lincoln Lore*, no. 790, May 29, 1944.

————, ed., "Lincoln's Return Trip from New Orleans." *Lincoln Lore*, No. 472, April 25, 1938.

————, ed. "A Riverside Lincoln Memorial." *Lincoln Lore*, no. 553, November 13, 1939.

————, ed. "A. Lincoln and J. D. Johnston—Step-Brothers." *Lincoln Lore*, no. 964, September 29, 1947.

————, ed. "A. Lincoln Manner of Buoying Vessels." *Lincoln Lore*, no. 1439, January 1958.

————, ed. "Factors Contributing to the 1816 Lincoln Migration." *Lincoln Lore*, no. 657, November 10, 1941.

————, ed. "Lincoln in New Orleans." *Lincoln Lore*, no. 333, August 26, 1935.

————, ed. "Lincoln, Miss Roby, and Astronomy." *Lincoln Lore*, no. 1349, February 14, 1955.

————, ed. "Lincoln's Return Trip from New Orleans." *Lincoln Lore*, no. 472, April 25, 1938.

————, ed. "The Railsplitter and the Railroads." *Lincoln Lore*, no. 484, July 18, 1938.

————, ed. "The Relatives of Lincoln's Mother." *Lincoln Lore*, no. 479, June 13, 1938.

Weik, Jesse William. *The Real Lincoln: a Portrait*. Boston and New York: Houghton Mifflin Company, 1922.

Whipple, Wayne. *The Story of Young Abraham Lincoln*. Philadelphia: Henry Altemus Company, 1915.

Whitney, Henry C. *Life on the Circuit with Lincoln*. Boston: Estes and Lauriat, 1892.

Wilds, John. *Collectors of Customs at the Port of New Orleans*. United States Customs Service, 1991.

Wilson, Douglas L. "Herndon's Legacy," in *Lincoln Before Washington: New Perspectives on the Illinois Years*, edited by Douglas L. Wilson. Urbana and Chicago: University of Illinois Press, 1997.

————. *Honor's Voice: The Transformation of Abraham Lincoln*. New York: Alfred A. Knopf, 1998.

———— and Rodney O. Davis, eds., *Herndon's Informants*.

Wilson, Samuel Jr. "Maspero's Exchange: Its Predecessors and Successors." *Louisiana History* 30, no. 2 (Spring 1989): 191–220.

Winston, James E. "Notes on the Economic History of New Orleans, 1803–1836." *Mississippi Valley Historical Review* 11, no. 2 (September 1924): 200–226.

Woolfolk, Margaret Elizabeth. *A History of Crittenden County, Arkansas*. Marion, AR: Margaret Elizabeth Woolfolk, 1991.

Wright, C. E. *An Illustrated Historical Atlas of Spencer County, Indiana*. Louisville, KY: John P. Morton & Company, 1896.

Wright, Gavin. *The Political Economy of the Cotton South*. New York: W. W. Norton & Company, Inc., 1978.

~Maps, Prints, and Ephemera~

Blanchard, Rufus. "The Republican Standard." Broadside published by Rufus Blanchard, Chicago, Illinois, 1860. Alfred Whital Stern Collection of Lincolniana, Library of Congress.

Grobe, Charles. Sheet Music, "Lincoln Quick Step, Dedicated to the Hon. Abraham Lincoln," Philadelphia: Lee & Walker, 1860. Alfred Whital Stern Collection of Lincolniana, Library of Congress.

Hall, Basil. Engraving, "The Mississippi at New Orleans." Engraved by W. H. Lizars, 1828. The Historic New Orleans Collection, Accession No. 1974.25.30.576 P.C. 30-11-A.

Hammond, J. T. *Map of New Orleans and Environs, Engraved Expressly for Cohen's Directory-1850.* The Historic New Orleans Collection, Accession No. 1974.25.18.111.

Hirt, L. *Plan of New Orleans with perspective and geometrical Views of the principal Buildings of the City.* The Historic New Orleans Collection, Accession No. 1952.4.

Melish, John. *Map of Mississippi, Constructed from the Surveys in the General Land Office and other Documents, 1820.* Library of Congress.

Moellhausen, Henry. *Norman's Plan of New Orleans & Environs 1845.* Map originally published in *Norman's New Orleans and Environs* (1845) by Benjamin Moore Norman. Baton Rouge and London: Louisiana State University Press, 1976.

Persac, Adrien. *Norman's Chart of the Lower Mississippi River.* New Orleans: B. M. Norman, 1858.

Pike, Charles J. *Coast Directory 1847* (Ribbon Map), The Historic New Orleans Collection, Accession No. 1953.3.

Wide-Awake Vocalist or, Rail Splitters' Song Book. New York: E. A. Daggett, 1860.

Wilie, John. "Exports of cotton and tobacco from the port of New Orleans during the last seven years . . . [1821–1828] Imports from the interior . . . Exports of sugar and molasses. . . ." New Orleans: Benjamin Levy, 1828. Broadside stored at Tulane University, Louisiana Collection, 976.31 (380) E96.

Zimpel, Charles F. *Topographical Map of New Orleans and Its Vicinity, 1834.* Southeastern Architectural Archive, Tulane University Special Collections.

Index

ABOUT THE AUTHOR

RICHARD CAMPANELLA (pictured above at the grave of Lincoln's cousin and fellow flatboatman John Hanks) is the author of *Delta Urbanism* (2010), *Bienville's Dilemma* (2008), *Geographies of New Orleans* (2006), *Time and Place in New Orleans* (2002), and *New Orleans Then and Now* (1999). A research professor of geography at Tulane University, Campanella has won two Louisiana Endowment for the Humanities Book of the Year awards, two New Orleans-Gulf South Booksellers Association awards, four Best Book selections from the *New Orleans Times-Picayune*, and the Excellence in Teaching Award from the Newcomb College Institute of Tulane University. He and his wife, Marina, live in New Orleans.

ABOUT THE COVER IMAGES

New Orleans: Taken from the opposite side, a short distance above the middle or Picayune Ferry, William James Bennett, watercolorist; Antoine Mondelli, draftsman artist; Henry John Megarey, publisher. Courtesy of New York Public Library.

Young Abe Lincoln by Thomas Hart Benton. Courtesy of the C. Benton Testamentary Trusts/UMB Bank Trustee/Licensed by VAGA, New York, NY.

This illustration was used as the frontispiece of Virginia L. S. Eifert's *Three Rivers South: The Story of Young Abe Lincoln* (New York: Dodd, Mead & Company, 1953), which featured several drawings by Thomas Hart Benton. It is reproduced here from the original artwork, which is owned by Kiechel Fine Art of Lincoln, Nebraska.

7c